THE
REITH DIARIES

THE
REITH
DIARIES

Edited by
CHARLES STUART

COLLINS
St James's Place, London
1975

William Collins Sons & Co Ltd
London · Glasgow · Sydney · Auckland
Toronto · Johannesburg

First published 1975
© The Trustees of the late Lord Reith of Stonehaven
and Charles Stuart 1975
ISBN 0 00 211174 8
Set in Monotype Garamond
Made and Printed in Great Britain by
William Collins Sons & Co Ltd Glasgow

For J.C.M.
who made this possible

Contents

Illustrations

Editor's Preface

For the last ten years of his life John Reith was concerned with the possibility of his diary being used for publication. For most of this time he was incapable of reaching a decision about it; he knew what he did not want and he knew whom he did not want, but he could not reach a positive position. The friend of many years standing who eventually coaxed him into decision was Sir John Masterman; 'What a very good friend J.C. has been,' he noted in 1967 after one of their numerous discussions about it. It was on Sir John Masterman's advice that the diary was entrusted to me to edit and it is to him that I have dedicated it in affectionate gratitude.

John Reith made this decision early in 1969 and I was able to have several talks with him in the spring and summer of that year while making a preliminary assessment of the diary which I continued in the following summer. But it was not until I was granted sabbatical leave in 1971 that I obtained the whole corpus of diary and enclosure volumes and was able to start working through them methodically. By that date I had submitted a general plan for the work and gained his approval for it. The time-consuming process of selection, transcription and editing occupied the next three years.

In constructing this edition I have been greatly helped by the readiness which many of John Reith's correspondents have shown in allowing me to quote from their letters. I am particularly grateful to Sir William Haley who has consented to the publication of extracts from twenty-one of his letters written between 1946 and 1964. I am grateful, too, to those who have given leave for one or more of their letters to be printed, notably to Sir Arthur Fforde, Sir Ian Jacob, Sir Hugh Carleton Greene, Sir Charles Curran and Mr Oliver Whitley among Reith's BBC contacts; to Sir Roy Welensky, Sir Robert Tredgold, Mr Garfield Todd and Mr Evan Campbell of his friends in Rhodesia; and to Lord Molson, Lord Stamp, Mr Philip Noel-Baker and Mr H. T. Hopkinson from among his other surviving correspondents. I have also been helped by being able to publish extracts from letters addressed to John Reith by distinguished men who are now dead, thanks to the permissions granted by their literary executors. Dorothy, Viscountess

Addison, Lady Gaitskell, Lady Normanbrook and Lady Nicolls gave leave for letters from their husbands to be printed, as did the late Mrs R. M. Barrington-Ward just before her death. Earl Baldwin of Bewdley and Lord Howick of Glendale authorized the publication of letters written by their fathers and the Earl of Selborne part of one written by his grandfather. The Earl of Harrington gave his consent for the publication of a letter from the late Lord Stanhope and Mr Max Rendall for a letter written by Dr M. J. Rendall. Finally, the First Beaverbrook Foundation approved the publication of a letter from Lord Beaverbrook, C. and T. Publications Ltd. of one from Sir Winston Churchill and Lord Moyle of two from Earl Attlee.

The system of selection which I have adopted has been to choose the main themes of John Reith's life and to collect in turn passages from his diary relevant to them. I was encouraged to find in his diary that when, in 1961, he was particularly concerned with the problem of its publication he approved this method. A purely chronological treatment would not have been feasible on grounds of length as well as of interest. It would have involved perhaps as many as four volumes (this was the estimate once made by Professor Briggs) and even then the outcome would have been shapeless, tedious and altogether too lifelike to be acceptable to most readers. As it is, the selections have been made with the object of indicating the course and purpose of John Reith's life as well as of providing immediacy and readability in themselves.

The adoption of this method has involved the risk of somewhat distorting the overall picture of Reith's character. It has unavoidably emphasized his quarrelsome side, his self-centred concern for his worldly position and for his inner spiritual state, his jealousies and his resentments. It must always be remembered that he did not write his diary for publication; he used it to let off steam at the end of the day. So the dark side of his character predominates in it. There is little to indicate his nobler and gentler qualities – his courtesy, his generosity and above all his unselfish readiness on innumerable occasions to help others. His own tendency to assess such help for others in practical terms obscures the extent to which he also sustained them mentally and spiritually by encouragement, even by inspiration. In the same way his diary rarely revealed his lighter side – his humour and his sense of fun. He is often mistakenly thought of as having been wholly without humour, a man like Barrie's Scotsman, for whom it would have needed a surgical operation to get a joke into his head. He himself confessed in his *Face to Face* programme in 1960: 'I have a sense of humour but not as much as I wish I had.' In the sense that he did not relieve his anxieties or ease his tensions by 'seeing the funny side' of situations, this is true. Nevertheless, when he was not deeply concerned, he could appreciate comical situations even when they involved laughing at himself. So, in July 1945, he recorded with relish as 'very funny' the occasion when Sir Alan Barlow, at a government reception and after talking with him, confided in Lady Reith whose identity he had foolishly failed to establish, 'I have always liked Reith but he is the most vain man I know.'

If these qualifications are kept in mind, the extracts may be read as giving not only an informative account of some public affairs but also an accurate inner view of the workings of the mind of an exceptionally talented, unusual and interesting man. No attempt has been made to collate the extracts systematically with other contemporary sources, so this edition is not a work of scholarship in the accepted sense of that term. But every effort has been made to assemble and to edit the extracts in a scholarly manner. Except where indicated the words printed are John Reith's words, although in some cases their order may have been changed to ease continuity. Marks of omission have been used sparingly; for the most part an extract within one day has been printed as a continuous whole. John Reith's numerous abbreviations have usually been preserved but editorial prejudice has led to the expansion of 'I've' into 'I have'. Similarly, the better known abbreviations for officers of State such as PM and PMG have been left, but office symbols, particularly within the BBC, have generally been translated into the name of the person concerned. Finally, the introductory and linking passages in each chapter have been constructed with the single purpose of clarifying the chosen extracts, placing them in their context and giving them shape. If the path between the fussiness of too much editorial direction and the obscurity of too little has at times been difficult to find, it is hoped that the picture of John Reith's life and achievement has not in consequence been spoiled. This is his story.

Christ Church, Oxford   CHARLES STUART
September 1974

Introduction

1. Early Years, 1889–1914

John Charles Walsham Reith was born on 20 July 1889 in Stonehaven where his parents, George and Adah Reith, were on holiday for the summer. In the summary of his early life which John Reith dictated in April 1929 he quoted his father's memory of 1919 that he had 'arrived earlier than was expected'. If this was so, it had no ill effects on him or his mother; within a week of his son's birth George Reith wrote in reply to anxious inquiries from his own parents, 'Adah is uncommonly well, and Baby is lively.' At this time George Reith was 47 years old. He was a minister of the Free Church of Scotland and had long been established at the College Church in Glasgow. He had started his ministry there in 1866 as the colleague of Dr Robert Buchanan, a veteran of the Disruption of 1843, and on his death in 1875 had become the sole minister. John Reith's mother, Adah Mary Weston, was 41 years old when he was born. She had met her husband in August 1868 when staying in Scotland at the house of friends who were members of George Reith's congregation. George Reith had proposed marriage in a matter of weeks, and in October his prospective father-in-law, a London stockbroker living in some style in Westbourne Terrace, summoned him south. It seems probable that they did not share the same attitude towards the world. By the standards of the time George Reith's views and outlook were markedly radical. In March 1869 he confessed in a letter to his future wife:

> I am getting more radical every day. I believe I should make my debut as a reformer of abuses in our social system. The fact is people have no business to be living in West Ends keeping up luxurious establishments with their poor brethren lacking a bit of bread.

But he ended this letter with some reassurance:

> Don't be alarmed at my radicalism; it is Scriptural. It is Jesus Christ's.

Adah Weston was not alarmed. In July 1870 she married George Reith at the Presbyterian Church in Argyle Square, London.

R.D.—B

Over the next ten years George and Adah Reith had a family of six children, four boys and two girls, the eldest being born in September 1871, the youngest in January 1880. The arrival of John Reith nine and a half years after his nearest brother, an unexpected addition to an existing family, meant that his early life was effectively that of an only child. By the time he was eight years old his elder sister had gone to train as a nurse in Edinburgh and all four brothers had begun their careers; one had been ordained into the Church of England, a second had completed his training as an engineer in a Clyde shipyard, a third was training as a chartered accountant and was soon to suffer a mental breakdown from which he never fully recovered, while the fourth had begun his theological studies at Glasgow University with a view to going to India as a missionary. Thus only his younger sister, Jean, remained continuously at home during his schooldays and she resented her young brother and was passionately jealous of his place in her mother's affections – feelings which he heartily returned. Later in life John Reith wrote and spoke of the absence of family life in his home, of the atmosphere of gloom which hung over the manse at Lynedoch Street and of the loneliness which he experienced in this situation.

It was all rather unhappy [he wrote in 1929], but I am sure it was due in large measure to my father and mother being both so fully occupied with good works.

In writing this he does not seem to have appreciated that his loneliness was as much a natural consequence of his isolation as the only child amid a family of grown-ups as it was the result of his parents' way of life. He acknowledged this in part when he later admitted that by his twelfth birthday one brother and one sister had left the manse and even the others were only there 'off and on'.

In any event John Reith's memories of his childhood, where they can be checked, are often unreliable. He believed, for example, that he could remember his summer holidays, which for the first ten years of his life were mostly spent in the Highlands, as far back as 1891 when he was only two years old. He was mistaken. In 1967 he found among his sister Jean's papers a list written in his father's hand recording for his mother the different places where they had celebrated their wedding anniversary in July between 1871 and 1911; this shows that his own memories of the period before he was eight years old are, as is only to be expected, inaccurate. Later in life he compounded and extended these errors, attributing to all his schoolboy summers the romantic associations of the Highlands, of Rothiemurchus and Aviemore, whereas he was as often simply at the seaside in Ayrshire or Angus. The conclusion to be drawn from this innocent romanticizing is that we should treat John Reith's later recollections of his early life, particularly his meanderings in interview and conversation in his last years, with caution as well as sympathy. The most reliable sources on this period of his life are the few letters of his parents which survive and his own summary of 1929; these were the foundations of the account of his early years given at the beginning of his autobiography.

The outline of his schooling between the ages of seven and seventeen is, however, clear. After a kindergarten year at the Park School for girls,[1] which was next door to the manse, he entered Glasgow Academy in September 1896. He had been preceded there by all his brothers, mostly with distinction. He remained for eight years but, as he wrote later, this was a 'most unsatisfactory' time.

I scraped through. I had no inspiration to excel. I lacked scholastic ambition. I might have done worse had it not been for periodic promptings from my father, but he could not talk the language I would have understood. How deplorable and what a waste.

The only school activity which he enjoyed was the Cadet Corps and he was a founding member of this. Yet he made no real friends and although, afterwards, he saw himself as 'more bullied than bullying', his contemporaries plainly viewed him as proud and stand-offish indicating this in their nickname for him – 'Lord Walsham'.[2] Undistinguished at school, he was difficult at home.

I had a violent temper and was disrespectful to my father and mother. I was continually threatened with a boarding school, and it was a considerable terror to me.

In the summer of 1904 this threat was fulfilled. His eldest brother, now married, had a living in Norfolk. He recommended Gresham's School at Holt and there John Reith arrived in September 1904 and there he was to remain for the next two years. He was just fifteen, 'far too old', as he wrote afterwards, 'to go to a boarding school for the first time'. Worse, he was 'the only Scotch boy in the School' and, by ill-luck, 'in the worst house'. Not unnaturally, he was lonely and unhappy, so unhappy that in his second term he ran away to his brother's vicarage ten miles off. But his unhappiness did not last.

As time went on I began to enjoy myself. In my last year I got fairly well on top of things and as a prefect would stand no nonsense from anybody.

He continued his enthusiastic military activities, became a sergeant in the Cadet Corps, shot for the school in the Ashburton Shield competition and attended the Public Schools camp. At the same time he made great progress at rugby football, winning a place in the school XV as full-back in the winter of 1905–6. His intellectual progress was equally great. Placed twenty-second in his form on entry, he was top of it by the end of his first term. Within a year he was in the Upper Sixth and before he left he won the German prize for the whole school and came near to winning the Latin Prose prize.

In spite of this excellent progress John Reith was taken away from Gresham's in July 1906, a week after his seventeenth birthday. Later in life he deplored this decision. It was an affront to his intelligence; if he had been allowed to go back for another year he would have become set on going to Oxford or Cambridge and his parents would have let him do it. He could then have developed his intellectual gifts. In his view, it was his father and his missionary brother Douglas, not yet on his way to India, who were to blame. They had concluded that he would never be a student, and they decided to put him into engineering, 'that dreadful dumping ground for indeterminates', thus stunting his intellectual development. He was unjust to them both. It was almost certainly not contempt for his intelligence that led to his engineering apprenticeship but simply lack of money. George Reith, though 'Minister of the wealthiest church in the West of Scotland' and working, as a Glasgow journalist wrote in 1899, 'in a limited and cultured section of merchant princes', was never himself financially well off. Nor could he rely on any help from his wife whose father had lost most of his money in the 1870s. In a letter he wrote to his wife, when taking their elder daughter to start her nursing training in Edinburgh in 1897, he admitted and deplored his poverty.

> Being a poor man I must share a poor man's trials and send my daughters into the world to work their way. Poor ministers! It exasperates me sometimes when I think of things but I must submit to God.

It is an example of John Reith's egotism that he never considered this fact as a possible cause of his father's conduct even though the evidence was later available to him. When he came to understand his father's financial difficulties during the war he showed extraordinary generosity, and when his father died and he saw how little money he left, he was greatly shocked. Yet he never seems to have understood that these circumstances applied in 1906 as much as in 1916 and that, accordingly, another year for him at Gresham's and three or four more at Oxford could not be arranged, whereas an engineering apprenticeship at the Hyde Park Works of the North British Locomotive Company, offered without a premium 'out of respect for father', was in the latter's eyes a great opportunity. Nor was engineering selected for him as a low-level occupation suitable to his limited abilities, as he thought, but rather the reverse. His father opposed his pleas to be allowed to enter the management side of the Hyde Park Works for fear that, without any qualifications, he would find himself in a dead end job – a railway clerk all his life. George Reith wanted his son to train as an engineer as a road to better things. His brother Douglas tried to explain this to him some years later writing in May 1924:

> Did it ever occur to you whether bluff alone, *minus* the practical experience in Hyde Park, would have been certain to secure you such a succession of remunerative jobs,[3] and all, be it noted, connected with engineering? At the worst engineering has been a peg, and a mighty useful one on which you have hung your more native and original gifts. And does it matter a damn now whether you hated it or not? Engineering was the jumping off ground for you. It is always easy to see how vastly better we would have arranged our youth than the way some blunderers arranged it for us.

In any event, insofar as his father and brother judged his qualities, they were almost certainly right to think that they would flourish more in the world of action than in the realm of speculative thought. All along John Reith was to see himself as a scholar-manqué, a potential philosopher, an imaginative thinker; but he deceived himself. His brother Douglas sought to explain this also in his remarkably perceptive letter.

> To be perfectly candid [he wrote], I do not think your main interests are really literary or deeply intellectual even though you may suppose they are. I take you to be more a man of action but one who has an instinctive sense of values. You are a man in love with good and right but whose special gift lies in the direction of embodying those ideas *indirectly* while engaged on your *direct life task* which to my idea consists in *getting things done*.

At the time that the decision to launch him into engineering was taken John Reith 'did not make any great protest'. He had 'no definite alternative' to offer; he was only certain that he was unsuited to engineering. Before starting his apprenticeship he was sent to study at the Glasgow Technical College where he attended three sessions between September 1906 and April 1908. Afterwards he described this period 'as something of a nightmare'; his interests were not engaged, except in mathematics and physics, and he was mixing for the first time with 'men from board schools' whose sole concern was with engineering technicalities which he could barely understand. Even so, he obtained second class certificates in most subjects. Later, between 1910 and 1912, he returned to the Technical College for night classes, at the end of which he obtained first class certificates with an average of over ninety per cent in his examinations, thus showing, as he himself put it, that he had begun to develop powers of study. It is clear from this that his theoretical studies were neither as unhappy nor as unsuccessful as he was inclined to claim in old age. In the same way, once he was started on his apprenticeship in April 1908, he did not find his practical work intolerable although his working conditions were hard and the hours long. In 1929 he recalled:

> The general manager was very kind to me and got me shifted from one place to another when I asked. I was very fortunate in getting through so many departments. I was very well known in the works and I think quite well liked.[4] I used to argue a great deal against socialism, and in fact generally rather asserted myself, but nobody seemed to mind.

In short, as he admitted himself, he found 'enjoyment and interest' in these years and was proud to be told that he was 'one of the best apprentices they had ever had through the shops'. It was only much later that he brooded more than momentarily on the mental stagnation of his five years as an apprentice. At the time, and by December 1911 his diary is available as a guide to his feelings, he was far from discontented with his work. In 1912 he was working in the Erecting Shop in charge of a little squad and noted that he was 'thoroughly satisfied with his experiences' there. His chief task at this time was 'fitting all the complicated pipe arrangements' when finishing off the engines that were being assembled. He was 'particularly expert' at this and exceptionally proud of his prowess, so much so that nearly fifty years later he could recall the voice of his foreman saying, 'Oh, aye, John does a very good job with the pipes.' In November of this year he moved to the Drawing Office to complete the final six months of his apprenticeship. Once again, he was well content, writing in his diary, 'I like working in the Drawing Office immensely,' and he was to stay there until February 1914, well after the six months were up. In 1947, when he wrote his autobiography, he dismissed this additional period in the Drawing Office as 'nine stupid months' but his diary shows no sign of impatience until August 1913. The truth was, as he noted in 1969, he was hoping to be offered a decent job by the North British Locomotive Company.

John Reith's unhappiness during his apprenticeship arose then not from his work but from his continued loneliness, which was aggravated by his 'fixed and settled conviction' entertained from 'early school days' that he was 'to do something considerable' in the world. Throughout his time at Technical College and in the Hyde Park Works he suffered 'a periodic longing to have a friend'. He had, of course, made one or two friends at Gresham's but they lived far from Glasgow. He stayed with one of these in Norfolk at Christmas 1910, while his parents were in Italy where his father was looking after the Scottish Church in San Remo. Here he met his host's sister and had a brief three months' flirtation with her, conducted mostly by letter. But his great desire was for a friend at home in whom he could confide. His military interests gave him an opportunity to satisfy this longing. He had joined the Glasgow University OTC when it was set up in 1908 and attended its summer camps with his company. On one of these occasions he met a medical student, George Harley, three years his junior, with whom he often walked and talked. Later he was to say of Harley, who was killed at Loos in 1915, that they had 'little in common except things military', but his diary suggests that their friendship was wider ranging than this. One of his first entries, dated December 1911, concerns George Harley; he wrote:

We seem to have pretty much the same views on nearly everything. I like him very much but he is confoundedly reserved.

Earlier in that year he had spent his summer holiday with another Gresham's friend, this time in Kent. Once again there was a mild flirtation with the sister, and although this came to nothing, he stayed with them again in 1912 and 1913. None of this fully satisfied John Reith's craving for friendship and when his brother Douglas, forced home by ill health, arrived back in Glasgow early in 1912 he was soon aware of John's state of mind and did his best to fill the need himself. At the time John Reith was not grateful.

I find him touchy and opinionative [he wrote of Douglas], and I would prefer to have some pretty girl to keep me company.

Then, just before his apprenticeship ended, he met Charlie, the man who was to replace George Harley as his friend, younger than himself but with the same interests and background. For the next nine years, until both were married, their friendship was the most important thing in his life. He could now become the older brother, as it were; he took the lead, gave the advice, guided the discussions, decided on the outings. Poor Douglas, with his vagueness and poor health, was forgotten, but he behaved in this situation as always, with unselfish understanding, and in 1922 when the friendship had ended he wrote to John:

> When Charlie came between us I never grudged him because I believed he was sent by God to fill a niche in your life at a time when I was incapable of it.

In September 1913 Charlie moved to London where his father's business had taken him. John Reith was miserable. Worse, his hopes of an excellent position with the Glasgow and South Western Railway, which had been virtually promised him, were disappointed. He was 'in an awful state' about this; his father interceded for him with 'various people' – help he ungenerously ignored in his autobiography – particularly pleading with the Reids of the North British Locomotive Company to give him a proper opening, but without success. The Reids were afraid that John Reith wanted to get on too quickly. He had other interviews but no offers. So, in February 1914, feeling he had waited enough, he took 'the decisive step of giving notice to the North British Locomotive Company'. He decided to go to London. His father was opposed to this, probably suspecting, what John Reith later admitted to himself, that 'to be in London near Charlie was what was dominating me as much as the conclusion that I had little future in Glasgow'. Once in London he used the letters of introduction he had prudently obtained with good effect and quickly received two offers of work, one in India, the other in Leeds.[5] He took neither. Charlie's father had given him another introduction, to E. W. Moir of Pearson's, and when this produced a third offer urged him to take it as 'the chance of a lifetime', even though the pay was a mere thirty shillings a week. So when the war came, six months later, John Reith was in London, working with S. Pearson and Son Ltd on the Royal Albert Dock Extension.

2. First War: finding himself, 1914–19

It was during the first war that John Reith discovered his powers and proved himself. Hitherto he had only dreamed that he was 'to do something considerable'. By the time he was thirty he knew that he could and had. There were three distinct stages in his wartime experiences. First, between August 1914 and October 1915, he was a regimental soldier, for most of the time at the front. Then, between March 1916 and August 1917 in the United States he was in charge of a newly built rifle factory near Philadelphia. And, finally, between May 1918 and April 1919, he was at Southwick in Sussex in his capacity as an engineer working on an Admiralty project building immense floating towers which were to form a hydro-electric submarine barrage in the Channel.

The story of his life as a regimental soldier is told at length in his book *Wearing Spurs* and, more briefly, in his autobiography. His enthusiasm for everything military had cooled in the last years of his apprenticeship. He had left the OTC and accepted a Territorial commission in the 5th Scottish Rifles early in 1911. He had not enjoyed this and when, early in 1914, he moved to London he had even written to resign his commission. But his letter was not acknowledged; it had been mislaid or not delivered, so in August 1914 he was automatically mobilized with his old battalion. He was to remain on active service until he was severely wounded in the cheek and jaw in October 1915. At first he was kept in Scotland on home defence duties; then early in November 1914 his battalion was sent to France where he remained, except for a short period of leave in February, until July 1915. Severe dysentery, occasioned by drinking polluted water, then sent him home for six weeks, but late in September he returned to France. By now he had transferred to the Royal Engineers. Sent up the line immediately, he was involved in the battle of Loos and, on 7 October when accompanying his commanding officer on an inspection of damage to the front trenches, was shot by a sniper. He was quickly moved back through a casualty clearing station to hospital in Wimereux, where the doctor warned him he 'wouldn't have any more war'. Next day he was moved again; this time to London. Although severely wounded, he made a rapid recovery. Less than ten days after he was shot, his London doctor, who had spoken first of the need for stitches and a silver plate, told him that his wound was 'healing extraordinarily well on its own'. When he was released from hospital early in November he noted, 'I have recovered in a third of the time they expected.' Even so, there was no question of an early return to the front.

In his twelve months of active service John Reith had revealed the traits and the talents which were at once to distinguish and to frustrate his public life for the next fifty years. His friends who read *Wearing Spurs* in 1937 saw this and warned him against publication. F. A. Iremonger told him that he had written 'the most complete personal revelation since the confessions of Augustine', and Warren Fisher said that it was not 'seemly to bare his soul in public'. For his account does not only illustrate his virtues – his executive capacity, his independence of mind, his strength of will and his gift for inspiring leadership – it also epitomizes his weaknesses, his readiness to quarrel with authority when in his view it rested on 'red-tape' and habit, his obstinate adherence to personal grudges, his inability to let bygones be bygones and his rigid refusal to compromise when he felt principle was involved. Here was what he later called 'the curse of temperament', which was to afflict him in every task he attempted throughout his active life just as much as his virtues were to help him. He could diagnose his temperament as 'the key of failure' but he could not control it.

His power to organize and what his brother Douglas called 'his special gift of getting things done' quickly showed themselves in his fulfilment of his duties as Transport Officer. From the start he was remarkably independent in his attitude and he admitted in a gloss of 1931 on his war diary for September 1914, 'I did all sorts of things I had no right to and I suppose HQ just resolved to put up with it.' Equally, he exercised a remarkable personal influence on the sixty or so men in his immediate command, commenting under the same month, 'I treated them as very few officers would or could – discipline very strict but every sort of privilege.' Six months later, at Easter 1915, he noted in his diary:

> After a short service the Minister admitted twenty-two of my men into the Church of Christ, giving them the right hand of fellowship. It was most impressive and I was profoundly grateful that I had been able to influence so many.

But while his men acknowledged his inspiring leadership and his efficiency impressed brigade headquarters, his battalion commander and adjutant found him hard to control. He had no patience with the 'usual channels' or the 'proper way' of doing things. He outraged his adjutant's conventional assumptions and in so doing earned his vigilant animosity. The outcome was his removal from his prized position as

Transport Officer in April 1915; he had short-circuited the formal channels of responsibility once too often. His answer was to apply for transfer to the Royal Engineers, for which his peacetime training equipped him well. But this took time to go through and, in the meanwhile, he pursued a remorseless vendetta against his commanding officer and adjutant alike. He had told his father even before he had been relieved as Transport Officer and sent back to company duty:

> If we had a *man* for a Colonel, the Adjutant would never be allowed to treat officers and men as he does. It is absolutely outrageous and I may say that everyone would rejoice immensely if a stray bullet picked him off. As for the Colonel, he is more despised than anything else . . . For *inefficiency, stupidity* and *bullying* we have found no equal anywhere in civil or military life to the Adjutant. *Can nothing be done for us?*

John Reith's resentment on this occasion, as on most others, had some solid cause. His second-in-command, in an unguarded moment, called the Adjutant 'the vilest blackguard on God's earth'. His father wrote privately to the Colonel to protest when he was removed as Transport Officer. So there were rational grounds for criticism acknowledged by others. But John Reith's violent and uncontrolled expression of this criticism was unbalanced in its intensity. His new company commander did not like it and urged him to stop it. His Transport sergeant, who was the nearest to being a close friend at the front, appears to have made much the same plea. Yet even after a talk of an hour and a half with him John Reith noted in his diary:

> *4 June 1915* If I could convince myself that the strongest and most Christian thing would be to forgive the blasted CO and Adjutant and not to continue to cherish such feelings of intense hatred, I would bring myself to it. But I cannot so convince myself.

He consulted his father on this who added his sympathetic counsel in the same direction, writing in July:

> If you will be advised by me you will cease to fulminate where you are against the Colonel and Adjutant. I don't mind your letting your soul out to me but it would be wiser, and more gentlemanly in truth, to be quiet among your comrades. Let them speak but be you silent. Do your duty and bear slights. There are 'Adjutants' everywhere and we have to put up with them. The discipline is good for ourselves to teach us how to bear and say nothing.

None of this had any effect. Eight months later, when he was on embarkation leave in Glasgow before setting out for America, he gave evidence of this. His diary records the incident:

16 February 1916 I was standing talking to Robert [his brother] in Union Street when I saw the gallant Colonel approaching. I had time to collect myself: one of the biggest exercises of will I have ever put through. He saw me some way off – smiled broadly and changed his course to speak to me. I just stared at him and gave no recognition at all. The smile faded from his face and blank bewilderment took its place as he changed his course again and passed.

When he told this story in *Wearing Spurs* John Reith admitted that it was 'a silly thing to do and wrong every way'. But, sadly, it illustrates an aspect of his character which he was never to change. In part, of course, his intense, almost frenzied, feelings of this year of active service reflect the tensions of trench warfare. In part, also, they reflect his renewed sense of loneliness. He missed his friend Charlie and found no substitute among his fellow officers. He explained this in a letter to his father at the end of November 1914:

I have never in my life been so much in need of a friend as now. Charlie is my only real friend. He is one in a million and it would make all the difference in the world if he were here. It is very, very lonely for me here. I can't tell you how much I feel this. I am absolutely 'alone'. Do you know what I mean?

His father answered sympathetically and tried to ease his loneliness; he praised Charlie and added, 'I have no doubt you have both helped one another.' Charlie, for his part, loyally sustained his friend; they exchanged letters regularly, John writing sixty and receiving almost as many between his mobilization and his departure for America. But John Reith remained 'alone' and at the same time intensely dependent on this one friendship.

John Reith's service in America in 1916–17 demonstrated to others, as well as to himself, how effectively he could work in a position of responsibility requiring the capacity to organize and to manage large numbers of men. It was no longer to be a matter of a Territorial subaltern being in charge of 60 men; he now had a department of 200 under him, rising to 1500 before he left, working in and with a factory employing 13,000. Later in life he was aware of his remarkable success in carrying this burden without any comparable previous experience to help him, and in February 1957, in a mood of forty years on, he wrote in his diary, 'I have done nothing at any age compared to what I did then.' His talents flowered while his temperamental weaknesses were momentarily not apparent. He had no quarrels with authority, except in his first few weeks, and these were impersonal with distant departments in London and not with men on the spot. Even his sense of being 'alone' was temporarily abated by the numerous friendships he made in his work and, more important, within the community where he settled. As he wrote in his autobiography, 'it was as happy a time as I have known'.

The opportunity for him to go to America arose by chance and he seized it. Two days before he was wounded he had written to his old employer at Pearson's, E. W. Moir, giving an account of his first independent civil engineering work in the army – the repair of a bridge over the La Bassée Canal which had been destroyed by shell-fire. It was a venial boast from one who had been taken on in February 1914 'to see what he could do'. Moir was intrigued and wrote kindly in reply; but, naturally, he addressed his letter to the front whence it followed John Reith back, eventually reaching him in hospital in London. He acknowledged it and explained where he was and what had happened to him. Next day, 'Mrs Moir came sailing in.' He had met her in July 1914 and been invited then to her house, which he had thought 'a great score', but his mobilization had intervened before he could go. Now, as a wounded officer, Mrs Moir paid him flattering attention, sending him flowers, taking him for drives and entertaining him at her home. Nor was this all; E. W. Moir himself was interested and ready to talk. At the end of October he remarked over the family lunch table that Lloyd George had asked him to go to America to organize munitions supplies. John Reith pricked up his ears . . . 'I thought I might come in on this and had some talk with him.' For more than two weeks nothing transpired. He had now been discharged from hospital, subject only to medical examination after three months. As he needed work, he pursued an alternative opening, drawn to his attention by some of his old colleagues at the Albert Dock. This was a project of Pearson's to build a huge munitions area at Gretna. Then, on 15 November 1915, came 'a letter from Moir. There is quite a chance of my going to America.' He was overjoyed and then cast down, noting on 24 November:

America still unsettled. I suppose I shall go to Gretna, not being the least keen on this. I want to go back to the Front, but America is not a thing to be missed.

So Gretna it was at £350 a year – 'supposed to be equivalent of a RE lieutenant's pay'. But Moir had not given up. In January 1916 he wired from New York asking Ernest Pearson to release Reith for 'rifle inspection'. To John Reith's great disgust Pearson at first said no, then relented and finally agreed that, if the War Office approved, he could go. He did not dally. Early in February he went to London 'to hunt up my American job'. In two days he had it all arranged; passage, pay ('£500 p.a. plus £730 extra American allowance') and high level briefing in the Ministry of Munitions including 'two interviews with G. M. Booth, Lloyd George's superman'. Characteristically he had less time for contacts on a lower level. He only arranged to visit the small arms factory at Enfield when the postponement of his ship's departure gave him an unexpected extra four days. Even then he 'never got there'; he had taken the wrong train.

He arrived in New York in the first week of March 1916. Moir told him there that his task was to supervise the inspection of rifles which were to be manufactured at the newly built Remington works at Eddystone, near Philadelphia. The British government had ordered two million such rifles. Unfortunately, Moir had neither cleared John Reith's appointment with the Army Inspection Department in London nor with that department's representative in America, a Major Smyth-Piggott, based at New Haven. As a result, for nearly six weeks he could not take over at Eddystone. From the start, however, Smyth-Piggott was friendly and did his utmost to secure Reith's confirmation. In his autobiography John Reith drew a picture of initial hostility from Smyth-Piggott which was gradually modified. His diary does not support him, recording that when they met in New Haven, two days after he had landed, 'S-P received me very kindly indeed.' Be that as it may, the authorities in London were not to be easily won over. For a time, early in April, it even looked as if Reith would have to return to England. But then Smyth-Piggott was struck down by acute appendicitis and Reith was asked to take charge temporarily at the Remington works until a general officer, on his way from England, could arrive and adjudicate in his case. London now gave way; on 14 April John Reith was confirmed in his appointment. The next day, at the moment of their triumph, his new friend Smyth-Piggott died. He wrote in his diary: 'It was a tremendous relief that the business had gone through, but I was very upset at S-P's death.'

In less than twelve months the production of rifles at the Remington works rose from 50 in April 1916 to 84,500 in February 1917 – the equivalent of over 3800 a day for the twenty-two working days of that month. Such mass production inevitably meant falling below the peacetime standards of accuracy still being demanded in London and Enfield. For a month or two rejections were as high as seventy-five per cent of production. In June 1916 changes were made in the design and rejections were reduced, but only to between thirty per cent and forty per cent. The continued rejection of such a high proportion of their output naturally aggravated the manufacturing company. In mid-October this produced a crisis; the company suspended deliveries altogether. John Reith kept his head, protested vigorously, on the one hand, to general manager and company president, while, on the other hand, urging common sense on the Army Inspection Department and its representatives in America. His wise intercession was successful. The company resumed deliveries on 8 November and a week later the British government took over all expenses arising from its rejections. In March 1917 the contract was reduced from two million to 600,000, a foreseeable target, and the next month, when America entered the war, it was a natural development that the US government should give notice of its intention to take over the whole of the factory's production for itself. In May, John Reith heard that his work was to be taken over by the US Ordnance and in July he met the officers who were to replace him. He prepared to return to England beginning with a massive clearing-out of his files, a process he was to follow at the end of every job he completed in life. He noted in his diary:

This [destruction] is quite contrary to the usual government procedure, but I am not going to be party to the absurdity of sending crate upon crate home.

Early in August he handed over to his American successors and sailed from New York at the end of the month. He landed in Liverpool on 3 September. He had done some remarkable work.

It was not simply in the practical sphere of factory organization and administration that John Reith proved himself. America also afforded him opportunities to exercise his powers of moral leadership. The issues of the war and the possibility of American participation in it dominated public thinking in the area around Philadelphia. In course of time he was invited to speak on these issues at those peculiar social gatherings which are a feature of American culture to this day – Rotary clubs and business associations, church banquets and Scottish societies, gatherings of university alumni and of ex-service men. Naturally, he was not invited immediately. In his first nine months he appears to have spoken only twice, but by February 1917, when he had been in America for a year, he was receiving more invitations than he could possibly fulfil. He refused most of these – as many as thirty in March and April alone; he was resolved not to become a professional speaker. As he explained to his father, 'it is not what I came here to do'. Nevertheless, in the first seven months of 1917 he spoke fifteen or sixteen times, substantially more than he afterwards claimed but still never more than three times a month. His message was simple. Fight on; no negotiated peace; no talk of reconciliation or fellowship 'as long as there is desolation in the land, piracy on the high seas and flying murder in the air'. Wherever he spoke, to select clubs or to large dinners or, after the American entry into the war, to very large gatherings of soldiers in training, he had immense success. After his first speech, in June 1916, he told his father:

> When I sat down there was some scene . . . They all came crowding on to the little platform to shake hands, dozens of them. I have never had such a time.

Nine months later, after speaking to the Princeton Club of Philadelphia, the situation was much the same:

> There were about two hundred there. At the end it was a positive ovation, people standing up and shouting and cheering.

The rhetoric which produced these excitable scenes has a strange flavour today, but it was certainly effective then. When he returned to England he was delighted to read 'a reference to my work in USA in *The Times*, a letter from the editor of the *Public Ledger* [of Philadelphia]. It said my speeches had got the public ear and assisted in moulding pro-Ally sympathy.'

John Reith's stay in America also saw the completion of his growing up. He was aware himself that he had been slow to mature and had admitted this to his father when he wrote from the front, 'I was very young for my years [as an apprentice] and I didn't grow up till about three years ago.' His bitter struggle at the time of this letter with his colonel and adjutant showed that this process still had some way to go and America helped him in this direction. Early in his stay he greatly impressed the millionaire president of the Remington company, S. M. Vauclain, and through him he made the acquaintance of other business leaders who were similarly impressed. He stayed in their houses, made himself agreeable to their daughters, and, helped by what he described as his 'very conservative views on Labour questions, Trades Unions and the like', gained their complete confidence. They approved a young man who could summarily dismiss thirty-four men who had petitioned for an increase in pay. He described the scene to his father in a letter of February 1917, 'I went down personally and they were out of the gate in a minute and a half.' At the same time that he learned to move easily among the rich and powerful of Philadelphia, he gained confidence and serenity from his daily life in the quiet middle-class suburb of Swarthmore where he was quickly integrated into the community. There he made many new friends while in no way losing touch with Charlie, to whom he wrote over two hundred letters while he was away and received as many back. Thus by the end of 1917 John Reith returned home happy, relaxed and confident – ready to move on to greater things.

For nine months following his return from America John Reith was to meet frustration and disappointment in his search for responsible work within the Army. He hoped at first that he would be able to 'get straight back to France – preferably in railroad work', but he could not arrange this. Instead, he was posted and cross-posted within the Royal Engineers. When, eventually, he did get attached to the Railway Operating Division and was on the point of leaving for France, another posting sent him back to his starting point. Small wonder that he noted in his diary in commenting on all this at the end of October 1917, 'it is really childish'. Then it seemed as if his luck had returned; he was sent to a site in Yorkshire where an aerodrome was being built. Here he 'fairly made things bustle' and was well content. Unfortunately, his commanding officer, 'a dead man and scared of his own shadow', was not. By the middle of January 1918 John Reith had been ordered to hand over to his deputy on the aerodrome site and to return to another RE depot. Here he was, once again, 'infuriated all round with the jealousies, incompetencies and absurdities' of a home base at a critical time in the war. He was contemptuous of his immediate superiors and even when he got an interview with his corps commander he found him to be 'an absolute dud – the Regular type at its worst, the sort which is responsible for so much bungling and waste and a good example of why we are doing so badly in the war'. So he was constantly on the look-out for more active work and in March he heard of an engineering project being managed for the Admiralty by the Royal Marine Engineers. He dashed to London to find out more details, taking care to say nothing of this to his superiors. The next month he

R.D.—C

was offered a transfer to the RME, accepted at once and in the middle of May 1918 arrived at Southwick, the site of this project. In his autobiography John Reith wrote of his 'frosty reception' here at the hands of the colonel in command. But, as with his tale of initial hostility in America, his diary does not sustain the story. The extent of the colonel's hostility was minimal; he only expressed a doubt at their first interview as to whether Reith could be 'much help', but readily accepted the advice of several other senior officers who were 'very friendly' from the start, to let him try. Certainly, John Reith was very soon on excellent terms with his colonel. He quickly proved himself on the job and by the end of August was working with immense zest, controlling 1800 men and directing the construction of eight great floating towers. He was in fact a great deal more than just 'relatively content', as he later alleged, noting in his diary for October 1918, 'this is one of the most interesting and exciting times of my life'.

The background to this satisfaction and contentment in his work was that it was also a time of great happiness in his private life. In the first place he was now in close sympathy with his parents. He had drawn steadily closer to his father throughout the war. While still at the front he had opened his heart in his letters home about his hopes of a political career. At first his father had discouraged him but in the light of his son's success in America he had changed his mind. By February 1918 he had withdrawn his objections. At the same time John Reith's selfless concern to look after his parents touched their hearts. He had been remarkably generous to them while he was in America. From concern for his feelings, his mother had not told him of his father's serious operation in July 1916 until it was safely over. But as soon as he knew of it he sent money to help with the expenses of convalescence; and when he found himself unable to get home for his father's jubilee at the College Church later that year, owing to the crisis at the Remington factory, he made every effort to bring his parents over to America. That these efforts came to nothing was because his parents were unwilling to go. When he did get back to England, he continued to help in the same spirit, improving the facilities of the manse and paying for his parents to rest at Exmouth. Then in July 1918 he brought them to stay near his work in Sussex. Here they quickly got to know his fellow officers and made themselves a centre of happy sociability and cultivated discussion. They loved it; as his father wrote on his return to Glasgow:

It was a very happy time as well as full of interest to us both. You were so kind and thoughtful in every possible way and your friends made themselves as agreeable to us as it was possible to be. Need I say how grateful we both are to you for your immense goodness which only God can repay.

Besides the happiness which came from this closeness to his parents – his father wrote that his 'affection was our great comfort' – John Reith was also overjoyed in these months to have the company of his great friend Charlie. While he had been in America, Charlie had been commissioned in the Royal Engineers. John Reith's hope on his return was that they could work together, and in the autumn of 1918 he was able to arrange this. So now he had exciting work, able and congenial colleagues, and the company of his one intimate friend whom he found 'ever ready to discuss serious things' and whose friendship he felt 'touched high levels of spirituality'. It was an added joy that his father now fully approved and accepted their friendship – 'Give my best wishes to Prince Charlie,' he wrote at Christmas 1918, adding in the context of his son's extravagant generosity, 'and tell him to take good care of his money and yours.'

Finally, this was a time of great personal happiness for John Reith because he was in love. He had first seen Muriel Odhams within a fortnight of his arrival at Southwick.

26 May 1918 I went to evening service in Kingston Church. I was shown into a box pew in which there were already other people. One was a girl in uniform. I liked the look of her and wondered who and what she was.

He soon found out. She was the driver of his commanding officer's official car. Before long he was talking with her. Then, while his parents were staying, the colonel let him use his car and with the car he saw more of its driver. He liked her and he thought 'she rather likes me'. When his parents left, however, he had less occasion to see her. Towards the end of September 1918 he was complaining in his diary, 'I have not seen Miss Odhams for exactly a month.' He put this to rights and by the end of the month 'Miss Odhams' had become 'Muriel'. From now on they met regularly. Then, to his horror, he discovered that a fellow officer was equally smitten. He felt he must not stand in his way and in January 1919 confided in his diary, 'Miss Odhams is an awfully fine girl and should make an excellent wife for T.' Happily, he could not maintain this noble posture. He became jealous and renewed his suit. He wrote her 'a little piece of verse'; she gave him her photograph and told him of her fiancé who had been killed in France; most significant of all, he consulted his father, in very general terms, about marriage. His father answered with an evangelical earnestness, begging him to ask himself:

> Will she [the girl you are attached to] help me to love and serve my Saviour more than I do? Shall we go hand in hand in the things that are of profoundest import?

So in February John Reith told his friend T. that he would no longer hold back from courting Muriel. He now saw her every day. By mid-March he could write in his diary:

> My heart is just full of the happiness which will be mine if the way can be opened up for Muriel and myself.

Nevertheless he held back from getting engaged. The war had now ended and John Reith had quickly lost interest in the work at South-wick which he had already resolved to leave. He was worried about his future and he did not want to commit himself to marriage until he had obtained secure employment. Further, although Muriel and Charlie were friendly, he feared lest by winning the one he would lose the other. So for the moment he dithered; he bought an engagement ring but would not ask Muriel to marry him. Charlie urged him forward; so too did the local parson whom he consulted. Then he wrote to his parents for their guidance. His mother was, at first, much distressed; she would 'lose her boy'. She knew, what John Reith was not to admit to himself for several months, that her husband was sinking and she feared to be without both husband and son. Her reaction made John 'very unhappy'; he was more uncertain than before. Fortunately, his father's saintly character overcame his mother's fears. Together they sent their son a telegram – 'Love and blessings to you both. Heartily happy in your happiness.' The next day, 5 April 1919, John Reith offered marriage to Muriel Odhams and was accepted. For the following fifty years his diary was filled with anniversaries, birthdays and death-days, the day he was wounded in one war and the day he was dismissed from the government in another war, the day his parents were married and the day he was married, but among all these his engagement day held pride of place. It was a turning-point in his life and he knew it.

3. In Search of a Career, 1919-22

John Reith's engagement lasted just over two years. He was not married until 14 July 1921. This long delay arose in large part because he did not wish to marry until he had settled employment. He was looking for an opening in life which would allow him to realize his high ambition for service and he did not find it. He left Southwick in April 1919 but he was not demobilized until the end of August. Then for just over seven months he worked in the Ministry of Munitions where in his own judgement (expressed when summarizing his diary in 1931) he did 'remarkable work for the country'. But his work there, the running down of war contracts, in its nature could not be lasting and although he was offered the opportunity of an established post, he did not believe that his call was to the civil service. So at the end of March 1920 he agreed to start in May as general manager of a factory at Coatbridge which was controlled by William Beardmore and Company. He did not regard this as his long-awaited opening any more than he had the Ministry of Munitions. He accepted it because 'nothing else had turned up' or, to be more precise, because his hopes of other openings at home had fallen through. In fact he had had one firm offer of an engineering post abroad in Bombay at a salary of £2500 a year. When this possibility was first raised in October 1919 his father, in his last two letters before he died, urged him to take it as a 'big opportunity'. It would enable him to marry at once. But the offer was not made firmly until March 1920. In spite of its attractions John Reith turned it down in favour of Coatbridge. His reason was characteristic and was to recur in other situations throughout his life. If he could have the directing position he would take it, but he 'did not wish to be second'. Thus he came to Coatbridge still looking for his big opportunity, still waiting his call. In the meantime he would do his best at the work he had taken on even though, as he noted just before starting at Coatbridge, 'this factory work doesn't interest me greatly.' At least it had brought him back to Scotland, where he could be near his widowed mother and where he could look for a house to set up home with Muriel.

When John Reith took over at Coatbridge he found things in 'a ghastly state'. There was, he noted:

> no sort of coordination in the factory; oil engines, steam engines, pumps, motor-cars all were running quite independently and many things were urgently in need of attention.

It was a great shock because, as he complained, 'no one gave me any idea of this'. He met this challenge with two answers which he was to give consistently in the future when faced with comparable situations. First, he improved organization. Almost immediately he arranged for 'a complete survey of the works from the point of view of planning' to be conducted by an outside expert. The outcome of this was that in six months he was able to send Sir William Beardmore (soon to become Lord Invernairn) 'a report on the whole position at Coatbridge'. Secondly, he raised morale; he found the spirit among the work force low and he determined to raise it. To help himself do this he read systematically about psychology with particular reference to industrial efficiency. At the same time he 'lined up discipline for works and offices'. Shop stewards were forbidden to call meetings in working hours or to leave their work without their foremen's permission, and their meetings with the management – that is with John Reith himself – were to be by appointment only. Time-clocks were introduced and workmen were to clock in or be dismissed; but the same rule was applied to the office staff who were also expected to stay on Saturdays until their work was done. With tighter discipline on the one hand there went improvement of amenities on the other. Clubs were formed, regular lectures and dances arranged, football matches and canteen concerts organized so that by October 1920 he felt there was 'a very good spirit being developed'. This process continued and in January 1921 he noted with pride:

> things in the social way are really very satisfactory in the Works and I think I have effected a great change since I came.

Nor did he limit his efforts to changes within the factory. In October 1920 he had the Provost and Town Clerk of Coatbridge entertained 'with ulterior motives, namely twenty of the new council houses for our staff'.

Most of the workmen accepted the new regime happily. Less than six months after taking over John Reith was even able to win the consent of his shop stewards and of their district Trade Union secretary to the dismissal of their 'Bolshevist' convener. This unfortunate creature, who seems to have been more of a wind-bag than a revolutionary, was no match for the new general manager. Inside three weeks he had been summoned to the office, where he had been made to take his hat off, isolated from his colleagues and dismissed. He left without making trouble, solacing himself only with 'a farewell speech after the whistle blew'. Although this has an authoritarian touch which is not in keeping with the spirit of the age today, it was acceptable and successful then, more particularly because John Reith never acted from principles of mere repression. His purpose was constructive. As soon as the agitator had been removed, he accepted the shop stewards' choice of a new convener and immediately appointed a labour supervisor to work with him in the factory. He sought the efficient co-operation of management and labour. When, almost a year later, he left the factory for his wedding in Sussex, he was given a royal send-off:

> The Works were decorated in tremendous style, great lines of flags with streamers. I had to walk through every part of the factory. The whistle went at 4.45 and everybody assembled below the main office steps. The Convener of Shop Stewards made a speech which any general manager would have been proud to hear. Then the presentation was made and there was a great scene afterwards with the car being drawn down to the gate by the men, others being lined up on each side, cheering.

It was a remarkable achievement to have attained such excellent labour relations at a time of widespread labour troubles in the country and it gave John Reith a reputation outside Scotland, as he was to learn, to his immense gratification, when he visited Gresham's School in November 1921 and heard the headmaster from the pulpit draw attention to his success in establishing good relations with his workmen.

Unfortunately for John Reith all his good work at Coatbridge was wasted by the inefficient management of the parent company. The London office failed to produce orders to occupy the reorganized and revitalized factory. As John Reith became aware of this situation he began to feel restless and frustrated. His diary reveals this state of mind building up throughout 1921. In February he noted:

> I am not really getting enough to do in the Works and feel that it is a horrid prostitution of my abilities to be going there every day.

Then, in April, he recorded that he was 'very bored in the factory', repeating this in August and adding, 'I want to get back to London and if I cannot do that I should much rather be in Glasgow.' It was an added aggravation that throughout 1921 he was forced to dismiss 'various members of the staff to reduce costs'; and it was little comfort in this painful predicament to be told by his shop stewards that he had 'done more for the men at the Works than any manager for thirty years'.

By November the writing was on the wall that the factory could hardly continue in production:

> *14 November 1921* Financial meeting. Most awful revelations have come to light about the result of past inefficiency in management as well as over-ordering to meet London office demands.

Two months later closure was being openly discussed:

> *20 January 1922* Worked all night to get the balance sheet out. There is a meeting with Lord Invernairn on Tuesday [24th] to discuss closing down at Coatbridge. We have been abominably let down. The loss is £82,000, including £9800 London Office and £9756 Head Office. What good do we get from either?

He was confident that in the adverse trading conditions of 1921 he had done well to limit the true loss at Coatbridge to a finally agreed figure of £49,000. But there were no orders for the future to put this right and in February 1922 he was informed that Head Office had decided to close down the oil engine department at Coatbridge. It was clear to him that he was no longer wanted and that he should go, even though he was technically guarded by his contract. He confided furiously to his diary:

> It is really a filthy firm to have any connection with. It has been an awful job to get accounts paid for a year past – little people being kept out of their money for months. If I were only on a month's contract they wouldn't have had the slightest compunction in putting me out. They would give a general manager no more consideration than an unsatisfactory and drunken foreman. I left the Head Office feeling lighter and happier than for over a year. I shall soon be quit of these skunks.

He stood by this resolve and on 1 March 1922 he wrote giving six months' notice according to his contract. This assured him of his salary for that period, but it was agreed that he should leave the factory at the end of the month.

> What a relief [he wrote on the day he left], to be clear of them. I am setting out on a new quest. I should never have left London.

John Reith's reasons for leaving London, as we have seen, had been largely personal. He wanted to be near his mother; he wanted to be in a position to find a home and to get married; and he wanted to keep his friend Charlie working with him. He had fulfilled all three of these aims during his two years at Coatbridge but none wholly in the manner he had anticipated. He had certainly been near his mother and had seen more of her than at any time since leaving the manse in February 1914. In so doing, however, he had awakened the latent jealousy of his sister, Jean, who had resented him while he was young as much as he had come to resent her. After his father died, his mother set up home with Jean and refused John's suggestion that, when he had found his home, she should live with him and Muriel. She was aware that at this time Jean was passing through a period of stress and unhappiness and she felt her daughter needed her more than her son. Like Shaw's Candida, she gave herself to the weaker of the two. John Reith did not appreciate this implicit compliment. In his eyes his sister was selfishly imposing her will on their mother and, further, was making every effort to exclude him from her company. He saw Jean both as a barrier to his affection and as a costly incubus, since he gave generously towards his mother's living expenses. His mother tried to persuade him otherwise and begged him to be kinder towards Jean so that on one such occasion he noted crossly in his diary, 'all through life I have been badgered to say I am sorry to Jean'. Thus by settling and working in Scotland he had come nearer to his mother in terms of physical distance but he had not achieved that exclusive spiritual closeness for which he had hoped.

Just as his hopes in respect of his mother were disappointed, so too were his plans for early marriage. It had probably been an element in his mother's decision to settle with her daughter Jean, that she wished to remove herself as a possible barrier to this; John Reith certainly went to Coatbridge with early marriage in mind and he immediately set about house-hunting. In July 1920, two months after he started at Coatbridge, Muriel had come north on a visit and together they had found a house near Dunblane which they 'liked tremendously'. It had 'a magnificent view and was very cosy'. They decided to buy it and early in October John noted, 'Dunardoch is now mine; we like it awfully.' But at this very moment when he could at last envisage marriage he became aware, as we have seen, that all was not well with the future of the Coatbridge factory. He felt bound to postpone his wedding by six months. It was a decision which nearly robbed him of Muriel altogether. Their engagement had now lasted eighteen months and had been under considerable strain earlier in the year when he had decided to take the position of general manager at Coatbridge instead of staying in the civil service. Muriel had felt that this was needlessly postponing their marriage. So in April, before he set out for Scotland,

John Reith had spent a day of explanation with her. His diary account of this was characteristically detached:

> To Brighton, Friday midday. Met by Muriel. We were a bit strained with each other and it was an unusual sort of time and trying. After tea we went to the West Pier where we sat for two and a half hours. It was raining all the time and very cold. The discussion was rather bitter at times on her part and perhaps callous on mine. I told her I had often said that I would be unsettled with an engagement when I was not settled otherwise, respecting a job, house etc., and I had also said that I would not be likely to act in what was the usual way for a *fiancé* but that that was no indication whatever of my feelings. I reminded her that she had often said that I was differently constituted from other people and that we had talked about this before and she had said she would not be distrustful again, but it had always come round that she was. She asked me if I wanted to break off the engagement. I said I did not wish to do so, but what would bring it about would be a distrustful attitude on her part. I was loving her very much and felt most awfully sorry for the condition things were in, and it all seemed quite unnecessary. Things seemed to finish off satisfactorily and she to be happy again. In the station I said I would like to kiss her, but of course she said 'Oh no, not in the station.' She went back to Southwick and I to Town.

Now, six months after this, Muriel again asked if John wanted to break off their engagement. He was horrified; he blamed Muriel's parents for making her feel uncertain. She was 'under the yoke of parental domination' and 'would never be happy or believing' as long as she remained so. She must develop self-reliance. He wrote; he met her in London; and in the New Year of 1921 he visited her at home in Southwick where, he noted with relief, he had been able once more to reassure her. From then on the preparations for their wedding progressed without a rub; 'correspondence with M. about banns and furnishing' was his brisk note in May, and in July they were married. They settled in their new home at the end of that month, after a short honeymoon in Skye. Once again John Reith had fulfilled one of his aims in coming to Scotland in that he had found a home and he had married, but only after painful delay and with the growing prospect, because of the situation at Coatbridge, that he would soon need to find another job.

The final disappointment of John Reith's two years at Coatbridge was the ending of his long friendship with Charlie. Once again, as with his mother and his marriage, things did not turn out wholly as he expected. When he left Southwick in April 1919 he left Charlie working there. Their friendship was as strong as it had ever been and John Reith's engagement to Muriel in no way changed it. Charlie, by remaining at Southwick which was Muriel's home, was able to look after her for his friend. In July John Reith visited Southwick on the occasion of his thirtieth birthday; he noted in his diary:

> Today was called a Peace Holiday. With Muriel and we had an affectionate time. A serious talk with Charlie about our spiritual state. My 30th birthday. C. gave me a beautiful Bible. I hope to have it by me for the rest of my life. All wisdom centres there, all comfort, all hope.

Very shortly after this John Reith had been demobilized and had started work in the Ministry of Munitions. He determined at once to get Charlie, who was also due to be demobilized, to join him there. His father, now near to death, warned him gently against doing too much for Charlie, writing on 10 October 1919:

> You won't run the risk of shoving Charlie in over some man displaced. That would lead to trouble. Charlie can fend for himself.

The warning was unheeded and Charlie began work later that month. It is, however, important to recognize that Charlie was talented and able. He could indeed stand on his own feet. Whatever job came his way through John Reith's friendship he did well. It is unlikely that John Reith would have remained his friend for long if he had not had the quickness of mind to go at Reith's pace. Certainly, Charlie proved himself at the Ministry of Munitions, and on leaving there John Reith was able to recommend him for the OBE, which he was awarded twelve months later. As he noted in his diary when the news came through, 'an OBE is a poor thing but it is quite good to get it at his age'.

It was not difficult, then, for John Reith on moving to Coatbridge to make an opening there for Charlie. Charlie was a good man to employ on his record of achievement. So in August 1920 Charlie started work at Coatbridge. Once again his natural ability proved John Reith's judgement to be correct. He did so well that in less than a year the head office 'were anxious for him to go to China under the joint auspices of Beardmore and Jardine Matheson'. John Reith was gratified that his friend should have made so favourable an impression. But although, while working together at Coatbridge, the two friends continued in their accustomed intimacy, there were signs in 1921 that their friendship would need to take account of new developments if it was to endure. Not only was John Reith himself about to get married, but Charlie in his turn had met his future wife in April 1921 and become engaged to her three months later. Furthermore, Charlie, now nearly twenty-five, was old enough to want their friendship to be more on a basis of equality. Hitherto, as we have seen, John Reith had always taken the lead and dominated his young friend; in the spring of 1921 he even organized Charlie's courtship, contriving opportunities for him to see his future wife, warning her of the possibility that he might be swept away to China and noting when these activities led to their swift engagement, 'the whole credit for this is with me'. In the months that followed their engagement it was natural for Charlie and his fiancée to find this dependent status unacceptable. John Reith acknowledged this to himself, writing in his diary a week before his own marriage: 'I cannot see how our friendship is to continue with things as they are now shaping.' But while he could see this, he could not bring himself to let go of his friend even when he became aware that his concern for Charlie and for Charlie's affairs distressed Muriel, who told him towards the end of 1921 that she 'could be happy when she was stupid enough to forget about Charlie'. He was the victim, and not for the last time, of his peculiar temperament. He acknowledged that his first loyalty was then, and for the rest of his life, to Muriel; this alone must alter his friendship with Charlie. Yet he could not accept such an adjustment calmly.

In any event, setting aside John's marriage and his own engagement, Charlie was, as we have seen, outgrowing the dominating nature of the friendship which John Reith had given him. John's diary reveals this in relation to their work:

> *10 February 1922* Charlie for supper. Sat and talked about business. He has become infernally dogmatic. I can't teach him anything these days. He seems to resent any suggestion from me. But I am as fond of him as ever.

The next month Charlie married, John organizing him to the last and supervising the seating in the church. Then, three weeks later, Charlie wrote him a letter which John Reith noted 'broke off our friendship finally'. The abrupt and unfeeling nature of this break did Charlie little credit. It was an act of weakness, not strength. Yet John's own inflexibility had left his friend little choice. As ever with John Reith, who was temperamentally incapable of compromise, it was 'all or nothing'. In March 1922 Charlie chose nothing. To the outside eye each was to blame – John for making any adjustment of their friendship difficult, Charlie for making the break unnecessarily wounding. Perhaps John Reith made the fairest comment when he summarized his diary for these months in 1931: what a silly blasted business it all was.

Thus by the end of March 1922 John Reith had lost his job and his friend. The second caused him much greater concern than the first. We have seen that he had never regarded his position at Coatbridge as a permanency and when he lost it, so far from regretting this, he looked forward to renewing the search for his life's work. He had no immediate financial worries as the terms of his contract gave him six months' salary. He celebrated this freedom from financial constraint in May 1922 by taking Muriel on a summer holiday to Jersey. His only concession to his jobless state was to travel third class and even this economy was abandoned on reaching London, when he saw the crowds bound for the Channel Isles. In fact he was never in any doubt that he could obtain another job of some sort; his concern was lest it should fail to be of the kind that would fulfil his sense of destiny. He summarized his state of mind when back in London early in June:

I am living in great anxiousness overshadowed with the sorrow of a ruptured friendship . . . Here I am, conscious of abilities which almost overwhelm me and yet with nothing to do. I am dreadfully perplexed as to where my future work is to lie for I would use my power of organization in some high place and yet I am eager to pass on the force of inspiration which burns within me. God grant me deliverance in His good time and in the waiting keep strong and high my faith.

It was the 'sorrow of a ruptured friendship' which was the essence of his distress at this time. When, later in the same month, he went to give a talk to the sixth form of his old school on 'Choosing a Career', he inserted in his prepared text a digression that reveals his state of mind at this time. He wrote:

A great deal might be said on the subject of friendship but I haven't time. I would recommend one real friend rather than a dozen lesser ones. It may be the divinest thing in your life. Few attain it. Take care, however, that the loss of it, for any reason, will not destroy your mental equilibrium. I speak from experience.

His wife, his mother and his brother, Douglas, all in their own ways sought to solace and sustain him in this unhappiness. In a letter, which has already been quoted in part, Douglas had written soon after the breach with Charlie:

29 March 1922 Now you are married and Charlie is married the operation of natural forces is in process and is not to be regretted. If Charlie is doing you an injustice at the moment, he will repent. But in justice to him I must say that I know he had for months been feeling qualms about the exclusiveness of your friendship. When you first met, Charlie was so much younger than you that he could not supply that independence of mind and will which is needed for the best kind of friendship. That Charlie is manifesting this now should give you a sense of satisfaction.

In his conclusion Douglas urged John to turn to his wife and to get another job but 'without worrying about it'. This was good advice and John Reith did his best to follow it.

So it was in the spirit that his brother Douglas had urged on him that John Reith returned to his home in Scotland with Muriel in mid-June 1922. He was determined to find a good job and almost immediately he was greatly encouraged to receive a letter from one of his American contacts in Williamsport asking him for particulars of his recent qualifications. This more than made up for the disappointment of hearing from another of his wartime industrialist friends that he could not help. His pleasure was short-lived; a month later he noted in his diary, 'the Williamsport job is off'. His friend had been ordered 'to go off for a year for his health'. To make matters worse he was plagued by toothache. Disappointment and poor health turned his mind back to his unhappiness over his break with Charlie. At the end of July he wrote, 'I am still in a dreadful state of worry about C. and my future'; a week or so later he returned to his dual theme of broken friendship and frustrated ambition, commenting, 'it is dreadful trying to be without work but that is nothing to the other sorrow.' He was aware that in harking back to this unhappiness over Charlie he distressed his wife but persuaded himself that this was her fault, confiding to his diary that 'Muriel can't or won't help now.' What he regarded as Muriel's rejection combined with his own inactivity to lead him into a tepid and superficial flirtation with a local tennis partner. This had one good result – he forgot about Charlie, but, as he admitted to himself 'the cure was perhaps worse than the disease'. He soon pulled himself together:

Awfully worried that Muriel is so unhappy [he wrote towards the end of September], and very sick with myself at how I have been behaving generally.

He now decided to return to London and seek his fortune there as he had over eight years earlier. His objective was a career in politics. He thus returned to the idea he had first outlined to his father in letters from the front in 1915. For two months at the end of 1922, as the extracts in Chapter I reveal, he was closely involved in the electoral arrangements of the Coalition Conservatives. Then, out of the blue, he was invited for interview for the position of general manager of the British Broadcasting Company for which he had applied soon after reaching London. Early in December, as is shown in Chapter Two, he was appointed to this position. His great opportunity had come and his search had ended.

4. Between the Wars, 1922–39

In so far as John Reith was capable of happiness and contentment he attained them while he was with the BBC. Of course, given his temperament, he was often yearning in these years for more testing tasks, and in the awkward period when he was at odds with Lord Clarendon as chairman of the BBC he was genuinely distressed by his situation. But, overall, this was a time when he achieved that serenity of spirit which, despite the gentle and loving support of his wife and the constant efforts of his friends, seemed always to escape him after 1939.

The foundations of this serenity lay in the happiness of his home life. Early in 1923, within a month of starting with the BBC, Muriel joined him in London. At first they rented a furnished flat in Queen Anne's Mansions; then, in the summer of 1924, they moved to a hotel in Weybridge and subsequently to a service flat in Buckingham Gate for two months. This was because they had now found a permanent home in London, at 6 Barton Street, Westminster and it was being prepared for them. In the autumn they brought their furniture south from Dunardoch, selling that house in February 1925, and from September 1924 until March 1930 they lived in Barton Street.

It was at Barton Street that their son, Christopher, was born in May 1928. Up to this point John and Muriel Reith had travelled together regularly in Europe as well as within Britain. In December 1923 they had visited Rome and spent Christmas at Bordighera; in the summer of 1924 and 1925 they had had holidays in the Highlands, preceded in 1925 by a visit to Cornwall. In 1926 they toured in France, visiting the area of John's wartime service and the war graves of Muriel's brother and fiancé. Then, in 1927, it was the West country and Scotland again. These jaunts united them and refreshed him at a time when he was working hard. John Reith was fully aware of his good fortune, telling Muriel with touching self-depreciation when they visited her first fiancé's grave:

> I supposed if he had appeared she would readily go with him and leave me.

Muriel, for her part, was equally content, telling John in September 1927 that she was 'very happy' in a way which left him 'quite affected'. The arrival of their first child forced an adjustment in this exclusive happiness. So, although they still travelled together – to France and Italy in 1929, to Germany and Poland in 1931 and even to the United States and Canada earlier that year – there were now occasions when John went on his own, as at Christmas 1928, when he visited Switzerland, and in the summer of 1930 when he went to Germany. Moreover, when they were together uncertainty over her son's health, as in 1929, could lead Muriel to cut short their plans. This adjustment to a family relationship was made the more necessary after the birth of their daughter, Marista, in April 1932. By this time they had left Barton Street and moved to Harrias House, near Beaconsfield, where they were to stay for twenty-five years from 1930 to 1955. Family holidays by the seaside, generally in Norfolk or Cornwall, now became an annual fixture. John Reith loved his family; in 1934 he noted that he was finding his children more and more attractive and interesting, while two years later he observed:

> . . . for me, as for Muriel, the future is so much, more and more, concentrating on these two children.

But for all this he was unable to relax in the circumstances of a holiday by the sea, so much so that in some years he would work in London during the week and visit his family at weekends. At other times he would resolve to sit it out. In July 1936 he wrote in this context:

> I am in an awful worry about the holidays. I hate not to be with Muriel and the children for their five or six weeks at the seaside, leaving them all alone; and yet it is not a bit the sort of holiday I ought to have. It is dull and provincial. If only Muriel was prepared

and anxious to go off somewhere with me it would make all the difference, but she never wants to do anything and wouldn't leave the children. I expect I shall just stay at Thorpeness.

This, in fact, was his decision.

But whatever John Reith wrote in 1936, there had been occasions when Muriel had agreed to leave her children and travel with him, visiting the United States for a second time in 1933 and going to South Africa for nearly three months in 1934, in addition to making trips to Scotland in 1932 and 1933. She also encouraged him to travel on his own when she felt he needed rest and she was unable to escape. So, after some ill health, he had enjoyed a spring holiday in Scotland by himself in 1935, while in the summer of that year he had cruised with Lord and Lady Iliffe in their private yacht. Later, in 1937, he accepted Sir Dudley Pound's invitation to travel as far as Gibraltar aboard his flagship, HMS *Barham*, a trip which he described as 'the most interesting and enjoyable five days I have ever spent'; and early in 1938 he accompanied Montagu Norman on a cruise to the West Indies. By 1939 he had found a solution to this apparent conflict between his family's needs and his own; this was to take them all to Canada in August of that year and it was ironical that this should have been the occasion of his most painful separation from them for the first three months of the war.

If the adjustment by John and Muriel Reith to the demands of home and family in these years was one factor in his fundamental serenity, another was undoubtedly the closeness which he achieved with his mother up to the very moment of her death in December 1935. Paradoxically, his move to London helped rather than hindered this. It removed him from his sister, Jean, whose jealousy of him – and his of her – had poisoned his relationship with his mother while he had been at Coatbridge. Now that he had a home in London, and later at Beaconsfield, it was natural for his mother to visit him and Muriel for two or three months in every year. Equally natural was their regular correspondence. In person or by post her influence was moderate and her advice wise. When he had been in a state of frenzy over his breach with Charlie in the summer of 1922 she had written with great understanding:

> Your first duty is to make Muriel happy by being strong and patient for her sake. Commit Charlie and the whole business to God, not forgetting your own mistakes in it but by no means being discouraged by them, 'forgetting those things that are behind, reach forward'.

R.D.–D

How often Father said that – never go back upon the past; learn what it was meant to teach and go right on.

It was advice which John Reith was not normally able to make himself accept, but in this case his removal to London and his busy life there allowed him to apply it. By the time he was summarizing his diary, nearly ten years later, he destroyed or returned all Charlie's letters with the cool comment, 'I do not care a scrap about him now.'

As over Charlie, so in the case of his sister Jean his mother urged him towards charity and common sense. But even to please his mother John Reith could not moderate his resentment towards Jean. He considered that his mother's 'happiness and comfort' had been 'dreadfully prejudiced by Jean'. His mother begged him not to think in this way. On one occasion she wrote that 'a few lines to Jean or even a little message would add truly to my happiness'. He would not comply. Jean herself had suggested as early as 1925 that they should 'try beginning over again' and asked him when next they met 'to be natural and not to say one word about past days'; a little later she made the pathetic plea, 'don't act to me as if you despised me utterly'. It was to no avail, for with John Reith in private life, as in public, bygones could not be bygones.

This unforgiving attitude, however painful, did not spoil his relationship with his mother. She was too sensible for that. She saw his faults and urged him to correct them; but she also saw his virtues and his great capacity for good. So, while her early letters had contained simple moral admonitions against finding fault and in favour of looking for the good points in people, by the time he was seeking appointment to the BBC she could write:

> ... my only ambition for you, as I know it was Father's, is that you should find a sphere in which you can have the best opportunities of service, helping to make men and women happier and better, and to find your own happiness there.

Thereafter she sustained him with constant encouragement and by her keen interest in the substance of his work. She made positive suggestions which sometimes bore fruit. So, in September 1930, John Reith wrote in his diary:

> Listened to the first of the *Religion and Science* series by Huxley and it was very good. The series would never have been undertaken if it had not been for Mother.

Their letters show that they discussed social and religious questions with serious intelligence. When the Lambeth Conference of 1930 published a statement on marriage and birth control his mother wrote:

> I disapproved of the Lambeth pronouncement . . . It is my strong belief that decision as to the rightness or wrongness [of birth control], in doubtful cases, should be left to medical men and women. The Church's duty is to urge self-control for the sake of the family . . . I may be mistaken but I am afraid that the Church *Imprimatur* on the whole subject, just because it *is* the Church, will do more harm than good.

A little more than a year after this letter, when already eighty-four years old, she wrote about the Resurrection:

> I do not believe that Christ's *Body* had a Resurrection but that legends did in time grow up about the Tomb and the Ascension as well as [about] His appearances to the Apostles and to St Paul who had never seen Him 'in the flesh' but to whom that one vision was proof enough that He was alive. (That is *the* all important fact.) The early Christians believed in and needed them – it was the childhood of Christianity, and how many visions and appearances in which God spoke to them they had read of in their Old Testament scriptures . . .
>
> I wish I had time to write more about this great subject. From Calvary Christ said He would be 'this day' in Paradise with the dying thief. That in His spiritual Body He appeared at various times, I do believe – How, is unimportant except for those who need crutches or those whom God is leading by a different path to have faith in the glorious fact and certainty of the Resurrection and Immortality.

Thus John Reith drew intellectual stimulus as well as moral support from his mother, and he certainly inherited some of his strong qualities from her. On this last point she took the opposite view, believing that his chief inheritance was from his father, telling him so in a letter written early in 1929:

> I believe that you have inherited from Father a great deal that had no, or but little, outlet during his Ministerial life. It is a joy to me to think that this partly accounts for the wonderful success you have had, and that he lives again through you. This may not account for everything, for you have special qualities of your own – but certainly for much.

Others saw his debt to her as being the greater. In the same year that she wrote this letter John Reith took her to a reception given by the new Labour government where she met Lady Astor who, in usual fashion, went straight to the point: 'she asked Mother if it was from her that I had my Mussolini traits.'

Contentment and satisfaction in his private life, however, were not the only factors in John Reith's well-being in these years. He also enjoyed and was inspired by his public success at the BBC. This brought him in touch with the leading figures in Church and State, men such as Archbishops Davidson and Lang and the prime ministers of the day, Baldwin and MacDonald, with all of whom he found himself in close sympathy. His self-confidence was further sustained by the numerous and flattering offers made to him by the leaders of commerce and industry. In the dozen years between 1924 and 1936, at one time or another, he was approached by the Marconi Company, by HMV and by RKO; he was considered as possible chairman for both the Central Electricity Board and the London Passenger Transport Board; and he was invited to become chairman of Waring and Gillow's, managing director of Standard Telephones and Cables and a vice-president of the LMS railway.

Another gratification for him in these years was the recognition of his public work shown by the honours he received. He became a Knight in the New Year's Honours for 1927, was appointed GBE in the Birthday Honours for 1934 and GCVO in the New Year's list in 1939. In addition he received honorary degrees from Aberdeen, Manchester and, in 1935, Oxford. This academic recognition delighted him and he wrote of his Oxford DCL as 'the greatest honour in the world'. But his attitude towards his other honours was ambivalent and illogical. He wanted to be offered them, but on his terms. As he wrote late in life:

I do not care two hoots or one hoot about honours, and often wish I had never taken one. What I do care about is the injustice of not being given or offered them.

He seems to have felt that the honours he received were devalued by the fact that they were also awarded to others, often automatically. In 1931 he confided his thoughts on this point to his diary:

It always rather infuriates me when I see people wearing rows of medals and sashes and stars which I know they have only got on some sort of ration system without doing a hundredth part of the good I have done.

Yet in 1934, when Ramsay MacDonald proposed to recommend him for appointment to be GBE, he wrote 'to implore' him to substitute the name of Noel Ashridge, the Chief Engineer of the BBC, for whom he had been seeking a knighthood for two years, and it was the prime minister who, in his answer, made John Reith's point that the 'growing assumption that Honours are attached to offices is a thoroughly bad principle'.

John Reith had shown the same contrariness over his knighthood on which he had set his sights from the start of his service with the BBC, telling his mother at Christmas 1922, 'I wanted her to live to see me a knight,' and openly placing this honourable ambition before his influential friends between 1924 and 1926. Yet when, at Christmas 1926, Baldwin offered him the long-sought honour, he was slow to accept it, complaining in his diary:

An ordinary knighthood is almost an insult. The PM has never comprehended the importance of our work.

In the same way when appointed GBE and later GCVO, initial coyness was followed by irritation in the first case that, through ignorance, it was not widely recognized as 'a high honour and a very unusual one', and in the second case that there was 'no excitement because people don't notice VO appointments'. Even when he was elected a member of the King's Bodyguard in Scotland, the Royal Company of Archers, towards the end of 1937 he was far from fully content, mixing remarks of amazement and delight with the complaint that 'it was for the landed aristocracy and not for the likes of me'. On balance, however, the recognition of public achievement which his honours represented acted on John Reith, up to 1939, as a calming and quietening force. It is possible to see the seeds of his later violent feelings on this subject, but they were not to grow until his sense of insecurity developed during and after the second war.

Another feature of John Reith's sense of fulfilment before 1939 was his conviction that he was serving the Christian cause at the BBC and that his religious attitude was shared and supported by those governing forces in the country which are today embraced by the pejorative cliché of 'the Establishment'. This allowed him to feel that so far from standing alone he was supported by tradition and authority. His own religious stand-point was simple and evangelical; he enjoyed complete faith in

Christianity and wanted others to share in it. He had demonstrated this in the trenches, where his Presbyterian zeal had influenced the men under his command, and again during his time in the United States where he had immediately participated in the religious life of the community in Swarthmore. On arriving at the BBC one of his first decisions had been that broadcasting services would observe Sundays and one of his first acts had been the establishment, with the help of Archbishop Davidson, of a Religious Advisory Committee for broadcasting. He believed that religious broadcasting served a national purpose and a national need. He agreed with his mother's view that the short daily service was 'a boon to thousands of people, especially the invalids and elderly'. For his first ten years at the BBC he even imposed upon Sunday morning programmes that strict observance of the Sabbath in which he had been brought up, following the tradition which Dr Johnson once described as allowing 'relaxation but not levity – walking but not throwing stones at birds'. But by the 1930s it was clear that this was in conflict with new ideas and John Reith, for all his intensity of feeling, was ready to accept the movement of the times. So, in April 1934, he noted:

> Lunched with the Bishop of Winchester with regard to the Programme Revision Committee's recommendation for Sundays, in particular that there should be a secular alternative to the national religious service. I felt passionately against this some years ago, but not so today, although on the whole I would regret it.

Four years later, on the eve of his departure from the BBC, he adopted the same position:

> I am perplexed as to whether there is anything against what I have always stood for in letting them run a programme on Sunday morning. I don't think so. I am distressed but it is no case of my being weaker than I used to be. The Religious Committee had no views on it.

Although happy in the company of bishops and archbishops, John Reith's personal preference was for the religious forms of the Presbyterian Church. He was a regular churchgoer but a rare communicant. Before he could partake in a communion service he believed that he must achieve a state of mind worthy of it by long preparation. When staying with the Bishop of Winchester (later Archbishop Garbett) in June 1935 he recorded in his diary:

Went to the Communion Service at eight o'clock in the Chapel, the first time I have been to Communion since our visit in 1933.

In fact he would attend mid-morning communion services on Sundays more often than this suggests, although he would rarely partake at them. But the weekly early service of conventional Anglicanism did not appeal to his sense of worship; indeed he wrote of it on one occasion as 'barbarous and upsetting', and on another as 'a silly and quite unnecessary affliction'. He liked a church service with good music and good singing, but one in which the congregation took a full part, and above all he liked a sermon with intellectual content. When in 1937 he attended a service in New College chapel at Oxford as the guest of Warren Fisher his comment in his diary made this clear:

It was very high-brow; no sermon; the music certainly very fine, but I can't see what good it does.

Four years before this he had been to a Quaker meeting at Jordans. His comment on this occasion was equally revealing:

The silent part of it I quite liked; but however snobbish it may appear I prefer to be spoken to by people in whom I can recognize some intellectuality; spirituality, no matter how deep, does not make up to me for lack of the other thing.

It was this insistence on intellectual foundations that made him doubtful of the Buchmanite Group movement; for two years he thought about it without being able to make up his mind. He felt that it was 'genuine Christianity' but he also felt that there was 'something about the system' he did not like. The outcome was a suspension of judgement; as he wrote in July 1937, 'I wish I knew what to think about that concern.'

If John Reith was puzzled and uncertain about the Buchmanites, he entertained no such doubts about the conduct of British foreign policy in the years leading to the outbreak of war. Here he combined great self-confidence in the correctness of his opinions with very little sign that he had much knowledge or understanding of the realities of foreign affairs. It was a posture he shared with other leading figures and his attitudes are of more interest as symptoms of the times than illustrative of any great originality on his part. Thus his diary shows him in 1932–3 to be 'very much anti-League of Nations' and, a year later, to have felt that the British governments had been 'too pro-French for years'. All his inclinations were in favour of Germany; in August 1936 he acknowledged this in his diary, writing, 'I have a great admiration for the German way of doing things.' This meant that when, thanks to his friend Dr Wanner, the head of the broadcasting company for South Germany, he had early warning of the evil and aggressive nature of the Nazi régime, he would not accept it.

> *9 March 1933* Dr Wanner to see me in much depression. He said he would like to leave his country and never return. I am pretty certain, however, that the Nazis will clean things up and put Germany on the way to being a real power in Europe again. They are being ruthless and most determined. It is mostly the fault of France that there should be such manifestations of national spirit.

Even when Dr Wanner was later 'too terrified to say much about conditions in Germany and said he would be shot if he did', John Reith was reluctant to acknowledge the truth about the Nazis, actually arguing in their favour with another German contact in November 1933.

He maintained much the same position throughout 1934. After the infamous 'night of long knives' he wrote in his diary:

> *2 July 1934* I really admire the way Hitler has cleaned up what looked like an incipient revolt against him by the Brown Shirt leaders. I really admire the drastic actions taken, which were obviously badly needed.

A few days before this he had dined at Cliveden, meeting there the American Minister in Vienna of whom he wrote:

> After dinner he more or less monopolized the conversation and gave a most interesting, and, as I thought, extravagant account of the situation in Vienna, particularly about the Nazis whom he abominates.

It was not until 1936 that he fully accepted Dr Wanner's 'tale of awful happenings in Germany' and when Hitler reoccupied the Rhineland in March of that year he passed his private information to the Foreign Office through Lord Stanhope. Even then he did not wholly reject the Nazi régime and on the occasion of the German seizure of Austria two years later he wrote gleefully about the Germans getting away with it. He admired Nazi achievement in spite of Nazi wickedness and as late as March 1939, when Prague was occupied, his only comment was that 'Hitler continues his magnificent efficiency'.

His views on Italy were very similar. In November 1935, at the time of the Abyssinian war, he told Marconi, who was visiting England:

> I had always admired Mussolini immensely and I had constantly hailed him as the outstanding example of accomplishing high democratic purpose by means which, though not democratic, were the only possible ones. I didn't add, what I believe, namely that if I had been Foreign Secretary I could have got Musso to stay his hand in Abyssinia.

He was often to return to this last point; in 1937 he recorded his belief that Eden had unnecessarily sacrificed the friendship of Italy in 1935 and that if he 'had been otherwise the whole course of European politics would have been different'. On those grounds he welcomed Eden's resignation in 1938 nor, on this occasion, did he keep his view to himself, making the point to Montagu Norman and more fully to Maurice Hankey.

It was of a piece with this conviction that England had no need to oppose the dictators that John Reith should have been convinced in 1938 that there would be no war over Czechoslovakia, and that even as late as July 1939 he should have been ready to accept Horace Wilson's advice, in preference to Vansittart's, about the wisdom of taking his family to Canada for their summer holiday. Yet his views were not the product of fear or cowardice; he was cranky but not craven. So at the time of Samuel Hoare's resignation over the Abyssinian peace plan of December 1935 he wrote in his diary:

> Certainly they [i.e. the government] had information that Mussolini would regard oil sanctions as an act of war but they should have risked it. It is pathetic, and Stanley Baldwin and England have lost caste throughout the world.

He felt that while the policy of antagonizing Italy was mistaken, once it had been embarked upon it should have been followed through.[6] It was this attitude which was to carry him forward when war did come.

5. Second War and After, 1940–70

When John Reith wrote his autobiography in 1947 his first choice for a sub-title to cover the ten years which followed his departure from the BBC was *Adrift*. It is not clear why he changed it; perhaps he felt that it was excessively revealing, for he was certainly adrift in those years.

His public life in this decade covered a variety of tasks. First, there was his period at Imperial Airways in 1938–9 when, though far from contented with his situation, he had solid grounds for thinking that a greater opportunity would soon appear. Then, between 1940 and 1950, he was successively a cabinet minister, a naval officer working in the Admiralty and, after 1945, part-time chairman of three public concerns, the Commonwealth Telecommunications Board, the Hemel Hempstead New Town Corporation, and the National Film Finance Corporation, all important and useful post-war tasks but none requiring the application of the whole of his formidable energies.

The sensation that he was adrift did not stem, therefore, from unemployment in the strict sense of that word. Except for three months in 1942 he was never without a job. It arose because he was constantly hoping, and was constantly disappointed in his hopes, for positions of greater responsibility and status. He sought these, not for their own sake nor for the public recognition that they would bring, but so that, in his father's words, he could do 'as much good to his fellow men as he possibly could and so serve God in his generation'. That he did not have such opportunities he ascribed to the ill-will of Winston Churchill. His feelings towards Churchill are the key to his sense of frustration and failure during the second war. There is no doubt that by 1940 Churchill had built up a strong dislike of him. He associated him with his opponents within the Conservative party, particularly Baldwin and Chamberlain, and he blamed him, unjustly, for having prevented him from broadcasting his views on India in the early 1930s, which he later described with typical exaggeration as keeping him off the wireless for eight years. On the other hand there is equally no doubt that John Reith disapproved of Churchill long before he became prime minister. This is plain from his diary during the General Strike and, ten years later, during the Abdication crisis, and it is confirmed by his references to Churchill in the brief period at the beginning of 1940 when they were Cabinet colleagues under Chamberlain. It was then, and not only when Churchill became prime minister, that his diary contained references to him as 'a horrid fellow' and that he exclaimed in fury, 'how I dislike him'. They were plainly incompatible, being at once too alike in their domineering egotism and too widely separated in their attitudes to life, the one cheerful and hedonist, the other pessimistic and suspicious of pleasure. The fierce patriotism and determination to win the war which they shared were not enough to overcome their wider differences of temperament.

It was, therefore, unlikely that when Churchill became prime minister he would spare much thought for Reith, nor did he. John Reith's reaction was an intensification of his dislike which he made no effort to conceal. Such conduct was exceptionally unwise in one who craved for political advancement. Some of those in Churchill's confidence, particularly Beaverbrook and Brendan Bracken, to their great credit, were aware of the loss to the government in this failure fully to use Reith's talents at a time of national emergency. Although he disapproved of them fully as much as of Churchill, they tried hard to coax him into greater cooperation. John Reith refused to be coaxed. Throughout the summer of 1940 when he attended the regular meetings of ministers outside the War Cabinet to hear the prime minister's reports on the progress of the war, he went in a mood of resentment and irritation. He regarded these meetings as 'farcical affairs and damned insulting' having 'nothing to them' and he deplored the sycophantic remarks made at them by the majority of his colleagues. Even when the business of his department forced his attendance at a genuine Cabinet meeting, as at Christmas 1940, his comments in his diary were no less critical:

The PM called a meeting about [air-raid] shelters which had nothing to do with me. For an hour and a half I sat opposite him, watching him and his tricks.

For his last year in the government he would not even attend what he termed 'the below the second salt kind of ministerial meetings'. By November 1941 he noted in the context of the opening of Parliament:

The sight of Churchill naturally bothered me. I absolutely hate him.

And in January 1942 when informed that some ministers were going to welcome the prime minister on his return from Washington he replied that he 'certainly wasn't going'.

John Reith's dismissal from the government in February 1942 must, then, be seen against the background of his conduct as a minister. For nearly two years he had done nothing to help himself with Churchill and a good deal to harm himself. Once dismissed, he quickly made things worse, rejecting the offerings of goodwill made to him and concentrating his bitterness against Churchill personally. It is true that he refused to give vent to his ill-will in the Press or in Parliament, but he did not stop himself talking. So, in October 1942, he recorded that he had expressed himself 'with some freedom about Churchill and his rotten gang'. It was natural, in these circumstances, that Churchill should turn a deaf ear to the pleas of John Reith's friends for his reinstatement in some ministerial or quasi-ministerial position. He was left to make his way in the Admiralty as best he could. As it turned out, his work there was of outstanding importance while he was in charge of the department responsible for the supply of all materials needed for the invasion of Europe. The achievement of this department still awaits its official history. When D-Day came it had attained almost one hundred per cent efficiency; of the landing ships asked for, ninety-nine per cent had been available, of the landing craft, ninety-eight per cent, involving in absolute numbers, 126 ships, 777 major craft and 1570 minor. Even Churchill recognized the magnitude of this work when he made special arrangements for John Reith to receive the CB (Military). Reith was genuinely pleased by this award but it did not long moderate his hatred of Churchill. When the general election of 1945 led to the catastrophic defeat of the Conservatives and of their leader there was 'no question about his jubilation'.

John Reith was to remain adrift for another five years but Churchill had no part in this. Reith's hopes of being appointed to the management of one of the newly established state monopolies, such as Transport or Steel, or even to the chairmanship of the BBC were frustrated by the decisions of Attlee and his government. None of this was the work of 'Churchill and his rotten gang'. Nevertheless his hatred remained as strong as ever it had been and was sustained by the publication of the early volumes of Churchill's memoirs, each one of which aggravated and irritated him more. When Churchill returned as prime minister he wrote in his diary, 'I suppose I do positively hate that man . . . he is an unprincipled and unscrupulous megalomaniac.' And when, in April 1955, Churchill finally retired he noted:

Good Friday, 8 April 1955 I wrote to the wretched Churchill thus:
'Here is someone who worked faithfully and well for you, but whom you broke and whose life you ruined. You were kind enough, some years later, to agree that you had misjudged; you wrote that you were very sorry and that the State was in my debt.[7] I couldn't remind you of this while you had opportunity to put things right; but I can now, and say that I am sorry to feel as I do.'
Of course people would say it was awful to have written such a letter, undignified and all the rest of it. But if I hadn't done it I should be much more bothered than I am likely to be having done it.

Yet he had not worked faithfully in any political sense nor had his life been ruined by his dismissal in 1942. When he wrote this letter he was chairman of the Colonial Development Corporation and had just signed its annual report in which it was stated that the 'really significant development' for that body was that its emphasis had 'now swung to looking forward instead of backwards'. Within six months he was to accept renewal as CDC chairman. So this continued harping on the evil consequences for him of Churchill's hostility was no longer rational. Indeed, his hatred of Churchill had by this time lost any foundation in reason. It sprang, to use Sir William Haley's words in another context, 'from an unhappiness really based elsewhere' – in himself.

This unhappiness, which continued and even increased in the 1950s while he was chairman of the CDC, had its roots in his private rather than his public life. We have seen that in the years before 1939 his sense of well-being had been founded on the happiness of his home with his wife, his mother and his children, a happiness which had helped him to overcome such troubles as arose in connection with his work. After 1939, however, he was overwhelmed by private worries as well as by public troubles. In the first place his dismissal from the government in 1942 plunged him into financial difficulties. His income, which in any event had been halved when he left Imperial Airways to enter the government, virtually disappeared on his joining the Navy as a lieutenant-commander and was no more than fractionally replaced when, after a year, he was promoted to the rank of captain. His only resource was to live on an overdraft from his bank which steadily mounted even when, after the war, he restored his income to £5000 p.a. He was able to pay this off in 1949, when an insurance policy for £10,000 matured, but his gloomy comment in his diary on this was 'it only just clears overdraft'.

Besides being constantly troubled by the uncertainty of his finances he was also burdened by the responsibility of his large house, held on lease, at Beaconsfield. Before the war this had been a source of great satisfaction to him; but in the servantless days of the war and in the immediate post-war era of austerity it grieved him to watch his wife, Muriel, tied down by domestic duties. In the same way he was saddened by the sight of the declining state of his grounds. To make matters worse, his home in Beaconsfield became increasingly inconvenient for his work. Without an official car and faced by a poor train service and stringent petrol rationing he felt bound to stay in London during the working week, either in his club or, for three years after the war, in a small flat. In this way his expenses increased along with his separation from his family.

These material problems, however, although they added to his unhappiness, were not its main source. This much is clear from the fact that when, by the mid-1950s, he had substantially improved his financial position and had also successfully moved from his home in Beaconsfield to a flat in Lollards Tower at Lambeth Palace, his mental distress was not reduced thereby but rather increased. One reason for this was his reluctance to accept his age. He could not bring himself to admit that his career was drawing to an end. He was determined to prove to himself and to others that his physical endurance and mental determination were as great as they had ever been. To this end he would work all night and congratulate himself afterwards – 'glad to find I could still do an all-nighter' – even if he required the help of benzedrine to do this. In the same way he would set himself tests of physical endurance; when on holiday in Scotland in 1949 at the age of sixty he recorded in his diary:

> Today I did what I was beginning to doubt my capacity to do – go for a really long walk. I set out at 10.30 in lashing rain and strong wind and walked fourteen miles. Matter of will. I got there about 2.00, had lunch and started back at 2.30 reaching the hotel at 6.30. It certainly was a mighty effort – twenty-eight miles and with no training. After dinner I did Gay Gordons, Petronella and Dashing White Sergeant till 11.00 – two hours of it.

Ten years later he was still anxious to prove his 'endurance and determination' by walking ten miles in an afternoon while staying at his son's farm near Perth. Soon after this, just three weeks following his seventieth birthday, he spent seven hours climbing Cairngorm with his son, noting at the end of it:

> A most successful day in every way. I was so very glad that Christopher and I did this together.

This entry reveals, perhaps, the innermost cause of his lack of serenity in the 1950s, which was his craving for, and his failure to find, a comfortable relationship with his children in which he would enter closely into their lives. Just as he was not prepared to accept that he was growing older, so he could not adjust himself to the fact that his children were becoming adults. He pined for their affection and longed to share in all their doings, to advise them and to discuss with them. He bombarded them with letters – he wrote forty-five letters to his daughter in her first term at the university – and he was chagrined at their not being answered in equal profusion. He could not see that his children were of an age to want independence and freedom from parental guidance, nor that the best way to give them help was to wait to be asked for it. When they tried to break away from his overpowering personality, he felt that they were treating him cruelly and that they were rejecting him. So in September 1954 he confided sadly to his diary:

> I wish to God I knew what I have done to make myself so much disliked by the children – for I am sure they do dislike me. Terrible. Terrible . . . It is not all my fault; but nearly all and it must be my responsibility to try harder. I am so tremendously fond of dear Christopher and dear Marista.

He wanted his daughter's affection even more than his son's, yet he was the more cut off from her. In 1956 he complained, 'she won't talk to me about anything, never consults me'. As always, his wife supported him in his unhappiness with kindness and understanding and urged him towards a better frame of mind. So in 1958 he noted:

> Muriel admitted that Marista had treated me unkindly [but that] I ought to have forgotten all about this and that I was so unforgiving. Yes, I am unforgiving to those who have wronged and hurt me and who have not asked for forgiveness and who have expressed no sort of regret.

Thus he was the victim of his temperament and his rigid refusal to compromise in his home life as much as in his work and with the same result, that he lost what he most treasured. Towards the end of 1958 he wrote in this context:

> I have been thinking so much today about the dear children as they were at Beaconsfield; and, oh God, what I missed and how I have suffered for it since.

Unhappiness in his work, as revealed in his departure from the CDC, and unhappiness in his home over his daughter's engagement and marriage combined in the early 1960s to intensify his mental misery. For most of 1961 he was on the edge of nervous breakdown, suffering from depression and 'feeling quite awful; one can only describe it as a need to be pumped up, tyres flat and such like'. At the end of the year he agreed to treatment but found this so disturbing that he quickly abandoned it. For the next five years he continued to suffer from periods of depression. In 1963 he consulted a psychiatrist and for a brief period attended his 'class' but, once again, he soon detached himself. In 1966, just after retiring from British Oxygen, he judged himself 'not far from insanity'; his doctor told him it was 'an attack of depression'. He struggled to free himself and on this occasion with success, recording within a week that he was 'feeling better – quite fit and well and happy'. The remarkable feature of this distressing time in John Reith's life was his capacity to work efficiently thoughout it. Not only was he vice-chairman of British Oxygen in these years, but he was also vice-chairman of the North British Locomotive Company, chairman of the Labour party's commission of inquiry into advertising, and the driving force behind the successful liquidation of the State Building Society. This power to rise above his worries and to concentrate effectively on the numerous daily tasks before him is wholly admirable. However depressed, he would never give up.

His courage was rewarded in the last years of his active life. His election as Lord Rector of Glasgow University at the end of 1965 saw the beginning of a happier time. The publication of his first war memoirs, *Wearing Spurs*, in the next year and its warm reception from the critics further restored his sense of well-being. Then two honours came to him which finally removed most of his resentments and went far towards bringing him serenity. First, in 1967, he was invited to be Lord High Commissioner to the Church of Scotland, the honour which he had refused at Churchill's hands in 1942 and which he had been ready to accept, if offered, since 1963. This invitation was renewed in 1968 so that for two successive summers John Reith held court at Holyroodhouse. He welcomed this opportunity, primarily, as a means of testifying to and reaffirming in the Assembly his Christian faith and of commending it to all. On a less exalted level he took a simple pleasure in the grandeur of the office as the Queen's representative, writing after his first year:

> *5 July 1967* I find myself thinking about Holyrood occasionally and I realize that it was the only time in my life when I was adequately circumstanced; extraordinary how completely naturally I slipped into vice-regality.

Then, early in 1969, Her Majesty the Queen appointed him to the Order of the Thistle. Here was an honour he could relish which placed him among the sixteen most distinguished living Scots. If his military CB in 1944 had been in his eyes 'a squaring off' for the work he had done in the Admiralty, his becoming a Knight of the Thistle twenty-five years later represented a final balancing of the books for his life of public service.

So, by 1967, John Reith had fought his way with courage and willpower through the recurrent unhappiness and distress of a quarter of a century to calmness and serenity in old age. There were still to be occasions when he would exclaim in his diary: 'What a terrible mess I have made of life and of myself,' or, particularly if he was by himself in London while his wife was in Scotland, when he would bemoan his loneliness and think 'how dreadfully I have misused them – Muriel and the children'. For the most part, however, he was now at rest, accepting that his active life was over. He might dream that 'God maybe has some tremendous work for me to do – even at eighty', but he knew in his wiser moments that this would not be so and that he was, as he phrased it in August 1969, 'now almost wholly *passé.*' He found solace increasingly in thinking about the past and remembering his father and mother and in the simple pleasures of his home in the company of his adored Muriel. 'Oh, so glad to be home,' he wrote in March 1970, after a trip to Scotland. Above all he found serenity and peace in the loving care of his wife. Her sympathy and understanding never failed him, nor did his concern for her. One of his last entries in his diary pays touching tribute to their fifty years of love and loyalty:

> *21 February 1971* I am most awfully worried about dear Muriel's leg; [Lady Reith had had an operation for varicose veins in her legs in 1964.] I don't know what to do. I am very anxious indeed to arrange a really good holiday for her. Several times this evening, when she was laughing, I thought I had never seen her looking so pretty.

6. The Man and his Achievement

When John Reith retired from the Colonial Development Corporation in 1959 he received among his valedictory letters one from a former colleague of forty years before at Southwick. In this his friend wrote:

> Whereas most of us have to be content with one career, you have had six or seven and been outstanding in them all.

He was not far from the truth. Reith's work in the BBC had certainly been outstanding but, if this was his *chef d'œuvre,* his other careers in peace also involved original and constructive work. At Imperial Airways he had supervised the organization of civil aviation under a single public corporation; with the CTB he had negotiated for Commonwealth cooperation in the field of telecommunications; and he had rescued the CDC from the brink of disaster and set it on the lines which it was to follow with increasing success after he left. In war he had

R.D.—E

first revealed his talents in the United States in 1916–17 and fulfilled them at the Admiralty in 1943–4. Only in his ministerial career had he failed to stand out; even here he showed flashes of far-seeing originality in diagnosis, as in his attitude towards a nationalized system of railways and, later, in his efforts to grapple with the problems arising from the change in the use of land, so that he was far from being a total failure as a minister.

Nevertheless John Reith was convinced, against all the evidence, that he had been a failure not just as a cabinet minister but in life. He came to say this so often in old age that a recent biographer has taken him at his word, at at least half his word, and has dismissed his life after 1938 as 'an accelerating anti-climax' during which he had 'an increasingly negligible impact on men and events'.[8] That John Reith wrote and spoke in this vein is undoubtedly true, as is the fact that he sincerely believed it. The interesting problem is to discover why he should have persisted in asserting this demonstrable falsehood. One explanation is that he was not thinking in absolute terms and that he did not in his innermost heart consider that he had done nothing in life; what he deplored was that he had not done 'a tenth of what I might'. This was what tormented him; the feeling that he could have done much more. And in thinking this he convinced himself that what he had done was, relative to what he might have done, of no account, even though, as Sir Arthur fforde wrote in 1962, it was 'enough for most men'. Another possible explanation lies in his engineer's conception of mechanical efficiency. He felt that, in engineering terms, the output of his powerful mind and talents was being artificially held down and that this would not be acceptable in terms of the use of any machine. The waste would be plain; the machine would be put right or removed. So, in his eyes, for him to function at a high level of inefficiency was indistinguishable from total failure.

None of this, however, takes away from John Reith's real achievement in life. As Sir William Haley wrote to him in 1962:

> What you have done is there for all to see. It does not need display or justification.

It is probable that with greater opportunity he would have had greater achievements, though not in the positions he often dreamed about such as viceroy of India, for which he had no qualification by experience, or even ambassador at Washington, but rather in the management of public corporations which was his particular field. He greatly resented the decision of both the major parties not to appoint him to the Transport Commission in 1947 and in 1953 respectively (he even hoped for it in 1960), and his hostility to Lord Boyd of Merton dates from the 1953 decision which was taken when he was minister of transport. But such 'might-have-beens' are not relevant to an assessment of what he did which is 'there for all to see'.

John Reith's contrary attitude towards his achievement was part of his general character. He was a mass of contradictions. As he once admitted to himself, 'I am an odd fellow,' adding on another occasion with wry self-knowledge, 'there are some respects in which I haven't grown up.' Nothing demonstrates this better than his curious attitude towards honours which became more illogical as he grew older. On the one hand he aspired to ever greater recognition for himself; so, in 1963, he noted in the context of the New Year's list that 'the honours that I have abundantly earned and not received would take a whole page'. On the other hand he was always reluctant to wear his decorations and regularly recorded his dislike of wearing them. He wanted honours for himself and at the same time resented the awards made to others. As early as 1944 he aspired to a step in the peerage, telling Sir John Anderson on the eve of his visit to the Normandy beach-head in August 1944 that if he should fail to return he expected his son to be made a viscount. He felt, to use a Gladstonian phrase, that he 'ought not to be lost in the common ruck of official barons'. And as he was disappointed in this so he came increasingly to resent the elevation to the peerage as viscounts of numbers of his wartime colleagues; nor was he solaced, when in reply to his resentful inquiries in 1954, Sir Anthony Bevir, then appointments secretary to the prime minister, explained the conventions that normally led to this recognition of former secretaries of state and senior ministers.

A similar ambivalence marred his relationship with the civil service. In principle he hated what he called the civil service mentality and on occasions he would transfer this distaste to all civil servants. When in office himself he had deplored the slowness and timidity of his permanent officials; when out of office he resented what he regarded as their bumptious insistence on interfering in matters which were not their responsibility. He deplored their excessive influence over weak ministers and their craven toadying to strong ministers. But this hostility was always directed against civil servants as a group. Where individual civil servants were concerned he was on comfortable and often on friendly terms. The roll of distinguished names in his diary demonstrates this – Sir Warren Fisher and Sir Robert Vansittart before the war; Sir Edward Bridges, Sir Thomas Gardiner, Sir Patrick Duff and Sir James Rae mostly during and after it, and Sir Alan Barlow at all times, are but a selection of the leading civil servants with whom he worked on confidential terms. Except for Sir Horace Wilson in the years leading up to the war and one or two at the top of the Colonial Office in the 1950s there were no individual civil servants towards whom he entertained any of the bitter feelings of hostility which he directed against them as an order.

In general, John Reith did not recognize his inconsistencies. But in respect of his religious outlook he felt in his later years that his strong distaste for mankind in the mass (he could scarcely endure the physical inconvenience of a crowd) did not accord with the Christian ethic in which he strongly believed. Here he thought he might be guilty of humbug. In 1964, after reading a paper by Lord Stamp, he wrote:

> I have said for years that I believe profoundly in the Christian ethic, but that I am a very poor practitioner; I have said also that, to such extent as loving one's neighbour is an essential criterion of admission to the company of the elect, I absolutely fail to qualify. I do not love, or even like, my neighbour; in fact I dislike him more and more as he hooliganizes about the roads with open exhaust . . . glorifying in being a damnable curse to the whole community . . . Ought I therefore to disown the Christian ethic because I am incapable of observing it in what appears to be an essential particular . . . and am too old and set, and too experienced in the beastliness of human beings, to begin to try?

Lord Stamp's answer was comforting and urged him not to confuse intolerance with unchristianity:

> I think we all have felt at times that the world would be well rid of some of its inhabitants, but I am prepared to maintain against all the odds that if one of those same hooligans were to come to grief on his pestilentially noisy bike in your presence, John Reith would not pass by on the other side. And surely that, finally, is the essence of Christianity.

John Reith's inconsistencies of attitude and opinion were accompanied by several personal foibles and quirks. He was, for example, burdened throughout life by a compulsive tidiness which would not let him, or for that matter his wife, rest. He 'abominated' untidiness and associated tidiness with intelligence. On one occasion, after successfully rearranging a store-room, he wrote with some self satisfaction:

It is, maybe, a trivial but quite definite form of intelligence which enables a very few people to arrange a room like this in the best way.

At the same time he loved to rearrange his working room, admitting that he gained 'satisfaction even from so small a change of scene as exchanging the reference books which were to right and left of the paper-rack' on his desk. With this neurosis about tidiness there went a hatred of unnecessary or unused possessions. As he once confessed to Stanley Baldwin, he never missed an opportunity of presenting visitors to his home with discarded books and possessions. But even while he devoted himself to this clearing-out process, he would preserve, often for years, trifling keepsakes of personal or family interest; it was one of his inconsistencies that despite his hatred of rubbish and his merciless destruction of the letters and papers of the past, he was always looking back. However much his parents had begged him, 'never go back upon the past', he could not prevent himself doing so. His visits to Glasgow would often be accompanied by self-conscious rambles through the haunts of his youth – 'loitering with intent in Lynedoch Street' is how his lifetime friend Professor Loudon once described it. He would re-read his diaries with clockwork regularity and live upon the past.

Yet placing these inconsistencies and foibles on one side, accepting his vanity and his impatience (he once admitted that he was 'constitutionally almost incapable of waiting'), allowing for his rigidity of outlook and for his refusal to compromise, he remains, none the less, an outstanding figure of his time in original achievement, in dedication to principle and in the power to inspire those who worked under him. The principle that he championed in all he attempted was efficiency, which he sought to attain through organization and moral leadership. His first thought in taking on any task was its organization. One of his earliest keepsakes is the organization chart he constructed for the Eddystone factory in 1916. But organization by itself was not enough in his eyes; it had to be accompanied by moral force. This did not mean mere exhortation and clap-trap; he was well aware that empty words, however noble, would have no effect. 'People are reasonable, if reasonably treated' was one of his basic tenets, appearing in his diary in the context of post-war labour troubles in both the 1920s and the 1940s. So his moral appeal was designed as a reinforcement of practical success, not, as is often the case in the political world, as a shroud to conceal practical failure.

The quality which he regarded himself as possessing in particular was what he called 'wisdom'. He meant by this the power to foresee how events would turn out and how best to direct the actions of his corporations or companies as well as of his friends to meet them. 'How often I have been right against all comers,' he boasted in his diary in 1967, 'and how infuriating this is.' But he seemed incapable of applying this wisdom to his own actions, however successfully he used it for others. He gave excellent advice to all but himself. At the end of his life he ruminated on this:

> . . . the almost intolerably sad thing for me about it all is that wisdom isn't worth anything as it is rarely on one's own behalf that it is exercised.

It was, indeed, rarely that he guided his own actions with wisdom; this was where his temperamental weakness betrayed him. He relied overmuch on instinctive judgement; as he wrote to his father in March 1914:

> I believe greatly in trusting to one's instinct. First comes instinct, then opinion, then knowledge. Trust instinct.

And while this intuitive approach never failed him in his dealings with others, it often led him into disastrous courses for himself. The tragedy of his public life was not, as he often claimed, that he had failed in achievement, but rather, in the words of his great enemy, Winston Churchill, when writing of the French General Michel, that 'his personality and temperament were not equal to the profound and penetrating justice of his ideas'; just as the tragedy of his private life did not lie in his failure to accept the simple truth that 'life was for living', as he put it, but rather in his disregard of another truth, equally simple, that virtue is its own reward.

NOTES

1. John Reith commented on this in 1929: 'Park School and Glasgow Academy was the obvious sequence for those socially and financially up to it in Glasgow.'

2. John Reith had been given the additional names Charles Walsham after the minister of that name who had charge of Holy Trinity Church, Westbourne Terrace, at which his mother had worshipped as a girl and where she had been confirmed.

3. The 'succession of remunerative jobs' which Douglas Reith had in mind were John's position in America (£1230 p.a.), his general managership at Coatbridge (£1200 p.a.) and his position at the BBC (starting at £1750 p.a.).

4. His recollection of being 'quite well liked' was confirmed in June 1934 when he spent about an hour and a half going round the Hyde Park works. His visit was

unofficial and unannounced, and he was delighted to find 'how many of the men whom I knew were there . . . I shook hands and had a yarn with all I could see.'

5. John Reith wrote Manchester in his summarized diary, but the letter he wrote to his father on 22 February 1914 said Leeds; he accepted the latter in his autobiography (*Into the Wind*, p. 14) but raised the salary offered from three to four guineas a week.

6. He had taken a similarly vigorous view four years earlier on hearing that Persia had refused 'to renew the agreement whereby Imperial Airways can fly over Persia on the way to India'. His observations on this were:

It is really dreadful that England takes all this sort of thing lying down. It could never have happened in the old days but our foreign policy today is utterly pusillanimous . . . and it seems now as if any dago republic can wipe its feet on us.

7. For Churchill's letter of 1946 see John Reith's *Into the Wind*, pp. 526–7.

8. Andrew Boyle, *Only the Wind Will Listen*, p. 297.

CHAPTER ONE

Politics and Politicians (1)

1922-35

1. Introduction: the nature of the Diary

When John Reith died his diary consisted of eighteen volumes of text, the last volume which covered the period January 1969 to March 1971 being only half completed, and twenty-three volumes of 'enclosures'. The narrative volumes are loose-leaf in form and each contains two or three years of diary. It seems probable that late in life Reith took advantage of this loose-leaf form to spread the material over a greater number of volumes than he had originally used. So the twelve years 1952-63 are spaced over six volumes whereas the previous twelve years are concentrated in four. In 1961, when he advertised in *The Times* seeking advice on what to do with his diary he stated that it then consisted of twelve manuscript volumes and ten so-called enclosure volumes. In fact, by his death, the material for the years 1911-61 had been spread between fourteen manuscript and fifteen enclosure volumes. In the same way, he noted in 1965 that he had arranged his diary into thirteen and fifteen volumes, although in its final arrangement this had become, for the period up to 1965, sixteen and seventeen. This continual adjustment of the diary's arrangement must put one on one's guard against accepting his own occasional references to its size and shape. No doubt his observations were true when he made them, but that is all that can be assumed.

If John Reith's *obiter dicta* on the size and form of his diary must be received with caution, so also must his claims for its regular, daily composition. In his 1961 advertisement he asserted that there was 'not a day missed for over 50 years'. This was certainly an exaggeration. The diary itself shows that in his early BBC days he was as much as two months behind in March 1923 and again in January 1924; then in May 1926 during the crisis of the General Strike he was 'a fortnight out of date' and almost as much again in 1940 when minister of information; later, in 1943, when at the height of his work in the Admiralty, he fell three weeks behind. All these breaks were caused by the pressure of work. Later interruptions, sometimes as great as two months in the

1960s, were the consequence of sickness or depression. But these occasions of delayed composition were comparatively few. Far more important is the fact, which he never explicitly acknowledged in public, that his diary for its first nineteen years from December 1911 to December 1930 is not in its original form. He had begun with longhand volumes and by January 1931 he had already filled forty-four of these. He appears to have had almost as many 'cuttings books', as he termed his enclosure volumes, writing of 'Book XXXV' in February 1929. Overwhelmed by this bulk of material, he took in January 1931 what he called 'the momentous decision' to summarize and condense the whole. This process took him four years. When he had finished he had reduced the forty-four volumes of his original narrative diary, which he appears then to have destroyed, to five hundred and ninety pages most of which could be divided into two loose-leaf volumes, the last fifty pages forming the start of his third volume. At the same time he reduced his thirty-five or more 'cuttings books' into his first five enclosure volumes.

The pattern he chose for this summary was the pattern he was to follow for the next forty years. While it may have suited him, it is not convenient for an outsider to read or use. Each page runs continuously without break or paragraph, and in the 'Summary' years before 1931 often without clear indication of the days of the month. The only intermissions are for months, normally indicated by a small space on the same page, and for years which invariably secure a new sheet. Most of his summary for 1911–30 was dictated. This produced typed sheets of an average of sixty lines in single spacing, but for his journal at the front of 1914–15 and again for the period between his return from the USA in September 1917 and the end of 1919, and for a part of 1922, he wrote his summary longhand 'in incredibly small writing' which produced sheets of over eighty lines. While he was busy with this huge task he also dictated his current diary in very similar form; then, in August 1935, with his summary at last completed, he reverted to longhand. From then until the end of 1959 he maintained the same pattern, writing on close-ruled paper using sheets of forty-nine lines until the end of 1948 and after that, his old paper being no longer obtainable, on slightly smaller sheets of forty-five lines. It is probable that he continued to write his diary in this form for the next six years but in 1965 he arranged for it to be copied so that it is in type-written sheets for the period January 1960 to February 1966. The effect of this decision was to increase the number of lines on each sheet from forty-five to fifty-five. Finally, from February 1966, the diary was left in its original longhand pattern.

Putting all these together we have a narrative of nearly four thousand pages totalling over two million words. John Reith, himself, calculated in 1961 that he had written over one million five hundred thousand words. His earlier calculation, made in his autobiography, that by 1947 his diary extended to 'about four million words' is misleading because he plainly included in this estimate the materials in his enclosure volumes. These materials were selected by him in the first instance and then put together by the dedicated work of Miss Josephine Stanley. John Reith, in his 1961 advertisement, described them as containing 'letters, photographs, newspaper cuttings and such like' which was certainly true. What he did not add was that they are without tables of contents or index and, except for a very rough chronological arrangement, without any clear principle of selection or pattern of subject matter. Letters from the Archbishops of Canterbury and York appear next to a programme of the BBC Amateur Dramatic Society, and letters from Stanley Baldwin are flanked by family snapshots. Picture-postcards and first day issue postage stamps, Cabinet papers and Admiralty orders, Christmas cards and birthday greetings, cuttings from *The Times*, dinner-party menus, extracts from Hansard, even old railway tickets all are jumbled up together. For a man who prided himself on his orderliness and his hatred of rubbish these twenty-three enclosure volumes are an astonishing and contradictory memorial.

Another paradox in connection with John Reith's surviving papers is that in spite of his vast output of letters to family and friends he preserved no organized body of correspondence. From 1917 to 1927 he kept a letter register but gave it up as 'increasingly troublesome'. The concept of a 'Reith Correspondence', which has been cited as a source in a recent biography, is wholly Gilbertian. The only series of letters which he preserved were those he exchanged with his father and mother until their deaths in 1919 and 1935 and, after 1948, the letters he received from Sir William Haley, and even these were selected. Of course, many other individual letters are preserved throughout his enclosure volumes, and he always had recorded with meticulous care the names of those who wrote to congratulate him on his honours and offices, but there is no continuous theme binding any of these together. He was conscious of this gap in his papers at the end of his life and noted in February 1970:

I am greatly concerned about the Diary business, there being so much that would be helpful to Charles Stuart that is nowhere available to him.

One difficulty arising from the form of the diary is the question of precise dating, particularly in the period of the summarized diary when days of the month have not always been inserted. Here one man's interpretation may differ from another's. Professor Asa Briggs, who had the use of the diary for 1922–38 when writing the first two volumes of his *History of Broadcasting in the United Kingdom*, is the only person to have read it carefully over an extensive period and there are some two dozen occasions when it is possible to dispute the days given by him to selected extracts.* Nor are differences always limited to days; John Reith was occasionally himself the victim of the obscurities of his diary. For example, as we shall see, he placed his letter to the Labour leader, J. R. Clynes, in April 1922 although, in fact, it had been written in March 1920. This confusion of years could affect anyone; even Professor Briggs has mistaken the year of an entry on five occasions. Months are equally easily muddled. John Reith himself, in his autobiography, telescoped his last meeting with Ramsay MacDonald and his lunch with Baden-Powell as falling on the same day, though they were a month apart. Such mistakes were unintentional errors arising from the obscure and unmanageable form of the diary. But John Reith was also capable of contrived error for artistic effect. So he vastly exaggerated the speed with which he wrote *Wearing Spurs*, the account of his service in France in 1914–15, which he published in 1966. He claimed in his autobiography that 'the first draft of eighty thousand words was finished in a fortnight' while he was on holiday in Cornwall in August 1937. This was not true. His diary shows that he began writing four years before, had written three chapters by February 1934 and then put it to one side until January 1937. By the end of July of that year he had written another six chapters making a total of fifty thousand words. So the fortnight of composition in August had produced thirty thousand words – not eighty thousand.

John Reith's decision to summarize his diary in 1931 did not only govern its future form but also its future content. He did not intend this to be the case. He had hoped to escape from his early addiction to

* No continuous study of the diary after 1938 has been made before this edition although several scholars have been granted a sight of short periods. In August 1961 Mr H. M. Harris spent two days assessing the diary as a whole up to that date as a potential historical source for purchase by Lord Beaverbrook who did not in the end make an offer.

detail because, as he wrote at the time, he was 'disturbed by the increasing space' that his diary occupied and because it contained a 'vast amount of trivialities' and 'things which I would not care for people to read now'. Unfortunately, in spite of these hopes, his diary remained in its revised form, as he admitted in 1936, 'too much a record of doings only'. Nor did he ever change this. In 1967 he regretted the same fault – the inclusion of 'inconsiderable details of doings' and the absence of reflections. His method of composition was in part to blame. He appears to have kept daily engagement forms, noting all his movements, and to have written his diary with these before him. Hence the detailed timing of each interview and meal, the recording of the trains which took him to work or brought him home, and the lists of names of those he met during the day. But while he recorded when and where and with whom he spent his days, the substance of talk or action was often allusively dismissed with tantalizing phrases such as 'much interesting talk', or 'he told me much that was confidential', or 'I gave them my usual anti-Parliament line'. Only on those occasions which he felt at the time were important or significant would he give a full account of conversations and comment directly upon them. Even then, each day would also have its record of trivia; the state of the weather; the condition of the garden; the doings of his children when they were at home, news of them when they were away; servant problems before the war, food and petrol problems during and after the war; family problems at all times.

Thus the content of his diary accurately reflects John Reith's busy life with its mixture of the public and the private, of the significant and the trivial, of the permanent and the ephemeral. Although, as this chapter shows, he had many contacts with politicians while he was at the BBC, his diary contains no continuous political narrative for this period or, indeed, for any of his life. This was partly because he was not deeply interested in political news or gossip and partly because his method of composition, as well as his intense egocentricity, prevented his recording political events except when they directly affected himself. Towards the end of his life he became aware of this limitation. So, after reading his friend J. C. C. Davidson's papers in November 1969 he wrote:

I am suffering from a Diary inferiority complex. I have lately read Davidson's memoirs and I am afraid he has a good deal more of high level interest than I have.

The diary shows a similar lack of continuous social comment. John

Reith's life was not of a kind to make possible a narrative of London society such as appears in the diary of 'Chips' Channon or even that of Harold Nicolson. His world and theirs barely touched. Lady Colefax and Lady Cunard, rival protagonists in their pages, get scant notice in Reith's diary, the one being dismissed as 'a crashing bore' (the occasion was when they sat next to one another at a dinner for the King and Queen of Siam in June 1934), and the other being condemned as 'an evil woman'. But on this point John Reith was not afflicted by any inferiority complex – rather the reverse. When he read the 'Chips' diary he was aroused to strong moral disapproval. 'Finished *Chips*, the diary of Sir Henry Channon MP,' he noted in February 1969.

– a terrible story, full of the sordid life of the Upper Ten as it used to be called. I was honoured by the mention that he disapproved and disliked me.

While John Reith's diary was far from comprehensive as a political or social record of his times it contained extensive material on all his varied public employments. The requirements of selection for this edition have involved omitting much of this matter. For example, no extracts have been made directly covering his brief service at Imperial Airways in 1938 and 1939 or his subordinate work in the late 1940s on new towns in general and Hemel Hempstead in particular. These experiences gave him a continuing interest in civil aviation and town planning but the nature of his references to them in his diary, at once allusive and disjointed, make coherent treatment of either impossible. Another aspect of his life to find no place in this edition has been his experience with industrial companies such as Tube Investments, British Oxygen and the North British Locomotive Company which occupied a good deal of diary space between 1953 and 1966. He himself, when summarizing his life's work in 1969 as a guide for a possible biographer, gave little mention to his industrial activities. Indeed, he wholly omitted his time with Tube Investments and the North British Locomotive Company which between them covered ten years, probably because both ended unsatisfactorily in his eyes. Even in respect of British Oxygen, where he was content and from which he retired on excellent terms with his colleagues, he regarded the most significant part of his work to be his 'periodic trips to different parts of the world' which, fortunately, it has been possible to include in this edition in the context of his imperial interests. Two further omissions concern undertakings in the last part of his life of which he was particularly proud. These were, first, his success in salvaging twenty-one shillings and sixpence in the pound for the shareholders of the State Building Society of which he was the chairman, 1960–4; and secondly, his chairmanship of the Labour party's commission on advertising, the unanimous report of which was, to his great chagrin, quietly buried when Labour came to power after 1964. John Reith's diary was not, however, a record of his public life alone. He also wrote copiously on personal and family matters. Room has only been found for selections from this part of his diary when his private concerns influenced his public life. Otherwise personal and family entries have been excluded. But their intrinsic interest is naturally so slight that their exclusion is doubly justified on grounds of content as well as of space.

To sum up, the diary in its surviving form is both long and dense. For a third of the period which it covers it is in the form of a summary of an original which no longer exists. Additional materials, as lengthy as the diary they sustain but with disappointingly few letters, are collected in an unpaginated and unindexed jungle of 'enclosure' volumes. From all this the present edition has been extracted.

2. Hopes for a political career

The extracts from John Reith's diary given in this chapter begin with his arrival in London in October 1922 when he was hoping to find his vocation in a political career. This was not the result of sudden impulse; he had long entertained political ambitions and had indulged himself in dreams of this sort as a schoolboy and as an apprentice. Just before he left the Manse for London in February 1914 he had taken his first practical step in this direction, noting in his diary:

> I went to see Gulland, the Chief Liberal Whip for Scotland. I was awfully keen to go into Parliament.

But although he had this general ambition before the war it was not until he was at the front in 1915 that he gave it precise expression. He then wrote to his father putting his case to be allowed to go to Oxford after the war so as to be 'ready and equipped to enter politics'. He developed his argument in a long letter:

> *27 March 1915* The intervention of this war in my 'career', forsooth, may have very good effects because, as you know, I have for now long had the idea very firmly fixed that I was to go into Parliament some time and that I never would consider that I was on the right tracks in life until I had.

He went on to plead to be allowed to develop his intellectual powers which he believed were being given no opportunity in his civilian work. He wanted to make money for his parents but not at the cost of stifling his intellect. For him intellect meant more than 'brains':

> intellect is the only one more precious possession than strength of will that a man may have. Strength of will may be developed; to some extent so may brains; but never intellect.

His 'horrible difficulty' was that if he went to Oxford he would be 'of no use financially for four or five years' and if he did not he 'would not be doing justice to the intellect with which he was born'. He begged his father to help him.

> What on earth can I do to decide? You see the ambition on the one side and the desire to use my higher abilities of intellect on the other . . . I shall eagerly expect some helpful words.

His father's answer was kind but discouraging. The intellectual life was not the highest; 'the eternal model for man's life is Christ's'. John could develop his intellect in Pearson's. As for the university . . . 'remember what Carlyle said that the best university is a good library'. Finally, he questioned the effectiveness of a life in politics:

> Let me caution you that Parliamentary life is not the desirable thing which you seem to think it, and a talk with some of the men already in the House might surprise you. What are you anxious to do in the world? To do as much good to your fellow men as you possibly can and so serve God in your generation? That *may* be attained by going into Parliament but only for the *very, very* few.

John Reith was not convinced by any of this. He rebutted each point with vigour and asserted the purity of his motives:

> Very few men have felt at an early age as I do that their life's work lies in the political field. My motives and my desires are based on very deep set convictions which you don't seem to credit. There is no *glamour* to me in the prospect of a political career but I think I see my duty very plainly marked and the greatest amount of influence is held by a Cabinet Minister. There are various things which I wish to do in the world, and to do them I have first to obtain the necessary influence.

Nevertheless, although not convinced, John Reith was for a time turned away from his political hopes by his father's discouragement and he did

George and
Adah Reith on
their wedding-day,
July 6, 1870

Lynedoch Street,
Glasgow, ca. 1914,
showing Park School
and Manse

John Reith as a baby

not revert to them for eighteen months. By this time he was settled in the United States and, perhaps reflecting his surroundings, he now felt that his entry into politics would be through the agency of money rather than intellect:

11 October 1916 If I ever do rise to the position in the State to which I aspire I think you will not be ashamed of your son. I know you will say that to be a good Christian is the most important thing and no doubt of it, but I also say this that a very strong Christian is terribly badly required in the State. We want a Gladstone-Cromwell combination mightily. In the next few years, however, I have more desire to make as much money as possible for your sake and mother's – not for my own sake by any means.

Once again his father sounded a warning note. 'Don't be ambitious for great things or much money,' he wrote in reply, 'and don't be in a hurry to make it.'

Notwithstanding this second dose of parental discouragement, John Reith clung to his political hopes. In February 1917, after dining at a table near to the American Secretary of State, he wrote again:

I am fully certain that I shall find my chief work in politics, either here or in the old country. I cannot ever be President of the United States as one must be born a Citizen. Politics are pretty rotten both here and in England but good men are therefore all the more needed.

He continued in these political aspirations when he returned to the United Kingdom in the autumn. His father, impressed by his achievements in America and convinced of the seriousness of his vocation, now accepted the situation. In February 1918 he told his son, 'I would be far from discouraging any legitimate ambition if you feel called to it,' only adding the proviso, 'don't forget that political life is full of snares and disappointments.' But John Reith was next faced by a graver obstacle than his father's discouragement. His wound had affected his hearing. He consulted a specialist who gave him bleak news:

12 November 1917 Doctor said nothing could be done for my deafness; it may stay as it is for ten years, but at 45 or 50 he expects me to need a battery affair. This was a terrible blow especially as I still have a political career in mind, which he advised me to give up. Then I felt that God could always stop the trouble.

This threat of deafness, although in fact it did not materialize until

R.D.–F

the last two years of his life, was enough, together with his other concerns while at Southwick, to push politics to the back of his mind for the whole of 1918. Then, as his demobilization approached and his engagement emphasized the need to find employment, his political interest revived. Already, a few days after his engagement in April 1919, he had taken advantage of his American experiences to call on Lord Bryce in London. They 'talked about America and Parliament and all', but John Reith 'wasn't impressed' by this distinguished former Cabinet minister and ambassador, and certainly nothing came of their meeting. Two months later, he made another move towards the political world:

17 June 1919 Saw Kenworthy [Liberal MP, later Lord Strabolgi] in the morning, he having advertised for a secretary and having liked my reply out of a thousand. Could have had the job but he isn't enough of a personality for me; his views too radical, salary too low.

After this, he once again placed politics behind him and concentrated on his job in the Ministry of Munitions. Then, as this job came to a close, he flirted yet again with the idea of a political career. This time he aimed at the Labour party and towards the end of March 1920, just before he had the offer of the job at Coatbridge, which he accepted, and just after he had the opportunity of going to Bombay, which he rejected, he wrote to J. R. Clynes who was soon to be the chairman of the parliamentary Labour party:

Letter to J. R. Clynes, March 1920[1]

I am not known to you but I take the liberty of addressing you on a matter which is of very deep moment to me.

I am a civil engineer and the fact of my having just received an offer of most exceptional professional and financial attractiveness in India has made me resolve to lose no further time in writing to you, a project which I have had in mind for some months.

The matter is that since boyhood I have been of a mind that I might do the best service (I use the word in its highest significance) by entering politics . . .

My father was a clergyman in Scotland – Moderator of the Church – famous for his impassioned advocacy of righteousness in every department of human activity. Is this what the Labour Party of today stands for, or is it not? It seems to me that it is and that is why I write to you. Further, I am most anxious to know if you agree that this can best and quickest (and I think *only*) be attained by an unqualified, deliberate, manly and aggressive adoption of the principles expounded by Christ . . .

I have made no political connection because I have looked for the party which builds on such ground. One grows weary of hearing of parties and sections of parties each building on ground more unstable than the others, and I have thought that yours has at any rate the reflection of the true light.

I am only 30 but I have handled some big work already [and] the further I go the more do I become obsessed with the thought that my service should be on the lines along which I venture to write to ask your advice.

Much of the seeming failure of Christianity is due to the weakness of its exponents and to their failure to show its absolute practicability to the problems of today and that it alone contains the solution. I believe a strong exposition of its wonderful principles would cause a profound impression . . .

Letter from J. R. Clynes, House of Commons, 12 April 1920
I regret that owing to great pressure of work a reply has been delayed.

It is difficult to advise on the outstanding point in your letter. A more reliable opinion than I can give might be expressed by Mr Arthur Henderson, MP [the effective parliamentary Labour leader at this time]. He has been more in touch with the work of religious bodies in relation to Labour movements.

Personally I share the view you express respecting the relation of the Christian doctrine to our own objects, and perhaps I could talk with you if you send in for me sometime at the House of Commons.

If his Christian convictions drew John Reith towards the Labour party, Clynes's cool reception of his approach prevented anything from cementing this alliance. In any event Reith's experiences at Coatbridge, as we have seen, sharpened his distaste for organized labour. His diary reflects this process. So when, at the end of 1920, Labour increased its representation in the Glasgow Corporation elections Reith's terse comment was 'a rotten business'. A few months later, when the coal strike of 1921 began, his view was that it was 'dastardly'. It was the inefficiency arising from Trade Union action which shocked him; he was not simply a boss's man and he viewed the inefficiency of employers' organizations with equal distaste. He made this point in an anonymous article which he contributed to the *Glasgow Citizen* in April 1922; he then wrote:

> Personality counts. There is no personality in either a union or a federation. Managers and men are often compelled to act contrary to their inclinations and judgement in order to conform to the instructions of organizations, of their own making perhaps, which, however beneficial in some respects in their original functions, seem now to have become one of the greatest deterrents to the harmonious conduct of industry.

So it is hardly surprising that when John Reith returned to London in October 1922, looking once more for a political opening, his contacts and his sympathies were with the supporters of Lloyd George's declining coalition government and not with Labour.

3. The General Election of 1922

John Reith's political contact in London was Sir William Bull, Conservative MP for Hammersmith since 1900 and the chairman of the London Unionist MPs. He was a solicitor with offices in Lincoln's Inn. Bull's son, Stephen, had met Reith at Gresham's in June when he had given his talk on 'Choosing a Career' and had visited him in Scotland, along with others from Holt, in September just before he set out for London. This had been the occasion for Reith to write to Sir William who, as is explained in Chapter Two, had given him an interview on his arrival and encouraged him ten days later by the offer of the post of secretary to the London Unionist MPs. But it was Lloyd George's resignation on 20 October which, leading as it did to a general election, enabled John Reith to participate briefly in political activity. His first assumption was that 'the political situation was so awful that Sir William Bull will not be able to do much'. And his first reaction, as his diary shows, was to contact the Central Unionist Office which was, of course, loyal to the new prime minister, Bonar Law. Only when Sir William Bull invited him to act as his personal assistant during the election and he accepted, did he transfer his loyalties from Unionist headquarters and Bonar Law's government to the Coalition Conservatives loyal to Austen Chamberlain, of whom Sir William Bull was one. The following extracts give his account of this period; the politicians to whom he refers divide into two main groups. On the one hand there were those serving under Bonar Law or well inclined to his government such as:

Reginald McKenna, former Liberal minister,
[Sir] Leslie Wilson, Conservative chief whip,
and W. C. [later Lord] Bridgeman, home secretary.

On the other hand there were those who followed Austen Chamberlain in loyalty to Lloyd George's coalition, such as:

Sir Warden Chilcott, Conservative MP,
Lord Birkenhead ('F.E.'), formerly lord chancellor,
Edward Goulding, Lord Wargrave,
Lord Long of Wraxall,
Sir Leslie Scott, formerly solicitor-general,
Sir Robert Horne, formerly chancellor of the exchequer,
Sir Ernest Pollock, formerly attorney-general,
Sir Philip Sassoon, Conservative MP,
Sir John Gilmour, Conservative MP,
Commander Oliver Locker-Lampson, PPS to Austen Chamberlain
and Walter Elliott, Conservative MP.

Between these two groups there were those who settled with Bonar Law, or his successor Baldwin, after an initial period of loyalty to Chamberlain, such as:

Colonel G. A. Gibbs,
Sir Laming Worthington-Evans, formerly at the War Office,
and F. C. Thomson, PPS to Sir Robert Horne.

23 October 1922 Went to a meeting in Cannon Street Hotel – McKenna and City Members. Wrote to Colonel Leslie Wilson and had a very nice reply from him. The Independent Liberal Manifesto is really very good. Went to the Central Unionist Office and saw one Vesey who was very decent and asked me to return and see the chief organizer, but I did not see much use in this. I wrote to Bridgeman, who is the new home secretary, receiving a very nice reply the same night. He wants me to take some part in the Election.

26/27 October 1922 To Unionist headquarters again. Sir William Bull phoned up to ask me if I would come and help him, which I was very glad to do. Next morning [27th] went to his office at Hammersmith and started in as a sort of personal ADC. He immediately began to shove work on to me. We went to St Stephen's House to see some rooms, and then to see a man Chilcott, a wealthy member of the Coalition party who are now co-ordinating themselves round Austen Chamberlain. Bull told me he declined a peerage but accepted a baronetcy. Wrote a good part of W.B.'s election address for him.

30 October 1922 Went with W.B. to see Chilcott. There is evidently no lack of money for this little party and it seems to be in the hands of one Colonel Gibbs,[2] and W.B. is apparently meant to look after them and he is having me do that for him. Getting to Lincoln's Inn we found a message saying that W.B. and I were expected to be at Lord Birkenhead's house at 5.00. The house was full of books and beautiful pictures. He was wearing a tweed suit and red and white tie and kept pacing up and down the room. He said Lloyd George and Chamberlain and he were to speak at a big meeting in London [see below, 4 November]. Ll.G. wanted W.B. to take the chair, which I could see pleased the latter, although he was not sure of his position with the Conservative party, as this sort of thing was apt to get him in bad with the Unionists. Chilcott arrived and a rather objectionable fellow, Thomson, Lloyd George's chief agent for the National Liberals. We adjourned to his office where Goulding also was and went through arrangements.

31 October 1922 Finished election addresses and went to take possession of the new offices in St Stephen's House. Nobody seems to know what is happening.

1 November 1922 Heard that Colonel Gibbs had deserted. W.B. asked me to go to Birmingham to see Chamberlain.

2 November 1922 Sent up W.B.'s letter to Austen Chamberlain and was immediately received by him in his sitting room in his dressing-gown. I liked him and he was very civil to me. I put various questions to him and got it definitely that he did not want to create embarrassment or dissension in the Party, but that he did want W.B. to keep things together in London. He thinks it is most unfortunate that in these days moderate-minded men should not be united in face of the Labour menace. Returned to London and went to W.B. who was much pleased. Tea at Lord Long's house and told him about the visit to Chamberlain. After I had gone he said to W.B., 'I am impressed by that big man of yours; where did you get him?'

3 November 1922 We went to Vincent Square where Lloyd George is staying. I was quite thrilled by being introduced. Only W.B. and I there. He was very polite and most interested, questioning me about what Chamberlain said yesterday. He was criticizing Bonar Law's absence of policy.

4 November 1922 To the meeting in the Stoll Opera House, where I met a great many interesting people and was thanked by Lloyd George, Chamberlain, F.E. and others. To the Savoy to meet W.B. A questionnaire is to be addressed to all candidates to see if they are favourable to co-operation again [i.e. to a renewal of the Coalition].

5 November 1922 Was going to go to Church but W.B. phoned before I was out of bed and I had to go to see him. He wanted me to sign a letter to be lithographed to all candidates asking for their election addresses, but I was not on for that, so he got someone else to do it and I was to organize the affair.

6 November 1922 Early to printers and put this letter idea in hand. Sir Leslie Scott phoned three times from Liverpool; finds need for Chamberlain to speak for him. Many phones from the National Liberal headquarters asking for speakers. Tried to get McKenna for Scott, who had said that Birkenhead was no good as people were furious with him for his attack on Lord Derby.[3] The Unionist headquarters are trying to get all Chamberlain's supporters won over. Phoned to Sir Robert Horne in Glasgow to get him to go to Liverpool. Chilcott phoned to say that he had been returned unopposed at Liverpool, and had travelled with Lord Derby and would make it up with him and Birkenhead. He said he bluffed a Labour candidate out of standing by offering to pay his expenses and give him £1000 if he polled one vote in three. Thomson of the National Liberals, I dislike, and he makes a mess of things.

9/10 November 1922 I got out a list of Chamberlain's supporters in various categories. I suggested a questionnaire should be put out after the General Election. They have been trying to get one round now. Sent copies of list to various people like Scott, Worthington-Evans, Horne and Pollock. To a meeting of W.B.'s in Hammersmith which was made pretty rowdy by Labour people.

15 November 1922 Election Day. W.B. wanted me to distribute handbills in the street, but that is beyond me. However I took an immense pile and presented them to a boy in the street, who was delighted. To the Town Hall [Hammersmith] to watch the count. Pandemonium – with the gallery full of Labour rowdies. The poll was declared at 1.30; W.B. in with a majority of 4,400. Tube to Dover Street – thick fog – and watched the returns till 4.00 a.m., Glasgow being almost wholly for Labour.

16 November 1922 Results put Bonar Law in with a good majority. The Unionists got 20 more, Independent Liberals 50 less and Labour 40 more than expected. We should have preferred a very small Unionist poll so as to have had another election soon, which would have left Chamberlain in a strong position. Birkenhead phoned to ask me to arrange a dinner for tomorrow night at Sir Philip Sassoon's, so I had to telephone all over the country and had it all fixed by 7.15. Back to office at 9.00 and then to Ll.G.'s house to go through lists of Chamberlain's supporters with Cope and Miss Stevenson.[4] Ll.G. is trying to get Chamberlain's people in his pocket. I was asked if they would stand pressure and so on. I was very careful.

17 November 1922 Visited 11 Downing Street to see Chamberlain with W.B. Chamberlain said I had been of immense service to him.

18 November 1922 Birkenhead sent me the names of 58 peers whom he wanted to dine with him next Wednesday [22nd November]. I was very fed up as I was alone in the office and wanted to get off. I did the job by 3.15 p.m.

22/23 November 1922 To see Lord Wargrave (as Goulding now is) with W.B. about a dinner list for the 30th. Chamberlain, Gilmour and Worthington-Evans called. Much confabs. Whitehall was stiff with police for the opening of Parliament for fear of the unemployed, who appeared to have gathered from different parts of the country. Nothing happened.

30 November 1922 W.B. passed all the seating arrangements for the dinner which took place in the House [of Commons]. Birkenhead had left Balfour's letter at home.[5] Fortunately I was taking no chances and had a copy which he read out. Chamberlain's speech was good and the whole affair went excellently. I told Chamberlain that I had always been a Liberal but that I liked his line and thought it the only possible one if people did not want Labour rule.

5 December 1922 F.E. is running a candidate at Portsmouth against L. Wilson.[6] Locker-Lampson said that the first time he saw Bonar Law as PM he was wearing brown boots, tweed trousers, morning coat and a soft hat.

13 December 1922 Called a meeting at my office. The following attended Austen C[hamberlain], F.E., Horne, Pollock, Scott, Worthington-Evans, Locker-Lampson, Chilcott, Elliott, and F. C. Thomson. I stayed in the room during the meeting. They were discussing what attitude to adopt towards Bonar Law's government which is in an embarrassing position owing to their standing aloof. A.C. definitely did not approve of any of them taking office. They agreed to keep quiet but to come to the rescue of the government if necessary and when good occasion offered.

4. Politics and the General Strike, 1923–6

The directors of the British Broadcasting Company had interviewed John Reith as their prospective general manager on the very same day that the leaders of the Coalition Conservatives had met in his office. His appointment to the BBC the next day marks the end of his flirtation with the idea of a political career. Broadcasting was to be his 'great opportunity' and his dreams of entering the House of Commons were forgotten. His concern now was to use his political contacts and his political experience to keep well with all three parties for the better development of broadcasting. So although he retained his position as secretary to the London Unionist Committee until July 1924 he did this for Sir William Bull 'personally' and he took no active part in the general elections of 1923 and 1924, such as he had in 1922. But broadcasting was soon seen to be a political weapon of some importance so that John Reith, as its effective head, was naturally brought in touch with the political leaders of the time, particularly Baldwin and MacDonald, the prime ministers of the period, with both of whom he was to establish a sympathetic relationship. The extracts which follow show how this developed.

31 May 1923 The Labour party are showing considerable hostility to us so I had a talk with Ammon [Labour whip] in the House of Commons for an hour and did very useful work.

21 June 1923 Lunched with William Bull at the House of Commons.

Tea there later with Ammon and [Herbert] Morrison and made them very friendly. Also dined in the House with Locker-Lampson and took him afterwards to see our place.

20 October 1923 Met Sir Reginald Hall, chief agent for the Unionist party. He hoped we should be able to broadcast the prime minister from Plymouth; but I am sure this will not come off.

[Parliament was dissolved in November and a general election was held on 6 December. The outcome was MacDonald's first Labour government. John Reith immediately set about to try to make its members friendly to broadcasting, particularly the new postmaster general, Vernon Hartshorn, with whom he thought he had been 'quite successful' by February 1924. But the government was in a minority in the House of Commons and soon came to grief. On 9 October 1924 Parliament was dissolved yet again. This time there was a substantial Conservative majority. In Reith's opinion Baldwin's superior use of the new medium of broadcasting greatly helped him.]

11/12 October 1924 The government whips rang up in the evening to say that we could have one political broadcast from each party but suggested I should phone the PMG in South Wales to confirm this, which I did. The PM wants his speech at Glasgow on Monday night 13th broadcast. This will be a great mistake, and the PMG agreed, but said we had better go ahead. I warned the Whips' office, but they could, or would, do nothing about it. This is the first occasion on which we have broadcast political speeches.

15 October 1924 Baldwin came at 5.30 to see what he had to do when he broadcast, and was very agreeable. MacDonald's, the day before yesterday, was quite hopeless. It will do him considerable harm.

16/17 October 1924 Dined with Mr Baldwin, Mrs, daughter and Colonel Storr [secretary to the Conservative shadow cabinet] at the Savoy. Then he gave an excellent twenty minutes talk, which will, I expect, win the election for him. Asquith's broadcast from Paisley was not good.

28 October 1924 Much political excitement. I hope the Unionist party have a really decisive majority as otherwise things are so unsatisfactory. I have been having some sympathy with the Labour lot, but not now, having been much put off by MacDonald's speech.

[Baldwin was now prime minister again.]

3 December 1924 The PM sent for me about broadcasting the King's Speech [i.e. at the opening of Parliament]. I saw him in the Cabinet Room and he was very nice. Evidently he would like to have it done. He said the last time we met had been on a momentous occasion, to which I said 'Yes – and a highly auspicious one.' I felt rattled in a way being summoned to see him.

5 March 1925 First meeting with Ramsay MacDonald in his room at the House. I quite liked him and found him interesting.

Lunch with Tom Johnston [Labour] MP. I was glad to meet him. A rough sort of fellow but straightforward. Anyhow he will be friendly to the BBC.

13 March 1925 Took Mother to meet Ramsay MacDonald who gave her tea in his room at the House.

27 March 1925 Muriel and I dined at No. 10 with the PM and Mrs Baldwin; no one else there. They were very friendly. I think I did some useful work for Broadcasting. Going to Savoy Hill [BBC headquarters] there was a detective in the front of the car and the PM was very funny about him. He said it was one of the great perquisites of the office and that he thought he had obtained true eminence when his car drove down the wrong side of Piccadilly one day when he was in a hurry. I suggested that my ability to broadcast from my own study was also greatness in a form, to which he agreed. The PM said he would like to have had a set at Chequers, so I said we would supply him with one, or would he prefer to pay for it. He said he did not like sponging on anyone but quite frankly he would like to have it given to him, and that he was overdrawn at the bank. He said he used to be quite well to do but there was no money in his present job.

8 May 1925 Met Ramsay MacDonald and had much talk with him. He was very affable.

[By the end of 1925 Reith knew that the prime minister held him in high regard from the reports of Sir Ronald Waterhouse, (Baldwin's private secretary), and of his old friend and political patron Sir William Bull. The events of the General Strike in May 1926 were to bring him into close touch with Baldwin on a matter of critical national importance.]

23 April 1926 A general strike is brewing so I phoned J. C. C. Davidson, who is vice-chairman of the Emergency Committee. [His official position was parliamentary secretary to the Admiralty.]

30 April 1926 It was certainly as well I was in touch with Davidson; at 11.45 the coal stoppage was announced and I received an intimation from a Cabinet meeting at No. 10 which, having had the dance music cut off, I announced from my study at midnight.

[Writing seven years later when he was summarizing this part of his diary Reith noted that his entries for the period of the General Strike were a fortnight late. He added: 'I was most happy throughout. I do not say that I welcome crises, but I do welcome the opportunities which they bring. The story would be much fuller and more interesting had I been able to write it daily.']

1 May 1926 Communicated with the PM's office with a view to his sending us a statement tonight. Davidson phoned to say that the TUC were meeting the PM at 8.30 and that the PM wanted to suggest this message to me – 'Keep steady; remember that peace on earth comes to men of goodwill.' I gave this myself at 9.40.

2 May 1926 The Chief Civil Commissioner [Sir William Mitchell Thomson, the postmaster general] phoned asking for a list of the power stations supplying all our power. I took it round after tea and told him I was keeping in touch with Davidson. I kept our transmitter open, making announcements every half hour; the messages mostly came by phone to me from Davidson. At 1.00 a.m. he told me negotiations had broken off and he said he was bringing round a statement from the Cabinet. At 1.10 I broadcast this from my study.

3 May 1926 Everyone was on edge today. I went to see Davidson at the Admiralty and then to the Home Office to see about the protection of BBC premises all over the country. Davidson gave me authority to arrange news bulletins at any hour. The telephone was ringing all evening and I was up till 2.00 in the morning.

4 May 1926 With Davidson to the Admiralty as he was anxious to have me there. His special job is the control of all news. Things were very mixed up at the Admiralty and Davidson with no clear ideas of what he wants me to do, nor what he is supposed to be doing himself. A government newspaper, called the *British Gazette*, is to be produced.

Caird of the War Office is to edit it. He apparently thought that the BBC news was to be regarded as a kind of off-shoot to that. I told him I was not going to have that at all. Our news bulletins today were pretty rotten as things were not working properly at the Admiralty. Lunched at the Travellers' Club coming upon the PM there. He said we had the key situation now and everyone depended on us. He asked if we were properly protected and I said we were everywhere. Savoy Hill is hotching with policemen and special constables. He said the government had no alternative but to break off negotiations. I said he ought to broadcast soon. Home at 8.00. Davidson came in at 1.00 a.m. with a first copy of the *British Gazette*. He was pleased with it, but I told him I did not think much of it.

5 May 1926 Admiralty most of the day. The news was coming in better. To Savoy Hill for a short time where the emergency news service is getting under way. I am vetting every item of every bulletin. A long talk with Davidson and Storr late at night regarding the whole news question. Things are really badly muddled and Churchill wants to commandeer the BBC. I met 'Jix' [Sir William Joynson-Hicks, the home secretary] at Savoy Hill who made an appeal for 50,000 special constables. I had a talk with him after about the BBC position and got him to agree to what I wanted.

6 May 1926 I went with Davidson to see the PM about the BBC position immediately after breakfast. He walked up and down the Cabinet Room while Davidson and I leaned against the mantelpiece and explained our views – at least I said what I thought and Davidson joined in. Every time I made a point the PM stopped in his perambulations and faced us. He said he entirely agreed with us that it would be far better to leave the BBC with a considerable measure of autonomy and independence. He said I ought to go to the meeting of the Cabinet committee which is called the S+T meeting. I got Davidson to see Mitchell-Thomson beforehand and then went to the meeting at the Home Office. 'Jix' was in the chair; he told me that the PM had sent for him immediately after I had left and told him that he wanted to leave the BBC to me. He told me it was all right, but he was not strong in the chair. Churchill, Birkenhead, Mitchell-Thomson, Hoare, Worthington-Evans, Cunliffe-Lister, Bridgeman and several other ministers present,[7] most of them with their permanent secretaries. I had got Bridgeman to go although he had not intended to. Jix said that as I was there they would take Broadcasting first, and asked Davidson to start off. Jix then said that he had been authorized by the PM to say he preferred to trust the BBC in particular Mr Reith the managing director, to do what was best. He agreed with that. Winston emphatically objected, said it was monstrous not to use such an instrument to the best possible advantage. Jix then weakly said he would have it discussed at a Cabinet meeting if anybody felt strongly about it. Churchill then launched out on other matters without asking the chairman to say anything, and at this stage I thought I better clear out as they had apparently finished with broadcasting. Went home and drew up a statement[8] regarding the BBC position which I took along to Davidson for him to give to the PM tonight.

7 May 1926 There is a muddle up generally and we are not getting news as quickly, nor in as good shape, as we should be. Winston was making a nuisance of himself at the *British Gazette* offices. The Cabinet was supposed to discuss the BBC position but did not get to it. The Archbishop of Canterbury [Randall Davidson] phoned to me to ask to be allowed to broadcast a manifesto drawn up by the leaders of all the Churches. I asked him to let me see it and when it came I found it was a suggestion that the Strike should be called off and negotiations opened concurrently. As the PM had said he would not negotiate until the Strike was called off, I was sure the manifesto should not be broadcast. The Archbishop had sent a copy to the PM so I phoned Waterhouse to find out what the PM thought. He got on to Fry [Baldwin's personal private secretary] who said that the PM had told the Archbishop that he would not stop it being broadcast, but would prefer not. In view of what Fry said, I said I would turn it down on my own, and I told the Archbishop by telephone, putting it as nicely as I could. He told me that he supposed the PM had objected, but out of loyalty I said I was not going by that. The BBC is in a very awkward position. Davidson told me later in the evening categorically that the Archbishop's statement should not be broadcast.

On Wednesday evening [i.e. 5 May] I had been visited by a deputation from the executive of the parliamentary Labour party, [Charles] Trevelyan and [William] Graham. I explained the situation as best I could and they seemed satisfied that we were doing all we could in the circumstances. Today I had a letter from Graham asking if one of their people could speak.

8 May 1926 A letter from the Archbishop, very worried about our not letting him broadcast. I thought I had better go and see him. Mrs Trevelyan brought a Labour man about the Archbishop matter –

[Hugh] Dalton. I thought I made him understand the position. A long talk with the Archbishop in the afternoon. He is still worried and so am I. He asked about his sermon tomorrow (to be broadcast from St Martin's) and said he would like me to see his notes. I said I did not want to. Waterhouse rang up to say that the PM was taking my advice and could he speak tonight. I said, yes, at 9.30 and that I would call for him at 9.10. By 8.00 everything was in order for the broadcast from my study. I thought it was much better there than going to Savoy Hill. I collected the PM, a police tender with about a dozen policemen close behind us all the way. Muriel talked to him for a bit after he arrived, then he had a voice test, then gave me his manuscript asking me what I thought of 'this tripe' and to make any comments. He said he thought of ending with something personal, and I said yes, something about trusting him. Then I said, 'What about this – I am a man of peace; I am longing and working and praying for peace; but I will not compromise the dignity of the British constitution.' He said, 'Excellent; write it down if you have a legible hand.' Then he said 'surrender' not 'compromise' and that he might say that he had been returned to power eighteen months ago by the biggest majority for many years, and what had he done to forfeit that confidence? 'Have I done anything?' I suggested. He was sitting at my desk and I announced over his shoulder. Davidson was sitting in one of the big armchairs. I began to think of what I had written; I did not like the word 'dignity' at such a crisis. I wrote this on a bit of paper to Davidson and he suggested 'safety' or 'security'. The PM had reached the second last page but I took the last from under his hand and wrote in 'safety and security'. When he came to this, he paused but almost imperceptibly. He spoke for under ten minutes. He was anxious to hurry back because Mrs Baldwin would be worrying about him. In the car going back he indicated quite clearly that his anxieties were not lessened by some of his colleagues.

9 May 1926 Saw the Archbishop's chaplain with the sermon for tonight. He reverted to the Church's manifesto, but it was quite innocuous. Grey of Fallodon [former Liberal foreign secretary] spoke tonight, and I had a message asking if I would collect him from Churchill's house, No. 11. I had not met Winston before. Hearing that someone had come to collect Lord Grey, he came out and asked me in to have coffee. He asked me if I were connected with the BBC. I said I was the managing director. He swung round with 'Are you Mr Reith?' – almost shouted out. I said I was. He said he had been hunting for me all the week. I said I was on the job all the time and he could have asked me to come

along, and that he ought to do so when he was feeling indignant with us. He was really very stupid; his wife backed him up but Lord Grey approved the idea of keeping the BBC to some extent impartial. He was quite polite throughout, but I certainly kept our end up. I told him that if we put out nothing but government propaganda we should not be doing half the good that we were. He came to the car with us. He said he had heard that I had been badly wounded in the war. I said that was so but that had no bearing on my actions at present, which embarrassed him.

10 May 1926 I have been reading some of the news bulletins myself as the result of complaints that our announcers had been sounding panicky. I spent a lot of time yesterday making arrangements for better and quicker working of the news. Ramsay MacDonald telephoned twice to me today, so I rang him up at 6.20. He was reasonable enough. He said he was very anxious to give a talk. I said we were not entirely a free agent, but that he might send his manuscript along. I got it with a friendly note offering to make any alterations which I wanted. I sent it at once to Davidson for him to ask the PM, strongly recommending that they should allow it to be done. I do not think they treat me altogether fairly. They will not say we are to a considerable extent controlled, and they make me take the onus of turning people down. They were quite against MacDonald broadcasting, but I am certain it would have done no harm to the government. Of course it puts me in a very awkward and unfair position. I imagine it comes chiefly from the PM's difficulties with the Winston lot.

11 May 1926 The Cabinet were to make a decision at long last about the BBC. Davidson was going to it. I primed him up with all the arguments and he came to see me at 7.15. As he was smiling broadly I saw it was all right. The decision was not a definite one, but at any rate we are not going to be commandeered. The Cabinet decision is really a negative one. They want to be able to say that they did not commandeer us, but they know that they can trust us not to be really impartial. Davidson came round again at 9.15 and we were supposed to draft a notice defining the BBC position. I wanted the inconsistencies in our acts so far squared up, setting us right with the other side. Davidson, however, thought the Cabinet would only agree to a statement that we could do nothing to help the Strike since it had been declared illegal. This does not seem to me straight.

John Reith 1913/14

Adah Reith ca. 1913
George Reith ca. 1913

12 May 1926 Davidson came round with a statement, but I did not like it. He then went to the PM and later to Savoy Hill. We discussed the statement and finally agreed on one which I did not think nearly comprehensive enough.

[The preparation of this statement was not completed in time for the lunch-time news bulletin so John Reith did not read it.]

I had just begun to read the news, when I was told I was wanted urgently on the phone from Downing Street. So I broke off and said I would stop for the moment as it might be more important news was coming. Waterhouse gave me a message, which I went back to the microphone and read, to the effect that the TUC leaders had visited the PM and announced their intention of calling off the Strike forthwith. It was rather wonderful to have been the first to give the news. So the Strike has lasted nine and a half days. I cannot pretend that I am not disappointed in some ways, and I have no doubt this is wrong. It is, however, great fun running a crisis . . . Back to the office at 9.00. A message was sent to me from the PM. There was a message from the King also. I read the King's message, and then the PM's and then a little thing of our own, and then Blake's 'Jerusalem'.

14 May 1926 J. H. Thomas [general secretary of the NUR] telephoned to ask if he could broadcast tonight – an appeal to railwaymen to go back to work. I told Davidson about this and he phoned Downing Street, with the result that I told Thomas it would be all right if he said something nice about the employers and sent in his manuscript. It came at 7.00 and was quite unexceptionable. I met him at 9.15 and found him very cock-a-hoop. He said he had been instrumental in getting the Strike called off and a railway agreement reached.

18 May 1926 Correspondence with Ramsay MacDonald and William Graham. We are properly in bad with the Labour party. I suppose they are utterly humiliated and their judgement and outlook warped. I was rather surprised at Graham, although I knew that our explanation could not sound very conclusive.

28 May 1926 I am still in fatuous correspondence with Ramsay Mac-Donald and Graham, though the former is much less unreasonable than the latter. Visited by Miss Ellen Wilkinson, Labour MP, and had some discussion with her.

5. Conservative decline and the second Labour government, 1926–31

In the aftermath of the General Strike John Reith worked hard to restore the BBC's good relations with the Labour party and its leaders. In the three years that followed he was to draw closer to Ramsay MacDonald without in any way losing touch with Baldwin so that by the time of the general election of 1929, which led to the second Labour government, he was helping both men with their broadcasts. At the same time he worked to free the BBC from the embargo on controversy in broadcasting, an embargo which was eventually lifted in 1928. As for himself, as his discontent with the new chairman and board of the BBC grew so his hopes of a political career revived; he looked now not to the House of Commons or the Cabinet but to some high diplomatic or imperial appointment.

3 October 1926 In the afternoon by tube, which I had not been in for over a year, to Upper Frognal Lodge, where I found Ramsay MacDonald tying up rambler roses. Went for an hour's walk on the Heath with him. He knew about Mrs Snowden's appointment to the new Corporation[9] and was furious about it, saying she did not represent the Labour party at all, is loathed by them and is held to be responsible for most of Philip's stupidities. We had much talk about the BBC. It is a pity the Labour party generally are so thin-skinned and suspicious. Apparently MacDonald thought it was owing to us that he had not been allowed to give a talk from the studio in the last General Election. I told him it was the fault of his own people, and that I had recommended his talking from a studio. Later Oswald Mosley [at this time a Labour MP] and his wife came; said to be the most unpopular man in the House of Commons. Left 6.30. MacDonald goes on holiday to the Sahara. I have booked him for a talk on his return.

12 December 1926 I collected MacDonald at the House of Commons and took him to Savoy Hill where he gave his Sahara talk. He was most affable.

22 December 1926 Home at 6.55 and found Ramsay MacDonald already there. He stayed till 10.30 and we had quite an interesting evening and I liked him.

14 June 1927 In the House of Commons about a place for the new BBC headquarters. Quarter of an hour's talk with Winston Churchill in a corridor, he sitting on a table and holding forth about controversy in broadcasting. He was glad to find that I was all for it, and I ditto with him.

11 July 1927 Ramsay MacDonald for lunch. Very successful. He agreed that big jobs were still very largely the perquisite of Etonians and said that most Foreign Office jobs were going to RCs. He said the RC influence was extending to the Consular Service also.

4 February 1928 I cancelled my dancing lesson tonight because I thought the PM might send for me, which he actually did. I was with him for about 40 minutes. This arose out of my telling Waterhouse that I thought it was time I went to another job. I told the PM I thought I should be doing something busier now and that the BBC would not suffer. He said I did the right thing in coming to tell him. He said Winston was always wanting more results from the government, but that no matter how much imagination, vision or courage he had (he said) it was like being stuck in a glue-pot. He was sure I would not be happy in a purely commercial job and asked me very closely if my going would not affect the BBC. I said I should not have thought of it if it would. He talked about the coming generation. I said they lapped up any advice on idealism etc. and he agreed. He is talking to students of Cambridge and Aberystwyth shortly. He spoke of governor-general-ships and agreed how poor a job they were. When he asked if I had any job in mind I said the only ones that seemed suitable were the Electricity Board and the Canadian high commissionership. I said if he thought I should stay on and wait I would do so. I mentioned Washington and India and he said it was very odd my mentioning India as he was going to speak to the students about that. He asked me to let him have a fortnight or so to think things over.

13 April 1928 Winston Churchill asked me to go and see him at the Treasury this afternoon. I was there for about an hour, he giving me tea. Churchill was anxious to know what we were going to do about the Budget. I said we were ready to broadcast from the House of Commons direct, but it had been turned down. He asked me to have another try for this with the PM and added that I had a great influence with him. I told him what we were going to do otherwise, and he said he would like to come to the studio and speak for 15 minutes the next night, factual and non-controversial. Much discussion about the handling of political controversy. He asked if the rumours of my leaving the BBC were true and said he was very thankful that they were not. He said he thought I had about the biggest job in the country.

25 April 1928 Collected Winston Churchill at the House of Commons at 9.15 and took him to Savoy Hill, where he delivered a good defence of his Budget, supposed to be non-controversial but was not.

11 December 1928 Saw Sir Maurice Hankey [secretary to the Cabinet] and told him I was worried about my future, wondering what I ought to be doing. He was most sympathetic. We spoke of India and Washington, his views being as one might expect, opposition from the 'regulars' with respect to the latter; but as to India, he thought I might begin via East Africa, where there may be a new job going. It is obvious that political service and payments to the party and such like are more important than efficiency.

14 February 1929 Lunched with Ramsay MacDonald. He wanted to talk about political broadcasting, the Labour party being so dependent on the wireless. I told him we would agree if the three parties agreed among themselves. We might even make arrangements if two of them did. He said the Labour party were ready to agree to almost anything.

21 February 1929 Saw the PM who seemed to be in much better form generally. He asked me if I could give him some ideas for his inaugural address as Chancellor of St Andrews, which appointment he said pleased him very much. He was the first one who was not a peer, and his great-grandfather had fought at Culloden; now he was succeeding the Duke of Cumberland as Chancellor. I suggested various lines and said I would send him something along.[10] This started him off on the opportunities for young men today. As to India, he said he sometimes almost wished England could leave there for twenty years, except that we should never get back; also that he sometimes wished that the Gurkhas and Sikhs would come down from the north and teach the others a lesson. Where would the baboo politicians be then? I mentioned the East African job and said it was an opportunity of ensuring that a bastard democracy did not get hold of things as in India. I said that I was on the look-out for a job and hoped he had not forgotten our talk last year, and that a thorn in the spirit was worse than a thorn in the flesh. He was much amused and asked if I felt that I must burst.

26 February 1929 To the House of Lords for tea with Clarendon [chairman of the BBC] and Ramsay MacDonald over the rota for political speeches. MacDonald winked at me once in obvious derision of Clarendon, and it was well deserved, however improper. Less was accomplished than when I talked with MacDonald alone.

1 March 1929 Clarendon came in to say that he had been sent for by the PM, Davidson and Eyres Monsell [Conservative chief whip] being present, to talk about the political speeches rota. I was very annoyed about this and thought it must be Davidson's doing.

4 March 1929 House of Commons 4.00 to 8.15, and 8.45 to 9.05. The attack which the PMG expected from the Liberals did not materialize. What a ridiculous waste of time Parliament is.

23 and 26 March 1929 Much correspondence with Davidson and Samuel [chairman of the Liberal party] re political speeches. The political speeches matter is all muddled up, Davidson being more obstinate than usual. A long talk with Ramsay MacDonald on the telephone.

28 March 1929 Carpendale [Reith's BBC deputy] and I visited Vansittart [principal private secretary to the PM] and told him the whole story about Davidson's obstinacy too. Vansittart phoned to say Davidson agreed with me and everything was OK. Davidson then spoke to me. The government did not want two rotas during the Election period and Davidson suggested one extra to them which is weird. It is a pity that the PM is associated with people like this.

4/5/6 April 1929 A long letter from Ramsay MacDonald, he being much incensed about the political arrangement . . . Lindsay, Secretary of the Labour party to see me. Admitted his people acted too quickly. Samuel very decently agreed to change the second rota from *Conservative-Labour-Conservative-Liberal* to *Conservative-Liberal-Conservative-Labour* to meet the Labour party . . . Letter from Davidson saying the Conservatives cannot agree which is monstrous.[11]

8/9/11/13 April 1929 Met Worthington-Evans for the first political address. He was not very good, and I told him so . . . Still racketting about the political business and I am sick of it. To see Philip Snowden re the muddle and had an interesting talk. I found that his conception of nationalization was on BBC lines. I consider this applicable in many different ways[12] . . . Met Arthur Henderson broadcasting . . . Spoke to Ramsay MacDonald who had not behaved at all well over the political broadcasts.

Letter from Stanley Baldwin   13 April 1929
I should be very glad of some information before I broadcast on the 22nd, though I am doubtful if you can give it to me.

I want to classify my potential listeners, e.g. what proportion may be working class? Does wireless go to the workman, or is the workman listener an exception, or would he be likely to listen at a club or a pub?

Letter to Stanley Baldwin   14 April 1929
. . . As to classification, some believe that broadcasting is used by the different classes in the same proportion as those classes bear to the total population. If this is not so, it is used to a greater extent by the lower-middle and settled working classes. The social centre of gravity is much nearer the bottom than the top of the social scale. In the broadcast audience it is probably rather lower still.

You will have every sort of individual listening to you, and a large proportion of working class people, mostly in their homes, not in clubs or pubs. The workman and his wife will certainly be there, but so will the ordinary middle-class fellow and his, mostly at the fireside.

16/19 April 1929 To the office to meet Neville Chamberlain [minister of health] in the evening; he was very poor; he said he had had no time to prepare his address. I asked him what more important he could have had to do all week. We listened to Lloyd George from Plymouth and thought him very poor.

22 April 1929 Davidson phoned that the PM and Vansittart and he would be along at 8.45 and that the PM wanted to talk things over beforehand. I thought the PM would quite likely say he had not got an ending for his speech as he did when he broadcast during the Strike. I had therefore dictated three or four minutes of a peroration. He did ask me how he ought to finish up, so I said I had put something down. He was awfully pleased with it, but said it was too good for tonight and that he would use it on his second broadcast before Election Day. He was very friendly; said he was feeling horribly nervous, couldn't believe that anyone would be listening etc. He spoke from a few notes and did quite well, certainly better than anyone else in this series.

30 April 1929 The Liberal chief agent phoned to say that Lloyd George was very annoyed at not having a date in the same week as the PM and MacDonald, and said he wanted me to go along and see Lloyd George. I said I was not going along to be abused, nor to be kept waiting. He said Lloyd George would receive me at once and be civil, so I went and was there for about half an hour. He was quite amenable but I did not like him or his entourage. Dined at 11 Downing Street with Winston Churchill, Mrs C. and Boothby [PPS to Churchill] there. Quite an interesting evening. They all came to Savoy Hill in my car. His talk was very good and he stayed for some time afterwards. He seemed to think people might be murdered here as well as in India by the Swarajists. We had quite an argument about democracy, he criticizing parliamentary systems and being very inconsistent.

Letter from Mother   21 May 1929
I stopped in writing this letter to go and hear Mr Baldwin's address in the Drill Hall [Dumfries] – it was really very good. He had an enthusiastic reception and Mrs Baldwin looked so nice. I wish he and Ramsay could join forces; not LG. *Who* or *what* am I to vote for? For 'who' B; for 'what' R! Instead of a final speech of thanks he took out his watch and said, 'This is just the hour when I want to go and have a pipe.'

28 May 1929 To Newcastle. To the studio at 8.30 to meet MacDonald. He was very hoarse and tired. A lot of rehearsing and adjustment before he began for which he was very grateful. He spoke for 36 minutes and got very declamatory and bitter towards the end.

29 May 1929 To Manchester. The PM came at 8.45, Mrs Baldwin with him. He produced the two sheets which I had given him at Savoy Hill and asked if I remembered them.[13] He was very friendly.

[The General Election took place on 30 May. Baldwin was narrowly defeated and MacDonald formed his second minority administration. In spite of his friendly contacts with the new prime minister, John Reith grew increasingly out of sympathy with the Labour government. So when it broke up in 1931 he was firmly on the side of the national coalition which succeeded it, and in the negotiations over the political broadcasts for the General Election of that autumn he appeared to weight the balance in favour of the National government. Paradoxically, it was in these years that he was attacked for what were thought to be the left-wing tendencies of the BBC. From his own point of view these years were a time of relaxed tensions, once Lord Clarendon had been replaced as chairman of the BBC by J. H. Whitley; and while his dreams of viceregal or ambassadorial glory remained they were no longer actively pursued. His last diary reference to these hopes in this period was in November 1929, when he greeted the news of Sir Ronald Lindsay's appointment to be ambassador in Washington with the sad comment: 'another job for me gone'.]

20 March 1930 In the evening went to receive Mr Baldwin who was broadcasting an obituary about Lord Balfour, who died yesterday. He said he was very pleased that I had come to meet him; he lay on the sofa for twenty minutes beforehand. He said he always felt so safe with me and that it was very nice to be mothered.

1 June 1930 I have lost any sympathy I ever had with the Labour party, largely on account of MacDonald and Snowden; but the Conservatives are pretty hopeless too.

15 June 1930 Dined at the Royal Academy – an Imperial Press Conference dinner; Mr Baldwin spoke and said a good deal about the sense of responsibility in the Press which was badly wanted; I had two conversations with him in the evening and got his coat for him from the cloakroom, which he thought very kind. He said he needed all the goodwill he could get. I am now quite definitely hoping for his return to power as I am so disgusted with MacDonald, Snowden and the like.

8 August 1930 Fuss on with the PM over political broadcasting. Whitley approved a letter which I had written for him to sign to the PM's secretary. It preserves the dignity and autonomy of the BBC and might cause a row between the PM, who is being very unreasonable, and us.

13 October 1930 Lunched at Lord Stamfordham's [private secretary to King George V]. He is not in sympathy with Baldwin at all. I said the Conservatives probably needed a new leader altogether and one not now in Parliament, as it seemed likely otherwise there would be a split or if not that at best only a luke-warm policy. I am all against governing executives having to serve their time in Parliament.

30 October 1930 Baldwin got a vote of confidence at the party meeting today. What a sorry business it all is. I know how very difficult it is to decide whether to support the man out of decency, which he certainly deserves despite his lack of ability and energy, which again is certainly equally urgent today. I expect I would put loyalty to person above loyalty to cause but it is about the worst decision which anybody can have to make.[14]

5 November 1930 A letter from the prime minister, grumbling about a speech from the Bonar Law College.[15] It is odd that in the midst of all the numerous crises he should bother about such a matter. We had been assured that Baldwin's speech would be non-controversial before we agreed to take it. When MacDonald was in opposition he told me that a number of his people were complaining of the number of opportunities which Tory ministers had and asked whether he could not make a fuss about it. Now, of course, the boot is on the other foot.

12 November 1930 Muriel and I dined with Sir Herbert Samuel, a rather disappointing party as there was nobody specially interesting. I do not enjoy parties unless there are bigger people than myself present.

18 November 1930 Meeting in the House of Commons with the political party leaders 6.00 to 7.00. They had some sort of minutes of the previous meeting and in this it said that the BBC would not proceed in this matter without their agreement. I said we could not accept that, and after some discussion they agreed to eliminate it. I was asked to write an aide-memoire to cover the last meeting and this one. They accepted my schedule for the political broadcasts in toto; also for next year. I am always better at meetings of this sort when I am by myself.

27 February 1931 The *Morning Post* has been taking a very silly line against the BBC. The attack was to some extent personal against me on the grounds of Socialist bias, forsooth.

19 March 1931 I had to go off to see Lloyd George. Apparently there was some chance of the Liberals making an attack on us. Lloyd George spoke to me about our work in Wales and would like to join our Religious Committee. He said he had been critical but that now he was absolutely converted, and had a great admiration for our organization, policy and work. I always feel how magnetic his personality is, and can understand his hold on those immediately around him. It is difficult to keep in mind one's indignation, dislike and even contempt for a lot that he does when one is with him.

mid-June 1931 Lord Lloyd [chairman of the Navy League] to see me. I was interested to have a conversation with him, having heard so much about his style and methods. I rather think he thought he could 'put it across' me, but he did not bring this off. He came to talk about the Navy League in particular, and about BBC left-wingishness in general.

21 July 1931 Whitley and I saw Winston Churchill. He had renewed his application to be permitted to broadcast his views on India.[16] I asked Churchill to put himself in our place, gave him the whole situation quite frankly and asked him what he would do. Of course he still said that, in view of the extreme urgency and gravity of the situation, he would permit the extreme right view to be given, even against the India Office objection. Whitley asked him what his idea was about subsequent talks, but he said he did not mind what happened. I then said that we might have somebody from the extreme left and then finish up with a representative of the Round Table point of view. Whitley thought this was a very good idea. Churchill obviously wanted to talk to me afterwards, so I walked with him to the lift, and he said 'I can tell you are a friend.' Whitley and I both felt that the matter was worth investigating on the lines I had proposed, so we arranged to see Wedgwood Benn [secretary of state for India].

24 July 1931 Whitley and I saw Wedgwood Benn and Stewart [permanent head] of the India Office at the House of Commons. They are very anxious that we should not have the proposed series before the Round Table Conference. They do not seem to mind so much if we have it afterwards.

[Early in August John Reith set out on a short European tour, visiting Germany, Austria and Poland.]

24 August 1931 Warsaw. From a newspaper which someone else was reading I gathered that there was something by way of a political crisis at home, so when I got to the hotel I put through a call to Admiral Carpendale, who told me what had happened. A little later a wire which Miss Nash [Reith's BBC secretary] had sent informed me that the Labour government had resigned, that MacDonald was prime minister of a National government, and giving the names of the Cabinet.

2 October 1931 I had to travel home on the 8.30. Sir Donald Maclean [a Liberal minister in the National government] came into the carriage until the first stop and told me he had just succeeded in getting Lord Grey to write a letter containing admonitions to Liberals and Conservatives alike. I should think this would be an important contribution and I arranged to have a summary of it broadcast next night.

6 October 1931 Business about General Election speeches. Dr Forgan, the Whip of the Mosley party came to see me. I told him that if they were putting 50 candidates in the field, as they said, I thought they would have a claim. Duff [private secretary to the PM] phoned to ask if the PM could broadcast tomorrow, and was pleased when I said it could be done from the Opera House. At 5.15 Carpendale and I went by request of Major Ralph Glyn, the PM's parliamentary secretary, to the House of Commons. There we met him and Eyres Monsell and the PMG [W. G. A. Ormsby-Gore]. We were there for about two hours discussing what to do about the political speeches. I said they should have both Samuel and Kennedy[17] in, but they evidently did not want this. They were all Conservatives and I was sure there would be a racket later. Some of them had ridiculous ideas, but eventually I produced a draft. Eyres Monsell kept going out and seeing one or other of the Leaders with it and eventually he said the PM, Baldwin and Samuel all thought it would do.

7 October 1931 Most of the day occupied with the political leaders all telephoning. Eyres Monsell and Glyn both seem to think that I should be able to carry the matter through. I said that was not my job. However I proceeded to ring up various people to find out if they had all agreed to what was proposed. When Samuel heard that Simon[18] was in as one of the Liberals he went off the deep end and said he had not been told that the night before. Kennedy was quite reasonable but unfortunately has no authority to settle matters. Glyn had told me that the prime minister would like me to go to the Opera House for his broadcast and also that he would like to be sent to America. He made a very good fighting speech. He said the American Ambassador had been very nervous about this being taken by the States. I showed him a letter I had had from Samuel signed by all the Liberal cabinet ministers asking for two dates and nominating Samuel and Maclean for the purpose. MacDonald said that Samuel was very nice personally but was awfully difficult when it came to matters of arrangements like this. Glyn is to tell him that the PM won't have it.

8 October 1931 A great deal of this day was occupied with the politicians, but Henderson is not back in London yet. Glyn has, however, let in another Opposition speaker. The original allocation was supposed to be on a Party basis, but with Lloyd George and Simon, whom Samuel does not recognize as a Liberal. It is all very complicated. Henderson phoned in the evening to say that the list was quite unacceptable to him. He was trying to make out that there ought to be as many speakers against the government as for, and at this rate he wanted for his Opposition as many as all the others together.

10 October 1931 Samuel rang me up. He had agreed to withdraw Maclean but now he told me only if Lloyd George was going out on the same lines. He was very indignant about the way the Conservatives were acting in this matter. I told Glyn what Samuel had said and that he was insisting on another reference to the PM. I said I did not see how the list could be altered, and I wired Samuel that everybody was claiming an extra date and that there seemed equal discontent on all sides.

13 October 1931 I had dinner out and then came back to meet Baldwin. He was as affable as usual, arriving half an hour early and lying on the sofa talking about things in general. I thought his speech not much to the point, as there was far too much about past events leading to the formation of the National government, and told him so. He said he would be much more polemical in the next one. He is giving both the Conservative speeches himself.

14 October 1931 Dined with Lord Camrose [the newspaper proprietor] sitting next Lord Londonderry [first commissioner of works and soon to be air minister] who was quite interesting about politics. He said that there was no need for the National government ever to have been formed. I did not gather definitely whether he thought it was the King's doing or MacDonald's or both, certainly one or the other. He said what could people do when the King came to them with tears running down his cheeks saying 'Who is going to stand by me?' Also that it was not difficult to be patriotic when you are offered £5000 (a year) for doing it. He said Baldwin had failed because he was bourgeois and he seemed to have a very poor opinion of him. If he meant that the government ought to be aristocratic in the intellectual and administrative sense, I quite agree with him, and if he meant that Baldwin was bourgeois mentally, I agree. Londonderry said he knew the BBC had the reputation for being biased to the left, but that he had never thought this justified.

15 October 1931 Duff phoned up about the political speeches going to America. The Americans had asked for Lloyd George, but I had said they must take all the leaders or none. This they had agreed to do. Duff said the PM did not have any objection but had suggested his consulting the American Ambassador. He phoned later to say that Dawes deplored it, feeling that it would have a bad effect on sterling, so I had them all cancelled but said not to let the reason leak out. Left the office at 6.00 o'clock and drove to Churt. Miss Stevenson had said that Lloyd George would be very grateful if I went. I was surprised to find him so well having so recently had a serious operation.[19] Although I abominate his attitude at the present time, I had a most interesting and enjoyable evening. I have never met anyone with a more magnetic personality. I always used to feel during the War that if I had got in touch with him I could have had some very big job, for which even then I felt myself capable. Nowadays I feel my capacity is going down, but I hope this is not so. His broadcast was, as far as delivery went, quite first class. I had purposely not drawn attention to the time, and we were actually still sitting at the dinner table five minutes before we were due to start, thus keeping his mind off it. He said that he could cure unemployment in the country in a year if I was seconded with him, and as some of the others said he had made the same remark some time ago it was obviously not made then for my benefit. I could not help feeling upset as a result, feeling that I had lost so much time up to date.

16 October 1931 Had an interview with the New [Mosley] party organizer. Glyn had left it that they would have a place next Monday [19 Oct.], if they had 40 candidates, but they only have 23 so they are out. The line I have taken throughout is that the list seems to create equal discontent in every party and hence is perhaps as satisfactory as it could be. The Labour party are being very unjust about it, as one would expect, and they have certainly least cause.

26 October 1931 I have passed an announcement to be made in all news bulletins today pointing out the duty of people to vote and that the future prosperity etc. of the country depends on them. I have no doubt that this will be regarded as tendentious by the Labour party.

27 October 1931 General Election Day. I had said the exact way in which the announcements were to be made and all the arrangements worked most satisfactorily. It was really quite thrilling – a tremendous sweep for the Conservatives, gigantic majorities, every member of the late Cabinet turned out – altogether most thrilling indeed. Next morning it was quite obvious how bucked people were feeling about it. There was obvious satisfaction in people's faces and one felt it even in the air.

28 December 1931 Saw Duff at No. 10 about political broadcasts and also gave him my view about the state of affairs. He said he thought the government were hanging together very well and that the more opposition there was the more they would do so. He thought it rather difficult to imagine the old party divisions coming into effect. He thought we should be in a better state this time next year.

6. The National government to the General Election of 1935

John Reith's enthusiasm for the National government soon waned. He was disappointed by MacDonald's weakness as prime minister and by Baldwin's laziness as his deputy. In addition he deplored the personal calculation of other ministers, particularly of the postmaster general, Kingsley Wood, with whom he found himself at odds over the renewal of the BBC's Charter. Thus towards the end of this period he noted that it was 'utterly damnable that the BBC should be made the political catspaw of a little bounder like K.W.'. Nor was he any more enamoured of the Labour opposition. This disillusion with all politicians was sharpened by his experience of the first discussions of preparations for a possible war. He found himself in alliance with the two leading civil servants of the day, Sir Warren Fisher, head of the home civil service, and Sir Robert [later Lord] Vansittart, now at the head of the Foreign Office. In spite of his prejudice against the civil service mentality he found both these distinguished men more sympathetic, because more ready to get things done, than his ministerial contacts. These years also saw a revival of his own ambition for ministerial or proconsular office and at the end of 1935 his diary shows him once again looking for a new task and a new challenge.

5 April 1932 To a meeting with the postmaster general [Sir Kingsley Wood]. He made some ridiculous remarks about people being worried about the BBC, Constitution, etc. He said he was afraid there was a lot of dissatisfaction, that an enquiry might be necessary, and so on. He really is a feeble little creature, particularly as he personally must approve practically all we do. He talked a lot about giving the public what it wants. I was quite disgusted with him.

[Tuesday] *27 June 1932* Warren Fisher rang up to ask if I could see him at 4.15. He told me without any introductory warning as to secrecy that on Friday in the House of Commons Neville Chamberlain would announce the conversion of the whole two thousand million War Loan from 5% to 3½%. I really felt rather dazed to be in possession of such a secret which was not even to be communicated to the Cabinet until 9.00 p.m. on Thursday. This of course is a first-class scoop for us.

6 and 7 July 1932 I had word that the idiot minister of labour was raising at the Cabinet the question of our U-boat talk[20] on Saturday. I wrote a letter to Fry which he said Baldwin would have before the Cabinet meeting. However at 6.00 o'clock the postmaster general phoned that he had been asked by Baldwin to say that the Cabinet had unanimously decided that the talk should not be given. I had quite an argument with him saying that he would be doing us a very good turn by declining to interfere. Then General Seely [a former Liberal war minister] wanted to see me and said he had an important message from the Cabinet to give me. I met him as I was leaving at 7.00. He seemed to expect me to cancel the talk then and there, and said that if we did not he would have an audience with the King next day and suggest that the royal visit should be cancelled. I told Whitley all about it and we agreed that we would both go to the PMG next day. In the morning he came round and suggested having Gainford [vice-chairman of the BBC] in on it also which was unfortunate as I was sure he would be inclined to give in. We could not get out of the PMG what he would do if we refused to cancel. Eventually the three of us went into the room next door. I said that it was the most important issue that had ever come before us, but I saw that Whitley was inclined to yield, so I said I would stay out of the argument. In fact I immediately wrote down the reply to be given to the question in the House in the afternoon to the effect that the talk was a serious contribution to the elimination of warfare but that in view of the Lausanne Conference we had decided to cancel it. There was a tremendous downpour as we left and I said this expressed my feelings with regard to the matter.

8 September 1932 Whitley and I went to see Duff with a view to having the political talks taken out of the hands of the PMG and in general to prevent his interference with our work.

26 September 1932 I had a letter from Sir Herbert Samuel saying that he and Lord Snowden were likely to resign at the Cabinet meeting next day and that they wanted to broadcast. I referred them to Duff but he could get nothing out of the PM except that he was averse to the whole thing. I felt that if the government was unwilling to participate, we would not be right in putting on the other side but that the government were making a great mistake all the same.

29 September 1932 Lord Trenchard [at this time commissioner of the Metropolitan Police] to see me and stayed two hours. He did not like Sir Herbert Samuel and told me he had been consulted as to the new home secretary, Inskip [attorney-general] Gilmour [minister of agriculture] or Ormsby Gore [first commissioner of works], Gilmour being appointed. He said Samuel could say a nasty thing more charmingly than anybody he had met.

11 October 1932 At 3.00 o'clock the chairman and I had a meeting with George Lansbury and Attlee [leader and deputy leader of the Labour party]. I had not met Lansbury before, although I have had periodic correspondence with him. They are still very annoyed about the resignation speeches, and they are all fussed up about our Political Committee. They may come into line on this. It is pathetic how apprehensive Labour leaders are of their followers, and how little control they seem to have over them.

7 December 1932 Dined with John Buchan [novelist and Conservative MP] at the Athenæum. A propos of nothing he said there was a tremendous shortage of men for big jobs and would I consider taking a governor generalship or the British Embassy at Washington. He said something to the effect that Baldwin and MacDonald had been talking to him about the matter.

30 January 1933 I lunched with Geoffrey Dawson [editor of *The Times*] at his home and had a very satisfactory talk with him, and we agreed we should meet every now and again. He confirmed what Buchan had told me about the awful trouble in getting good men for jobs, and in particular he spoke about the governorship of Bombay. I said the chief difficulty in that job from my point of view was that there was a viceroy over the governor. I dropped a hint about Washington, but he said he thought it would be disastrous if I left the BBC.

25 March 1933 [staying with Sir Edward Iliffe, newspaper proprietor] Long talk with Ralph Glyn who came with his wife for dinner. He told me that the prime minister had asked him to see me about what we could do in connection with the World Economic Conference. He was very pleased to hear that we had already arranged a series of talks. He told me that he had secured the establishment of a so-called co-ordination committee to represent the various parties in the government. I asked him whether this was with a view to abandoning the party labels and he said this was so. At dinner he remarked that things were very well with the government. I told him later that I was surprised to hear this. He said they were not but did not want to say so in front of others. I told him I thought MacDonald had the opportunity of being almost as much a dictator as Hitler and yet within the constitution. Two of his chief troubles were, I said, a sort of inferiority complex and not knowing how strong his position might be, and secondly that he had not the capacity for choosing people and then trusting them.

5 July 1933 I have been handling the arrangements for the political series which we are to run in the autumn, chiefly with Margesson, the chief whip. Our advisory panel decided that it should be five to the government, three to the opposition and one to Samuel; but Margesson of course wanted six for the government.

11 July 1933 Whitley, Norman [the new vice-chairman of the BBC] and I saw a [Labour] deputation consisting of Lansbury, Greenwood, Morrison and Middleton. They went over an absurd memorandum rehashing the old stuff with one or two bits of new spicing about the TUC and workers' organizations generally. Whitley said they were not going to have an opportunity of replying every time a government speaker broadcast on a national occasion, but said he would refer their protest against the 5–3–1 allocation, proposed for the autumn political talks, to the Board. They were hopelessly confused between election and non-election procedure.

19 September 1933 Today I went along to see Hankey to tell him I was a bit concerned about my own future in which I saw three alternatives: (1) that at 44 I would just have to reconcile myself to the attitude of a man of 60 and be content to stay on in the BBC for the rest of my life;

R.D.–H

(2) that I might stop on for a bit feeling that some other big job was to come along; (3) that I might go to some more remunerative job. I said the first and third alternatives did not appeal to me at all, and with respect to the second there were very few jobs indeed that I would really like to go to. Hankey was very decent and told me that my name had been mentioned more than once in connection with some big appointment, but that people had then said that I had no experience of Parliament, etc. He thought that this was an almost insuperable objection to such a job as that of viceroy of India. It was he who mentioned this, not me. He seemed to assume that the Bombay job would not interest me, but he said I would have much more chance of being viceroy if I had been in Bombay. The same thing more or less applied to the Washington post, but he thought I might quite likely be asked to take on something like railway nationalization, and he mentioned cotton too. I told him the sort of job I might take if offered and mentioned the Post Office if there were to be a permanent post-master general, and I it, but I should not feel much enthusiasm. I also told him I thought I ought to know exactly what I would have to do in the event of another war, or even a national emergency like the general strike. He asked me if I wanted a mobilization job, and I asked him 'Would I not be minister of munitions, or something of that sort?' He said that two of the biggest problems would be that of manpower and that of air-raid action. Incidentally, he said that he thought the government some time ago should have taken some steps to prepare the country for what they would have to do in the event of air-raids and that he thought the best means of doing this would be through a series of talks on the BBC. I am very worried and annoyed on both scores, that is both what I am going to do in the future and what I should be doing in the event of an emergency of any sort.

16 October 1933 [Germany had left the Disarmament Conference on 14 October; the BBC had reported this and then included a commentary on it by Vernon Bartlett; the prime minister had protested by letter – 'one of his really wild and stupid ones . . . as if we were getting Europe into a war'. John Reith drafted a reply, 'rather snotty for a prime minister, but he certainly deserved it', but before this was sent the prime minister telephoned . . .] He said that he, Baldwin and Simon [the foreign secretary] were sitting together and they would like Simon to give a fifteen-minute account of what actually happened. I said that we had arranged for Lloyd tonight but that we could easily cancel that and let Simon talk putting Lloyd next night. It was a most extraordinary conversation, the PM saying that we were turning his hair grey and that he wondered which was the government, we or them. The conversation lasted 10 or 15 minutes, after which I got Whitley to send the letter, we waiting to give it time to be delivered and read, and, then, in accordance with his request, going along ourselves. We found the PM, Baldwin and Simon sitting in front of the fire. They were very civil. The PM spoke for a long time about the German behaviour at Geneva, how Lloyd George had complicated things by coming down on the German side, etc. At the end of it all he just asked if we could let Simon talk that night. I said at once that I had suggested this on the telephone.

27 October 1933 Saw Barlow [private secretary to the PM] by arrangement at the Athenæum, I having asked him to think over some arrangements by which we could be kept better informed of government policy, particularly international developments. He said we would be welcome to send a representative to No. 10 and FO daily conferences, and that if at any time I wanted to know more than these people, I should let him know and that in the case of an unexpected crisis he would communicate with me.

30 November 1933 Dined with Stafford Cripps before his contribution to the political series. He had some extraordinary opinions, but I think I got him to agree that the Post Office should be de-nationalized to the BBC type of constitution, but he persisted in trying to make out that the conduct of a service like the railways was different in nature from that of the BBC, but I believe he would be for the BBC sort of control over that and anything else. We argued also about the state of the electorate in regard to responsibility and intelligence. It is odd that I should be almost entirely socialist in my outlook in regard to the point on which the socialists put so much importance, namely the nationalization of public services.

3 December 1933 It infuriates me to think that for eleven years I have been in the same job, making no progress whatever, and that there is increasingly less chance of any progress.

12 December 1933 Postmaster general for tea in my room with the chairman. We asked his opinion about our building a concert hall with government approval and the government releasing our so-called voluntary contribution for three or four years, but, as I anticipated, he was very doubtful about it, and it was finally left that it would be wiser to wait till the next Budget. He said that the chancellor's attitude would determine the Cabinet, quite irrespective of what the PM wanted. We just touched on the new Charter business and found that he felt that a public committee would have to be appointed, so I said I presumed he and we should try and agree certain changes beforehand.

21 December 1933 Went to dine with Barlow. We had a very interesting talk about the BBC, particularly its relations with government departments and the best procedure to adopt with respect to the future constitution, new Charter etc. Barlow strongly urged me to have a talk with Warren Fisher on the whole matter and said, what I had not imagined, that he would have considerable influence in the matter.

24 January 1934 Lunched at Brooks's with Warren Fisher, who is very friendly. I told him what I had in mind and he suggested that he, Banks [director general of the Post Office], Barlow and I should meet very soon and discuss procedure. He told me that he was the 'shop walker' of the civil service and that although head of the Treasury could not do anything with figures when they were put before him. He told me that he, Hankey, Ellington [chief of the Air Staff] and Massingberd [CIGS] were all busy producing for eventual public consumption a document to show, what he said every other country was aware of, the immense unpreparedness of England to meet any sort of war emergency. We also spoke of the matter of better government department contact with the BBC which he said he would set about to arrange.

26 January 1934 Meeting from 4.50 to 6.30 in Warren Fisher's room at the Treasury. Barlow and Banks present, primarily to discuss the best tactics for getting our new Charter and Licence. Barlow said that Simon had the BBC on the Cabinet agenda ever since the Vernon Bartlett German affair. They all agreed that if the matter was properly handled no public committee would be required. My suggestion was that we four should get things into shape; that the PM should then appoint a small committee of the Cabinet; then, if the Cabinet agree, the new Charter and Licence could be debated direct in the House of Commons.

2 February 1934 I went to the House of Commons at 12.45. The PM was in a somewhat distraught state. We lunched in the Strangers' Room, then I accompanied him to No. 10 in his car, and on to the Oxford and Cambridge Club. He mentioned Vernon Bartlett, which gave me the cue to talk about our liaison with government departments generally. He agreed that we could have a much better liaison without any prejudice to our autonomy. He said they were still afraid of us, which is true, but I said they were quick enough to come to us when they wanted publicity; that if we were better informed we might do more good and cause less complications than apparently we sometimes do. He said that he was not trusted in the FO, and that there had even been suggestions that he had been suborned by the Nazis. A propos of ministers continually wanting to see him, MacDonald said that often he really wished that this country was run by a dictator, which gave me the opportunity to make my usual remark about democratic principle and method, and also to say that although people often know the right thing to do they are afraid to do it because of the effect on votes.

14 February 1934 Meeting with Vansittart and Warren Fisher, which was very helpful, as relations between ourselves and the FO have been a bit strained. I told Vansittart that I thought this was due to a general dislike and distrust which was as stupid as it was undeserved. He was in very good form from halfway through onwards – most affable and anxious to arrange all sorts of contacts.

2 March 1934 4.30 to the Treasury [to see Warren Fisher] and there till 7.30; interesting and amusing as usual. It really looks as if we would be better to reckon on having a public committee, but of such a sort as we would be quite happy with and sure of. Fisher was funny about Baldwin. We were saying that the PM, PMG, and Baldwin would have to be told what our ideas were. I asked how they thought Baldwin would take it, and Fisher said that S.B.'s tendency whenever he saw what looked like a job of work or some responsibility was to bolt, and he added 'I must admit he does it with remarkable skill.'

28 March 1934 Saw Vansittart at the Foreign Office and had an interesting talk. We are to have these monthly. He thinks affairs in the Far East have quietened down and that neither Russia nor Japan, however much they hate each other, is prepared for war in the near future. He thought Germany is a real menace. He was very much in favour of a clear enunciation of policy on the part of the British government, and said he had tried to bring this about. The indecision and indefiniteness of 1914 was a salutary example in this respect. An inevitable sequence would, however, be a considerable increase of armaments.

20 April 1934 Lunched with Geoffrey Dawson, of *The Times*. He has a very poor opinion of the Foreign Office, including Vansittart, who he says runs about all round the place and never has a mind of his own.

30 April 1934 Visited Vansittart at the Foreign Office in the afternoon. He had specially asked me to go along but had not much to say. The Foreign Office are furious with *The Times* for two leaders which they think were too pro-German. He would not agree that we had been too pro-French for years nor that the Germans would have taken all sorts of things from England had they been entirely English and not a re-hash of French policy.

1 June 1934 To the Cabinet Offices to a meeting with Hankey, General Dill [director of military operations and Intelligence], Colonel Hill and Colonel Hind. I was prepared to be somewhat bristly, but Dill and Hill were so very civil and friendly that there was no need. Not only do they fully realize our importance in time of war or civil emergency, but they had also come to the conclusion that we should be properly represented and as a part of the family so to speak.

25 June 1934 Meeting with the PMG and Banks about the BBC future. It was most unsatisfactory. I have never seen such political expediency as the PMG showed at this meeting. There is no courage or determin-ation, for with these I am quite sure the whole affair would go through as we want it. It is a sorry affair that a man should be so timid and his whole outlook be determined by considerations of popularity, avoidance of trouble, etc.

14 August 1934 I saw the PMG today about the committee; Warren Fisher having suggested McKenna as chairman, which I thought an excellent idea. He also suggested Buchan as the Conservative back-bencher, but, as I expected, the PMG did not like this idea. Further the committee has grown to seven – it was five – because he has discovered that both the 1923 and 1925 committees had one member from each party and then outsiders. The PMG is set on having an accountant even if McKenna is chairman. He had discussed the matter with Baldwin and wanted also to talk to the chancellor of the exchequer [Neville Chamberlain].

[Between September and November 1934 John Reith was on his South African mission.]

22 November 1934 To see Warren Fisher. McKenna can't or won't do the committee chairmanship and the PMG is apparently stuck with the idea of inviting Lord Ullswater. He is 79 and I do not know him.

5 December 1934 I went to 10 Downing Street at 1.00 o'clock and took the PM to lunch at the Athenæum. I did not think he was very much different from what he had been before his holiday, and practically all the information about South Africa was of my giving and not of his extracting.

11/12 December 1934 Vincent [private secretary to the PM] phoned to me from No. 10 in the evening to say that the PM was anxious to see me next morning. As I had seen him so lately and he had talked about the BBC, I really thought this might be something interesting. However, it was only that the Cabinet wanted him to broadcast a New Year's message. He said the National government was misrepresented so much in the newspapers that the Cabinet thought they had better tell the public their point of view over the wireless. I said that of course they were able to do this by order, but I did not think it would be very advisable.

14/17 December 1934 I drafted a letter to send to the PM making him, as chief trustee in the national interest of the impartiality of our Service, the judge as to whether or not he, as PM, ought to broadcast on New Year's Day. I sent this letter by hand to Vincent and he thought that it was a very good one. It is in fact a very good one indeed. Perhaps the PM will feel it is too good. It is an awkward position. I am quite ready to take a strong line with anybody on certain occasions, but to oppose the government in a matter like this is of doubtful expediency.

Vincent came to see me as the PM was very fussed about my letter. He told me that both he and the PM thought we ought to allow him to say the sort of thing he was going to say, so of course I replied that that settled the matter. He rang up next morning to say that the PM was very grateful and that he would broadcast on January 5th.

5 January 1935 The PM's broadcast was not at all bad and certainly will not cause anything like the antagonism with the Labour people that it might have. He seemed very pleased about it.

17 January 1935 As a result of a remark that I made to Geoffrey Fry that I was sorry to see so little of Baldwin, I was asked to go along this morning at 10.00. He said he knew I had just come for a chat, and that he was delighted I had done so. I told him that it was a great pity that people like himself did not take an active interest in our work e.g. the Empire Service and Schools. He said he was beginning to feel that he had lost some of his energy and enthusiasm and that he would be very willing to hand over to younger men if they were available. He read me an extract from a letter from an old Russian woman with respect to the application of Christian principles in political life. I have often wondered why he is not more positive on this matter, and I said I thought the country is waiting for an out-spoken expression of opinion from such a one as himself.

29 January 1935 Came back after dinner to meet Winston Churchill, who was very pleasant and seemed to appreciate my staying to meet him. His talk on India was awfully disappointing – a string of bombastic phrases with little sincerity at the back of it. Finished up by borrowing 5/– from me.

5 February 1935 Baldwin came to broadcast on India, half an hour early as usual. He asked me what I would do if I were in his position about taking Lloyd George into the government. He said he did not have the same objection to Lloyd George that he used to have, and that in fact he thought he rather liked him. I told him I would not do this before an election. He said would I go ahead with it if I thought it might split the Conservative party, and I replied that if he was really keen on a thing he could do extraordinary things with his party. I said that Lloyd George would probably behave fairly well being so anxious to re-establish himself, but that the whole matter was probably better decided by his own instinctive judgement. He was quite amusing about Churchill. He said one of the best things he had ever done in his life was to put Churchill in charge of the *British Gazette* during the General Strike. With regard to India I asked him if he really was happy with the way things were going, and he said he was not but that he thought it was the lesser of two evils.

21 February 1935 Saw Margesson in the House of Commons and explained to him the idea of a Speaker's committee to advise us on political talks, both when Parliament is sitting and at election times and said it must be clear that the initiative came from us. He said he liked the idea but was doubtful whether it would work since, according to him, the Conservative party would insist upon his being on it; this would mean that other parties would nominate similar representation and they would never agree about anything.

30 April 1935 Bridgeman [chairman of the BBC] and I to see the PMG in the afternoon. He informed us that he had been appointed chairman of a committee to advise with respect to the control and use of Broadcasting in war. I asked him if we were to be on the committee and he said not. We had a thoroughly unpleasant twenty minutes, with for the first time a definitely and openly hostile attitude on both sides. He is quite beside himself with conceit nowadays, and it is unfortunate that he stands at the moment pretty well with people generally. I indicated that if we were not put on the committee I did not feel disposed to give a bunch of colonels and civil servants the benefit of all our knowledge and experience. All through my dealings with him I have been aware of the fact that he would never be decent to us if it would damage his own popularity. Now I know that he will sacrifice the interests of this great public service to serve his own miserable political ends. He is thoroughly despicable.

4 July 1935 Dined with a very distinguished company at Claridges, a party given by Lord Greenwood for Beattie [chancellor of McGill University]. I sat immediately opposite him and Neville Chamberlain. I left at 10.30 giving a lift to the National government in miniature, Thomas, Davidson and Belisha, and so on to Beaverbrook's party till 12.[21] This was a very good show, interesting people, plenty of room and plenty to eat.

17 September 1935 To tea with Ramsay MacDonald at Upper Frognal Lodge. He wasn't in very bright form, but had been having teeth out. I told him about our lord president idea, and he was quite agreeable.[22] He said that we ought not to be under the PMG any longer. My view and his of K. Wood quite tally. He said he should never have been in the Cabinet as PMG. He observed that there was a great intrigue going on to capture everything worth having for the Tories. I said I didn't think Baldwin had anything to do with that and he agreed, adding that apart from anything else he was too lazy. That was the trouble with him – laziness and not taking any interest in his work. How many people have said this and what a pity it is.

20 September 1935 I to lunch with Malcolm MacDonald, colonial secretary. What a very poor figure he seems for such a job, walking back with his hands in his pockets and no stick or gloves and a grey suit. He would normally be mistaken for a Division II clerk. I think, however, that he is pretty capable and hard-working. He gave me a long dissertation on broadcasting and the Colonial Empire – in fact I finished a large helping of steak and kidney pudding without saying a word. I then remarked that what he had been saying, I had been saying since 1930. But it is certainly a good thing that he feels as he does, though he was a sore sight for a secretary of state, poor little man, no presence at all.

4 October 1935 Two hours with Warren Fisher; he said I wouldn't be allowed not to be fully busy. Usual outspoken comments on people. J. C. C. Davidson an amiable ass, completely unreliable, and his influence with Baldwin very unfortunate. Told me about this committee of himself, Hankey and head of three fighting services for liaison purposes; also about another similar committee to co-ordinate contract work and the like. Trial runs with bits of the War Book. Just managed to stop an Emergency Powers Bill with much too drastic provisions for any Italian trouble.

21/25 October 1935 Invited by Hankey in a very nice letter to join a committee of Imperial Defence sub-committee to deal with organization of a Ministry of Information on outbreak of war. Colville [parliamentary secretary for Scotland], who is called Minister-Designate is chairman, Warren Fisher represents the Treasury, Dill the War Office. So its calibre is all right . . . To the first meeting of the CID subcommittee. W.F. told me that this was as strong a CID committee as had ever been called. I was pleased to be on it. I was asked to give my views so had to give them though I would have preferred to be silent at this first meeting. I asked what had happened to the other silly committee which K. Wood had said it would not be proper for us to be on. The reply from Hankey was that it had been short-circuited.

25 October 1935 Great rows on about the election talks. I had a letter from Snowden this morning and it appears that Samuel is not only giving Lloyd George one of his 3 periods but also Snowden. Margesson is furious and regards this as a breach of contract wanting us to stop it. We told him we aren't going to intervene. I was surprised that Margesson suggested 5: 4: 3. Now he regrets it.

1/5/8 November 1935 [1] The political talks go on; hopeless; and there

is very little interest in the election. Snowden's performance was awful. ... [5] [Arthur] Greenwood's political talk was really disgusting. I felt it was a prostitution of broadcasting. MacDonald began well but deteriorated. I told Geoffrey Fry that S.B. must stir people up to vote; there is so little interest.
... [8] Baldwin gave the final political talk. Very earnest, impressive and emphatic, but he didn't tell people to vote as he should have done.

24 November 1935 I keep wondering what I am to do. I should like to retire and live much more simply. There is so much that I want to write, but I don't think that I'll ever do it if I am in a job. Alternatively, I would like some new job if it were distinguished enough, but it doesn't look as if I should ever have one. And I have been such a ghastly mediocrity compared to what I wanted to be and could have been.

12 December 1935 MacDonald's secretary has been ringing me up about mobilizing ministers in Scotland in aid of MacDonald's candidature for the vacant University seat.[23] I phoned and got things moving. I don't like it but I am sorry for the man. I lunched with Lady Bridgeman and we talked about Baldwin (with whom she is to spend next weekend) and politics. I said I would like to be minister of defence. I said she could tell S.B. that I could do some odd job.

NOTES

1. John Reith mistakenly dated this letter as April 1922 in his autobiography (*Into the Wind*, p. 80) and in his letter to Lord Addison in January 1946. His diary shows that he lunched with Clynes at the House of Commons in July 1923.
2. The scale of the funds involved may be inferred from John Reith's final accounts presented to Sir William Bull in July 1924. He then reported the expenditure of £7642, of which the largest amount paid to any individual was £650 to Lord Birkenhead. In his autobiography he added payments in to payments out and concluded that '£15,000 passed through my hands'.
3. Birkenhead had accused Lord Derby, who had taken office under Bonar Law as secretary of state for war, of appealing to Liberals to help in keeping Lloyd George out. The quarrel was patched up by the end of the month through the agency of Winston Churchill.
4. Sir Alfred Cope was secretary of the National Liberal Federation and Miss Stevenson, later Countess Lloyd-George, was at this time Lloyd George's confidential secretary.
5. The dinner was 'given to Mr Austen Chamberlain by some of his friends in both Houses of Parliament'. It had been hoped that Balfour would take the chair at it but he was detained in Scotland and sent a letter to William Bull instead.

6. Birkenhead's scheme was unsuccessful; Leslie Wilson was elected MP for Portsmouth and retained the seat until becoming governor of Bombay the next year.

7. Winston Churchill was chancellor of the exchequer, Lord Birkenhead at the India Office, Sir Samuel Hoare at the Air Ministry, Worthington-Evans back at the War Office, Bridgeman at the Admiralty and Sir Philip Cunliffe-Lister, later Lord Swinton, at the Board of Trade.

8. John Reith published the central portion of this statement in his autobiography (*Into the Wind*, pp. 108–9) with one or two verbal amendments which have the effect of making his claims on behalf of BBC independence somewhat stronger than, in fact, they were. What he did not publish was his final wise warning that 'public confidence in the BBC' should not be dissipated by extreme government action.

9. Mrs, later Viscountess, Snowden had just been appointed a governor of the BBC. Her husband, Philip, had been Labour chancellor of the exchequer in 1924 and was to be again, 1929–31.

10. John Reith sent a long letter of suggestions in August 1929. His theme was that Baldwin should address himself to the young men and 'stimulate in them a determination to excel' by emphasizing the qualifications 'which make for real success' – personality, character, efficiency and wisdom 'in a high sense embracing idealism and faith' – and showing that success should be 'measurable in terms of service'. He concluded: 'I feel that this kind of thing would be more helpful than an address on Education or Democracy or things like that.'

11. The final settlement was on the basis of two rotas of four talks, giving the government four talks and the opposition parties two each.

12. Two years after this John Reith was arguing in favour of the nationalization of the iron and steel trade on the basis of a corporation 'with definite control'.

13. The peroration which John Reith had given to Baldwin on 22 April was used by him practically verbatim in this final election broadcast. In particular the final phrase, 'You trusted me before; I ask you to trust me again,' was Reith's.

14. John Reith's own later comment on this passage in his diary was pointed and personal. 'I certainly did,' he wrote, 'and to my great hurt. Chamberlain *v* Churchill, 1940.'

15. MacDonald complained that the Bonar Law College was 'the property of the Tory party and is used for the purpose of training their tub thumpers. It has no *raison d'être* except for the party.'

16. The problem of the government of India was a dominant theme of British politics in the early 1930s. In an attempt to bring Indian opinion to accept the recommendations of the Simon commission which had been published early in 1930, the Labour government had summoned a Round Table conference in London. Its first session had been stultified by the absence of representatives of the Congress party. Accordingly, in the spring of 1931 the viceroy, Lord Irwin (later Lord Halifax), came to an understanding with the nationalist leader, M. K. Gandhi, under which he and other Congress representatives agreed to attend the second session of the conference due to open in September. Churchill opposed any abdication of British power in India and was outraged by the Irwin-Gandhi pact, protesting in memorable phrases at the 'nauseating and humiliating spectacle of this . . . seditious fakir striding half naked up the steps of the viceroy's palace there to negotiate and parley on equal terms with the representative of the King-Emperor'. His purpose in wishing to broadcast was to mobilize public opinion

against concessions in India; the purpose of the government was to keep him muzzled. Once again, as during the General Strike, John Reith was to bear the burden of Churchill's disapproval for a decision which was not his.

17. Thomas Kennedy was chief whip of the Labour party, 1927–31, and John Reith clearly considered that he should have been allowed to speak for his colleagues in this matter. Professor Briggs appears to regard Kennedy as the spokesman for *National* Labour on this occasion. See Briggs II, 138.

18. Sir John, later Viscount, Simon had formally left the Liberal party in June 1931 before the fall of the Labour government and had now established himself as leader of the so-called Liberal Nationals.

19. Lloyd George had had an emergency operation for the removal of a prostate gland early in August.

20. The BBC had advertised a talk by a former commander of a German submarine. The minister of labour was the Conservative politician Sir Henry Betterton, later Lord Rushcliffe.

21. It was some weeks before this that Beaverbrook approached Reith with a view to his becoming president of McGill, see *Into the Wind*, pp. 218–19. The only reference to this in his diary is a note of April 1935 . . . 'Found myself composing a fine inaugural for McGill on *Politics.*'

22. Ramsay MacDonald had made way for Baldwin as prime minister in June 1935 and continued in the government as lord president of the Council. John Reith's idea was that the BBC's contact with government should be through the lord president in place of the postmaster general.

23. Ramsay MacDonald had lost his seat at Seaham at the general election in November; he was successfully elected for the Scottish Universities early in 1936.

CHAPTER TWO

John Reith and Broadcasting (1)
The BBC Years; December 1922 — June 1938

The most creative period of John Reith's life and the time for which he would most wish to be remembered was the fifteen and a half years he spent at the BBC, first as general manager and, subsequently, managing director of the old company, and finally as director-general of the new corporation. Yet, paradoxically, his diary is, by itself, an inadequate source for these years. This is partly because he himself was ever too ready to record the details of his quarrels rather than his achievements, using his diary in this way as a means of releasing his passions and resentments. But it is far more because of his decision in January 1931 to summarize and then destroy his original journal up to that date. Further, in the process of summarizing his diary he also much reduced the additional material that went with it; thus two volumes of enclosures cover the period December 1922 to December 1930 as against four volumes for January 1931 to October 1938. In consequence much of the material concerned with the BBC is highly allusive and can only be made significant in combination with the BBC archives. Fortunately, this process of collating the diary with the official records has already been completed with great sensitivity and skill by Professor Asa Briggs in the first two volumes of his *History of Broadcasting in the United Kingdom* and needs no repetition here.

It is, therefore, reasonable, to treat the BBC period in John Reith's diary in episodic form dealing with a selection of the issues which feature prominently in it and at the same time supplying the evidence on certain points of controversial interpretation in his career.

1. John Reith's appointment at the BBC

One matter of recent controversy is the story of John Reith's original appointment to the BBC in 1922. He himself was always convinced that he had obtained this on his own. When King George VI asked him in 1938 to what he owed his appointment he jokingly ascribed it to 'Aberdonian favouritism' on the part of Sir William Noble. Earlier, in

May 1933, when Lord Inverforth claimed that he had given him 'a general recommendation for the BBC job', he had noted: 'I was quite sure he had not and that I had not asked him or anyone else to do so.' But it has now been suggested that he owed his appointment to his kindly political patron Sir William Bull who, it is claimed, called his attention to the BBC's advertisement, advised him to apply for the position of general manager, and smoothed his way with Sir William Noble, the chairman of the selection committee, before he was interviewed.[1] John Reith's diary reveals this to be largely invention.

Reith arrived in London on 1 October 1922. Before leaving Scotland he had written to Sir William Bull, as we have seen in Chapter One, seeking an interview for advice on a political career. Sir William saw him on 3 October and he came away much encouraged that there was a chance for him 'in the political line at last'. A week later, having heard no more and 'feeling depressed but trying to keep up faith', John Reith wrote to Bull and was delighted to have a reply on 12 October offering a small political position as secretary of the London Unionist MPs which might 'lead to other things'. But the very next day he saw the BBC advertisement and applied immediately. If Sir William Bull included in his offer of 12 October the totally disconnected advice to apply to the BBC, there is no sign of it in Reith's diary. Moreover, owing to the political crisis occasioned by the resignation of Lloyd George, John Reith did not hear again from Sir William until 26 October when he invited him on the telephone to act as his personal ADC during the general election campaign then in progress. The next six weeks, as we have seen, were filled by Reith's political activity in close association with Bull who was certainly delighted with his young assistant. Indeed, early in December, Reith was encouraged to hear Sir William Bull say that 'if the syndicate which has bought Richborough go ahead with it, he will put me in as general manager at £2 or £3,000 a year'. But throughout this period there was no mention of his BBC application. Only after John Reith had received his invitation to go for interview for this is there evidence that Sir William Bull knew of it. The diary takes up the tale:

7 December 1922 Letter from Sir William Noble received asking me to call and see a committee of the British Broadcasting Company [in formation] with reference to an application for the general managership which I had sent on October 13th. Most exciting. It seems an excellent job for me. [*1932 note by John Reith*. Actually I had little idea what it was.]

Sunday, 10 December 1922 William Bull phoned so I went to his house but left in time to go to Regent Square in the evening. W.B. said he knew Sir William Noble and was ready to go and see him but thought it probably not advisable. He gave me a vast historical survey about a Congregational church in Hammersmith to do! I was slightly reconciled by finding that a minister for 40 years there was supposed to have come out in 1843 with Chalmers.[2] I dictated hours of it and got it into good shape and W.B. was very pleased.

13 December 1922 This morning I had the interview about the BBC. Sir William Noble came out to get me and he was smiling in a confidential sort of way. Present, McKinstry, Binyon and one other [representatives of the wireless manufacturers]. I put it all before God last night. They didn't ask me many questions and some they did I didn't know the meaning of. [The fact is I hadn't the remotest idea as to what broadcasting was. I hadn't troubled to find out. If I had tried I should probably have found difficulty in discovering anyone who knew.][3] I think they had more or less made up their minds that I was the man before they saw me and that it was chiefly a matter of confirmation. McKinstry made a remark about the letters of complaint which were coming in. They asked what salary I wanted and I said £2000. Noble came to the door with me and almost winked as if to say it was all right.

14 December 1922 Bull phoned Noble and Sir A. Duckham wrote to Hirst of the GEC. But the Lord is mightier than all the influence in this way I could bring. At 3.45 Sir William Noble phoned to ask if I would come along to see him at once, so took a taxi and went. He received me very nicely, was going to Leamington tonight and wanted to see me before he went. The Committee had unanimously recommended that I be offered the general managership of the British Broadcasting Co. He said he had tried hard to get the salary at £2000 but some of the others didn't want it to start over £1500, but that if things went OK I should get a rise soon. Later he recommended me to take £1750 as he thought he could get that approved. After a cup of tea and a general talk, I departed. I am profoundly thankful to God in this matter. It is all His doing. There were six on the short list.

15 December 1922 Went to see Godfrey Isaacs, head of Marconi, according to a letter received from Noble. He didn't want to agree to £1750 without seeing me. He was very cordial indeed and it seemed most satisfactory. He said he would inform Noble at once that he agreed to £1750. As Noble's request I telephoned to him at Leamington.

28 December 1922 [In Scotland] I told Mother I wanted her to live to see me a knight anyhow. I feel if this job succeeds and I am given grace to succeed in it, I might not be so far off this. I do want a title for dear Mother's sake and Muriel's and other similar reasons. May I never forget dear Mother's prayer. I must take Christ with me from the very beginning and all through this difficult work. I cannot succeed otherwise. 'Without me ye can do nothing.' I can do all things through Christ.

29 December 1922 [On the way to London] Newcastle at 12.30. Here I really began my BBC responsibility. Saw transmitting station and studio place and landlords. It was very interesting. Away at 4.28, London at 10.10, bed at 12.00. I am trying to keep in close touch with Christ in all I do and I pray he may keep close to me. I have a great work to do.

[While it is plain from the above, particularly from the entry for 10 December 1922, that before John Reith's interview Sir William Bull not only did nothing, but judged it better to do nothing, to promote his appointment at the BBC, and that his intervention afterwards was, as Reith wrote of the interview itself, 'a matter of confirmation,' none the less both men retained a warm regard for one another. John Reith was fully conscious of the general support Sir William Bull had given him since October 1922 and he was delighted when, in March 1923, he was able in some small way to repay this.]

21 March 1923 Statutory meeting [of the BBC] at the Cecil; went off very well. Two directors had to be appointed to represent the wireless trade generally, apart from the other six. I arranged for Sir William Bull's nomination so carefully that he went through at the top of the poll and he and Lady Bull were very pleased about it. The other director was Burnham, chairman of the N[ational] A[ssociation] of R[adio] M[anufacturers].

[Thereafter John Reith remained on close terms with Sir William Bull both over broadcasting matters, until the end of 1926 when the old company came to an end, and, socially, right up to Sir William's sudden death in January 1931.]

24 January 1931 I had a bad shock today on reading that Sir William Bull died at Frome last night after speaking at a dinner. I have had

R.D.–I

many interesting experiences with him, and I regret his death very much. I had just read *Between Thames and Chilterns* which he sent after his visit last summer.

2. The 'Company' years, 1923–6

[In these years one of John Reith's main concerns was the constitutional position of broadcasting. Later in life he persuaded himself that from the very start he had expounded the idea of broadcasting as a public service controlled by a public corporation. In fact, as Professor Briggs has shown, this was not the case; Reith's ideas in this direction grew slowly from experience. But he was imbued from the beginning with what he called as early as 1924 a 'high conception of the inherent possibilities' of broadcasting, particularly in relation to religion. To fulfil this he looked to a national broadcasting service, centrally controlled, which would be as independent as possible of pressures from government, Press or trade. He early achieved the form of internal organization of the BBC which he wanted and his conception of regions working together under guidance from the centre was soon illustrated by the technique of simultaneous broadcasting which allowed national coverage when wanted. He won an early victory over the Press with the launching of the *Radio Times* in the autumn of 1923, and was successful in quenching the initial hostility of Lord Beaverbrook. The wireless trade was, on the whole, far less troublesome than the Press, accepting the end of its hold on broadcasting with the disappearance of the Company in 1926. Even the government, although maintaining a ban on 'controversy' in broadcasting and showing a greedy inclination to limit the BBC's income from licences, imposed no drastic pressure until the General Strike. Thus John Reith carried forward his ideal to the end of 1926.]

31 December 1922 I had told Burrows [director of BBC programmes] – my first order to him – that we would observe Sundays and that we should ask Dr Fleming of Pont Street to give a short religious address tonight. I went along to Marconi House to the top-flat studio. I hadn't met Fleming before.

15/16 March 1923 Lunched at the Caledonian Club with Iremonger [editor] of the *Guardian* and Bell, chaplain to the Archbishop of Canterbury.

Bell arranged for me to see the Archbishop at Lambeth and I had an hour's talk with him. He is very much interested in the possibilities of wireless. I wanted his cooperation in some sort of control for the religious side. He had never heard wireless so, with some diffidence, I asked if he and Mrs Davidson would dine with us next Monday [19th].

19 March 1923 This day we moved into the new offices at Savoy Hill. (I had the sense to take an option on about four times the accommodation we actually needed.)[4]

I had a weird and awful pain in my back, so bad that I could hardly walk. Lumbago; I was most annoyed. It was most embarrassing the Archbishop coming as I could not possibly go down to meet them at the door as I otherwise should have done. I arranged to be engaged on the telephone so Muriel went down. I was in awful pain but I do not think they noticed anything. Before dinner I was standing talking to them with the wireless set at my back and I pushed the switch without saying anything about it. The Archbishop and Mrs Davidson got a great surprise – thunder-struck in fact. The whole evening was most successful. There was no piano solo so I rang up Stanton Jefferies and got him to play Schubert's 'Marche Militaire'.

23 March 1923 A very nice letter from the Archbishop enclosing correspondence he had had about the establishment of a Religious Advisory Committee.

27 March 1923 The *Daily Express* is running a great ramp againt the BBC, very largely on the monopoly issue.

9 April 1923 Saw Beaverbrook about the stunt he was running against us. I was not a bit afraid of him as I imagined he expected me to be. He said I had impressed him very much. He said all he was out against was manufacturers taking control of broadcasting.

[Between May and August 1923 John Reith was much occupied with the Sykes committee appointed by the postmaster general to report on the BBC's constitution.]

21 August 1923 We are just about to bring off the connecting up of Savoy Hill to all the stations by telephone line at 6.00 p.m. each night. This is the beginning of S[imultaneous] B[roadcasting] and will bring wonderful results all over.

29 August 1923 I read the news bulletin at 7.00 p.m. – the first real SB. The switchboard is quite thrilling. Everything went successfully.

10 September 1923 Everything is now in shape for the BBC magazine and from various alternatives I chose *Radio Times* for the title.

28 September 1923 The first issue of the *Radio Times* appeared and was sold out.

[The report of the Sykes committee was published on 2 October 1923 and arising from this the government effectively confirmed the BBC's monopoly until the end of 1926.]

3 October 1923 Godfrey Isaacs phoned to congratulate me on all I had done [i.e. as a member of the Sykes committee]. He was tremendously emphatic and said he could not find words to express his admiration and so on. I was most surprised as he is usually so undemonstrative.

7 October 1923 The second copy of the *Radio Times* was sold out on Friday; 285,000 copies.

25 October 1923 Very busy on new regulations for SB. There have been dozens of letters in favour of it but I am leaving it more to the Station directors.

14/27 November 1923 and 6 December 1923 I sent Carpendale to Buckingham Palace about the King's [wireless] set.
The King is accepting a set from us.
I got Burnham to give a wireless set to the Archbishop of Canterbury, much to the latter's delight. He has agreed to broadcast on 31 December.

11 December 1923 Station directors here; I started the meeting off. I indicated we were going to tighten up things considerably. Lunched with them and others at Simpson's. Having heard that some of them were inclined to jib at the tightening of control, I attended most of the afternoon meeting and delivered myself of some remarks with great emphasis.

23/26/30 December 1923 [Staying in Bordighera] Joynson Hicks [outgoing Conservative minister of health] is here and I had some talk with him. He is much surprised at the attitude Asquith and the Liberals have taken up [i.e. making possible a Labour government].

A long talk with 'Jix' about various things. There are some Germans here who rather annoy us, particularly one young couple who turned 'Jix' out of his seat tonight.
Expatiated to 'Jix' on the advantages of unified control for broadcasting.

9 January 1924 Marconi's are making trouble about the relay stations. They want to do them all themselves, but we are doing it departmentally, more or less.

11 March 1924 Lunch with Sir Frank Newnes at the Savoy, discussing matters about the *Radio Times*. I put it that profits must be reduced and more money put into the magazine.

12 April 1924 Saw Grierson of Newnes about *Radio Times* – £5500 profits for the first six months.

22 April 1924 Opening of Wembley Exhibition. Everything went most successfully, including the broadcast which went out all over the country and was the biggest thing we have done yet.

28 April 1924 Sent circular to all member firms [i.c. of BBC] inviting programme criticisms. Reorganized the Programme department.

[During 1924 numerous relay stations were opened, as well as new regional stations at Belfast and Manchester, and a start was made on the high power transmitter at Daventry. By 1925, John Reith was beginning to look forward to the freeing of broadcasting from its connection with the trade.]

26 February 1925 The *Daily Mail* and *News* are running a stunt against us just now. Apparently the work of a cub reporter of whom Smith [publicity officer of the BBC] had been unduly considerate. Smith left last Saturday [21 February] to be publicity chief of the new Liberal party.

12 March 1925 Board meeting. Salary increases approved including my own. Increase of £750. It was not as much as I expected and I felt annoyed, but did not think they could have given me any more. To have £3,700 at 35 is not bad and I wish I could appreciate it better. Decided to have a special meeting next week to discuss constitution of Board.

18 March 1925 At 6.30 with Sir Robert Donald [chairman of the Empire Press Union] to meet Beaverbrook in the Hyde Park Hotel, the *Express* having started a mad scheme called the Wireless League with all sorts of wonderful plans. They say it is not meant to be hostile to the BBC. I am quite sure it will not be a success.

19 March 1925 Special Board to discuss the line to be taken with respect to the change of constitution. I tried to make them see how anomalous and absurd the present constitution is, but of course they have their own positions to think about and mine is one of great difficulty and embarrassment . . . The trade are a nuisance so long as they think they can control the BBC, which of course they do not actually, but might do, and so long as other people think they do. The directors were not all enamoured of the idea of increasing the number of stations and power which I brought up last month. This is a good argument for a public service board. The meeting was very stupid, lots of them talking at once. Noble said nobody else could manage the BBC as well as they did, because of their knowledge of wireless, which was of course humbug. It is not a knowledge of wireless that is required; and in any event, they have never managed it. I am very glad they have left me to do so, but I think they should recognize and face up to the position now. Eventually I was told I could write to Murray [secretary to the Post Office] and say I was ready to discuss the matter with them at the GPO.

23 March 1925 Conference at Post Office about our development schemes which they systematically turn down with no adequate reason. After much argument we managed to make an impression – Peter Eckersley [chief engineer to the BBC] and I.

Beaverbrook rang up and asked Muriel and me to dine with him and go to *No, No, Nanette* which we did tonight, with supper afterwards in the Savoy, talking till 1.00. Lady Beaverbrook and her sister from Canada there also. Beaverbrook said he had to stop his attack on us whenever I came to see him. He assured me his silly Wireless League was to be friendly. He said he had made up his mind that there must be monopoly in broadcasting, but that he had to be in it.

17 April 1925 Sir Arthur Stanley, chairman of the Wireless League, Lord Derby's brother, to see me. A very decent bluff sort of fellow and very anxious to have friendly relations and cooperation with us. I said it depended entirely on the line they took, and they would have to be independent of the *Daily Express*, which he says they will be. He asked me if I could suggest the names of the committee for him.

[Later in the year John Reith heard that there was to be another committee of enquiry into broadcasting. This was the Crawford committee which led to the establishment of the BBC as a public corporation.]

23 July 1925 We dined with Lord Wolmer [assistant PMG] in Regents Park. Very interesting talk with Lord Robert Cecil. Also some with Wolmer about the broadcasting committee which, I gather, is practically settled. Lord Crawford is to be chairman, Lord Blanesburgh, Lord Rayleigh, Kipling, forsooth, Dame Meriel Talbot, Sir Henry Hadow and Sir Thomas Royden.[5]

24/25 September 1925 Lunched with Bull and talked with him on the same subject as with Gainford [now chairman of the BBC] last night, namely the BBC constitution after 1926.

Dame Meriel Talbot, a member of the new committee, to see me and very friendly. Lunched with McKinstry and Burnham, so another talk about the constitution.

8 December 1925 To GPO and saw Dalzell and Weston [secretary to the Crawford committee] who thought things were going very well indeed on the committee. It appears that if we wanted it to be so there might even be a chance for the Company to continue as it is. It would be satisfactory to bring this off but I know it would be quite wrong to retain trade control. The directors' references to their management of broadcasting always amuse me.

10 December 1925 Board meeting. I had expected it would be rackety and had warned Gainford. It was pathetically dreadful. They are reacting to my evidence, which I do not believe they like at all and are beginning to try to assert themselves. Bull, of course, is quite all right. Gainford is often too weak.

26 January 1926 To see Fraser about the committee. I gathered pretty completely what their proposals are likely to be. In general things are OK and as I should wish. I should have been on the committee to keep clearing things up and prevent woolliness and misconceptions. I cannot control this sort of thing from outside.

1 February 1926 Gainford in and talking about the future constitution. He has the same views as I; I having persuaded him to them. It must be put on a public service basis, but I cannot say this definitely in evidence, so I suggested that he should be examined privately after me. I gave him various notes to keep him right but very much doubt whether he will put the thing properly.

4 February 1926 Home for tea and then to the committee, where I was examined for over an hour. Everything went excellently. I am quite sure that if I had been categorically in favour of a continuation of the Company this would have been achieved. Blanesburgh in particular was hinting at this.

5 February 1926 As I was leaving the House of Lords last night and before Gainford went in to give evidence, I saw Lady G. talking very emphatically to him in the corridor. I suspected that she was putting him up to protecting his own position, and I expect he was silly enough to say all sorts of things that I did not give him to say, and that he did not say half what he should say.

8 February 1926 Dame Meriel Talbot told me that she was not at all impressed by Gainford's evidence, so what I feared has happened.

10 February 1926 Gainford in to go over things for the Board. I was much surprised when he told me that it would not be quite right for him to show me the verbatim report of his evidence. He told me what had happened, but I was certain he did not tell me everything.

11 February 1926 Gainford did not tell the directors anything about giving evidence. *Radio Times* advertisement rates go up, as they should have long ago, but the Board have held out against this. Binyon wants to get us to spend a vast sum of money on advertising, but it fell through owing to my opposition. What a rum lot they are.

16 February 1926 Ian Fraser came in at 10.00 and talked about the committee. He said that Gainford had cracked himself up a good deal, even saying that it was very good for me to have him to come in on important issues. He said he had not been nearly as loyal to me as I to him.

4/5 March 1926 Lord Wolmer in the evening. Very friendly and hopes the PMG [Sir William Mitchell-Thomson] will consult me fully about the new constitution.

Got 20 of the senior staff together and told them the main features of the report which will be out tomorrow. I also spoke to several station directors about it. I told them all I was quite satisfied.

8 March 1926 The report came out on Saturday [6th] and has been quite well received on the whole, but a good deal of ignorant disquietude on the idea of our being a government department, which of course we are not. The report is liable to misinterpretations of all sorts and is very woolly in parts.

12 March 1926 Saw the PMG and found him very ready and even desirous of discussing who the Commissioners [i.e. the governors of the new corporation] should be. I was there for an hour and a half. There is apparently no chance of Gainford being chairman, although I put in a very strong plea for him. He suggested Lord Forster, lately governor-general of Australia. He thinks I might be on the Commission myself. I suppose there are reasons against, but it is likely to be misconstrued and I don't want to be.

26 March 1926 To see the PMG again for an hour and a half. I made another effort to get Gainford chairman. They are actually going to give the chairman £3000, which is ridiculous.

[In May 1926 John Reith and the BBC were faced, as we have seen, by the challenge of the General Strike. After it was over Reith felt that the government's policy of using the BBC without taking full responsibility had damaged its independence and he hoped for a strengthening of the BBC's constitutional position against this happening again.]

17 May 1926 The Strike would certainly have lasted much longer had it not been for us, and all sorts of panic might have come. The PM's speech may have broken it, but that was via the BBC from my own study. The verbatim messages from the meeting at Downing Street with the TUC when they agreed to call off the Strike were important services, and there were many other such. Today I circulated heads of departments, station directors and engineers-in-charge a message of some length explaining what we have done and how difficult our position has been.[6]

18 May 1926 First Control Board since the Emergency began. I think some of the directors are very peevish that they have not been consulted in any way through the General Strike. If so, they are very stupid. It was no time for humbugging with them and they could have done absolutely nothing. I am sorry that the BBC was put into such a weird position through the Strike, as it has rather prejudiced our work and the exceptional progress of the past three and a half years.

[Although the General Strike was ended, the coal strike continued· Working behind the scenes J. C. C. Davidson encouraged Gladstone, Murray and C. F. Atkinson [director of BBC publicity] to broadcast 'editorials' urging moderation on both sides; the result was much resentment in Press and Parliament. John Reith's diary records his view on this at the time.]

25 May 1926 [On long week-end in Norfolk] Sorry to be leaving. I telephoned to the office as there is a racket on about some wretched coal editorials which Murray has allowed Atkinson to do. I was afraid that Murray would be unduly influenced by Davidson but I felt I could rely on his judgement. It is most annoying. I phoned him again and told him to come along after dinner and bring all the coal stuff with him. Some of the newspapers have violent attacks on us, but I am not troubled by this. What I was angry about was that Murray's judgement should have been so utterly at fault and in spite of the undertaking given me about no controversy over the weekend. I was amazed that he should have let Atkinson write five coal editorials, which, in the latter stages anyhow, were obviously controversial. He tried to make out that they were not and, of course, the things themselves were quite clever.

Davidson came round from 11.30 to 1.00 and read the things which he said were quite unexceptional, but he tried to disclaim any responsibility for them, and tonight my suspicions about him were confirmed – he cannot be trusted. Of course he has no idea whatever of organization and is very weak, but this is much worse, that he should let us down when it is entirely owing to him that the things were done. He finally hedged on the point of our control through the Emergency, trying to make it appear that because we were not definitely commandeered we were not interfered with. His form of the notice which we were to broadcast the day the Strike was called off was also a great surprise to me, being all talk and no good. I am very surprised that the PM should be on such friendly terms with him. Of course he is always very nice and plausible. He had told Murray that we could still get all sorts of things through him; but as soon as any trouble comes he will shuffle out. I gave him my views about the new Commissioners etc., and he said he would have a talk with the PM, 'Jix' and the PMG regarding our position in the future, which ought to be much stronger than it is, but I do not expect he will do anything about it.

26 May 1926 Saw Davidson at the Admiralty for an hour and a half. Very vague but seemed to think he could fix things so that we were not reverted to pre-Strike conditions [i.e. about no controversy in broadcasting]. About 6.00 a letter came from [Sir Evelyn] Murray of the Post Office; he had had a talk with Davidson who had entirely agreed to dropping out of the picture and to our reverting to non-controversy, etc. This was not at all in accordance with what Davidson had said at lunch-time. However, Davidson later confirmed that Murray was right.

27 May 1926 I went to see Davidson again at the Admiralty. His chief anxiety seemed to be to get back from me the notes on the suggested coal editorials which he had given to [Gladstone] Murray last Friday [21 May]. He made fatuous reasons about their really having been intended for himself only, his writing being well-known, etc. – really dreadful. I said he could certainly have them back. I gather he has been told to keep off us and does not like to say so.

23 June 1926 Dined with Lord Wolmer at Chester Gate and afterwards to Savoy Hill with some of his party. In my room I trapped him into letting out the name of the new chairman – Clarendon, now Dominions [Under] Secretary. Wolmer said he thought he would be very nice and suitable and that he would not interfere at all.

1 July 1926 Very busy in connection with financial matters with respect to the new Corporation as I have the Post Office proposals now – absolutely rotten and ridiculous.

2 July 1926 Meeting with the PMG at the House of Commons, Wolmer, Gainford, Clarendon, [Evelyn] Murray and self. Clarendon took no part. I argued very emphatically against the iniquity and absurdity of their financial proposals.[7] Also with respect to the continued ban on controversy. Their attitude is dreadful.

Gainford raised my personal position in a half-hearted way. I said I thought it might look rather invidious if I were not on the Board, although personally I did not much care. The others thought that my position would be as strong as ever, irrespective of that. I certainly do not like the idea that the Board should have the power to co-opt the chief executive. No one is looking after my interests and I am not being treated well at all.

3 July 1926 I rang up Clarendon and asked him what he thought of things and whether he proposed doing anything. Evidently he did not in the least understand what was happening yesterday about money. I am afraid he is a stupid man and weak. I do not see him taking a strong line on anything. If he interferes I am afraid it will be through fear that trouble might come if he did not. I am afraid he might turn out to be a nuisance. I think he is a decent enough sort of fellow, but I ought to be very wary of him.

3. 'An awkward period', 1927–30

[John Reith's fears of a troubled relationship with Lord Clarendon were more than justified. The new governors included Mrs (later Viscountess) Snowden, an interfering busybody anxious to earn her generous stipend but unable to see how best to do this. Without the pressure on the Board of Mrs Snowden as a goad, Lord Clarendon would probably have given Reith as free a hand as was compatible with his higher policy of elegant surrender to government demands; certainly John Reith concluded in his autobiography that he could 'have got on with Clarendon if Mrs Snowden had not been a member of the board – and with Mrs Snowden if Clarendon had not been chairman'. As it was, while both were present, Reith had to endure what he later described as 'an awkward period' of personal friction. Behind the personalities – Clarendon thought of Reith as a 'Mussolini', while Reith wrote of Clarendon in his diary as 'Silly Bertie' – there was a genuine institutional problem caused by the rapid growth of the BBC which created the need for larger offices to contain it and an expanded organization to control it. Neither need was to be met until Clarendon had been replaced as chairman by J. H. Whitley.]

18 October 1926 Lunch with Lord Blanesburgh at his house and told him the way things were going. He said I should make a great fight about finance but that on the whole he did not think I need worry about protecting my own position, which was the advice I hoped for, but I am not at all certain it is right.

28 October 1926 To the Post Office at 12.30 with Gainford, meeting there Dr Rendall [formerly headmaster of Winchester] and Mrs Snowden for the first time. Both very cordial, but I could not understand the latter at all. She said she was 'so proud to meet me', and both said they had already met many friends of mine. Rendall mentioned the Archbishop, and Mrs Snowden, Lord Stamfordham, who I know dislikes her intensely. We met the PMG, Wolmer, [Evelyn] Murray and the parliamentary secretary. We were handed out copies of the Royal Charter and went through many points, particularly regarding finance. The position is most unsatisfactory and the new body is not getting any more autonomy than the old, which is a deliberate ignoring of the Crawford recommendations, apart from anything else. The treatment of finance is abominable. Practically all the conversation between the PMG and myself. Gainford butted in occasionally in his anxiety to get in a point which he knew I was going to make. Mrs Snowden spoke quite a bit in a way which amazed me.

29 October 1926 To GPO at 5.00 and struggled with the PMG and Murray till 7.30. They were very annoyed about our attitude on finance. I said the Governors would at least put in writing that they were very doubtful about the adequacy of the arrangements. The PMG said he had better get five other Governors. But I did a very good evening's work, and left feeling that if Clarendon wrote a proper letter to the chancellor [of the exchequer] on finance things might go fairly well. The PMG outlined a feeble kind of letter which he could accept and the whole thing is abominably one-sided.

1 November 1926 Heard today to my infinite disgust that the PMG had got Clarendon along on Saturday [i.e. 30 October] after all my work the evening before and threatened him with getting five other governors if they did not agree. What a sickening affair it is. Clarendon is so weak and stupid that he immediately accepted the terms. This confirms my suspicions of his appalling weakness.[8]

16 November 1926 The PMG put the Broadcasting business up in the House of Commons last night, but there was very little comment about it. I cannot express my opinion on the way that the Post Office has treated us; they have been unfair, arbitrary and positively dishonest. They have printed outside the document [i.e. the Charter] that the terms were mutually agreed. I wonder whether I should not make some public protest about it. The constitution was to be changed to admit of more scope and more autonomy, but none of these has materialized. I think the PMG and Murray have behaved in a very caddish way, and it is most unfortunate that Clarendon and the others have not more guts to stand out against this treatment.

17 November 1926 There were several references to me in Parliament on Monday [15 November]. Wolmer said that without me things would not be as they are and that the country owed me more than it realized. Personally, I do not think it realizes anything at all.

[At the end of the year John Reith was told of the prime minister's intention to recommend him for a knighthood, which, after much introspection and wide consultation, he wrote to accept. When this honour was published in the New Year he was delighted by the enthusiastic reception given to it, noting the arrival of some 400 telegrams and almost 1000 letters.[9] But there was little else to give him pleasure over the next three years in connection with the BBC.]

4 January 1927 New Board met at 11.30. Mrs Snowden immediately made herself most disagreeable to the chairman when he said that the first thing to be decided was with respect to a secretary and suggested that they should use Miss Shields [Reith's BBC secretary]. She said she ought to have had notice of this question.

11 January 1927 Mrs Snowden has written to Clarendon that she considers the minutes [of the Board meeting] very unsatisfactory and making various other complaints. A thoroughly nasty letter. What a poisonous creature she is.

25 January 1927 Beginning to feel that I ought not to be long with the BBC, but it is extremely difficult to find what the next job is to be. So few good jobs or ones that I would like at all. What a curse it is to have outstanding comprehensive ability and intelligence, combined with a desire to use them to maximum purpose.

4 February 1927 I drove to Daventry with P. P. Eckersley and Clarendon. Clarendon talked a lot about Mrs Snowden on the way back and said that if she had her way the BBC would burst in about ten minutes. If one could trust Clarendon it might be all right, but I cannot.

12 February 1927 What a stupid ass Clarendon is. A letter from him today referring to:

(1) A Foreign Office complaint re: the Emperor of Japan;
(2) A set for his daughter;
(3) A hospital appeal;
and (4) An ex-butler of the Duke of Portland.
He does not begin to understand what a nuisance his friends can be, and when any one of them wants a hospital appeal he thinks it should be given; or a job for one of their protégés. To have to put up with such a man and with a creature like Mrs Snowden is quite wrong. I am very annoyed with the PMG for not letting Clarendon understand what a chairman was meant to do and not to do. He actually told him apparently that it would be a three-quarter time job and told the other Governors half-time.

5/9 March 1927 Mrs Snowden thinks there ought to be a Board meeting every day.
Board for two and a half hours and an abominable exhibition by Mrs Snowden. A truly terrible creature, ignorant, stupid and horrid.

16 April 1927 [On a brief Easter holiday in Devon] A glorious day. Walked to Lynton, sat on the north walk till 12.15 and then back by the Valley of the Rocks. For some reason the valley rather frightens me. Sat in the sun in the afternoon and then down to the bay. I was worried about the future, thinking I ought not to stop longer with the BBC. Of course I should have been chairman with the opportunity to do other things, but the whole thing has been abominably done by Mitchell-Thomson. The chairman and Board are a humbug. Clarendon has been quite decent up to date but he is quite incompetent to handle Mrs Snowden.

2 August 1927 [On holiday in Scotland] Sir Robert Bruce [formerly controller of the London postal service] told Muriel that my creation of the BBC was genius and that he thought I ought to go to some much bigger job. What on earth can I go to?

26/28 September 1927 Feeling very disgusted with the Board and my invidious position respecting them. Clarendon is so weak and stupid.
Board for two and a half hours, but peaceable. Clarendon very irritating.

12 October 1927 The 'Red Woman' [i.e. Mrs Snowden] surpassed herself today at the Board, making most insolent and unfounded statements.

If Clarendon had either guts or decency he would have pulled her up, but he has nothing of either. It was left to me to take exception and be very outspoken and even rude to her. I am determined entirely to change my attitude to Clarendon. To call him a broken reed would be complimentary, as he has none of the strength of the ordinary reed, broken or unbroken.

[Early in 1928 the differences between John Reith and Mrs Snowden came to a head over her mischief-making indiscretion in making a statement of her own to a daily newspaper about a dispute between the BBC and one of its authors. After promising much, Clarendon did nothing. Reith felt that the Board had completely withdrawn their confidence from him and he considered resignation, feeling 'that I do not care a hoot about the BBC Board now'. Among the Governors, M. J. Rendall now tried to coax him into a better frame of mind.]

Letter from M. J. Rendall   14 January 1928
I believe you have, in the BBC, a superb bit of work, than which there is none greater at the moment. I believe you are doing it superbly, and I believe that no one could do it better and more efficiently.

If this is true, it cannot be right, in the sight of God or man, even to contemplate throwing it up for reasons which are, as you admitted to me, trivial.

Indeed, I would go further and say it cannot be right to allow your general attitude to the Board to be modified in consequence of one not important issue.

I beg you to see things in their just proportion . . . I ask you to get clean away from personalities and look at the question as a broad impersonal issue. We all have to march through life with a few people we should like to discard but cannot. That is, perhaps, the position now . . .

I don't want to argue or even explain. I only want you to prove your greatness by rising above personal issues (though I admit freely you have received not once only great provocation) and to trust the good-will, the judgement and balance of, shall we say, nearly all your Board of Governors.

[Rendall's intervention was temporarily successful. John Reith's diary, though still containing irritable references to both Mrs Snowden and Lord Clarendon, was less preoccupied with these personal issues throughout 1928. Board meetings, he noted in June of that year, were 'peaceable but stupid' and again, a month later, 'very placid'. Important things, such as the arrangements for the site of the new BBC headquarters which were finally settled in November, 'went through without any trouble'. In October, helped by the advice of Archbishop Lang who was on the point of moving from York to Canterbury, John Reith noted that he felt 'reconciled to staying with the BBC for a bit'. Then, early in 1929, came the battle over the publication of the *Listener*. Reith was on holiday in Switzerland when this came to a head. The newspaper proprietors wished to prevent the *Listener* being launched and appealed to the prime minister, Baldwin, to help them. The diary takes up this story.]

7 January 1929 [In Paris on the way home] Phoned Miss Nash in response to a wire. She told me that there was much row on in connection with the publication of the *Listener*. Apparently every newspaper in the country is trying to prevent our publishing it. I was not in the least bit worried if only the damn silly governors would keep out of it.[10]

8 January 1929 [Back in London] Conversation with Vansittart, the PM's secretary, by phone about the *Listener* affair and sent him a memorandum.

11 January 1929 Saw the PM [Baldwin] at 11.00. He said he had not seen me for a long time and was very glad to do so now. When I went in I wished him 'a year of high content'. He noticed the expression at once and said 'God only knows what content means to me.' I gave him our point of view relative to the *Listener* and our publishing activities generally, to which he listened carefully. I made a good deal of their [i.e. the newspaper proprietors] not having come to the BBC which he said was a big point. As I went out I met J. J. Astor [proprietor of *The Times*], and I said what a silly thing it was their not having come to me, and he quite agreed and said he did not approve of this deputation. I then got Duff out to see him, having suggested that he should propose that the matter be referred to the BBC or that he should accept such a proposition from the PM.

Vansittart phoned at 2.00 to say that the PM wanted me to see the leaders of the deputation that afternoon, and that they could then meet our Board on Monday (14th). I rang up Riddell [chairman of the Newspaper Proprietors' Association], who had been told the same thing, and he said he could arrange a meeting between himself, Iliffe,

Graham of the Newspaper Society and myself. I said I did not mind coming to the Newspaper Proprietors Association's offices so long as it was kept quiet and no deduction drawn from it. Actually I met more than ten of them. I purposely went alone, listened to them for about an hour, making notes, and then started off. They immediately began to interrupt, which I said was not fair and they apologized. I made a general statement of our policy and attitude and then turned to their points, most of which were absurd. I had to take a strong line, which fortunately I can take, and what a good thing it is that I can say 'I won't have that.' It all came to a most anti-climactic conclusion as to what I would accept. Drove back with Riddell feeling mildly pleased that I could put it across such a gathering. But, of course, it is the Lord helping me.

14 January 1929 Sent a note to Vansittart at No. 10 with an account of the meeting. I also asked for his advice on a specific point. I said I had told the PM that we were not a bit disturbed by the opposition to the *Listener* and our publishing activities, but that we did not want to embarrass him and realized that he was in a difficult position. If we considered ourselves only we should yield in practically nothing. Their appeal to the PM altered the matter, however, and I wanted to know whether the PM was hoping very much that we would come to an agreement, even if it involved going further than we otherwise would. I also asked 'Ought we to be conciliatory lest government *force majeure* be exercised?' Vansittart asked me to come and see him at lunch-time. He said the PM had great difficulty in answering my questions, but he himself felt it would be 'diplomatic' for us to settle as there was no knowing what might happen if the matter had to be discussed at the Cabinet or in Parliament. This is all wrong.

The silly Board met from 2.00 to 3.00 and I got them to take the line I wanted. The Press deputation arrived at 3.30 but were not ready till 4.30. I had another hour with them alone. They had drawn up a different document, three times as long as mine and full of things which I said I would not and could not agree to. I got my memorandum through practically unchanged. The Board had agreed certain concessions if necessary, but none of them were. At 6.00 the deputation saw the Board; Riddell made a speech; Clarendon also; ten minutes total. Miss Nash phoned Vansittart to say that all was well and he told the PM just as he was leaving. It is really a great victory and I have done it all alone, but I cannot say I felt the least elated. There was not a word of appreciation from the Board. I surely prayed for help before going down for the meeting with the deputation this afternoon. I am much burdened with a sense of my own ability, and this is not conceit.

[A month after this agreement over the *Listener* was announced Baldwin sent for John Reith to tell him personally that he was 'very grateful' for having the matter settled 'so that he was not bothered'. Reith was pleased by this notice but felt that the prime minister 'ought to do something' for him. He was, once again, 'feeling horribly unsettled' at the BBC and thinking of announcing his resignation at the end of the year. Indeed, as 1929 progressed, his discontent with Clarendon and Mrs Snowden broke out again, particularly over the painful issue of the departure, occasioned by divorce, of the BBC's chief engineer, P. P. Eckersley, and by midsummer he was on even worse terms with the Board than two years previously. Throughout that autumn the situation deteriorated. In September, Clarendon summoned John Reith for a full discussion of their differences to a meeting which Reith thought 'made things infinitely worse'. Eventually, at the end of October, their differences were papered over and Clarendon agreed to let bygones by bygones; but the Board's meetings remained bitter and in January 1930 Reith noted that 'the ice was very thin and skating difficult but no break'. Then in February came the wholly unexpected news that Clarendon was to be Governor General of South Africa. The 'awkward period' had come to an end.]

14 May 1929 I am to an extent responsible for the way in which things are [at the BBC] but the abominable Board is responsible for it all. The wells of satisfaction and inspiration were polluted by the wretched woman [Mrs Snowden]; the idiocy and futility of Clarendon did the rest.

22 May 1929 Clarendon in 11.45 to 1.00. Went through Board stuff and then tried to get him to understand that I was sick of things and that he and the Board had pretty well taken the heart out of me. He was incredibly stupid. He was worried because Eckersley's resignation was to me and not to the Board, and could not at all see why people should work to me and my inspiration and leadership and thought it should all be to the Corporation. He is a perfect ass.

12 June 1929 A superficially peaceable Board and no reference to the Press rackets [over the resignation of P. P. Eckersley]. I thought it very odd that they all sneaked off hurriedly at 1.00. I discovered subsequently that they had betaken themselves to Clarendon's house and confabbed there till after tea like mice conspiring against the cat, but without coming to any conclusions. What a miserable lot they are.

25 June 1929 Board meeting; they did not turn up till 3.00. A peaceable meeting lasting for an hour and a half, during which I thought they were all surprisingly civil to me and I was sure there was something brewing. At the end of the meeting Clarendon said there were three small things he wanted to mention: that governors should attend meetings of advisory committees sometimes; that I should let them know of resignations and appointments of the more important people; and that I might devise some scheme whereby governors could know a little more of the work of branch chiefs. They were all obviously feeling frightened that I would make a scene about this. I debated within myself whether it was worth while pointing out that they could have had all these things from the beginning and had been frequently reminded of the fact; or whether it was better to give the impression of conceding something. I decided on the latter and just said 'Oh Yes'. A sort of sigh of relief went up, they having kept their eyes studiously on their blotting papers meantime. It was really pathetic. I suppose this was the result of the afternoon's confabulation after the last meeting.

[Letters and minutes between Clarendon and John Reith exacerbated their relationship in July and August. On 12 August Reith received 'such a letter from Clarendon' that he asked another governor, Sir Gordon Nairne, to come and see him about it. Nairne was 'understanding and very decent' and, while John and Muriel Reith were on holiday in Italy between 13 August and 5 September, he did his utmost to calm Clarendon and moderate his criticisms, but without much success. When John Reith returned Clarendon was still in a critical frame of mind.]

20 September 1929 Carpendale told me of a three hours' conversation he had had with 'the lord' on Wednesday [18th] and another two hours' yesterday morning. He had gone to see him about the relationship between me and the Board. I wrote a long letter to Nairne giving him a summary and told him the situation was more serious than I had thought.

Carpendale had told 'the lord' that I felt there was no trust or support from him; that mistrust was shown in his having letters sent on unopened and that there were undercurrents and happenings we knew nothing of. I had cited as typical the case of an announcer which had come to the knowledge of the Board in some underhand way. 'The lord' had written to him himself and admitted it was wrong in principle, but justified it on the grounds that there was so much discontent. Yet this case had been carefully investigated and the man himself had told Graves [assistant director of programmes] that he had been very sympathetically treated. In an organization of this size there are bound to be malcontents and disgruntled ex-employees and it is amazing that they should have the ear of the Board and their complaints investigated without any communication with us. 'The lord' spoke about my being a Mussolini; the Board did not like this and were afraid of it; I was very hard on the staff. Carpendale did not feel he had persuaded 'the lord' of the absurdity of all this – he even said my two secretaries were terrified of me. He also told Carpendale that the governors were not entirely satisfied with the administration, but Carpendale could not get any elucidation of this. It has been obvious all along that 'the lord' does not understand the necessity for responsibility in executive management in a concern of this sort and he has completely misjudged the atmosphere.

[Clarendon's confrontation with John Reith came four days later. At this interview, which was conducted throughout in an unfriendly fashion, Clarendon said 'as one speaking to a subordinate requiring chastisement' that he held Reith 'entirely to blame' for their troubles, that he mistrusted him, and that he required him, if things were to continue, to acknowledge the absolute supremacy of the Board. Reith replied that he did not see how anyone could dispute the Board's supremacy and that he 'certainly never had'. He then endeavoured to rebut specific complaints; but Clarendon cut short the interview and refused Reith's request that it be continued next morning. In this situation John Reith returned to his office 'feeling furious about everything'.]

25 September 1929 Nairne called and told us that he had been thinking a great deal of what we had told him [of Reith's interview with Clarendon] and said that he had made up his mind to do more than he originally intended. We felt that he was getting down to business, but were disappointed when he said that the line he was going to take with the Board was that the thing must stop and would I be willing to let bygones be bygones if Clarendon was. We told him that this was an extraordinary proposal as all the magnanimity would be on the one side. I said, however, that I would go to the Board as he asked me and I attended from 3.00 to 4.30 as if nothing were wrong.

I cannot say that I have been to any extent considerably worried or upset by all this miserable business. Carpendale has been of great assistance, and so has Miss Nash. We feel pretty sure of our ground and perhaps, in a way, we are spoiling for a row. None of us feels that there is the least chance of things being satisfactory so long as 'the lord' is chairman.

[In spite of his immediate reluctance to accept Nairne's proposal, John Reith agreed the next day [26 September] to try to end the quarrel by writing to Clarendon regretting their difficulties and suggesting that 'in the interests of the service' the whole matter be dropped. He felt the letter was 'much too polite' but he sent it. Clarendon, to Nairne's great disappointment, refused this olive branch. He wanted Reith to submit a memorandum to the Board 'not on past troubles but on difficulties due to lack of definition' [the words were Rendall's]. Fortunately, though such a memorandum was prepared, Nairne, now supported by Gainford, was able to prevent it being presented to the Board when it met in the middle of October, without Clarendon or Reith being present. They wanted Reith to write 'something that would save the chairman's face' but he felt that his letter of 26 September had done this. They also wanted Clarendon to meet Reith half-way, and in this they were more successful.]

30 October 1929 Letter from 'the lord' saying he deplored as much as anyone what had taken place recently; that he had had an opportunity of some talk with his colleagues; like them he was prepared to let bygones be bygones with a view to starting *de novo* in happier circumstances. I suppose this means that the others have made him climb down about his silly memorandum idea. People here are pleased about it, and I suppose I should be too, but I have always said that there was no use putting a patch on the sore until you have eradicated the poison.

Board peaceable, but infernally boring. All sorts of things are going wrong now which are a direct result of my being sick with the Board and all their muddling and wanting to interfere. My sickness with them is for causes outwith my control. It is all their doing. I can handle difficulties they cannot, and the difficulties are of their own making. I wonder whether I should hang on in the hope of being made chairman at the end of 1931. It is a long time and the process puts a greater demand on me than anything that has yet come. I suppose I should welcome this further experience and in some ways I do – however annoying and silly it is. I suppose too that the cause of broadcasting is worth it.

6 February 1930 Letter from 'the lord' to Miss Nash sending down some ridiculous alterations in the minutes about new appointments, resignations, and terminations; also about my writing articles and making speeches on BBC matters. They are still hammering away on this silly business about staff, and what rot it all is, particularly about my rare speeches and articles.

7 February 1930 At 4.00 [Gladstone] Murray told me that the editor of one of the news agencies had a story that 'the lord' was going to South Africa as governor-general. I heard a gasp from Miss Nash who was listening on the parallel. I answered quite calmly that I had heard nothing about it. What terrific news! We could not contain ourselves and did not know what to do to show our delight.

Nairne came in. I told him I wanted to be chairman and he said that would be quite acceptable to him; but I said I would not put myself up against Gainford because, though I had no reason to be grateful to him since 1927, I had what mighty few would have, an obligation for his decency from 1923–'26.

18 February 1930 To see the PM [Ramsay MacDonald] at 9.30. He asked what he was to do about the BBC and I said it was all rather awful; he said he heard that Clarendon did nothing at all and I agreed. He asked if I had anybody in mind as chairman; I said Gainford, but MacDonald said he would never do; too old and other objections as well. I, however, had cleared my conscience by doing all I could for him. So I said I would like it myself and how silly it was to have a highly-paid chairman as well as director general; the PM said he might appoint a committee to look into the whole thing, but I put him off that. There had been an argument with the PMG as to whether the appointment was the PM's or the PMG's; settled by the law officers that it was the PM's.

[After this interview John Reith wrote to the prime minister emphasizing his advice that there be either 'a well paid half-time chairman with a chief executive with half my salary', or 'a well paid chief executive and a trustee type of chairman', and suggesting that 'the indefiniteness on this point had caused a lot of the trouble in the past'. At the end of the month he repeated this advice to Lees Smith, the postmaster general; and early in March he saw the lord chancellor [Lord Sankey] to make the same points. But his arguments were in vain.]

21 May 1930 Heard that Mr J. H. Whitley, late Speaker of the House of

Commons, is to be chairman of the BBC. It is very annoying, and another instance I suppose of the damage done by the Red Woman. Miss Nash went along to Downing Street where she had a talk actually with Duff, the PM's principal secretary, who agreed that I had been most abominably treated. I wrote to the lord chancellor that I was very disappointed. I am feeling very disgusted with the PM.

4. Comparative quiet, 1930–5

[John Reith's initial disappointment over the nomination of J. H. Whitley as chairman of the BBC was soon to be removed. Whitley's influence from the start was just and soothing. The pressures which Reith met during his chairmanship were not from the Board of Governors but from outside the organization – from the Press and from Parliament. In combating these John Reith owed much to his chairman's loyal support. It was in these years, too, that the problem of physical space for the BBC was met by the move to Broadcasting House in May 1932. The associated problem of the internal organization of the fast growing corporation was approached through the creation of a new post in 1933, that of output controller. This officer was immediately responsible to the director general and had charge of all creative departments; he was co-equal with Admiral Carpendale who was left in charge of all administrative departments. The filling of this new post dominated John Reith's thoughts and his diary during the early months of 1933. His choice fell finally on a soldier, Alan Dawnay. The quality of the field from which he made this choice was outstanding; almost every person he considered subsequently attained a position of high responsibility. Unfortunately Dawnay's health broke down and he gave up the post in 1935. He was effectively succeeded by the promotion from inside the BBC of Cecil Graves. But by this time J. H. Whitley was dead and John Reith was about to enter on his final period with the BBC.]

11 June 1930 Mr Whitley, the new chairman called. I did not find him as impossible as I had expected, but he has a quiet dignity and I am not without hope that things will go satisfactorily; he was very nice to me, and although I am sure he has been filled up with all sorts of stories about me, I expect he will try to make up his own mind.

15 June 1930 Mr Whitley in, 3.00 to 5.00. He seems to have very much the right attitude about things, in particular our religious responsibilities and on the activities of the Board and myself.

11 July 1930 Mr Whitley in for an hour. He was very decent and I often wonder what he is thinking.

[At the end of September 1930 J. H. Whitley left for India for six months to complete his work as chairman of the royal commission on labour in India.]

14 April 1931 Whitley attended the Control Board [the weekly meeting of the chiefs of departments] and is to do so regularly with my full concurrence. I had told him that Clarendon thought that governors could attend as a matter of right. Whitley was very pleased at being invited.

21 April 1931 Control Board as usual. Whitley present. Some of the others have reservations about his being there, but personally I quite approve it, as it is good cover for us with other members of the Board [of governors], and he hears things that interest him and we show him how much work we have to do.

[One of John Reith's complaints in respect of Clarendon's period of office was that the annual increases in his salary of £750 p.a. which had been promised him for 1 January 1928 and 1929, had not been paid. In April 1931 he told Whitley 'the whole story for the first time'. By the end of that month Whitley secured that his salary should be immediately raised to £7500 which was £1000 a year more than John Reith felt he was entitled to but which took no account of his past losses. Characteristically, Reith was more affronted that his past expectations were not exactly acknowledged than gratified by the immediate increase.]

Early May 1931 After Control Board I told Whitley that I had not changed my mind with regard to the salary question and that I was £3750 down at the end of last year on Clarendon's promise. I said the Board had lost a great chance of making me feel happy with them. He was very embarrassed and I gathered he had wanted something done to make up for the arrears, but he is not strong enough to put it through. It is a most unfortunate affair and I cannot feel as I might otherwise have done towards them. They are quite hopeless, but I suppose one had better reconcile oneself to feeling a resentment and irritation towards them and not to have anything in the nature of friendly relations. Whitley repeated that he was anxious for me to regard him as a friend, and he hoped I would not say anything more about the salary matter. Probably I shall say nothing more, which will leave him guessing and at their next meeting he may tell the others what I thought.

[In May and June 1931 John Reith visited the United States.]

Late July 1931 Lunched with George Gordon, the President of Magdalen, at the Athenæum, and told him of our proposal to appoint someone senior over all the talks. He was eminently suitable to consult, since apart from his knowledge of people he has the same outlook as I have on things. Whitley is very set on our getting such a man, and has been talking of it a great deal, always in terms of the relief it would be to me. I must say his attitude to me so far is everything that one could wish. I told Gordon that the man we want was such a one as himself, and he said that if he had been offered it three years ago, before he became President of Magdalen, he would probably have accepted it.

16 November 1931 Whitley showed me a letter he had had from the PM saying he would like to see him very soon about the BBC. Of course despite all the cordiality between Mrs Snowden and myself at the moment, the whole thing is artificial and a great strain. Whitley and I agreed, however, that the best plan was to try to have the present Board re-appointed, not necessarily for five years, but I am afraid the PM will want to put on one or two new people. There is such a ridiculous misconception of what governors are supposed to do. New blood and what not.

18 November 1931 Whitley saw the PM this morning about governors. He asked me to draft a document indicating what the governors' responsibilities were, which I naturally did with much pleasure. He accepted it as it was and sent it on to the PMG.[11] They have made up their minds that one governor should retire, and that this must be Nairne. Whitley agrees with me that this is most unfair as he did more good than any of the others, and in fact practically saved the concern from being wrecked in the days of the Clarendon-Snowden troubles. Whitley is to do his best to get him retained. The idea is that the other three should be re-appointed for one year only.

14 December 1931 Whitley lunched with me and then we went to see the PMG. We saw him primarily about our growing apprehensions about the detriment to our monopoly by way of wireless exchanges, foreign transmissions etc., but he was not strong enough to do anything about it. The point is that ethical policy cannot stand competition. The only ultimate unfailing powers are, unfortunately, force and money, and ethical policy put across by virtue of one of these (our monopoly arises from the former) may be approved but cannot establish itself on its own.

16 March 1932 Whitley lunched with me at the Athenæum. I had a talk with him about the succession and about my present over-burdened position. He said that he thought I had far too much to do, and not half enough free time. It is really due to the fact that Carpendale has become increasingly ineffective as No. 2. He is worrying me a good deal. Whitley wants me to take in an outsider and work him up for this post.

2 May 1932 Yesterday was my last day in Savoy Hill. It has been getting rather depressing as so few of us have been left, so that on the whole I have little regret at leaving it, although naturally I feel that it was something of an occasion. I packed the little things in my room and bade it an affectionate farewell. It has been the scene of an enormous amount of work and I suppose considerable achievement. It really has a kind of romantic interest and the only period I should like to forget is that during which the miserable Clarendon was a visitor.

[In November 1932 the BBC celebrated its tenth birthday.]

21 November 1932 About 760 sat down for dinner at Grosvenor House, the office boys in a separate room but joining in after their meal. Dinner lasted from 7.30 till 9.00, then the entertainment for an hour and a half and then, after the main room was cleared, dancing until about 2.30. It was in every way most successful and thoroughly enjoyable. I was feeling quite nervous about it in the afternoon but all right when I got there, although horrified at having to speak. However my speech was apparently just what was required and I certainly made them laugh a great deal.

10/11 January 1933 Lunched at the Langham with Whitley who made a somewhat laborious speech and handed over three salvers to the ex-governors. I could not help feeling profoundly relieved that Lady Snowden was no longer on the Board.

Norman[12] came in and spent two hours in the morning asking all sorts of questions, some arising from the Board report. He was very pleasant indeed. The Board meeting was almost rowdy, certainly quite amusing. Mrs Hamilton was very articulate. It lasted about two hours.

6 February 1933 Lunched at the Bath Club with Gwynne of the *Morning Post*. He had written some days ago to ask if I would meet him. He brought his two deputies and we had a very interesting and amusing time. Of course they thought that the Siepmann [director of talks] crowd was chiefly responsible for our left-wing bias, as they see it, but they also thought that I was a bit of a socialist. Quite naturally and in the course of conversation I was able to give them some of my views, which seemed to surprise them very much. I told them pretty straight what I thought about the *Morning Post's* attitude, saying that it was quite possible to be critical without making fools of themselves, and having so warped an attitude which rendered what would otherwise have been helpful, nugatory. Gwynne was very pleased and said he thought the attitude of the *Morning Post* would be considerably changed.

[John Reith had been pondering the problem of the reorganization of the BBC since the beginning of 1933. In January he noted that he dictated a long memorandum on the matter. In February he turned to the difficult task of finding a suitable man for what he came to regard as 'the big job'.]

23 February 1933 Lunched with Ernest Barker [professor of political science at Cambridge] in the Athenæum. He had a weird idea that the appointments of our staff should be done in some way as civil service appointments are, but I convinced him that this would be quite impracticable for a long time. Then I told him some of the things I had in mind with regard to reorganization, and he was immensely interested and showed me that among one or two things of which he had made notes to talk to me about was the suggestion of an output controller. I almost offered him the job. At any rate I told him I had almost given up hope of getting someone from outside, but that if he could find someone I would be glad to consider him.

2/3/4 March 1933 [2] Interviewed Pickthorn, from Cambridge, and felt sufficiently interested in him to ask him to come down for the weekend.
   [3] Interviewed another suggestion of Barker's, Vellacott, also from Cambridge but did not think so much of him.
   [4] Pickthorn and his wife arrived at teatime and for the rest of the day and most of Sunday morning we were talking shop.

13 March 1933 Got Geoffrey Dawson to come and see me to consult him about our new big appointment. He had not heard of Pickthorn, but had various suggestions to make, including one Masterman, of Christ Church, Oxford, and W. S. Morrison, MP.[13] He seemed very fully to realize how important the job was.

I thought I would like to see Baldwin about it, but on second thoughts decided to tell the story to Fry. I accordingly called on him. [Some days later he wrote to say that S.B. could only think of Pickthorn, Sellon and Roberts of the Cambridge Press, whom Barker did not think suitable.]

20 March 1933 I had a long talk on the telephone with Barker the other night with reference to Pickthorn in particular. He still feels that he is as good as we can get and that he could not think of anyone else up to the job.

21/22 March 1933 [21] This evening I assembled Carpendale, Goldsmith, Graves and Nicolls, outlined the reorganization scheme and told them to work out details.

[22] At the Board I had them go into the whole scheme very carefully and, giving as little lead as possible, I was glad to find that they independently arrived at the same sort of conclusions as I. They felt very strongly that there should be only two people dealing direct with me.

24 March 1933 Visited W. S. Morrison and asked him if he would like to consider and be considered for the big job. I had not met him before but had heard very well of him. I was not much impressed and not surprised when his first question was 'what is the job worth?' To my relief he wrote later to say he should stay where he was.

To see the Archbishop [Lang] at Lambeth at 5.30 and told him about the big job and also the religious one. He was very affable and said he was as complimented as if the prime minister had consulted him about Cabinet appointments.

27 March 1933 Letter from Lord Eustace Percy [former Conservative minister] in which he says that if I were thinking of him for the job he would be very glad to consider it. When I phoned him the other night and told him of our need for a big man I wondered whether he might do himself. But I do not think so, as he is so much associated with politics and unpopular with the Labour party, and probably very opinionated and difficult.

3/4/5 April 1933 [3] Bridgeman and Norman in to see Pickthorn, Carpendale also being present. Campbell Stuart called to see me as I had spoken to him to enquire about Bickersteth, of Hart House, Toronto, whom Masterman, of Oxford, had recommended. He had also recommended one Colonel Dawnay, whom I asked Norman to get a line on.

[4] Norman and Bridgeman in to see Vellacott, but he is definitely out.

[5] Norman and I saw Masterman, whose first recommendation was Dawnay, with a view to cross-examining him on this, so surprising was it that a don should recommend a soldier. Norman also wanted to see whether Masterman's observation to me as to his not having crusading zeal applied to the change of career, or to the new career. Obviously it was to the latter, so no more was said.

Yesterday I rang up Sir Herbert Creedy, of the War Office, on Bridgeman's suggestion, so that we might tap the civil service field. Today he phoned to recommend first Spencer Leeson, head master of Merchant Taylors and said to be in the running for Eton; second Sir James Grigg, chairman of the Inland Revenue, and third Austin Earl, one of his own assistant secretaries at the War Office. Yesterday I had also got Norman to ring up Guy Dawnay, brother of the Colonel, with the result that he saw Colonel Dawnay at the War Office that evening. Dawnay was definitely interested, although his brother had told Norman he would recommend him not to have anything to do with it, he being alleged to have a distinguished career before him. Today I managed to get Norman to go along to Somerset House to see Grigg. He telephoned me to say that he had gone at the psychological moment, Grigg being rather dissatisfied with his present job and prospects, although he might quite likely succeed Warren Fisher in seven years. At 5.00 this afternoon I got Tallents [secretary to the Empire Marketing Board] along, Barlow having spoken highly of him and found him most interested and anxious to be considered.

7 April 1933 Norman and Brown saw Earl and Tallents, Carpendale with them. They do not think that Earl would do, and he had apparently said that he would prefer Creedy's job to this one, which I think puts him out. Both Grigg and Dawnay have written to say that they would like to look into the matter further; so I saw Grigg at 1.00 and Dawnay at 4.15. Grigg is an odd little fellow, obviously very capable and very self-confident. I think he might be difficult to handle and there is not the similarity of outlook with me on some things that I should have liked. I have been making it quite clear to everybody that although I would like to give an immense amount of rope to the new man, I propose to be director general, and that they will have no statutory powers. My confidence in them will largely be a matter of similarity of outlook and the confidence will determine the freedom they have. Colonel Dawnay I liked very much.

10 April 1933 J. C. C. Davidson to see me. He proposes to appoint Iremonger[14] as the Savoy Chapel Minister. The Archbishop had suggested Iremonger for our job and Davidson thought he might hold both posts. I told Davidson we did not think a parson would be suitable. I also told him about our search for a man, and after making various suggestions he thought Barrington-Ward of *The Times* was the best we were likely to get. I told him that Geoffrey Dawson had said he did not think Barrington-Ward would do for this, in reply to a question of mine, B.-W. being my first idea of all. I got Davidson to lunch with Barrington-Ward and ask him whether he would like to be considered. Davidson phoned later to say that he would, so I met Barrington-Ward for three-quarters of an hour in the Athenæum.

25 April 1933 Whitley and Brown saw Tallents and Dawnay and they put Tallents right out.

5 May 1933 Saw Barrington-Ward's Oxford brother [a tutor of Christ Church] and sent him along to Whitley. He might have done as a talks director some years ago, but not for the big job.

11 May 1933 Lunched with Ernest Barker at the Athenæum and told him about Dawnay; also that I had written to put Pickthorn off and had a nice reply from him.

19 May 1933 Long talk with Norman and lunch at the Athenæum. I told him I had done nothing about Dawnay for three weeks. Both Whitley and Brown had left me to fix it if I was entirely satisfied. I told Norman that this was not due to my being too busy, and I said I wished he could get hold of someone who knew Dawnay well; also that he could question Dawnay about his feelings towards me.

25 May 1933 Norman called having lunched with Dawnay. Dawnay he said mentioned at once that one of the great attractions was his desire to work with me. I told Norman that I supposed I should go ahead and appoint him. He said he thought so, and that the War Office were very anxious to know as they have some other big job in view for him if he does not come to us.

26 May 1933 I saw Dawnay from 6.00 to 7.00. I told him this was a most momentous interview, but apparently he had come quite uncertain as to whether he was to have the job or not. In a very short time I told him he could have it, and he was very pleased. He is by no means Grade A in intelligence and quickness of uptake, and I told him that if he made up his mind to become so he might, and that this was important, being one of the things upon which he would be judged. I could not help taking account of the fact that an incalculable amount depends upon this decision, to me personally, to the BBC, and to the country generally. I do not by any means pretend to be satisfied. I do not mind his being an Army officer – in fact there are many advantages in this from the point of view of working. I wish, however, that his interests were wider, that he were more cultured and perhaps above all that he were quicker intellectually. I had a horrible fear that very soon after I would happen on the very man who would have filled the bill completely. It is dreadful to have been in the position of having so magnificent a job in one's gift – a job with such effect on me and on the country – and yet have been quite unable to fill it otherwise than in the odd way in which this has been filled.

[Alan Dawnay now joined the BBC and within a few weeks John Reith was well satisfied with 'the way he had taken hold'. By the end of the year, however, he had begun to feel that his new scheme was not working as it should; yet he could not see how to 'alter things without upsetting the organization and in particular the position of the two Controllers'. Then, during 1934, Dawnay's health was seriously affected by the strain of his new job and when, in August, he was invited to return to the Army he indicated to John Reith his wish to accept. Reith was much upset by this and managed to bring Dawnay round to staying with the BBC. But on his return from South Africa, where he was for the latter part of the year, he found that Dawnay's health had again collapsed and with it his resolve to stay. So, by January 1935, John Reith was resigned to the need to find a replacement for his 'big job'. Once again he surveyed the outside field; he hoped momentarily that J. C. Masterman might change his mind; then he considered John Maude [deputy secretary in the Ministry of Health], at the instance of Geoffrey Dawson and of Archbishop Lang; neither wished for the post. Next he interviewed

S. C. Roberts, head of the Cambridge University Press, but did not take to him. Finally he faced reality and settled for Cecil Graves from within the BBC. But as Graves was himself on sick leave it was agreed that Dawnay should continue for some months to allow Graves to take over on his return.

Through much of this period John Reith was much concerned with the renewal of the BBC's Charter, which led on to the Ullswater committee, and with the attacks on the BBC in the Press and in Parliament. He was to handle both of these with some skill.]

18 February 1934 The Rothermere and Beaverbrook papers have had instructions to attack the BBC and apparently also myself personally. I do not think it will matter much and of course it is largely because of our increasing influence. I wrote to Riddell about it tonight.

23 February 1934 Went to Riddell's house at Walton Heath. Much discussion about the BBC and the Press, with reference particularly to the attitude of Beaverbrook and some others, and the malicious and libellous things they are putting in about us. I told Riddell that I thought we might quite effectively defend ourselves if we were driven to it. He would not admit that the primary cause was jealousy of our advertising revenue [through the *Radio Times*]. I was glad that he did not suggest that it was in any way genuine.

16 March 1934 Geoffrey Lloyd [PPS to Stanley Baldwin] has been very anxious to help us in connection with press rackets etc.: so I had an hour's talk with him this morning. He appears to have a great deal of influence with the press, and he told me he had spoken to Baldwin about the whole thing and that S.B. had said he would love to make a great defence of the BBC. I said I did not bother with these attacks except insofar as they might indicate any internal disloyalty or inefficiency but that I did feel we were entitled to have a great deal more support from people who should be, and probably are, grateful to us.

[John Reith's answer to the attacks upon the BBC and himself was to explain his position to the influential 1922 Committee of Conservative MPs.]

19 March 1934 We have never had such a sustained and malicious press attack – Beaverbrook, Rothermere and the *Herald* – very much on personal issues which makes it all the more upsetting.

The meeting was held in the biggest committee room in the House

R.D.–L

of Commons; and when I went in several people like Astor and Ellis came to shake hands. Morrison, the chairman, was very friendly. Unfortunately the division bell rang, so the room which was already half-full, emptied. I had to wait in Geoffrey Lloyd's room for some time and when I went back to the committee room they were all assembled and the room was crammed. Morrison introduced me in a few words and then I started. I had purposely looked less austere than normally, smiling and very content with my surroundings as if I were rather amused. This was the first good move. The next was that I said it was a terrifying ordeal; the third was in speaking for under ten minutes. I said I could talk for as long as they were ready to listen but I thought that it would suit them better if I were very brief, leaving more time for questions. [Waldron] Smithers, an objectionable fellow, was the first to get up and rapped out a difficult question about financial control. I got through this well and then for 55 minutes answered one question after another. I thoroughly enjoyed it and only wished the meeting had gone on for two hours longer. As a matter of fact the questions were not particularly good and I could have suggested much more searching ones and would have done so had I had time. One question was about staff discontent which several newspapers have made a particular stunt about. I said it was not the kind of thing I could well answer personally, but that I would hand to the chairman (which I then did) a paper in connection therewith. This was a document signed by about 800 of the staff, the signatures very hurriedly collected in the morning, which was given to me just before I left. It was worded as follows:

> The undersigned members of the staff of the BBC, thoroughly disgusted with the false and malignant statements about the Director General being published in certain newspapers, wish to record their detestation of the action and methods of the newspapers concerned, and to reaffirm their loyalty and gratitude to the Director General.

I think the staff will be pleased that their action had so much effect.

27 March 1934 I am more than impressed by the goodwill shown to us in the press [in the context of the 1922 Committee meeting]. I should think that every newspaper in the country has had a leading article and all that I have seen are most complimentary and friendly.

8 May 1934 Muriel and I dined with the Newspaper Society, I being so pleased with all their friendliness to us recently. On Lord Riddell's urgent advice I had declined to speak, although I was rather sorry. The prime minister [Ramsay MacDonald] did quite well for the first part of his speech, but then rather wandered. He said all sorts of things about the London stunt press, but he did not say them very well.

[John Reith now applied himself to the parliamentary Labour party and to the Liberal party in opposition.]

10 May 1934 At 5.30 to the House of Commons where I had tea with Margaret Bondfield [former Labour minister], Hicks, Malone and others, and then to a meeting in the same committee room as for the 1922 Committee, but it was still more crowded. I adopted the same procedure, speaking for under ten minutes and answering questions for an hour and a quarter. Many were silly and vicious, and I did not feel nearly so happy as with the Conservatives, but this was quite natural. The result seemed equally successful and the meeting was on the whole very cordial. Attlee was in the chair.

29 May 1934 Collected Warren Fisher and went to lunch with Beaverbrook, much against my will but I could not decline to do it as Fisher was so keen on it. It was the fact of our refusal to let him give a special talk about Isolation, in answer to Vernon Bartlett, which caused all the attacks. He said he was much annoyed at this especially after having defended us so frequently. It was quite irrational and all rather amusing.

4 July 1934 To the Liberal party lunch in the House of Commons. This was quite a good affair, about 40 present, Sir Herbert and Lady Samuel, Lothian, most of their MPs, Walter Rea [Liberal chief whip] in the chair and some of the senior Liberal lobby correspondents. I spoke for about ten minutes and then answered questions but there was not nearly enough time. It seemed to be tremendously successful.

[In the autumn of 1934 John Reith was in South Africa.]

15 January 1935 Lunched with Beaverbrook at Stornoway House – an embarrassing kind of affair as one never knows what to make of him. He said he wanted to know whether I had any complaints against any of his newspapers, and I could hardly tell him that I never read any of them. Being pressed to supply some criticism, I said that our people were worried about a ridiculous paragraph on the motive behind my visit to South Africa – saying that the idea was to turn the BBC into the British Empire Broadcasting Corporation. He told his butler to get his secretary in and told the secretary to get the *Evening Standard* editor along. He said that he approved our policy and wanted to support it. He really is a weird fellow, and of course one is better with his friendship than his enmity and I said I was very grateful.

[J. H. Whitley had now been in bad health for more than a year and when on 18 January John Reith visited him in the nursing home to which he had been taken he said that he felt 'he could not last long.' His premonition was correct; within less than three weeks he was dead.]

3 February 1935 Oliver Whitley phoned at 11.45 in the morning to say his father had died at 11.30. Of course I am glad that he has gone because he was so anxious to be off and was so tired of it all. Apart from this, however, I am very sad indeed and can never be grateful to him enough for all that he has done for me. It began when he arrived bringing peace and comparative happiness again in place of our so miserable state under 'the lord' and 'the Red Woman'. It seemed that one of his main objects was to make me happy, and if he did not succeed I suppose it was because nothing would make me happy, but he certainly removed completely the major cause for my unhappiness in the two or three years preceding 1930. He was a great comfort officially as he was never the least worried about the machinations of our enemies and one felt certain of his backing in everything.

[Whitley's death and Dawnay's departure together marked the end of a stage in John Reith's career with the BBC. He was still to be 'fully stretched' by great occasions and moments of crisis, notably by the Abdication in 1936, but in his last three years as director general he was, in a Palmerstonian phrase, increasingly 'on the kick and go'.]

5. 'On the kick and go', 1935–8

[Whitley's successor as chairman of the BBC was Lord Bridgeman who was already a sick man when he took over and who died six months later. He was succeeded by R. C. Norman, another sitting governor, whom John Reith would have preferred for the job in the first instance. They worked well together for the remaining three years of Reith's time at the BBC, dealing with the report of the Ullswater committee and government decisions arising from it, meeting the familiar problems of parliamentary pressure and administrative reorganization, and carrying the burden of preparations for war. But John Reith suffered from ill health throughout 1935 and much of 1936; he endured a heart murmur and, when this cleared up, persistent indigestion which was eventually diagnosed as being caused by an incipient ulcer. Bad health made him difficult and, as he put it in April 1935, 'snotty to everybody'. It was certainly an attack of 'coli-cystitis' that made him offer his resignation in writing in November 1937. But, health apart, he had been seriously thinking of giving up as director general of the BBC for practically two years before this. What he hoped was that he would succeed R. C. Norman as chairman and so be able to use his great executive powers on governmental tasks without losing touch with the BBC. But in December 1936 Norman was renewed as chairman for a year and continued a year later. It has recently been suggested that it was Norman who, as the 'prime mover', stage-managed John Reith's eventual departure in June 1938, having resolved early in that year that he must go, and that even as early as November 1937 he was convinced that 'Reith had already outlived his positive usefulness.'[15] This theory is more ingenious than convincing. Until December 1937 Norman thought that it was he who was going – not Reith. On 20 December he wrote a letter of generous gratitude in this sense; then, hearing of his second renewal, scribbled at the top: 'I wrote this before I knew about staying on but that is a temporary business . . .' Later, between mid-March and mid-May 1938, Norman was away from his duties altogether, recovering from an operation. So if, as is alleged, he 'applied himself assiduously to the problem' of removing Reith during that period, it is hard to see how; and when, in June, it was settled that Reith should go, the latter noted in his diary 'R.C.N. is awfully depressed at my going.' In fact, as Reith's diary shows, no particular intrigue was necessary to persuade him to leave the BBC by midsummer 1938; so in March he noted in his diary his wish to *announce* that he would be leaving at the end of the year. What distressed him, when eventually he left, was not his going but the manner of his going and the position to which he moved. He felt, in respect of the first, that he was woundingly excluded from participating in the choice of his successor as well as denied the continued contact which appointment as a governor would have given him; while in respect of the second, he felt that the task of chairman of Imperial Airways was not sufficiently central to the national life to merit his being tied exclusively to it. Here his feelings were like those of the Duke of Wellington when he was approached to be lord lieutenant of Ireland in 1821 – that the government were letting off a great gun against a sparrow.]

22 March 1935 Went to the Post Office where Banks told me that Bridgeman was to be chairman and H. A. L. Fisher [Warden of New College, Oxford] the new governor. I said of course Norman should have been made chairman, but that I was pleased it was Bridgeman and not an outsider, but that with regard to Fisher, if the PMG wanted to strengthen the elements in the BBC that he had often deplored to me he was going the right way about it. Banks was upset about this and said he would try and get in touch with the PMG over the weekend in case something might be done, but I am sure it will be too late. I rang up Norman who was very decent indeed about it, much more so than I would have been in like position.

. . . April 1935 The four of us [i.e. R. C. Norman, John Reith, Admiral Carpendale and Alan Dawnay] met for an hour on the organization today, and the two controllers and I later again in the evening. I think we are near a solution and Dawnay went off tonight to spend the weekend with Graves at Falloden.

30 April 1935 A long telephone conversation with Tallents in the evening, finishing at 11.15. I was wondering whether he might do for the central public relations job, and he was evidently very keen indeed to be considered for it. I am arranging for him to see Norman.

7 May 1935 Norman and Carpendale saw Tallents with a view to his being in the public relations job, central to myself.

8 May 1935 With Bridgeman and Norman to the Ullswater committee. I was examined for over two hours and got on quite well, supplying a vast amount of information apparently out of my head and being treated in quite a friendly way until the miserable cad Selsdon [formerly Sir William Mitchell-Thomson] got on to our proposed changes in the constitution. It is outrageous that he should be on the committee and all our anticipations were realized and more. I do not know when I have felt so indignant.

16 May 1935 Another morning with the [Ullswater] committee with Norman there and he thought it had gone very well. Attlee shows his hand very much as a left-winger and tried to put across trade-unionism for the BBC.

24/26 May 1935 [24] [Dining with Lord Iliffe] I was feeling very much in the mood to resign, and in fact during dinner occupied myself in drafting a letter of resignation.

[26] Getting a bit worried about the amount of work I have to do and thinking I ought to resign soon. I feel that the BBC is such an all-absorbing monster – no home life and no time for any interest in wife or children, or in pursuits and interests of one's own. One wonders if it is worth it, however important it is.

3 June 1935 Lunched with Tallents and had a good talk about the 3rd controller job. I am not at all sure that he is the man for it.

11 June 1935 In the afternoon a meeting with Carpendale, Ashbridge and Nicolls about broadcasting and war. Hodsoll of the Air Defence has sent along a preliminary document about our air-raid precautions, and this will want separate and careful handling.

17 June 1935 Hodsoll, who is now established at the Home Office in charge of air raid defence, to see me and talk things over generally. He realized how very important all our plans are. I said we would do whatever he advised. I cannot help wishing we had built the roof at Brookman's Park with air raids in mind, but this would have needed $2\frac{1}{2}$ feet of concrete, 2 or 3 feet of sand and then another 2 feet or so of concrete with more earth on top.

25 June 1935 Muriel and I lunched with Lord and Lady Bridgeman to meet Tryon, the new PMG, and Mrs Tryon. He was very civil. He said the personal publicity which his predecessor had indulged in was not at all in his line.

2 July 1935 Board Meeting. I reported that I was not enthusiastic in the least about Tallents, but that I thought he had better be appointed. This they approved, also that Carpendale should give up the controller (administration) job and become deputy director general early next year.

5 July 1935 I saw Tallents in the afternoon and fixed him up. I hope profoundly that it will be a success.

17 July 1935 To the Ullswater committee at 11.00 being examined by Selsdon, Attlee and Graham White [Liberal MP]. Selsdon tried to get me to agree that it would be better not to fix on the lord president [as minister responsible for BBC policy] but have the prime minister nominate a minister with each new government. I said I thought this was most unsatisfactory even if the other plan might mean that [J. H.] Thomas was lord president as he foreshadowed. Attlee kept on about publishing details of our accounts, artists fees etc., and I wrote him something of a snorter when I got back, telling him that if he was ratting on the BBC system for the management of public services I was going to cease advocating it in public, no interference in management being a cardinal principle of the system.

24 July 1935 I sent the PMG our War Memorandum last night. This recommends the abolition of the Board [i.e. of governors] on the outbreak of war.

[In August Lord Bridgeman died. John Reith was on holiday in Scotland where he had gone on the assurance that Bridgeman, though seriously ill, was not in immediate danger. So the news was 'an awful shock'. The next month R. C. Norman accepted the chairmanship.]

10 September 1935 Monstrous yarn in the *Daily Mail* that I asked the Ullswater committee to combine the chairman job with mine. Not only untrue, but I completely disapprove this combination. It is ridiculous that nonentities should be in the position to write utter rot about us day after day and to deal with matters quite beyond their comprehension.

16 September 1935 Lunch and a talk with Mrs Hamilton. I am wondering how I am to get through as I am sure I shall not be busy with the four controllers and the deputy DG functioning. I told Mrs Hamilton that I was perhaps not the type to keep things going after they had been put more or less on an even keel. I told Graves, however, that I was likely to take much more interest in programmes than I used to.

[On 1 October 1935 the new organization of the BBC was put into operation. The Control Board was revised and now embraced besides John Reith and his deputy Admiral Carpendale, the controllers of administration, engineering, programmes and public relations. In addition R. C. Norman was invited to attend, as Whitley had been before him.]

11/12/16 November 1935 [11] Not busy and wondering if I can put up with this. I have, it seems, organized myself out of work – desirable and the right thing to do but trying.

[12] I am beginning to feel that I have organized and developed myself out of a job. This is very satisfactory in one sense but I don't know how I shall get on as I probably can't reconcile myself to slack days.

[16] I do feel so tired of the BBC.

24 December 1935 A copy of the miserable Ullswater report was delivered to me at the station. It gives all we want but it is a wretched document with several silly and annoying things in it.

26 December 1935 I started on the Ullswater report yesterday about 10.15 and worked on it till 12.00. Continued today and had 7 pages in small writing and about 100 notes. These and the Report I sent by a motor-cyclist to Norman at 12.35 and he had it at 2.15.

[Norman and his vice-chairman, H. G. Brown, both thought that John Reith 'had been too severe on the wretched Ullswater committee', while R. M. Barrington-Ward of *The Times* assured him that the report was very satisfactory from the BBC's point of view, even if the victory was 'more real than apparent'. These moderating counsels, combined with the diversion of his interest occasioned by the death of George V, brought Reith to a more balanced view. But the decision of the government to refer the report to a special committee of the Cabinet and the early indications that this committee was not prepared to accept the full BBC case, turned his fury against ministers. In April 1936 he even briefed the Labour opposition before the report was debated in the House of Commons. But this had no effect and at the end of June the government's White Paper revealed that on two issues – the effective extension of the BBC monopoly to cover wireless exchanges and the establishment of the lord president of the Council as minister responsible for broadcasting policy – it had rejected the Ullswater recommendations. These commotions occupied most of the year 1936.]

11 March 1936 The blasted Cabinet has decided that the Ullswater report should be published on Monday [16th March] but that a committee should discuss the recommendations so there will be no decision with the report. This is deplorable and is of course largely the result of commercial lobbying about the wireless exchange business.[16]

24 April 1936 Hearing that the Labour party had the right to choose the subject for debate next Wednesday and that they were likely to choose the Ullswater report, I phoned Attlee with the result that Lees Smith [PMG in the Labour government] is coming to see me on Monday. I told Lady Bridgeman [now a governor of the BBC] that it was distasteful to me and something improper to be scheming with the Labour opposition but it is the Cabinet's fault. She seemed to think she would tell the PM how disgusted we were.

27 April 1936 Lees Smith for two hours and then I passed him on to the chairman. He came back in the afternoon and had two hours with the Control Board! I asked him if he would like this and he said he would.

28 April 1936 Treasury 3.30 to 5.00, Sir Horace Wilson[17] being there also. The chancellor [Neville Chamberlain] had paid no heed to Warren Fisher's views and had supported the little cad Wood. Result, the Cabinet committee had recommended against the control of wireless exchange and against the lord president point. Fisher and Wilson were very disgusted about it all. Wilson had had two goes with the PM and had made some impression on him. He had an idea of a sort of committee of the lord president, president of the Board of Education and the PMG as a compromise, but the wireless exchanges will have another three years.

13 May 1936 To the GPO at 11.00 with all the governors. PMG was accompanied by assistant PMG [Sir Walter Womersley], ex-pawnbroker and looked it. To our amazement we were informed that he could not tell us what the government decisions were; he was going to go through the other matters – i.e. things which affected the internal administration. We were given a six-page document and spent two hours going through it – largely a waste of time. There was only one serious point and that was serious enough; PMG said the government were strongly in favour of a civil service commissioner or deputy sitting on all our appointments boards. This is an insult to past management and a monstrous interference with governors' authority. I was very snotty and reserved with the PMG who was being conciliatory and civil. At the end we had a bit of a flare-up about their not having given us the chance of talking things over before the Cabinet discussed the report, nor of briefing the PMG before the 'debate' recently.

I was so sick of everything I kept clear of the governors at lunch. At the Board, afterwards, they went through the PMG's document again. On the 'decision' issues, such as wireless exchanges and lord president, I asked if they didn't think an eleventh hour appeal to the PM worthwhile, but they didn't. I don't know that I did, but I felt annoyed and Norman said at the end that he thought I was as angry with them as with the PMG!

19 May 1936 I have been reflecting a great deal on the hopelessness of trying to hold out for the right in these days – moral issues or anything. There is no support from quarters whence one should have it. Most everything goes by default, or by a combination of default on the part of those who should care, and of active hostility and propaganda from the other side. Look at what we have in the King [Edward VIII]. This is bound to have an effect on all grades.

20 May 1936 The chief cause of discontent with the BBC in Parliament is its efficiency which is undemocratic!

9 June 1936 Board till 5.00. Lots of important things and much talk. But when other people are all pow-wowing about the right course to take on something or other, my mind seems to leave functioning and I don't have much opinion of my own, if any. If I were doing things on my own I should have no difficulty in coming to decisions. Similar problems arise with regard to devolution. If one devolves it probably means all sorts of things being done (and oneself permitting them) which wouldn't have been done otherwise.

22 June 1936 Very disgusted with everything and feeling that I simply cannot stand things longer in the BBC. If I leave at the end of the year all I would say would be that 14 years was probably as long as was good for the BBC or me. Norman came in and wanted to send off a letter capitulating to the PMG on the civil service commissioner ramp. At the last moment I got it altered to a suggestion that he should simply announce that we were prepared to confer with the commissioner with respect to the general principles of staff recruitment, including one of them being a member of our appointments boards when any useful purpose would be served thereby.

30 June 1936 Brown and I went through the miserable White Paper this morning. [R. C. Norman's wife had just died and he was away from the office.] It is as expected, though not quite so offensive. There are bits of rank humbug and hypocrisy in it. They reject the lord president idea because they say it is inconsistent with the desire to keep the Corporation free from political interference!

10 July 1936 Feeling annoyed with Tallents' apparent futility; our press relations are quite rotten. Most newspapers write more or less congratulating the government on its decisions. They are ignorant and have been hoodwinked.

26 August 1936 Wrote to Lady Bridgeman. I told her I was concerned about the future and thought I might be chairman after R. C. Norman and so have time for other things.

[In September John Reith discussed his ambition to succeed as chairman of the BBC with R. C. Norman and Mrs Hamilton but this idea was not acceptable to the government which, in any case, was preoccupied for the latter part of the year by the Abdication crisis.]

17 December 1936 Mrs Hamilton reported that she had been asked if she would be willing to carry on if asked! Norman said he had been rung up by the PMG and asked if he would carry on for a time but go if and when they found a chairman they really wanted! He gathered that some politician might go out after the Coronation and a job be required for him. He had agreed and of course I am awfully glad. PMG asked Norman if [H. A. L.] Fisher would do as vice-chairman but eventually decided not to offer it to him. Anyhow Fisher would not have accepted. Ian Fraser and Mallon [Warden of Toynbee Hall] are to be announced tonight [as the additional governors] and the vice-chairmanship left over. All I hear of Mallon is good. Fraser will take up a lot of time and his blindness is otherwise awkward.

[During 1937, John Reith concerned himself mainly, once more, with the problems of internal organization within his fast expanding corporation, problems which were sharpened by the approaching retirement of his deputy, Admiral Carpendale, who had been with him from the start. Externally, he had to face parliamentary accusations of bias over the Spanish civil war, which had begun in the summer of 1936, and he successfully dealt with these by his well-tried method of meetings with the backbenchers of all three parties. Meanwhile, his hope of succeeding Norman as chairman was finally extinguished so that by the beginning of 1938 he was determined to leave the BBC.]

10 February 1937 At the Board Meeting this afternoon Fraser talked as much as before and almost always the first to express an opinion. The deputy director general job was the only important item. I didn't give my views about this till almost the end. They decided unanimously and definitely that there should be the post and a proper occupancy of it. Mallon, talking to me after the meeting, suggested that governors might departmentalize! I tactfully and gradually pointed out that this was contrary to what the PMG gave him about governors' jobs and anyhow that this would be a ridiculous thing to do. I said, however, that I thought he might take a special interest in staff matters.

16 February 1937 There have been several questions in Parliament by backbench nonentities stimulated by the *Daily Mail* rag about bias re: Spain. Gardiner [director general of the Post Office] has been trying to get the PMG to take a proper line and stamp on them.

24 February 1937 Invited to meet Conservative MPs same as 1933 [in fact, 1934]. Thoroughly bored but PMG anxious that I should accept.
   Discussed deputy director general question at the Board and decided to make a decision in a month's time and that it should take effect 1.4.38, Carpendale staying on till then. He will thus have the next chairman to cope with.

27 February 1937 Wrote a long letter to Norman about the DDG job. I said I could gladly accept Graves if they fixed on him; but that I would not happily accept Tallents.

15 March 1937 Tea with PMG who was very civil and friendly. I had mugged up stuff for the Conservative MPs' meeting – a silly ramp. There was a big crowd but not so many as in 1934. I really ought to have read out the silly bias charges and the replies, but I only spoke for seven minutes and then answered questions from 6.25 until 7.40. They were a poor crowd. It seemed to go very well but owing to their fault not nearly as well as it should have done.

23 March 1937 Captain Ramsay, a Tory MP who has been taking the lead about Spanish news, to see me. Very decent, simple sort and I think it did good.

21 April 1937 I lunched with the Liberal party in the House of Commons, seventeen or eighteen there. I answered questions and they seemed very pleased.

4 June 1937 Lunched with Lord Cadman [chairman] and Fraser [vice-chairman] of Anglo-Iranian Co. in Finsbury Circus where I don't think I have been before. Odd that I should have so different an outlook now on men like them from fifteen years ago. I don't like their organization – five working directors including chairman and vice-chairman and lots of others, including two government directors, at £3000 p.a. or so and nothing to do. The BBC is the best system I know.

23 June 1937 To House of Commons, 6.00 to 7.00, to meet Labour MPs, members of Labour Executive and TUC. About two hundred there, E. Shinwell in the chair. I spoke for about quarter of an hour and then questions. It seemed to go excellently and I made them laugh several times. Once I answered a question in broad Glasgow.

14 July 1937 Busy morning. About 12.30 I rang Gardiner to ask if we were clear of National Defence Contributions as the Finance Bill was being put through finally this afternoon. He didn't know; said they had tried to find out last night and wished me luck in any effort I might make to find out from the Treasury. I rang Hopkins [second secretary at the Treasury]; he didn't know but said he would find out. Rang me a little later to say that the BBC was specifically exempted. This was good news. We now proceed to thank various people who helped – however feeble was such help. It would have been monstrous to tax us.

[While on holiday with his family in Cornwall, during August, John Reith was involved in a car accident but he was fortunate not to be seriously hurt. When he returned to work in September he soon heard from the newly appointed vice-chairman, C. H. G. Millis, that he was being talked about 'in connection with Imperial Airways', while it was also plain that he was not being considered as the next chairman of the BBC.]

11 October 1937 Gardiner of Post Office to see me so I didn't get off till the 7.20 train. He is still against Clark [high commissioner in South Africa] as chairman and asked me for suggestions. I thought of Fitzroy, Speaker.

13 October 1937 Long talk with Tallents. Told him I was going to recommend Graves for deputy director general as the job as conceived was more in his line. He would like to be controller of programmes and thinks it in the public interest that he should be but I think his qualities are more useful where he is. At the Board Graves was chosen by 5 or 5½ to 2 or 1½. Introduced sequential changes.

15 October 1937 Lunched with Woods Humphery [managing director of Imperial Airways]. Can't make out whether he knows about my being run for Imperial Airways chairmanship. He said he wouldn't have a full-time chairman!

[Between 6 and 15 November John Reith was away from work because of illness.]

10 November 1937 Various telephone conversations about Board agenda. There was nothing of any importance. Chairman read my letter offering to resign and apparently everybody was very complimentary and didn't take the offer seriously!

24 November 1937 Gardiner to see me. Fitzroy has said he doesn't want to give up the Speakership yet, so there is no one in view for chairman.

1 December 1937 Fraser to see me re: my being chairman so that I could do other things as well. Quite right this.

15 December 1937 To GPO rather unnecessarily, to see Gardiner. PMG apparently very upset about a play by us on the Russian Revolution. I said I hadn't read it and wasn't going to and wasn't concerned with *Daily Mail* stunts and MPs. He said S. M. Bruce [Australian high commissioner in London] was being offered the chairmanship. This made me angry as I had heard nothing of it.

21 December 1937 Heard from the chairman of his visit to the PMG this morning when he was asked to carry on – *sine die*!

31 December 1937 Fifteen years since I went to the BBC – what a time and how doubtful I am about staying much longer.

[In January and February 1938 John Reith was cruising in the West Indies as one of a party made up by Montagu Norman, the Governor of the Bank of England and brother of R. C. Norman. He returned 'feeling most unsettled about the BBC' and seeing 'no solution to the job question'. In this situation the publication in March of the government enquiry under Lord Cadman on Imperial Airways made him consider again whether he would take on this task. Over the next three months his speculations were to become realities.]

4 March 1938 Perplexed as to whether there is anything against what I have always stood for in letting them run a programme from 10.45 to 12.30 on Sunday mornings. I don't think so. The Lord seems to have done nothing whatever in the matter of English advertising competition from Luxembourg all these years and soon we fear that this horrid place and others like it will hold English listeners even when we are operating. I am distressed but it is no case of my being weaker than I used to be. The Religious Committee had no views on it.

9/10 March 1938 [9] I am very tired indeed of the BBC. Ghastly Board meeting. I don't think I have ever shown so much irritation. Awful waste of time.

[10] R. C. Norman very funny about yesterday's Board meeting; he said I had been very naughty and that I wasn't helping him at all. In the early days he had so much admired my handling of the Board and now I wouldn't do anything with them at all. He asked what I thought of his handling of them and I said I thought he was far too gentle with them. He said he would promise to reform if I did, but I said I couldn't do that. He was very decent and rather pathetic.

17 March 1938 Chairman told me he had developed a suplière and would have to have an operation in a week. He was so apologetic about it, poor man. I like him very well.

20 March 1938 [Sunday] Glorious sunshine. Sir Thomas Gardiner, wife and sister came out for the day. I met them in the Wolseley – not without some hazards as I hadn't driven for so long. I told him I wanted to announce now that I would leave the BBC at the end of the year.

28 March 1938 R. C. Norman operated on for rupture this morning – successful and straightforward I gathered.

18 May 1938 Norman in again and awfully nice to me. I have a little to do – maybe an hour's effective work daily.

1 June 1938 Norman asked me at lunch if I were really very tired of the BBC. I said I really didn't know.

[On 3 June John Reith was summoned to Downing Street to be told

John Reith, summer 1915, before he was wounded

John Reith in the United States, May 1917

that he was wanted to go to Imperial Airways immediately. His hope, as he told the prime minister in a letter of 14 June, was to avoid complete severance with the BBC by being placed on the Board of governors. Unfortunately, after making this request, he heard through Sir Warren Fisher that one or two of the governors were opposed to his joining them; worse, R. C. Norman had to tell him that they wished to choose his successor, in which he had already taken some part, without his being present. He was deeply hurt by this double rejection. On 22 June he telephoned Warren Fisher to withdraw his request to be made a governor; a week later he refused to attend his final meeting as director general with the Board. He resolved to cut himself off completely from the BBC. It was, as he wrote to R. C. Norman on 3 July, 'a melancholy end to an epic 15½ years'.]

8 June 1938 Board meeting for which I wasn't in much form. I told them of Imperial Airways and they were very decent and all much shocked. They wondered if I couldn't be seconded but I said this wouldn't be fair to my locum. Also talked about my succeeding R. C. N. as chairman.

10 June 1938 I was with Warren Fisher, and for part of the time H. J. Wilson, between 5.00 and 6.45. I told them the position to date and they then tried to convince me that Gardiner of the Post Office should succeed me. All wrong.

16 June 1938 At 12.30 we had a very silly meeting in Warren Fisher's room at the Treasury – Norman, Millis and I, Horace Wilson being there also. I arranged it so that Fisher and Wilson could have the chance of putting direct their plea that a civil servant should succeed me! I had made my doubts about Gardiner (so like Graves as he is) so clear that they suggested three others, Vansittart, Barlow and Grigg. I said there were two serious objections to a civil servant; that it made it look as if the job were in the gift of the government; and that a civil servant couldn't be relied on to keep the corporation where it should be constitutionally. They made an awfully poor show of it.

22 June 1938 A quite fatuous Board to discuss the succession. There is little chance of a civil servant getting the job.

[It appears to have been after this meeting that John Reith telephoned

R.D.–M

Warren Fisher to withdraw his request to be placed on the Board of governors of the BBC.]

27 June 1938 Interviewed Ogilvie, vice-chancellor of Queen's University, Belfast, as he had said he would like to be considered for the job. R.C.N. saw him too, he being more impressed with him than I, probably because less affected by externals. I had another hour and a half with him in the afternoon. He was so impressed with the importance of the job that it is likely he would come for less pay than he is getting now.

29 June 1938 I did not go to the Board meeting as I had intended because I just couldn't. The reason was that Norman came in about 1.35 to say that some of his colleagues felt they should decide on my successor by themselves. He said he didn't approve, but there it was. I said I thought it was dreadful. I was already annoyed enough by having heard that some of them thought it wouldn't be fair to my successor if I were on the Board – what a reflection on the successor. He was in an awful stew and when I said I wouldn't come to the Board he begged me to. I would perhaps have done so but I got more upset and broke down later. He came in two or three times and it was all awful.

30 June 1938 I saw Norman this afternoon and he was in a state. I said I wasn't angry with him, though I thought he could have prevented it all – but that I was very incensed against the others and that I was cutting out of everything – my wireless set and television were being recovered and I had cancelled all magazines. It is all simply damnable. I expect Ogilvie will get the job. I said goodbye to a very few and left at 5.45.

Later with Graves and two others went via Broadway to Droitwich, where we had dinner, and then to the transmitter which was most impressive. I closed down one of the oil engines. All over. I signed the Visitors Book – 'late BBC'. To Daventry – dawn breaking and things looking beautiful – all the red mast lights, most romantic. Reached Broadcasting House at 6.45. Went to my room to collect the last of my gear and that's the end of that.

NOTES

1. See Andrew Boyle, *Only the Wind Will Listen*, pp. 120–1.

2. The Free Church of Scotland, to which John Reith's father had belonged, had been formed by the ministers who followed Thomas Chalmers out of the established Church of Scotland in 1843. John Reith had a lifelong interest in Chalmers and there is among his papers an unpublished essay on him which he wrote in the 1950s.

3. The passage in brackets was probably inserted by John Reith in 1932.

4. This is probably another insertion of 1932.

5. This was not the full composition of the Crawford committee which also included the Labour MP, William Graham, the future Conservative MP, Ian Fraser, and the future Lord Strathcarron. John Reith's distaste for Kipling, who in fact resigned from the committee because of illness, was to continue. He met him when staying with Lord Stanhope at Chevening in 1935 and 'did not feel at all friendly'.

6. This message is printed by Briggs I, pp. 364–6.

7. The Post Office, supported by the Treasury, aimed to take a part of the BBC's licence revenue as taxation over and above their legitimate costs of collection.

8. John Reith pencilled against this passage in his diary the comment, 'here was the beginning of the miserable time with Clarendon'.

9. In his autobiography John Reith raised these figures to 500 and 1200 and related them to the end of the 'Company'.

10. The last sentence was probably written in 1934.

11. The postmaster general was now Sir Kingsley Wood. The document was what came to be called the 'Whitley document' and was circulated to all new governors until 1952. See Briggs II, p. 431.

12. Besides Lady Snowden, the retiring governors were Rendall and Gainford. R. C. Norman replaced Gainford as vice-chairman. The other new governors were Lord Bridgeman and Mrs Mary Agnes Hamilton; Sir Gordon Nairne had already been replaced by H. G. Brown.

13. All four of these men went on to important positions – Sir Kenneth Pickthorn as a member of parliament, P. C. Vellacott as headmaster of Harrow and Master of Peterhouse, Cambridge, Sir John Masterman as Provost of Worcester College and vice-chancellor of Oxford and W. S. Morrison, later Lord Dunrossil, as a cabinet minister, speaker of the House of Commons and, finally, governor-general of Australia.

14. F. A. Iremonger had given up the editorship of the *Guardian* in 1927 and was at this time a parish priest. John Reith was soon to appoint him director of religious broadcasting in the BBC.

15. See Boyle, *op. cit.* pp. 289, 293.

16. Wireless or relay exchange (also called rediffusion) was the practice of wiring broadcast programmes to individual subscribers by commercial companies operating under licence from the Post Office. By the end of 1935 nearly a quarter of a million subscribers, mostly drawn from the poorer sections of the population, were availing themselves of this service. John Reith wished the BBC to have control of the programmes relayed by this method and the Ullswater committee recommended just this although one of its members, Lord Selsdon, dissented. Reith's fear was

that political interests in the Cabinet, anxious not to lose votes among the sub-scribers, and the commercial interests of the relay exchange companies, anxious not to lose their profitable and expanding enterprises, would combine to overthrow the committee's recommendation. His foreboding was fully confirmed.

17. Sir Horace J. Wilson, chief industrial adviser to the Government since 1930, had been seconded to the Treasury for service with the prime minister in 1935. John Reith was to have much contact with him in the years leading up to the War.

CHAPTER THREE

John Reith and the Monarchy

1. Between the Wars, 1923–39

John Reith was quick to see the opportunities which broadcasting offered as a means of personal communication between the Sovereign and his subjects at home and overseas. As soon as he took over the BBC he tried to put the case for this at the Palace. By the end of 1923 he had arranged for a wireless set to be presented to King George V; and, as we have seen, during 1924 the King's speeches at important occasions such as the opening of the Empire Exhibition at Wembley were broadcast. But George V was not to be easily won to a more direct exploitation of the microphone. Fortunately, in 1926 John Reith found an ally in Lord Stamfordham, the King's long-serving and influential private secretary. Stamfordham seems to have made some efforts over the next two years to break down the King's reluctance to broadcast, but without success. Then, at the end of 1928, the King's severe illness made further progress difficult. In April 1929 John Reith noted that Stamfordham had told him that 'the King was still very weak and not fit to broadcast'. In 1931 Stamfordham himself died and Reith took up the issue with his successor Sir Clive, later Lord, Wigram. The next year his long-pressed case was accepted. At Christmas 1932 George V gave his first personal broadcast. Thus it took ten years to break down the barrier of royal conservatism in respect of broadcasting. Thereafter, in spite of some apparent resistance at court, the King's Christmas broadcast was continued until his death.

2 February 1928 Stamfordham rang up to invite me to lunch, saying he was to be alone. He was very agreeable. He said the King still thought everybody ought to be wearing silk hats in London and did not at all approve of the way the Prince of Wales dressed. But it is evident that he believes in keeping the King on a pedestal.

10 November 1928 Lord Stamfordham phoned in the evening and read a message issued by the Queen, the last paragraph of which said she wished her voice could reach every woman in the country with a message of love and sympathy on Armistice Day. I had written to Lord

Stamfordham to say that either the King or Queen could broadcast a message, and he telephoned to say that he had been trying to get hold of someone in the Palace but could not. He agreed that this would have been very effective on the 10th anniversary, but he did not think they would do it and that it was difficult enough to have got a message out of the Queen. He said he would send the letter over first thing in the morning. It is extraordinary how conservative they are.

13 October 1930 Lunched at Lord Stamfordham's. Exchanged views with him of what the King might, or rather ought, to do if conditions go on as they are and parliamentary government becomes much more farcical.

[The BBC's move to Broadcasting House was the occasion of the first royal visit.]

7 July 1932 The King and the Queen arrived punctually. Whitley introduced the governors and the ladies and then I took on. The reception in the concert hall was most impressive, the national anthem being excellently sung as the King likes it, the second half much louder than the first, and the cheering afterwards was very hearty. I actually got them round in 50 minutes. I found the King much more talkative than the Queen, in fact at tea she was rather heavy. They left at about 4.45, and the people with them said that the visit had been a tremendous success. At my suggestion we all fell to and had a good tea after the King and Queen had gone, in the middle of which Clive Wigram rang me up and said it was exactly as he had wished, that they were not only not bored but felt they could have seen more of the place.

10 October 1932 Saw Clive Wigram about the King opening the Empire Service. He said he had had two sleepless nights about it, and was it a religious service? Eventually he said he was in favour of it, but that he found the King difficult to manage. The King was frequently saying that he was too modern. He asked me to get the PM to endorse it.

17 November 1932 Visited Wigram at Buckingham Palace about the King on Christmas Day. He is always very genial, but it seems to take a good deal to make him understand things.

25 November 1932   History of the fixing of HM the King's broadcast on Christmas Day 1932

On two or three occasions I had broached the matter with Lord Stamfordham – the first time for Christmas 1927 . . .

The idea of the King's opening the Empire Service occurred probably to several of us, as well as to the chairman and myself.

It was mentioned to the King (not as for Christmas Day) by the chairman when he was invested with the Kaisar-i-Hind Medal.

When Sir Clive Wigram came here about the King's projected visit, it was mentioned to him then, and he advised not saying anything about it meantime until the Broadcasting House visit was over.

In October, I ascertained that the Empire Service would start operations about December 19th. It struck me at once that, if the King were to broadcast, we should suggest this for Christmas Day rather than for the opening.

I wrote Sir Clive Wigram on 6th October and I saw him on October 10th. He said that it might help if there were a strong recommendation from the prime minister. I accordingly wrote to Duff the same day.

I heard later from Duff that the PM had written.

Wigram wrote me on 18th October, saying that he thought it would be all right.

25 December 1932 After lunch we listened to the Empire broadcast, which was most impressive and excellent. The King was evidently quite moved and spoke more personally and effectively than I had ever heard him.

12 October 1933 I went to see Sir Clive Wigram at 11.30 on the Christmas programme. Wigram thought it was very good. He told me he had had a lot of opposition among his colleagues to contend with.[1] He had told the King that as he was 68 he had not got many years to look forward to, and had also got material assistance from the Archbishop of Canterbury and the prime minister at Balmoral.

[Lord Wigram's fears for King George V's survival were well-founded and his frank warning to the King that he had not many years to look forward to was sadly confirmed. In November 1935 he told John Reith that 'the King had no reserves of strength' and later that month, when both men attended a meeting in the Cabinet offices to consider arrangements for the demise of the crown, it was

plain that this was now accepted in governing circles. By January
1936 the King was dying.]

18 January 1936 Alas! Graves told us last night that the King was ill and
that the Prince of Wales had gone to Sandringham. This morning the
bulletin said there was cause for disquiet. Neither Vincent nor Cleverly
[private secretaries to the PM] was on duty at No. 10. Dunnett said the
latest news was that it would be at least a matter of days. Found that
the PM had no warning till I gave it that he was supposed to broadcast
when the King died. The recent meeting about the demise of the crown
and its decisions hadn't been passed on to anyone. Our arrangements
which were supposed to be all taped up were by no manner of means
so.

Dunnett phoned at 5.45 to say the PM would like to see me. I was
taken straight to the library. He was reading the new More biography[2]
and immensely impressed with it. Got talking about the number of
books he had so I gave my usual observations about getting rid of
rubbish. He was much amused. Said he was waiting to hear from the
Dean of Westminster if Kipling (who died this morning) could be
buried in the Abbey and what did I think of that. I said it was the
obvious thing and rather absurd that the Dean had the yea or nay in the
matter. Worried about the King dying as things were so critical. Agreed
that kingship never stood higher in this country and that broadcasting
had a lot to do with this – that, as I said, it had brought the solicitude of
fatherhood in where before was the aloof dignity of the throne. He said
he had had many serious talks with the Prince of Wales and his brothers.
He asked what I thought he should talk about; said he hadn't begun to
think about it.

19 January 1936 Omitted to say that Sir Ralph Verney [secretary to the
Speaker] came to see me yesterday to ask us if we would announce the
House of Commons meeting which would be today (Sunday) if the
King died yesterday. I asked about the House of Lords, saying we had
better cover both. He wasn't interested in that but I got Sir H. Badeley,
the Clerk of the Parliaments, on the phone and framed a joint one.

20 January 1936 Went home on the 5.16 there having been no news all
day from Sandringham. Just as I got home the news came through with
the statement that the King's strength was diminishing. Muriel thought
I should go back at once so, after talking to the office, she and I just
did so. At 9.30 came 'The King's life is moving peacefully to its close.'

We got it out at 9.38 as we had to collect all the Regionals and Empire. It was repeated at 10.00 with a special epilogue which included the 23rd Psalm chanted. Repeated at quarter-hour intervals till 12.00 – Big Ben also. At 12.08 Dunnett rang me from No. 10 to say that the PM had just been informed that the King died at a few minutes before 11.00. Dunnett thought that I should wait for Sandringham, but since I had it from No. 10 I put it out at 12.15. I hated having this to do.

21 January 1936 PM decided to do his broadcast from No. 10 and said he would like me to go along if I didn't mind. Later he asked me to dine there with him. To No. 10 at 8.00. My top dental plate was very loose and bothered me all evening – most unfortunate. Mr and Mrs Baldwin were alone and were very cordial. We had dinner, a very nice one, in a little room where I hadn't been before. Much talk and jesting. He told Mrs B. of what I had said about pushing rubbish into people's cars when they came to H[arrias] H[ouse]. Spoke of the bitterness of Snowden's broadcast, when he should have been preparing his soul for eternity. I said what I thought of Greenwood's[3] also, and S.B. said perhaps he was drunk at the time. They hope the Queen will live with the new King and keep an eye on him and act as hostess. Hoped Wigram would be taken by the King, but didn't know. S.B. told me about the King in a conscious interval yesterday opening his eyes and asking Wigram, 'How's the Empire?' I said he certainly should mention this, but 1 said also that he should make it clear that this incredible, legendary sort of story, was actually true. He said he would – but didn't, just told it rather badly. When Mrs B. went off he produced some sheets of paper – said someone had done five pages for him and that he was going to use the last three, but had made his own notes for the beginning. He asked if I would mind reading what he had. I made various suggestions and changed bits of the typed stuff – bringing in the moral authority, honour and dignity of the throne being enhanced; also 'God guide him aright' at the end. The broadcast was in the Cabinet Room at 9.30, Mrs B. in an armchair at the fire. It was good but nothing to what it might have been. I do wish he would prepare. I said goodbye afterwards and they both thanked me again for coming. It is interesting to have dined with the PM on this particular day.

[Stanley Baldwin's reference to 'serious talks with the Prince of Wales', whether they took place or not, and John Reith's insertion into the prime minister's script of the phrase 'God guide him aright' indicate the intense concern felt behind the scenes at the new King's growing attachment to the then Mrs Ernest Simpson. John Reith's feelings about this and about the monarchical system in general were often confided to his diary culminating in a detailed account of the Abdication crisis.]

15 November 1932 The Prince of Wales arrived at 8.25, instead of 8.15 and I took him a hurried tour through the building.[4] He said he would like to come again when there was more time, which would certainly be much better. He broadcast quite a nice birthday message about the BBC. Then for about five minutes in the vaudeville studio, where a special show was put on. He had to leave in five minutes to get a train to Liverpool on his way to Belfast. Prince Arthur of Connaught and his wife were present. I spoke to them afterwards and then they went for a tour round the building. I thought them particularly dull and did not care for them. I am not in the least diffident about dealing with Royalties, but the trouble is that they always seem so shy and nervous, it puts me at such a disadvantage. I was reflecting on the way home how long the monarchical system would survive without more definite personality in the Royalties. Certainly if they have a lot of it, it has to be largely suppressed, but how much better it would be if they had such presence and personality as would automatically command respect, and above all the ability to appear at ease and to put other people at ease.

6 January 1933 To the office to meet the Prince of Wales who was introducing the unemployment talks. He was in better form that I had ever known him. He said at the end that he loved broadcasting and wished he could give all his speeches in this way. He did very well and I told him that, speaking quite honestly, he was a first-class broadcaster.

3 July 1933 Went to meet the Prince who was to have broadcast from the Dominion Day dinner but decided he did not want to do so and came to the office instead with Bennett, the Canadian prime minister. He was in good form and sat talking for some time, but he is very difficult to talk to, going from one subject to another and having fixed ideas of all sorts. I am sure he must be very difficult indeed to manage, and I can foresee troubles of one kind or another later on.

[John Reith's forebodings were soon to be fulfilled.]

20 June 1935 Lady Constance Gaskell[5] for lunch. Talked of the terrible way the Prince of Wales carries on. It is indeed very tragic. Mrs Simpson has been figuring in *Time*. It is damnable.

3 November 1935 Miss Bigge[6] to lunch. She said the Prince of Wales's reply to people who spoke to him about his morals was that he did his job and that his private life was his own. This is not so and never can be. It is deplorable and wretched that he carries on as he does. It is common knowledge.

[Once the Prince of Wales had become King Edward VIII events moved swiftly to the crisis of December 1936.]

29 January 1936 Wigram phoned. Asked how long notice we needed of a talk by the King [Edward VIII] as they were going ahead with that now, though he added that he hadn't seen the King all day. He hoped that Queen Mary would stay on at Buckingham Palace and take her part as of old. Also that the King would live there which he didn't seem to want to do. If he didn't, he said that would be the beginning of the end of the British Empire, as Buckingham Palace was the centre of it. He said the Queen had gone to communion on Sunday – which led me to say how deplorable it was that the King hadn't gone to church last Sunday. He quite agreed and said that it was even worse that he hadn't gone the Sunday before.

22 February 1936 At midday Godfrey Thomas [private secretary to King Edward VIII] rang up to say that the King would broadcast on March 1. The *Radio Times* went to press last night but we stopped it and there will be a picture of the King on the front. Fixed 4.00 as the time and told G[odfrey] T[homas]. The King would have liked it earlier but this is best for the Empire.

1 March 1936 The King arrived at 3.40. There was a great crowd and much cheering. To my room for five minutes or so and then he said he'd like to go to the studio. He and I were in [studio] 3B alone for about 12 minutes. He was in very good form, read over his speech; asked if I thought he should say 'Ladies & Gentlemen' or anything like that and I advised definitely not. He said he felt far happier coming to Broadcasting House than doing it in Buckingham Palace. I made the announcement myself, stood by the door to make sure that he would start when the green light came on and then left. When he was finished I went back and he asked if I minded his having a cigarette despite studio regulations; I had to get him a light from outside. He sorted his hair with a pocket comb and then I handed him over to Tallents and G. Thomas who saw him through the photograph. This took about ten minutes and then I fetched him along for tea. He stayed for about 25 minutes. We played back the whole performance to him and he was awfully pleased to hear it.

6 March 1936 Wigram rang up at 10.00. He said the King was very pleased with last Sunday; he would have liked to come with him to Broadcasting House but wasn't invited. Said his position was difficult and very tiring but the King very nice indeed to him . . . 'You can't do it, Sir, it is not constitutional.' Thought the 'young fellow' was getting on quite well; diversities of gifts but the same spirit, he hoped; other times, other manners . . . Said he was feeling a bit depressed so had rung me up to get cheered up. I was surprised at his saying so much on the telephone.

8 April 1936 Warren Fisher said Wigram had been to see him about the King; that it was arranged that the PM, Speaker and Halifax [lord privy seal at this time] would visit HM over his 'private life' affairs but that S[tanley] B[aldwin] had been too lazy to do so. Agreed that the fate of the Empire was involved. It is a terrible affair this. It seems as if we might be back in the days of Henry VIII.

28 May 1936 The Times today had the most serious news that it has had for many years. The King gave a dinner-party last night: his first. The PM and Mrs B[aldwin] were there. Lady Cunard, an evil woman who was never at the late King's parties. Mr and Mrs E. Simpson. It is too horrible and it is serious and sad beyond calculation.

30 May 1936 The King has made the Victorian Order open for women in all grades. Will the first GCVOs (female) be Lady Cunard and Mrs Simpson?

10 July 1936 The King has given another dinner-party with the Simpson woman in it. Reflecting on all this I came to the conclusion that it wouldn't take much to make me a republican and that it should be possible even so to devise methods for keeping the Empire as much together at least as it is now – perhaps make the ties more definite. It would be great fun to devise a completely new system of Empire co-ordination, involving for instance much greater status for the Dominion high commissioners and their association with the home government as a unit of Empire policy. As to the crown it is not possible today, in my view, for the crown to be thought of independent of the wearer and King Edward VIII is setting an example which will be disastrous to himself and to the country. I do not object to kingship *per se* and the dignity and majesty of it are essential. These attributes might be retained in republican form. The King might be elected for life, but certainly the position would need to be kept clear of the disgusting circumstances of the American presidency and should never go to one who has been a politician.

6 October 1936 Lunched with Geoffrey Dawson. He feels as I do about the King and Mrs Simpson, an overhanging depression. He said he couldn't feel any personal interest in the Coronation and didn't want to have anything to do with it . . . He said the King's popularity was suffering clearly. He thought some Scots minister might break out on the subject, which is just what I have thought too.

29 October 1936 Lunched with Harley, in charge of Fox Film here . . . He told me that Coronation insurance risks had risen from four to twenty-one per cent in two and a half months. This is all due to the wretched Simpson affair and it is most significant. It was good news to me.

3 December 1936 Times leader about the King and Mrs Simpson and all the papers have the affair in the open now. I sent a letter first thing to Warren Fisher asking advice if the King rang me up to say he wanted to broadcast. Soon after this left, H. J. Wilson phoned to ask if he could come to see me on behalf of the PM. I said certainly, but he had better wait my letter to Warren F. Later I was asked to go and see them both. W.F. said he and others had been wanting to get leave to work on the 'mechanics' of abdication etc., but they hadn't been allowed to, and now the thing had burst on them and he regarded this as a crisis of the first magnitude. The Dominion governments had been asked on Friday [i.e. 27 November] what line they would take if the King insisted on marrying the woman: (1) accept her as Queen (2) tolerate a morganatic marriage (3) insist on abdication. They had all replied No. 3. Winston Churchill had been badgering H. J. [Wilson] about the necessity for consulting Parliament, but no one was clear as to whether this was so or whether it was simply for the Cabinet. He and Esmond Harmsworth [later Lord Rothermere] (a friend of the King's) were to some extent responsible for making the King think he might get away with a morganatic marriage . . . When Baldwin saw the King last night, the King was 'foaming at the mouth' about the *Yorkshire Post* article[7] and accused the government of having inspired it. Baldwin convinced him that this wasn't true. He hadn't been truculent with S.B., 'rather pathetic' in fact. At 10.30 the King himself had rung *Whitehall 1234* [i.e. No. 10 Downing Street], being answered by the old doorkeeper man. He asked to speak to the PM and was told he was probably in bed. 'Who is speaking?' – 'The King.' So S.B. was produced and the King said he had heard that Geoffrey Dawson was printing a leader and that would be very harmful. Would the PM please stop it? S.B. said this would create a very bad impression that the King was trying to muzzle the Press. So the King asked him to get hold of the leader and control what was said in it. Another communication goes today to all Dominions informing them tactfully of what the British government think is proper procedure on abdication. H. J. [Wilson] said he had hunted for my telephone number at midnight! This was in case the King tried to broadcast. They said he might quite likely. I was to say we must consult the PM before agreeing. It was hoped he would abdicate voluntarily, not that it would have to be on the advice of the government. King now at Belvedere; Cabinet not to meet today.

Office at 4.50. Godfrey Thomas phoned and asked if he could come and see me. Arranged for him to give his name as Smith. I was very sorry for him. He was in a dreadful state. I got a whisky and soda up for him. Asked if, in the event of the King wanting to broadcast, we could arrange it at short notice and from Windsor Castle. I said we probably could do it very quickly – even tomorrow night. I asked if the PM would know of it, and he said yes, the King was going to talk to him about it tonight and would only do it if the PM agreed. He seemed to want to talk. Said the King was quite 'insane' on this issue – wouldn't listen to anyone, but that he got on well with the PM and had said this morning how fortunate he was to have a man like S.B. as PM. He said the King had refused to discuss the matter with any of his staff except [Walter] Monckton. He said he had done his best to 'keep the flag flying' all these years and now it had gone for nothing. He was sure that even if the King now did everything he was advised, he could never recover the ground lost. He said he had not met Mrs Simpson till he went on the yacht.[8] He said he was surprised after all the stories he had heard about the woman's familiarity with the King, that she treated him quite properly in public, curtsy and 'Sir'; in fact if she hadn't had a husband . . . he wouldn't have seen anything wrong. She was smart in talk but not the least clever. He was full of condemnation of her; blaming her infinitely more than the King. He confirmed what I heard earlier in the day about E. Harmsworth and said the King was surprised at the Dominions' replies. He didn't think the King had ever really thought he could make the woman Queen.

Just as I was writing this Godfrey Thomas phoned that the King probably would broadcast tomorrow night – the PM agreeing. Anyhow it was advisable for us to get Windsor Castle fixed up on chance. This was at 11.55 p.m.

4 December 1936 I phoned both Fisher and Wilson informing them of Godfrey Thomas's midnight message; also asking that any news should be given to us quickly. Warren F. and H.J.W. phoned jointly that Godfrey Thomas was quite wrong in saying that the King and the PM were in agreement over the possibility of a broadcast by the former. G.T. was being entirely honest but no one could believe anything the King said; he was very difficult – encouraged by Winston Churchill. They were a bit alarmed by the news that the installation in a room at Windsor Castle was proceeding. They said the King was quite capable of crashing in, but I said this was impossible. W.F. and H.J.W. were quite happy about this so long as there was no chance of the King broadcasting without the PM's permission.

5 December 1936 To see Wilson at 4.30. He was with the PM so I talked first to [T.L.] Dugdale, the PPS. He said there had been drawn up a document pointing out that the King could only broadcast on the advice of his ministers. The PM had taken this to Fort Belvedere last night. The King had been 'rather pathetic' about it; had read it and said all right. 'That's what your advisers say; I have no one to advise me.' There was no chance of his broadcasting at all. Ministers wouldn't give permission. They think it would be very difficult. I suppose they are afraid of trouble. The stunt press are campaigning for the King to be allowed to marry and to stay King. They quote 'the public' as usual. It is dastardly. H.J. said it was the lowest depth to which they had sunk. Of course I am very sorry for the King. What a ghastly position he has put himself in.

6 December 1936 I suppose anything might happen in the country now; it might be the end of the monarchy; or we might have the King as a sort of dictator, or with Churchill as PM, which is presumably what that worthy is working for.

9 December 1936 Abdication is all the talk today. I wrote a note tonight to H.J. and sent it to No. 10 first thing in the morning saying I hoped I would have information quickly.

10 December 1936 Wilson phoned to say he would do this as soon as he had got it all himself. I went along at 12.00. The PM came in and seemed in very good form. He said he still wouldn't change jobs with me, however difficult a time he might have been having. After H.J. had started telling me about things the PM came back into the room with a pencil letter he had just received from the King, which he referred to in his House of Commons speech. He implored me not to get up because he said I seemed never to be going to stop. I said I was sorry about my length but I liked to show respect. H.J. said he was suffering from violent emotion which prevented him from being as coherent as he could wish. [Wilson said that] the King, after giving assent to the Abdication Bill, was to be called 'His former Majesty' and was to be allowed to broadcast then. We were to be very careful not to get any confusion between old King and new and not to play the national anthem at all. Also to go slow on Irish Free State news as there was a fear of a republic being proclaimed there.

To see Sir John Simon [now home secretary] at the House of Commons at 5.00 and was there till 6.15. He said the King wasn't sane. He had asked him [Simon] to see me about his broadcast; he would like it to be at 10.00 p.m. So I said this could be fixed. Simon said he would be helping him with his talk which would say something about his personal trouble; make clear that no one had tried to rush him; that he would do nothing to split the country; best wishes to his successor. Simon asked me if I didn't think the abdication announcement was very good. I said 'Yes – you wrote it didn't you?' He said he had. He said the King had wanted other things in the Abdication Statement, particularly a reference to the Navy.

11 December 1936 Godfrey Thomas liked my idea of having London announce at 10.00 that we were going over to Windsor Castle, and then letting the King start without further intimation; but he said the King would probably have his new title by then. Soon after Cleverly of No. 10 said we should call him HRH Prince Edward, and that the new title would not be conferred today. I told Godfrey T. and he was surprised. 5.51 home. At dinner Sir John Simon was announced on one phone and Buckingham Palace on the other. Simon said that King

Muriel Odhams on her engagement, April 1919

John and Muriel, July 1919

A Southwick tower, 1918

George [VI] was very particular that his brother should be called HRH Prince Edward.[9]

Left at 9.05 and got to Windsor at 9.30. I was expected and the car took me to the door of the private quarters. Here were a red-coated footman, the major-domo and the housekeeper. Went up to the room where the broadcast was to take place. It was in a little corridor of three rooms, bedroom at end. This was the suite the King [i.e. Edward VIII] always used. The microphones were in the centre room. I had just looked around when I got an agitated message to go down to the door to receive the King. It struck me as rather odd that I should receive him in his own house. No one knew who was coming with him. Actually it was Monckton who has stood by him so well in recent days. He had on a light suit, fur coat and was smoking a big cigar. Seemed very glad to see me. (I should have said that Godfrey T. had found that the King wanted me to be there myself.) Next thing I considered was whether I should announce him myself; decided to do so. He didn't seem any different from usual. 'Good evening, Reith; very nice of you to make all these arrangements and come along yourself.' I said he had better have a trial for voice; next door I found an evening paper. I carefully turned the pages to racing news so that he couldn't read anything about himself. Actually he went across the page and read about Sir S. Hoare and some lawn tennis meeting. After only two lines I got the signal that it was OK, so I told him. He continued, however, because the next part was a remark of Hoare's that the new King was a keen and skilled tennis player. He seemed to think this very funny. I saw Wigram in the passage. He wouldn't go into the room so I took him into the bedroom where there was a portable. Monckton told me the King had actually wanted to say goodbye to his family before the broadcast, but he had persuaded him to go back after. The King went to pump ship in a place between bedroom and sitting-room, saying he didn't know when he would use that place again and leaving the door open. I announced; then left the chair on the left side having got him to stand to the right of it. In sitting down he gave the table an awful kick which came over quite clearly. I didn't think much of what the King said. I listened in his bedroom. After he finished I waited for a while and then went into the room. He and Monckton looked as if they had been having an argument. I said Wigram was next door and the King went to find him. Monckton said he was glad I had come in when I did and that I got the King's mind off himself. He said there would be a ghastly reaction in a week or so, and the King didn't in the least realize what he was doing . . .

R.D.–N

It surprises me how ready all these people are to talk freely about this business. Monckton especially. I said I ought to get off; he said I mustn't go without seeing the King. He was talking to Wigram so Monckton told him I was going. He came into the big corridor with me and thanked me again. He said he hoped very much he would be able to use the BBC again; he had found it very useful – the medium I controlled. I said I hoped he would – though I could not well see how. I said 'Good luck, Sir,' shook hands and bowed. He smiled very nicely and rather sadly, so I bowed again and left. What an occasion. What that young man has thrown away – a greater opportunity than any King or any man ever had. I felt very sorry for him.

13 December 1936 We all went to Hedgerly church. We felt as if a cloud of depression of which we had been almost physically conscious had lifted. Poor Edward. But thank God he and his ways have passed and there is a new King and Queen. The effect was quite extraordinary. It seemed as if the old England was back. Tonight there was a special service at which the Archbishop[10] spoke. I thought he did excellently – some hard things about the late King and his set, much needed. No doubt he will be much abused.

[The new reign quickly fulfilled John Reith's hopes. He greatly approved what he regarded as the serious approach of King George VI and, more personally, he appreciated the recognition of his own work implicit in the invitation he received to dine at Windsor Castle in April 1938, and explicit in the award to him by the King of the GCVO at the end of that year. Before this, however, he had been closely involved in the arrangements made for the King's broadcast after his coronation.]

14 January 1937 Went to give Lascelles, King's second secretary, wife and son tea in my room. He said the King was more fussed about his Coronation Day broadcast than about anything else. He wondered if any recording arrangements could be made. I said the King should decide if the deception mattered and anyhow he would need to go through the process of actually broadcasting at the time.

[Amidst the preparations for George VI's coronation broadcast John Reith still thought about Edward VIII's abdication. In April he dined with Stanley Baldwin, then on the eve of his retirement as prime minister, and in the course of a long conversation with him (part of which is given in Chapter Four) he heard more details of that extraordinary crisis.]

16 April 1937 [After his broadcast] Stanley Baldwin told me things for forty minutes about the new King and Queen – with whom he is very pleased – and about the late King and his abdication. George VI is, he thinks, very like his father. In a letter that week he had said that he liked being at Royal Lodge because he had time to rest and think – two things of which his brother was quite incapable. S.D. told me a funny story about de Valera. Someone from the Dominions Office had gone to see him about the abdication and de Valera had said that as a Catholic he couldn't recognize divorce so no question of morganatic marriage could be relevant and he didn't care what happened and he wasn't going to pass special legislation. It had been pointed out to him that at that rate Edward would be left King of Ireland and nothing else, so de Valera had hastily changed his mind. S.B. said on the Wednesday [9 December] he was terrified lest Edward changed his mind and didn't sign the abdication instrument. He had been with him from 4.00 to 11.00 on Tuesday [8 December]. About 7.00 the King rang for a whisky and soda – the first he had had – and S.B. said he would like one too. When the footman went to get it, S.B. said he wanted to tell him that whatever happened he and Mrs B. hoped he would be happy. The King had told somebody later that the PM was the only one who had ever expressed such a hope. How miserable, S.B. said, with all the sycophants round him.

[On another occasion] when S.B. came to see the King, he was talking to Mrs Simpson (on the telephone). When S.B. came into the room the King's face was as if he had seen a vision; he walked about in ecstasy saying 'She is the most wonderful woman in the world.' It had been on S.B.'s advice that Mrs Simpson had left the country; he had told the King that harm might come to her. S.B. was afraid that the King might fly out to her, so they had arranged that no aeroplane could be available. If he went, S.B. said, 'the crown would go down the drain'; but how awkward it was on the other hand if the government could be accused of keeping the King prisoner.

S.B. said he had first tackled the King in October. People had wanted him to do it earlier but there was no real occasion before the divorce. At that time the King had thought he needn't abdicate, that a great many people would be sorry if he did. S.B. had said the crown was much more important than the King. The King had asked him if he hadn't behaved with dignity in his public appearances and S.B. had said yes, but that would count for nothing if the English papers had any of the stuff the American ones had.

To my surprise both Mr and Mrs B. seemed to think that he might have 'lived' with Mrs Simpson provided it had been kept quiet – a special dispensation for the King established by usage since he alone couldn't marry the woman he wanted to. I said I didn't think that would do; it would surely be an overhanging depression to those who knew and always the danger of its getting out.

S.B. said the King was absolutely devoid of any appreciation of his responsibilities, physically and mentally incapable of appreciating an iota of them. I asked if this was simply in respect of Mrs Simpson, but the PM didn't know; he thought he had the mind of a child. He didn't think he would ever realize what he had done himself. S.B. said he was going to write the full story of his dealings with Edward and would probably present it to Cambridge University.

4 May 1937 To the Palace at 5.30. With Hardinge [private secretary to King George VI] for a while. Logue, the King's stutterer curer in. He is much more in charge than anyone else. King in very good form. We got a desk fitted up so that he could talk standing. He recounted an amusing Coronation rehearsal at the Abbey this morning with the Dean of W[estminster] and the Archbishop cannoning into each other and tripping over things. The two Princesses came charging down the passage followed by a little brown dog and then by a stout nurse. They came into the room where we were, said they had overheard the talk in the news room and generally played about. The King paid no attention to them.

5 May 1937 To Buckingham Palace at 11.00. The King went through his speech twice completely, it being recorded and then played back. There was also an intermediate attempt when he coughed and spoilt 'the bloody record'. The Queen came along and the King and she and Logue and I listened to the first attempt in the King's bedroom. It is quite a small room and the only odd thing in it was a glass case with about one hundred jewelled cigarette cases. There were a good many stutters so they tried again. Didn't get away till 1.00.

12 May 1937 [Coronation Day] To Palace by police car at 6.00, arriving far too early and sitting in Hardinge's room. Logue came to Buckingham Palace at 7.00. Listened to the Empire Homage programme – very good. King got through much better than at rehearsals and really did quite well. I was for going off without seeing him but he sent for me and the Queen arrived at the same time. They were both in much delight over everything. Talked for five minutes or more. He said that it was a whole hour between his crowning and the Queen's and that his crown was getting heavier and heavier meantime. Talk about 'what a day'. I said he had given a final end to it by his broadcast. He was wearing a light suit without waistcoat (which seems to be a custom of all the brothers).

28 May 1937 To Toscanini concert to receive Duke and Duchess of Kent. I sat next the latter and found her quite nice and easy to talk to. He seemed exceedingly stupid or gauche. It is extraordinary that the Royal Family should be so lacking in ordinary qualities of personality and character. They always seem the most awkward people in the room.

19 October 1937 Straight to Buckingham Palace. Hardinge said that N. Chamberlain [the new prime minister] had felt that it was impossible for the King to broadcast every Christmas as they couldn't produce an interesting enough talk. How pathetic. Almost unbelievable. How typical of the attitude of politicians. His talks would get dull and people wouldn't listen to them. This – with the enormous benefits of a Christmas message on the other side. Hardinge then said that he and Lascelles had thought of a compromise – that the King should read the 2nd Lesson and wish people a happy Christmas at the end of it. I said this wouldn't do by itself but to take the whole Sandringham church service would be effective. They are not much concerned over the Duke of Windsor's 'working man interest' stunts in Germany or USA (where he goes soon). They think it is too obvious and that he would have been far more of a danger if he had sat quietly in Austria for 18 months.

13 April 1938 Invited by telephone to dine at Windsor on Saturday night. Rather funny because I had been thinking it was time we were.

16 April 1938 Dined at Windsor Castle. The invitation had said I was to bring knee breeches and trousers so I phoned Hill Child [Master of the Household] and he said it was a mistake. I had enquired if one were meant to turn up in pants with both alternatives ready; if not which would he tip. At 7.45 I suddenly thought that, with ordinary breeches, buckles wouldn't be worn on pumps. Phoned up – told yes. Much relief. A few minutes later phoned back – bows. Much consternation. I got the governess to use a black evening tie. It was excellent and there was much amusement at the Castle when I told them about it.

In to dinner, one long table. I sat next but one to the King, immediately opposite me Queen Mary, then the Archbishop and then the Queen. The men didn't stay in the dining room; they went into a room beyond the one in which we had first met. The King should have spoken to me in this room but the Archbishop stuck to him for about an hour. An equerry of the last reign, Dick Molyneux, looked after me. He told me lots of interesting things – Edward was quite hopeless as King irrespective of Mrs Simpson. He said it was providential the woman turning up but that they had played their cards very badly; they might have got married on the quiet and then Edward could just have produced her as Queen. When we went next door I was with Queen Mary who was rather heavy at first but got more at ease when she realized that I wasn't scared of her. Talked of the visit to B[roadcasting] H[ouse] in 1932 remembering things about it. Next I spoke with the Queen. She was really awfully nice, speaking so sympathetically and earnestly about my work, not to be bothered by critics and so forth. She said they all listened as a family as often as they could. She really was most delightful. I was waiting to speak to Queen Ena [of Spain] when the King came up and took me to his sofa. He spoke of left-wing influences and wished I would talk with the American Ambassador [Joseph Kennedy] who had said that the School of Economics was the source of information for US journalists. I said it was a plague spot. Spoke of propaganda etc., I giving my experience of left-wing progressiveness when filling jobs or arranging talks. He asked how long I had been in the BBC. Told him I wasn't busy and wanted to do something else and when he asked what, I said I imagined it would be what the PM or himself wanted. Asked how I got the job and I told him – Aberdonian favouritism. I then talked with Queen Ena – about Edward VIII and my last visit to Windsor. She said he was the only English king who had never slept at Windsor. We left at 11.30 the King and Queen shaking hands all round.

20 December 1938 I received a letter from Hardinge saying the King would like to give me the GCVO for my work in connection with him, his father and brother. Very nice as not many have this decoration. It is entirely personal to the King.

2. Epilogue, 1940–69

John Reith's period as a cabinet minister between 1940 and 1942 brought him in touch once again with King George VI. He enjoyed the audiences and the formal visits which political office entailed and he appreciated the personal encouragement and understanding which he received from the King. This was particularly the case while he was minister of works and the satisfaction expressed by both the King and the Queen, when he was finally established in that office with extended powers over post-war planning, gave him intense pleasure. It was, therefore, particularly galling when after his summary dismissal, which was within ten days of a formal audience, he was obliged to go again to the Palace 'to take leave of the King'.

For the next quarter of a century his contacts with the monarchy were to be few and distant. Indeed, after he received the CB at the hands of King George VI in 1945, he was not to enter Buckingham Palace again, apart from occasional attendance at royal garden parties, until his appointment as Lord High Commissioner in 1967–8. In the late 1940s, when he was nearly sixty years old, he protested to Sir Alan Lascelles, the King's private secretary, that he had been dropped and received the crushing answer that 'the explanation was simply *anno domini*'. He was as reluctant to accept this unpalatable truth from the Palace as he had been to listen to his American friend, David Sarnoff, who told him about the same time that 'we have had our day'. He explained his feelings about this in a letter in the middle 1950s which he sent to a long-standing friend at Court:

What bearing has *anno domini*? I think it irrelevant. I have done and am doing enough work for the State to have been taken notice of.

This sense of having been forgotten at Court was greatly intensified after his retirement from the Colonial Development Corporation in 1959. His negative 'lack of interest' was replaced, momentarily, by a more positive rejection of the whole conception of monarchy. In 1963 he could still write, 'I believe in monarchy, subject to some conditions', but by 1966 he was noting in his diary: 'I am beginning to wonder if I am a monarchist.' This was not to last. The next year he was appointed Lord High Commissioner to the General Assembly of the Church of Scotland and the appointment was renewed in 1968. This involved him in reporting personally to HM the Queen in each year. His sense of rejection was quickly removed, his sense of loyalty as rapidly renewed. When, in 1969, he was appointed a Knight of the Thistle he felt that his long service to the State had, at last, been fully recognized. A final act of royal bounty was to grant him, as his last home, a grace and favour house in Edinburgh – the Queen's House – where he spent the last year of his life.

[On becoming minister of information John Reith was made a privy councillor.]

16 January 1940 [After War Cabinet meeting] I drove to Buckingham Palace arriving at the private door in the inner yard a few minutes before the Royal Family back from Sandringham. Clarendon, Stanhope, Oliver Stanley and Gilmour were the others present as privy councillors.[11] We all went upstairs, Stanhope having preceded us to tell the King what the business was. The King shook hands with us as we filed in and then we stood in a row while he stood behind a round table. The oath of allegiance was read, I kneeling with Testament in hand. Then I went forward to another stool beside the King and 'kissed hands'. After that I went back into the line and the impressive privy councillor oath was read, after which I shook hands with the other privy councillors. And so I became the Right Honourable. Next Stanley kissed hands as war secretary and received the seals of office in a little red box. Then other business, which I didn't understand, was done and after this the King dismissed the gathering saying he 'wanted a word with Reith first', meaning that he would see Stanley later. We sat in front of a fine big fire and conversed easily for fifteen minutes or so. Very agreeable. He asked various things about the job. Didn't think [Lord] Macmillan had been at all suitable. Said he would like to see me again when I had taken hold. I said I was honoured to be in direct service to him.

2 February 1940 Saw the King from 11.30 to 12.15. It was in the same room as the other day. He was in very good form. Spoke with vehemence about boys not getting some proper training to fit them for the Army life which was asked of them now, or for whatever their life's work was to be. I asked if I ought not to go at 12.00, and whether someone came or would a bell ring or what? He was much amused. He agreed that we ought to have some of the efficiencies of dictatorship states.

9 February 1940 Lunch with Hardinge, the King's secretary, at Brooks's. He was very interesting and frank about things. Clarendon is about the stupidest man he ever met. H. J. Wilson he can't abide, distrusts him profoundly and says his influence is sinister and all wrong. Talked about Tweedsmuir [John Buchan, governor general of Canada] who is dying and I said I didn't at all want that job. He said HM was coming on all the time but was inclined to jump to conclusions and then he sometimes got things wrong.

4 March 1940 Dined at Buckingham Palace sitting on the Queen's left. Oliver Stanley was on her right. Interesting evening. Assembled in the room where I had been twice of late. King and Queen and two corgis came in about 8.40 and we went to the dining room through two or three other rooms, one of which had been George V's study. The Queen talked to me till the course before the sweet. She had greatly enjoyed her week in Scotland and said she felt a sort of return of sanity there. She was miserable in London when there was nothing to do. She agreed emphatically with me that the Christian ethic should be the basis of post-war policy and thought the King ought to make a pronounce-ment about it – 'he believes it, you know,' she added. Afterwards the Queen went out of the room and the King and we sat for ten minutes or so. He was in very good form, talking very loudly as his father did. In the sitting room afterwards there was the usual exchange of con-versation and I sat with the King for a while. At 10.00 a tray with tea and cups was brought in and the Queen poured out and handed it herself. All very nice. Home about 1.00 as they didn't say goodnight till 11.45.

[In the autumn of 1940 John Reith had been moved to the Ministry of Works and given a peerage.]

22 October 1940 To see the King. I was announced as *Lord Reith of Stonehaven* and I thought it really sounded rather well. He was very cordial. I told him about the difficulties of definition [of the respon-sibility of the Ministry of Works for post-war planning].

9 July 1941 Dined at Buckingham Palace with about ten others – in day clothes! Sat next the King at dinner, cold jelly soup, ham mousse and cold chicken, strawberry ice and strawberries and cream but I wish I hadn't taken that. The King said: 'I can talk to you about these things. You understand me.' This was apropos regionalism and local author-ities on which he was informed. I told him what a job I had with departmental particularism and so forth. Went outside afterwards and conversation with the Queen in turn. Left at 10.30.

[On 11 February 1942 John Reith was able to announce in the House of Lords the establishment of his Ministry under its new title of Ministry of Works and Planning.]

18 February 1942 Saw the King at 12.00. He asked me what I did in the last war. With him half an hour; I always get up after that time or less.

Nothing special. Met the Queen in the passage rushing along. She said, apropos my new job, 'I am so glad it is you.'

[On 21 February 1942 John Reith was dismissed from the government.]

27 February 1942 I had to go to London 'to take leave of the King'. I tried to get out of this embarrassing business – especially having seen him so recently. He was very friendly as usual. I said I hadn't expected to be back so soon and for such a purpose. He said, 'No – and you had just got things going too.' I said I didn't understand it and I would be glad to know any reason but I didn't say this as if putting a question to him. He said later that he was very sorry indeed. I told him about meeting the Queen last time and what she had said. I said I had taken that home and that now I wished she hadn't said it. Last time I was there he asked me about my past. This time to get off an awkward subject I gave him stories of the Greig family.[12]

[From July 1942 John Reith was at work in the Admiralty.]

31 March 1943 I was dreading the Buckingham Palace party. Talked with the Duke and Duchess of Montrose about this year's General Assembly [of the Scottish Church] and advised him to read up some of the Disruption books. I wondered what they would have thought had they known that it was offered to me. The Queen said as we shook hands: 'I haven't seen you for ages.' We spoke to her at the end of the party. She said I looked very nice in uniform, as if I had always worn it. She also said nothing had happened about planning since I left. She thought it would benefit me to have been out of things for a year. Very friendly, she was. I was glad for Muriel's sake.

[On leaving the Admiralty at the end of 1944 John Reith had been recommended for the award of the military CB which he now needed to receive from the King.]

17 October 1945 I have to go and see the King tomorrow to get the military CB. I am not at all wanting to; but an official investiture was an abhorrent idea. I used to like seeing the King but I am now simply overwhelmed with my self-depreciation, feeling that everybody dislikes and despises me.

18 October 1945 Buckingham Palace at noon. Talked with Lascelles before seeing the King and with Michael Adeane [assistant private secretary to King George VI] afterwards. With the King for thirty-five minutes. When I went into the room, after shaking hands, he said 'Wait a minute; I have got something for you': and he shot next door and came back with the CB military which he handed to me. He said he always thought it was the best of all the decorations. Talked about my Admiralty experience. He knew I had began in Coastal Forces. I told him what I had done elsewhere, how I came to be DCOM and what I did there. He was much amused by the Mark Twain remark about a dog and its fleas,[13] and I said that that applied to me when I was in the Admiralty. He asked why the Navy should be the best and happiest service to work in. Talked about my Empire tour and also about the New Towns committee. He asked about Christopher and said that the Navy was the best life for him to do his service in. He said army life would drive him mad. It was all very nice.

[Over the next few years John Reith came to feel that he had been dropped. By 1948 his attitude towards the Court had much changed. The delay in obtaining clearance from the King for certain passages in his memoirs, the particular omissions eventually asked for, and most of all, the general and highly perceptive criticism made by the King of the memoirs as a whole all enraged him.]

25 August 1948 [On holiday in Scotland] Letter from Lascelles at Balmoral which irritated me greatly. He says the King would prefer that four things mentioned in the memoirs were omitted. One about Mrs Simpson I quite felt would have to come out; the sections about the abdication which are most interesting and which I won't take out; a bit about the rehearsings for his Coronation broadcast which I don't mind altering; and the account of the Privy Council first meeting which I can't see his point about at all. He goes on that the King was much interested in reading the whole thing but he seemed to think it wasn't in general a strictly accurate account of English public life; nor, in particular, that it does justice to your own long and varied service to your fellowmen. Infuriated, I felt.

[In the published form of his memoirs John Reith contrived to conceal this resentment. He even stated in his moving final paragraphs that he had completed the composition of his memoirs while listening to the broadcast of the 'wedding of the King's daughter'. This was far from being the case. He did not finish the first draft of his memoirs until five days after the wedding. He did not write this final section until January 1948. And he had refused to listen to the broadcast of the royal wedding on 20 November 1947, noting in his diary under that date:

> Miserable royal wedding day. Didn't get up till 10.30. Completely out of phase with everything and everybody through not being asked to the Abbey.

He was to continue in this unhappy state of mind towards the monarchy for another twenty years until his appointment as Lord High Commissioner in 1967.]

28 June 1967 Saw and spoke with the Queen for the first time since her father's coronation when she and her sister were little girls. Quite extraordinary that I have never met her.

I was early and had to wait for ten minutes or so behind a screen in the big room that gives on to the terrace. The Queen was moving about in the middle of the audience room when the Master of the Household took me in. She didn't smile until I did, and then she definitely did, and I thought she looked relieved. We sat on similar chairs about a yard apart, and I talked almost without stopping for a quarter of an hour or twenty minutes – anyhow till 12.30 when I got up. I had a page of notes but didn't look at them at all. Mentioned the bodies which had specially sent messages of loyalty and devotion; I made clear how much loyalty and devotion there was to herself. The Queen said she was grateful to me for taking the job on at short notice. She was much amused to hear I had been offered it twenty-five years ago. I really don't know how much she took in nor whether she was really interested. I asked once if I was boring her and she said No, indeed.

[A year later John Reith made his second and final report to the Queen as Lord High Commissioner.]

25 June 1968 I had audience of the Queen this morning for about forty minutes. I had made out a list of the ten or twelve most important things in the Assembly. I gave Michael Adeane a copy of this afterwards. The Queen said she had watched my performance with Muggeridge and she thought it was very good.[14]

[John Reith's last audience was after his appointment to be a Knight of the Thistle early in 1969.]

28 February 1969 Buckingham Palace at 12.30 and a very agreeable time. The Queen was most friendly. The first thing I said was for the honour she had done me for two years in making me her representative as Lord High and now in appointing me to the Order of the Thistle. She said it was very good of me to do the Lord High twice. I nearly said we would do it a third time if she wanted us to. I reminded her that last time I had said the Lord High was 'great fun'. She might have thought that a very odd expression to use but it was a kind of summation of the interest and responsibility and other sentiments. She said 'summation' was a good term to use.

NOTES

1. In February 1936, after the death of King George V, Lord Wigram confirmed this, writing to John Reith that 'some of my colleagues were narrow-minded and used to urge HM against broadcasts which they said were becoming too familiar.'

2. This probably refers to *Thomas More* by R. W. Chambers published in 1935.

3. The reference is to the political broadcasts before the general election of November 1935. Arthur Greenwood had by this time become deputy leader of the parliamentary Labour Party.

4. The Prince of Wales visited Broadcasting House on the tenth anniversary of the start of broadcasting.

5. Lady Constance Milnes-Gaskell was Woman of the Bed Chamber to Queen Mary, 1937–53 and lady in waiting to Princess Marina, Duchess of Kent, 1953–60.

6. Miss Margaret Bigge was a daughter of Lord Stamfordham.

7. The *Yorkshire Post* had been the first paper to break the silence of the British Press on the King's plan to marry.

8. The King had cruised in the Mediterranean during the summer of 1936 aboard a private yacht, the *Nahlin*.

9. John Reith was 'sickened' to find in the biography of King George VI by Sir John Wheeler-Bennett published in 1958 that the new King was convinced that he had wanted to describe the Duke of Windsor on his farewell broadcast as 'Mr Edward Windsor'. These extracts show that there was no truth in this allegation.

10. This was Archbishop Lang. He deplored the fact that King Edward VIII 'should have sought his happiness in a manner inconsistent with the Christian principles of marriage and within a social circle whose standards and ways of life are alien to all the best instincts and traditions of his people', adding, 'let those who belong to this circle know that today they stand rebuked by the judgement of the nation.'

11. Lord Clarendon, John Reith's old enemy of 1927–30, had returned from South Africa in 1937 and was now lord chamberlain. Lord Stanhope was lord president of the Council; Oliver Stanley had been president of the Board of Trade

and was in course of being transferred to the War Office; Sir John Gilmour had returned to the cabinet in 1939 as minister of shipping.

12. Sir Louis Greig had served King George VI as Duke of York and King since 1920. He and his family had been well known to John Reith in Glasgow.

13. See *Into the Wind*, pp. 462–3; 'Mark Twain wrote that it was good for a dog to have a reasonable number of fleas; it prevented him from worrying overmuch about being a dog.'

14. This refers to the television programmes 'Lord Reith looks back'.

CHAPTER FOUR

Politics and Politicians (2)
1936-9

In the years leading to the outbreak of war in 1939 John Reith was constantly hoping that he would be invited to participate actively in the government's defence preparations. As has been seen, he was unsettled at the BBC and had been thinking of leaving there as early as May 1935. Twelve months later he returned to the same theme, observing in his diary that he was 'longing for some new job'. But at the same time that he hoped for a high task in the centre of affairs, he became increasingly disillusioned by the weakness and indecision of the politicians. His attitude in this respect is illustrated in an article he wrote for the *Glasgow Academy Chronicle* early in 1937. He wrote then:

> The older one gets, the more one sees of men and affairs – politics and politicians especially – the more one may be given to reflect (though even this isn't profitable), the less to counsel or prophesy. Why counsel, when nobody wants it, and no attention would be paid to it, if given? And why prophesy? With things as they are, what's coming is coming and cannot be averted, and won't be any the more agreeable for having been foretold. Vanity and vexation of spirit.

This state of mind was aggravated by the fact that his old friends in high places were now in decline. MacDonald could not help him; Baldwin would not. In any event, during 1937 the one died and the other retired, while Neville Chamberlain, prime minister from May of that year, though not unfriendly, was distant.

John Reith's reaction in these circumstances was to find solace in the company of men of affairs who were 'in the know' but outside politics – men such as Sir Warren Fisher, with whom he had been on close terms for two or three years, and, after the end of 1937, Montagu Norman (later Lord Norman) the governor of the Bank of England. He was able to get on terms with Montagu Norman through the good offices of the Governor's brother, Ronald, who was chairman of the governors of the BBC, and from 1938 onwards Montagu Norman became his chief political mentor.

Reith's own hopes were of two kinds. On the one hand he dreamed of Cabinet office or ambassadorial glory; on the other hand, more realistically, he hoped for an administrative position helping to co-ordinate defence or reorganize the War Office. For the last of these he had, for a moment, the enthusiastic support of Leslie Hore-Belisha, the then secretary of state for war. But in so far as other members of the Cabinet wished to make use of his talents they looked towards the embryonic Ministry of Information as his ultimate niche. None of this, in fact, was to come his way for the time being and as things turned out in the summer of 1938 Neville Chamberlain pushed him with the assistance of Sir Horace Wilson, the *eminence grise* of No. 10 Downing Street, into the chairmanship of Imperial Airways. John Reith's brief was to reorganize civil aviation by merging Imperial Airways with its competitor British Airways. The bait was the opportunity to form a public corporation such as the BBC. He swallowed it most reluctantly, making the move, as he put it, 'feeling like a lamb led to slaughter'. He went in duty, not enthusiasm. If the prime minister asked him and Montagu Norman urged him, then he must obey.

The worst consequence of his move to Imperial Airways from John Reith's point of view was the fact that he was now cut off from all inside knowledge of political developments. At the BBC it had been his duty to keep in close touch with government. At Imperial Airways it was not, except in respect of civil aviation and here, as a further irritation, his new political master was his old *bête-noire*, Kingsley Wood, newly promoted to the Air Ministry. So during the final twelve months before the war John Reith was politically isolated, so much so that he noted during the Munich crisis of September 1938 that he had not 'the least idea of what was happening'. A year later he was no better placed. In August 1939, against the advice of Vansittart but with the confident encouragement of Horace Wilson, he had taken his family to Canada for a summer holiday. When he returned in mid-September to a country at war 'no one at all was interested'. His task at Imperial Airways was finished; his family was still in America. He was to endure three months of this 'inactivity and separation' before, at long last, Neville Chamberlain invited him to join his government.

6 February 1936 Dawnay [now back in the army] to see me to ask if I would really go to the new Imperial Defence job as he had asked some weeks ago. I told him I might, but I don't know how I should feel. Anyhow I said I was sure there was no chance of my getting it.

16 February 1936 Alan Dawnay rang up. Seems if they do anything about this defence business it will be a political ministerial job. This is hopeless.

22 February 1936 Dawnay to see me. There will be some wretched co-ordinating defence minister and either one or two people like Hankey for defence and for industrial mobilization work. He said people were anxious for me to have this. Hankey will probably keep it himself. It would be interesting if things were to be done properly, but how am I to drop from £10,000 to £3500?

28 February 1936 Ministry of Information committee 4.15 to 6.30. Colville was in the chair, but isn't good. I got Tallents nominated as DG. They wanted me to have it but I have either greater or lesser ideas for myself for the next war if it comes.

7 March 1936 The office rang to say that Hitler was denouncing Locarno and had sent troops into the demilitarized Rhineland. Vansittart is on leave(!) so I spoke to Sargent [deputy under-secretary] telling him we were ready to put on a special talk tonight if FO liked, to offset scare headlines etc. Hitler says now he can negotiate on parity and he offers a twenty-five-year non-aggression pact with France and Belgium. Seems to me that this is really the crossroads for Europe and despite his tearing up of Locarno and all the rest of it, he means business now; that the French should accept; that England should decline any support if they don't; that our £80 million armaments programme might be checked; and that English foreign policy can really now break off from French influence and dominate. Spoke to Sargent in these terms but he was full of doubts; Hitler had sunk lower than ever, couldn't be trusted and so forth.

11 March 1936 Dr Wanner[1] turned up. He said this was Europe's last chance; there was nothing in Hitler's twenty-five-years promise; long before then he would be in Alsace, Austria and elsewhere; other countries should do to Germany as she has done to them – namely the virtual embargo on foreign travel – bank loans also. He said that Schacht [German economics minister] told him ten days ago that he was reckoning on having two hundred million marks out of visitors to the

R.D.—O

Olympic Games alone. Said fifty out of the sixty-five million people in Germany were really anti-Nazi. I passed on his views to Stanhope [parliamentary under-secretary] at the FO.

12 March 1936   Letter from Lord Stanhope
I am so grateful for your letter. We had much the same from other sources but with less definiteness.

I showed your letter to Eden [foreign secretary] (who showed it to the Prime Minister) and I also showed it to Vansittart, so it has had considerable effect.

The problem is an extraordinarily difficult one and, whatever we do, we are open to blame, as in this case the right course depends on the point of view.

The right course is obviously to support the moderate against the gangster and to uphold the sanctity of treaties.

Is it right however to risk the chances of war for a provision in a treaty which many people think should in fairness have been abolished long ago?

In any case we are only one of those with whom the decision lies and, although we need not bow to other people's opinions, disunion is *not* strength.

27 March 1936 To FO to see Vansittart. He is in a high-strung state and was fuming against politicians for their timidity, etc. Only about six worth a place in the Cabinet and would like to see me in it. He wasn't very coherent about foreign affairs though he was talking a great deal about them. Said he wasn't going to retire nor take an ambassadorship. Very thankful he had private means. Poor Van.

8 April 1936 Warren Fisher 5.00 to 7.00. He was violently indignant with Kingsley Wood who is acting as I was sure he would on the Cabinet committee about the BBC [Ullswater] report. It consists of Chamberlain, Stanley, Ormsby-Gore, M. MacDonald, Tryon, K. Wood and one other.[2] K. Wood is doing his utmost to get the Cabinet to throw out the report. W.F. was lurid in his language about him. He said he had never had such a hopeless Cabinet to deal with; that they had started running properly in December (Hoare-Laval issue)[3] and hadn't stopped since. He despises the present lot as much as Van does. Said ministers were jealous and afraid of me.

6 May 1936 Lunched with Ramsay MacDonald bringing the chairman [of the BBC] with me. Norman had to leave at 2.00 but I was with J.R.M. till 2.30 and he was much more definite when Norman was gone. He spoke in terms of contempt of Kingsley Wood, a crooked rascal, but said he had Neville Chamberlain in his pocket because he was running him for PM, and himself to be chancellor. He agreed that the Cabinet was jealous of our power and efficiency and that some of them were jealous of me, though he said it was more that I was a good lightning conductor. Most of the Cabinet cared nothing at all for the serious issues of broadcasting. I asked MacDonald if I should perform the Jonah stunt, since it looked as if I were responsible for a lot of the bother brought on the BBC. He said certainly not; implored me not to.

6/15/16/20 June 1936 Hoare is back as first lord of Admiralty. I have no use for any politicians these days.

. . . To the office. I wasn't at all happy to be back; I am so hating everything nowadays.

. . . I am very anxious to leave the BBC at the end of this year.

. . . Stanhope has joined the Cabinet as Office of Works minister. I wrote him a letter, congratulating the Cabinet not him and had a nice reply this morning.

23 June 1936 To see Warren Fisher at 4.30. As usual very outspoken about politicians. He said he thought every department chief was, as he is, more disgusted than ever before with them. He is longing for his three more years to pass. He implored me to hang on and not even to leave at the end of 1936. He thought K. Wood would overreach himself in due time. I felt some comfort as usual after seeing him.

2 July 1936 To see Warren Fisher. He told me about the Foreign Office deficiencies and how Cadogan and Oliphant had both been made deputy under secretaries. He had agreed to there being two on the understanding that Craigie would be one to bolster up Cadogan.[4] He has no use for either C. or O. Van is in a flat spin about everything.

8 July 1936 Lunched with Ramsay MacDonald at his request. Poor man. His memory is hopeless. He wants to help us but it is too late now. He was very sarcastic about his colleagues. He is a great problem, I believe, to them.

20 July 1936 To Warren Fisher 4.50 till 6.50. He went through the Cabinet list, making his usual pungent comments on them. The only ones who survived were Chamberlain, Hoare, Swinton [air minister] and Stanhope. He thinks Chamberlain and Hoare would make a good pair in Downing Street. Baldwin completely ineffectual. Vansittart expects the Germans to start their bomb throwing after the Olympic Games; W.F. says he is in a hopeless condition.

29 July 1936 To see Vansittart at the FO. He said Lady Cunard had asked him to help her with me, and had urged him to get me appointed a governor general or something of that sort because I was such a marvellous administrator. I said I might like to be Ambassador in Washington, and that would give him something to snort about after I had gone. He said it wasn't the appointment of people like me which he and the diplomatists objected to, but to dud politicians.

3 August 1936 Damnation. It may be something to have got a Grand Cross from nothing at all, and still more a DCL of Oxford when one is comparatively young though ten years older than one should have got them at; and getting older every year and therefore such things of less and less significance. I wanted these things when I was so young that no one could have believed I had them. Have I ever been young? Not since the war anyhow. And the war didn't make me old. I made myself so by longing for the responsibilities and authorities of twice my age. And I could have carried them too. What is it worth? A few years ago I still had ambitions. Now none, but an aftermath of ambitions which makes me dissatisfied and if anything big came now I should only feel that it was the sort of thing I ought to want to take because I once wanted it.

1 September 1936 Long letter from Lady Bridgeman. She stayed a night with the PM recently and he visited her. No allusion to politics or the BBC either time. Says he was utterly fagged out.

16 September 1936 Had nearly two hours with Warren Fisher. He implored me to stay on in the BBC for two years yet, even if I wasn't fully busy. He said I would likely be badly needed after that.

16 October 1936 Lunched with Lady Reading at Claridges. She has been in USA and Canada. She thought it was awfully important for us to have the right sort of representative there. I said that I thought sometimes I might like to be British Ambassador at Washington. She said if I were, Anglo-American relations would be very different in a short time; but that she had another job in mind for me. 'What's that?' I asked out of politeness. 'Dictator of England,' she replied!

18 October 1936 Mr and Mrs Martin of Johannesburg to lunch and tea. I really think I would like to be governor general of South Africa – not what I would choose, but what else is there?

19 October 1936 To see Ramsay MacDonald at 11.00. He was grumbling about the government; it wasn't a government at all; to such extent as it was, it was a partisan Tory one and very bad at that. He talked about the iniquitous handling of the Ullswater recommendations. Said Ormsby-Gore had been casting aspersions on me at a Cabinet committee about dictatorship and he [J.R.M.] interrupted him and said he wouldn't stand it.

29 November 1936 I reflect sometimes on 'politics'. The whole horrid technique should be abolished. Government of a country is a matter of proper policy and proper administration, in other words efficiency. It need not be different in nature from the government of a business – only in degree. And the policy should be set according to the Christian ethic. I wonder if I shall be called to this. I do not wish to be a dictator, but I should appreciate this chance of magnifying Christ – but of course I am not fit for this.

15 December 1936 I am very sick of London and politics and politicians and other cads.

[John Reith's political disenchantment continued throughout 1937, although he was momentarily put in better humour by Baldwin's sympathetic treatment of him in the earlier part of the year. But Baldwin was in process of retiring from public life and so could offer him no positive help. It was Neville Chamberlain who mattered now and in the autumn John Reith heard with dismay the first rumour that the new prime minister might ask him to take over at Imperial Airways.]

26 February 1937 Lunched at Lambeth Palace. Great fun and much badinage at lunch. Settled details of our May 9 Service afterwards.[5] The Archbishop was very insistent on my not leaving the BBC. He said in no way could I better and more fully serve God and the country. He doesn't understand. 'God bless you and your work,' he said when I said goodbye.

5 March 1937 To the Home Office to see Sir John Simon and Geoffrey Lloyd [parliamentary under-secretary] and fixed up for a proper contact between Broadcasting House and Home Office [i.e. in case of war]. I made it clear that we must be told ahead of things that might cause trouble. They were both very civil. I saw a standard gas mask for the first time.

9 March 1937 To see Van at the FO. I think he is unbalanced in his attitude. He is awfully apprehensive about any references to communism and fascism.[6] Says no one believes abroad that we are independent of the government. Thinks there is no improvement in the foreign situation. Very apprehensive lest Franco (owing to *The Times* and BBC) feels unfriendly to this country and so is dominated by Italy and Germany. Nice position for France then. He would like us to get pro-Franco in our news and even stop using the word 'insurgents'.

16 April 1937 To Chequers, arriving 8.02, the door opened by a maid and the PM appearing behind her. There was only himself and Mrs B. We had dinner at once. He and I went to the housekeeper's room for the broadcast at 9.15 and then we sat in the gallery from 9.40 till 10.20. I was for going away at 9.40 but they made me stay. They both asked if I didn't think he was right to retire and I said absolutely from his point of view but that I felt sad about it as, though I didn't see him often, I felt in a way that I was working for him and that would be a great loss. He said he appreciated that very much. He was going to do nothing much for six months. He wanted to keep in touch with Labour. He thought he might travel round the Empire and I said that would be very good and effective. He said I had done a great work; he would never have done creative work; I had created the BBC. People wouldn't realize for thirty years what I had done. He said Winston used to be worried because he wasn't getting credit for his work and he had told him the same thing. He said quite out of the blue 'Would you like to go to the Lords when you retire?' I said I had no idea. He said he had told Montagu Norman and Hankey that they would have to join him in the Lords and that we might all sit on the cross-benches. He spoke about his Albert Hall speech to youth next month. It is on his mind a bit. He said he was sure I was full of ideas on it, so would I send him some suggestions. At dinner, after Mrs B. had left, I told him I had hoped I should have had a summons from him to do some big job and that I should have done anything he asked me to; he said that certainly was the right spirit. I said I wasn't ambitious personally – only to do as much work as capacity demanded.

25 April 1937 Muriel made me stay at home to do the PM's speech. I worked at it 10.45 to 12.45; 2.00 to 4.00 and then 6.15 to 6.45. Finished and I hope it is good and useful.

Letter from Stanley Baldwin 3 May 1937
I am ashamed to think of the trouble my simple request has put you to!
But I am grateful and you have given me much to think over and work on.
I have to do it in my own way but it is a real help to have such a contribution to bite on.

18 May 1937 Listened to Baldwin talking to youth in the Albert Hall. His first two or three sentences were as I wrote them and there was a good deal elsewhere in the first part of his speech which was verbatim mine. It was odd to listen to one's own stuff coming over like this and to realize that it was the PM speaking on a big occasion. I thought he would have done better to stick to what I gave him but he went off on brotherhood of man.

29 May 1937 I had to go to Hertford to Christ's Hospital as Phyllis Reith [niece] is head girl and this was Speech Day. The Lord Mayor of London spoke and in the course of his speech quoted a considerable part of Mr Baldwin's Albert Hall speech. I thought it was very funny.

5 June 1937 To lunch with Lord and Lady Trenchard. He is as disgusted as everyone else with the recent jugglings with Cabinet offices, Navy and Army particularly. Said S. Hoare wanted to leave the former because it wasn't a secretaryship of state and because he didn't think he could hold his admirals over the Fleet Air Arm row. Inskip [minister for co-ordination of defence] has never consulted him about anything and he is now doing no public work of any sort. Agreed with me about a single Defence Ministry. Said Hankey was in the way of any proper system and had managed to sidetrack Inskip on the munitions. We are similar in many ways.

1 July 1937 With Warren Fisher at the Treasury 5.00 to 7.00. He told me, what I knew, that the PM had offered the BBC chairmanship to Runciman but he had declined it, and that previous to this Clark, high commissioner in South Africa, had been asked if he would like to be considered. W.F. said that he and H. J. [Wilson] thought this would suit me as he wouldn't interfere etc. I said he wasn't a big enough man. Fisher spoke of my being wanted for some other job in a year or eighteen months, but I don't think it is at all likely.

14 September 1937 Millis [vice-chairman of BBC] came back with me after lunch and told me he had heard my name in connection with Imperial Airways chairmanship and apparently I shall be regarded as the only one to take charge and clean that mess up. I shouldn't like this but I suppose I should have to do it if I was asked by the PM.

27 September 1937 Ramsay MacDonald in my room for three-quarters of an hour this morning. Very gaga, poor man.

1 October 1937 To Warren Fisher 4.30 to 6.00. He told me that Kingsley Wood had been so pleased with a line I had put at the end of the note I sent him acknowledging his letter after our car smash that he showed it to W.F. ahead of all the business he had to do with him. It was to the effect that I regretted that we had parted brass rags after some years of satisfactory association. Apparently I was nearly offered the chairmanship of Imperial Airways (which I shouldn't have wanted) on a full-time basis, but Swinton approved Beharrell[7] on his own.

4 October 1937 To the Cabinet committee on foreign languages,[8] my first meeting with the little crook Kingsley Wood for several years. The chairman [R. C. Norman] spoke first and then I pretty well finished the matter. To my surprise Leeper of the FO said I had more or less set his doubts at rest – the FO having wanted to run Arabic on their own from Cyprus. I made it clear that we would require finance and independence.

18 October 1937 Visited H. J. Wilson at No. 10. The PM and Eden had Citrine [general secretary of the TUC] and another TUC man who came to report an urgent request from some Spanish communist that England should send a mission to a town which Franco is expected soon to capture and where are forty thousand communists whom he will shoot. The presence of a mission might deter him, it is said. H.J. deplored the way Cabinet ministers read all the criticisms about them and are all out for popularity. Damnable.

5 November 1937 To see Warren Fisher at the Treasury. He said our not being made to have any written agreement with respect to the Foreign Office in foreign language broadcasts was a great tribute to us and he gave Kingsley Wood credit for it. Eden had wanted something definite but the Cabinet minute referred only to a gentleman's agreement between Vansittart and myself.

28 November 1937 To Athenæum dinner to Baldwin. On one side Dawson of *The Times* who was very complimentary and said there would never be a *Times* attack on me or the BBC so long as he was there. Baldwin spoke for about 45 minutes. He spoke mostly of the Labour party and justified his attitude of courtesy and forbearance to them; otherwise they would have been much more bitter and iconoclastic. Something in what he was saying. Rather striking in some ways. Critical of his own party in places.

7 December 1937 Lunched with Muriel at the prime minister's (No. 11). Quite pleasant. Chamberlain looks straightly and pleasantly at one.

[In the first half of 1938 John Reith was concerned with the critical events in Europe as well as with his personal prospects. This was the time of Hitler's occupation of Austria, in March, and of the first Czech crisis, in May. His attitude to both of these was naively confident. He admired the German efficiency in carrying through the Anschluss and he wholly discounted the possibility of war over Czechoslovakia. At the same time he hoped that the impulse to Britain's defence preparations occasioned by these events might offer him the personal opening he sought. Here he was to be disappointed. His immediate future was to be with Imperial Airways – not with the War Office.]

24 December 1937 Montagu Norman phoned and nothing could dissuade him from coming out to see us this afternoon! He was very genial and amusing but I can't help being rather frightened of him.

17 January 1938 Along to Eaton Square to see Baldwin at his request. He seemed in good form. He told me a story about Balfour and himself on Epstein's *Rima* – 'conceived by a drunkard in a brothel' – 'too hard on the brothel'. I was sure he only wanted to see me about a job for someone, and so it was. He was trying to get his papers into order – innumerable tins he had brought from No. 10. Very friendly.

Later to see Kingsley Wood. He said he was sure some new big job would come soon for me. Very critical of the Air Ministry and of Cunliffe Lister [Lord Swinton] who did the detail work he ought to leave and not much else.

[Between 19 January and 22 February 1938 John Reith was on a cruise of the West Indies and the Panama Canal in a party made up by Montagu Norman.]

27 January 1938 Usual talks with Montagu Norman. Tonight I told him of my ultimate despairing hope of an appeal to Christ for the country and I found him definitely sympathetic. He is so against piling up armaments. He says that is his main problem – where the money is to come from to pay for it all. I hope if I were PM I would have the strength to stake all on Christ.

29 January 1938 M.N.'s sole solution for European troubles is an understanding with Germany, which I have said for years.

5 February 1938 M.N. said I should stay at the BBC only till my new job turned up.

18 February 1938 Thinking about my future and whether I should stay on in the BBC.

20/22 February 1938 [20] Eden has resigned. A good job I'm sure.

[22] Some excitement on owing to A. Eden's resignation which I took as meaning that for the first time there was to be some reality and sanity on foreign policy.

3 March 1938 Saw Halifax [now foreign secretary] at House of Lords 5.30 to 6.30. It was about our debate on colonies for Germany initially but we covered a lot of ground and had a friendly and satisfactory talk. He told me that Hitler had said at once that it was no use trying to do business with democratic countries, so he replied that he might as well go home but Hitler then said he meant France. He remembered our conversation about the Christian ethic at Chevening. I said I wasn't a Socialist.[9]

10 March 1938 To a party at the German Embassy by Ribbentrop and wife. I made myself very agreeable to lots of people and quite enjoyed myself. I told Ribbentrop and the Embassy Counsellor to tell Hitler that the BBC was not anti-Nazi, and I invited them to have my opposite number come over to visit us. I said I would 'put the flag up for him'.

11 March 1938 Germany seems to have annexed Austria!

12 March 1938 I told the FO and No. 10 where I was and spoke to Halifax after lunch. Things are all quiet and the Germans have got away with it. Halifax said he did not believe Ribbentrop knew it was coming. Marvellous people, he and his wife going to see the King and Queen yesterday and lunching with the PM and this *coup d'état* taking place simultaneously. Leeper said last night that he had been told in very clear terms what this country thought of it. Before or after lunch, I asked!

21 March 1938 To see Sir Sam Hoare [now home secretary] at the House of Commons at his request. Very pleased with the result of his appeal for a million ARP volunteers; wanted to know if we would let him have a series of talks, and if so should he do them himself. I said we would certainly arrange this. He thinks the ARP business of determining importance in the next year since the enemy would reckon on finishing a war against England in six weeks. He said we had no anti-aircraft guns worth talking about. There was no discussion in the Cabinet over Germany and Czecho-Slovakia; thought useless to do anything as bluff would so easily be called. Advocated Germany and C-S coming to terms. Very civil and friendly.

To see H. J. [Wilson] at No. 10. Very friendly also. Talked about a job for me but I can't see what can come of it.

29 March 1938 House of Commons and had tea with PMG and then met representatives of the 1922 Committee who were vexed with our news bulletin references to the PM (Labour party attacks) on Sunday a week ago.[10] I said if they charged us with bias I would defend the BBC to the last ditch; if they asked if it were expedient and decent I would say definitely not. Some argument but I think I was a match for them all.

26 April 1938 4.00 to 6.00 with Hankey. I am putting him and the US Ambassador[11] into touch with each other. He agreed with my verdict on Eden, the most costly experiment England has ever had and that the Italian agreement could have been made early in 1935 with European history since vastly different and hundreds of millions saved. Talked about myself. I told him I had offered to take a Territorial Army job and he was quite annoyed; said I would have to be a Minister if war came and that was using a steam hammer to crack a nut. In the evening I had to go to meet the chancellor (who put another 6d. on to the income tax today). Gave him and Lady Simon dinner and went over to Broadcasting House at 9.00. Very pleasant and successful. I tried my opinion of Eden on him at dinner as he had said (quite insincerely I'm sure) that he hoped Eden would be back in the Cabinet before long. He obviously agreed with me and then gave his own reception in Italy after Stressa as indication of the friendliness to England in Italy at that time.

3 May 1938 Newspaper Society dinner at Grosvenor House. I sat next Mrs Chamberlain and told her what I felt about the lack of aliveness of the Conservative party.

6 May 1938 To see Horace Wilson but only as I had expected because the PM had told him something of what I had been saying to Mrs PM on Tuesday. Wants me to see K. Wood. Wilson said they had a lot of bother with the PM trying to get him to go to the Derby or to lunch with the Australian cricketers. He never wanted to do anything 'out of character'. They had managed to get him to go into the smoking room of the House of Commons a few times but he had given that up. I spoke with a good deal of emphasis on the need for producing him. Sickening that this was all he wanted to see me about.

11 May 1938 [After attending a charity matinee] I heard that H. J. Wilson was anxious to see me as quickly as possible. It took twenty-five minutes to get there – so dreadful was the traffic. To my utter amazement this summons was about some criticism of the Air Ministry in the news bulletin on Sunday night. I suppose I ought to have controlled myself, but I did not to any great extent. To make matters worse, having accepted his view about what had been broadcast, I discovered that it was all grossly exaggerated. I am sorry to have had this racket with Horace Wilson as he has always been so decent to me, and of course he is a great power in the land, but it was quite monstrous that a man like H.J.W. should take the line he did.

17 May 1938 Saw K. Wood [now air minister] to tell him (by request) what I had said to Mrs PM the other night. Told K.W. how slack I was. I said politicians didn't like me – he didn't because I had kept up my own point of view about the BBC in opposition to him. He denied this in rather a flustered way and said I was a 'genius' and that I certainly must be properly employed. To the War Office to see the military secretary about the possibility of my doing a Territorial Army job. He was very civil but obviously embarrassed, and he eventually gave me a form to fill up. Dined with the American Ambassador – his first dinner party – to Halifax. Hore-Belisha [war minister] among those present. I told him about my visit to his place and he asked me to lunch next week.

22 May 1938 [Staying with Lord Camrose at Hackwood Park] Scare on over Germany and Czecho-Slovakia. I was sure it was only a scare. H. J. Wilson wanted me on the phone; wanted to know my movements and how long it would take me to get to London. Soon after this Warren Fisher phoned to ask if we could carry on if Broadcasting House were bombed! I said it wouldn't matter. Fisher and Wilson said they didn't think it would be necessary for me to come to Town.

23 May 1938 Scare almost finished. To the War Office at 3.30 to see Hore-Belisha who expressed great appreciation at my offer of help (!) and asked if I had anything special in mind. He said they could easily make me a major-general. He sent for the CIGS [Gort] and deputy CIGS [Adam] and spoke of my offer to help to my much embarrassment. It transpired that there had been some idea of an enquiry into the War Office organization generally and of course I was the very one for this. I kept trying to put a brake on them – things were moving too quickly, terms of the announcement of my appointment even. I said it would be far better if no public statement were made, which wasn't the right thing to say as H.B. has such a craze for publicity. I said also that I was sure there would be a great deal of jealousy – W. Fisher and Creedy [permanent head of the War Office] to start with. Of course the War Office badly wants reorganization.

29 May 1938 Went up early to bed but was rung up by Hore-Belisha. He said he had been to see W. Fisher immediately after I saw him but had been implored not to do anything about it – my 'reorganizing the War Office' for two or three days because I was probably going to be offered the chairmanship of Imperial Airways. I said I didn't want to go to IA and that even if I were going there I could do his War Office job first. He said if I did his reorganizing job he expected that would lead to something else as there were so many reforms 'we could put through together'.

3 June 1938 To No. 10. H. J. Wilson said on behalf of the PM and secretary for air I was instructed to go to Imperial Airways as chairman and 'tomorrow' at that. I thought this was pretty rotten – left to me to get rid of the present managing director[12] and to settle salary and all the rest of it. I said I wanted to be told direct by the PM. I accordingly saw him. I asked if he was instructing me to go. He said he wasn't using that word. So I asked if he wanted me to go. He said again that was maybe too strong but that if I went he would be very glad. I asked if he thought I might later try to take advantage of him and he said certainly not, but that he was being cautious. Later he did say he wanted me to go and the government did. I told him I didn't want to go to IA and would very likely regret it. I left after only four minutes. H. J. Wilson was too casual about it altogether.

6 June 1938 Hore-Belisha telephoned. He had twice seen Warren Fisher and the PM. His great idea turns out to be that I should be under secretary of state – head of the War Office! (£3500 vice £10,000). He said W. Fisher approved and that it would happen if I turned down Imperial Airways.

8 June 1938 Last night I had been to Thorpe Lodge to see Montagu Norman who was very ill with shingles. He was very keen on my going to IA but advised me to insist that the government support me in turning the concern into a public utility.

17 June 1938 Saw Montagu Norman for three-quarters of an hour. He is recovering slowly. I told him how things had gone. He said he would stand by me to the greatest extent I would allow him to. That is something for anyone to have from the Governor.

23 June 1938 Had a very pleasant hour with Lord Baldwin this afternoon. He said he did not think he would have made me go to Imperial Airways. He told me – something that I had never known before – that MacDonald had chosen Gorell for viceroy of India, and his name had even gone to Buckingham Palace. S.B., however, had managed to stop it. He did not think Gorell was suitable for us at all.

24 June 1938 Banks [now permanent head of the Air Ministry] to see me and talked for an hour and three-quarters about Imperial Airways. He wanted me to think of the job as a far bigger one than I had imagined it; sitting at the centre of a vast aerial communication system, almost as if I were chairman of all the English shipping companies. I hope he is right.

[John Reith was unhappy at Imperial Airways from the start and shocked his friends by talking of giving it up. Fortunately, this was no more than talk. In fact, he worked hard to achieve a 'corporation structure' for all British civil aviation and this was eventually established by act of Parliament in August 1939. Nevertheless, although he completed his task at Imperial Airways, he hoped all the time that he would not be long tied to it. He still hankered for a place in the Cabinet, or the embassy at Washington, or the permanent headship of the War Office. In April 1939, a few weeks after failing to persuade Warren Fisher to accept a peerage on his retirement as head of the civil service, he wrote to him again. This time he proposed himself for a peerage:

I should like to go to the House of Lords and do not mind saying so. I should like the additional interest and it would lead to others.

He was unsuccessful. Sir Samuel Hoare indicated delicately that the road to Cabinet office was through the House of Commons. Thus, as war approached, John Reith was at a dead end, cut off from political affairs and political information. Even when war came and he returned from his holiday in Canada, things looked no better. Then, with the New Year, the longed-for call from Downing Street came.]

7 July 1938 To Treasury with Barlow and H. J. Wilson and Banks. Talk of an early act of parliament to enable Imperial Airways to change its constitution and to absorb British Airways – all as I wished but Wilson is quite silly and weak over anything that might upset MPs and he didn't want to make IA altogether like the BBC.

11 August 1938 To see Warren Fisher and gave him all my news – including what I proposed doing with myself. He is very odd to discuss things with. He didn't want me to give up the chief executive job for three years!

15 August 1938 Dined at Thorpe Lodge with Mr and Mrs Montagu

Norman. Told him what I was doing and of my plans for getting out of Imperial Airways. He didn't approve of this at all (and Warren Fisher sent me a note today enclosing a paper he had meant to give me and explaining that he had been 'so flabbergasted at my naughtiness' that he had forgotten). M.N. said someone had to give 'blood and tears' to make IA come right, but I said I didn't see why this should be me and that anyhow I would have done a great deal before I left. Very jolly time.

22 August 1938 To dine at Thorpe Lodge. Much laughing. The Governor said he hoped I would come often and come early. When he asked me what job I would like in the country (the Hitler one excepted) I fairly floored him by saying his! It is very odd that I should have gotten on such friendly and familiar terms with him after all these years.

29 August 1938 To the Air Ministry (unwillingly) about the silly 'investigation' which I am supposed to make into charges made in the House of Commons by irresponsible MPs. Something of a dilemma over this as on the one hand the Company should be cleared and MPs brought to task and on the other it is undesirable to stir up a lot of mud again.

30 August 1938 To see Kingsley Wood. Got confirmation from him that I was safe in going ahead [with the amalgamation of Imperial Airways and British Airways]; also told him about my desire to get out. He says he hopes I won't have a new chief executive until the middle of next year.

10 September 1938 Considerable war scare on over Germany and Czecho-Slovakia. I can't see anything for me to do if war came. I'm not sorry to be out of the BBC as that will be so subservient to the Ministry of Information.

13 September 1938 Today I had a letter from the DG Territorial Army offering me command of a searchlight company! Very funny this after all the scorn from CIGS and DCIGS on the military secretary for making me fill up a form when the secretary of state was talking about giving me major-general rank – or alternatively appointing me to reorganize the War Office!

14 September 1938 War scare continues. I wrote to W. Fisher, sending a copy to H. J. Wilson, asking what I was to do if war came. Announced this evening that N. Chamberlain was going to see Hitler tomorrow – just what I had been thinking all along I would do if I had been PM or even foreign secretary.

15 September 1938 PM's visit (accompanied by H. J. Wilson) hailed as courageous and magnificent. I simply can't understand it. It is all annoying to me as I have so much more ability than these PMs and Wilsons and such like. I suppose it is too late for me ever to get to any position such as I should have. I ought of course to be dictator.

18 September 1938 We went to the Kemsleys for lunch. He said I ought to be in the government and I quite agreed with him! War secretary he suggested. He said it was inexplicable how Chamberlain had kept so many dud political hacks.

24/25 September 1938 I sent a message to Hore-Belisha that I had so far nothing to do in the war and got one back that he would telephone after the Cabinet at 5.30. I didn't hear anything and then his secretary rang at lunch-time next day to apologize. Seems odd that I haven't the least idea of what's happening.

27 September 1938 Awful war depression and I felt for the first time a personal apprehension for Muriel and the children. Quite awful to think of them in danger.

28 September 1938 One of the very few I am who feels that something will happen to prevent the war. Announced that 'Musso' was to mediate – so that's the War off.

29 September 1938 Felt certain that the crisis was over so stopped a pantechnicon of gear going from the office to Pembroke. To Middlesex Territorial Force Offices to be interviewed. Really very funny. They were most civil. Left it that I might accept a battalion command (searchlight).

16 October 1938 Very angry about Kingsley Wood's expected double cross on the constitution of Imperial Airways point – he having remembered that he opposed the creation of the LPTB.[13] How foul.

R.D.–P

20 October 1938 Treasury to see W. Fisher. H. J. Wilson has asked me to come and see him but later arranged to join up in W.F.'s room. Said the PM wanted plans for a Ministry of ARP by next day – to satisfy public clamour. About an hour's argument on this. Decided that a Minister of Home Security could be arranged. Then my job – this feeling rather small beer. Warren in a great disgust with the politicians.

28 October 1938 Saw Kingsley Wood in the morning for about three-quarters of an hour. Bally crook he is. Posed as having been in favour of the corporation constitution all along and of having been very clever in getting together the ministers whom he expected would oppose it. Sickening exhibition. Lunched with another of them – Hore-Belisha – at a charming little house in Stafford Place. Still very keen to have me as head of the War Office. Don't care for him either – such conceit.

31 October 1938 Lunched with Kemsley – no one else there. Said he had lunched alone with the PM last week and had told him that he ought to take me into the Cabinet. What avail?

4 November 1938 Went to see Lord Baldwin and stayed about an hour. He said how unsettled he had been when the crisis developed. He thought the PM had done very well. He himself had thought a personal visit was the only thing to do. Worried about the future as there was no one to succeed Chamberlain.

2 December 1938 Dined at the Swedish Legation to meet Crown Prince and Princess. Good party: [Lord] Macmillan, Speaker, Hoare. I felt almost surprised at being in such company. The minister said he wasn't surprised that politicians should dislike me or be afraid of me – 'because you are too near a possible alternative'. Pretty smart that.

11 January 1939 Lunched with Warren Fisher at Brooks's. Hore-Belisha had been to see him recently still wanting me to be under secretary of state when Creedy goes. 'Bloody nonsense,' Warren said, that I should have such a footling job when I ought to be in the government. He wants P. J. [Sir James] Grigg for that job. Talks of leaving himself in April. Very bitter about things, he is, and it is such a pity.

18 January 1939 Lunched with Creedy. He is utterly sick of his present man [i.e. Hore-Belisha] with his fuss about cameras and receptions and such like. Much fun over Hore-Belisha wanting me to succeed him. Surprised that I would even consider it. I said it was a fine job to me from where I now was. I wondered if my newness to civil service methods and my unorthodox outlook might not carry me through and make a bigger thing of that job than ever before.

13 February 1939 Warren Fisher 4.45 till 6.00. He said H. J. [Wilson] didn't dislike me at all and that he agreed I had to get into the Cabinet.

16 and 29 March 1939 Wrote to Warren Fisher at [Lord] Cadman's request, in effect to urge him not to decline a peerage. He has obviously had a considerable row with N. Chamberlain.

   . . . Warren Fisher had me along to tea. Outlook for me entirely blank I should say. He seems to have tried hard to get me into the Cabinet and of course H. J. Wilson wouldn't wish that to happen. Hopeless, and I have so little an opinion of H.J. W.F. was greatly touched by my letter. He says he doesn't want a peerage.

11 and 15 April 1939 I am tired of the sort of life I now have in which there is so little of interest to record and even what there is I haven't any inclination to write about . . . I have lost caste and gone down in the world.

17 April 1939 Beaverbrook phoned and I went to see him in Stornoway House. He said Sam Hoare had been along and had asked his advice about the Ministry of Information. He had remarked that he had wanted me in the Cabinet for some other job but now there was this chance. I couldn't imagine that there was any serious idea of my joining the government, especially on such a job, but I let him talk away.

18 April 1939 Saw Sam Hoare for an hour and a quarter. All he seemed to want from me was advice on the handling of the wireless side of this Information Ministry. Quite interesting and a good deal about the BBC – whether to take it over, or 'reform' it, or take all this foreign language activity away from it. To meet him and Halifax and Chatfield [the new minister for co-ordination of defence] in a few days.

21 April 1939 Saw Sam Hoare from 3.15 to 4.15 and then we went to the FO. Meeting in the foreign secretary's room, where I have never been before. Present: Halifax, Chatfield, Hoare, Cadogan, Leeper, CID secretary and Admiral Sinclair, the hush-hush SIS chief, odd-looking fellow. I read out my piece [recommending that Cecil Graves be director general of the new Ministry while remaining at the BBC], Halifax listening very closely. Some questions and some discussion, and then they all agreed with what I had said and the PM is to be asked to approve. Quite interesting but it is all *weird*. And the new Supply Ministry is to be given to Burgin! [minister of transport] Warren Fisher wanted me to have that job. Really dreadful.

25 April 1939 Feeling profoundly depressed especially since Lindsay's successor at Washington was announced this morning – the job which I should so much have liked to have – Lothian.

26 April 1939 Saw Hoare in the House of Commons at 4.30. He said there had been a little difficulty in getting Graves agreed for the M of I job, but that all was in order now.

27 April 1939 To the Royal Academy dinner. Spoke with various bigwigs whom I don't think bigwigs at all. Hoare told me his interview [about Graves] with Ogilvie and Powell [the new chairman of the BBC] had gone very successfully – sticky at first but he had taken the line I recommended. He was to see Graves next day, so I gave him the line to take with him.

2 May 1939 Graves has declined the M of I job. I shall have nothing more to do with him.

5 May 1939 Saw Sam Hoare. He said he was thinking of getting Lord Perth set up as a sort of umbrella DG of the M of I in the Foreign Office. This is a silly scheme. I said the only way to handle this business was from the top down by a proper DG – part or full-time. He said he wanted me to do the ministerial part in war. I said I didn't fancy the job. He said I ought to be in the House of Commons and I said I didn't like that at all and that if ever I had to stand my election address would probably be unlike any that had ever been issued before. He seemed to think (despite Chatfield and Halifax) that it was impossible for any minister of any importance to be in the House of Lords.

2 June 1939 Lunched with Barrington-Ward. He was sure I should be in some proper job in a year or two.

3 June 1939 A year today that Wilson told me about Imperial Airways.

How I dislike and distrust him and what a poor miserable creature he is to carry such power. Typical of England.

5 June 1939 To dine at Thorpe Lodge with Montagu Norman and wife. Great fun as usual. He is worried by attacks on him in the matter of German claims on Czech gold in the Bank of England. Very disgusted he is with Simon, the Protestant Jesuit. Telling me some of his troubles trying to find men. I think he was wondering if I would take the chairmanship of the Hawker Siddeley group. I said I didn't want any industrial job of that sort.

7 June 1939 To tea with H. J. Wilson. He was very civil and decent and was fairly outspoken about politicians. Said Simon took an hour over things that didn't need more than ten minutes, and that Kingsley Wood and Belisha checked up on each other's publicity. Said he had a few people reserved for war jobs which couldn't be foreseen, I one; but this wasn't very convincing as I don't imagine the best people are there. I asked how he thought I stood with politicians and he said I had a name for being forthright which was of course very different from their way of doing things – always thinking of their constituents and trying to say something which later could be interpreted as required. Contemptible all this. I said I preferred work on Olympus and that I wasn't keen on industrial jobs. He had said ICI badly needed taking hold of. I should really have been depressed by what he said, or didn't say; but I don't think I was particularly. Perhaps it was that through reading my diary for October 1922 I have been trying to get a better outlook on things and trust in God.

10 June 1939 Letter from Brownrigg, the military secretary and Territorial Army chief to be. He said he didn't think there was going to be a job for me in the TA after all which disappointed me but I don't know that I might not have greatly regretted having one.

15 June 1939 Each day I seem to get more unhappy and unsettled and on edge. I have been trying lately to forget, as it were, that ever I had a place of influence and dignity.

19 June 1939 In very bad form – frightfully depressed about the future. Contributing to this is the new fact that Kingsley Wood is taking all the credit for the Airways Bill and also for the Civil Aviation Planning committee which was of course *entirely* my idea. Self-seeking little cad.

Dined with Montagu Norman. He told me not to accept a Midland Bank directorship or LMS or anything; I would have to give them up. Sure I was going to be properly occupied.

27 June 1939 Beaverbrook says he doesn't think I would be made information minister in war though Sam Hoare would wish it so. I suppose that little swine Kingsley Wood is at the back of that. What a fool I was ever to get into his clutches again, though for my consolation I imagine he would always have had a stranglehold on broadcasting.

27 July 1939 Lunched with Citrine. Said he was shocked and angry over the narrowness and absurdity of Labour outlook – e.g. over Ministry of Information matter. He thought there should be a coalition Cabinet on the outbreak of war and he would obviously join if asked.

[In August 1939 John Reith was on holiday in Canada. On 25th he received a warning telegram from Sir Horace Wilson of the approach of war but indicating, by a code agreed before he left, that he should travel by train and ship and bring his family. On 30th he reached New York and after painful heart-searching, decided to sail back alone, leaving his family with his first-war friends in the United States. On 6 September he landed at Southampton.]

8 September 1939 Lunched with Barrington-Ward at Wyndhams. He was quite sure I would be happy soon – adequately employed. To Thorpe Lodge for dinner. Montagu Norman said things were all in a shocking state of muddle. He realized how awful it is for me but only counselled patience, as had Barrington-Ward.

12 September 1939 I wonder if I can stand this much longer – inactivity and separation. Prayed and called on God for rescue.

13 September 1939 Saw H. J. Wilson from 3.30 to 4.10. He said he had had me in mind all along – whether to telegraph and what to say and then what I was to do when they did get me home. He had suggested various things such as Information and Supply Ministries that I should be minister of – 'but "they" wouldn't have it' – even that I should have Perth's job when it was decided that he must go. Macmillan [the minister of information] welcomed the idea, he said, but the Press thought I would be too partial to the BBC. The talk was completely unsatisfactory in that there was not only nothing arising from it but seemingly very little prospect thereof. He was very decent and civil and sympathetic. Said nothing had happened yet to show up inadequacies of present system; seemed fully to expect this to happen and that then I might do something really big. Didn't think anyhow I would be happy in a bunch of politicians such as the present.

21 September 1939 Went to see the Governor at the Bank of England, 2.50 till about 3.50. Palatial quarters of course. He talked about my being unemployed. He had done all he could, so had Wilson, but nothing had come of it and clearly there was some prejudice but he didn't want me to examine him on what it was or why or anything. He didn't think it was serious and he thought things would happen which would make me busy. Anyhow his advice was to have patience and keep quiet. It was most discouraging and upsetting.

4 and 8 October 1939 Peace proposals in the air as I expected . . . People are really divided on the peace issue arising from Hitler's Reichstag speech.

6 October 1939 I couldn't stand going to Brooks's [for lunch] so I went to Kensington Gardens and walked round and round and up and down from 12.30 to 2.45 wrestling with myself. I tried to establish contact with God. I went over all my sins of past days asking forgiveness. At the end I thought I was a little comforted. My loneliness and my unemployment – these two awful trials. I asked to be made patient and to wait in trust.

16 October 1939 I wrote a letter to Street [permanent head of the Air Ministry] giving warning of state civil aviation will soon be in and how dreadful not to be preparing for post-war conditions and competition with other countries. I think it is monstrous that only this country and France should be opposing Germany and Russia. Diplomacy has been at a discount for years past, as well as crass inefficiency and timidity and vote-serving at home.

19 October 1939 Saw Trenchard at his request. In response to his offer of service to Kingsley Wood he had just had a note from the Ministry of Labour saying it was much appreciated and would be referred to a panel shortly to be established to deal with such offers from highly qualified people. Almost unbelievable.

15 November 1939 Lunched with Kennedy, American Ambassador. He is fed up with things including his job. The interesting part has gone, he says, and he has to do the silly things he did twenty years ago. Didn't care much for him this time. I think the adulation he has received has gone to his head. To Vansittart at the FO, he having invited me. Extraordinary. Advice systematically disregarded for years; most unhappy since 1930; knew the war was coming; read an extract from a note he wrote on a Rumbold despatch in January 1933. Finally they had sacked him, giving him nominal rights as diplomatic adviser to the government with direct access to the PM (in fact he hadn't seen the PM once since then). Kennedy had never been to see him, probably because he had been told he was unpopular with the government. His job was a complete sinecure. He thought all this would help me to endure my inactivity, which he was sure wouldn't last long; he expected me to be in the Cabinet. I asked if he didn't think more should have been conceded to the Germans, and he said he would have given more to the Weimar Republic but the trouble was that we had lost influence with the French through not supporting them in the Rhine valley affair when the Americans backed out. Had we done that we could have insisted on better treatment to Germany later. Of course he is generally regarded as responsible for the war maybe more than any other owing to his strong pro-French sympathies.

[At the end of November (in spite of much official discouragement) John Reith sailed to New York to escort his family home and on 17th December they were all safely back.]

4 January 1940 As I was finishing dressing for dinner Muriel came to talk to me. She said she saw that Tweedsmuir was leaving Canada at the end of this year and she wondered if we would be going to that job. I said it was most unlikely and that I wouldn't like it anyhow. She said she was sure I should do whatever I might be asked to do. At that moment the telephone rang and I wondered if it were No. 10. It was – the PM's secretary to say could I manage to come and see the PM tomorrow morning. Oh well . . .

NOTES

1. Dr Wanner had been chairman of the broadcasting company for South Germany; he and his family had made friends with John Reith in 1930 and were to remain his friends for forty years.
2. The other member of this committee was the home secretary, Sir John Simon; see Briggs II, p. 509.

3. In December 1935 Sir Samuel Hoare, then foreign secretary, and Pierre Laval, prime minister and foreign minister of France, met in Paris and agreed a plan to end the Abyssinian war under which Italy was to be ceded two-thirds of Abyssinia. Public outcry against this plan forced Baldwin to disown it and to sacrifice Hoare who resigned as foreign secretary.

4. Sir Alexander Cadogan later succeeded Vansittart as permanent head of the Foreign Office. Sir Lancelot Oliphant became ambassador to Belgium in 1939 and Sir Robert Craigie ambassador to Japan in 1937.

5. This was part of the Coronation celebrations.

6. In March 1948 Lord Vansittart wrote to John Reith, who had used this passage as the basis of a paragraph in his autobiography (*Into the Wind* p. 273): 'What I meant was that I did not wish to *discriminate* between fascism and communism.'

7. Sir George Beharrell was chairman of the Dunlop Rubber Co. and acting chairman of Imperial Airways in place of Sir Eric Geddes who had died in June 1937.

8. The story of foreign-language broadcasts is told in Briggs II, pp. 399–401.

9. Halifax had visited Hitler in November 1937. John Reith had spent a week-end at Lord Stanhope's home at Chevening in May 1937 and had met Halifax there. They had talked 'about the Oxford groupists and this had led to a discussion about the application of the Christian ethic in politics and elsewhere'. In later life John Reith somewhat inflated this incident, see Boyle *op. cit.* p. 289.

10. A BBC news programme had given extracts from three personal attacks on Chamberlain. John Reith was annoyed, noting, 'it is the sort of thing one cannot discuss in terms of pro-government speeches mentioned. It is just wrong – especially at such a time as this.'

11. The American ambassador was Joseph Kennedy. John Reith had lunched with him a week before this, noting, 'he kept me talking after lunch for an hour and a half and said he wanted people to tell him when he made mistakes'. Subsequently the ambassador was to be amply informed in this respect by British public opinion.

12. This was the more awkward because G. E. Woods Humphery, the managing director of Imperial Airways, was a long-standing friend of John Reith who had been best man at his wedding.

13. The London Passenger Transport Board had been set up by the National Government in 1933. The act of parliament was based upon a bill drafted by Herbert Morrison as minister of transport in the Labour government of 1929–31 and was opposed by some Conservatives as a measure of socialism.

CHAPTER FIVE

John Reith and the Second War (1)

In Government

John Reith was a minister of the crown for just over two years, serving in three departments and under two prime ministers. He was minister of information under Chamberlain between January and May 1940 and then, under Churchill, he was successively minister of transport between May and October 1940 and minister of works from October 1940 to his dismissal in February 1942. He did not make a great success of any of these tasks. In respect of the first two he was given so little time at either that he can hardly be judged on his performance at them. But at the Ministry of Works he had a longer tenure and even there, though he was able to make his mark in some measure, he was dismissed, as he had been earlier from the Ministry of Information, just when he was in a position to make constructive progress.

His comparative failure as a minister was partly the consequence of the conditions of the time which would have afflicted anyone holding his positions. Whoever had succeeded the ineffective Lord Macmillan as minister of information in January 1940, would have needed to begin, as John Reith did, by seeking to reassert control over censorship and propaganda which had escaped from the infant Ministry's command. Whoever had been appointed minister of transport in May 1940 would have been forced to concentrate on the immediate problems arising from the disastrous course of the war during that summer, just as any minister of works in the winter of 1940-1 would have had to give priority to the problems created by the bombing of British cities in those months. Yet John Reith's ill success as a minister went beyond these external circumstances. It was also caused by difficulties of personal relationships. These, too, were not entirely of his making. He can hardly be blamed, for example, because Chamberlain would not give him full support until the last days before his fall; nor was he responsible for Churchill's unreasonable prejudices against him. But he was at fault in his obstinate refusal to recognize that if he wanted to participate in politics he must act politically. He appeared to think that because he was unattached to and independent of any party he was exempt from the ordinary rules of political conduct. He was contemptuous of Parliament and impatient with the established methods of the civil service. He considered that his duties as a minister would be more efficiently fulfilled if he ignored the one and overrode the other. He was wrong, and when Churchill dismissed him he was undefended in Parliament and unmourned in Whitehall.

Reith's political ineffectiveness was aggravated by two further facts. First, there was his own growing distaste for, soon to be hatred of, Churchill and his close associates. He did nothing to conceal this and so made it the more unlikely that he would win that support from the prime minister which a departmental minister requires at any time to be fully effective in his office. Secondly, there was his dedicated determination to keep post-war problems in the forefront of the minds of his colleagues. This was prescient, even statesmanlike; had Churchill listened he might have avoided the humiliation of the general election of 1945. But in the circumstances of 1940-1 it was wholly unrealistic. To expect plans for a national transport system to be seriously considered at the height of the Battle of Britain was naively innocent; and to seek Cabinet priority for the consideration of general post-war planning when the British Empire in the Far East was in process of collapse was little closer to reality. Thus the story of John Reith's period in government is one of small achievement and much personal disappointment.

1. Minister of Information under Chamberlain, January–May 1940

[Chamberlain included John Reith in his government unwillingly, yielding to the pressure of public opinion. For his part Reith joined with little enthusiasm. He longed to serve, but not as minister of information. As originally planned before the war, that office was to have had overall control of news and propaganda, and even in that form he had not wanted it. Now it controlled neither. So his first task was to try to reassemble the functions of the Ministry which had been dispersed in the first four months of the war. In this he was partially successful and, as he told his successor, 'after three and a half months we were getting somewhere near what the Ministry should be'. But to make it work he needed, first, the support of the prime minister against the secretive particularism of the service departments, especially of the Admiralty under Churchill; and, secondly, he needed complete information which could only be forthcoming if he was invited to attend regularly the meetings of the War Cabinet. The painful muddles over the Norwegian campaign of April 1940 persuaded Chamberlain that he should do both these things. Unfortunately for John Reith, at the very moment that Chamberlain gave him his confidence he fell from power.]

5 January 1940 Saw the PM for about three-quarters of an hour. He was clearly under strain and did not make a good impression on me at all. To make things worse he pretended to be very sure of himself and to be deciding matters. He began by saying that Macmillan was leaving the Ministry of Information as it was necessary for the minister to be able to defend himself in the Commons. Walter Monckton had been 'tipped' in the newspapers for the job so he had seen him and told him he wasn't well enough known to appear in the House of Commons as a minister. (PM actually told him that it was too much of a risk for him to take.) I asked how Macmillan had done and whether the House of Commons reason was the excuse only. The PM said this was so. Macmillan hadn't done well at all; he was much older than had been realized. He talked and talked and didn't give decision. I said I had hoped it wasn't the Ministry of Information job that he wanted me to take, but I imagined I would do whatever was wanted of me. I also said I was very sorry that it had to be the House of Commons and was that inevitable. He said it was – to cover Macmillan obviously. He said there was no political implication in the matter at all. I said there would need not to be since although I was more his way of thinking than any other, I wouldn't be in line on all points. I was a Gladstonian Liberal – as my father was. He said he also was a Liberal. Of course I had remarked how different the job was now from what it was at the beginning of the war, but as to what support he would give for a reassembly of the hived off parts, he was very 'cautious' – rather shockingly so. Timid. He hoped there wouldn't be a 'brawl' about it. Obviously he isn't going to oppose Churchill or the Service Ministries. He thought I might look around and then tell him what I recommended. He would see what he could do. (Quite likely nothing.) Most unsatisfactory it all is. One is told to do a job by a man who says one ought to do whatever one is asked to do, but who won't and can't tell you what the job is, nor what, if any, support he will give. He told me the Labour party had been very critical of the Ministry and he was seeing Attlee that day and would tell him about my appointment. I said I wasn't popular with political Labour – never having bothered much about them. He said he was taking some risk or anyhow all the responsibility in appointing me and

I replied that I realized that and that any decent fellow always had a sense of responsibility to whoever appointed him. I asked if the job carried War Cabinet rank and he said no, agreeing that it was 'below the salt' in that respect but on an equality with colonial secretary and the like. I asked if a privy councillorship went automatically with the job. He said not, didn't seem to have thought of this and certainly didn't know what to say. I said it would be a help with other ministers.

Went to see Montagu Norman; (I had asked the prime minister if I could talk to him.) Told him the whole story. He said I had no alternative, no matter how unsatisfactory it all was.

To lunch at the Travellers with H. J. Wilson. Told me Hore-Belisha was going into the wilderness and was to be succeeded by Oliver Stanley [as war minister]. What an appointment. Nice fellow but a cypher. Picked up later by Barrington-Ward in the car. Very sick to hear about O. Stanley and why ever hadn't I gone there. How differently I should have been feeling if I had been put in the other job. I can't say I felt any elation or satisfaction. The circumstances are very similar to June 1938 – extraordinarily so.

8 January 1940 Had a talk with Sir Walter Monckton. He is in charge of censorship in the Press Bureau and as such is now independent of the Ministry. This is quite wrong. I am glad to find that he is wholeheartedly in favour of return. It did not take me long to work out in my mind the sort of organization that I would like to see here.

10 January 1940 Much discussion with Lee [director general of the Ministry of Information] and Monckton about the organization. I would go quicker rather than slower, Lee the other way round.

To a meeting with Halifax and MacDonald [secretary of state for Colonies]. Halifax asked me to stay after MacDonald had gone and gave me advice in a very kindly way about the House of Commons. He advocated forbearance, humour, visits to the smoking room and so forth, and contrasted Chamberlain's position with the Labour party with that held by Baldwin, who appeared ready to suffer fools gladly in the House of Commons for any length of time (I don't think he did elsewhere).

13 January 1940 Lunched at the Carlton with Sir Charles Barrie, MP for Southampton, and he told me what would be required if I were to take his seat there. I am not at all enamoured of the prospect but I would certainly much rather have Southampton than say Bournemouth or any place that has no special interest.

15 January 1940 Saw Churchill about a ridiculous idea that he has put to the Cabinet that shipping losses should only be broadcast weekly. He said he would hold up that request. Of course he talked about my keeping him off the wireless 'for 8 years'. Gave disinterested and friendly advice about the House of Commons. Then saw Margesson [Conservative chief whip] and settled for Southampton – provided they'll agree!

16 January 1940 Munster to see me, one of Gort's ADC's, very bothered about a news film of Hore-Belisha and Gort in which Hore-Belisha was cheered and Gort received in silence. Went to War Cabinet meeting. Churchill said I had asked him to withdraw his paper on shipping losses to be given weekly. Next item was a long memo by Macmillan on propaganda policy. The PM asked me what I thought. I said it was very fine but might be more practical, so I was requested to produce a document of my own. Cabinet conducted in quite a smart way so far as I saw, and really rather reminiscent of my old Control Boards.

17 January 1940 To House of Commons to see Attlee. I had about an hour with him and went over past troubles between his party and the Ministry of Information. All unnecessary and silly. I think I can make him play but of course he is weak and won't do anything on his own. Then saw H. J. Wilson for a general talk. He agreed on our doing all we could on our own to get the M of I collected together again.

18 January 1940 Meeting of ministers at FO, Halifax answering questions. Nothing new but interesting and pleasant. Dined at Thorpe Lodge. Governor said in effect that he had staked his reputation on my doing well. He was most concerned that I should be patient and modest. Just that. It seems that people expect me to move on in politics.

19 January 1940 There is some confusion and upset about my standing for Southampton. It was clear all along to Margesson, Barrie and me that I was standing as a National for a Liberal-National seat. Margesson had not realized that there would be bother over this. It is not my fault at all. The Liberal National whip (Kerr) is at the back of it all. It came clear finally that I could stand as a National; I insisted on this. Margesson advised me to live up to my reputation and treat them autocratically. I really don't care much, but I was horrified to find that I was one of the Simon-Burgin-Belisha group.

20 January 1940 I only can believe that it is God's hand and Father's which has given me this Liberal association at the beginning.

23 January 1940 Saw Ronald Tree MP and fixed him for parliamentary private secretary. I imagine that he will be as good as the next one, so to speak, and no one else has suggested himself or been suggested.

24 January 1940 Very nice talk with Lord Baldwin. He is bothered by the majority of appointments Chamberlain has made. He had kept the Conservative party 'left centre' but Chamberlain was undoing much of that. Sorry I had fixed Tree as PPS as he had a general prejudice against Americans.

Lunch with Beaverbrook. What a dreadful man he is; one of the worst I ever met. Evil he seems. He said Churchill and I were in the government against the will of the PM. The country had demanded that I should be there and the PM had put me in to help cover Hore-Belisha going out. He told me I would quite likely be prime minister. 'Do I want to be' I felt like asking but didn't. I have an uneasy feeling all the time when I am with this man. I don't know whether I want to be PM or not. It certainly greatly diminishes in attractiveness the nearer one gets to it.

Saw H. J. Wilson with my propaganda objectives paper which he liked. I had another one saying the M of I needed proper co-ordination and a proper attitude from Service Ministries. H. J. thought I shouldn't put this in, but try to get all we wanted on the quiet.

29 January 1940 Saw a miserable election agent and had to give him £225 of which £150 is returnable. Loathesome.

30 January 1940 Attended War Cabinet. My objectives document was passed with slight amendment and they seemed to approve it all. I was there from 11.30 to 12.45.

Seeing Monckton and Lee [about reorganization of Ministry]. Too much shilly-shallying. How difficult it is to get things moving and to know whether to ignore the point of view of other people.

31 January 1940 DMI from France to see me, Major-General Mason Macfarlane. Very live wire. Strange to me to be called 'Sir' and saluted with normality by such like. He said troops in France were very bored and discipline not at all what it should be. Very much dependent on type of officers and some were very poor. Much discontent among those who knew that tank production was only single-shifted. The Germans had several armoured divisions and we none yet ready to go overseas.

Meeting at 5.30 with PM – non-War Cabinet ministers. He didn't tell us anything we didn't know, but some of his own views in answer to questions were interesting. He has little fear of Italy coming in on German side, but thinks there might be trouble with Russia.

Dined at Thorpe Lodge. Governor has no sort of opinion of Sir J. Simon; dislikes and distrusts him. Has a high opinion of Sir A. Duncan [president of the Board of Trade and newly elected MP for the city of London]. How I wish I had been City member instead of Southampton. I slipped up on that and so did others. Can't be helped now.

1 February 1940 A most important meeting with the three chief party agents at which I should think we definitely squared yards as between Ministry and parties. They said Macmillan hadn't thought it was any function of the Ministry to provide an umbrella under which the three parties should get together. I said I thought it was not only expedient but vitally necessary that there should be this co-operation.

2 February 1940 Gave lunch to Herbert Morrison. Unpleasant in appearance and manners but very friendly. Spoke about the House of Commons. Said I had lots of friends and some enemies.

5 February 1940 To Sam Hoare's [for dinner]. Chatfield was there. Learnt things about RAF – independence of Bomber, Fighter and Coastal Command and Chief of Air Staff not having much authority over them. Took too long – up to an hour Chatfield said – for action to be taken in raids.

[John Reith had been elected MP for Southampton unopposed on 1 February and took his seat on 6 February.]

7 February 1940 I had to be in the House of Commons this afternoon to answer a question – a quite fatuous one about staff. Later I took part in a division for the first time – about Hankey's salary [as minister without portfolio]. I expect I had better be careful about divisions. There are some I don't want to vote in.

8 February 1940 To a ministers' meeting at the FO. I quite like these meetings though I don't learn much. Halifax thought the 'peace' might well not be broken all this year. Gamelin [Allied C-in-C] had said if it wasn't broken in March he didn't think it would be at all.

13 February 1940 House of Commons, having a question but we didn't get to it. I think I enjoy being an MP as long as I don't need to bother with a constituency.

20 February 1940 Monckton had an entirely unsuccessful talk with Churchill yesterday. Churchill is a horrid fellow. Dined with Stanley Baldwin. I enjoyed it and we had much interesting talk.

22 February 1940 Talked with DNI about news from the Admiralty which is giving Monckton so much trouble. It is quite clear that Churchill is the cause of *all* the trouble, and that even D. Pound [First Sea Lord] has little to do with it.

28 February 1940 A really ridiculous and fatuous memo from H. J. Wilson about Enemy Propaganda. Monckton instead of 'control' was to have 'contact'. I was surprised at his putting up such a piece of jobbery.

Lunch with Campbell Stuart. He said he had told Cadogan that he would resign rather than work under Monckton.[1] Very awkward. To the House of Commons. R. A. Butler was around and was much embarrassed by the turn things had taken. He was as nice as could be but clearly Halifax hadn't been strong enough to put across what he wanted.

29 February 1940 Lobby correspondents' lunch in the Victoria Hotel. Most of the Cabinet there, Churchill speaking. How I dislike him. To House of Commons. Saw Amery [former Conservative minister] in my room about things in which he is interested. Then he asked how I was getting on. He said the government couldn't afford to have a row with me, and that I was bound to get what I wanted, so why didn't I enter an ultimatum. However unfairly the PM has treated me, and I think it has been very unfair, I don't feel I could do that.

5 March 1940 Attended Sam Hoare's Home Affairs committee for the first time. Anderson [home secretary] there too. Nothing affecting me and all quite formal. H. J. Wilson came to see me in my room at House of Commons; asked me to try to make things work without Monckton having authority over Campbell Stuart, but with him as deputy director general of my Ministry and also deputy under secretary of state at the Foreign Office. He was sure Monckton would agree if I did and if I said I wouldn't expect too much of him. Weird, it all is.

6 March 1940 Simon collared me for a talk. He is too jealous of the Governor [i.e. Montagu Norman] to let him come and meet the Press as we had arranged in connection with War Loan publicity, and too jealous of Stamp [as a director of the Bank of England] to like our scheme of having him talk weekly in explanation of financial and economic problems. This would have done much good. Pathetic that he should be like that. We shall drop it all.

7 March 1940 Lunched with Hore-Belisha. Odd experience. I found him very unattractive. He was anxious to know what I felt about his future. I said I imagined that in the long run it would pay him to comport himself with dignity, in which connection it was surely a pity to be writing in the *News of the World.*

Chatfield took the ministers' meeting and was as usual very informative and well documented. Two divisions are standing by for Finland.[2] Saw the PM for three-quarters of an hour at 7.00. He had seen Monckton last night telling him that he thought I would agree if he would, and he now told me the same thing the other way round. He asked me if I would try this scheme and I said of course I would though I didn't think it was a good one. I told him about our new Charter of Rights and it is clear that we shall have his support; I hope it will be determining.

12 March 1940 Home Affairs committee at which I brought up the two Orders in Council which are to go through transferring postal and telegraph censorship to me from the War Office.

13 March 1940 I had to dine with the Simonites. Simon introduced me quite nicely and I talked and answered questions.

14 March 1940 Ministers' meeting at No. 10. The PM gave us the Finnish story, especially the Swedish obstruction, but he puts the blame on Germany not on Sweden; also something about Italy and then his impressions of Sumner Welles [American under-secretary of state] whom he liked. Quite interesting. A USA peace proposal is to be expected. Talked with Bridges [secretary to the Cabinet] about the ridiculous position of the Ministry of Information. I said the thing might be of real help but to do so would mean its being taken seriously. He was very friendly and said he was going to send me all confidential annexes from the 'Standard File' of Cabinet conclusions, and that he would tell H.J. that I ought to attend meetings.

18 March 1940 Dined at Thorpe Lodge. The Governor said things in the Treasury were most unsatisfactory. He spoke as if he were going to bear a considerable part in changing them. He disapproves of H.J. holding two jobs.[3] Says there are going to be all sorts of changes soon. Told me that it was remarkable how much the PM had taken to me in view of how things started. He thought I was very wise to be going so quietly.

20 March 1940 Discussion with Lee and Monckton about Ministry organization. It is most unsatisfactory and we seem to go backwards as much as forward.

Attended a National Liberal meeting at which Belisha resigned the chairmanship – though some of them there thought he didn't need to despite his attack on the government. Rum lot this party is.

Went to an odd cocktail party at Oliver Stanley's house attended by the King and Queen. Duchess of Westminster, with whom I had considerable conversation, enlightened me about the others including Beaverbrook's mistress – disgusting.

21 March 1940 Lunch at R. Tree's house – where Haldane lived in Queen Anne's Gate. B. Bracken present. He said Churchill was very well disposed to me; I wonder.

23 March 1940 Lunched at Cliveden. Geoffrey Dawson there and some interesting conversation about my job which is so worrying till I get the authority to do it.

24 March 1940 (Easter Day) Very uneasy about the Ministry I feel, but 'the Lord God Omnipotent reigneth.'

25 March 1940 To Ronald Tree's place, Ditchley. There was a big party mostly of the very young with whom I feel less and less at ease – completely self-centred and cynical and blasé.

26 March 1940 A depressed day. I feel that I have lost two months, lost the easy opportunity of making all sorts of drastic changes, and more or less lost myself and my own value. Lee has been utterly ineffective; Monckton knows what is required but never seems to get any nearer to it. Anyhow I asked God many times today to help me and I must have the faith I need.

27 March 1940 Saw PM at 6.30. He said we weren't taking propaganda nearly seriously enough in this country, putting the blame on the Service departments. He said it was abominable how parts of the Press behaved, continually criticizing and so forth – making his task much more difficult. He said he thought it quite likely that the war would continue more or less indefinitely as it is now, the Germans may be being afraid to risk putting their people through the experiences of the last war; hence it would be a war of nerves. He said he was going to support me, but how he didn't say. I said he could abolish the Ministry altogether if he liked but it was an exotic and belonged to the dictator regimes – special care therefore had to be used if it was to be grafted on to democratic machinery.

3 April 1940 Cabinet changes tonight. Chatfield is dropped, S. Hoare and K. Wood change places and there is a weird shift-round elsewhere.[4] I wonder some of them stay.

4 April 1940 To Admiralty and had an hour and a half with Pound and Phillips [vice-chief of Naval Staff]. Very civil and amenable and I came away quite angry that I had been able to do so much which Monckton ought to have done months ago.

5 April 1940 Very angry with people and things in the Ministry. Incredible incompetence. Saw H.J. at 7.30. Told him things wouldn't come right till I was at least present at War Cabinet meetings. He said he and the PM had more or less agreed this, but felt it would be bad for me – jealousy of others and such like.

9 April 1940 Muriel telephoned me at the station this morning that the War Cabinet offices had been ringing for me. Hood [Reith's principal private secretary] was at Marylebone and I went to No. 10. Germany had invaded Norway and Denmark. The Cabinet met at 8.30 and were then discussing military measures. I was bid enter at 9.20 and had the privilege of witnessing the final efforts of this distinguished body.

Historic but unimpressive. They decided to have air reconnaissance, naval efforts to retake Trondheim and Bergen and military preparations and so on, but all vague and uncourageous. They tried to draft a statement round the table and then it was left with Halifax and me to finish it. We went into H.J.'s room. Winston came in. He thought he had the German fleet where he wanted them now – but however did they get all up the coast with almost the whole Navy around? Having got a statement drafted H.J. and I went to Halifax with it. He got the French Ambassador in and read it to him, asking if we could refer to the French government as well. 'I think so; I think so,' he said slowly. H.J. and I then took the thing in to the PM who made some more changes and it was issued at 12.00.

10 April 1940 Lunched with Churchill. B. Bracken was there and was very outspoken to Churchill about me and my job, saying it was all wrong that I should be as I was. He certainly seems most friendly and anxious to help.

11 April 1940 Dined at Lady Astor's. CIGS [Sir Edmund Ironside] was there. He was very forthcoming to me. He is sure of an invasion of Holland or Belgium within a fortnight.

13 April 1940 I think the incompetence of the Ministry of Information is greater far than that of Imperial Airways. And the hopelessness of the set-up inside together with there being no proper position for the Ministry in the political scheme makes me often inclined to chuck it up. The complication of being an MP makes this much more difficult.

14 April 1940 To K. Wood's office being joined there by H. J. Wilson. K. Wood said the Military Co-ordination committee was a farce – dreadful state Churchill had gotten himself and everybody else into. Admiralty in a state of jitters from top to bottom. Spoke as if it was very serious. Advised me not to mind if Churchill was rude or declaimed away, and urged me only to talk of two points: better staff at the Ministry and Ministry representation at Service departments. We went to the Admiralty and as H.J. said it was worth a seat in the stalls. Churchill said at one time that we weren't going to have a postmortem and at another that that was necessary. I had documents giving the lie to what he said. All ridiculous and very serious that this should go on in war. He looked as if he had been drinking too much – as he did last Wednesday [10 April]. However I suppose it was more satisfactory than it might have been. Churchill said to K.W. after the meeting that I ought to be in the War Cabinet. Oliver Stanley said so too.

18 April 1940 Attended a quite fatuous meeting of ministers taken by Hankey. I think I will stop going to these.

19 April 1940 Very angry indeed to get a letter from Bridges saying confidential annexes weren't being sent owing to their extreme privacy but that if I wanted to keep myself informed he would be delighted to let me see them if I called. Forsooth.

22 April 1940 Went with K. Wood to the War Cabinet as there was an alarm about the optimistic tone of news from Norway. The Cabinet had decided yesterday that K. Wood should consult with me and see the Press. Really ridiculous. Also of course ridiculous that I come to Cabinets once a month only. Felt disgusted. K. Wood's press conference was a farcical affair – a waste of time. Dined with H. J. Wilson. He said he still wouldn't press for War Cabinet attendance. I felt better after talking with him though there wasn't much reason why I should. Afterwards to Lady Reading's. She said she was greatly concerned as were many others that I should make a great personal success, as I ought to be PM.

24 April 1940 House of Commons. The PM read out the statement about the Ministry. What a time it has taken to get it and how little it is. Dined with Oliver Stanley. He said he thought we would have to clear out of Norway and he wished I would tone the Press down.

25 April 1940 Meeting at No. 10 with John Anderson and some others about the *Daily Worker* and such like. In the middle I was summoned to the FO by Halifax as he and the American Ambassador wanted to see me. I thought I had better go. Joe Kennedy let off ten or fifteen minutes criticism of the BBC, of Service Departments, of the Cabinet and of England generally. Among other interesting remarks he said there had recently been a meeting of US military attachés at which it had been agreed that England would be beaten. Of course most of his remarks were helpful to me. Halifax suggested that he should repeat them to the PM.

26 April 1940 PM at 3.30 to be told (what I had been expecting and fearing to hear) that the southern party in Norway was to be evacuated. Emphasis to be put on Narvik which I much doubt their being able to hold. He hoped we would do the best we could with the papers. What an awful shock this will be. Spoke about my job and I told him I ought to be at War Cabinet meetings, not because I wanted to be but because it was all wrong that I shouldn't know what was going on. I offered to let him appoint some senior minister to my job. Very amiable he was and seemingly in good form.

Collected Oliver Stanley at the Treasury and walked with him to the War Office. He was in great depression – almost as if he were drunk. I said I would like him to get Dill [vice-chief of Imperial General Staff] along which he did and I got all the news there was. Evacuation was inevitable. Oliver was in a very bad way and I was sorry for him. To the office and got Barrington-Ward along (though he was in sole charge of *The Times*) and told him. He is the only one we will tell the whole story to. Met Dill at the Carlton and dined with him. He was talking about Hore-Belisha, how awful he had been and what harm he had done. He didn't approve of the idea of bombing Ruhr refineries as well as marshalling yards in the event of an attack on the Low Countries.

27 April 1940 Spent from 4.15 to 7.15 in K. Wood's room waiting for news. Dill was with us for the last hour. The French are in a great stew about the evacuation and of course it will make an awful lot of trouble here. People think there will be a change of government.

29 April 1940 War Cabinet 11.30 to 1.30, till 1.00 being occupied with Norway. I wasn't asked my views though there was a lot I wanted to say – e.g. Sam Hoare's broadcast on Saturday [27 April] was quite inconsistent with evacuation; and Churchill has been seeing Press lords. Consideration was given to Italian situation also. Churchill brought up his paper recommending that shipping losses should be given out weekly. When the PM asked my view I just said I agreed. Churchill was so surprised. 'Oh thank you,' he said and pushed the paper back into his box.

Saw PM at 3.00. He was looking very alert. I went through my points – the thinness of the case; Narvik the sole salvation; eagerness of some papers to attack the government; need to avoid (1) inflation again by too much soft-pedalling of troubles and (2) charge of misleading if Narvik not held; difficulties owing to S. Hoare's broadcast and the direct dealings with the Press (how could I get someone along and then tell him a quarter of what he might already know). PM gave me his views and I wrote them down. He was very angry over S. Hoare and the like.

30 April 1940 Called off policy meeting as we had so much to do. Lunched with *Daily Sketch* Editor who was very pleased with the guidance points I gave him. Geoffrey Dawson to see me and talked for about an hour. Saw *Daily Herald* Editor, Powell and Ogilvie [of the BBC], Camrose and Beaverbrook. Arrived exactly an hour late for John Astor's dinner – a small party including David Margesson with whom I had talk about reactions to the PM.[5] To see K. Wood at 10.30 and then to the War Office to Dill's room where I got some bits of news which was telephoned to the papers and Broadcasting House. Beaverbrook stamped and roared about his room in fulmination against the government. He said he would overthrow them as soon as the evacuation was over, but till then his papers were ours and he would say anything at all we asked. Dreadful fellow. Of course it is awful to think of the way British troops in Norway have been sacrificed. CIGS came into Dill's room in his pyjamas. They have a great opinion of the PM. To the office till 1.30. Bed 3.30.

1 May 1940 PM at 6.30 till 7.20. Told me all sorts of things. The sea lords had been against a Trondheim attack and Churchill had accepted this and then put it across the other Service ministers. PM felt he was therefore virtually responsible. Also told me of new arrangements whereby what Churchill *has been doing* becomes constitutional – namely summoning chiefs of staff himself! I told the PM how carefully (as I had observed in minutes) he had always committed Churchill to decisions. He said he had done so deliberately. I told him what people were saying; I believed he could and would hold his place but that it was a pity he didn't make some changes in his Cabinet. I said the military people liked and respected him. He was frightfully pleased. It was really a most extraordinary conversation. He certainly trusts me.

2 May 1940 Leakage of Information committee, Hankey chairman. About Eire. Quite inconclusive and very badly chaired. Apparently the Free State government help in tracking German spies but they keep a German minister which is dreadful. There is a lot of leakage and though the SIS are at work I don't think they accomplish much.

3 May 1940 PM sent for me at 10.30 and I was there for half an hour. Light-hearted he said he was feeling – news of the successful evacuation of Namsos having come through. He seemed fairly confident of the political situation. He gave me further details of Churchill's changes of mind about Trondheim. On Wednesday [1 May] he referred to Churchill's reputation, so inflated and based on broadcasts (I said this latter), and said if there was to be a debunking it would have to be done by someone else. There is no doubt how he feels about Churchill.

4 May 1940 Attended a meeting in Oliver Stanley's room, Dill and others about returning Norwegian troops. I had said there ought to be controlled interviews which no one apparently had thought of. Almost unbelievable the muddle between War Office general staff and the public relations people.

7 May 1940 Monstrous affair – a two days debate on the conduct of the war. PM spoke first, not very well, mostly about Norway, but quite dispassionately and calmly. Attlee followed – doing no damage. The Whips made a great mistake by their choice of pro-government speakers – Sir H. Page Croft and Southby.[6]

8 May 1940 Ronald Tree said he would vote against the government if there was a division so that I would have to find another PPS. He was very sad about this. Hoare started the debate this afternoon but I didn't hear him. I heard Morrison who followed and who announced that there would be a division which apparently the PM hadn't expected. He jumped up saying he welcomed the challenge and that he had his friends in the House. A mistake that. I heard Lloyd George who was horrid. We heard Amery last night and he was very bitter but still more so Duff Cooper today. I had dinner with Ronald Tree and wife – rather fun and it was all exciting, though such a beastly business. I listened to the winding up. [A. V.] Alexander (who is a pompous ass) and Churchill. I felt throughout that Churchill was such a hypocrite as he was loving the criticisms against the government knowing that it was all helping to put him in power. Division 281 to 200 and thereafter a scene of disgusting jubilation – fellows like Harold Macmillan yelling themselves hoarse. I was sorry for the PM throughout and he stood it all very well. We stood up as he left and gave him a cheer. Sickening.

9 May 1940 I had to go to the House to answer silly questions at 11.00. Sam Hoare asked me to come into his room. Jackals, he said, they had been last night. Today he said he hadn't the heart to open his letters. I felt something like it myself only I had no doubt that I should be retained, whereas he and Simon had been specially attacked.[7]

10 May 1940 Saw the PM for quarter of an hour before War Cabinet. Things have broken suddenly in the land front, Holland and Belgium having been invaded in the night. PM said he has asked the Labour people, Attlee and Greenwood, last night if they would join the government under him or under someone else. They said No to the first part, Yes to the second. Then he had seen them this morning again after the Low Countries news, and I understood quite clearly that they had agreed to defer the political crisis and support the government in view of the other crisis. A Labour conference was on over the weekend in Bournemouth and confirmation would have to come thence. PM said he could put out of his mind what had happened in the last two days; Sinclair [the Liberal leader] had apologized and he had no feelings against Attlee, but of course he and Lloyd George would never be friendly. He was in quite good form and I thought how odd it all was, he and I sitting there with such colossal happenings across the North Sea. I shook hands with him and he was greatly touched and appreciative.

Attended Cabinet – there had been one at 8.00. Ironside was very snotty about a homing rocket which Churchill's tame scientist, Lindemann [later Lord Cherwell], was demonstrating on a side table. 'Do you think this is the time for showing off toys?' he asked me. At the meeting a bit of the tape was given H. J. Wilson and he passed it over with a note to me. It was a statement by Attlee and Greenwood which might have been written before the political crisis and seemed to me (and to H.J.) to leave things just as they were before the war blew up.[8]

[John Reith did not record the fall of the Chamberlain government. From lunch-time on 10 May to 11.30 that night he was occupied in getting a war-room properly established in the Ministry of Information. A later pencilled note in the margin of his diary records 'Resignation meeting on the 10th, p.m.']

11 May 1940 War Cabinet announced tonight, Churchill being defence minister as well as PM. Heaven help us. The three Service departments are Sinclair, Eden and Alexander. This is obviously so that Churchill can ignore them more or less and deal direct with the chiefs of staff. Awful.

12 May 1940 Whit Sunday Dill rang up and I arranged to dine with him at 8.30. Left for the office at 5.30. At 7.00 or so I phoned Barrington-Ward from Monckton's office. He said they were to receive a further Cabinet list at 8.00, and Monckton got this as I was on the telephone. Lord chancellor, Simon; chancellor of the exchequer, K. Wood; Lloyd, Colonies; minister of information, Duff Cooper – my first intimation of it. Quarter of an hour later the First Lord's secretary rang up to tell me the news but I said I had already seen it, which rather flabbergasted him. I handed over my Cabinet key and police pass, cleared up in my room in less than a minute, shook hands and departed, shaking the dust. How filthy this treatment – and what a *rotten* government. I got home about 9.15 having called off dinner with Dill. Brendan Bracken telephoned me at 10.15 or so to say I was 'to blame for all this' owing to my having no address in *Who's Who* and I would find a very nice letter from the PM at the Athenæum. Bracken said the PM thought very highly of me and had one if not two jobs to suggest. He said there certainly was no suggestion that I hadn't done my job very well, nor that I wouldn't be asked to do another at once. What to believe? A dirty business every way.

2. Minister of Transport under Churchill, May–October 1940

[John Reith's short period as minister of transport in Winston Churchill's coalition government was unhappy from the start. As he himself later observed his 'self-confidence was shaken'. He had been gracelessly removed from the Ministry of Information and, as he saw it, shunted into a less important office at a time of national emergency. It seemed to him that his endeavours to improve the efficiency of his new ministry were frustrated by the rigid conservatism of his departmental officials and that his attempts to look ahead to a national transport system for the post-war world were undermined alike by the weakness of the Labour members of the government and by Churchill's total lack of interest. In any event he was out of sympathy with Churchill and suspicious of those around him, such as Beaverbrook and Brendan Bracken, even when they tried to coax him into a more co-operative frame of mind. In the black days of 1940 his best informed contact was Sir John Dill, newly appointed CIGS, who was himself opposed to Churchill's methods and doubtful of their success. So the elements of his future political isolation were already visible – conflict with civil service orthodoxy, distrust and resentment of Churchill, and refusal to compromise with those who now held power.]

13 May 1940 No word from anyone. I think Chamberlain might have telephoned. We drove up, unwillingly, to dine at Thorpe Lodge. The Governor wasn't sympathetic or helpful at all. R. Tree phoned. Thought I was to be offered Shipping Ministry. Beaverbrook likely to get the aircraft production one! My trust in God is not at all what it ought to be.

14 May 1940 Hood phoned to say that the PM wanted to see me at 4.55. I called up Rucker [private secretary to the prime minister] who said the lord president [Neville Chamberlain] would be very glad to see me before I saw Churchill. I also spoke to Barrington-Ward who advised me to take even the postmaster general job. Saw Chamberlain at 4.40. He was looking and sounding *very* disgusted as well he might be. He said I was to be offered Transport. This was quite a shock as I had expected shipping or the new aircraft production job. I asked him whether I should take it. He said he hoped I would. I hadn't had any real chance in the last job. No question of not having made a success. This was a senior ministry and might be of vital importance. I said I should do as he advised. I said also I should like to keep in touch with him as it was he who had brought me into politics.

Interview [with Churchill] went all right. He rose to shake hands and said he had a difficult and important job which he wanted to ask me to do – put on his glasses to look at a slip of paper – Transport. Would I like it – pressed this question as I wasn't forthcoming in reply. Wouldn't that suit me – I had said at lunch I wanted a more definite job. (I think surely I meant that to refer to being given more power at the Ministry of Information.) I said I was probably referring to the Admiralty. He said that was the most thrilling of all and he missed his room across the way. Incidentally Neville Chamberlain, to whom I had said I would have preferred a Service ministry, looked at me very significantly and answered that I wouldn't like it now. There is no bit of doubt as to what Chamberlain thinks of Churchill.

Looked in on Kingsley Wood, chancellor of the exchequer. When he sits in one of the big chairs round the table his legs are clear off the ground.

15 May 1940 Talked with Euan Wallace [outgoing minister of transport] till 1.00 and then lunched alone. I felt frightfully lonely and greatly missing the nice fellows from the other place. Things here are completely different. Not the same type of fellows or anything. Talk with Hurcomb [former permanent head of the Ministry of Transport] after lunch. All the senior staff seem irreproachably efficient! I wonder. An hour or more with Browett, the Ministry of Transport secretary. Very well satisfied with everything and everybody!

16 May 1940 Attended the Civil Defence committee. Duff Cooper said he would attend all Cabinets, would get enemy propaganda under him and would control the BBC – Churchill has done everything for him which Chamberlain wouldn't do for me.

18 May 1940 A tremendous battle has been raging for some days now. Holland has capitulated and there is a German drive round the Maginot line. The position is serious. Discovered various things happening about demolition that the secretary and minister should have been in on and weren't, so I had a meeting including the Parliamentary secretary, Montague, a Labour man aged sixty-four who notified us of his own appointment this morning. Oh dear! Most unhappy about my job.

20 May 1940 I had to attend the Cabinet on shipping diversion – what a crew. Things on the western front are very parlous indeed and we are like to lose the channel ports and the BEF is all in danger.

21 May 1940 How I hate leaving each morning. The Lord God omnipotent reigneth – oh that I could keep that more in mind and that nothing more need or could be said.

Went to the House of Commons where I hadn't meant to go. It was horrid, I thought. Didn't sit down in the Chamber at all. Brendan Bracken spoke to me – usual style. Back to the office where I have very little to do. The news is about as bad as it can be. Germans are in Abbeville and Amiens and Arras. The Horse Guards are all barbed wire and machine-gun posts. Incredible.

22 May 1940 No pleasure at all in the House of Commons now and the Ministry of Transport is a backwater. Attended a meeting of the Liberal National party. Much argument round and about. It was monstrous and almost unbelievable that Churchill should have ignored this party and regarded Sinclair and his few followers as the real Liberal party, bringing in Harcourt Johnstone for instance and putting Shakespeare out of Overseas Trade where he had only been for five weeks.[9]

23 May 1940 Lunched with Stamp [chairman of LMS railway] and had an interesting talk about nationalization [of the railways]. Friendly he was. Trouble brewing, or alleged to be, in the railways. The Railway Executive will report to me early next week and I will inform Bevin, the Labour minister, of the position. Long talk with Tolerton [principal assistant secretary in the Ministry of Transport], endeavouring to shake him out of his complacency about the ports. He is a real civil servant in most ways. Dined at Oliver Stanley's. Oliver has declined the Dominions Secretaryship because of the abominable way he had been treated over the War Office and because of the terms in which the other had been offered.

24 May 1940 Saw Bevin with Montague [about railwaymen's pay]. 'Give them 2/-.' Tried to stir things up about the Home Defence Executive which is in a hopeless state – the body we depend on for defence against invasion. Started up the Transportation Corporation this afternoon – outlining my ideas to Sir A. Robinson [deputy secretary in the Ministry of Transport]. He is another typical and typically irritating civil servant. Talk, talk and so many difficulties. Almost unbelievable inefficiency there has been, and the people responsible: Hankey, Fisher, Wilson, Chamberlain.

26 May 1940 Attended Home Office meeting about evacuating East coast towns of children. Anderson told me that the BEF would probably have to be evacuated. Quite a chance of the French giving in. I thought I would like to be Chief of Staff to Dill if he was going to be GOC, Home, so phoned Rucker to see what was happening. Ironside is to do this and Dill becomes CIGS which he should have been years ago. All the same I think the Home job is the more important just now.

27 May 1940 Heard via Hill [principal assistant secretary in the Ministry of Transport] and Browett that the BEF was to be evacuated, starting today. This is awful and awful the slaughter that will be done them in the process. Very odd, I thought, that this information should reach me from below. Hill had it from an official of the GWR.

28 May 1940 Telegram sent this day warning all docks of diversions and emergencies. All road signposts throughout the country to be taken down – I gave this order tonight after approval by the Home Defence Executive.

Meeting in PM's room of ministers not attending War Cabinet. Told us of the happenings in France – dramatic; unreal; insincere. Ghastly losses, Dunkirk the only evacuating place left. Hitler would probably take Paris and offer terms. The Italians would threaten and offer terms. No doubt whatever that we must decline anything like this and fight on. Hear, hear, said everyone. Some rather humbugging and sycophantic remarks. I hate it all from my present useless position. I wish I were in better mind about everything. God help me to trust Him and to know that His will is best for me all times, all ways.

29 May 1940 Had an hour with H. J. Wilson. Very much deflated from his former state so I felt rather sorry for him. Of course he feels that he has been badly treated; he said he had never wanted to go to No. 10. Anyhow he is quite out of it now. He said he never wanted to go to the House of Commons again after the disgusting exhibition he saw there the night of the 281–200 vote.

30 May 1940 Lunched with Barrington-Ward who tried to console and encourage me. He has no use for Duff Cooper.
    Yesterday I had a meeting with Bevin. He had said we ought to give the railwaymen two shillings the other day, repeated it this morning but then when he saw them he was beaten up to three shillings. I suggested an offer of two shillings failing which arbitration but he didn't think this would do. Rather a ramp the whole business is.
    The Whips Office can't produce a proper PPS for me so I am going without one.[10] It is simply awful.

31 May 1940 Saw K. Wood and he said I should agree three shillings on to railway wages so I directed accordingly. Dinner with Oliver Stanley – he joining the army next Monday as a second-lieutenant. Duff Cooper and wife present – horrified and very bored I was to hear this but we had some amicable conversation. Lady Pamela Berry also there. She said people were sure I would not be long in a second-rate job like Transport. Spoke in very friendly and interested terms, surprising me and rather encouraging.

3 June 1940 Usual meeting – fatuous as usual – in Anderson's office [this was the Home Office meeting of ministers concerned with the home front]. Most ministers try to answer questions themselves and then get stuck and have to appeal to their officials. I don't answer in details. The day dragged by, slightly encouraged by lunch and a talk with Anderson at Brooks's. I told him I wasn't busy and asked his advice about intervening in organization [i.e. of the Ministry] and about doing something drastic about traffic allocation instead of establishing a mild advisory committee. Ministers meeting with PM at 5.00. Nothing to it and I disliked it very much. Sycophantic remarks by so many of them and Beaverbrook preening himself and being flattered for increase of production for which he is probably not at all responsible. Oh, so lonely, so jealous and so unhappy.

5 June 1940 I wish I had had to make the sort of speech Churchill did yesterday.[11] I felt I couldn't go to hear it. Jealousy. I *could* speak.

Liberal meeting at 5.00. I left at 6.15, there being great argument as to whether or not there should be a leader and if so who. Talk of the party being split!

7 June 1940 This morning I spent an hour and a half at a meeting of the Railway Executive. The relationship between it and the Ministry is all wrong and never should have arisen.

3.00 to 5.00 in the Ministry on my traffic allocation ideas and on general problems of control. Hopeless they are and I wish I knew whether I ought to push my ideas over.

Dined with Dill, CIGS, in his little flat. General Percival [assistant chief of the Imperial General Staff] and his ADC there. He thinks Hitler will get to Paris and the French will give in.

10 June 1940 Montague and I went to see Attlee. He gave me very definite encouragement to do all the post-war planning I was inclined to.

12 June 1940 Last night in the train I wrote some notes for a memo on the future organization of transport. Today I dictated three and a half pages on it. Maybe the beginning of an immense and revolutionary reorganization.

13 June 1940 Home Office meeting. When Anderson asked if I had anything to raise, I answered 'bus fares'. Worked on memo and went through it with secretary and deputy secretary after lunch.

14 June 1940 Saw Attlee with my memorandum. He liked it but hadn't given much thought to it and wanted to discuss it with Greenwood. Ministers meeting at No. 10 at 5.00. The French no longer exist as a nation. Churchill didn't know whether they would make peace or

John Reith and
Ramsay MacDonald,
1928

King George V
and Queen Mary
arriving at
Broadcasting House,
1932

John and Muriel Reith, June 1931

preserve some sort of national existence from Africa or England. Much flattery of Beaverbrook – disgusting. How I wish I were bearing my proper part in these awful days. So much I could do, so little doing.

15 June 1940 When I think how badly, very badly, I have been treated by Chamberlain and then by Churchill and how unhappy I am in my present state, I think I would despair if I didn't keep always in mind that the Lord God omnipotent reigneth.

16 June 1940 I ruminated a good deal today on the future. I was wondering whether God wouldn't show his hand now in some unmistakeable way. I believe He may. Indeed I hope so.

18 June 1940 On Sunday [16 June] the British Cabinet adopted what seemed to me a panic sort of measure in the hope of keeping the French in the war – a declaration of union between Great Britain and France, not two countries but one. Quite meaningless I should say. Churchill made a statement in the House of Commons this afternoon. Not very good.

25 June 1940 To see N. Chamberlain. I have been feeling so sore with him that I thought I had better see him and then I might feel less so. He said it was very galling for me to see [Duff] Cooper so much in things. He said he had that day been told by Hacking [chairman of the Conservative party] that his position in the country, in the party and in his own town has deteriorated. Short memories, Chamberlain said, people had. Astonishing. He does not seem to realize what he has been responsible for. Then went to see H.J.W. and said a thing or two about the new Works and Buildings Ministry proposed. R. Assheton [parliamentary secretary at the Ministry of Labour] had thrown a fly over me about it earlier in the day. I don't know whether I would like it or not, but it would be a change and although no more interesting than the present and still less in the heart of things, as information was, it would be busier. I said I could do both together.

Dined with Dill [CIGS], he having asked me this afternoon. Dill is evidently not at all happy with the Churchill system of doing things.

27 June 1940 Attended a Production Council meeting – Greenwood in the chair. A weary business only enlivened by Beaverbrook's two proposals about plywood and alloy steel control being rejected. How I dislike that man. I think I would oppose anything he wanted.

R.D.–R

3 July 1940 At Civil Defence committee and later meeting at Home Office there was a good deal of criticism about lack of co-ordination and such like. Bevin made a personal attack on Beaverbrook which everyone present seemed to endorse. Bevin said he was incapable of teamwork. Horrid it is to have that evil and disgusting man a minister. The immediate delegation of powers to regional commissioners was hotly opposed. I did not say anything all through.

CIGS phoned inviting me to dine. His two ADCs there, and a very pleasant and interesting time. He told me of the battle between British and French fleets off Oran[12] – how awful and it will probably mean that France will declare war on England. Much talk about leadership. Dill doesn't think success will come to us till we have our stand on moral issues and our outlook and intentions clear. Of course this is what I feel strongly, and always have. We spoke of the distrust of Ironside – universal he said and asked why. Character, I replied; and said that explained why people trusted him. He finds the PM very trying of course. I told him that if there were anything of a dictatorship here it would be with Army support and that would be his look-out. Very interesting, and such a conversation about the Christian ethic as was very encouraging.

4 July 1940 House of Commons. PM spoke explaining French fleet business. He got a tremendous reception, everybody standing up afterwards. It wasn't anything in the least remarkable. Oh dear, I am so confused and vexed. I dislike him officially so much – chiefly on account of his association with people like Beaverbrook and Duff Cooper. I don't think he is at all worthy of or due this sort of tribute from the House of Commons. His reputation and his place in the country are due to his speeches, not his acts nor his character.

Tea with Horne [chairman of Great Western Railway] and another argument. I told him that my legal advice was contrary to his and was to the effect that I had full power over the railways in every respect. I had the better of him, I think.

5 July 1940 Meeting at No. 10, PM in the chair; Chamberlain there; also honoured with the presence of the following Olympians: Eden, Sinclair, Ironside and Haining [vice-chief of the Imperial General Staff]. *Terribly* irritating to me. The only thing I remember is Churchill saying (whether truly or not I don't know) that however burdened he was he realized that it was harder for those who knew a little but only a little, especially if not fully engaged. Oh, how true. It is almost more than I can bear. Tired today – the tiredness of inactivity and discontent.

9 July 1940 Every morning in the tunnel before Marylebone I say the Lord's Prayer and the 23rd Psalm. Another ghastly day – one of the worst I have had.

10 July 1940 Saw Bridges and told him how I felt about things. Lunched with J. Rae and Douglas [under-secretaries in the Treasury] – both very kindly and anxious that I should get on well. I had been suggested for charge of all American purchases. I wonder if I would have liked this.

19 July 1940 I told Browett the other day that I disagreed with his organization but that I did not want to say in what way as it was obvious he didn't expect me to interest myself in it. I dictated a note about this today. I am really disgusted with what I have seen of the civil service.

22 July 1940 Ridiculous meeting at Air Ministry, K. Wood giving us his budget proposals – ghastly but nothing makes sense nowadays. He obviously knew nothing at all about his own budget. Then Sinclair held forth on banalities about the RAF. I felt today I couldn't carry on in this ridiculous position.

29 July 1940 Dined with Dill, CIGS. He said Beaverbrook and others of the PM's *galère* made him shudder, as they would any decent fellow. He said he was anxious about the Near East situation where the enemy have so much more strength.

30 July 1940 Lunched with Woolton. He isn't very happy in the government and doesn't propose to stay after the war but he feels we must certainly set our plans on the Christian ethic.

31 July 1940 Attended the farcical Civil Defence committee. I haven't been going to meetings recently. I keep thinking about post-war conditions.

3 August 1940 Went to the silly Home Office meeting which I haven't attended for a long time. Complete waste of time. Went to see Attlee afterwards as I was feeling simply disgusted at an announcement this morning that Beaverbrook was joining the War Cabinet. I told Attlee I wasn't happy because I wasn't nearly busy enough. He seemed quite sympathetic. Wilfrid Greene[13] may be asked to do some post-war planning. I should like to do this.

5 August 1940 It is dreadfully difficult to trust in God as I should. I feel all deteriorated. More disgusted than ever with the Ministry. Lunched (by accident) with Trenchard who said Churchill had offered him the commander-in-chiefship but he had been put off from the beginning of the interview by Eden's presence – just a film star, he said. He had declined to be under him stipulating for deputy defence minister. They had both lost their tempers, so that was that.

6 August 1940 Called on Cross [shipping minister] and asked if he would like to take the Shipping Diversion Room and the Port Committees from Transport. He didn't. I should have in his place. Perhaps he saw all sorts of congestion troubles coming.

7 August 1940 Swotted up endless papers about road transport. Deputation at 11.30, twelve of them. Three read out speeches full of complaints. They charged the Ministry with failure to consult and of disregard of advice where given. I surprised them by admitting first and by saying I could argue second if they liked, but they could have a consultative committee and leave detailed arguments to them. I said we would send terms of reference next day. This may be the beginning of a rationalization of the goods hauliers.

10 August 1940 Saw Attlee. I had had a note from him saying he had told Churchill that I wasn't busy enough. Also that he had told him I had a paper about rationalization of transport. The PM had said I should go on with this.

12 August 1940 Attended meeting in First Lord's room with various people about south coast convoys which are now to go by night hops only and that means only 50,000 tons carried instead of the 150,000 required. Went into Dudley Pound's room afterwards for a talk. Minute from Churchill asking what steps had been taken to see that ports did what was required of them. I suppose he is trying to catch me out. Went off to No. 10 to a meeting of ministers there. I hated it – Kingsley Wood and Simon and most of the others so sycophantic.

Churchill said he didn't think there should be any thought to the post-war state – better world or anything – till the war was won. How silly and short-sighted.

16 August 1940 Dined with CIGS and his two ADCs, contributing some peaches. He sees no hope in the Middle East and is afraid Egypt will be overrun also. There are 250,000 white Italian troops in those parts and 50,000 British. 'Does it make sense?' he said, and it does not. He clearly was in favour of making friends with Germany years ago, as I have always been. How right. And equally wrong therefore the present PM who urged preparations for war against Germany. Churchill now cashes in on this whereas it is all part of the wrongness. There is no doubt what Dill feels about Churchill and the present regime or rather *galère*.

20 August 1940 Gave Muriel lunch at the House of Commons. She went off shopping and I listened to Churchill and thought little of him. Of course he made the usual revolting reference to Beaverbrook which was received in silence.

24 August 1940 Greenwood and Attlee asked me to go and see them about railway rates. They are very scared about it and although I agreed with a good deal it would be silly to renounce everything as Attlee suggested. A post-war planning committee has been established: Chamberlain, Attlee, Halifax, Sinclair, Bevin and [Duff] Cooper! I should like to have been on this.

26 August 1940 Saw Attlee and Greenwood again about the railway agreement. They are certain that we oughtn't to proceed with another increase in charges. Their attitude to the whole thing is superficial and unreal – Attlee much more than Greenwood. I asked Greenwood if he knew how the war was to be financed and he replied: 'I gather the general idea is that we should go into pawn to the USA.' I thought that very funny.

I saw Beaverbrook this morning. He said I would soon have plenty to do and generally was very civil and encouraging.

27 August 1940 Very busy on paper for Cabinet about railways. Saw Dr Coates of ICI and gave him preliminary general instructions about planning for nationalization. Then Montague and I went to another meeting with Attlee and Greenwood, H. Morrison also present, and they went through my paper. They urge proceeding at once with nationalization.

28 August 1940 Sent in my paper for the Cabinet about the railway agreement. Saw Stamp and told him what was happening.

2 September 1940 To a meeting with Attlee and Greenwood at 5.00. Went over points for me to make about railway public ownership next day at the Cabinet. They clearly want me to take all the responsibility and odium! Saw Beaverbrook who said that he would oppose public ownership and advised me not to advocate it as it would damage me with the Conservatives. I had a talk on the telephone with David Margesson about this. He wasn't horrified at the thought of public ownership. Saw K. Wood at 8.00. He had no view of his own.

3 September 1940 Saw Beaverbrook in his garden (telephone and bell-push being carried about after him) 10.00 till 11.00. Weird the influence he now has – deputy PM of course. He said he recommended me for political promotion and was very anxious that I shouldn't spoil myself by the public ownership business, which, of course, I know to be the right course.

At the Cabinet I had to hedge, to my disgust, between Attlee and Beaverbrook and so was indefinite in recommendation. An hour and quarter of argument, Churchill saying – no rise in fares, no more profits than pre-war. K. Wood kept chipping in with, no subsidy, but Churchill didn't agree. Really dreadful it was. An awful exhibition for the country's management. Then a brief argument about compensation for war damage – £2000 maximum for houses etc. but nothing for business. PM didn't care about shareholders, he said. Extraordinarily inconsequent.

4 September 1940 Feeling very disgusted with the Churchill-Beaverbrook regime and their attitude to government ownership. Wondered if I might not resign on this – a convenient peg. Lunched with Barrington-Ward. Nice talk. He says Eden has no future. I was fed up about his speech yesterday – straight jealousy.

8 September 1940 [Sunday] Damage in London on a scale bigger than ever before.[14] Browett spoke to me last night and advised me to come to Town today. Left at 8.30 and there was a meeting at the Home Office at 11.00. Invasion is expected on the 12th or 13th with intensive bombing of the south-east beforehand. The military want all the coast towns cleared! Home after lunch and then back to the office and another meeting at the Home Office at which I contributed the decisive point – if there was to be evacuation people should be told to move by the first train rather than wait for plans to be prepared since railways would catch it first.

13 September 1940 Busy on the draft of a memo for the Cabinet about bomb disposal, Churchill having telephoned me at 11.00 last night. Home Office meeting which Anderson had to leave and then the 'imminent warning' came. Instead of going to the basement I went back to the office, having to walk there. Bomb had just fallen and I found the Ministry on fire, smoke pouring from the roof. I went up to my room to settle the minute for the Cabinet to which I went at 11.30 in the underground place. I was pressed by the PM on the subject of tube stations being used for refugees. I said that I thought it was inadvisable, admitting that as minister of transport I couldn't be completely impartial. A message was handed to him. Buckingham Palace had been dive-bombed. King and Queen safe. PM said he was sure that this indicated that they meant business. I read my paper and Eden said he was getting more men to London. I asked if I could have some units attached to Transport. Anderson shook his head violently. PM said that my request seemed to him entirely reasonable. More argument, Anderson being very emphatic but Churchill continuing to say I ought to have it. Eventually left for Eden and Anderson and me to settle.

14 September 1940 Churchill rang me up again – 11.55 this time – to ask how I was getting on. Great confidence he said he had in me. Apropos the discomforts after fire he remarked that the adaptability of the English was one of our great assets. Odd.
    Went to see Beaverbrook on my initiative – about airfields, I said. Told me he was urging Churchill to appoint me to a bigger job.

17/18 September 1940 To a dreadfully boring meeting with Anderson and others on tube refugees. I was dreadfully sick of it.
    To see Beaverbrook who said he was giving me the fifty aerodromes to build.

19 September 1940 Though warned to speak for the government today I made no preparations. To the House of Commons and went through notes and sketched outline. Shinwell led off; I followed, speaking for three-quarters of a hour – my maiden speech. I twice offered to stop, thinking people might be getting bored, but they shouted for me to go on. Sat till 4.15 listening to the rest of the debate without lunch.

20 September 1940 War Cabinet at 12.30 on a report about more lighting for streets and shops. Some argument about this. PM said the streets and shops should be brightly lit for people going to cinemas and theatres. Argument also about the red warning not being given for single aircraft. Some of them (Anderson and Sinclair) thought this ought to be done. Churchill said they had already decided not and they mustn't go back on it.

Visited Holborn Tube. Ghastly crowd of refugees; five thousand there they reckoned. We went into a disused tube where the LPTB had offices and bedrooms and feeding arrangements and all. Sat in the cabin reserved for the chairman and talked business. They asked for police control of refugees and for local authorities to take care of litter and sanitation. Asked me if I approved some risk being taken re stations which were shut in raids owing to proximity to sewers or river. I said yes.

21/22 September 1940 Silly 'Action this day' memo from PM about tubes to me and Anderson.

Another silly PM memo caused by a blasted woman fussing about bus queues.

23 September 1940 Dictated reply to one of the PM's silly minutes and then went to the Home Office and settled draft of the other reply with John Anderson. Returned to office to do some work and then to a meeting with the PM about shelters generally – a pointless affair lasting an hour. Lunched with Sir W. Wood of LMS and then visited the damage at St Pancras, and a bridge at Dalston and then Blackwall Basin railway warehouses – awful destruction – and Hayden Square, an old East India Company barracks, high and low level. Attended a fatuous [ministers] meeting at the Admiralty where we heard of what seems an utterly pointless attack on Dakar[15] which won't come to anything.

25 September 1940 Great destruction wrought in London last night – west end shops in particular. Much the most disturbed night we have had here also – guns and bombs and flashes and shell-bursts and searchlights.

26 September 1940 Chairman and general manager of the Southern Railway called for me at 11.30 and I did a sort of tour returning at 4.30. Went first to see the Charing Cross damage. Then a bridge at Lambeth. Then to Clapham Junction where I visited two signalmen who had carried on with awful disaster near them – terrible sight it was. Special train to Leatherhead; then Dorking and by car to Deepdene. Here there was much Home Guard ceremony which I didn't at all like but think I carried through all right – my first guard of honour. Saw the special traffic room and then lunch with about twenty-five senior executives. I made them a minute's speech. Then train to Redhill, where I saw the Divisional Control room, and back. As we got near Victoria the sirens went again.

Meeting with PM 5.00 to 6.45 about shelters and such like. Interesting though very discursive. He didn't think Hitler could do any worse and thought he might switch off London as like as not. General criticism of Sir A. Sinclair's saying we wouldn't go in for reprisals.

28 September 1940 Saw Attlee about the railway agreement telling him what the committee had recommended. His advice was quite fatuous. I told him I was making progress in the nationalization matter; he said I couldn't have urged it on the War Cabinet that day last month.

30 September 1940 Dined with CIGS. Anthony Eden also there. Eden told me he had been asked by the PM to be lord president, Chamberlain having resigned. What did I think he should do. I said I should have preferred to stay war secretary. He showed me a letter he had written saying he would do as wanted but would be content to stay where he was. Dill know about the offer already and Eden had also told P.J. [Grigg] [now permanent head of the War Office] whose advice had been to go where he could most restrain Churchill. Dill agreed with me that in that letter he would be appointed to the new job. It was clear to me that he was going to accept and wanted to. And I said so. Arguments around his having to take charge of the Home Front – and he said Attlee and Greenwood were quite incapable of it. Said PM wanted someone to hold his hand and he was clearly the one to do it and he could more or less stipulate to be on the Defence Council and have a hand in settling strategy. He said the PM had once thought that Beaverbrook would succeed him, but not now; that would be himself (Eden). I said no one had ever gone to the lord presidency who was on the way up.[16] I said I should like to be war minister.

1 October 1940 [Ministers] meeting with PM in Cabinet War Room. Told us about Dakar. A sorry story. Command of the seas doesn't mean what it ought – by a long way. He didn't think it was such a sorry tale and was very indignant at press criticism. He thought things were going well – despite the destruction of London. Invasion by no means improbable. Eden told me last night that K. Wood and Bevin join the War Cabinet.

2 October 1940 Message to see PM at 5.00. Told Beauchamp and Montague what was in the wind. PM meeting put off till 5.15, then 5.30, then come at once at 5.20, and then waiting in the secretary's room till 6.00. I went to the Athenæum at 6.00; then, come at 7.00, then at 6.35 come at once. Works Ministry job and Lords. I told him I didn't think much of it and that I thought I might have stayed in the House of Commons after the war. I said I wanted a Service ministry and he replied that the war might go on for a long time, with Japan and America in. I said I had wanted to be more in touch with him and that he didn't really like me. He said he had a great admiration and respect for my qualities. I said I would do what he wanted me to do and he said he would command me.

3. Minister of Works under Churchill, October 1940–February 1942

[John Reith's first few months as minister of works were occupied with such immediate problems as the provision of an alternative meeting place for Parliament in Church House, Westminster, and the creation of bomb-proof strongholds for the prime minister and other members of the government. This meant that his consideration of post-war planning was temporarily placed on one side. In any case he could not consider this aspect of his ministerial work until he had obtained clear terms of reference and Cabinet approval of them. Even while he struggled for these, he continued to hope for some great task outside the government. A kindly note from Lord Beaverbrook aroused his dreams of becoming viceroy of India. Then, early in December 1940, the sudden death of Lord Lothian concentrated his hopes on his other long-cherished ambition – the embassy in Washington – and he was cruelly disappointed when Lord Halifax was appointed to it. After this, he accepted that he would get no outside appointment for the moment and turned his whole attention to the problems of post-war reconstruction and planning.]

4 October 1940 Lunched with Assheton and heard his account of the birth pangs of the new Ministry. Saw Bridges who was about to issue a press statement but we stopped that. Arranged with him about getting proper papers including Cabinet minutes.

5 October 1940 Treasury at 9.30 to see Douglas and eventually told him I would like to be in charge of the new Ministry. On the way up I had done some thinking, arriving at a clear idea of the organization I wanted. Thereafter talked with Barlow and Duff [now secretary at the Ministry of Works]. Duff is a very decent fellow I have always thought. Went over terms of reference. Saw H. J. Wilson who was horrified at my idea of taking Douglas.

Letter from Lord Beaverbrook   6 October 1940
    I hope you like your new job. It is full of possibilities. You can become the building arbitrator of Great Britain. In that capacity you can perform an immense public service, most beneficial to all of us.
    And do not turn your back on public life in the future. You will have a big administrative job before long.
    When Naaman went up to Jerusalem Elijah told him to bathe in the Jordan three times. Naaman would not take the advice.
    Now at Thames House there is a good swimming bath. Will you please play the role of Elijah, telling our Naamans to bathe in it at least once a day, if not three times. It is on your permission only that we can open up the way for our Naamans.[17]

7 October 1940 Lunched with John Anderson; he said he was very sorry indeed to leave the Home Office [he had become lord president of the Council]; he felt he had been put out and that Morrison [now home secretary], who had not done well at Supply, thought he had been promoted. Told me Churchill remembered silly things against me such as the old rows about the allocation of political time on the radio. He evidently regards Churchill as a menace in some respects.

8 October 1940 Saw Beaverbrook and thanked him for his letter. In it he said 'you will have a big administrative job before long'. Maybe he was referring to India.
    Saw H. J. Wilson about Douglas but he won't let him go and I don't know that I care as I shall just act as director general myself and leave Duff as secretary.

9 October 1940 Meeting with Greenwood and Assheton at the House of Commons. I thought I should like Assheton as parliamentary secretary and that he would be better than anyone else owing to the work he had done. But Bevin doesn't want to let him go.

11 October 1940 Dined with CIGS. Bombs dropping and at dinner the nearest I have heard. Something fell in the kitchen next door and I heard there was some damage to the building. We went placidly on with dinner. I do like Dill.

15 October 1940 Saw Bevin about the Ministry terms of reference. Position most unsatisfactory and Beaverbrook ratting on his previous assurance.

Saw H. J. Wilson about staff at his request before and after a Cabinet which I attended at No. 10 about cement – silly performance.

16 October 1940 Called on Joe Kennedy who asked to see me. He is going to US on Tuesday [22 October] by air and quite clearly doesn't intend returning. And he might be a tower of strength in this country's hour of need. I told him it was a good thing to have an American Ambassador even if he was only 'sitting around'. The US military attaché whom I met said he had refrained from drawing Kennedy's attention to his French colleague's remark that a dead US ambassador in Paris was better than a live one in Bordeaux. He evidently despised J.K.

17 October 1940 PM's meeting [of ministers] 5.30 to 6.45. He never shows any friendliness to me and I therefore dislike him intensely which is a pity – especially as he reminds one so much of myself in his methods.

18 October 1940 Message at 8.00 a.m. that the Treasury had had a direct hit. Saw Barlow and Duff about the Ministry terms of reference and felt very angry about them. Saw Anderson and Barlow about this and determined on action – paper by me for Cabinet. Went into the Treasury and saw the damage. Ghastly. Three or four fellows killed including one who was to have come to the Ministry.

19 October 1940 Beaverbrook wanted to find a place where Churchill could live safely. He phoned me twice last night – such a fuss all out of proportion. I was back and forth several times. We went to look at the new Scotland Yard building much to P. Game's [commissioner of police] concern.

20 October 1940 Sickening to have to go to town [on a Sunday]. Same silly job. I picked up Beaverbrook and from 11.00 till 2.00 I was on this job; Curzon Street, Faraday House, Evening Standard building, Horseferry Road.

21 October 1940 A rotten day. Sickening meeting about the terms of reference – Attlee at 10.00 and 12.00 – and Beaverbrook badgering about building plans for Churchill's flat.

22 October 1940 Busy as usual. Visit to Beaverbrook to hear about buildings for the Cabinet.
    Another meeting with Attlee and Greenwood at which Malcolm MacDonald [minister of health] (accompanied as seems inevitable by Sir J. Maude [now permanent head of that Ministry]) was also present. I was a bit angry but we agreed a sentence about the future as follows:
    'It is clear that the reconstruction of town and country after the war raises great problems and gives a great opportunity. The minister of works and buildings has, therefore, been charged by the government with the responsibility of consulting the departments and organizations concerned with a view to reporting to the Cabinet the appropriate methods and machinery for dealing with the issues involved.'
    This is pretty comprehensive and I felt pleased about it.

23 October 1940 An awful lot of time wasted over Beaverbrook and his building for the prime minister and such like. He tried to put Trollope and Colls to work at Faraday House on top of the proper contractors. Apart from the blasted interference they are the people who are going so slow on the Evening Standard flat and the one in the Board of Trade as to call for special reprimand! Impossible fellow. Really the china shop bull.

29 October 1940 Went to see Faraday House and had to pay a second visit with Beaverbrook; also Church House with him and stirred things up so that Parliament can meet there if it wants to next Tuesday [4 Nov]. There was alarm today because bombs fell near Parliament. Don't know where I am with Beaverbrook and his buildings.

31 October 1940 [Ministers] meeting at No. 10. I don't think much of my 'colleagues'. No indeed.

2 November 1940 Saw Beaverbrook – usual business of several interviews proceeding simultaneously. The chairman [Sir Allan Powell], director general [F. W. Ogilvie], Ashbridge and Tallents of BBC arrived and there was an exceedingly funny meeting about commandeering Broad-casting House. I quite enjoyed it. I was moderately civil to Powell but stood off from the others. They made a poor show.

6 November 1940 I had to go to a Cabinet about Faraday House. Silly business, but interesting. The PM spoke most bitterly about the BBC – enemy within the gate; continually causing trouble; more harm than good. Something drastic must be done with them, he said. Duff Cooper (sitting next me) agreed – more control probably and they ought to be civil servants (!), but Broadcasting House should not be commandeered; already a bomb there and seven people killed. He said this twice but fortunately the PM knew about the bomb and said it was their own fault that people had been killed. Anyhow the Broadcasting House point is to come up next week and meantime Faraday House is to be used as Beaverbrook and I were arranging. The whole thing is ridiculous.

7 November 1940 Went to Church House – remarkable the work done and very odd to see the two Chambers – Woolsack, speaker's chair, mace brackets and all.
Saw also the old Office of Works place where Mr and Mrs Churchill are having a flat built.

13 November 1940 Saw Beaverbrook and made him very angry by telling him that Churchill had given orders direct to some Ministry of Works people to build a strong post. Dreadful the way Churchill splashes about.

14 November 1940 Meeting with Greenwood and many other ministers about the Production Council. An hour and a half and the confusion is ghastly. Much criticism of Beaverbrook as usual. Bevin said the PM had called him a magician, so he had replied that the magician's chief stock-in-trade was illusion. Beaverbrook told me he hoped I would be air minister.

15 November 1940 Dined with CIGS (with ADCs there). They are all very bored with Churchill and his 'Action this day' notes of which forty or fifty go out daily – seven or eight to CIGS.

19 November 1940 Nearly an hour watching the Beaverbrook circus this morning. He told me Churchill thought of appointing someone of ministerial rank to Washington for the purchasing. I wondered if I would like that job and thought on the whole not.

20 November 1940 Irritated all day. Beaverbrook barging in on other people's work. I sometimes think it is almost hopeless. The country is not free from blame for the inefficiency but it deserves a better government than it has got, and much better management.

22 November 1940 Beaverbrook told me I should go to USA as ministerial representative for purchases. I should like this except that Muriel does not like the country.

26 November 1940 Churchill inhabits the Faraday House flat tonight and Beaverbrook dines there. He might have asked me but hasn't the decency or grace to do so.

27 November 1940 One of Churchill's women snoopers was over yesterday for two hours badgering Beaver and Wolmer[18] about cement – his Gestapo. Disgusting it all is.

29 November 1940 Meeting with Greenwood about cement. He said Beaverbrook was Public Enemy No. 1 and Churchill's Gestapo No. 2.
    Dined with CIGS. He is very fed up with Churchill and everybody loathes the whole Churchill entourage. PM goes away on Thursday now. Beaverbrook told me yesterday that he was in a highly nervous state. So I can well believe.

2 December 1940 Lunched with Barrington-Ward. He told me there was a growing dislike of Churchill's entourage. Each evening on the journey home I am mostly occupied in trying to get into proper adjustment with God. Tonight I felt sure this country could only be saved by the Lord and that that would only be if the country were worthy of it. We need the fear of the Lord upon us – not the fear of the enemy. I keep wondering if there is something I might do.

4 December 1940 Feeling *very* disgusted with Churchill and his cabal and the government and the system and everything. Feeling as if I would not stay in the political racket, and very bloody-minded about everything.

9 December 1940 Sent PM a note about my Reconstruction paper. To my surprise I had a memo from him approving it and asking me to arrange with Bridges how it should be handled.

13 December 1940 It was a considerable shock to see in the papers this morning that Lothian had died. I would like this post more than I can say. Laid my desire before the Lord. After a good deal of doubt told Beaverbrook. I hope I shan't be disappointed.

16 December 1940 Couldn't put my mind on anything properly with the USA business. Had an appointment with Halifax but he had to go to see the PM; I was very disgusted having resolved to say something about USA. Saw Butler and had a talk with him and he said he would tell Halifax I wanted to go to USA. Went home at 4.30 and straight to bed having no dinner. Didn't sleep.

17 December 1940 Meeting of ministers to hear a very complacent story from Churchill. At the end Woolton said there was a serious situation coming over food but Churchill didn't take it up.

18 December 1940 Keep trying to be in touch with God about this USA business. I ought not to ask to go, but having said I want to go, ask to be reconciled to God's will.

19 December 1940 Dined with CIGS. Very disgusted at PM having apparently forgotten that a few months ago he had tried to sack Wavell [C-in-C Middle East], whom he now cracks up so much, Dill just saving him. Halifax is expected to go to USA.

23 December 1940 Halifax goes to Washington, Eden to Foreign Office and Margesson to War Office. Weird this last, but it confirms that Churchill only wants sycophants in the Service ministries.

31 December 1940 Weird memo from the PM, which John Anderson hadn't seen, recasting the committees, abolishing Production and Economic Policy Councils – possibly to get Greenwood shelved, but

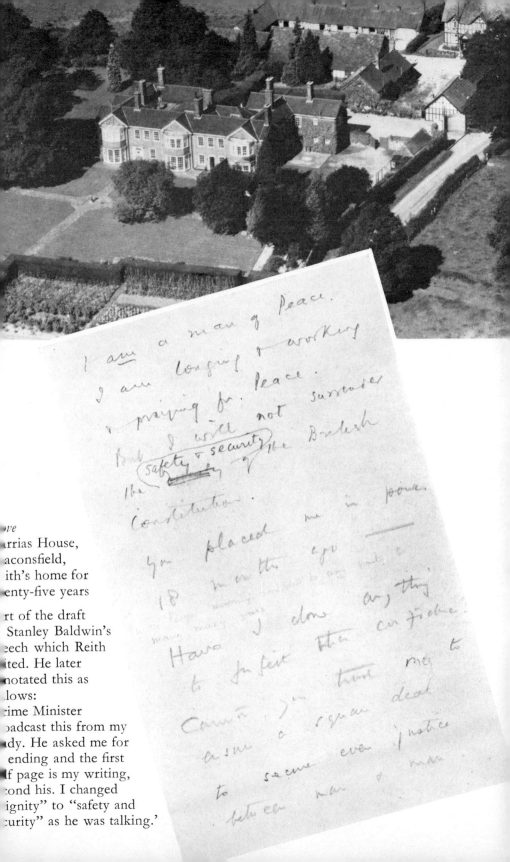

ve
...rrias House,
...aconsfield,
...ith's home for
...enty-five years

...rt of the draft
...Stanley Baldwin's
...eech which Reith
...ited. He later
...notated this as
...lows:
...ime Minister
...oadcast this from my
...dy. He asked me for
...ending and the first
...f page is my writing,
...cond his. I changed
...ignity" to "safety and
...curity" as he was talking.'

John Reith and Sir John Simon, February 1934

John Reith and Montagu Norman, February 1938

putting him on to post-war problems – apparently absorbing Attlee's fatuous committee, but with what effect on my job wasn't clear. Anderson said this was all very disquieting – the Labour racket and Churchill's personality. I added to it by saying I had already suspected that the Labour people were wanting to collar the kudos of my job.

Committee meeting 3.00 to 4.15, Attlee, Greenwood, MacDonald, Brown [secretary of state for Scotland], Anderson and I. Muddled but fairly satisfactory end as I was asked to get legislation to stop speculation in land and to get an enquiry going into development acquisition. So ends 1940. I suppose the worst year of my life in many ways.

[In 1941 John Reith entered on his final period as a Cabinet minister. He seems now to have cut himself off from the progress of the war. As he himself later admitted: 'I knew little or nothing about what was happening in spheres other than my own.' Nevertheless he remained profoundly critical of Churchill, finding support for his disapproval from Sir John Dill and to a lesser extent from R. M. Barrington-Ward of *The Times*. At the same time, his long struggle to establish his Ministry as the central authority for post-war planning brought him into conflict with both political parties. The Conservatives feared that he would undermine the rights of property in land; the Socialists that in so doing he would steal their thunder. The Conservatives wanted nothing done; the Socialists nothing done save by themselves. Yet John Reith stood, above all, for getting things done and in his own way; so a collision was inevitable. Nor could he call on any large store of goodwill within the civil service to soften this ministerial clash because here his relationships had been worsened by struggles over the staffing and organization of his ministry. In all this he had a new friend in Sir John Anderson who, as lord president of the Council, supervised the departments of state concerned with the home front. Anderson helped and guided him and above all cautioned him against his contemptuous treatment of his ministerial colleagues. Unfortunately, he would not listen. When, early in 1942, Churchill's government was shaken by disasters in the Far East, John Reith, for all his success in launching the Ministry of Works and Planning, was isolated and expendable.]

8 January 1941 Went to see Greenwood whom I found in much depression about himself. He was very sick at the way he had been treated by the PM – having had a note about the changes only when they were settled and about to be issued. He had written a very feeble paper about my ministry, war and post-war. I asked him if he had had any reply from Churchill about my joining the War Aims committee; he hadn't. I said if he gave me the proper scope for my work I would carry on all right in conjunction with him in his comprehensive brief. He said certainly. He said also he thought Anderson's committee should fade out, but I said No – it should first get me into proper perspective vis-à-vis the other departments – institutionalizing me and my ministry. He agreed but he was almost inconsequent. Blames Beaverbrook.

Later I gave Anderson an account of the Greenwood meeting. He said Greenwood saw considerable prejudice to his political career 'whereas neither you nor I care what happens'.

10 January 1941 Meeting 11.15 to 12.15 with LCC people, with Malcolm MacDonald and Moore Brabazon [minister of transport] present. Likely to be exceedingly important. I suggested a committee of officials from LCC and Ministries of Works, Health and Transport – also with City included. Immensely significant this – the first real move to a planning of London.

3.00 p.m. meeting of Reconstruction committee. It went quite well and people see that I am getting ahead.

14 January 1941 Reconstruction committee 3.00 to 4.30. Such a lot of talk and I never spoke at all till directly questioned by chairman and then I said I didn't understand. Greenwood was trying to get himself into a proper job.

27 January 1941 Lunch with Camrose. A US editor there, over with Willkie.[19] Absolutely damning about Halifax's appointment and voicing every criticism of it which I had myself in mind. The man's own opinion was prejudiced by the fact that he seemed to have formed a favourable opinion of Bracken! Heaven help us.

28 January 1941 Went with Anderson and H. Morrison to Claridges to find almost all the Cabinet there, guests of Beaverbrook to meet W. Willkie from USA. I had imagined there would only be ten or so. Don't like gatherings of this sort. Churchill flamboyant and hollow. Willkie glib and rather patronizing and kept shaking his head while talking.

31 January 1941 Dined with CIGS. He told me he had tried hard to get me made secretary of state for war. I thought perhaps he might have done so. He said the PM dealt far too much with detail and seemed often unable to appreciate or understand major issues. One minute out of ten was perhaps useful – occasionally very good. A great part of the time of responsible ministers was taken up in dealing with silly minutes from the PM. He himself was continually having to argue with him. I asked if on balance the PM did more harm than good – i.e. more nuisance and upset to those running the war than benefit from public opinion of him. He thought it a very moot point – in fact if I hadn't switched off that point I am sure he would have said more harm than good which is what I feel.

17 February 1941 Lunched accidentally with Malcolm MacDonald. He is very sick at being pushed off to Canada by Churchill [as UK high commissioner]. He says Churchill doesn't approve of various things he has done and that the Labour minister wanted him out as revenge on his father.

8 March 1941 Talk with Kingsley Wood, who had asked me to come and see him, mostly about the War Damage Commission and its relationship with me and my job. Saw Anderson also who said he was always delighted to see me. I asked if I should tell the PM I wanted to see him but he thought not unless I had something I wanted him to do, which I certainly have not. 'Curious fellow,' Kingsley Wood said he was.

15 March 1941 Talked with Anderson about the Ministry of Health people's intention to stimulate local authorities to produce plans; he said he would absolutely stop that. So far so good. But we must get the form of the new authority through quickly.

17 March 1941 Greenwood's Location of Industry committee. They talked for an hour and then he said, 'Lord Reith has been silent as usual.' This was at 4.05 and by 4.15 the room was empty. They all agreed with me and I got what I wanted.

18 March 1941 Silly note round from Churchill about committees saying that he had discovered that about eight hundred were meeting so the number had to be reduced by twenty-five per cent and the number of persons attending ditto. Designed for publicity of course.

25 March 1941 Saw H. J. Wilson who told me that Churchill was emphatic that there ought to be a civil servant at the head of my Ministry. But Beaver could be equal with the official head. Dyarchy.

They had resolved that Sir G. Whiskard should be brought back from UK Commissionership in Australia to be secretary of my Ministry. I asked if he was being moved to permit some ex-minister being appointed there but was assured this wasn't so.[20]

1 April 1941 Meeting with Anderson and Ernest Brown [now minister of health] – quite useless – Brown being so quick-tempered and the whole Ministry of Health attitude to planning – 'sidetracked' he called it – quite hopeless.

7 April 1941 Budget – though I didn't know about it. There was a meeting of ministers to hear details but I had the American Ambassador [J. G. Winant] at that time and I wouldn't have gone anyhow.

14 April 1941 I suppose my diary has seldom been so uninteresting as it is these days. There are various reasons for this – one that I am so disgusted with politics and politicians and have such a dislike and distrust of the present 'direction'. I may be (though I know I am not) in a minority of one but that would make no difference to the strength of my views that Churchill and the Churchill entourage and method are a menace to the country.

15 April 1941 Lunched by accident with Geoffrey Dawson. He was very disgusted with the government and wishing Smuts [prime minister of South Africa] could come to this country. He says (as I know) that the War Cabinet is no use at all. We have a war lord and a press lord in control and he thinks it most unsatisfactory and so do I.

16 April 1941 Dined at the Athenæum where I had a room for some nights. An air-raid warning went at 9.10 and it was odd that this should have been my first night in town since war began as it was the worst night London had had. Bombs were dropped all night long. I looked out at various times and then went somewhat puzzled to bed about 11.00. The other members staying had gone down to the bunks in the billiard room corridor. There were several bombs quite close and three times I hastily transferred the pillow from below my head to above it. I went out in my dressing-gown and pyjamas at 12.00 and again at 1.00, on the latter occasion going with a policeman into the middle of Waterloo Place where, on his giving the alarm of the advent of a whistling bomb, I left one bedroom slipper in the roadway. Went to the bunks at 2.10 as nobody could sleep on top. Got up at 7.00.

2 May 1941 Disgusting news that Beaverbrook has been made 'minister of state' – a sort of No. 2 to Churchill presumably. I don't know whether this is primarily to have him away from the Ministry of Aircraft Production where he has caused such confusion or to have him as No. 2. Moore Brabazon goes to MAP where he will certainly be interfered with by Beaverbrook. Really revolting it all is. Shipping and Transport are to join which is in line with what I suggested nearly a year ago.

Sunday 11 May 1941 The fact of no telephone communication to London sent me in. Pall of smoke and dirt. St Columba's gutted. Houses of Parliament in an awful state. The Commons anyhow won't be used again. Didn't have breakfast or lunch. Walked over the ruined House of Parliament and then to the Abbey.

12 May 1941 Went over the House of Parliament with Churchill, calling for him at No. 10. His henchman Beaverbrook accompanied and B. Bracken arrived in time to rush up and be photographed with the PM, I having got out of the way. He said it was typical of Hitler's fury against any democratic organization that he should have destroyed the House of Commons – as if the Germans had been able to direct their bombs so accurately as to get the chamber itself. He was certain he would never speak again in that place.

16 May 1941 Set to do a bit of lobbying about the silly Greenwood committee next Wednesday [21 May] on the Uthwatt report.[21] Saw Henderson, Greenwood and Brown today. Hudson [minister of agriculture] thought I would be wise to go very slowly. Greenwood had infuriated me by issuing a paper without any word to me – a hopelessly wordy thing too – and had a long-winded excuse for doing so. Brown tried to be agreeable.

19 May 1941 Saw Anderson about the Greenwood committee and what I should do at that. I told him I imagined he might be prime minister. Saw Greenwood again. Talked with Leitch [deputy secretary of the Ministry of Works] about the organization and told him it was like pushing a hay-stack. Hopeless the civil service and politics.

21 May 1941 Greenwood's silly committee 3.30 to 5.00. They all sheep-like followed Kingsley Wood in resisting the early establishment of a central authority. This would be a good thing for me to resign on. Anderson may get the thing through but I doubt it.

22 May 1941 Saw Anderson at 6.30. He really agrees with me that Greenwood's handling of the central planning business is lamentable as to chairmanship and contemptible as to weakness.

27 May 1941 Balfour of Burleigh[22] in and talked about the line I was to take with that blasted Greenwood committee. He said I should certainly resign rather than read the draft statement which Kingsley Wood and Greenwood had prepared.

9 June 1941 Dined with CIGS who is in a little maisonette in the same block now, having had a narrow escape indeed. He thinks we will lose Syria and Egypt and all the Mediterranean. He thinks we might [not] be invaded till September and that meantime Germany will be at war with Russia.

10 June 1941 Lord president's committee – quite weird. Listened to arguments from ministers who had opposed me before and were now quoting my own remarks. Dirty work. And Greenwood has issued a shockingly dishonest document. And he is trying hard to collar the job I have in planning and reconstruction. Dirty work indeed.

12 June 1941 The minutes of Anderson's meeting [i.e. lord president's committee] say that he would consult with Greenwood and with other ministers concerned. I told [Sir Norman] Brook [personal assistant to the lord president] that if he agreed it was inaccurate and unfair but tactful, I would not mind. He said it was certainly the first and third.

17 June 1941 Spoke to Brook and said I wanted to see Anderson. Saw him at 7.15 and he told me what had been happening – how he had got the silly Kingsley Wood, Brown and Greenwood to eat their words and come to the conclusion they did at the lord president's committee; how since he had tried for a committee [i.e. on planning and recon-struction] with myself as chairman, but that Brown was objecting and also the Conservative party. Oh damnable.

He said he would be most uncomfortable and unhappy if he had to be PM. Not at all the man for it, he said.

22 June 1941 Germany marched against Russia today! Churchill is broadcasting at the moment and the others are listening to him. Not I.

23 June 1941 Dined with Barrington-Ward at the Athenæum. Quite interesting talk. Churchill's credit impaired and considerable uneasiness.

4 July 1941 Dined with Montagu Norman at the Athenæum. Very critical of everything. Said we weren't beginning to get organized for war. Kingsley Wood was quite useless and never had any ideas of his own.

[On 17th July 1941 John Reith announced in the House of Lords the government's decisions for post-war reconstruction. The recommendations of the Uthwatt committee on compensation and betterment were adopted and a Council of Ministers was established consisting of himself, as chairman, the secretary of state for Scotland and the minister of health with the responsibility of seeing that planning legislation should proceed in conformity with long-term planning policy pending the establishment of a central planning authority in its final form.]

7 August 1941 Prepared for first meeting of Council of Ministers which I hadn't exactly looked forward to but it went very well. Fifty minutes only and I did well in the chair.

8 August 1941 Southwood [chairman of Odhams Press] informed me the day before yesterday that Churchill had gone to meet Roosevelt off the American coast. Nice for a minister to be told this by a press man, but I let on that I knew.

25 August 1941 Saw Greenwood and found that he was in favour of no central authority but only a board of ministers, all the departments retaining executive power! Upside down this is. I wrote to Anderson about it.

26 August 1941 A meeting of ministers was summoned for tonight at 5.00 to be addressed by Churchill. I did not go. I simply couldn't bear to sit and listen to that impostor and menace and see all the sycophantic smilings and noddings of heads around me.

27 August 1941 Council of Ministers: Brown had all sorts of objections to my appointing the regional chairman for planning purposes but I said it was within my personal authority and I was going to do it. I got the thing through quite amicably but very firmly.

2 September 1941 Dined with CIGS. Scathing comment on Churchill's invariable habit of putting the blame on the chiefs of staff whenever he could but of giving them no credit when things went right and contrary to his expectations. CIGS said he had never known subordinates treated as Churchill treats them. Contemptible he said.

4 September 1941 Went all over the Great George Street underground. Churchill and his favourites will be safe from any bombing.

16 September 1941 Lunched with Lord Bennett [former prime minister of Canada] at the Savoy and had quite an interesting talk – most damning it was. He said Beaverbrook was as much a puppet in the hands of Churchill as anyone else. Churchill would have only yes-men about him. Of course I could do far better than most any of them. He said the war was a very secondary consideration with lots of them. (It is No. 5 in my view: (1) their own interests personally; (2) their particular preconceptions, prejudices and partialities; (3) their political party; (4) friends and relatives; and (5) country.) He said that though power might be concentrated in the executive rather than in Parliament, it was an executive of twenty or thirty which is absolutely true. I can't get things done because of blasted departmental particularism.

I have been asked to approve £450 odd for wines etc. on the *Prince of Wales* for Churchill and Co., under guise of entertainment of foreigners. I wonder how much of it Roosevelt drank. Today I was asked to approve £1300 for a special train for Beaverbrook and Co. going to the north of Scotland en route for Moscow. I hope Beaverbrook gets killed en route. It would be a splendid release and escape for this country. And this also is under guise of entertainment of foreigners.

18 September 1941 Saw Anderson and got a little lecture from him about not going to ministers' meetings and leaving things to Hicks [parliamentary secretary to the Ministry of Works] to do that I wasn't interested in. All with some point but absurd that a senior minister should have to footle about with detail. He said he thought my memoranda were too abrupt and harsh! Oh gosh, how bloody it all is. He said other ministers liked me personally but not as a colleague. So they damn well shouldn't.

25 September 1941 Saw Kingsley Wood for three-quarters of an hour. He was very friendly and agreed that there had better be a statutory authority for control planning and that it might be done by the end of the year.

29 September 1941 Dined with Barrington-Ward at Travellers. He assumes the editorship of *The Times* the day after tomorrow. I told him what I thought of that job – unique and with a prestige, dignity, responsibility, authority and independence quite of its own. My job at the BBC as I left it is the nearest comparable but that is quite a new one. Talked about the Churchill-Beaverbrook racket. He counselled me still to be patient.

1 October 1941 Went for the first time in a year to the Civil Defence committee. Morrison sent a note to Hicks – 'Very glad you have brought your boss but don't look so glum.'

2 October 1941 Dined with John Dill. He showed me an album of pictures of the Atlantic business. I shuddered with anger and irritation and disgust at the pictures of Churchill and Beaverbrook. Dill said, 'Our empire is worth saving. We must save it if we can from what others may do with it.' – 'What do you mean?' I asked. There was a picture of Churchill on the page before us. He stabbed it with his thumb. 'That.'[23] And he feels to Beaverbrook as I do – Evil – though he gives him a duality, one of which is Presbyterian.

9 October 1941 Council of Ministers at which we discussed the Town Planning Bill. There is not to be a finance clause so I shall probably start it off in the Lords which I should like.

10 October 1941 Saw Greenwood about a paper he had circulated recommending a council for policy and a ministry for planning. This is a great principle advanced. We need to make many alterations to give more power to the ministry and to eliminate messiness.

20 October 1941 Beaverbrook – to no one is the vulgar designation shit more appropriately applied – telephoned about park railings and annoyed me very much. I will tell Anderson about it.

28 October 1941 Letter from the swine Beaverbrook about park railings which I answered in similar shape telling him he had no power over crown property. GOC London doesn't want the railings down anyhow.

3 November 1941 Kingsley Wood asked me to see him about Greenwood's paper. I told him what my objections were and he said he would read my paper very carefully. He has evidently heard from Greenwood that I was objecting. As Brown has written to Bevin in protest against my remarks about local authorities and ARP, I am in trouble all round!

6 November 1941 Greenwood's miserable committee taking the paper on the Development Council and the Ministry. There were about thirty people there talking a lot. Bevin made an utter ass of himself not having read the papers and being incapable of understanding what was said to him. I didn't say anything till called on by Kingsley Wood. He supported me against an absolutely idiotic remark by Greenwood that the Ministry should not be specially named as part of the central authority.

19 November 1941 Went to see Jack Dill whose retiral from CIGS was announced today. He had known nothing about it a week ago. (He announced that he went with regret but no bitterness – which made it obvious that he wasn't going of his own volition.) He said it would not have happened if Eden had been at the War Office still. I said it would not have happened if I had been there. He had not wanted to be made governor of Bombay at all but thought that Churchill felt this would lessen criticism of his action. He had also asked not to be made a field marshal as there was no vacancy but they had put this through. He said the Army Council knew nothing of it till they saw it in the papers today. He said Wavell and Auchinleck [the new C-in-C Middle East] were delighted when he said, 'Don't worry, you have my complete confidence.' If the new CIGS [Sir Alan Brooke] said that they would tell him to go to hell. He is very sorry and disgusted. The Bombay job isn't vacant till 25 September 1942. 'I can't join the Home Guard,' he said.

26 November 1941 Meeting with Greenwood, Kingsley Wood and John Anderson about Greenwood's draft for the Cabinet. I secured by the help of Anderson and Wood the insertion of several sentences which had been left out and the elimination of an objectionable paragraph. Greenwood is a bad lot. At the end Anderson said he objected to the terms of reference of the 'Executive' [i.e. the proposed Development Council] as making the new ministry much too subordinate to it. Well this is what I had said all along.

28 November 1941 Saw Churchill at 6.00. He was wearing overalls – a kind of battle dress – of dark blue. Odd sort of conversation as it began by his asking if I had read Anderson's report. I said his proposals were mine. He said he thought it wasn't necessary to go beyond me for the additional responsibility and I said I was glad. It seemed to me that he didn't really know the matter at all. I don't think he had any idea of the amount of building the Ministry of Works does. I said I would take on all building if he liked and that it would be better if I did. Gave me a direction to read which seemed all right. I was friendly and smiled and he beamed at me. Damnable that I should feel to him as I do and that he has so deserved it.

[On 8 December John Reith noted baldly 'War with Japan now', adding 'Parliament met but I didn't know of it.']

10 December 1941 Saw Anderson who is very worried about the war and agreed that it was a tragic mistake to cancel the Anglo-Jap alliance. *Prince of Wales* in which Churchill did his pompous American stunt was sunk today by the Japs. Also *Repulse*. Awful.

14 December 1941 Thinking about a 'suicide' speech – suicide politically or anyhow as a member of this government.

17 December 1941 Dined with the Governor of the Bank of England. Very interesting and dignified. I told them what I thought of things and about my suggested speech on democracy, politics, politicians, local authorities, education and civil service. They were delighted with my views.

21 December 1941 I was in a vile temper with the hopelessness of things at home and in the office. I was feeling in dreadful bad form, inclined to scrap my whole diary. I kicked this volume across the study last thing at night.

23 December 1941 Saw Greenwood about the Ministry bill. He said he thought I should have another parliamentary secretary on the planning side. He was muddled about finance.

Lunch with Swinton and R. A. Butler about reconstruction issues generally, the latter being chairman of the Conservative party reconstruction committee. They were impressed by my views about democracy and such like.

31 December 1941 Co-ordinating minister required for Washington. I don't think I want the job.

13 January 1942 Lunched with London Master Builders but left at 2.50. I think it didn't finish till about 4.00. Huge crowd. I had been asked to speak but declined. Probably I ought to have.

14 January 1942 Lunched with Balfour of Burleigh. I asked him if he thought I was wrong in so much resenting the below the second salt kind of ministerial meetings such as I did not attend yesterday. He thought I was.

16 January 1942 Miserable day. I went to lunch at the Athenæum but was in too bad form to have it. Disgusted almost beyond endurance and very unhappy. I often wish I were dead. What leadership is needed – and I might have given it – a lot of it, but I don't feel I want to now, nor able. I am amazed at the condition in which I am.

25 January 1942 Reading *Berlin Diary* [by W. L. Shirer, the American journalist]. Amazing how Churchill – the one chiefly responsible for the Norway fiasco – should have ousted Chamberlain over it. He is due some trouble now for unpreparedness in the Far East.

28 January 1942 Churchill made a long and according to Anderson dull speech yesterday on a vote of confidence. More criticism of the government all day today. The beast Beaverbrook was to broadcast which is obviously an attempt to influence the end of the debate. We turned off quickly to avoid the pollution of a word by him in this home.

30 January 1942 Cripps[24] to be minister of supply and Beaverbrook production minister – absolutely damnable. Spoke with Duncan, Bevin and Moore-Brabazon in the afternoon. Brab said he hadn't been consulted and knew nothing whatever. Said he had a beastly time with Beaverbrook criticizing his output – apparently as I had expected when Beaverbrook left the Ministry of Aircraft Production he retained some supervisory powers over it. Brab spoke with great feeling. 'We might have been playing golf for a fortnight past judging by the comments.' Bevin said he had been sacked from Production. He thought Beaverbrook would do what the Production Executive had done about priorities so that I would have to work to him on that. Duncan has some personal angle on the matter but he did not think the Board of

Trade of the Works Ministry would be affected as such. I wonder whether he is going up in the world.[25] Felt absolutely miserable all day. Gosh, how bloody awful everything is.

2 February 1942 No announcement about the miserable production minister business and all kinds of rumours.

5 February 1942 Saw Beaverbrook at 12.15. How loathesome. He showed me his terms of reference [i.e. as minister of production]. He has been defeated by the Admiralty. But he has a reference to building programmes all right. He said he wanted to help not hinder. I said I hoped he would support Greenwood's paper at the Cabinet tonight; he didn't know about it. I left after ten minutes.

Met Attlee and told him I had read his paper on India with interest. Attack on Amery [secretary of state for India] and viceroy. Saw Alexander (First Lord). He told me about his struggle to keep Beaverbrook out of the Admiralty. Bombastic but very friendly. Dinner in the Athenæum as I had been asked to stand by at short anchor for the Cabinet. But as I expected with India and Russia on the agenda the buggers (that is how I feel) never reached my item. Infuriated to think of the bunch that were settling our Indian policy and Russian. Ghastly. Bloody awful.

6 February 1942 Got the terms of reference for Beaverbrook's job for comment – the paper he had shown me yesterday. It is a muddled document and the whole situation is hopelessly muddled. But I am well out of it in the document and I am not drawing anyone's attention to the confusions and indefinitenesses.

9 February 1942 Blasted Cabinet about Greenwood's paper. Churchill was against a separate ministry but almost all the others were in favour of it when Morrison arrived and quite inconsequently, arising out of the complexity of dealing with local authorities, said a new ministry wasn't necessary but the planning power should either stay with Health or go to Works. I said I would rather have had a separate ministry but could do with the powers being transferred to me if the name of the ministry was changed. When asked if I thought the Samuels and such like would be satisfied, I said I supposed it was up to me to make them. The Development Executive got toned down greatly – but it really wasn't clear to what.

10 February 1942 Lunched with Barrington-Ward. I gave him the official statement about the Ministry. He said Beaverbrook was in his last job and he seemed to think that Churchill was in a pretty poor way. The announcement about Beaverbrook had gone badly – as it damn well ought.

11 February 1942 Much arguments yesterday about the official statement. It is very good and Greenwood's 'National Development Executive' has been dropped altogether. The emphasis is all on my job. Lobby conference at 12.15, then lunch at House of Lords before the debate which lasted till about 5.00.

> [John Reith's statement in the House of Lords announced the establishment of his Ministry with extended powers under its new title of Ministry of Works and Planning and the dissolution of the Council of Ministers set up in July 1941. He was 'institutionalized' at last.]

12 February 1942 Discovered that Greenwood was trying to get the nomination of the chairmanship of my committee [this was to be a committee of senior officials representing all departments of state affected by the new ministry's planning powers]. Anderson told me to tell Greenwood to go to hell.

13/14 February 1942 Trying to get a move on about the new Ministry. Whiskard moves much too slowly and is far too soft.

Very angry with H. J. Wilson and pretty disgusted with everything. Sometimes I think I can't stand the civil service and politics for another week.

17 February 1942 Churchill's stock is low now. He had a bad show in the House of Commons today.

18 February 1942 6.30 to 7.50 at No. 10. Churchill (who was looking awful) gave us bits of news about the war. Six divisions against the Jap twenty-four. 106,000 troops in Singapore; 60,000 captured. Where are the rest? And very bad work in letting the Japs in so quickly and easily. Duff Cooper there, just back.[26] Churchill asked him to talk in the secret session obviously with a view to his saying there were plenty of troops in Singapore so that it shouldn't have been taken. He said it was obvious that his job must come to an end when a generalissimo was appointed.

Churchill said he was making considerable changes but did not say what they were. He said he was going to give up the leadership of the House of Commons and that it was better to yield to public pressure. Such sycophantic attitude on the part of Simon, Woolton, Leathers [minister of war transport] and all. Leathers has the manners and attitude of a shop walker. I loathe these meetings. I expect Churchill will have his favourites around him still.

20 February 1942 The blasted War Cabinet changes announced today. Beaverbrook, thank goodness, seems to be dropping out – going to the USA.

Saturday 21 February 1942 Busy morning. I felt last night that I might like my work; but not this morning. 3.10 home. Very cold. Letter from Churchill giving me the sack. Telephoned to Anderson who was greatly shocked; also to Balfour of Burleigh ditto. Anderson asked me to come and see him which was decent of him. I got to him at 9.15 and left about 10.30. He was awfully nice and I was grateful to him. He urged me, as Balfour of Burleigh did, to write a note at once to Churchill resigning. I wondered if I should not do nothing, in which case I should have to be dismissed by the King. But I wrote the letter in the office – my last visit there I imagine. Read it to Anderson and he had me put in another two lines.

NOTES

1. Sir Campbell Stuart was head of the department for propaganda in enemy countries subordinate to the Foreign Office. John Reith wanted to bring him and it under the Ministry of Information.

2. Russia had invaded Finland at the end of November 1939 and the Finns had successfully defended themselves. The British and French were uncertain whether or not to send troops across Norway and Sweden to support Finland, finally deciding to do so only to find that the Finns had accepted Russia's terms.

3. Sir Horace Wilson had succeeded Sir Warren Fisher as head of the Treasury and Civil Service while retaining his special service with the prime minister. Churchill soon ended this.

4. Lord Chatfield gave up as minister for co-ordination of defence and the office lapsed. Hoare became air minister and Kingsley Wood, lord privy seal. The only other important change was the introduction of Lord Woolton as minister of food.

5. In his autobiography (*Into the Wind*, p. 379) John Reith claimed that he told Margesson 'the government would fall in a week or two, or at any rate have to be radically reconstructed'. This is hardly consistent with his own version of what he said to Chamberlain the next day.

6. Sir Henry Page Croft, soon to be Lord Croft, had been a Conservative MP

since 1918. His loyalty to Chamberlain did not harm him as he was parliamentary secretary at the War Office, 1940–5. Sir Archibald Southby, a former government whip, had been a Conservative MP since 1928.

7. In 1948 John Reith corresponded with Sir Samuel Hoare, then Viscount Templewood, about the fall of Chamberlain's government. Reith appears not to have preserved the letters but in March 1950 he recorded in his diary:

Sam Hoare's letter to me of 5.5.48 said he had welcomed a drastic reconstruction of the Cabinet in May 1940 after the attack in the Commons, even though he was sure that he and Kingsley Wood and Simon would be dropped . . . 'The whole time that I was in the War Cabinet I pressed for it. Unfortunately several of the people around Chamberlain obstinately opposed me. Time after time I told Chamberlain that I myself was prepared to go and to make way for someone more suited to war conditions. Between you and me K. Wood was one of my chief opponents. He wished things to remain as they were so long as he remained in the Cabinet.'

8. John Reith's account of the events of 9 and 10 May 1940 was privately challenged by L. S. Amery in 1954. The story is clarified with masterly precision by A. J. P. Taylor in *English History, 1914–45*, p. 474. Chamberlain saw Attlee and Greenwood on 9 May but not on 10 May. They did not answer his question, whether they would join the government under him or under someone else, but said they would put it to their National Executive in Bournemouth to decide. Their answer was sent from Bournemouth on 10 May; Labour would join the government but under a new prime minister. It is plain that the message at the morning Cabinet to which John Reith refers was not this answer; Attlee and Greenwood had not reached Bournemouth by then. Amery's conclusion was that:

the tape message may well have been some statement by Attlee and Greenwood or one of them as they left for Bournemouth in answer to a pressman who asked if the invasion of Holland had changed their attitude towards serving under Neville [Chamberlain].

9. Harcourt Johnstone had been out of parliament since 1935 and had to be found a seat. Sir Geoffrey Shakespeare was solaced by being transferred to the Dominions Office.

10. John Reith was provided with a parliamentary private secretary on 13 June; this was Sir Brograve Beauchamp, 'a decent fellow and very anxious to help', of whom he later added with characteristic contrariness, 'he is rather an embarrassment as there is nothing to do.'

11. This was Churchill's speech promising to 'go on to the end . . . we shall fight on the beaches' etc.

12. Two French battleships and a battlecruiser were sunk in port at Mers-el-Kebir by a British force under Admiral Somerville after protracted negotiations had failed to secure their surrender or transfer to the French West Indies.

13. Wilfrid (later Lord) Greene had been Master of the Rolls since 1937. John Reith wanted him to be chairman of the committee of enquiry he set up in 1941 into compensation and betterment, but was frustrated by the lord chancellor.

14. The German air bombardment of London at night began on 7 September.

15. The joint British and Free French expedition against Dakar had met with a series of misfortunes from the start and the war Cabinet had wished to abandon it on 17 September. John Reith's expectations of ill success were unfortunately fulfilled when the attack was made on 23/25 September.

16. John Reith's comment contains much truth. In the twentieth century only Baldwin and Attlee held office as prime minister after being lord president of the Council, but both Baldwin in 1935 and Attlee in 1945 were exceptional cases.

17. Lord Beaverbrook's memory played him false. Naaman went to Samaria, not Jerusalem; the prophet he sought was Elisha, not Elijah; and the therapeutic advice he obtained was to wash in the Jordan seven times, not three. See II Kings 5.

18. (Sir) Hugh Beaver, who was a consulting engineer with Sir Alexander Gibb, was John Reith's particular choice to be responsible for all technical work in his new ministry. In February 1941 he became director general, though not sole head. See *Into the Wind*, pp. 409–10. Lord Wolmer, later 3rd Earl of Selborne, was director of cement. Churchill's 'gestapo' was Lord Cherwell's statistical department.

19. Wendell Willkie had been the Republican candidate in the election for president of the USA in November 1940.

20. John Reith's suspicions were swiftly fulfilled; the merging in May of the Ministries of Transport and Shipping resulted in Sir Ronald Cross, the outgoing minister of shipping, being appointed to Whiskard's post.

21. John Reith had set up an expert committee under A. A. (later Lord) Uthwatt in January 1941. Its purpose was to report on the thorny problems of the payment of compensation and the recovery of betterment 'in respect of the public control of the use of land'. The committee made an interim report in April and John Reith was then faced with getting agreement on its recommendations from his ministerial colleagues.

22. Lord Balfour of Burleigh had become friendly with John Reith as a result of their common interest in planning and reconstruction. Over the next few years he was to give Reith much help and advice.

23. A month later John Reith recorded Dill's single exclamation 'Poor England'.

24. Sir Stafford Cripps had just returned from his service as ambassador in Moscow. He did not accept the offer to be minister of supply but was able to demand to enter the War Cabinet which he did as lord privy seal and leader of the House of Commons.

25. John Reith was right. Sir Andrew Duncan became minister of supply on 4 February. Moore-Brabazon was equally right; he lost his place in the government along with John Reith.

26. Duff Cooper had been replaced as minister of information in July 1941 and had been sent out as minister of state to the Far East. He proved no more effective in the second than in the first task.

CHAPTER SIX

John Reith and the Second War (2)

1. Interlude: Between Government and Admiralty, February–June 1942

IN the three months following his abrupt dismissal John Reith's diary is of particular interest for the light it throws on the extraordinary loss of confidence in Churchill's government now felt by those who were politically knowledgeable – a loss of confidence probably far in excess of that felt by the general public. Sir John Anderson and R. M. Barrington-Ward, the one a member of the Cabinet, the other by now Editor of *The Times*, both urged him not to commit himself to long-term employment on the grounds that the government could change at any moment. At the same time the diary reveals in poignant form the intense personal distress which John Reith suffered in his cruel situation, going to London daily *'just in case*, like other kinds of unemployed' and hearing from his friends how he was being 'sort of hawked around'. He hated politics, and yet he craved for political office. He was too proud to accept the consolatory crumbs offered by Churchill and too honest, perhaps also too politically naive, to follow the advice of the Editor of *Picture Post* and give himself nuisance value by attacking the government. The most he would do was to initiate in June a debate in the House of Lords on the future organization of public services. But already by mid-May he would wait no longer. If he was not wanted in government he would bury himself in some war work. So he offered, through a naval friend, to work in the headquarters of Coastal Forces command. Anderson and Barrington-Ward approved, arguing that if the political situation changed, he could be got out. John Reith was less hopeful and events were to prove him right. He did not leave the Navy until December 1944 and he never held political office again.]

27 February 1942 Invitation from Churchill to be Lord High Commissioner [to the General Assembly of the Church of Scotland]. I saw that there was a letter from his office but I didn't open it; took it up to

Muriel in bed with the others. Next time I went up she told me there was something to refuse 'from that cur'.

1/2 March 1942 I have no doubt that we were moving too fast and too far for other ministers concerned, so that they could cabal about lack of team spirit and such like. No doubt about it – the good work and growing authority of the Works side with consequent interference with freedom of other people – *delendus est*. Similarly with the planning side – still more *delendus*. And taken together the job was obviously very important and the most important of all after the war – so why should I have it – *delendus* urgent. Also Greenwood's going more bearable if I went too.[1] And no one to speak for me – no party.

Anderson has written, to my horror recommending that I accept the Lord High Commissionership but I certainly can't do it – not this year.

5 March 1942 Bracken [minister of information] asked me to do a job – wireless apparatus co-ordinator under Ministry of Supply. Insulting almost. I asked Anderson. 'Chickenfood,' he said at once, and to have nothing to do with it. He said things were in a most involved state and he thought I ought not to take on any commitments.

10 March 1942 Feeling absolutely awful and on razor-edge of frenzy. I am no company for home these days.

[From 18 to 29 March John Reith was seriously ill. 'What put me to bed,' he noted, 'was a very sore throat but it was my recent shock which made me liable and has prevented recovery. Always listening for the telephone . . .']

31 March 1942 I went to London feeling pretty awful. Met Balfour of Burleigh who said he was going to get busy and find me things to do. I told him not to bother; it is awfully kind of him. Then with Anderson for over an hour – his doing. Very decent and kindly but of course nothing out of it. He had thought Churchill might be out of office by this time and still thinks any major disaster such as the loss of Ceylon or a big naval defeat (Bay of Bengal) or occupation by Japs of Madagascar would effect this. (He added that in spite of everything he thought it would be a great misfortune as Hitler would have a triumph over it and Roosevelt and Stalin would regret it. I said nought.) Apparently he seemed sure I would be in any new administration. (Do

I want to?) I told him how I felt. And how easy is Woolton's job or Grigg's [as newly appointed war minister] and for quite different reasons – that the former has no civil service to bother about and the latter has brought the civil service under himself by having two under secretaries. He hoped I wouldn't attack Churchill in the House of Lords though he admitted I could say a few things. He still thought I would be well advised to hang on but that I could take some director-ships maybe – the sort that aren't offering. Said I certainly shouldn't take Bracken's job or anything under a minister. He told me that Churchill hadn't even seen Greenwood to give him his congé. What a coward he is.

16 April 1942 Lunched with Balfour of Burleigh. He had had a long talk with Montagu Norman who hoped I would keep clear of politics and go into an industrial job. I told B. I would be miserable in this line. Montagu Norman had said no civil servant would work with me if he could help it – which is as I would imagine and most creditable.

17 April 1942 Lunched with Barrington-Ward. He didn't think I ought to go into an industrial job. Thinks Cripps will be prime minister soon.[2] How dreadful. He urged me not to feel there was any prejudice or anything.

23 April 1942 Lunched with *Picture Post* editor and was very forth-coming with him. He said it was a great pity I had not done some advertising of myself. He thought I ought to create a nuisance value for myself. I said it wasn't in my line at all.

3 May 1942 Thinking of trying to get up energy enough to make a speech in the House of Lords about nationalization and civil service and corporations. I could work a lot into that.

15 May 1942 Saw Montagu Norman for an hour and a half. I tried three times to get away. He said no Boards that he knew of or thought any good would look at me. Quite hopeless position, I said. Fatuous interview, but he was very kind.

16 May 1942 Phoned Charles Meynell[3] to see if he could get me into Coastal Forces as a warrant officer – chief clerk or storekeeper or something like that, at a post where there was excitement and danger. He phoned me in the evening to say he had spoken to his Admiral and they wanted me to come and organize the command but I would need to be RNVR sub-lieutenant. I said I couldn't have a commission.

18 May 1942 I lunched with Charles Meynell and his Admiral Kekewich and I said I would join them if Anderson gave his OK. Commander RNVR he thought. I think it would be rather fun but I would have to keep nine-tenths of my mind frozen up. Spoke to Barrington-Ward who quite approved.

19 May 1942 Saw Anderson at noon in his House of Commons room. He said the PM was well disposed to me – forsooth – the cad. At lunch three or four weeks ago he had asked if he had made a mistake in putting me out. Anderson had said yes, and Kingsley Wood had assented. Churchill had said he must find something for me. And what is that worth? Anderson approved of my House of Lords motion and of my going to the Coastal Forces job. He said it wouldn't prejudice me at all and in no way contravened his desire that I shouldn't do anything that might, such as taking an unsuitable job. He said I could easily be got out – much chance.

House of Lords all afternoon. Quite interesting. And I wrote to Dudley Pound as advised by Kekewich. Oh well, it will be like a nightmare in which I think 'Have I really come down to this?'

21 May 1942 Lunched with Balfour of Burleigh in the House of Lords. Talked with B. about railways. There is a job that I would like to do, turning them into a corporation, but they wouldn't have the sense to get me to do it.

27 May 1942 Charles Meynell phoned. The Admiral saw the Second Sea Lord and the Admiral commanding reserves. They said I couldn't come in higher than lieutenant-commander. Damnable. Meynell was awfully disgusted with them.

28 May 1942 I phoned Meynell. He said his Admiral was quite frightened about my coming and had said today, 'We are playing with a strong personality and we must get things started right.' He said also that the deputy controller at the Admiralty had said it was a marvellous coup.

29 May 1942 Spent the whole morning with C. Meynell and Maurice, the maintenance captain.[4] They said they wanted me to organize their jobs for them. The muddle and confusion is quite dreadful and the position between them and the Admiralty is monstrous. Felt tired after five hours absorbing stuff. There is such microscopic detail for me to get down to. Oh gosh, what have I come to – that blasted thug Churchill responsible for it all.

30 May 1942 I feel I must rid myself of this House of Lords thing this weekend. It is frightfully hard to get down to it.

I got on quite well and finished the first draft of my speech. Worked on it till 2.10 a.m.

9 June 1942 To Town. Saw Barrington-Ward. He made several rather drastic amendments to my speech.

17 June 1942 Lunched at the House of Lords feeling very jittery. My speech was apparently a tremendous success. Selborne [minister of economic warfare] said that House of Lords debates had been on a high level but that a new level was reached today. I could have done much better – which just shows. Moore-Brabazon, Balfour of Burleigh, Bledisloe, Strabolgi and Samuel spoke.[5] And they all hoped I wouldn't be sitting on the cross-benches long.

Sunday, 28 June 1942 Muriel and I went to church – first time I had been since February. I was glad to go with her. I tried to get down to a wretched article for *Picture Post* but I couldn't write about what he wanted.

2. Admiralty: Coastal Forces and Naval Assistant to the Third Sea Lord, July 1942–July 1943

[In spite of the pessimism about his political future which had led John Reith to join the Navy, he continued to harbour hopes of gaining some important appointment for another twelve months. For a time, these hopes were nourished, as before, by the advice of Anderson and Barrington-Ward; but by the end of 1942 Anderson had changed his tune and even Barrington-Ward's encouragement had lost much of its confidence by early in 1943. As Churchill's government weathered the disasters of 1942, so John Reith's chances of political resurrection declined. He retained some political interest, as in post-war planning and civil aviation, and he even spoke in the House of Lords on the second of these in April 1943. But for the most part he withdrew from political activity as he lost hope of political employment,

It was against this background of disappointment and near despair that he completed his first tasks for the Navy. Within six months of joining he had secured the rationalization of Coastal Forces, organizing his Admiral and the chief staff officer who had recruited him out of their jobs and getting the supply side of this important functional service established as a department within the Admiralty. Then, after a period of inactivity, he was transferred to the staff of the Third Sea Lord, the Controller of the Navy (Admiral Sir William Wake-Walker), with the task of extending his reorganizing powers to the whole of the Admiralty departments subordinate to that officer. Thus, ironically, he was appointed to do for the Admiralty from below what, five years earlier, Hore-Belisha had hoped he would do for the War Office from above. But the essence of both these tasks was that, although important, they were short-term and, for one of John Reith's immense powers, almost part-time. Despite his low rank and minute pay he was working virtually as an expert adviser from outside. This was wholly changed when, at the end of June 1943, he agreed to take on, with the rank of Captain, the directorship of a new Admiralty department, the terms of reference for which he drafted himself, in charge of the material side of the Navy's part in Combined Operations. As this involved preparation for the invasion of Western Europe he was now committed to full-time, responsible and vitally important work 'for the duration'.]

7 July 1942 Feeling very depressed and so insensately jealous of the blasted politicians and so awful to be doing nothing at all myself. Lunched with Portal [the new minister of works] (or he with me, rather) at Brooks's. He was very forthcoming throughout and complimentary; wished we might meet weekly etc. Said someone had told him today that Churchill had said he wished so-and-so would happen for then he would be able to bring me back into the government.

4 August 1942 Awful day at the office with very little to do and I was seething with indignation about it all. Saw E. R. Stettinius [Lend-Lease administrator] at the US Embassy. He had never met anyone with a good word for Beaverbrook. He said he was all bluff and would give figures that meant nothing. As to Lyttelton [minister of production] he said he wasn't making a success of it at all and he didn't consider Eden the calibre for PM. Poor show all round and it made me feel more angry than ever.

14 August 1942 Lunched with John Anderson. He said he had suggested to Churchill I might go to the West African job Swinton went to. But he had sent Swinton because he wanted him out of his old job [as chairman of the national security executive] in order to put Duff Cooper into it. Disgusting. He said Churchill had asked him to put Duff Cooper on the lord president's committee but he had declined. Also said Churchill was afraid of Beaverbrook. Thought I should hang on in hope. Very decent and slightly encouraging.

18 August 1942 Saw Dudley Pound for nearly an hour. He was awfully friendly and forthcoming. I asked if he wanted me to talk frankly and he said he did. I told him they were making a fool of Rear Admiral Coastal Forces – that Coastal Forces should be a functional service with all that Submarines had. I went over all the points I had thought of in the morning – how important Coastal Forces were, how keen everybody was from Rear Admiral down, but feeble commanding officers at some bases, no tactical appreciations and so much responsibility without authority. He was most receptive and said he would deal with the thing himself. It seemed to be a most satisfactory interview.

27 August 1942 The Admiral had been summoned to see Dudley Pound who told him that the Deputy First Sea Lord had been given terms of reference to look into the Coastal Forces position which covered all the points I had given him.

2 September 1942 Went to see Jack Dill.[6] He was waiting on the pavement for me. His job is to ask for things from the US government and he said he had not had anything since he started asking. He said the ghastly inefficiency of British colonial government was now public property in America.

4 September 1942 Terribly weary of my ten foot square room and the footling work I do.

18 September 1942 Lunched with Barrington-Ward at the Travellers. He said there was great discontent in the government itself about Churchill. How ludicrous it is that people say 'who can succeed him?' It is highly undesirable that he should be succeeded. Nobody wanted who will behave as he does. Beaverbrook is high in favour, which is utterly damnable. B.-W. said that even Churchill-toadies like Leathers were very unhappy. He said he had no opinion now of Lyttelton (and

I reminded him that I had never had any at all); that Duncan had quite lost his nerve and that Alexander and Sinclair were nonentities and so forth. How awful it all is.

8 *October 1942* Balfour of Burleigh made me dine with him at the Great Northern and with someone who is in the so-called Production Ministry. I expressed myself with some freedom about Churchill and his rotten gang. I don't believe we can win the war with this essential rottenness at the centre, and Churchill is essentially rotten. He is the greatest menace we have ever had – country and Empire sacrificed to his megalomania, to his monstrous obstinacy and wrong-headedness. I am finding it more difficult to restrain myself in expression about him.

31 October 1942 Kennedy-Purvis, deputy First Sea Lord, telephoned to ask me to draft terms of reference for the Coastal Forces Maintenance Department in the Admiralty. A difficult job that. Charles Meynell thinks that I might be director of Coastal Forces Maintenance.

5/6 November 1942 I fairly got down to the miserable DCFM thing. It was a case of driving and forcing and by evening I had a draft all typed out. Phoned the maintenance captain [Maurice] about 10.15 and was astonished to find that he thought my document excellent. Much relief.

I had the whole thing nicely typed and gave it to the Admiral as I thought this would be polite though Kennedy-Purvis had asked me direct. It was a tremendous relief to have the whole thing done.

13 November 1942 I told Maurice that he ought to go and tackle the vice-controller [Vice-Admiral Sir Thomas Tower] who seems to be blocking the reorganization of Coastal Forces. (I met him yesterday at the Senior.) Maurice rang him up and he asked us both to come and see him. We argued for an hour and he changed his mind and had the decency to say so. He also said that he would tell Kennedy-Purvis so this afternoon. This he did for K.-P. rang up Meynell to tell him. We got a CFM Department inside Admiralty now. Charles Meynell is rather sad about it all. He has been very decent to me.

19 November 1942 Very slack in the office. Lunched with two members of BOAC at their request. 'When are you coming back to us, Sir John?' was how they introduced the subject. I said I did not want to go back except that such as they wished me to. I must do something about this with Anderson I suppose.

Went to the House of Lords. It was a farce. I was so angry that I nearly spoke and I could have made them laugh and the opposite. Dinner with Barrington-Ward. He was much disgusted with the government's attitude to reconstruction. As to myself he urged me to have patience.

22 November 1942 Changes in the government announced tonight. It gave me a great shock. Llewellyn goes to Washington, Cripps to Aircraft Production, Morrison in the War Cabinet, O. Stanley, Colonial Secretary and Cranborne, Lord Privy Seal.[7] Absolutely weird.

1 December 1942 Lunched with Portal and Balfour of Burleigh in the House of Lords. I hate going there and it brings out the worst in me – seeing people like Simon and Woolton and Cranborne and all the rest of them. I felt completely bloody-minded. Sat in the House of Lords to hear Portal announce a separate Ministry of Town and Country Planning. There is no chance at all of my being offered this job and I don't think I would take it.

6 December 1942 J. Colville has been appointed governor of Bombay which is a job I had come to feel I would be quite glad to have. So that is another disappointment. I might be excused for feeling that the situation is absolutely hopeless and for shooting myself.

7 December 1942 John Anderson phoned; he said the thing had dragged on long enough and he was going to ask Churchill whether he had any intentions about me. And what if he hasn't? Two people offered Bombay declined. He had thought of me for it but had rejected the idea as not being up to my style. This is satisfactory – but where does it lead to?

16/17 December 1942 Feeling in lower depths than ever before; almost complete despair.

Very slack and in the depths of despair. I hope every time the bell rings that it is a message.

19 December 1942 Letter from the chief whip of the National Liberal party inviting me to a dinner to discuss Beveridge's Report [on social security], Mr Ernest Brown to be present and 'our leader' intending to circulate some notes beforehand. I am inclined to say that I am not a member of their dirty little party as evidenced from their side by the fact that 'the leader' did not even write to me when I was sacked.

24 December 1942 Very little doing in the office. I wished the Admiral a happy Christmas and said I greatly sympathized with him in the break-up of Coastal Forces of which I was, of course, the unintending instrument. I told him that I wasn't happy about going to the Admiralty in the Materials Department and he said he is going to see Kennedy-Purvis about what I should do.

31 December 1942 Saw J. Anderson by request. He was as kindly and as irritating as he could be. I really don't know if he had spoken to Churchill at all. He said he was sure I would not have anything in the political field. There was something he was working on which would suit me; but he did not know if it would come off. The talk might have been about someone else. I was there for over an hour and it might have been five minutes for all I can remember of it. I was in a terrible state this evening. I would welcome death. I wondered if I might not start again and go through *King Alfred* [naval base for the training of officers] with a view to going to sea. Feeling utterly hopeless and in despair.

1/2/4/6 January 1943 [1] Asked the Admiral if I could be trained for sea. Too old, though I am fit for sea service.
[2] Having a tremendous struggle with myself not to be in absolute despair but I was feeling very depressed for all my resolution to struggle on and not give in.
[4] I lunched with Portal at White's which I had been looking forward to in a way, but I much regretted it. He sailed off in the car I had, leaving me to push about in bus queues and such like. I had a great struggle with myself. Tears flooded my eyes several times.
[6] I am still an Olympian. I reflected a lot on this today and was considerably comforted.

1 February 1943 Very boring day and in very bad form. I found myself in fury of hates and resentments against people like Stuart, the chief government whip, who probably more than any other was responsible for my being thrown out. Trying hard not to feel like this, but when I survey the scene, I can't see how I can ever do anything decent again.

[In mid-February 1943 John Reith moved with the reconstructed materials section of Coastal Forces from Hampstead to Queen Anne's Mansions where the section was now lodged as part of the Admiralty.]

22 February 1943 Lunched with Barrington-Ward. He is still sure I will have a proper job! He said he was shocked beyond words at the levity with which affairs of state are handled.

8/9 March 1943 A terrible day. I don't think I ever felt in such despair about my state. I went to Brooks's for lunch but couldn't eat anything.

I don't sleep at night but have weird mixed-up dreams. Every time the telephone rings I pray it may be a message from Anderson.

10 March 1943 Maurice told me that the controller and vice-controller both asked about me recently and that the Fifth Sea Lord had specially inquired about me in conversation with the possibility of my joining him to help reorganize the Fleet Air Arm. Maurice had said I wouldn't like it because it meant dealing with politicians. He might at least have told me about it! Tonight he signalled to me to listen on his parallel to a Combined Operations man inquiring if I were available. He said I wasn't!

24 March 1943 Absolutely nothing to do all day long. I look at my empty table and take up a pencil or my pen but have nothing to write, or I go out of the room as if I were going somewhere, walk down the corridor and then turn back; and I don't like to be out of the room for long in case my telephone rings . . .

There was a White Paper issued today by the wretched Sinclair [air minister] announcing the BOAC resignations.[8] Miss Stanley telephoned and read me a telegram and a letter sent by the BOAC staff asking for me back; round robin also being produced. I don't at all want to go there – not from any point of view except money. I should simply hate it.

25 March 1943 Lunched with T. Johnston, secretary of state for Scotland. He was very decent. He is very bothered by Bevin and other English ministers who do things affecting Scotland without consulting him. He thinks there is a great danger of Scottish Nationalism coming up, and a sort of *Sinn Fein* movement as he called it. The Lord Justice

Clerk had said in a letter that if he left off being a judge and went back to politics, he would be a Nationalist.

26 March 1943 Controller's secretary rang to ask if it would be convenient if the controller came to see me! I said I would go to see him. He was very civil; wanted help with his organization and explained it. I asked various questions. I said I would need to ask Maurice. Out of loyalty to him (mistaken probably) I did not show any enthusiasm. The vice-controller told Maurice in the afternoon (I listening on the parallel) that the controller had spoken to him after seeing me. V.-C. seemed terrified of it all. I don't know that I care much whether I go or not. Miss Stanley rang to say that Sinclair had sent a message that he was embarrassed by the letter which the BOAC managers had sent him so would they withdraw that and write him individually. There had been a staff meeting and this idea had been put to them and they rejected it. I was asked what to advise. Most embarrassing. I suggested an intermediate measure.

31 March 1943 [At a Buckingham Palace party.] Spoke to Kennedy-Purvis who said I was going to the Third Sea Lord as Extra Naval Assistant. I think I am glad of this but it will be an awful sweat. He told me that Alexander had been fussed about Coastal Forces being abolished and that he had not told him about it before it came up.

1 April 1943 A myrmidon from No. 10 rang Maurice this afternoon to say that an MP had a question down – what was I doing in the Admiralty. Funny that it should take a year to be asked. I wonder if he thinks I am not worth £600 a year!

6 April 1943 Lunched with Rothermere about the motion in House of Lords next week about the Airways Corporation. I wonder if I can speak; I doubt it.

Saw Anderson 3.00 to 4.00. There was nothing of any encouragement at all. The job he had in mind was to do with cinema control but that, he said, is now in cold storage. The other thing he had thought of was Airways, but Sinclair, Kingsley Wood told him, was against offering that to me. Of course I am not surprised but it is just another item of indignation and resentment. J.A. said he had told Kingsley Wood that I did not want to go there. K.W. came in as he had a date with J.A. for 3.30 but he went away again. I had shown J.A. my 'testimonials'[9] and he told me to show them to K.W. Also he told him about the Controller's job. Anderson said K.W. had told him he could not sleep for thinking about me. What humbug. J.A. said he had spoken again recently to Churchill about me and that he would like me to be fixed up. What humbug again. He wants me to write to Churchill; he had always said No to this before. It would be the most distasteful thing I ever did and humiliating but I suppose I must try. It will be terribly hard to write it, apart from sending it. I hardly think I can. The situation seems quite hopeless to me. As usual I did not say a tenth of the things I meant.

Home at 7.15 and not able to talk to poor Muriel at all. I am in a terrible state. Went for a walk about 9.30 and when I came back I got down to a letter to Anderson and then one to Churchill – the most difficult and distasteful ever I wrote. By the end, however, I was feeling quite pleased with it. I worked all night.

8 April 1943 I wrote a very brief note to Churchill's secretary saying I knew nothing of the question in the House of Commons about me. This evening I had a wire . . .

I was sure you had nothing to do with the question.
                                                    Winston Churchill.

10 April 1943 Letter from Anderson; he did not like my draft of the letter for Churchill which is most disappointing, and I did not like his.[10] I felt inclined to do nothing at all, and anyhow it is a bit odd to be going to this new job and at the same time sort of intriguing to get out of it.

11 April 1943 Wrote the miserable letter to Churchill according to Anderson's draft verbatim.

15 April 1943 Could not get down to doing proper notes for civil aviation speech today and absolutely loathing the idea of speaking. Wretched House of Lords business did not start till 4.45. Rothermere made a feeble speech: I came next and went down to the reporters' room to correct the draft, so I did not hear Sherwood's [parliamentary secretary at the Air Ministry] reply which I am sure was utterly feeble. Rothermere very weakly and stupidly thanked him for it.

I am feeling desperately and almost despairingly anxious and depressed about my future. Although I didn't at all want to go to Airways it is quite monstrous and also very worrying that I was not asked to.

22 April 1943 Lunched with Wilshaw who asked if I would like to join Cable and Wireless Board, and who also said he thought he ought to retire soon [as chairman] and leave someone else to put to rights the anomalous position in which that concern is.

[On 23 April John Reith moved into his new office as extra naval assistant to the controller. He had already started on his first task of inquiring into Admiralty organization in Bath as well as in London.]

3 May 1943 Managed to make a second draft of my memorandum which the vice-controller will, despite his reluctance, be given.

4 May 1943 Felt more of a down and out today than ever – sneaking along by the side of walls and feeling as if I should be in the gutter really. Made worse by limping owing to a sore foot. Avoiding people I know and so on.

The vice-controller had my retyped memo today and we see him about it tomorrow. He told Bateson [naval staff officer] that the more he read it, the more he hated it – which Muriel said is complimentary.

5 May 1943 Meeting with the V-C this morning on my memo. It was what I expected and thought. Lasted from 11.15 to 1.15 and I converted him. It was a most agreeable and interesting meeting and he sent me a note afterwards saying I was right. I reminded him of his conversion to my terms of reference for Coastal Forces Material Department.

13 May 1943 Lunched with Mrs Hamilton [former governor of the BBC] whom I had not seen since I was cast out. I was in very bad form. Said how disgusted I was that no Labour minister had raised a hand to help me.

17 May 1943 Controller sent me down a bundle of papers about the navalization of the Royal Corps of Naval Constructors, asking my views. Very important business.

18/19 May 1943 Saw the director of Naval Construction about his papers and he agreed with my view that the whole organization of technicians should be gone into.

The papers about the Royal Corps of Naval Constructors have come back to me to write a memo for the Board [of Admiralty] on the whole subject of technicians. What a job.

23 May 1943 Not a good day in any way. I am getting more and more embittered against everybody and everything. It is awful and very serious. Enormously worried about myself.

4 June 1943 No work all day. Thought about the dreadful state I was in and decided to try to pull myself together and behave differently.

8 June 1943 I fairly got down to the memorandum about specialist officers and finished it with great satisfaction, taking it in to Bateson about tea-time. It is a most revolutionary document but to my surprise Bateson liked it. He made some suggestions and we went through it later.

11 June 1943 Gave controller my memo; also vice-controller who came into my room in his shirt-sleeves and talked for an hour about it as I hoped he would. I like him very well.

Trying to feel in better shape with myself and everybody and everything and in large measure succeeding. This is a great achievement.

12 June 1943 Very nice note from the vice-controller beginning: 'As you may have noticed, I am inclined at first sight to view the several proposals you have made with antagonism, but after further thought and explanation find you are right!'

I saw the controller for three-quarters of an hour. He likes it all but is *non possumus* about getting anything done.

19 June 1943 Wavell has been made viceroy – so that has gone again. I have been a bit happier the last two or three days but I am feeling very down tonight.

21 June 1943 Talked with Engineer Rear Admiral Warde who was very forthcoming about engineer officers. He said that he had never felt that he really belonged to the Navy. A very significant remark this.

24 June 1943 Bateson telephoned last night that he had something to keep me busy. It was the Combined Operations racket clean-up. I read through several very muddled papers and then saw the vice-controller who talked to me for about two hours in his usual modest way. About 1.00 o'clock I asked if he thought I could do the Material Directorship for Combined Operations. He said he had thought of me but was sure I would not want it. He was sure I could do it and no one so well. I said I didn't want it at all, but that if he was stuck I would do it out of regard for him. He said that was 'a hell of a sheet anchor in case a gale blew up'.

26 June 1943 Vice-controller said the controller welcomed the idea of my doing the job. He had told the controller that they could go through ten pages of senior officers and the whole lot wouldn't be as good as me. He asked if I were still prepared to do it and would I think about it over the weekend. I said I wasn't going back on what I had said.

28 June 1943 All morning on DCOM [i.e. Department of Combined Operations, Material] terms of reference and a meeting all the afternoon. I pretty well took the meeting and the text of it was *my* terms of reference for DCOM.

When I got back from the meeting I asked if Tower would like to see me, and he said 'nothing better', so I gave him an account and he was very pleased. He then told me that the controller had said definitely that he wanted me to do the job, so Tower had told him he should see the First Lord and get me proper rank.

30 June 1943 Vice-controller is very disgusted with controller for havering about instead of going for the rank for me – Commodore First Class.

1 July 1943 Controller asked if I would do the DCOM job and as Captain RNVR. He asked if I thought they were making use of me unfairly in not giving me Commodore First Class RN rank as strongly recommended by the vice-controller. I said No, but that I thought he ought to have been able to put the other thing across. As to taking the job, I said I would do as I was told. He was obviously embarrassed. He is not half the man the vice is. I felt inclined later to say I would do the job as a lieutenant-commander.

5 July 1943 Just before leaving the office I heard that the blighted Alexander had referred my appointment to Churchill. If he says yes, it carries the devastating significance that I am off his agenda and in this

R.D.—U

job for the duration. I don't know what I want and I am feeling
sickened of the whole business. I wrote to John Anderson telling him
the whole story.

6 July 1943 Vice-controller showed me a copy of Alexander's minute,
made after seeing Churchill, that he approved my promotion to
captain. He added that 'if Lord Reith gives satisfaction' he thought I
could be put up to commodore. V-C was much amused by this expression. 'A.V. Alexander,' he said, 'My God.'

3. Admiralty : Combined Operations Material (DCOM), July 1943–December 1944

[John Reith used his new position and the heavy work it brought to
anaesthetize his worries and to turn his mind away from his resentments. He rejected a second opportunity to attack the government in
print, offered by the editor of *Picture Post*, and, though he kept in touch
with Anderson and Barrington-Ward, acknowledged to himself that
little or nothing would come of this. His work intensified as D-day
approached and in the first half of 1944 he often found himself in his
office until the early hours of the morning. In all this he was helped and
encouraged by the sympathetic support of the vice-controller of the
Navy, Vice-Admiral Sir Thomas Tower. Nevertheless his resentment
of the past and his concern for the future were only submerged – not
removed.

At the end of 1943, eight months after the first tentative approaches
from Sir Edward Wilshaw, John Reith had been elected to the board
of Cable and Wireless. Lady Reith wisely urged him to accept the
prospect of the succession to the chairmanship on Wilshaw's retirement and to turn his back on politics. He could not bring himself to
accept this. He had earlier been in correspondence with the Tory
Reform committee and, in March 1944, at the instance of Lord Astor,
he took part in a debate in the House of Lords criticizing the government's lack of progress on post-war planning. But, fortunately, the
problem of integrating the communications of the Empire roused his
interest and involved him fully in the future planning of Cable and
Wireless. He proposed a characteristic solution – an imperial corporation. This was blocked by the fears of interested parties and the outcome was a Cabinet committee to consider the problem. By now the
invasion of Europe had been successfully launched and the work of his
Admiralty department largely completed. His friend, Admiral Tower,

had ceased to be vice-controller; plans for the war in the Far East were uncertain; and he himself was made no definite offer to continue in the Navy. Then, on Churchill's personal recommendation, he was told he was to receive the CB (Military) for his work. It was a fitting completion to his naval service. When, therefore, at the end of the year, the Cabinet committee reported in favour of something like his single corporation idea and recommended that he lead a mission round the Empire to secure agreement to this, John Reith was ready to accept, even though it involved him in giving up his directorship of Cable and Wireless.]

7 July 1943 Found out that accommodation [for the new department] had been settled in a ghastly building between Holborn and Tottenham Court Road with no daylight or natural air. I wrote a protest about it and got busy on the matter.

13/14/15 July 1943 I went to look at the Paymaster's old building and quite liked it.

I spent some time in the PMG building which I have managed to get all of.

It is very irritating being on the edge of this new job with so much happening in it.

21 July 1943 To Portsmouth, quite comfortably, arriving 12.30. To the *Victory* for lunch, everything being very well done. Meeting at 2.45, with C-in-C in the chair, when I expounded my new job. They are worried about the amount of Combined Operations repairs they will have to do.

29/30 July 1943 Saw Walsh, director of Establishments, and was civilly treated. He said (in answer to a question) that they were not in the habit of letting directors vet their chief civil servant; in fact had not done so before. He is getting one Huckle up from Bath tomorrow.

Saw Huckle and quite liked him. I so informed Walsh.

4 August 1943 Letter from the Editor of Picture Post

Can I persuade you to come out in public with a strong article about the trifling and almost frivolous way in which the government is handling the basic problems which underlie post-war planning?

The last time we talked this over you felt, I know, that such an article coming from you would have the appearance of personal feeling. Surely after this lapse of time, any suggestion of that sort must now have gone.

11 August 1943 I am very busy now and presumably will stay so. Lunched with Hopkinson, editor of *Picture Post*, who wanted me to write a strong article attacking the government. I wouldn't and anyhow as a naval officer can't.

15 August 1943 I wasn't feeling at all happy. I have made such a mess of everything and I wish I had never been born.

16 August 1943 DCOM started officially today. Vetted my first minute reducing the number of words quite considerably.

17 August 1943 Lunched with Woolton and told him what I thought about things and the way I had been treated.

22 August 1943 I began a letter to Woolton at 10.00 this morning and did not get it done till 1.30. It wasn't any good really. I sent him my 'testimonials'; and told him of the children wanting me to come and play with them and of my wanting to shout at them that I wished to God that they had never been born; and that we had to break up this home.

I must busy myself in this job of mine and forget about the family and everything that has ever been. Of course I shall have the most ghastly remorse about all this. I have not done my duty by the children. It isn't all my fault. They are fond of me, but I am no use at all to either of them. Here is the house and grounds they have enjoyed so much, and in which Christopher has worked so hard, passing from us. We should have left it long ago. My overdraft is now about £3000 and it mounts every month. It seems the end of all things.

I must busy myself, as I have said, in this job. I cannot do it properly if I am always wanting to get home to them and always burdened with the worry of the expenses here and of the awful life which Muriel has to live. There is so much to think of and settle. I wish a bomb would eliminate us all. It is the only way out. And all of this, or most of it, is due to that loathesome cad Churchill. I feel like disposing of all my books, burning my diaries, and selling most everything we have. God Almighty, whatever that or he may mean, has completely cut us off. There is no hope anywhere. I find I still can't contemplate suicide, chiefly because things would be so muddled and difficult for the family.

think. Molson MP sent me a copy of a statement issued by the Tory Reform group, asking my comments.

12 October 1943 Letter to Hugh Molson MP [honorary joint secretary of the Tory Reform committee]
    I could wish your statement were shorter and more definite.
    I could wish I had felt able to agree, definitely and pugnaciously with more of it – provocative, controversial sort of statements.
    I should like you to have said more, or rather to have been more definite about, for instance, the control of public utilities.
    I should like to have seen something about the exercise of power without responsibility – such as in the Press.
    Perhaps most of all I regret that there is no reference anywhere to an ethic, presumably the Christian ethic on which political policy and conduct should be based. What is the inspiration and ideal? Bread is not enough; nor freedom from want; nor independence.
    Another thing I should like to have seen is a statement that statesmen must lead and risk their return to Parliament in leading. What is the average politician's attitude and to what criterion does he submit? The vote? Too much – far, far too much, the vote.
    Fear of the elector is the root of most if not all the troubles that have come to us.
    When I was director general of the BBC I directed it. I made myself very unpopular. I was alleged to be dictatorial. I wasn't so. Governors of business and communities and countries are chosen to govern. Not to count heads as they too often do. The mass of people will accept government if they are governed. They won't accept if they are asked whether or not they will.
    Your fight in this Hinchingbrooke group is with your own party. The future of the Tory party depends on you. Your enemies are of your own household: the reactionaries and those ministers who are manœuvring for position. You have got some bad men among them. Look around for real character, foundations and principles.

18 October 1943 I lunched with Wilshaw who had wanted me to join his Cable and Wireless board but who had been given a sorry tale of objections to me of the usual sort. It doesn't depress me as much as it might have done, but it is very serious really.

28 October 1943 Letter from Hugh Molson MP
    I have shown your letter to Hinchingbrooke and Thorneycroft [of

the Tory Reform committee] and the answer I am sending you has in broad outline their approval.

It is quite true that our statement is not in a particularly concrete form nor is it provocative or controversial. It was not intended that it should be. It is intended to provide a basis of agreement for reasonably progressive people of all parties and none. We believe that there is a large measure of agreement as to the kind of reconstruction which is required. This should take the form of an extension and development of existing institutions rather than of an entirely new construction.

. . . With regard to the Christian ethic, it was the most active churchman amongst the draftsmen who was most opposed to any reference to religion in the statement. The pamphlet is a political statement and I do not see that it would have been appropriate to introduce into it anything about the code of conduct which should influence politicians. It is of course wrong for us to be unduly influenced on matters of right and wrong by consideration of electoral popularity, but on the other hand we can only work through the democratic machine.

Your paragraph regarding your work at the BBC is revealing. I knew you to be a direct and vigorous administrator to whom compromise does not make much appeal. But the whole spirit of democracy is compromise and I believe that is what the English people want.

3 November 1943 Saw the vice-controller at noon. He was very angry with the controller for having let himself be bullied by Churchill into agreeing to build seventy-five more LCTs [tank landing craft]. This causes an awful upset. Controller had not said a word to V-C about it.

10 November 1943 I wrote to Anderson telling him what Winant had told me. No good will come of this, of course, but he might as well know. I don't know what I want. I don't know what I should feel supposing I was asked to be minister for reconstruction even. It is rumoured that there is going to be one. I doubt if I could do anything like this – or anything at all. I am utterly miserable and so near utter despair. I am in an absolutely dreadful state, and I am becoming unfit for any sort of job. I feel I want to quarrel with everybody.

12 November 1943 Woolton is minister of reconstruction and in the war cabinet. The other changes are of the usual shuffling sort.

11/12 December 1943 Not so busy and therefore disgruntled. Managed to write to Hooper of the 'Forward by the Right' party commenting on Molson's letter to me.

[Dated *16 December 1943*] *Letter to F. C. Hooper, Political Research Centre*
Molson almost explicitly said my methods were not suited to democracy and that therefore I was not fit to govern. That is my point – or one of them. Another, is look what 'compromise' has brought us to – this war and our unpreparedness for it.

Is 'the whole spirit of democracy compromise'? Is it really? Largely as practised – yes. With the results we know.

I still feel that there are fundamentals which the statement does not touch and without which the result is disappointing. The main thing may be that more leadership, more courage, more 'right is right, to follow right were wisdom in the scorn of consequence' and *less* compromise are needed if democracy is to be safe for the world.

14/16 December 1943 Sir E. Wilshaw called to say that at a special Board meeting that morning I had been unanimously elected to all their Boards. Very nice of him. I didn't know if I wanted to do this, or if I would be allowed to.

Markham [permanent secretary of the Admiralty] rang me to say he thought my joining Cable and Wireless Board would be all right. I wrote to Anderson about it.

17 December 1943 Saw Anderson. He was not clear about my going on the Cable and Wireless Board and was reluctant to give definite advice. I am to see him again.

20 December 1943 Saw Anderson and was told that Alexander had spoken to him about my Cable and Wireless directorship. Alexander had said he would have to refer it to Churchill. How feeble. Anderson encouraged me to accept, but said they would look to me, as a privy councillor, to work in with the government schemes for reconstruction there. I was inclined to say that the offer had nothing to do with the government, I was under no obligation to them. Anderson seems utterly insensible to the iniquity of my treatment, or rather does nothing about it.

23 December 1943 Saw the secretary who told me what I already knew about the feeble Alexander waiting for Churchill's return. He said twice that the First Lord would be glad to see me if I liked, but I said I had no desire at all to see him. He could not tell me why reference to Attlee as deputy PM was not enough.

26/31 December 1943 Churchill has barged in again and the LSTs [tank landing-ships] from the Mediterranean are not to come back when originally arranged. What a curse the man is.

Picture of the loathesome Churchill in the paper – makes me want to put my boot through it.

28 December 1943 Dinner with Balfour of Burleigh at the Athenæum. He said he had spoken to Smuts about me and suggested I should be governor general of South Africa; he said Smuts evidently had a high opinion of me and had seemed much interested. Obviously nothing will come of it or else Smuts would have asked me to see him when he was here.

31 December 1943 Here is another last day of the year; I had hoped the end of 1942 would see the end of the worst I had ever had since 1922 but there is absolutely no lightening of the skies. But I expect I am as happy in my work as I have been in anything.

10 January 1944 The days get busier and busier. We are doing a tremendous lot and the staff side are envious of our order against their disorder.

Montgomery, the self-advertiser who is now in command of the British armies for Overlord, wants far more ships and craft, and Churchill has apparently backed him to the tune of ordering another hooh-hah about stuff from the Mediterranean. It is really shocking that there should be all this muddle with the date so close.

A lot of papers are flying around about what craft are to be built for the S.W. Pacific. Quite obvious that the Americans don't care whether we are there or not.

11 January 1944 Longhand letter from Alexander saying that Churchill had accepted his recommendation that I should be allowed to accept the Cable and Wireless directorship but had wanted it mentioned at the war cabinet. This was done last night. I had hoped it was to say I had been made commodore.

19 January 1944 Vice-controller told me that the blighted Second Sea

Lord [Sir William Whitworth] had opposed my being made a commodore for all sorts of red-tape reasons. V-C is very angry and does not think the controller will stand up to it. And yet the First Lord minuted that it was to be done.

20 January 1944 I rang Balfour of Burleigh and told him I was joining the Cable board and he was very pleased. He told me that people were much disgusted with the Churchill-Beaverbrook position, which I am delighted to hear. Apparently there are rumours that Beaverbrook is going to the War Office and Grigg to India Office. My goodness what disgusting things that evil man Churchill does.

7 February 1944 Very busy day. Vice-controller came over with latest changes about LSTs from Mediterranean. Anvil [attack on S. France] at same time as Overlord is off. Things in Italy are all bogged up and it looks as if the Germans can hold up the Allied advance there. I got a series of Churchill minutes about LST return. Differences of opinion with the Americans are obvious.

14 February 1944 Lunched with General Laycock, in command of Combined Operations, aged thirty-four. I was not greatly impressed and anyhow he has not much of a job and does not like it.

Worked till midnight and then got down to the paper with full details of Overlord, the most secret and interesting paper I have had. Left at 0350.

23 February 1944 I asked vice-controller about the commodore business and was most disgusted and disappointed to hear that Alexander had given in to the objections and difficulties raised by the blasted Whitworth, Second Sea Lord. How contemptible of him. V-C felt as much as I did, or more, and he has a contempt for Whitworth who, he said, had just been 'blown along' into his present rank. I really am very sick about it. I had not said much at the time but did when he phoned me later. I said my feelings were less than they might have been, knowing how he felt.

25 February 1944 Barlow spoke to me at breakfast [i.e. in the Athenæum] with much nervousness about seeing him and Rae about Cable and Wireless.[13] I was at the Treasury with them from 12.00 to 1.35. I said I wanted to know where I stood. Their answers were quite satisfactory. But my suspicions that Beaverbrook might come in on this matter were confirmed. Barlow said that he had made a ghastly botch of civil aviation and was now tired of it and was looking at oil and at communications. He said the Americans hated Beaverbrook and would not deal with him. Beaverbrook's excuse, of course, was that you cannot do business with them in election year.

6/7 March 1944 I wish I could be sure of leaving the Admiralty in the early autumn after the invasion is over. I cannot bear the idea of staying on for the Japanese business. If I got another £1500 a year somehow or other I would be no worse off financially.

I just don't know what to make of things and what, if any, future I can have. Can't something clear somewhere, somehow?

16/17/19 March 1944 [16] A letter from Lord Astor urging me to speak in the Lords next week on a motion by Latham. I said I might speak if I got a draft by lunch-time on Saturday.

[17] Getting bothered about speaking in the Lords. It brings up so many resentments, and my mind gets in all of a seethe of indignation against Churchill and his gang.

[19] Worked at the speech almost all day. It was a dreadful grind. And the most sickening thing is that I don't know whether there may not be some announcement by Woolton which puts a different perspective on it all. I greatly resented having to give up all of my precious Sunday to this business and possibly I shall not speak at all.

20/21/22/23 March 1944 [20] I sent copies of my speech to Barrington-Ward and Astor. Barrington-Ward wrote advising me to cut out the personal side. Back to the office after dinner to work on speech and left at 1.10 a.m. having recast it.

[21] Talked with Astor in his house. The debate is to go on for two days so I got myself moved to the second.

[22] Went to see Woolton at 10.45. He said he would like to talk to me as a friend and give me all the government secrets. He said W. S. Morrison [minister of town and country planning] had produced a plan which was too 'confiscatory'. He himself had then given him some other ideas which Morrison had developed and which he had on the whole thought should go to the War Cabinet. It had done so the night before but had been thrown out. He said he was in an awful jam. He had told his colleagues he would resign if he weren't given support. He had seen Churchill (but had not mentioned resignation to him) and had had some assurances. I wished we had had longer to speak. I had

a very rushed morning but was able to meet Muriel at the House of Lords for lunch. Woolton made an absolutely ghastly show. He had nothing to say except a feeble attempt to excuse the Cabinet because of their war preoccupations. He made a mess of it even given his rotten position. I went to Astor's for tea. I was awfully tired and sick of the whole business – so fatuous it is. Office till 8.15. No dinner. Club and not to bed till 1.30. I made some notes of what to say and will only use a page of what I had before.

[*23*] Lunched in House of Lords. I got on all right, but would have given a lot to have spoken after Beaverbrook who replied for the government. It was a disgusting performance but the government bench was crowded, also the steps, with ministers.

26 March 1944 Awfully unsettled and unhappy because I don't know whatever I want to do. Muriel said she did not want me ever to go into any political job but would like me to be chairman of Cable and Wireless. I don't want this; I couldn't be bothered with it – coming in, as I did with Imperial Airways, knowing nobody and nothing. I just don't know what I want to do.

31 March 1944 Attlee at breakfast time came to my table and said, 'Well, we had our spot of bother yesterday.' 'Yes,' said I, 'a deplorable affair.' 'It certainly was,' he said. But perhaps he didn't mean the same as I; or perhaps he did.[14]

An utterly ludicrous inquiry from Churchill in the office as to whether it would be possible to have operations in Burma and China and at the same time a considerable amphibious operation in the Indian Ocean.

4 April 1944 To my surprise and disgust Beaverbrook rang me. Very cordial and Christian name. I was distinctly frigid. Asked if I had had anything to do with international communications before the war. I said only in broadcasting. He said he would like to have a talk; was I in Town at nights; would I come to the government dinner next night to Berle [US assistant secretary of state] and Warner [vice-chairman of US civil aeronautic's board] from USA over here to talk about civil aviation. He hadn't rung to ask me to this dinner, so I don't know what his reason is. He said he knew that I was head of an Admiralty department and that Churchill had been talking about it with much commendation. When, by my rejoinder, I cast doubts on this, he repeated it with great emphasis.

5 April 1944 Went to this government dinner at Claridges. It was very well done – with champagne! Weird to be in this crowd again. People were very civil and friendly. Hudson [minister of agriculture] said I had been very sarcastic about Woolton and that it had upset him very much – 'got under his skin'. W. S. Morrison, on the other hand, said Hudson was 'mischievous' (and that is quite true) and that Woolton was pleased with what I said. I sat between Bruce of Australia and Morrison. Former talked to me about Cable and Wireless – the troubles they had. Latter said he had tried to get modified Uthwatt proposals accepted but was blocked by everyone. As Bruce was talking so much I had little chance to get all the information from W.S.M. which he was quite willing to give.

10 April 1944 There have been strong rumours that Eden was giving up the Foreign Office, for which of course he is utterly unfit; but now it seems he isn't. And if he had, the rumours are that Churchill wanted Beaverbrook in it, but would have had to put Cranborne. The one is a crook and the other a half-wit, so I don't know which would have been worse.

I am terribly distressed about my state and about my behaviour with the children. They don't know how to take me at all. And the years are passing so quickly. I had a bath before supper tonight for the first time for many years, I think. It made me think of the time when I had this regularly, and then dressed in dinner jacket suit, and sat down to my evening meal with Muriel like a gentleman. I don't suppose I shall ever do this again. I sometimes look at my old diary 'enclosures' volumes when I was 'the most powerful man in the country next to the PM' and such like. *Ichabod* indeed.

14 April 1944 Saw Barlow and Rae at their request about the position between Cable and Wireless and Australia. Negotiations for a tripartite merger there have been held up by Wilshaw for nearly two years now. They wanted him at least to reopen negotiations. I then went to see him and he quite agreed that he should start talking with them. I then tried out on him the idea of an imperial company and found him surprisingly receptive. He said he would put it to the Board. This is very good; it is the obvious thing to do – just what I had in mind for civil aviation. It would be a tremendous thing to achieve.

15 April 1944 Decided to tell Barlow about the imperial corporation idea. He said it was certainly the right thing and he hadn't expected it to come from the company.

17 April 1944 Lunched with Gardiner [director general of the Post Office] and astonished him with my suggestion about an Empire corporation. He finally described his attitude as one of 'modified rapture'. He thought the present Post Office representations on the Commonwealth Communications Council would oppose it, and the Labourites, and the Dominions. The first want Cable and Wireless taken over by the Post Office; the second would object to further Post Office services being handed over to the new corporation. The third are all for autonomy. I think I could achieve it but I am in no position to do so.

18 April 1944 Saw vice-controller 4.30 to 6.00. He said 'the controller is jealous'. People had been talking to him about what I was doing and he thought he was missing things and wanted to see something of our work and go on tours! V-C said he was going about the middle of July. This is sickening. I said I would not want to stay and work for someone else. I must get doing something about the future if I want to leave the Admiralty in July. The chairmanship of an imperial communications corporation might appeal to me.

19 April 1944 Wilshaw called for me and we went to the Treasury at 6.00 – Barlow, Gardiner and Rae. He propounded my scheme for an imperial corporation. It went very well. I fairly jumped on Rae's query about Churchill being too busy with the war, and also on their suggesting that UK political prejudice might crab it – an imperial scheme of such magnitude. Really monstrous – and I permitted myself a mild threat of publicity over that – sabotage of imperial interest by party prejudices.

24 April 1944 At Electra House 10.30 to 3.30. I saw Wilshaw's draft about an imperial corporation and made several alterations in it, getting it addressed to Barlow. After lunch Wilshaw gave quite a good presentation of the case and secured the unanimous approval of the Board. Courtauld-Thompson made the incredible suggestion that a paragraph should be added to propitiate Churchill, that this idea was not aimed against the Americans. It was a striking condemnation of Churchill, that he should be willing to sacrifice imperial interests in this way, and of course the thing *is* directed largely against US competition.

25 April 1944 Meeting at Treasury: Barlow, Wilshaw, Rae and Gardiner. We were told that the blighted ministers had considered the imperial project, but had nothing to say by way of encouragement; only would we put the matter to the Communications Council. And that body has adjourned for a week because of a bomb from the Australian and New Zealand members who are reporting to their PMs that they are in favour of national corporations in each country. Our scheme is infinitely better.

4 May 1944 To Electra House and went through my paper on the imperial corporation with Wilshaw. He seemed very pleased with it, but he is not sincerely keen on the idea and he does not know enough. Inverforth [deputy chairman of Cable and Wireless] and he and I went to the Communications Council; I didn't want at all to go, but the government side had hoped I would and Wilshaw had asked me. It quite infuriated me. We were sat like prisoners in the dock at a cross table some distance from the others. Wilshaw made an absolutely rotten show. He read out the first page and a half of my memorandum and then stopped. There were some questions but soon it all petered out. I was very angry. When at the end I was asked if I had anything to say I replied: 'Not at this stage,' and went off.

5 May 1944 I went in the afternoon to the Civil Lord's room to deal with the MP who had been making trouble about the cancellation of a contract. I had persuaded the Civil Lord to give up his idea of a further letter and to get the man along. I put it across him all right. I can do tremendous things when I get the chance. The Civil Lord said the man had been 'overwhelmed' when I saw him. What armament I carry – and getting no chance to do anything with it. Oh gosh it is awful.

6 May 1944 As I was passing the Athenæum after lunch the secretary of state for War [P. J. Grigg], whose flag I had recognized and was about to salute, jumped out of his car to talk to me. There was a five minutes concentration of libel (quite accurate) on some of his colleagues that was very gratifying. Beaverbrook, Bracken, Portal were all bloody crooks. Beaverbrook and Bracken were manipulating the BBC in their own interests, despite all Bracken's denials. In my day, he said, the place was under control. Now there was none and the young communists did as they liked. He said Churchill was visibly failing.

8 May 1944 Lunched at Cable and Wireless. I told Wilshaw I thought the Empire corporation scheme was dead and that the conference would recommend either nothing or the Anzac scheme.

12 May 1944 Feeling utterly disgusted – debates about civil aviation and education; empire conferences; parties of all sorts; and I am nothing and nowhere. It makes me seethe with indignation at the bloody and dastardly treatment I have had and still have. To hell and torture with Churchill and all the lousy swine of politicians and civil servants.

Sunday 14 May 1944 I am utterly alone. No one to help me; no one to talk to. All the swarming people that push against me in trains and tubes – they are all more or less happy. Anyhow none can be so utterly bereft and without hope as I. I just don't know what to do or where to turn. I really feel I could contemplate killing myself. I don't know how to do it decently. I am absolutely at the end of my tether and am making things terrible for poor Muriel also. There are three ghastly problems – if any one would be settled I might have hope; (1) my future; (2) money affairs; (3) the house. I just sit here and stare across the room or out of the window. I even rang J. Anderson's number but there was no reply. The situation is DESPERATE. I would write to Anderson but I just don't feel able to.

15 May 1944 When I am busy, as I have been today, I don't feel so desperate about things, but it is there all the time and periodically surges over me.

20 May 1944 I suppose I am and always have been almost completely self-centred and that nothing interests me at all except what I am concerned in. I expect it is too late to change. I have no ordinary human kindliness or tolerance. I have brilliance, intellect and all sorts of things like that, energy, conscientiousness and thoroughness. About the only passion I show is in reviling politicians, Churchill especially. Never rise to any heights. Scornful of patriotism and honest efforts to serve the country. Loathing the common people. I will rarely admit greatness in others. This is the kind of thing that might be said about me. A good deal is true. I am obsessed by my own fate and by a desire for revenge for my treatment; by a sense of injury. Is my ambition just lust for power? (I don't think so; I never have.) I think no one is so unhappy or has had such hard treatment or is in such a bad way. The greatness that used to be there never now appears – nothing that shines. I only show a hopelessness and almost an acceptance of my own shortcomings. I have always known I had a horrid character and disposition. And now I am querulous and embittered and small and shrunken and can't see even the near horizon. Believing nothing and without faith or hope; stifled and strangled and submerged by the pettiness of my own preoccupations. The inspiration and domination of my personality are gone.

23 May 1944 Lunched with controller. He said he could not object to my leaving in the autumn if I wanted. I said I wouldn't go if I could be properly busy, which seemed unlikely.

Went with Wilshaw to see Barlow, Rae and Gardiner. Told that our Empire corporation idea had been rejected in favour of a series of public corporations with interlocking directors and some sort of council to link them up. They did not think our scheme would have got through no matter how well presented. I don't agree, of course. Some sort of ministerial committee has now to look into the idea of Cable and Wireless becoming a corporation!

26/28/30 May 1944 [26] Wondering if I might not somehow be able to get back to my former faith . . . I have such longings for it. I do still believe, but I have been so hardly used by circumstances that everything is distorted.

[28] Feeling very unsettled now that DCOM work is so largely done and there will not be the impetus of Overlord.

[30] If I were to get a CB for this job, or even a CBE, I should feel not only very pleased but that that would put a sort of 'paid' to it.

6 June 1944 Invasion today, the D-day of long expectation. It seems to be going very well, with very little opposition. Controller rang to congratulate us on the serviceability percentage which was ninety-eight for craft and ninety-nine for ships. Very good. I picked up an evening paper at the Club, which is a most rare occurrence for me, and was revolted at the sycophantic stuff about Churchill making a statement in Parliament. He poses as disgustingly as any Hitler or Mussolini. He is of the same breed as they.

7 June 1944 Neither saw a paper, nor had any breakfast nor took any interest in the progress of invasion. I think I am beyond any help from anyone or any salvation.

10 June 1944 If I quarrel with Anderson, as is quite possible, that is my sole link (for what little it was worth) with the political world gone.

12 June 1944 Lunched at the Athenæum. I always go and sit by myself on the balcony afterwards, and I cannot help brooding on the ghastly injustices which have been mine. Today I got up and came back to the office where at least there is a chance of my mind being diverted.

14 June 1944 Very slack and I cannot get down to the S.W. Pacific stuff. The Americans don't want any British there anyhow.

19 June 1944 Went to the GPO for lunch. Gardiner said a committee of ministers has been appointed to deal with the nationalization issue – Anderson, Attlee, PMG [H. F. C. Crookshank] and – Beaverbrook, which is utterly disgusting. He said he hoped I would become chairman [i.e. of Cable and Wireless] in the autumn, and he thought I should get full-time busy on the job almost at once. I don't feel at all happy at this prospect. I feel I ought to get DCOM liquidated quite quickly, but I have no satisfaction at all in contemplating the Cable and Wireless job. I think I would like to stay in the Navy and go to the Far East.

21 June 1944 To see J. Anderson at 9.15. It wasn't a helpful meeting and too short. I asked what he thought of my going to Cable and Wireless. I said I would probably be leaving the Admiralty in the early autumn. He said I ought to write to Churchill or him saying this. He was quite vague as to what was likely to happen in Cable and Wireless. Very friendly but getting old.

5 July 1944 Busy day. Went through the list of ships for the Far East and the work to be done on them. No decision about the ones for the US Navy in the Pacific and I can't think why they don't make up their minds. Most things don't get decided, and I imagine it is Churchill who is responsible. It is quite disgraceful that there is still no decision as to where the war is to be in the East so we don't know what to be preparing for.

7 July 1944 The swine Churchill sent one of the Cherwell Gestapo notes to the First Lord about repairs to LCTs – an utterly ridiculous affair. He suggested Admiral Tennant being appointed 'to push people along'. Spy work and grossly inaccurate information.

11/12/13 July 1944 [11] Vice-controller told me that John Anderson had asked him to come and see him tomorrow. This arises from my having put a PS to the note I sent him the other day to the effect that I wished he would ask the vice-controller what he thought of my work.

[12] Vice-controller came to my room after seeing Anderson. As I expected, he was asked every sort of question about me and my work in the Admiralty. He fairly put it across. While he was in my room Anderson's secretary rang to ask if I could come and see him next day. I am afraid it is all about Cable and Wireless.

[13] Saw Anderson 9.45 to 10.30. He told me of Tower's visit which he said (re his remarks about me) had been very impressive indeed. He told me a great deal I knew about Cable and Wireless and said he was prepared to try to get me into 'some central position' but he could not specify what this would be as he did not know what would develop. I said I wasn't very keen on it, but that I would write to him. It looks as if the idea might be that I should leave the Admiralty very soon and go on to the Treasury pay-roll – if I do the thing at all.

21 July 1944 Admiral Tower said he had been summoned to see the wretched First Lord on termination of his appointment as vice-controller. The ass had yattered on about nothing relevant, switched on the one o'clock news and then dismissed him and his seven years outstanding work with 'much obliged – much obliged'. Ignorant ass, he is.

28 July 1944 I was in a black mood all day. I have practically no interest in this Admiralty work now. There was a meeting of the blasted ministers' committee about imperial communications at five o'clock yesterday but I have heard nothing, nor has Anderson acknowledged my note yet. How I wish I could tell him to go to hell.

3 August 1944 Rae told me that the minutes of the blighted ministers' meeting a week ago had no reference to me at all. He could not make out why I had heard nothing. What an inconsiderate cad Anderson is to have said nothing to me at all.

17 August 1944 Meeting this morning about bases for the Far East. There were twenty-five departments represented and about forty people. I fairly put the business through – one hour and a quarter only. I never saw a better prepared or better conducted meeting. It might have taken hours and hours.

18 August 1944 Meeting 3.30 to 4.45 in Treasury with Wilshaw, Barlow, Rae and Gardiner. We were given a note of what they wanted Cable and Wireless to do. Anderson has not seen Churchill and cannot do anything about me until he does. He might at least have told me so.

21 August 1944 Lunched with Gardiner at GPO. I told him I was in a sickening position not knowing where I was with either side.

Meeting later with Alexander (First Lord, forsooth) about the ridiculous weekly landing-craft returns to Churchill. Alexander was very cordial with me. I said he ought to get along whoever in the No. 10 gestapo was responsible and explain that the figures given to date were all hopeless and make a new start.

21 September 1944 Joyce Wilson [John Reith's private secretary] came in with some signals this morning and said, 'There is one bit of good news for you anyhow. You are getting a decoration of some sort.' She did not know what or where so I asked her to find out. Later she gave me a note: 'The PM is putting you up for CB (Military) in Overlord honours. Hurray.' Apparently it is Churchill's doing. The Admiralty complement was already filled, but he said I was to have this. I am very pleased about it as *very* few captains RN have it and it is for vice-admirals and some rear admirals. Mountbatten got it after being in command of Combined Operations as vice-admiral. It is a squaring off for the naval service I have done – adequate for that period and that is a relief.

3 October 1944 Went to a meeting to hear about the Ottawa conference. There was not much except that Dracula (Rangoon) is postponed till the end of the year chiefly, I suppose, on account of the difficulty of getting ships and craft out of Overlord. It is all hopelessly muddled.

6 October 1944 There is to be a civil aviation ministry. Ludicrous. I cannot understand how such silly things happen.

7 October 1944 Charwomen and the young sluts who are so much in evidence these days conduct their conversation in the shape of all screaming simultaneously and continuously at the top of their raucous voices, quite oblivious of what any others of the party are saying and periodically emitting hyena-like yells of laughter. There can be no attention to content – only volume and continuity. It is a melancholy and miserable spectacle.

13 October 1944 Wilshaw to see me and we went on to Barlow and Rae. Wilshaw said Beaverbrook had sent for him yesterday to check up the 'brief' he had prepared for himself for Anderson's committee. Apparently he is against the Americans and the Anzac scheme.

23 October 1944 Saw J. Anderson for half an hour. I hate these office interviews and if he had any decency or imagination he would not ask me there, nor have someone else in half an hour. I told him what I had done to get progress in the negotiation and about Wilshaw's desire for some kind of honour. I said he deserved this on merit and for reasons of expediency. I told him also of Beaverbrook's intervention. He said he had expected to be able to go to Churchill with a plan for Empire communications with my name attached long ago. This is quite inconsistent with what he had in mind before.

8 November 1944 Rae told me that the blighted ministers' meeting yesterday went very well, so my memoranda have been adopted. What a difference I have made by being in on this business. He said the thing was going to the Cabinet next week. Also he thought the ambassador of the scheme would have to go off round the Empire very soon.

18 November 1944 I wondered if I went on this touring job whether I could be minister without portfolio but with a less silly name – I ought to have ministerial status anyhow.

29 November 1944 Rae rang to say the emissary idea had been approved by the War Cabinet. It is left to Churchill, Anderson and PMG to decide who, and Churchill had agreed to my being asked. Anderson was to have seen me but has gone to Paris so he has asked Barlow to arrange a preliminary meeting for tomorrow.

30 November 1944 Awful racket of a day. Treasury 2.30 to 4.00 with Barlow, Rae and Gardiner. Informed of things to date. The Cabinet decided to reject the Anzac scheme and that a mission should go round the Empire to explain this and to try to secure agreement on something more like a single corporation. Anderson had then been told to consult Amery, Stanley and Cranborne and submit a name to Churchill.[15] I was invited to be the mission. I said I would have to think about it and that I would have conditions to make. They proposed that I should resign as a director of Cable and Wireless and be reappointed as a government director, which they have a right to do. I said I did not think that status would be sufficient.

11 December 1944 Spoke on the phone to the controller saying I would not agree to go on this mission if he had a proper job for me. He said he deplored my going but did not think he should object. Lunched at the Club feeling miserable. I am terribly worried about leaving Muriel. Saw Anderson at 4.45. I said I supposed I would do the job if I was wanted, continuing the amenability I had shown on each previous, similar occasion. He said it had nothing to do with people wanting me to have a job, so I said I had understood that. But I said it was necessary for me to be in proper perspective with the Dominions; hence I had wondered about ministerial status. He said he didn't like the idea, nor think it necessary. He thought there would be no doubt about my status. As to myself, I told him about my financial position and worry. He said nothing about the fee for the trip and when I talked about the long period involved before anything could be settled, he said he didn't see any difficulty in finding something satisfactory. So I said I would rely on him for this and leave it so. He annoyed me at the end by saying he could not be definite as he had not said anything to Beaverbrook and he must also talk to Cranborne again.

13 December 1944 Rae phoned that all was clear. Met him and Barlow at the club after lunch. They said Beaverbrook had waved his arms about with delight when Anderson spoke of my going.

Drove to Wilshaw's house at Haslemere and told him the position to date. He hated the idea of my resigning and taking the government directorship, was most pessimistic about its effect on the other members of the Board and said it would put me in a most invidious position.

15 December 1944 Rae approved the draft of a letter I wanted to give Wilshaw saying that I was prepared to resign without reappointment. Wilshaw came to see me and I gave him the letter. He said I could not have acted more straightly by him.

18 December 1944 Last day in uniform – and for this I was thankful about ninety-five per cent. Everyone was most cordial and grateful. I was really quite moved. I can surely look back with real satisfaction on my Admiralty service.

22 December 1944 Saw First Lord and he really was most agreeable. He said, 'Oh John, the Navy is terribly grateful to you.' Told me that Churchill was continually interfering in detail which he never ought to touch, and that the war effort was appreciably delayed as a result. He spoke with great heat on this. I was sorry I had to leave as he was in talkative mood. Said he was very worried about German submarines as they could now get air and charge up without surfacing and only five per cent were spotted.

31 December 1944 The last day of the year. The only satisfaction in it is that I have been very busy and relatively content in the DCOM job and that I left Admiralty with a great deal of good will. But it has been the most dreadful year poor dear Muriel has had with hard work and this is a continual distress for me.

NOTES

1. Arthur Greenwood had been one of the Labour members of the war cabinet since May 1940. He had supervised departmental planning for post-war reconstruction. He lost his position in the government in February 1942 also.
2. Sir Stafford Cripps had, in fact, passed the peak of his brief wartime influence by this date, having just returned from his mission to India where he had failed to persuade the nationalist leaders to co-operate in the war with Japan.
3. Captain C. W. L. Meynell RN had been a friend of John Reith since 1928.
4. Captain F. Powys Maurice RN was one of the three staff officers immediately under Admiral Kekewich at Coastal Forces HQ.
5. These peers represented all ranges of political opinion; Moore-Brabazon, now Lord Brabazon, and Lord Bledisloe represented the views of 'ministers out of office'; Lord Strabolgi had been Labour's chief whip in the Lords since 1938; Lord Samuel was, even at this time, the Nestor of the Liberals; and Lord Balfour of Burleigh was a back-bencher and a friend.
6. Sir John Dill had been designated the next governor of Bombay to take up office in September 1942. In December 1941, however, after the United States had entered the war, he had accompanied Churchill to Washington for further conference with President Roosevelt and had remained there as senior British representative on the combined chiefs of staff committee. Bombay was forgotten.
7. These changes marked the end of Sir Stafford Cripps's challenge to Churchill's authority; he now left the war cabinet and lost the leadership of the Commons. He was to remain minister of aircraft production until the coalition government broke up in May 1945.
8. Four of the directors of British Overseas Airways resigned in protest at the establishment of the RAF Transport Command which they contended was final

and culminating evidence of the government's hostility to civil aviation and which made their position impossible. Miss Stanley, who in 1938 had transferred from the BBC to Imperial Airways as John Reith's secretary, had returned to work there after he left the government.

9. John Reith's 'testimonials' were the glowing references which he had earned from Admiral Kekewich and Captain Maurice for his work under them.

10. John Reith's proposed letter to the prime minister was at once lengthy and tactless and seemed to be almost demanding his restoration to office:

14 months ago you dropped me from office ... but I am wondering if you are not now disposed to give me responsibility in line with what I have done and can do.

Anderson's draft was shorter and more modest:

I should be grateful for any suggestions you could give which would help me to decide what to do.

11. Lord Hinchingbrooke was chairman of the Tory Reform committee.

12. John Reith never abandoned this view of his removal from the government in February 1942. Much later, in November 1956, his friend Lord Selborne wrote with sympathy and truth what Reith acknowledged to be 'an extraordinarily kind letter':

I think you take Churchill's dropping you in 1942 too seriously; and are you sure it was at the behest of a *Tory* cabal? I have always thought it was simply because he was head of a coalition and had to find places for the 3 parties represented in the coalition, and people like yourself, not attached to any party, had no one to fight for them. I thought it was very ungrateful treatment, but he did the same to other people. Neither you nor I would have dreamed of treating one of our servants in the same way ... but I think some allowance must be made for a prime minister leading a coalition in a war where the nation's existence was at stake.

13. Sir Alan Barlow's nervousness arose from the fact that John Reith had refused to speak to him for over a year because of his sense of outrage at the Treasury's refusal to recognize his claim to £38,000 insurance on leaving Imperial Airways.

14. The incident here referred to was the defeat of the government on an amendment to the Education Bill calling for equal pay for men and women teachers. Churchill demanded and obtained the deletion of the amendment as a vote of confidence.

15. L. S. Amery, Oliver Stanley and Lord Cranborne were the ministers responsible for India, the Colonies and the Dominions so that it was natural to consult them before naming the head of such a mission.

CHAPTER SEVEN

John Reith and the Empire (1)

1923-50

1. Introduction, 1923-45

When John Reith agreed at the end of 1944 to lead a government mission with the purpose of establishing a single corporation to control telecommunications throughout the Commonwealth and Empire, he was picking up a thread which had run through his time at the BBC and later with Imperial Airways. This was the thread of imperial unity. He told Neville Chamberlain in January 1940 that insofar as he had any political affiliations he was, like his father, a Gladstonian Liberal. But filial piety led him to misplace himself; in fact, he was far closer to the tradition of the Liberal Imperialists. He approved the existence of the British Empire and wished to see it continue and flourish.

Very early in his time at the BBC he had noted the potentialities of organizing broadcasting in India but he had been frustrated in his attempt to exploit these by officialdom. Thus he noted:

10 April 1926[1] Read the official papers re: Indian Broadcasting Company and am more than disgusted with the matter. I had made two attempts to get things on the right lines, one two years ago with the India Office and then about a year ago with the viceroy. Then I gave it up. There is neither vision nor recognition of the immense potentialities of broadcasting in this affair; no ethical or moral appreciation; just commercialism. It is an unparalleled opportunity for service in India but they have let the chance go now.

Eight years later, when the India Act of 1935 was being drafted, he felt the same frustration:

5 July 1934 Meeting at the India Office. It was unsatisfactory as England has obviously given up all idea of governing India, and such government as is done from Delhi with respect to the Provinces is to be very slight. I said it was rather discouraging to have such a hopeless attitude to start with and that as broadcasting was quite new surely it could be reserved for the Federal Government. I came away very depressed. It would be interesting to trace the development of the democracy inferiority complex in Imperial affairs, from quite small beginnings, just a few men here and there beginning to yield, and far too much lip-service prematurely to democratic methods.

Then he had the good fortune to meet the viceroy, Lord Willingdon, who was home on leave, and to enthuse him on the subject:

17 July 1934 The viceroy of India and Lady Willingdon round in the afternoon; he most pleasant and intelligent and very much interested. He said he wished that they would let him govern and that the India Office would leave him alone and that Sam Hoare [secretary of state for India] were not so timid. I told him that I thought his job was one of the few in the world really worth having but only if he were left alone and were able to govern.

30 July 1934 An hour's talk with the viceroy this morning. He admitted that he had taken no interest in the matter, and that it has never been discussed on the Executive Council. He said he would get busy in the matter immediately on his return. He gave me a lift back to the office and his last words were, 'You and I together will pull this through.'

The viceroy was as good as his word. When he addressed the Indian Legislature at the end of August he 'made considerable reference to broadcasting' and early in September he wrote asking John Reith's assistance in finding a 'superman' who could go out to develop broadcasting in India. Reith's reaction to this request (he was in South Africa when it arrived) was to think of his trusted deputy, Admiral Carpendale, and he called London to suggest this. It was, he said, a job more important than his own. But on his return he found the opportunity was more restricted than the viceroy had at first envisaged.

30 November 1934 High commissioner and deputy for India came to see me with respect to our sending a man out there. The viceroy's letter to me gave quite an inaccurate picture of what they require. Instead of the superman, which he asked for and for which I thought only Carpendale would do, all they want now is a man to run the new Delhi station and to supervise the existing ones at Bombay and Calcutta.[2]

Disappointed in India (in August 1935 he had a letter from P. J. Grigg, then financial member of the viceroy's Council, saying that the only thing the organization there was fit to run was a school of intrigue), John Reith had greater success in South Africa. Here he was able to escape what he regarded as the suffocating hand of Whitehall and to make his recommendations directly to the government of the Union. Early in May 1931 he had met the South African high commissioner whom he had found 'immensely interested in broadcasting' and who had asked for a memorandum on it which could be forwarded to his prime minister. The high commissioner had also suggested that John Reith should visit the country. This suggestion was to be fulfilled in the autumn of 1934 and was to lead to a personal report on broadcasting policy and development in the Union. John Reith's diary for this, the first of his many Commonwealth journeys, gives interesting sidelights on the political situation in South Africa at the time and, in particular, on his own attitude towards the imperial connection and how best to preserve it.

South African Journal

26 September 1934 Left for Simonstown, arriving 12.15. Great ceremony of going on board – first time I had been on a warship – all very impressive. Escorted by various officers to the Admiral's quarters and received by him and his wife. Interesting talk with Evans [C-in-C Africa station] after lunch on the walk at the stern. He speaks Afrikaans and is on very good terms with the Dutch – he is incorporating them in part of his training. There was a party on board of farmers whom he soon put at their ease and had great sport with. Evans is very optimistic about British relationships; he says Stanley, the high commissioner, is the opposite. Much ceremony in getting ashore.

Very glad of the evening to ourselves. We listened to the King and Queen at the launch of the big Cunarder[3] and heard everything – a record.

28 September 1934 [In Capetown] Visited Gayer, editor of the Malanist *Die Burger* and had an interesting talk with him about politics. He said ideally he was a republican but he didn't see it coming here – nowhere in prospect – as the bulk of the people didn't want it. He said his republicanism was largely here determined as a corrective (I put this to him) to offset the English and the England-orientation of others; that he would not bother much about it if English South Africans could be relied on to put South Africa first and all the time. Even if they had the right of neutrality – which he firmly believes they now legally have –

he is not satisfied because of the effect of English sentiment operating against the interests of South Africa in an emergency. He thought (naturally!) that it was in South Africa's interests to remain within the Commonwealth – even as a republic he thought it might be possible.

6 October 1934 [In Pretoria] To see Madeley, leader of the Labour party – what we had at home twenty years ago, conceited and bigoted. Very pleased that I had wanted to see him. He said it wasn't so unlikely as might appear that he would soon be in power! He wants state management of wireless, but I shook him on that.

7 October 1934 My wounding day. To the high commissioner's for lunch – Sir H. J. Stanley, GCMG. Present Liesching and wife (political secretary and second-in-command). Stayed there till 4.00, having an interesting talk. He is *very* pessimistic, as I had expected, about the British connection. It is true that Hertzog [prime minister of South Africa] wanted the Governor General to cable the Status Bills to the King. He said the King didn't like them at all, but had to accept them.

11 October 1934 [In Durban] Saw Kingston Russell, the firebrand imperialist editor of the *Mercury*, who is tremendously anti-Dutch. I did not feel I had finished with him so arranged to see him later . . . Kingston Russell arrived at 6.00 and I had another hour with him. He really is extraordinary. Thinks Admiral Evans 'a damn blasted bloody bounder', toadying to the Dutch and very unlike what an English admiral should be. That the excellent idea (which I had myself) that the Duke and Duchess of York should have been here instead of Clarendon, to keep the Governor General clear of politics, was crabbed by 'that damn woman Mary' who did not want to lose Princess Elizabeth. That Clarendon was a consummate weakling and fool; that Smuts was as bad as any of the Dutch; that the English connection would soon be lost; all this and lots more. There are hardly two coincident opinions on anything in this country – Malanist future, Socialism, or anything.

16 October 1934 [In Johannesburg] I saw Barlow, editor of *Express*, Colonel Stallard, leader of the imperialist faction, and Tielman Roos. As usual I had radically different opinions on everything from them. Barlow was a republican and fought against England; now he is very much anti-Dutch and thinks the only salvation of this country is to get the British element dominant in number. His paper was Roosite but he said he was seriously thinking of backing Stallard. Stallard is of the die-hard Tory type and is terrified of any State ownership of radio or anything else. Roos strongly in favour of it and doesn't see the least danger of political interference.

18 October 1934 [In Pretoria] To see Pirow [minister of defence, railways and harbours] at the Union Building. It certainly is a magnificently situated place, wild country just behind, flowers all round and a fine view across Pretoria to the hills the other side. Pirow is anxious to have public ownership of broadcasting but, like Havenga [minister of finance], he fears unpopularity to the government. He admitted that he would like to see something approaching Nazi rule here and said that he would then hope to use broadcasting as an adjunct thereto. He gave me his views on several of their problems, admitting that they were ruled by the poor white, that they would have to reduce the franchise, put the native out of the towns to a large extent, fixing a minimum wage of 10/- a day for them and the semi-skilled white equally.

23 October 1934 Lunched with Hofmeyer, minister of education, interior and health, at the Club. After lunch I had about an hour with him and found him very interesting. He said he thought Pirow would put efficiency before racialism, though not a year ago, that he had greatly modified his ideas and attitude towards the British connection since association with the South African party ministers. He thought Pirow's attitude to the Empire was the *faute de mieux* one; Hertzog's had a bit of sentiment now; and his own, positive. I wonder. Some English South Africans believe this but others, the high commissioner included, are sure they are all out for themselves, i.e. South Africa only, Smuts included; they also think that they want to inherit the Rhodesias in Central Africa. Defence is another powerful factor, and Pirow, who is very anti-French, is sure that there is a war coming from the French in the north.

24 October 1934 To Johannesburg at 7.45 and had an hour's talk with Stallard – a fine man but too extreme in his actions. His Dominion party is gaining ground; he said he thought ten per cent were Dutch. Of course he is convinced that the whole policy of the Dutch is to subordinate the English and everything English. He thinks Smuts quite as bad as any of them and all out for an independent United States of Africa.

25 October 1934 Saw the prime minister [Hertzog] for about an hour. I had first to give him a little lecture on the importance of radio. Then I mentioned some of the advantages of state ownership. He got on to the same line as Havenga of course; said that in South Africa a very few people, and certainly any considerable interest, could stampede the government; that with things as they were governments could not really govern. In other countries vested interests off-set each other and also the franchise was so large that it needed a great many of them to produce any effect. Here fifty people could stampede a member. He said they would have to reduce the franchise if they were going to get anywhere in South Africa. He was very cordial and grateful to me and said he would study my Report very closely.

Saw Pirow again. More talk about my report. I asked whether it was a foregone conclusion that, through fear of unpopularity, they would do nothing for two years. He said he did not think that necessary, repeated what he had said the other day and said that he himself was in favour of immediate action. I said I was surprised at the fear of un-popularity bothering him of all the ministers. He admitted that his attitude to the 'British League of Nations' was of the *faute de mieux* order, but that he expected South Africa would be a member of it for one hundred years yet, largely on account of the defence situation. He is sure that there will be war sooner or later with the French, their native policy being different from the South African one. The native with them is equally a French citizen. He is more afraid of this than of Japan.

John Reith's report to the South African government was published early in 1935. In this he gave expression to his belief in broadcasting as an instrument of good in the world 'in the service of wisdom and beauty and peace' but only if it was 'rightly institutionalized, rightly inspired and rightly controlled'. For South Africa, in particular, he pointed out the potentialities of broadcasting as an agent of national union and education, drawing together English and Dutch, country and town, blacks and whites. So he drew attention to the part which broadcasting could play 'in amelioration and development of the social life of the native races'; he recommended 'special provision for the Asiatic section of the community'; and he urged the need for broad-casters to be aware of their 'high commission', not to 'bend to every breeze of criticism that blows' and to be prepared to lead. He con-cluded:

The loneliest plattelander may hear the statesmen of his own and other countries. He may be present at the function and participate in the crises of his day. He may hear the finest music and the greatest exponents of learning in his own home – enjoy in fact many of the amenities of metropolitan life and culture, and farm his land better than ever before. He may be in touch with and able to take a real interest in the movements of thought and the processes of action which determine the destiny of his country and of the world – this directly and not through an intermediary with his personal education and bias; for the statesman has the whole electorate before him as in the days of the ancient city-state.

Thus in his South African report John Reith enunciated his general ideas for broadcasting and for imperial unity and applied them in the context of a single Dominion. But he wished to see them operate throughout the Commonwealth and Empire. So in July 1935 he urged on the Australian authorities the need to control their so-called B-class broadcasting stations, which were largely owned by the local Press and permitted to advertise. He warned Mr [now Sir Robert] Menzies, then attorney-general in the Lyons government, that unless checked immediately 'the B-class would become so powerful that no one would touch them'. A year later he noted:

11 June 1936 Menzies, attorney-general of Australia, to see me. He said I had been quite right about the B-class stations getting out of control. He told me what they had tried to do. A member of the government had made a fighting speech, very rude to the B-stations and to the Press, but then everybody got cold feet about the next election – just as I predicted. I asked if they were ever going to put things right and he said, 'No, we haven't the guts.'

At the same time that he urged on the governments of India and of the Dominions the opportunities that they could and should take for themselves, John Reith also pressed upon a reluctant United Kingdom government (and on what he regarded as its obstructionist officials) the doctrine that broadcasting from England should be used as a 'consolidatory element within the Empire'. He made this point at the Colonial Office Conference in 1930.

30 June 1930 To the Colonial Office Conference at 11.00; it was quite an affair with Lord Passfield [colonial secretary] in the chair, he having come specially as I was speaking. I spoke for about twenty minutes and it was really all quite interesting as there was the

British Colonial Empire – fifty colonies mostly represented by their governors. A great many of them spoke and all seemed very keen to have an Empire broadcasting service.

Eventually, at the end of 1932, after more than two years of governmental delay, John Reith was able to launch the BBC's Empire Service. He continued to think in these terms for the remainder of his time with the BBC and throughout these years and beyond, the idea of helping to draw the Empire together was one which strongly appealed to him. So, in June 1938 when he had newly moved to Imperial Airways and was as yet still uncommitted in his mind to its work, Sir Donald Banks, then permanent head of the Air Ministry, skilfully appealed to these imperial feelings as a means of enthusing him in his new task. He urged Reith to think of himself as being 'at the centre of a vast aerial communication system'. John Reith swallowed the bait and in November 1938 he was writing in his diary of 'my ideas for Empire co-operation'.

By 1945, then, John Reith had been thinking and preaching dominion development and imperial unity through the agency of broadcasting and civil aviation for more than twenty years. Characteristically, he hoped always that this unity would be a means to achieve moral purpose. He was deeply disappointed during the war that little attention, as he saw it, was given to this aspect of the imperial war effort not merely by the Churchill government at home (he expected nothing of that) but also by the individual Commonwealth governments. So even within two weeks of D-day he found time to note:

22 May 1944 There was a pompous manifesto issued by the Empire prime ministers recently. Its content was nil, and there was no reference to anything spiritual or moral. A great chance was missed.

When, therefore, John Reith took up the task of negotiating with the governments of the Empire over telecommunications, he was, in a sense, on familiar ground. For the next fifteen years his Diary was to contain much on this imperial theme.

2. World Tour, 1945

[Before 1939 John Reith had probably felt more strongly about the decline in imperial leadership and purpose at home than about the aspirations of the Dominions to secure a proper recognition of their sovereign rights. But he had always appreciated the second, and, as we have seen, he could understand and sympathize with the feelings that led a South African journalist to tell him in 1934 that English South Africans should learn to put 'South Africa first and all the time'. After 1945, however, the emphasis of his thought changed. He now cared less for Empire and more for Commonwealth. He wished the members of the Commonwealth to be treated by the United Kingdom authorities as sovereign equals and to extract from this relationship the benefits of an agreed collaboration willingly entered into. This attitude explains his success in negotiations with the Commonwealth governments in the field of telecommunications. They could trust him to recognize their interests. For all the strength of his personality he appeared in their eyes less dictatorial and more understanding than the British ministers, who had no time for more than lip-service to their interests, or the British civil service which seemed only concerned to preserve the superficial appearance of co-operation.]

5 January 1945 To see Bruce, the high commissioner for Australia. After a sticky beginning in which he tried hard to get me to say what I was going to say in Australia, I got him talking and even succeeded in making him say he thought one corporation for the Empire should be acceptable.

8 January 1945 To see the New Zealand high commissioner. He was very friendly and forthcoming, but he knew nothing about the thing at all.

11 January 1945 Saw Beaverbrook at Arlington House where he apparently does most of his weird business. Bracken was there when I arrived and Sir A. Sinclair came as I left, shaking hands with me; I didn't want to shake hands with him. Beaverbrook said he was delighted I was going on this mission – absolutely the best man etc., so much so that he didn't mind my views on public corporations with which he disagreed and would fight against. Referred to my running the BBC and now what had become of it – it was just a sub-department of government. The public corporation system depended too much on someone like me.

Dined at Claridges with the Iliffes. Hamar Greenwood and Lady Willingdon among those present. Greenwood said I ought to take charge of the railways in Canada. Lady Willingdon took a cigar for her son, bones for her dogs, and a shilling from me for the cloakroom.

17 January 1945 Long talk with Machtig, head of Dominions Office. He cared nothing at all about imperial communications as such – only about some appearances of Empire co-ordination, and even if only in such an utterly specious shape as the Commonwealth Communications Council. He very much approved a draft letter of mine to Malcolm MacDonald [high commissioner in Canada]. Quite a useful talk generally.

Saw Attlee in his room in the House of Commons and he was very friendly, but beyond urging a cure for air-sickness had nothing specially relevant to say.

19 January 1945 Saw Bruce again unexpectedly. He read me part of a signal he had made to Australia. He gave me a great boost – in favour of public utility system, Empire co-ordination with proper share to the Dominions, independent minded, strong personality, and that I could be relied on to get the government here to agree to what I came back with. It should be most helpful and I am very grateful to him.

[John Reith now set out on his great tour of the Empire. His party included, besides himself and his personal secretary Miss Joyce Wilson, Sir Edwin Herbert, director-general of the Censorship Department, Sir Stanley Angwin, assistant director-general of the Post Office, and N. J. M. Buckley of the War Cabinet secretariat. An administrative officer of the Post Office, to handle business affairs, and a second secretary completed his 'splendid team'.

As his first objective was to explain the Government's decision to reject the so-called Anzac scheme, under which Cable and Wireless would have been superseded by numerous corporations in each of the Dominions and India, and as this scheme originated, as its name implied, from Australia, John Reith resolved to begin his negotiations at Canberra. This meant flying westwards, crossing Atlantic and Pacific, and the party which left Northolt on 22 January did not reach its first destination until the last day of the month having travelled via the Azores, Bermuda, Washington, San Diego, Honolulu and Fiji.]

1 February 1945 [In Canberra] We all went to see Ronald Cross, the high commissioner at 10.15. He didn't know anything and couldn't give us any help. While there I had word that the prime minister [John Curtin] wanted to see me at 11.30 so Cross and I went along. He came out of his Cabinet which seems to sit almost continuously. He suggested I might begin with an official committee and seemed to be diffident in making the suggestion. I said it was quite satisfactory and it was in fact what we had been advised to try to secure.

Committee from 2.00 till 4.45 with McVey (Post Office), McFarlane (Treasurer) and others. Made great progress and we were very pleased. Cabinet committee at 8.00 with prime minister in the chair, and Evatt [minister for external affairs], Ashley and Chifley [minister for post-war reconstruction]. I expounded the objections to the Anzac scheme. They agreed that central control was necessary. Prime minister was very civil and we felt very pleased again.

> [John Reith's early optimism was not to last. The choice, as he wrote in his autobiography, was between a multi-corporation system with maximum central control and a single corporation with maximum local autonomy; after lengthy discussions over the next week a compromise was arrived at. As he later wrote, 'though each country was to have its own corporation there was to be a central organization with the powers of a holding company'.]

3 February 1945 I went by arrangement with the prime minister to see his ministerial committee by themselves. I went quickly over the whole situation and made an effect on them. PM said he would direct that both schemes be examined over the weekend. He agreed that the single scheme was more efficient but said he simply could not get that agreed. Pathetic.

4 February 1945 At 2.45 we all went to the office and worked out a revision of our paper [for the single corporation]. Meantime McVey and Co. had worked on a paper which he brought to us at 5.00 p.m. As ours went much further I suggested a committee to try to reconcile the two. [John Reith left this to his colleagues as he was committed to giving a broadcast talk.] Herbert and Buckley came at midnight but there were substantial alterations in the paper, especially that the local corporations were to be more comprehensive. I made a mistake in not doing this meeting myself. Herbert had of course reserved points for me but there was nothing to be done. Possibly I wouldn't have got any more.

5 February 1945 Herbert and Buckley both strongly advocated my letting the document go in with a covering note to the effect that there was little between the papers. There certainly wasn't since ours had gone so far towards theirs, and ours began by being a considerable way to theirs anyhow. I wasn't very pleased with them. Cabinet at 12.00.

We had a great struggle but it came out fairly well. An agreed paper was drafted and at 7.45 I went to the office to read it. It wasn't bad as things were. We went into the committee at 8.15. It was the worst meeting we had had – almost incredible. They actually tried to get us to substitute for the agreed document one they had done on their own. It looked as if we might break up in confusion. Finally, I got them to work on our draft. There were several tussles still, including the most monstrous suggestion of all – an addition to the clause which gives the central body its power which would have vitiated that completely. We were furious with them. Meeting finished at 11.30; and I was feeling much better at the end than at the beginning. I had been tired through doing nothing all afternoon.

6 February 1945 Cabinet committee at 11.00 and there was a lot of argument. Curtin did his best to get things through. It took till 12.20 and then he delivered himself of one of his impressive exordiums about Empire unity and pooling of sovereignty.

Dined at Ronnie Cross's. Very pleasant party and very well done. McVey came for me and we went to the prime minister's Lodge. I signed my letter and a copy of the agreement and he did likewise – this interchange of letters between Curtin and me was a hopelessly formal affair but he then went off again very interestingly about the Empire.

[On 8 February John Reith's party flew on to New Zealand.]

9 February 1945 [In Wellington] This is very different place from Canberra being rather a mess-up of a town. I saw the prime minister, Fraser, and Nash, treasurer [in fact minister for finance], at 10.15 and was very civilly received. The PM made a speech of welcome and we got to work with their official committee. I made the same sort of statement as in Australia and hammered in the advantages of the single corporation idea. We worked till 12.45 and again 2.15 to 5.15 making very good progress.

12 February 1945 Prime minister and Nash from 9.30 to 10.30. I explained our views about local corporations and central corporations. Nash was now on to a holding corporation idea which suits us well. I was to see him and the PM again at 4.30 but they were not ready. They looked to a central body with more power than the Australians wanted. I arranged that the PM should telephone me at the Wellington Club when he was ready, and I dined there, Herbert and Angwin also, with about a dozen notables. It was an urbane metropolitan atmosphere, very different from that of the Parliament House. I wish we could have more of this. PM telephoned at 9.15. The letter from him to me is quite satisfactory. Went to the hotel, got the party collected and drafted our reply to the PM. We were all in the sitting-room till nearly 1.00. Most satisfactory.

13 February 1945 [In Melbourne] We left New Zealand at 8.15 and arrived Melbourne 17.45 – 15.45 local. To Athenæum Club for dinner. Very pleasant and I circulated about. It is almost pathetic how eager these people are to talk with us and get our views on things. It was very obvious in Wellington also. By not sending the right sort of people out to these Dominions we are losing an awful lot. Melbourne is a really fine city with broad, tree-lined avenues and fertile gardens.

[On 15 February the party flew from Western Australia to Ceylon.]

16 February 1945 [In Ceylon] The postmaster general here, Appleby, said there was no need to alter any of the ownership arrangements here, despite their intense desire for dominion status. Their constitution is the weirdest in the Empire. Soulbury [chairman of the Ceylon commission] and party are out here trying to improve it. They have universal male suffrage – even illiterates; ministers are thrown up as chairmen of committees, and the chief secretary presides over a board of ministers.

18 February 1945 [In Delhi] We left Ceylon at 8.45. It was extraordinary to be flying over India – India! We went over Hyderabad and Nagpur, where I thought of poor Douglas's years of devoted labour,[4] and then we went over Agra, which was the supreme excitement of the day – the first sight of the Taj Mahal away below us. We came down to about 2000 feet and circled twice round it, seeing also the famous old fort. Arrived at Delhi, 4.30, and were met by the viceroy's military secretary and two or three ADCs. Then two or three miles drive to viceroy's house and shown our quarters there. I have the Irwin suite which the viceroy and wife originally occupied. My bedroom is about 70 feet by 35 feet and the bed about 8 feet broad. We had tea and then, having sighted a bit of the gardens, we all, on my initiative, went out. It was quite indescribable, especially a circular terraced part at the far end. I never saw anything like it. The flowers were nearly all English – every sort and kind including all the lovely homely ones like pansies and mignonette. It got dark quite quickly about 7.00, by which time we were having a drink indoors. At dinner there was a gorgeously attired Punjab servant behind each chair; they made a great salute when the viceroy [Lord Wavell] entered. After dinner I was bid go and talk to the viceroy on a sofa. He wasn't very easy or forthcoming but quite pleasant; he told me that he thought the Anzac scheme was the farthest the Indian government would go by way of central control, which was most alarming, but I thought it could not be so bad as that.

[John Reith found negotiations with the Indian representatives 'very slow going' initially, but with the support of Sir Jeremy Raisman, the finance member of the viceroy's Council, and helped by the open-minded attitude of the chief Indian negotiator, Sir Gurunath Bewoor, he was able to achieve a considerable measure of success.]

21 February 1945 Worked in the office all morning. The Indian draft official letter was excellent and I had only one word to suggest should be changed. I lunched at Sir Firoz Khan Noon's [defence member of the viceroy's Council] house, meeting there the London high commissioner. Very interesting and amusing conversation. Noon was very critical of the UK government – its slowness and lack of guts.

[On 23 February the party left Delhi for Southern Rhodesia flying via Aden and Nairobi.]

26 February 1945 [In Salisbury] Met Sir Ernest Guest, senior minister next to the prime minister [Sir Godfrey Huggins], who apologized for the prime minister's absence. He had to handle some crisis in Bulawayo. We then went into conference. I went over all the ground as usual and they took it very well. They seemed quite ready to consider a single corporation. Of course Southern Rhodesia is quite differently situated from anywhere we have yet been, being in the centre of a continent. Finished at 12.30 and they said that was all they would need. On the drive yesterday [from Gwelo airfield to Salisbury] I had suddenly come on the idea that the central corporation should have most of the assets which we had always thought of as going with the UK corporation. This would enormously strengthen it. It would not only ensure its position by giving it something executive to do, but its position would get stronger and stronger, instead of local corporations acquiring more and more power.

[On 28 February John Reith took his party on to Capetown.]

1 March 1945 [In Capetown] We went to see Smuts [prime minister of South Africa] in the morning. He told me that they had been about to reject some of the Anzac proposals as giving too much central control! Smuts was most cordial in his welcome. I wasn't misled. Herbert and Angwin were with me. I spoke for about ten minutes and then Smuts said with great regret that he simply could not agree to anything that tied him up with my central body – it was quite impossible politically. It was hopeless talking to the officials under the shadow of this edict. I told Smuts of this at lunch and asked if he would tell his people they could at least discuss properly. He said he would, but it didn't have any effect. I didn't have much talk with Smuts at lunch. I was feeling disgusted with him that he hadn't the political courage to do what was right – especially when the difficulties of the position were so slight and the advantages so great.

5 March 1945 I was feeling tired today due to the utter disgust I feel with Smuts and this country and to our having failed to continue the success of elsewhere owing to Smuts's obstinacy, cowardice and dishonesty. The others thought we had accomplished a great deal. Saw the man after lunch. He assured me that we should get all we wanted by the consultation method and that he would fully co-operate. I was disgusted with him and wanted to be away. I then went to see the high commissioner [Sir Evelyn Baring]. He is very unhappy in his job and thinks anything might happen – e.g. Smuts demand the native protectorate; also encourage Southern Rhodesia to absorb Northern Rhodesia and other territories, and then South Africa absorb them. What a country; I should be frightened to live here. We took off at 7.00. I was delighted to see the last of South Africa, we mostly all were.

[John Reith's party were now on the last leg of their long trip, flying to Canada via Ascension Island, Brazil and Trinidad. They reached Ottawa 'exactly as scheduled' at breakfast time on 9 March but found that talks could not begin until 12 March, much to Reith's disgust. But as he suffered an acute attack of sinusitis the day after his arrival this delay enabled him to have some small rest.]

12 March 1945 Saw Howe [minister of munitions and supply], the minister concerned, for an hour and had a helpful conversation with him. If his will prevails we should emerge with the same sort of arrangement as in South Africa. Meeting at 3.00 with Howe in the chair and he supported us well.

13 March 1945 The morning meeting was terribly dragged out but at lunch I was able to suggest formulae which met all their points. At the afternoon meeting they accepted all our amendments to their draft letter and it is most satisfactory. I was really very pleased. We go home tomorrow on D+51 as scheduled. It is extraordinary.

15 March 1945 We had a very smooth passage, landing at Northolt just before 1 o'clock. I am very grateful to God for having brought me safely home and for keeping my darling ones safe. But no message about our return from anyone at all – Anderson or Cranborne or anyone. Lousy of them, it is.

3. Commonwealth Telecommunications, 1945–50

[John Reith's official report was presented and printed by the end of March. It included a characteristically allusive reference to his having formed some conclusions on Commonwealth and Empire affairs in general which were outside the terms of reference of his mission. To his intense chagrin those at whom this glancing shot was aimed ignored, or possibly failed to notice, it. Of the main content of the report, however, Sir John Anderson expressed warm approval and promised to try and hurry it through the Cabinet. But there were rocks ahead. Lord Beaverbrook had given notice of his hostility to the idea of public corporations before the mission set out and he was soon to give evidence of this both in Cabinet and by encouraging the directors of Cable and Wireless to change their minds about the whole scheme. Reith's idea, which had come to him in Rhodesia, of strengthening the proposed central corporation by lodging with it the 'oceanic assets' of Cable and Wireless (i.e. assets not situated in Britain, the Dominions or India) was feared by ministers for the very reason that he advanced in its favour – namely that it would give additional control to the Dominions, jointly, without compromising their sovereign rights, and extend the sphere of Commonwealth co-operation. Nevertheless, the Cabinet agreed to the calling of a London conference, as recommended in the report, and John Reith was appointed chairman of it. When this decision was made the wartime coalition government was still in existence; when the conference assembled Churchill's 'caretaker' government held office; and when the conference ended the Labour government had taken over. In this uneasy political situation John Reith was once again oppressed by introspective doubts and hopes for his future.]

4 April 1945 I have wondered if that cad Churchill offered me a job in the government when the Labour and Liberal lot walk out, whether I would take it. I cannot imagine his doing so, of course. If he did, I don't think I would accept and I don't think I should. Apart from my loathing of him, thereby making it almost wrong to serve under him, I think it would be an undignified thing to do; and what security is there in it anyhow?

5 April 1945 Lunched with Weeks, DCIGS. He said Churchill was a menace – always avoiding decisions – and he himself is terrified of what will happen when Germany is out. How I wish people generally could know what military and other leaders associated with Churchill think of him.

6 April 1945 I am not in the least keen to be in charge of the preparations for the [Commonwealth Communications] conference or to take the chair at it. I don't know what to make of myself. I simply don't know what to do or want to do. I am obviously still in full powers – as evidenced by the recent tour. I suppose I would like to be Ambassador in Washington, but really am not sure as there would be lots of things which would irritate me intensely.

11 April 1945 Miserable ministerial committee, to which I was summoned, in Anderson's room. There were present Attlee, Amery, Devonshire [under secretary for the Colonies] (attended or rather watched by a miserable bumpkin from the Colonial Office), Beaverbrook and Grimston [assistant PMG] (PMG being sick which was most unfortunate). Stanley (Colonial Office) was sick also. It was a miserable affair. Anderson asked if I had anything to add. I said my report was clear. Questions of me were invited. Very few. I said in answer to a typical, silly, waffling letter which Cranborne had written – no one from the Dominions Office there at all – that the 'oceanic assets' did not make a new problem. He said he was sure Canada and South Africa wouldn't accept it. Weak-brained, weak-kneed idiots they are. After half an hour Anderson intimated that they would discuss the matter 'among ourselves', so I left. Rae had told me last night that Beaverbrook had written saying the thing was no use at all. He said nothing this morning. It seems that they didn't come to any conclusions except to refer the matter to the War Cabinet.

16 April 1945 I saw Cranborne, 3.15 till 4.00. This was my first talk with him since I got back – very bad. Quite obviously he had not read my report, and this is simply damnable as it concerns him so much. He was very civil and thought I had done a wonderful job and all the rest of it. I told him what he ought to say in rebutting Beaverbrook's abominable and obscurantist line and he seemed to hoist it all in.

18 April 1945 Rae came up about 11.30 when I was sitting in my armchair reading Dickens. He brought the blasted Cabinet conclusions. Churchill, summing up, said it seemed to be the opinion that matters should be taken further on the lines recommended by me but that, since legislation was necessary, which couldn't be put through this session, there was no need for the government to come to a definite decision. Typical of his abominable cowardice and policy of indecision. A conference is to be called to work out a scheme after consideration of my report – what in heaven's name is the sense in this? – but it was then to be submitted to the governments – and all the Dominion governments have already agreed the principles and are expecting to come and settle details without more submittings back. I told Rae what I felt, and of course he is of the same view, but being more used than I to such contemptible wafflings, wants to make the best of it.

27 April 1945 Saw the blighted Anderson at 10.30. His self-satisfaction, conceit and pomposity seem to increase. He said he had great difficulty in getting the Cabinet decision he did; the whole thing was very nearly thrown out; although the other ministers had agreed to recommend the report he had had no backing from them; they left it all to him to argue with that devil Beaverbrook. He said it was quite painful to see Churchill's distress at not being able to agree with what Beaverbrook wanted. What an illuminating remark that is. Bracken had supported Beaverbrook (what business had Bracken to talk at all?). He hoped I would take charge of preparations for the conference and take the chair thereat. I suppose I shall have to do the job.

4 May 1945 I am dreading the victory celebrations and have no sort of heart for them. I am feeling absolutely rotten and utterly soured of everything even religion if an essential is loving one's neighbour and feeling kindly to them – for I hate and loathe them. It seems to me that anyone who has decency, unselfishness, kindliness, public spirit and such like is a fool. He is put on. It is the opposite sort of qualities which bring success and contentment. Everything is upside down. The undesirable are subsidized from birth to grave at our expense; they are given everything and nothing is expected of them. We who pay for it all are pushed about, insulted and soon will be driven out of existence.

6 May 1945 I am the worst possible example for the children in almost every way. I am so embittered and soured by the treatment I have had. The best years of life have gone and I have missed such a terrible lot when there was plenty of money and the children were young. I had so very much to be thankful for; but I was always wanting much more to do than I had to do, and never content. Oh God, what a disposition I have.

18 May 1945 I told Machtig of the Dominions Office that I thought it would be most discourteous if there weren't a minister in the UK delegation (for the coming conference). His attitude was typical and symbolic of the UK attitude to the Dominions: Clarkson (South African minister of posts) was a dud and as to Danziger, a Southern Rhodesian minister was nothing at all and was so treated here. Yes indeed. I got him to see that there was something in what I was saying. They are letting the Empire drift away. The King's visit to Parliament yesterday was made a purely UK affair, but they don't see this. They don't do nearly enough with the King.

24 May 1945 Saw Vincent Massey [high commissioner for Canada] and told him of my Ottawa visit. He thought the 'oceanic assets' idea was a brain-wave. But the Colonial Office are giving stupid trouble about this scheme. Things aren't moving fast enough.

The cad Churchill is making up his new government. I suppose I really should like to be offered a job – if it were a decent one – but I don't think it would be good for me to take it.

26 May 1945 Cabinet of 16 announced. Bracken is First Lord! It would have been fun in some ways to be that, but I don't think I could have stood it with Churchill minister of defence. And of course Beaverbrook is still in. I think I should only have wanted to be lord president, which Woolton is. I wonder if there is anything ahead for me. I have tried to take a better view of life. Five years from now I suppose I shall wish it were possible to return to 1945. I even wondered if I would go to the House of Lords with some regularity. The only job I know I want is ambassador to USA – or viceroy though what I saw of India put me off that a bit.

29 May 1945 The Dominions Office are making difficulty about the conference being held before the election results are known[5] arising unfortunately from Machtig taking seriously my observations about the UK delegation having a ministerial head.

31 May 1945 The postmaster general [H. F. C. Crookshank] to see me. He is an unimpressive little man. I told him exactly what I thought about there being no proper ministerial head of the UK delegation. He tried to base his objection on the election preoccupations, but it is really my not being a minister which is monstrous. None of these people seem to be able to appreciate Dominion susceptibilities.

8 June 1945 Meeting 3.00 to 4.30 in Anderson's room to deal with my papers [for the Dominions]. Amery, Stanley, Mabane [minister of state], PMG and Beaverbrook there. It was an absolutely disgusting affair, Beaverbrook making every sort of statement and objection he could to get them held up or not sent at all. Simply shocking and shameful. The others were all helpful. After interminable arguments in which Beaverbrook made a series of statements without foundation – definite obstructionism – Anderson managed to get the length of saying that they must be sent off at once but that high commissioners could be told not to release them till further word came. Very weak, I thought. A disgusting show.

9 June 1945 The Company [i.e. Cable and Wireless] have written rejecting the whole scheme, which was not what I expected. It is due to Beaverbrook having got in touch with them, and their letter might have been dictated by him.

Letter to Lord Beaverbrook 11 June 1945
In view of some of the things you said about me last Friday [8 June] I want to make my position clear.

You spoke as if I were solely responsible for abhorrent recommendations. I'm not . . . I hadn't a clear field. Other people had trampled all over it. I had to clean it up as best I could. I had a difficult time and was (relatively) pleased with what I brought back. It was a lot better than what was expected here.

Further, I should have thought you, of all people, would have welcomed the imperial co-operation element in what I brought back; and even if you loathed corporations generally that you would have welcomed the establishment of an imperial corporation – the first to be achieved (except War Graves).

13 June 1945 Minister's committee at 10.30. It wasn't quite so bad as last Friday but nearly so. There was no argument about the papers being released but a long, weary and ridiculous one about ministers being on the UK delegation or not. Also a long wrangle about oceanic assets caused by Stanley's stupidity. Anderson was awfully feeble.

21 June 1945 Meeting with Anderson, Inverforth and Wilshaw about the Company's letter. It was a rotten show. They were talking verbatim as Beaverbrook, and Anderson was very feeble. I really do feel more and more contempt and irritation with him.

24 June 1945 McFarlane from Australia telephoned. He was most sarcastic about the Dominions Office. He said they were very remiss in looking after 'their children'. Absolutely shocking.

6 July 1945 I felt rather apprehensive of the South African attitude but what Smuts said when I met him at the high commissioner's party at the Dorchester put that all right. He said, 'I think you will get away with it this time,' and repeated it.

[The conference opened on 16 July and there was a government reception at the Savoy that evening which John Reith thought 'a second-rate show'.]

17 July 1945 Danziger to see me. He obviously feels very peeved at the UK government not appointing a minister on the delegation. He had a lot to say which was most critical of the UK attitude to the Dominions generally. All of which I understand and sympathize with.

18 July 1945 We went to the Abbey Memorial Service to Mr Curtin.[6] We were put in the second row in the choir and then to my disgust I found people like Louis Greig and Ronnie Tree arriving with better tickets so I sent a note to Admiral Bromley [ceremonial and reception secretary to the Dominions office] saying I didn't think the Dominions ministers were properly placed. He came along and said Danziger was all right but Clarkson should come out. Apart from Danziger hearing him, the discrimination was quite wrong. Clarkson properly declined to move. After the service I took them round.

Oceanic Assets committee 2.30 – 4.15 resulting in an amicable agreement not to pursue the matter further. Perhaps I should have felt more disappointed than I did; my chief feeling was one of relief at getting the issue cleared. Some wanted it; others would have agreed to it after more examination; but the Canadians and South Africans were against it. This is another instance of vaccillation, since Howe in Canada and Massey here had both welcomed it and Forsyth (South Africa) had told me here that they would resent its being dropped.

25 July 1945 Lunched at South Africa House. Amery, Cranborne, Sandys [minister of works] and some other ministers present. I was in a bad temper but got out of it to some extent by Amery's sympathetic reception of my story about never having been questioned on the paragraph of my report about Dominion and Colonial affairs. He said it was typical and made a striking criticism of Churchill. If I had included anything about India in my report he said he would have been after me pretty quick to find out what I meant. Machtig said it was dreadful that the Dominions Office had nowhere to entertain people such as the South Africans had. It was interesting that he had sufficient imagination to make that remark.

26 July 1945 Election results at 11.00 made it clear that there was a tremendous swing over to Labour. I had thought that Churchill might have a small majority, but it was obvious at once that he had suffered a crushing defeat, and there was no question about my jubilation on this score, however little confidence I might have in Attlee and Co., and however much I might dislike the Bevins, Morrisons, and such like in office. What was particularly gratifying to me was that most of the thugs like Bracken and Sandys were put out.

31 July 1945 Barlow came to see me to say that everyone wanted me to be chairman of the new Board and would I accept. I said I couldn't give a definite answer, that I wasn't particularly keen but that I wouldn't turn the thing down.

3 August 1945 We had the signing meeting at 4.30. Later there was a meeting of heads of delegations to discuss arrangements for Bermuda [conference with USA] from which I was asked to absent myself. They were all very anxious that I should accept the chairmanship of the Commonwealth Communications Council at the end of August and go to Bermuda as such. I don't at all want to be appointed chairman of the CCC (in succession to Campbell Stuart forsooth), but I can see that the sooner this job is filled the more chance there is that the new central body collects its authority. It is a very difficult position for me. And, apart from not being keen on the job, I don't know what becomes of my present £5000 p.a.

[The Labour government did not give John Reith the opportunity for public service for which he pined. He felt totally rejected, noting at the end of January 1946, 'Here are all sorts of things in which I could be of the utmost use, but I am not wanted anywhere.' Almost two years later, when summarizing his position at the end of 1947, he wrote: 'it seems that everybody has now accepted my absolute negligence'.

Although he did not attend the Bermuda conference in the autumn of 1945, he did agree to accept the chairmanship of the Commonwealth Communications Council with the prospect of this leading to the chair of the new central body (the future Telecommunications Board) which the London conference had recommended should be established. This decision kept him in touch with Commonwealth affairs, and in all the long negotiations which led, first, to the signature of the overall agreement on Commonwealth communications in 1948 and then, in 1949, to the formal establishment of the CTB, he maintained his position as a champion of the dignity and sovereign rights of the Commonwealth countries, often, as he felt, in the teeth of the feebleness and indifference of the ministers and Whitehall departments concerned.

Labour ministers and their enthusiastic hangers-on felt, in the heady atmosphere of their temporary political ascendancy, that John Reith should join their party before he was given any important task. This was something he could not bring himself to do although he was well aware, as he noted in the context of the New Year's honours of 1947, that if you 'join the party, you get a peerage and jobs'. He despised the careerist turncoats of the time and when, at a sherry party at Christmas 1946, he was told that he had joined the Labour party his sarcastic rejoinder was that he had also become a Muslim. In these circumstances it is not surprising, though he himself was surprised, that Attlee, as prime minister, ignored or turned politely aside his pleas for full employment in 1946 and 1948.

But John Reith was too experienced and too efficient to be totally neglected. In September 1945, a month before he finally agreed to take on the CCC, he accepted the invitation of Lewis [later Lord] Silkin, then minister of town and country planning, to chair (unpaid) the committee of inquiry being set up to consider the development of New Towns. By July 1946 this committee had completed its work with admirable promptitude and, arising out of its work, John Reith then accepted the paid position of chairman of the board of the Hemel Hempstead development corporation which was one of the New Towns to be set up. At the same time he gave himself the task of writing his autobiography which he began in December 1946, finished in November 1947 and revised finally for the press by November 1948. The gap in his activities made by the completion of this work was fortunately filled in January 1949 by his appointment as chairman of the National Film Finance Corporation. For the best part of the next two years he thus had three jobs – CCC (or CTB as it became in November 1949); Hemel Hempstead; and NFFC.

While these activities and much besides kept him busy (these were also the years of his renewed association with the BBC through the sensitive management of Sir William Haley), John Reith remained as keen as ever he had been for 'a proper job'. In May 1950 he noted, 'I realized I have been unemployed since 1942.' Then in August, on holiday in Scotland and encouraged by hearing a sermon which he felt was the herald of 'real work and service' (as had been the case in 1922 before he applied for the position of general manager of the BBC), he wrote again to Attlee what he described in 1969 as 'a letter of appeal – almost an SOS'. This time the prime minister did not ignore him. Labour confidence was by then much reduced; Labour plans had not always been fulfilled. In particular this was true of the Colonial Development Corporation of which in October Reith was offered the chair. It was to be the start of over eight years of happy and fruitful work in the Commonwealth.]

10 September 1945 Pleasant talk with Addison [secretary of state for Commonwealth Relations] who was as emphatic as I could have been about the desirability of my being properly employed. He was very kindly and said he would talk to 'Clem' [Attlee].

19 September 1945 A particularly sickening, discouraging and upsetting day. I found I was not to be asked to attend the ministerial committee on my telecommunications report, and it was a decision, not a default. Listowel [postmaster general] was (apparently) much upset about it.

How I dislike and indeed loathe civil servants – their complacency, smugness, self-satisfaction, lack of initiative, cowardice and every sort of speciousness.

8 October 1945 Saw Dalton [chancellor of the exchequer] for half an

R.D.–Z

hour. He urged me to take the CCC chairmanship, leading to that of the new board, at £3500 p.a. Made complimentary remarks about the tour and the conference and all, and said all the governments wished me to be chairman and that it would be an awful bore if they had to try to find someone else. I made it quite clear that I wasn't keen on the job, but agreed to do as he wished, subject to his trying to keep my income up and to my not being prevented (or prejudiced) from taking other jobs.

23 October 1945 The Canadian government has accepted the report without any reservation, which is unexpected and most gratifying. That is the supreme achievement of the tour and of the conference. No one rang to congratulate me at all.

30 October 1945 Feeling absolutely miserable. If I am to stay at my present low level I shall go off my head, unless I am kept too busy to have time to think.

15 November 1945 Went to a party at South Africa House to meet the new governor general, van Zyl. Met a lot of people and avoided a lot. Spoke with Addison who sought me out. Various remarks about my joining the Labour party.

Sunday 2 December 1945 An unsatisfactory day as I did nothing whatever of any value or interest in it. Finished Napoleon's Life. It upset me all through, of course, as there was so much in it reminiscent of myself. For I might have been of such power in the world. Feeling quite miserable.

Letter to Viscount Addison 1 January 1946
I must give you some answer to your 'I invite you now to join the Labour party' at South Africa House.

Incidentally, I was shown a newspaper list of peers voting for the US loan in which I appear as a Tory. I have never been a Tory. Actually my first effort to settle political allegiance was in a letter to J. R. Clynes in 1922 [in fact 1920] so it is of old standing.

Do you despise one who feels as strongly as I do on many points, and yet hesitates to commit himself? Is it odd or discreditable that I should want to be properly and fully occupied and that this obtrudes when I try to answer your question?

Here are some of my thoughts:

(1) I do not know that I would be welcome or trusted,
(2) I do not think I would be given the position and responsibilities in the councils of the party which experience would seem to justify,
(3) It might look as if I were hoping for a job,
(4) I was disappointed with the talk with Mr Attlee in July and I hoped he would see me after you talked with him in October,
(5) I am wholly in sympathy with Labour principles – and other parties have none – but I do not know that I should agree with all the methods and procedures,
(6) My best service might be in loose rather than close association with the party, but with no doubt as to sympathy on all major issues. Because I have said openly for years what I feel on such matters as nationalization and because I have shown in my work (BBC, Airways, politics and telecommunications) the direction in which my allegiance lies, I have destroyed any chance of being offered the few private enterprise sort of appointments I might have considered. I am therefore dependent on your people – and unfortunately they know this.

I have been waiting a long time with increasing difficulty. I will continue to wait if told something that will reconcile me to it. Otherwise I feel it might be better to get out of public affairs altogether.

15 January 1946 Letter from Addison. At the end he wrote long-hand that he had had a talk with 'Clem' about my letter. What does that mean? No indication of what was said or whether I was going to hear from either.

17 February 1946 I wonder when England will be communist. I don't have much doubt that it will come. France will be so soon and it will spread all over Europe and Asia. How I wish we could all go and settle in America or Canada – with all our belongings, and I wish we could reduce our belongings a good deal.

1 March 1946 Wrote a note to Addison, there having been a debate about imperial relations, telling him about the paragraph in my tour report on which no question had ever been asked.

5 March 1946 It is simply shocking the delay there has been about telecommunications. There is no justification for the coming bill not dealing with the whole business instead of just buying the shares of Cable and Wireless.

6 March 1946 Addison replied today completely missing the point in my letter that no one had questioned me about the paragraph in my report about Empire relationships. I shall write to put him right about the business.

Letter to Prime Minister [Attlee] 9 March 1946
Your broadcast – I took it personally, as no doubt you wanted everyone to do.

But since last summer, I have not had two days' work a week and if it had not been for Silkin's New Towns committee I would have had nothing to do at all.

It does not seem right, especially in such times. And it is hard to bear.

Letter from Prime Minister [Attlee] 17 March 1946
You may be sure that I have you in mind as one whose services are not being fully utilized at the present time.

I shall not overlook you should the opportunity arise.

Letter from Lord Addison 14 March 1946
I was sorry to see what you said about the position after your return from your visit to the Dominions last year. I suppose that it is now too late for any action to be taken but if there is anything of importance which you think I ought to know, I shall be most glad to hear it from you.

22 March 1946 Barlow told me that the feeble Colonial Office was frightened to ask the Colonies to agree to my being chairman [of CCC] as the Colonial Office delegate. He urged me to agree to their putting the idea of my being UK representative round the world. He was sure that my taking the CCC wouldn't prevent anything else happening.

[John Reith was reluctant to accept the chairmanship of CCC not simply because he feared it might prevent him from getting a larger and more testing appointment but also because he felt that if he were the delegate for the United Kingdom as well as chairman he would lose his impartial position with the Dominions.]

29 April 1946 [On a tour of Sweden with New Towns committee] Mrs Felton [a Labour member of the LCC], *en route* for the bath, kept me talking for half an hour. She got on to politics which led to talking about myself which I didn't at all want to do. She thought if only I could make up my mind where I stood politically I might do tremendous things. This interesting, though untimely, conversation made us both late.

20 May 1946 Feeling utterly furious and disgusted with the Labour politicians. Dalton paid a long and fulsome compliment to Sir A. Duncan [as chairman of the Iron and Steel Federation] when introducing the Steel bill. When he introduced the Cable and Wireless bill, for which I am entirely responsible, he never even mentioned my name.

6 June 1946 Saw Barlow. I told him I was not able to agree to take the CCC chairmanship yet. I said it was better for me to do nothing than one or two days a week; I would take this job as part of a busy week. He said ministers evidently didn't like me. He had several times suggested my name to Dalton but always someone else had been chosen.

10 June 1946 Sometimes I feel I might still be something very big in the land. I certainly won't if I don't believe it; and so much has come to pass that I used to imagine – knighthoods, peerage and Oxford DCL etc. Perhaps I only feel 'it might still be' after a glass of sherry – I hope not. I wonder if it really does depend on whether or not I am able to 'believe' I shall.

18 June 1946 Saw Bridges [permanent head of the Treasury] 5.45 to 6.30. He had talked to Attlee about me with nothing definite, though nothing unfriendly. He urged me to take the CCC/CTB job and wanted me to feel there was more to it than I know there to be. It seems quite definite that there is no chance of my ever again having the sort of job I should have. It simply comes to this that I have too much ability and capacity for the only jobs I would get, namely government appointment ones. It is a terrible outlook for me. Met Horder [the distinguished physician] on my way out from dinner at the Ivy and he asked how I was. I said, rapidly qualifying for a mental home, and he replied, 'That is not a recent development, is it?' Very clever.

18 July 1946 Twenty-five minutes conversation with Bridges at 4.00. He urged me not to make any terms at all [in respect of the chairmanship of CCC/CTB]; he said it wasn't really me, etc. He agreed my condition that taking this job wouldn't prejudice another, but that is worth nothing. After twenty minutes I got up to go and moved to the door; he came after me and in a pleading sort of way said, 'Say yes.' 'Yes,' I said.

21 August 1946 [On holiday in Scotland] Government statement yesterday about the Iron and Steel Board. There was a note in the *Scotsman* that I might be offered this. I think I would rather like it but can't imagine it being offered to me.

2 September 1946 To Town – oh gosh. *The Times* on Friday said a chairman of the Iron and Steel Board had been appointed; this was a great disappointment after so much in the hopes that it would be offered to me.

23 September 1946 Saw Bridges from 3.00 to 3.40 and he was very decent – hoped I would take the new town job [i.e. Hemel Hempstead chairmanship]. He promised that this would not make it less likely that I would get a proper job. Silkin said he hoped I would take it so I said I would. I wasn't feeling at all pleased about taking the job, but I suppose it is as well. If Silkin had uttered any caveats or reservations I should have told him he need not waste his time.

28 October 1946 Lunched with Listowel at the House of Lords. I told him how important it was that the right sort of UK representative should be appointed [for the CTB] and I also explained about oceanic assets. I think he understood but he is most ineffective.

29 November 1946 [In bed with gastritis] Tired of lying in bed with nothing to do. The transport nationalization bill has been published. Of course this is the thing I would like to run as I did so much work on it in 1940. But I am sure I shall never have any really first class job like this to do. Apart from all the general prejudices against me, I am sure that utter swine Dalton would stop me having anything decent.

3 January 1947 Sir H. Shoobert [secretary to the Indian department of communications] from Delhi to see me for two hours this morning. He was most pessimistic about conditions in India in every way. It was the government's fault that the Muslim League had also gone for leaving the Empire.

9 January 1947 Shoobert in again today. They are not going to do anything to keep India in the Empire and would prefer them right out rather than half in and half out like Eire.

14 February 1947 There have been several receptions lately to which I ought to have been asked – Dominion ones; quite shocking.

20 February 1947 Lord Simon collared me in the evening about a decision the government had just announced about India. He was very upset. What upset me far more than their decision to evacuate by June 1948 was that Mountbatten had been made viceroy, Wavell being dismissed. So that is the job I most wanted on earth gone for good. It is not just a cleaning up. More can be done by the viceroy in the next year than in the last hundred.

26 February 1947 Dined with Wilshaw in his flat in Arundel House, an extraordinary place. He said that in his view I was the one man in England who, as viceroy of India now, might have brought about a satisfactory settlement. I could have done it.

28 April 1947 I gave dinner to C. B. Fanning, director-general of the Australian Post Office. He said some interesting and shocking things about the lack of hospitality or even courtesy shown by the Post Office here – all just as I have often remarked on.

29 April 1947 Saw Webster[7] about rationalization of the telecommunication systems in the colonial empire. Plans in hand.
    Dinner with Burke [South African postmaster general] from South Africa. This was much more interesting than last night. Talked about broadcasting about which a royal commission has now been appointed. Burke persuaded me to send a signal tomorrow to Smuts on his golden wedding.

12 July 1947 McFarlane from Australia to tea and supper. He was disgusted at the way he had been humbugged about by the Treasury, for four weeks now. It is just as I have heard so often before – the lack of common courtesy to visitors from overseas, and how silly and disastrous.

23 July 1947 We dined with Mr and Mrs McFarlane from Australia at the Savoy. They are still feeling very sore at their neglect here. I rang

Addison's secretary next day and he is to see him. The UK treatment of visitors from the Empire is absolutely shocking.

[Earlier in July 1947 John Reith received a letter from Vincent Massey, then chancellor of the University of Toronto, offering him the position of Dean of the Faculty of Engineering and Applied Science. This offer arose from Reith's inquiry about opportunities for himself in Canada. He had just been bitterly disappointed at failing to become chairman of the BBC and was considering whether to leave the country.]

8 August 1947 [On holiday in Scotland] I am beginning to feel more positively attracted by the idea of going to Canada and that not to go might be to miss a great and I suppose last opportunity offered.

29 September 1947 Dinner at Marlborough Club (amalgamated with Wyndham's) with Barrington-Ward. Told him about the Toronto idea; he is a great friend of Massey.

3 October 1947 Letter from Massey, most apologetic and embarrassed. I am too old. So that's that.

[John Reith was greatly disappointed by this fiasco and after acknowledging the news could not bring himself to write to Vincent Massey again till May 1948. Meanwhile he pursued the long negotiations for an overall agreement within the Commonwealth on telecommunications.]

3 November 1947 Began a series of Athenæum lunches with overseas visitors, Canadians today, Indians next week.

12 December 1947 Fanning from Australia was very helpful at the [CCC] meeting this morning by way of disagreeing with Townshend of GPO.

28 January 1948 Canada and India have agreed to sign the Overall Agreement which is a relief.

Letter to Prime Minister [Attlee] January 1948
After your broadcast on 8 March 1946 I wrote that I had taken personally your appeal that everyone should pull their full weight and that I was only too ready to do so.

You replied that you had me in mind and you would not overlook me should the opportunity arise.

Between the chairmanship of one of Silkin's new town corporations and the Commonwealth Communications Council only a small fraction of the week and of my energies are occupied. Such inactivity is increasingly hard to bear.

Maybe you feel now that no opportunity such as you had in mind will arise, but I should be grateful if I might come and have a talk some time.

19 April 1948 Letter from Fanning about the Australian representative coming to the CCC. He wrote:

> I have made it quite clear to him that I expect him to take an independent stand in some of the matters that will arise and in particular that in all things coming up for decision to be sure to approach them from the angle of what is best for the Commonwealth and Empire.

Quite remarkable that is.

30 April 1948 Fanning rang from Melbourne to tell me that the Australian Government had agreed to sign the Overall Agreement. This was a great relief. Rang the office and told them to get the Dominions Office to make plans at once for the signing party.

3 May 1948 Ismay [deputy director general of the Post Office] rang from the Post Office to ask if I would agree to preside over the signing of the Overall Agreement; he made out that this was intended as a compliment to me, but I wondered if it had anything to do with jealousy between the Post Office and the Dominions Office. He later assured me it hadn't.

11 May 1948 The office was very nicely arranged for the signing of the Overall Agreement – flowers and all. I spoke for one minute ten seconds and then there was the signing by the UK postmaster General and the six high commissioners. I am certainly relieved that that is done at last.

Letter to Prime Minister [Attlee] 24 May 1948
Last January I wrote you a note. I asked if you would let me come

and see you sometime. But I never heard any more. I wondered what had happened; perhaps the note went adrift.

Letter from Prime Minister [Attlee] 25 May 1948
I am afraid that I have no recollection of your letter but I should hesitate to put any blame on my secretary. It may be that I put it aside specially to answer and then under pressure of work forgot it. If this was so, please, accept my apologies. I should like to see you. Would you ring up my secretary and fix a time.

28 May 1948 Saw prime minister, Attlee, for half an hour at 10.00 o'clock. He was very friendly. I told him what and how I felt about my idleness. I wonder what will come of this meeting. I ought to have recorded it. I felt afterwards that it had gone well.

[As a consequence of the signing of the Overall Agreement a full meeting of the Commonwealth Communications Council was called in London early in June.]

1 June 1948 Various telephonings and preparations for meetings [with Commonwealth delegates]. I got the UK to agree to more generous terms for delegates in their signals home. They are unbelievably short-sighted and mean.

10 June 1948 No meetings because of the Trooping of the Colour, which was then cancelled though not a drop of rain since breakfast. A wicked decision. I wasn't going, of course, but most of the delegates had seats.

21 June 1948 The CCC met at 2.30. Just before the meeting began the Australians appeared with a most disappointing signal from Fanning. Fortunately we got that dealt with by inserting two lines in the report about their government's position being reserved. The final paragraph of the report which I drafted without thought and which wasn't changed reads:

We have had a most useful and satisfactory meeting. We have all profited from the interchange of experience and opinions. We have shown again that it is possible for the representatives of the Governments of the Commonwealth to concert happily together in their common interests.

21 October 1948 Much telephoning, mostly about other people's affairs.

A great part of my time is spent in trying to help others. Then to South Africa House party. Conversations with many people and I felt a considerable spurious inflation as a result. Herbert Morrison was one. He asked how I was. I told him, and fifteen per cent occupied. 'Yes, I know.' He said my day would come. Mistake to go to such things.

29 October 1948 Went with Shaw-Zambra [secretary of the CCC] to see Norman Brook [secretary of the Cabinet] from 3.00 to 4.00 to get news of the recent Commonwealth Conference forsooth, in connection with which the word 'British' is quietly dropped. Pakistan and Ceylon appear to have no qualms about the crown. India won't have it but wants to stay in. Ireland is going out. They are trying to devise something that will keep India in and have to settle whether Ireland is to be a foreign country. If they make a compromise with India, South Africa may want the same. Ceylon would be a member of UNO if it weren't for the present connection which Russia uses to veto their admission. Brook agreed with my views about the Commonwealth Relations Office; too timid for years, he added. What a melancholy position it is.

21 December 1948 Meeting with the Ceylon high commissioner about the wretched Cable and Wireless chief engineer's recent visit to Colombo. He was in much indignation about this – treating Ceylon as a colony and such like. I said I quite agreed with his making a signal telling them to forget all about it. The man had obviously been trying to frighten Ceylon off nationalization.

24 January 1949 Saw David Sarnoff [chairman of the Radio Corporation of America] at the Savoy at 4.45. I listened to him talking till 6.40 and missed the train which I had meant to get. Very depressed as Sarnoff spoke as if my work as well as his was more or less over . . . 'We have had our day' . . . He is two years younger than I, too.

8 February 1949 Saw M. Nicholson [secretary to the lord president of the Council's office] in the Cabinet Offices. He said Labour politicians looked on me as a Tory and gave the usual excuses for putting other people into jobs. He didn't mention anything about their being frightened of me, so I had to and of course he admitted it. He said I must have the record for near-misses. Asked if I would take a regional gas controller sort of job as it would be more executive and independent than others that looked better. Gosh.

[About the same time as this interview took place Lord Balfour of Burleigh was pressing the claims of John Reith to be chairman of the National Film Finance Corporation. Towards the end of March Balfour of Burleigh reported that Stafford Cripps, the chancellor of the exchequer, had stopped this; then on 29 March Reith was asked to contact the secretary to the president of the Board of Trade, Mr Harold Wilson. He was 'to be offered the chair after all'.]

30 March 1949 Went to see H. Wilson, sitting in Harry McGowan's[8] office, aged 33 but looking ten years older. Civil reception. Asked if I would accept the job, explained at length that it was much bigger potentially than what the new Act indicates. I questioned him closely about what sort of chairman he wanted – full-time, then said of course I could do other things though in the end and later I might feel that other things would have to go. I must admit that I felt somewhat enthused at the extent of the prospects.

3 April 1949 To the Board of Trade via the flat where I invited the aid of the Almighty. Wilson gave me a draft letter of invitation. I had him alter one paragraph. Talked for about an hour. Quite satisfactory I thought it. I asked him if S. Cripps hadn't tried to crab me; he said he had been inclined to boost someone else and that the Treasury had put me up – as I know. I later thanked Balfour of Burleigh for what he had done.

27 April 1949 Dinner at Lady Reading's. Exchanged comments with Machtig about Dominions Office parties. I told him what I thought of their neglect of the CCC.

[In the summer of 1949 the CCC was holding its final meetings in preparation for the establishment of its successor the CTB which was incorporated in the United Kingdom by the Commonwealth Telegraphs Act on 31 May; John Reith's concern in all this was to maintain the spirit of Commonwealth co-operation in the field of telecommunications and to persuade the Labour government and its Whitehall advisers to support him.]

9 May 1949 Council 10.30 to 12.30 and 3.00 to 5.15. It was most successful and one felt the original atmosphere had been gotten back. One Borland from South Africa was there to deal with an item on which everyone had expected a lot of trouble. He was said to be responsible for the periodic difficulties the CCC had had with South

Africa. I suppose it was my handling of the thing to some extent, probably considerably, but it not only passed off easily and with the utmost goodwill but was of immense advantage as it enabled me to write a cracking minute which got into intelligible terms some of the most important clauses of the Overall Agreement and, to my surprise, this was passed by the whole Council without amendment. Surely was a good day's work.

Letter to Secretary of State for Commonwealth Relations [*P. J. Noel-Baker*]
9 June 1949
I have just been reading the broadcast talk you gave recently about the Commonwealth Conference.

I could not help wondering why, and regretting that, you made no reference to the work of the Commonwealth Communications Council.

There is, I think, a closer, more consistent and more effective Commonwealth linkage in the telecommunications field than in any others. This Council is the only body of its kind.

An organization of some sort has been in existence from 1928. In 1945 plans were laid for the establishment of the Commonwealth Telecommunications Board while the Council in the interim exercised the wider powers of that Board.

On May 31st, following the Royal Assent to the Commonwealth Telegraphs Bill, the Board was at last officially incorporated – the culmination of several years of effort. But this passed without notice.

From every point of view the functions and responsibilities of this body are of immense Commonwealth importance.

Letter from the Secretary of State for Commonwealth Relations 21 June 1949
I am more than sorry that the official incorporation of your Board did not receive greater public notice. I would be more than willing to do another broadcast on the CCC if someone would invite me to. I fully agree about its importance.

Letter to the Secretary of State for Commonwealth Relations 25 June 1949
The idea of your giving a broadcast talk about the CTB is excellent, so excellent that I nearly rang up the BBC at once to ask them to invite you. You will agree with the reason which caused me to refrain – Pakistan. They have not yet definitely joined the party. They have been minded to do so ever since they became a Dominion; their high commissioner has been most helpful and has done his best to get a

decision. If and when they make the decision to join, then would be the time for your broadcast.

I will surely communicate with you when the Pakistan issue is settled. This should be in the autumn, as we shall be having another meeting then. Before that, in August, there is to be a conference between all the Commonwealth governments (including Pakistan) and the United States of America. The Americans want to rescind the 1945 Bermuda Agreement about rates and put them up – an interesting sidelight on the competitive system which is so strong there. I have to be in the chair, somewhat invidious; they probably think Marshall aid is keeping our rates down – nothing to do with it.

[The August conference to which John Reith referred duly took place and at this there was to be a striking demonstration of Commonwealth solidarity in face of the Americans which he made every effort to draw to the attention of the British authorities.]

5 August 1949 McIntyre of the US Embassy came to the club at 6.45 and got papers from Shaw-Zambra. We went to meet the Golden Arrow at 7.30. Most of the Commonwealth people were there and the Americans led by Wayne Coy, chairman of the Federal Communications Commission, who was not what I expected.

6 August 1949 Meeting of CCC people from 10.00 till 12.30 and 2.45 till 4.30. Lunched with Coy and McIntyre at the club and got, at last, a proper agenda out of them. All most complicated and confused, particularly owing to so many delegates having no authority.

8 August 1949 What a week. Heads of delegations met at 10.00 and agreed procedures etc.; conference began after coffee. The Americans got a considerable surprise at the rate at which I moved.

9 August 1949 Today there was a surprising demonstration of Commonwealth solidarity on the multilateral versus bilateral issue. It looked as if there might be no agreement at all; and this would not necessarily have been at all bad for the Commonwealth system. The Americans were clearly scared. I adjourned twice to give them a chance of considering the situation. Eventually a satisfactory compromise was reached.

12 August 1949 Delegates studying draft agreement today. Met at 10.30 p.m. with the Agreement in final form. Signed at midnight. The

Foreign Office made an absolutely monstrous suggestion that two reservations, one by New Zealand and the other by Southern Rhodesia, should be mentioned in the Final Act. They were of absolutely no importance and psychologically this would have been most unfortunate, giving a wholly misleading impression. I shot it down and Coy was very pleased. Speeches of mutual esteem and eventually out of the place at 1.15.

17 August 1949 Saw Bridges and gave him an annoyed account of the CCC business – no realization of what had been done, particularly over the USA business. He was apparently very interested and concerned. He wanted me to talk with Liesching [permanent head] of the Commonwealth Relations Office. I don't know that anything will come of that.

19 August 1949 To Commonwealth Relations Office and an hour and a quarter with Liesching. Unusual civil servant. Told him all about CCC and US meeting and all. He was greatly interested. Said he was having an awful time trying to get order into the combination of Dominions Office and India Office. I said exactly what I thought about the place from past experience. He agreed that it was Whitehall that had let the Empire go.

22 August 1949 Dictated a long memo for Liesching and was relieved to get this done.

[John Reith was on holiday in Scotland for the next three weeks and did not submit his memorandum to Sir Percivale Liesching until mid-September. This was a lapidary restatement of the points he had pressed since returning from his world tour early in 1945.]

Memorandum to Sir Percivale Liesching August/September 1949

. . . The object of this memorandum is to draw attention to the fact that in the Commonwealth Communications Council there has been, and is still, a great deal more than simply telecommunications even in the widest sense of the term – high policy implications not excepted.

. . . The Commonwealth Communications Council is unique; there is nothing like it in any Commonwealth sphere; it seems to show what might have been done elsewhere; what might, perhaps, still be done.

['Certain happenings' early in August demonstrated clearly the significance of 'this Commonwealth collaboration'.]

. . . For many years before the war the Americans had been highly envious of the Commonwealth telecommunications system; they were determined to break in on it wherever they could; the war had enabled them to do so; direct circuits had been established between the United States and several of the British Dominions and Colonies; the stage was set for a telecommunications war both in radio circuits and in telegraph rates. The American object was to shift the telecommunications capital of the world from London to New York.

[At the conference in Bermuda in 1945] an agreement was made between the United States and the Commonwealth governments which went a long way towards regularizing procedure and stabilizing rates. The Americans got a good deal out of it, but by no means all they wished. The future depended on how effectively the Commonwealth Communications Council functioned.

In the spring of this year the Americans gave notice of their desire to have the major provisions of the Bermuda Agreement revised. The explanation is that whereas the Commonwealth system pays its way, the Americans are finding it increasingly difficult to 'keep out of the red'. In that country there is no centralization of telecommunications; carriers compete with each other; and much extravagance results.

. . . The Bermuda Agreement was a multilateral one. One of the main objects of the Americans at the [recent] meeting was to get rid of multilateralism and introduce bilateralism, that is, negotiations to be authorized under the revision of the Bermuda Agreement between the United States and any one Commonwealth government bilaterally.

The issue was, in fact, so plain that the chairman specifically put the question to the head of each delegation – multilateralism versus bilateralism. The American answered bilateralism; every delegate of the Commonwealth governments – nine sovereign states – answered multilateralism.

This was a considerable shock to the Americans. They had discovered that there was more to the British Commonwealth than they had imagined; they were up against it. It seemed likely that the Conference would break down. But in point of fact a unanimous agreement was signed.

Although these facts are surely known at some level in the UK departments other than the Post Office, it is at least doubtful if their

John Reith as Minister of
Information, January 1940

John Reith at Ascot Races –
the day he accepted his move
from the BBC to Imperial
Airways, June 1938

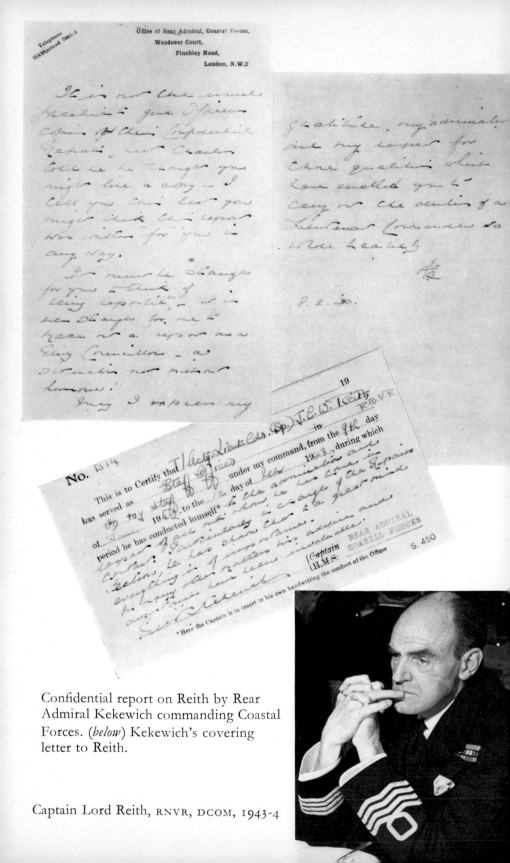

Office of Rear Admiral, Coastal Forces,
Wendover Court,
Finchley Road,
London, N.W.2

Telephone
HAMpstead 7661-4

No. 1514

This is to Certify that

(Captain
H.M.S. REAR ADMIRAL
COASTAL FORCES

S. 450

Confidential report on Reith by Rear
Admiral Kekewich commanding Coastal
Forces. (*below*) Kekewich's covering
letter to Reith.

Captain Lord Reith, RNVR, DCOM, 1943-4

significance is appreciated by the heads of these other departments and by their ministers.

By way of footnote to the above, the chairman of the CCC received a letter from the chairman of the Federal Communications Commission and also one from the latter's wife on their return to America. The former said the voyage had been somewhat rough; the latter said her husband had been flat on his back for most of the passage, adding that whereas he blamed the sea, she blamed the British Commonwealth.

Note by Colonel Shaw-Zambra, Secretary of CCC 15 September 1949

[This reported a visit of a principal in the Commonwealth Relations Office on the orders of Sir Percivale Liesching 'in order to try to agree some procedure for the future by which the CRO would be kept fully in the picture as regards CTB affairs'.]

. . . I said that it seemed to me there were two main points:

(1) that the CRO should appreciate the wider significance, in Commonwealth relations, of the work done by the CCC/CTB in its own sphere, and

(2) that the chairman of the CCC/CTB might expect to be kept confidentially informed by the minister of all important political developments in Commonwealth relations.

I believe he accepted the validity of both these points.

1 February 1950 One slips from a month to the next without knowing it; no comment; no jolt.

CTB meeting today with Stevens from Australia there. Quite a job to get things through. Canadians are being very bothersome.

2 February 1950 To see Bruce of Melbourne in Westminster Gardens; he had asked me to come and I had wondered if it were to see if I would be willing to consider going to Australia as Governor General; I think I hoped it would be that. It was only to ask if I could consider another chairman job – petro-chemicals or something like that.

[The General Election in February 1950 did not arouse John Reith's interest; 'I simply don't know which I dislike more, Labour or Tory,' he noted on election day, adding, characteristically, 'nor which, if either, would be any better for my doings'. But the reshuffle of ministers which followed brought him, as chairman of the Hemel

Hempstead New Town, into reluctant contact with Hugh Dalton, now minister for town and country planning.]

16 March 1950 Saw Dalton at 3.00 in his House of Commons room. Oh, gosh – couldn't have been more cordial. Very delightful that '*nous deux*' being friends should have this new association now. I just had to listen to it. How I dislike and distrust him; he couldn't have been more civil – nor more insincere.

23 March 1950 Feeling much better; maybe I could do a proper job of work again, if only one would come.

30 March 1950 Myers [South African member of the CTB] in for an hour and a quarter. He is very keen on the CTB taking more and more authority; particularly interesting that this comes from a South African

[During the summer of 1950 John Reith, though happily occupied with the details of his work at the CTB, and also for the NFFC, remained as anxious as ever for a larger challenge. This anxiety weighed heavily upon him when, on holiday, he was relieved of the burden of day-to-day work.]

Sunday 13 August 1950 We all went to church. The service began with the 23rd psalm to Crimond. There was a good congregation and the singing was splendid. The text was from the last verse of *Zechariah* VIII and the minister referred to the awful need for leadership, finishing by substituting 'Scotsman' for 'Jew' – 'we will go with you for we have heard that God is with you'. Impressed and moved me very much, this ending. I wondered if this text today was the heralding of real work and service, like Dr Ivor Roberton's text about the end of 1922.[9]

Letter from Sir William Haley 15 August 1950
As a nation we are going to go through as difficult and trying a time as ever we have had. It will call for all the wisdom and energy men of goodwill can muster. By comparison the war will seem an easy, un-complicated affair. And while I know all it means to you that your great gifts and energies are not directly harnessed to public affairs of a magnitude or importance to match them, you always seem to me to underrate what you can do and the influence you can have indirectly. And in fact do have. It is part of the British tradition that influence can achieve more than power. But even putting this on one side, I am still

convinced that you are simply in a waiting time. That, too, is part of our genius in public affairs. The greatest figures in our history have had such periods. Beaconsfield for nine years, Winston for ten. And there are many others. In retrospect they seem mere interludes when the spirit can subside from turbulence into serenity.

The needs of the country are going to expand once more at an alarming rate. Demands are going to be made to tax every single first-rate mind in the country. God knows how few there are. But they must be used and must assert themselves if we are not to go into the twilight of mediocrity and the rule of the second-rate.

You may wonder why I say all this. I do so because I believe the hour may come at any time, and the state of your mind not only at that moment but also before it, will condition all you then do. We are going to have a year ahead to test the hearts and minds of all of us and no one can tell – least of all yourself – what part you may be playing at the end of it.

21 August 1950 I had sent a line – one short page – to Attlee when leaving Scotland ending 'isn't there some big job you would like me to do? I could do such a lot, you know.' This morning very civil and friendly long-hand note from him.

[Two months after this John Reith was, at last, summoned to see the PM.]

16 October 1950 Just got to No. 10 [Downing Street] by 10.00 a.m. To my alarm a man whom I thought was the colonial secretary was sitting outside the Cabinet room, and I was afraid this meant I was going to be asked to go to M. MacDonald's job in Malaya. It was he – Griffiths. PM and Griffiths *most* friendly and civil. PM said they wanted me to do a job – chairman of the Colonial Development Corporation. I was quite surprised. He then asked 'Jim' to describe it to me, prompting him occasionally – 'give some examples'. I asked a few questions; then was it full time and £5000. Yes. That meant dropping all I was doing and I said I was worried about H. Wilson giving me the film job and also about the CTB. Moreover not happy about dropping £2500. I suggested I should talk to Bridges and the PM said yes – with relief in his voice. Some vague talk on generalities and then a most cordial farewell.

I am a little pleased about this.

27 October 1950 Saw Bridges at Treasury and had a straight talk with

him; result was that I left it with him to make the financial arrangements for me in the CDC.

30 October 1950 Message from Bridges that he had had to come out of
the negotiation about the CDC as ministers were determined to handle
it themselves. I saw him at 3.00 and he was very angry. Then saw
Gaitskell, the new chancellor, forsooth, and Griffiths and was told with
many regrets that they couldn't move the CDC job from £5000 and
that I couldn't remain with the CTB for more than six months.[10]
Absolutely sickening.

31 October 1950 Rang Lloyd [permanent head of the Colonial Office]
and said he could tell Griffiths that I would do the job.

8 November 1950 I got a letter from Dalton in answer to my note of
resignation [from Hemel Hempstead Corporation]. I had said the date
could be at his convenience. To my utter amazement the swine said
that as the colonial secretary was in a hurry the appointment would
terminate next day. Sorry that the Hemel Hempstead years should have
ended thus owing to Dalton's swinishness

9|14|19|27 November 1950
   [9] To the new job! 33 Dover Street.
   [14] CDC till 12.30. Saw legal man and intelligence woman. Keep
thinking about the organization.
   [19] The *Observer* 'profile' was very well done.[11] Rather frightening
in the importance attached to the CDC job. God help me in it, please.
   [27] The CTB people are planning a farewell for me. I am sad about
leaving them. Six of us were having a talk this afternoon and it was all
such good company and interesting to think that they were all of
different nationalities.

*Letter from W. A. Borland, minister of posts, Union of South Africa
29 December 1950*
   I feel that I must write a personal note to bid you goodbye in the
Commonwealth Telecommunications field and to wish you every
success in your new post.
   In my humble opinion you can be proud of the results which have
been achieved. You have made history once more and it is my guess
that the Commonwealth system, as now constituted, will stand for
many, many years.

NOTES

1. Professor Briggs cited this passage (Briggs I, p. 324) mistakenly as 1925.

2. In his autobiography, *Into the Wind*, p. 207, John Reith claimed that he had thought he ought to go to India *himself*; this was plainly not the case. The man chosen was Lionel Fielden.

3. This was the launching of the *Queen Mary*.

4. Douglas Reith had worked as a missionary and professor of English at Hislop College, Nagpur, between 1907 and 1912.

5. To allow for the 'forces vote' to be collected it had been arranged for the general election to be held on 9 July but for the counting to be delayed until 26 July 1945.

6. John Curtin, prime minister of Australia, had died on 5 July 1945.

7. G. H. Webster was the representative of the Colonies and Protectorates on the Commonwealth Communications Council. Six months after this John Reith noted of him that he was 'a most energetic custodian of the dud Colonial Office interests'.

8. Lord McGowan was chairman of ICI in whose offices on Millbank the Board of Trade was then established.

9. John Reith had attended evensong at Dr Roberton's church in Regent Square on the day of his return to London on 1 October 1922:

The sermon was from *Ezekiel* that the Lord could not find a man to fill the gap. He said in closing that perhaps there was someone in the church who would save this country and lead it to Christ . . . I still believe that there is some high work for me in the world but that it won't come till I have reconciled myself absolutely to God's way of working.

10. Hugh Gaitskell had succeeded Stafford Cripps as chancellor of the exchequer earlier in October 1950. John Reith's income at this time was £3500 from CTB, £2500 from NFFC and £1500 from Hemel Hempstead. So by abandoning all three and taking on CDC at £5000 he dropped £2500.

11. The *Observer* article referred to the great opportunity which was presented 'in the development of our more backward colonies' and suggested that John Reith could seize this and place himself, in the eyes of posterity, among such 'men of genius' as 'Clive, Hastings . . . Livingstone and Rhodes'.

CHAPTER EIGHT

John Reith and the Empire (2)

1950-70

1. Colonial Development Corporation, 1950-9

When he wrote a short summary of his life's work in 1969 John Reith described his years as chairman of the Colonial Development Corporation as 'a happy time'. Seen overall this was true, notwithstanding the bitterness at its end when he hoped to continue as chairman and was disappointed in a way that made him feel betrayed by his friends as well as victimized by his enemies.

Initially he was faced in the CDC with heavy financial losses and an over-centralized and top-heavy organization. As a consequence his first few years were concerned with cutting losses and reorganizing management – the process which he described in the CDC's report for 1951 with the homely Scots phrase of 'redding up'. By the end of 1954 he could report in respect of finance that CDC had 'come very near break-even on current operations'; and a year later he was able to point to a surplus of over £400,000 after paying all outgoings including a heavy charge of £307,000 in interest on loans. At the same time he reduced the administrative costs of the head office from nearly £340,000 in 1951 to under £194,000 in 1955, while the number of head office personnel was reduced from the 340 he inherited in 1950 to 171 in 1955. So in his fifth annual report he was in a position to claim that '1955 saw an effective end to the redding-up process'.

It was when he turned from the tasks of financial and administrative doctoring to the more constructive field of new undertakings that John Reith ran into difficulties. By the end of 1954 he reported that CDC's emphasis had 'swung towards looking forward instead of backwards', and that the corporation was by then capable of 'contributing fully to the planning and execution of large development projects'.

But when he came to apply this policy the outcome was nearly four years of wrangling and friction with the Colonial Office – over the legal right of CDC to participate in certain kinds of activity such as the building of houses and roads which were not strictly development 'projects' under the act of 1948 (this was happily settled by amending legislation in 1956); over the question of CDC's entitlement to launch new projects in the so-called 'emergent territories', i.e. those colonies about to become independent; and over the limitations of the capital structure of the corporation which saddled it with heavy interest payments on its early losses and left it tied down for the future by capital restrictions which John Reith described as 'a financial nonsense'. So, when, in his last report, he came to summarize the achievements of CDC under his chairmanship he concluded that though it had done some good, 'it could have done a lot more'.

There was, indeed, a fundamental divergence of principle between John Reith, on the one hand, and a powerful section within the Colonial Office on the other as to the value and purpose of the Colonial Development Corporation. It was argued from the Colonial Office that there was no need for CDC whose work could be done more cheaply and effectively by the Colonial Office itself. John Reith, for his part, felt that CDC had been set up as an 'instrument of government purpose' and that it was 'foolish and wrong to superimpose on it a higher civil service direction'. Further, he believed that when this was attempted the result was an abuse of the corporation system producing friction and frustration which impeded, if it did not prevent, the achievement of any objective. Each of these views was honestly entertained and strongly argued. The colonial secretary in these years, Mr Alan Lennox-Boyd (now Lord Boyd of Merton), tried his utmost to hold the balance between them but ultimately concluded, as anyone of political insight would have seen that he must, by coming down in favour of his department and terminating John Reith's chairmanship.

In the long run, however, it was John Reith's principles which triumphed even though he did not. For, after his retirement, his views on capital structure were largely accepted and his hopes of freedom of action in 'emergent territories' largely fulfilled. Finally in November 1968, nearly ten years after his retirement, the House of Commons Estimates Committee recommended that the sphere of operations of the *Commonwealth* Development Corporation (as it had by then become) should be extended to cover even those territories, such as India and Pakistan, which had been excluded in consequence of their early independence. It was on hearing the news of this last development that John Reith noted, with pardonable satisfaction: 'here is a most poignant justification of all my rows.'

(a) *Settling down with Labour, December 1950–October 1951*

[John Reith's early enthusiasm for his new task was soon moderated when he discovered the extent of the muddle and loss with which he had to deal. In this period he was himself chief executive, and he immediately sought to establish the sort of organization with an executive management board, such as he had created at the BBC, combining this with the devolution of responsibilities to regional offices. He also took trouble to clear the air for CDC with both political parties, and was sufficiently successful in this to make sure that when the Labour government was defeated in the General Election of October 1951 he was as welcome to the new colonial secretary, Oliver Lyttelton (later Lord Chandos), as he had become to the outgoing James Griffiths.]

7 December 1950 CDC all day. More and more irritation as to loose ends and such like; shocking bad management.

15 December 1950 Meeting at Colonial Office. I was very annoyed as Dugdale [minister of state for colonial affairs] had promised to reduce the numbers; absolutely sickening, two junior Colonial Office people, one of whom did most of the talking, and a junior Treasury man. Won't happen again.

20 December 1950 Saw Herbert Morrison at No. 11 – and this was really funny – he read me a little lecture about public corporation chairmen in their relationship with ministers – me! Everything he was tactfully suggesting I had known and practised for twenty-five years. Especially ministers' powers of discretion, which could be announced, but much better for the chairman to have an informal chat with the minister to see what he thought about any particular action. Ye gods!

22 December 1950 Saw Griffiths and Lloyd from 11.00 to 12.30, an hour and a quarter of the time being taken up with my explaining what I was going to do with the organization.

Lunched with Lennox-Boyd and the Tory adviser on colonial affairs. Very successful meeting.

16 January 1951 Very busy day. Lunched with Dugdale in House of Commons and achieved the abolition of the Colonial Office regular meeting.

24 January 1951 Terribly busy and really in considerable disgust and concern about the state of affairs in CDC.

7 March 1951 Lunched in House of Commons with Lennox-Boyd and about fifteen Tory MPs. A most successful affair, I thought; questions about the CDC which I answered with much more detail than they had expected.

8 March 1951 The Tories are having half a day on the Gambia hen affair[1] which is quite ridiculous. I offered to write a note to the secretary of state saying he was in no way to blame and the only right thing to do would be to sack the board or the chairman – or some such punitive action. This is a most important constitutional point.

30 March 1951 There is hardly a day but I get new examples of the shocking inefficiency of the CDC. Last night, for instance, I read a report about British Honduras and Dominica which was dreadful and no one in headquarters was watching what was happening; utter incompetence.

3 April 1951 Two whole hours with the Secretary of State and the wretched little Dugdale about the report; the late chairman, Trefgarne, having been to see them last night. One would almost think that they wanted a report which covered up his incompetence.

11 April 1951 Signal from Trefgarne that he was making a statement in the Lords today and that he was reluctantly obliged to express regret that I hadn't said anything in his defence. How could I when the charges against him were true?

16 April 1951 Each day I seem to come on some new sickness in CDC – some new underestimate, disloyalty, grumble, failure. I wish I could find occasional things to praise or even to feel relatively easy about.

23 April 1951 Saw Gordon Walker, Commonwealth Relations secretary of state. Very civil he was; most anxious not to seem interfering. I told him he could have all the information and contacts he wanted.

24 April 1951 Administration controller [A. E. Porter] started work today, and it was a comfort to know that another brain of some calibre was at work on the mess.

18 May 1951 First meeting of Executive Management Board – six months that has taken me. I feel great relief and satisfaction over this.

28 May 1951 Saw Griffiths 2.30 till 4.50 about the House of Commons debate on the CDC report tomorrow. The miserable Dugdale there for most of the time. I was thoroughly sickened by their purpose to exonerate Trefgarne at any price; I thought that they would rather I concealed the truth than that he were incriminated. I got a bit angry with them.

4 July 1951 No dinner at all tonight as my brain was in too much of a whirl after an hour and a half with the Colonial group of the Labour party in the House of Commons. I enjoyed this and got on very well indeed. I was informed at the end that I had the absolute confidence of the Labour party. One fellow tried to give Trefgarne a boost but he was crushed by his own people before I had even begun on him.

23/26 July 1951 Meeting with Griffiths in the Colonial Office about encroachments by the Treasury. Most successful it was.
[26] Away to see the secretary of state for half an hour at the House of Commons. He asked if I would like to be Governor of Kenya and I said Oh yes, if he liked.

> [In August John Reith was on holiday in Scotland, and needed to come south to see the secretary of state before he left for a tour of Africa late in that month. Their meeting was 'most successful' and their relationship was friendly and stable when Parliament was dissolved in October. The Conservative victory presented him with a new colonial secretary with whom to get on terms.]

26 October 1951 I said in July 1945 that I couldn't imagine the Labour government ever being out of office because fifty-one people out of one hundred would always vote for them – as giving more than any other party ever would and expecting nothing in return. More votes went to Labour than to the Tories, though the latter have about twenty of a majority.

27 October 1951 One of the Tories of whom I have a specially poor opinion is colonial secretary – Lyttelton. Sickening. I wish I could get out of it all. And Ismay at the Commonwealth Relations Office!

29 October 1951 Went to see Griffiths and found that Lyttelton had heard that I was coming and had asked to see me. I said some nice things to Griffiths, quite genuinely; he said he would like to be kept in touch. I was sorry that I had to see the new man but it couldn't be helped. When I went through the door he raised both his hands above his head as if welcoming a very old friend. Most cordial he was; bubbled over with cordiality; it was magnificent that I was there; I must come any time about anything; don't worry about appointments; he could clear out whoever was there. I said I would like to know if he wanted me to carry on or would he like me to resign; no, indeed. I could not respond fully without that insincerity which I cannot bring myself to.

(b) *Recovery and reorganization. November 1951–December 1953*

[In the immediate aftermath of the Conservative victory John Reith was depressed and disillusioned. He thought, once more, of abandoning public life and retiring to Scotland; yet again his friend, Sir William Haley, with whom he was regularly in touch at this time, sustained him and refreshed his spirit. But as events turned out, he was to find the new colonial secretary helped on personal as well as on corporation affairs. Reith had been appointed to CDC on the understanding that he would serve full time and receive no other stipend. This meant, in practice, reducing his income from £7500 to £5000 a year. He wished, understandably, to restore this. His idea was to become a part-time chairman with an executive general manager under him, along the lines of his arrangement in Imperial Airways before the war, which he believed to be the most efficient management system. He would then be in a position to accept some outside directorships. Thanks to Lyttelton's friendly support this was agreed during 1953. In April and May John Reith joined the boards of Tube Investments and the Phoenix Assurance Company; in October he handed over his executive duties in CDC to a general manager. His corporation salary was reduced but his directorial fees made up the loss and as much again. Lyttelton was no less friendly in appointments to the CDC board. In this more relaxed atmosphere it was possible for John Reith to start on his series of tours of CDC regions, visiting East Africa in September 1952 and South Africa in June 1953.]

5 November 1951 Saw Lyttelton. Beaver[2] was agreed for the board and when I said I objected, and had objected before, to the other name he suggested he said that was enough; didn't want to hear any reasons.

When I told him about my plans for regional controllers he said we were obviously out for the same thing, so I let it go at that.

10 November 1951 Apparently Lyttelton in a press conference recently, remarked, in answer to a question that he and I saw eye to eye. As I made my views quite clear I am glad he can say that.

22 December 1951 Feeling very bored indeed with CDC – disgusted really.

Letter from Sir William Haley 29 December 1951
It disturbed me you were again unhappy. But despite all the disgusting things there are in public life at the moment do you think you would be happier if you had withdrawn from it all, into a Scottish retreat?

Surely a great deal – the major part – of your unhappiness in recent years came from precisely the fact that you had not the opportunity to stretch yourself mentally. The CDC post at least partially remedied that. There was national relief when you went there. There is national satisfaction and a sense of security (in a positive, not in a merely negative sense) that this high responsibility is yours. It is clear to everyone that you have already performed a Herculean task. And although the work is wretchedly ill-rewarded, it does carry within its implications and responsibilities a reward which in the end means more than anything else.

I suppose that each generation thinks that a new world is in the making. To some extent it is. But there are widely differing degrees to the process, both as to its pace and extent. And never can there have been a generation in which life for the whole world, not merely for nations, classes and individuals was being so rapidly and so vastly changed. In all this picture Great Britain's colonial empire has a major role to play. Possibly the new fulcrums of the world are there. Unlike Canning, you cannot, in one proud gesture, call in the weight of this new world to redress the balance of the old. But it does lie with you to give it the momentum to acquire weight; and the work you are doing now, and the spirit in which it is conceived and carried out, may well decide much in the years to come. So it seems to me the only alternative to the CDC is something greater and even more important, not something less.

31 Janaury 1952 Lyttelton 5.00 to 6.15 about financial flexibility and other such matters. Surprisingly successful; contingency for over-drawing and he agreed that we should get all the Trefgarne legacies wiped off – tin can tied to tail with Trefgarne written on it.

28 Febraury 1952 Saw Lyttelton; he said he had been trying to get me a rise in pay. Very decent he was, but I never know where I am with him.

9 May 1952 Lunched by myself in the House of Lords reading an utterly fatuous White Paper on transport reorganization. A. Lennox-Boyd becomes minister of transport; I am sorry he is leaving the Colonial Office [as minister of state].

3 July 1952 Saw Lyttelton 3.30 to 5.30. He said he thought I was going to get on to a pension scheme and that from the beginning of next year I could take other directorships. Some talk about CDC organizational future; he is quite impractical. Then about the financial structure; at least we agreed that the attitude of the Treasury was plain silly.

Letter from Sir William Haley 13 July 1952
    Often since our last lunch I have thought about your own affairs and wondered how they were going. If Lyttelton is willing to allow the CDC post to become non-exclusive would that not perhaps best meet your problem?
    The great importance of the work to be done by the CDC remains. I know you say its scope is limited. No one but you can break through those limits. We have won and lost three empires; and the plain truth is that we cannot live without an empire. It is not simply a question of being a great power but of sustaining life in these islands. Our fourth empire must come out of the colonies. It must come enheart-ened and enlightened, enriching itself as well as us; avoiding the errors of the past. Doing that is a great thing in itself.

31 July 1952 Saw Lyttelton for an hour and a quarter. Very agreeable he was. I almost hoped he was going to offer me three or four years pay to leave the CDC. He said he was going to do all he could with the Treasury to get amortization off as well as interest, and on partial as well as whole abandonments. Said he would write me a letter which would give quietus to alarms that CDC might be abandoned.

[Between 5 September and 2 October 1952 John Reith, accompanied at his own expense by his daughter, was on a tour of CDC projects in East Africa, visiting Uganda, Kenya, Tanganyika and Northern Rhodesia (now Zambia). In his report to colleagues on his return he included some characteristic and entertaining details as well as drawing some serious conclusions.]

9 September 1952 [In Entebbe] A considerable storm blew up during lunch so we were not looking forward to the trip across the lake [Victoria] to Macalder [site of a CDC mining project]. Nor was the sight of the charter aircraft, hopping along the airstrip like a locust, re-assuring; nor the fact that the pilot could get no information about the weather over the lake. 'We can go and see what it is like,' he said. In fact the one hundred and fifty mile journey was in flat calm. Having made landfall somewhere near what we took to be Macalder, we were surprised to find the pilot giving it a wide berth and proceeding inland; soon it became obvious that he had lost his way. We found later that the explanation was that the map by which he was navigating showed the Macalder airstrip as disused; he was making for another about ten miles inland, shown as in use. Having reached this latter, but seeing no signs of life, he concluded he had better go back to see if there were any on the Macalder airstrip. All was well.

Sunday 14 September 1952 [In Nairobi] We attended service at St Andrews Church of Scotland, a most unusual building architecturally, both internally and externally. Large congregation; music good; sermon passable; visitors were invited to a cup of tea in the church hall after service. Hore-Belisha was there and spoke to me. He had accompanied his hostess to the adjacent Christian Scientist church but had thought he would get more good for himself from the Scots church. We signed our names in the church autograph book – I think it was only mine they actually wanted; he wanted me to sign first but he was pleased when I said that he was senior to me as Privy Councillor and so should sign first.

After tea we visited the game reserve; and having managed to get there before the usual Sunday evening crowd, were fortunate in being able to watch two lionesses and four cubs disporting themselves about fifteen yards off. Unfortunately there were soon about seventy cars in the vicinity. We had had enough and made off, but, in rounding a corner, came on one of the lionesses emerging from the bush into the open – the prelude to an odd scene. One frequently finds a policeman at the centre of a London traffic jam. Here there was soon a traffic jam but with a lion *vice* policeman at the centre. She kept moving around, sniffing the air; at last sat down, seeming oblivious of the cars now almost hemming her in. In ten minutes she got bored; edged her way round, passing immediately behind the car in which we were, and returned to the bush. It was not an edifying spectacle. In insouciance and dignity the lioness was superb; she had the gaping humans in obvious contempt.

20 September 1952 [In Mchuchuma, southern Tanganyika] On the way out to Mchuchuma [another CDC mine] we met a dozen leading Africans, charge hands and the like. I had Lady Twining [wife of the governor of Tanganyika] make a speech to them in Swahili; then she and I shook hands with each, she asking each what tribe he came from and what work he did. About two miles from Ngaka I received the head road ganger, an elderly man who had served in the German army,[3] so some conversation was possible; at the end of it, imploring us to wait, he rushed off to his hut returning with a basket of eggs.

21 September 1952 [en route to Njombe] We had to travel one hundred and thirty miles to Njombe where are the wattle estates. Every time this journey had been mentioned there had been looks of interest, even surprise; occasionally a 'rather you than me' sort of remark. We did the journey at an average speed of about ten m.p.h., up and down thousands of feet; across three considerable mountain ridges; for miles up (or down) steep escarpments where a few inches error – and literally so – would have sent us a very long way indeed off the road. I have never been on anything like it for scenery and hazard. The African driver of the car in which I travelled drove supremely well.

23 September 1952 [returning to Dar-es-Salaam] East African Airways had arranged to divert an aircraft to the Njombe airstrip where none had been seen for four months and we had a rather bumpy passage back. This journey, or rather the necessity for it and for one two days later from Dar to Nairobi, indicates the difficulties of African travel. As I had been in the extreme south-west of Tanganyika I imagined that from Njombe, or anyhow from Mbeya ninety miles away, it would be possible to fly direct the five hundred miles to Lusaka. And so it used to be; but now one had to go from Njombe to Dar, from Dar to Nairobi, and then a nine hour horrible journey from Nairobi to Lusaka.

[John Reith's last stop was Northern Rhodesia where he arrived on 26 September and spent the next three days discussing the Chilanga Cement works which had been launched in association with the Northern Rhodesian government in 1951 and was making a profit within twelve months.]

30 September 1952 [In Lusaka] Marista and I left at 2.00 p.m. on one and a quarter hours bumpy flight to Livingstone. Here we were met by the provincial commissioner who took us first to the site of the proposed CDC hotel; thereafter to the Victoria Falls, he showing us in one and a half hours as much as most people would have seen in one and a half days. This is an experience rather than a spectacle; stupendous and awful; and it is fitting that the statue of David Livingstone has its back turned on the jazz band of the Victoria Falls Hotel.

Conclusion and comments on visit to East Africa, October 1952

Much damage has been done in the past by the control little short of absolute, and by the absence of control, little short of absolute, exercised from London. For some time now there has been an increasingly reasonable sharing of responsibility and authority, and incompetence of control at home and overseas has been checked.

I am sure the regional control system was sound in conception and introduction and I am in favour of increasing somewhat the authority and responsibility of regional controllers.

Head office is nothing like as well informed as it should be on personal affairs; e.g. one feels foolish and annoyed when, on asking what a particular individual is doing, one is told he was sacked a year ago.

The tour was interesting and instructive; on occasions one felt one was earning one's pay and justifying the cost; but I do not know that that applied to the tour as a whole. Worthwhile to me – yes; worthwhile to the Corporation, the regional controller, the project managers and staff – I do not know; rather doubt it.

[On his return from Africa John Reith resumed his negotiations to secure the colonial secretary's approval of his accepting outside directorships (he had already been approached with a view to his joining the Tube Investments' board), with the implicit assumption that this would lead to his giving up his executive responsibilities. At the same time he kept up his pressure for the CDC to be granted greater financial flexibility.]

John Reith at the opening of the South African Parliament, July 1953

John Reith in South Africa again, this time with Dr A. Hertzog, December 1962

John Reith at the 75th Anniversa
celebrations of British Oxygen Co
June 1961

John Reith with the President
of India, Dr Radhakrishnan,
November 1963

16 October 1952 With Lloyd and Poynton [deputy under secretary, Colonial Office] from 2.30 to 4.00 about my African visit and things generally, and in particular the exceeding of capital sanctions. Fixed for Rendell [controller of finance, CDC] to talk with Poynton about a *modus vivendi*.

9 December 1952 Saw Lyttelton in House of Commons about Tube Investments job. To my amazement he said he hadn't said what I know he did say on 3 July – that I could take other directorships – but to wait until the smoke about the pension affair had settled; he said that that meant till the pension matter was settled. Just not speaking truth, but awkward to handle because he is trying to help me; I suppose he shouldn't have said what he did; and the wretched Treasury are being more difficult than he expected.

4 February 1953 Letter from Lyttelton that he was happy to be able to tell me that the principle of pension problem had been settled, though exact terms had still to be worked out; he hoped there wouldn't be much delay over this. When that was done – although the full-time condition still applied I was to ask him about another directorship if it could truly be said to be helpful to CDC work. This is really absolutely sickening.

3 March 1953 Lyttelton now calmly writes that any other directorships must reduce my CDC pay. It is shocking that he can't be straightforward and admit he has been misled.

5 March 1953 Tyser [a director of CDC] to see me 11.30 to 12.30. We talked all round the Lyttelton correspondence, agreed I should send him a draft letter for Lyttelton indicating that I couldn't stay on with the limit at £5000, but that I might agree to some reduction if they agreed to a part-time basis without check outside that. Helpful, he was.

14 March 1953 Most of the morning on a letter to Lyttelton about the directorships affair. Really wicked the *pro tanto* reduction the Treasury swine are insisting on as it means that if I get ordinary fees for one-tenth of the week, I should have to work the rest of it for nothing.

20 March 1953 To see Lyttelton. I said yes to both his suggestions as CDC directors. I had said in my letter, which Tyser had approved, that there were three alternatives in respect of myself:

that I should forget about other directorships;
that I would leave CDC now;
that I would become part-time.
He said he thought I should become part-time at £3500 and it would be nobody's business what directorships I had. He said the pension benefits were nugatory. I asked when this could happen and he said at once. I am glad I can do what I like about directorships.

30 April 1953 Saw Lloyd at the Colonial Office from 11.00 to 12.15. The Treasury had a sort of snarl about the £3500 compared with other part-time jobs – which is obviously silly as they are thinking of the £500 a year sort. I said just what I thought about it all.

[This compromise on John Reith's pay and outside activities was not made public till May, although he attended his first Tube Investments board meeting on 1 April and later joined the Phoenix board, for which he had been warmly recommended by his friend and colleague, Granville Tyser. In line with his general views on efficient organization he coupled the relaxation of his CDC commitment with a move towards giving up his executive duties by appointing Mr (later Sir William) Rendell, who had been CDC controller of finance since August 1952, as his deputy chief executive. But, inevitably, public announcement brought criticism in parliament and press. So far as the House of Commons was concerned, the colonial secretary was able largely to disarm this when it transpired that the previous chairman of CDC, the unfortunate Labour peer Lord Trefgarne, had been allowed to retain several of his other directorships. But by the time this little squall blew up John Reith had set out on the second of his tours of inspection, accompanied on this occasion by his wife, visiting South Africa, Southern Rhodesia, Bechuanaland and Swaziland. Earlier in the year it had been his intention to visit West, rather than South, Africa but this had been postponed 'because of political troubles and uncertainties about CDC's job there'.]

13 June 1953 [en route to Swaziland] We drove [from Johannesburg] to Ermelo for lunch, covering the last twenty-nine miles in twenty-seven minutes. Very good lunch and then on east on a rough road, crossing into Swaziland at 3.30 and reaching Usutu and Hubbard's house at 5.30. The position of this gave us a tremendous thrill – nothing like it in our experience except the Grand Canyon; fifty-mile view of mountain, moor and veldt; a four hundred foot precipice immediately beside the house.

14 June 1953 I drove round the job [i.e. Usutu Forests project] from 9.15 to 4.30. Then attended a tea-party of about twenty senior officials and wives in Hubbard's house [project manager]; here, and on similar occasions on other jobs, in addition to talking to each senior if not already met on the job, one felt obliged to hoist in the name of every man and woman present so that one could give everyone their name when saying goodbye; one wondered if it were worthwhile; whether it were not just the sort of thing one might be expected to do to create effect.

19/20 June 1953 Beastly drive [from Pretoria] to Mafeking arriving at 4.00. We were very pleased and rather thrilled to be here, staying at the Bechuanaland Resident Commissioner's house, which had a Union Jack flying.

Went to the 'Army Reserve' in which the resident commissioner's offices are, in the middle of which is an old fort which was one of the defended posts in the siege of Mafeking. It was all overgrown with weeds and in a shocking state of neglect, although one would expect to see it treated with respect.

22 June 1953 [en route to Bulawayo, Southern Rhodesia] On our journey through Bechuanaland I saw a railway station pillar-box with 'VR' on it; probably there were lots such. Border at Plumtree and into Southern Rhodesia. We had sickening forms to fill up and I was rather dreading the Customs at Bulawayo, though I had what amounted to a *laisser-passer*; in fact there was no bother at all; we were first through and straight through.

24 June 1953 [At Panda-ma-Tenga, Bechuanaland] After lunch we went to look at the agricultural land, over 7000 acres of it, apparently in good shape. This job [Bechuanaland Cattle Ranch] is one with as disgraceful a story as any in the Corporation, utter incompetence and criminal extravagances especially in machinery. Muriel went away in a Land-Rover with Van der Post[4] into really wild parts of the bush looking for lions – but never a lion they saw.

[After his return from South Africa, John Reith's only immediate problem was the completion of his plan to hand over his executive duties to a general manager. He achieved this with effect from 1 October and for the remainder of the year the affairs of the CDC moved smoothly.]

28 July 1953 Lyttelton wants two of his pet finance types on the board; utterly wrong. I asked if he would like me to resign.

3 September 1953 Saw Lyttelton 3.00 to 4.00 about more directors – sickening bore his wanting to put some of his thugs on. He seemed very reluctant to do it against my wishes.

9 September 1953 Worked till 2.30 a.m. doing a policy statement about CDC projects and full notes for the meeting with Sir T. Lloyd about capital write-off. With him 10.30 to 11.30. I think I got my arguments across all right on the inequity and illogicality of having a cut-off date in August 1952 and that this was contrary to Colonial Office statements to us. It is entirely a Treasury ramp.

Informal board meeting and dinner – all present. Discussed Rendell's promotion to chief executive and pay; and then a woolly commentary on the House of Lords debate in July. It was because I thought a sort of policy statement might go down well that I prepared the one last night and had copies to issue; but there seemed no point, so I said nought.

1 October 1953 Colonial Office 3.00 to 4.45 with Lloyd and Poynton about capital write-off, a pension for Rendell, and other matters. Most satisfactory.

Office Notice for Colonial Development Corporation, 1 October 1953

The Board has appointed Mr William Rendell to be chief executive officer of the Corporation from October 1, with title of general manager.

I think you know why I wished to have the offices of chairman (at reduced salary) and chief executive separated; and why the Board agreed. But it might be well that your responsible assistants should know also.

As with most public corporations, my appointment was as full-time, executive chairman and for a period of five years.

It was a political appointment, made by the colonial secretary of state after consultation with the prime minister; and perhaps other ministers were consulted also.

At the end of the five-year term the government in power could make – and owing to my age probably would – another appointment.

So, at the end of 1955, there might have been a new individual with almost plenary powers over the internal organization and general conduct of affairs.

He could have changed existing staff, system and procedure; he might have disapproved of everything and everybody.

Now there is a continuing chief executive, not subject to political confirmation or reappointment; he is appointed by the Board, responsible solely to the Board.

6 November 1953 With the secretary of state [Lyttelton] for over an hour and a very agreeable time. Talked about his ideas for the future organization of CDC. He was very apologetic but of course I said I had come to get his views. The major point is four or five subsidiary functional companies in London.

Letter to the governor general of Canada [Vincent Massey] 7 December 1953

I sometimes wonder if I would have taken on the Colonial Development Corporation if I had had any idea of the state it was in. Perhaps I would for I have always been very stupid. Anyhow I have been more liquidator than chairman and it has been a rather sickening time, but things are nearly in shape now.

(c) *The end of 'redding up', January 1954–December 1955*

[John Reith hoped that CDC would soon be able to follow a more positive policy and he believed that this would be made the easier when Lyttelton was replaced as colonial secretary by Alan Lennox-Boyd at the end of July 1954. But signs of future disagreements were not long in appearing, over the supervisory claims of the Colonial Office as well as in relation to the type and location of permissable operations by CDC. Nevertheless at the end of 1955 John Reith agreed to accept the extension of his appointment as chairman for a further three years from 1 April 1956.]

18 February 1954 To see Lyttelton and went through my rejoinder about his subsidiary companies scheme – quite absurd; he took it all very well. I showed him a letter very complimentary to him over Nigeria. He said Baring and Erskine [governor and commander-in-chief] in Kenya were not working as a team at all and he was going to knock their heads together. He agreed that something would have to be done about land in that country and soon.

30 March 1954 With Lyttelton, 12.00 to 1.00, about the [capital] write-offs chiefly; usual sort of blarney talk.

30 June 1954 To Rhodesia House to a party given for the new prime minister of Southern Rhodesia, Garfield Todd. I had special correspondence with him about loans. He was very good, I thought.

29 July 1954 Lyttelton has ceased to be colonial secretary – to nobody's regret that seems; Lennox-Boyd the new one; one wonders if he will put some discipline into the blasted civil servants there.

7 September 1954 Dictated a sort of climax of infuriation with Colonial Office, especially in their references, now official, to 'financing of losses'. I was relieved to get this done. I am really doing almost as much work as when I was full-time chairman.

9 September 1954 Long letters from Southern Rhodesian prime minister. Very annoyed that Southern Rhodesia cannot borrow from us equally with Nyasaland and Northern Rhodesia. [Sir T.] Lloyd at the Colonial Office is most puerile about such issues and lets himself be dictated to by his office boys.

15 September 1954 Weird hooh-hah about a meeting which I was to have with Lennox-Boyd tomorrow. It was to have been a private meeting with an official one later on, but the civil servants didn't like this and were working for some days to secure that one at least of themselves should be present. This had twice been denied by the secretary of state's private office but when I got home this evening Miss Shipton [John Reith's secretary] rang to tell me that the Colonial Office had said that Melville [assistant under secretary] would be at the meeting and so expected that I would bring Rendell. I got on to the secretary of state's office and the result was that Lennox-Boyd rang me to say no one would be there and would I bring my engagement book to fix a lunch or dinner and also the other meeting. So that is a minor Crichel Down[5] for me.

16 September 1954 To CDC. It was agreed that I should suggest to Lennox-Boyd that Rendell and Melville should try to settle the differences, now fairly serious, between CDC and the Colonial Office rather than all of us should be engaged now; we would come in if the negotiations were not successful. Saw him 11.30 to 12.30; most cordial he was. I didn't talk real business; generalities about the corporation and myself. Fixed a day for lunch and he welcomed the idea of our standing off to see if Rendell and Melville could settle the troubles.

23 September 1954 Lennox-Boyd rang me last night wanting to change the lunch-party from just Hume [deputy chairman of CDC] and myself to include Poynton and Melville; I asked for Tyser also. I am not at all pleased.

24 September 1954 Lunch at A. Lennox-Boyd's opulent establishment in Chapel Street; Hume and I there at 12.30 with an opportunity to tell him some things causing trouble between Colonial Office and CDC. Others came at 1.15. It wasn't a good party and I didn't expect it to be.

[At the end of the year John Reith embarked on his third tour of inspection on behalf of CDC – this time of the Caribbean area. In three and a half weeks he visited the Bahamas, Jamaica, British Honduras, Trinidad, Barbados and British Guiana as well as stopping en route between these places in Miami, New Orleans and Caracas. This involved him, as he later reported, in '38 take-offs and 38 landings in all sorts of aircraft, trying to be intelligent and well informed as to the continually shifting panorama of people and places and things', producing 'a rumbling mass of queries and impressions and opinions'. His conclusion was that CDC affairs were by no means yet right in the Caribbean but that the job of putting them right was 'a very hard one'. It was, he explained, 'the most difficult region of all to handle; many territories, spread over a great area, with inefficient transportation and no telephone service worth mentioning'. Nevertheless, he was hopeful that further improvement would be achieved.]

28 December 1954 [Staying in Government House, Nassau, with Lord and Lady Ranfurly] After dinner, having made clear that I could not and would not play bridge, I was introduced to a word-making game called Scrabble from which after much humiliation but tactfully assisted by the ADC, I actually emerged winner. Thereafter, I being hungry, the governor's wife, ADC and I went to the kitchen in search of biscuits. I have never seen so many nor such large cockroaches; I was thoroughly frightened.

29 December 1954 [On visit to Eleuthera Island, the site of an 8800-acre estate, an early CDC project] If I had come out here some years ago I think I might well have found some way to carry out this development, not directly but in conjunction with some private interests – such as A. V. Davis. An immense expenditure is required and the return will be slow; but I should think sure. I am sorry about it all; and I suppose I ought to have done a tour of the world, every job, in my first year. But the hopeless conditions of head office makes my not having done so entirely understandable. It seemed not the right sort of thing for the Corporation to be risking. When I asked Davis's manager straightly whether we had been wrong to withdraw, his considered reply was that he would have advised it.

[On December 30 John Reith 'visited Lord Beaverbrook at his request'.]

31 December 1954 [en route for Jamaica with the CDC Regional Officer] Arrived Miami at 6.30. Here met by representative of Bahamas Tourist Association who whistled us through medical officer, immigration and customs so quickly that the local BOAC manager only caught up with us after it was all over. An argument developed between him and the tourist gentleman as to where we should go. The reason was that annually, on the last day of the year, Miami goes carnival and our hotel was in city centre. It was not clear what was to become of us. Eventually a vast Cadillac car appeared; we were told that a very special driver had been procured and he would get us to our hotel. And indeed by a most circuitous route and by knowing every policeman in Miami who tried to turn him back, he did, travelling the last half-mile or so stern first. The reception clerks were much disturbed to see us; we had booked, by mistake, for the next night. Because of this carnival every bed was occupied; but after considerable telephoning two rooms were procured in a hotel only a block away, though we had to go several miles to arrive at it. Then we discovered that we could get nothing to eat that night and no breakfast before 8.00 a.m., so that was no good. After waiting three-quarters of an hour on the street we managed to get a taxi to take us back to the airport where we got back at 11.00 p.m. just three hours after we had left it. The largest steaks I ever saw were soon before us; I could only dispose of a third of mine. Bed 12.30 a.m.

7 January 1955 [Staying with the governor of British Honduras] At 3 o'clock, at the governor's request, I went to Government Information Office where a seconded BBC official is responsible, among other things, for broadcasting. I feel great regret at the neglect of broadcasting pretty well throughout the Colonial Empire. It is not my fault, nor the fault of Sidney Webb, colonial secretary in [1930][6] when during a Colonial Conference he asked me to come and speak about the importance of broadcasting to the colonial territories – which I surely did but might as well have kept silent. There are few projects on which money might more profitably have been spent – a service conducted, if not by the State, at any rate under the ægis of the State and for the benefit of the State.

8 Januuary 1955 [In New Orleans] It is a commentary on Caribbean transportation that, having gone from Jamaica to British Honduras due east to west, one has to go north on an isosceles triangle with sides about three times longer than the base to New Orleans (and then to Miami) in order to get back to Jamaica and Trinidad.

New Orleans at 3.00 p.m. and into the medical officer's room with fifty others. American citizens taken first; then an almost plaintive 'No more US citizens?' We were in no hurry, but when all were through, we were left alone on a wooden bench. Regional controller and I moved towards the desk; a commotion sprang up; something was wrong. The doctor shot a remark between us, not sure which was which, 'Say, are you Lord Reith?' I said I was and here a clerk took over. Why hadn't I come up to the desk at the beginning; it was too bad; we ought to have been taken first; they were very sorry. I said it was perfectly all right but in a matter of seconds we were shot past and found ourselves on a boulevard of New Orleans with nothing to do for three hours.

17 January 1955 [In Georgetown, British Guiana] Flew up to Tumatumasi [site of CDC hydro-electric project] and there hardly seemed room for the aircraft to come down on the Potaro river. After lunch went across to the dredge at work and then to the other bank to see the beginning of the hydro-electric dam. Then, after a false start, the river bank looming too close, we made for the Kaiteur Gorge despite some mist, the captain 'pretty sure I can find the entrance to it'. He found it all right – precipitous bastions, and as we flew up the gorge it seemed that the aircraft's wing tips must scrape the precipices on either hand. In twenty minutes the Kaiteur Falls came in sight, higher than Zambesi and Niagara combined. Flew up over them, then turned and back to Georgetown by 6.00 p.m. after an hour's stop at Konawaruk on the Kuribrong river.

[On his return, John Reith found himself called on by Sir Godfrey

Huggins (later Lord Malvern), the prime minister of the Central African Federation, to give advice on 'the hydro-electric plans' which were later to produce the Kariba dam, and later in the year he met Sir Roy Welensky on the same subject. But for much of 1955 CDC affairs did not bulk large in his diary. He was occupied with his work for Tube Investments (he had helped to restore its aluminium division to profitability) as well as with his move from his home in Beaconsfield to a flat in the Lollards Tower of Lambeth Palace at the end of March; and he was, once again, in a state of depression about himself. 'Very unhappy,' he noted at the end of May, 'about my quite useless life,' and then again in September, 'feeling that I have now forfeited my right to another life'.]

7 September 1955 Much alarmed to see in *The Times* that the public works loan rate was up from four and a half to five per cent, and the CDC drawing £3½m at noon today. I rang Rendell and then Melville at the Colonial Office getting him to agree to put it across the Treasury that the old rate would apply. When I got to the office Melville had already rung to advise drawing the £3½m. I was sure that this meant that the old rate would apply but Rendell was frightened of it. I spoke to Melville again and all was well to my vast relief.

21 November 1955 Saw Lennox-Boyd for three-quarters of an hour and more or less agreed to carry on for three years from 1.4.56 which would bring me near seventy! It wasn't a coherent talk at all and I was a bit disgusted with it.

(d) *Battling with the Colonial Office, January 1956–December 1957*

[Within a few months of his agreement to continue as chairman of CDC John Reith was involved in major disputes with the Colonial Office. It was in this period that the argument over the statutory right of CDC to be involved in projects for house and road building came to a head. The amending legislation of August 1956 resolved much of this difficulty by validating existing projects of this type but, unfortunately, it also introduced a new principle of limiting the areas in which CDC could work. Thus, as the CDC Annual Report of 1956 phrased it, the 1956 Act was construed 'as affording the secretary of state no discretion to authorize CDC to participate in a Southern Rhodesian undertaking' because, though it would be of *value* to the Northern Territories, it was not *needed* by them. (The undertaking in question was the Rhodesian Iron and Steel Commission.) This strict construction of CDC's legal mandate presaged further restrictions – notably by the Ghana Independence Act, which excluded Ghana after independence from CDC's area of operations. It was, indeed, government policy to exclude future CDC projects from being started in all 'emergent territories', and in November Malaya was so excluded. But on the financial front, it appeared, after long arguments, that CDC was to be granted an increase in its borrowing limit and even the possibility of a new financial structure. So when at the end of 1957 John Reith set out on his fourth major tour of inspection to Nigeria – in 1956 he had made short visits to the Bahamas and to Central Africa – he felt 'a bit better pleased' with the Colonial Office.]

25 January 1956 Letter from the secretary of state about the housing nonsense [i.e. about CDC's right to be involved in house-building projects]. He asks me to accept the Law Officers' ruling and to get down to devising an amending act! Not likely with such an opinion as we have. It is a sickening business.

26 January 1956 I had to see Lennox-Boyd in Lancaster House at 11.30 to tell him we were not going to do as he suggested and accept the Law Officers' ruling. I had prepared rather carefully what I wished to say and I said it. He couldn't have been more agreeable.

[In spite of his brave words John Reith appears soon to have accepted the idea of an amending act.]

20 February 1956 Colonial Office at 5.30 and the meeting wasn't over till 7.30 – re housing, most weird and it showed how exceedingly badly the whole matter had been handled at the Colonial Office.

28 February 1956 Lunched with House of Commons Labour party colonial committee; a big lot there. I think it went quite well.

Long talk on telephone with Melville of Colonial Office, morning and evening; quite helpful about what was needed in amending bill clause.

12 March 1956 To see Lennox-Boyd in the House of Commons with Beaver and Rendell. Waffling meeting; all that is required is some courage and strength on Lennox-Boyd's part.

[In April John Reith made a quick visit to the Bahamas, returning via New York. His purpose was to complete the selling off of the CDC estate on Eleuthera Island to the financier A. V. Davis.]

5 April 1956 [On Eleuthera Island] We met in Davis's room, sitting in a circle. I said nothing, so Davis said, 'Well, what is the position?' and asked his manager to put his map on the table and explain it all. This took fifteen minutes or so. The first jolt was when Davis thought that the figure for Section A of the 3000-acre plot (of which 1500 was marked as swamp) was the total instead of just half. The manager – carrying on because I had said nothing – said he thought it worthwhile Davis considering exercising his option on the whole lot if a figure could be agreed. Davis immediately said there was no point in his buying 1500 acres of swamp at the far end of the property. Here I said that the whole 3000 acres were in at £20 per acre which seemed to take account of the swamp half averaging out as other farm parts were down at £30 per acre. After a good deal more Davis said we could have all the property back if we liked, which, of course, was designed to prevent my trying to beat him up. I spotted that, and assured him that this would not be decent and we would not do it. He said all right, he would buy – what was the figure? £305,797 the manager said. £60,000 this year, Davis said, and £30,000 for the next eight – the balance at two per cent interest. I said, 'Did you say two per cent?' Yes, he replied. I waited about a minute before saying anything; very odd silence this was. Then I spoke thus: I would have thought that he would prefer to settle the whole affair now and be finished with the CDC. From my point of view, we would far rather he paid us now for the whole – no hangovers or anything of that sort. Would he make an offer for liquidation immediately in cash? He looked at me for a bit and then said he and his agent would have a word together. Regional controller and I then went out. It was a relief that he was willing to consider what I had said but I was chiefly conscious of the vast gap between the £290,000 (which was the best I thought possible) and his offer. We walked in the sun for fifteen minutes or so and then the manager came out for us. I left regional controller behind. Davis said, rather aggressively, that he had an offer to make, the very most he would do – (oh gosh!) – £280,000, £10,000 today and the rest in June. I said I would like to tell him what I had had in mind – five per cent discount for cash, £290,000. All right, he said, he would go half-way. Thank you, I said. It was all done in about three minutes.

6 April 1956 I am of course quite sure that God was with us yesterday.

I could hardly believe that the deal had really gone through at £280,000; maybe a dream.

[Back in London on 10 April, John Reith's main concern in the summer of 1956 was the amending legislation authorizing, retrospectively, CDC's various housing and road-building projects. Then, in August, he went on another tour of inspection in Central and Southern Africa, concentrating for the most part on CDC projects in the Central African Federation of Rhodesia and Nyasaland.]

11 June 1956 I had to meet Lennox-Boyd and the attorney-general [Sir Reginald Manningham-Buller] and others in the House of Commons at 8.00 and didn't get away till midnight – about the CDC bill. It was a most successful evening and a pity they hadn't done this earlier.

26 July 1956 Secretary of state's dinner-party in Chapel Street 8.15 to 11.15. All the CDC board and Rendell present besides Lord Lloyd [parliamentary secretary], Poynton, Melville and Galsworthy [head of finance department] from Colonial Office. Very good indeed. We went through thirty (Labour) amendments after dinner.

2 August 1956 Called to say goodbye to Sir T. Lloyd who retires tomorrow. I have had no hard words with him in near six years. The CDC bill had the royal assent today; signals had gone to all regional commissioners for removal of hold-up of schemes.

4 August 1956 [In Salisbury, Southern Rhodesia] Lord Malvern and his wife were walking in their very nice garden when I arrived. They had tea for me and I was very glad of it. He talked almost without stopping from 5.00 to 6.00. He talked mostly about Colonial Office and Commonwealth Relations Office and the recent London Conference, being obviously much disgusted thereat. The arrangement of a Federation with a prime minister and a governor general, and three territories with three governors and one prime minister is also quite ridiculous; and there is a silly mix-up of what the Colonial Office is responsible for and what the Commonwealth Relations Office is. He seemed to agree with my occasional remarks about the sickening inefficiency and timidity apparently inevitable with democracy, and that it was time the politicians in England gave a lead instead of doing only what they imagined the voters wanted. As there is no chance, things as now, of the Conservative government being returned three years from now, they might as well make up their minds to govern for this period

– and that quite likely would bring about their re-election. I don't now feel about Malvern as I was inclined to before. I am now afraid that he is really like the rest – following not leading on the important issues.

5 August 1956 After lunch we went off with the prime minister [Lord Malvern] and his wife for what he called a tour of the village. This was quite interesting, particularly the Kopje where the pioneers had stopped to survey the countryside. Only five houses before the war with more than three stories; now several dozen. Forty-four years ago when Malvern came here, the population was 3000, now 60,000 white and double that black.

6 August 1956 We were ten minutes late at the Southern Rhodesian prime minister's house, Garfield Todd. This is another delightful house and garden. Two other ministers there and after tea we went off with them to see the Highfield African houses built with CDC money. The quarters were quite good. The most interesting feature is that Africans can own the freehold, this being hitherto unknown.

7 August 1956 Garfield Todd gave a dinner for me – about forty there. To my great disappointment he made an entirely *Who's Who* speech about me. But it was a distinguished party – all Southern Rhodesian ministers except one who had had to go to Kariba because of some native troubles there.

8 August 1956 [visiting the Kariba dam site] About a dozen men lined up to meet us, including the agent and deputy agent of Cementation. I had not realized that Cementation were to hand over to Impresit at the end of this month, the new Italian agent and sub-agent being of the party. I was very sorry for the Cementation people; nothing of this sort has happened in British civil engineering before. We drove first to the dam site where one of the coffer dams was just visible and the suspension bridge for foot traffic; then to the diversion tunnel driving into this first one end then the other. Odd to think of the Zambesi running through it in a year's time. Across the bridge to the crushing plant, where we had a welcome tea; then back and visited the African quarters, the European temporary camp and the beginnings of the European township which might well become a permanent summer resort beside a new lake, 200 miles long by 35 broad and 2500 to 3000 feet up. The last thing we saw was the brickmaking plant which singularly failed to make bricks while we were watching it.

9 August 1956 [en route to Mzuzu, Nyasaland, site of the CDC Vipya Tung Estate] Arrived Mzuzu at 1.15 and was met by the Northern Provincial Commissioner and the Vipya Tung project manager. I was amazed at the setting of the latter's house with a magnificent view and the lake behind; it seemed as if we had come for a nice weekend in the country. Unpacked, lunch, visited office, works and stores and then to tea with a RC bishop, Monseigneur St Denis, a French Canadian, in charge of a White Fathers' Mission nearby. He had taken over many of the surplus houses of Vipya Tung and the provincial commissioner had also taken over a great many, so CDC got out of its early monstrous extravagances better than it deserved to. Very jolly he was and full of schemes. I told him CDC might be able to help him.

10 August 1956 [In Mzuzu] Went round estates all morning and lunched with provincial commissioner. He knew a lot about Livingstone and I was delighted to find among his books *Among the Wild Ngoni* which I remember so well as a child. More estates in the afternoon and then an African senior staff tea-party. They were all lined up which seemed very odd and unnecessary, so I walked down, shook hands with and spoke to them all. They were all very civil and friendly, but too much time was taken up by a non-employee, a local agitator and vice-chairman of the Congress party. The party wasn't well done at all – e.g. only half the number of seats required and those all kitchen chairs. I got everybody's names; Kaunda[7] was the agitator's.

16 August 1956 [Staying at Blantyre, Nyasaland] Went to Michiru of which I couldn't remember hearing before. Regional controller was sure it was mentioned as a project in the Annual Report. It wasn't but it seems to have become attached to regional office accounts. I was full of wrath when I saw it. Fifty acres on a hillside without light or power or water. At the top was a £15,000 house for the 'regional director'; another a little lower for the 'finance director' and on lower slopes still other dwellings and a big office block. The houses are let and there is £1200 or so annual loss. Better financially to have the houses empty. Nobody could tell me what the place was supposed to be, nor why it should have been built several miles from Blantyre on a rough road leading nowhere.

[Back in London, John Reith soon found that his good-will mission was to bear little fruit, at least in respect of Southern Rhodesia. The Colonial Office's interpretation of the new Overseas Resources

Development Act excluded that territory from future CDC assistance. Further, it was in the last months of 1956 that the Colonial Secretary made it clear that it was the Government's policy to exclude all newly independent colonies from CDC's sphere of action. In all this John Reith was as much concerned at the way in which the struggle developed as he was at its outcome. He felt a lack of trust and brooded over it.]

1 September 1956 Lennox-Boyd wrote yesterday suggesting that the CDC shouldn't put new money into jobs in territories which have been given self-government. There will be a great argument about this; a most unfortunate move it would be.

6 September 1956 To Colonial Office to call on Sir John Macpherson, the new permanent under-secretary. I told him I was greatly concerned about the secretary of state's letter suggesting that CDC shouldn't deal with countries after they got independence; very friendly and outspoken he was.

6 October 1956 I am wondering whether I ought to have a campaign to secure the continuance of the CDC in territories after they become independent.

18 October 1956 Infuriated to hear that RISCOM [i.e. Rhodesian Iron and Steel Commission] is being turned down presumably at blasted Treasury instance. The case for rejection derives from a clause introduced at the end of the negotiations as to Southern Rhodesian jobs, whereas this is quite irrelevant as it was a moral obligation to let RISCOM through irrespective of what is in the blasted act.[8]

19 October 1956 Macpherson rang to say that 'ministers' had decided they must act at once on the RISCOM matter because of a statement in Salisbury. I said he had promised to hold things up until a statement from me arrived. I asked if he was prepared for Board resignations.

25 October 1956 Colonial Office letter on RISCOM row was a real shocker of equivocation and deceit. But as I have often said civil service and politician morality carries an automatic discount of fifty per cent on what applies among decent people.

26 October 1956 I declined to have anything to do with the drafting of a rejoinder to the wretched Colonial Office but I had a final draft given me late in the afternoon.

29 October 1956 I was to have lunched with the New Commonwealth today, Lennox-Boyd making a speech about help to colonial territories! I cancelled this.

30 October 1956 Very angry at having the letter to the Colonial Office about RISCOM dropped back in my room and spent most of the day on it.

23 November 1956 To the Colonial Office to see Lennox-Boyd. He talked about ill-feeling between CDC and Colonial Office, appointments to the board, and RISCOM.

27 November 1956 Saw Lennox-Boyd 3.30 to 5.00; quite sickening but I managed to keep quiet.

17 December 1956 Meeting with secretary of state at 6.30 lasting till 8.00. Beaver, Tyser, Hall, Rendell and I, Poynton and Galsworthy. I should think it was the most sickeningly unsatisfactory meeting I have ever been at.

28 December 1956 When I was asked yesterday (by deputy chairman) what was the minimum I would accept I said I couldn't specify in any way; perhaps I would be willing to accept what was recommended to me by people whom I trusted and provided that they really understood how abominably the corporation had been treated.

> [John Reith's colleagues now tried their hands at repairing the breach of confidence between CDC and the Colonial Office which had been caused by the decisions over RISCOM and 'emergent territories'; but they had little immediate success. John Reith, himself, was deeply hurt and, as often happened when frustrated in his work, he suffered another bout of pessimistic introspection.
>
> In the end it was the government decision in the middle of 1957 to ease the CDC's financial restrictions which relaxed the tension.]

16 January 1957 Hume rang me to give an account of the meeting he and Beaver had had with Macpherson and Poynton – two hours and nothing but talk.

R.D.–2C

27 January 1957 [Sunday] Wishing I could have some objective for the remaining part of my life, which can't be very much. I wish I could make dear Muriel happy; that would be a good objective. I have really come a most awful crash in life.

31 January 1957 Went to see Home [secretary of state for Commonwealth Relations] in the House of Lords. I certainly said a good deal. He said he and I and the chancellor [Peter Thorneycroft] and the colonial secretary should get together about the future. He was friendly and open.

5 February 1957 Saw Perth [minister of state for colonial affairs] and was thoroughly disgusted at the sophistry of the case he had to put to me on the Ghana bill. The lawyers had been asked to see if they could approve the elimination of clause 3 of the bill, and I intervened to say of course they would say they could not. The argument actually was that a *general* direction to keep off Ghana would not be legal! The other main point was that the CDC would not be prejudiced in the review which is to take place And that, I told him, had a sinister sound.

20 March 1957 Colonial Office want all reference to RISCOM and emergent territories taken out of the CDC Report. What idiots!

2 May 1957 CDC 1956 Report was published yesterday. The wretched Colonial Office put out a sort of rejoinder to some of the things on the Report, including the statement that CDC comments about Ghana and Malaya were 'overstated'.[9]

11 June 1957 To see Perth 3.00 to 4.45 re the future which he told me about with great solemnity (privy councillor to privy councillor) but nothing I didn't know. I asked what he was going to do about the points I had raised in April (i.e. about fresh capital and CDC's part in emergent territories).

3 July 1957 4.30 to 7.15 with Perth. It looks as if the tensions between the Colonial Office and CDC were loosening.

17 July 1957 Went to the House of Lords after lunch as there was a debate on about CDC on Ogmore's motion which censored the government for its treatment of CDC. It was a most boring and irritating affair, especially for me having to sit there for five hours (which I certainly won't do again), hearing questions asked and not answered and many inaccuracies.

23 July 1957 Lunch in House of Lords. Perth said CDC was to have another £30m from the government and £20m by borrowing; this is much better than expected.

21 November 1957 I went to the Colonial Office at Perth's urgent request at 5.15; he had wanted to come and see me. It was chiefly about a possible complete financial reconstruction which would be very welcome.

> [John Reith now set out on his tour of CDC operations in Nigeria; he had been warmly pressed to make this tour earlier in the year by the governor general, Sir James Robertson, when he was home on leave.]

23 November 1957 Airborne at 1615. The older one gets the more conscious of the affliction of one's height; not beds or lintels or anything special – one can deal with them; it is the inadequacy of the ordinary chair in the room, above all in the aircraft. Best place in the Stratocruiser is on the port side immediately aft of the ladder to the wretched bar. These two seats have more leg room than any others but they are subject to an incessant yatter from the bar till midnight, a continuous clatter of opening and shutting of adjacent lavatory doors and the inevitable glare of light from within them. In the air it seems necessary for people to go to the lavatories at two-hourly intervals all night long.

24 November 1957 Kano in Northern Nigeria, 6.10 to 7.25 GMT. At intervals, but without obvious reason, a man from the sands tilted a seven-foot bugle and put cacophony on the air. After twenty minutes he shuffled indignantly from the scene; but five minutes later, reappeared mounted on a camel with another one in tow. At his first salute thereafter at least three parties gave him alms; he had been trying to do his act without the scheduled props; the public had not responded; something had been accomplished in Nigeria.

25 November 1957 [Staying in Lagos with the governor general] State of main roads in colonial capitals and scale and style of amenities at Government Houses depend largely on whether or not the Monarch has visited there. I had never slept in air-conditioned room before. It was a bit primitive as the air-conditioned rooms exhausted into the passage; so, to get to one's door, it seemed as if one had to move through the accumulated smog of a dozen different occupants; but there was great relief on opening the door.

26 November 1957 Large dinner-party at Government House. Governor general had asked me to get hold of the Federal prime minister and talk about CDC requirements for coming in on Cameroons Development Corporation; we had about half an hour before dinner. He said he wanted us to come in. I said I thought it would be a good thing for Camdev if we did, but that CDC would require a lot of freedom. He said the local people were interested; it was about the only thing they had to be interested in; they would be very bothered if control passed to CDC. I said I understood that; but special measures were urgently needed and it would be for a limited period. CDC fully realized it was asking him to agree to something that looked undemocratic, about which there might be a row in UNO. I said in effect that two things were required – confidence in CDC and courage on their own. Prime minister then said he was rather worried about public corporation; he had federal ones for railways, electricity, ports, etc. Did I think they were better than departmental management. I said I surely did; and for many reasons some of which were not complimentary to politicians or civil servants. He said he had set up a committee of six of the most experienced civil servants, all English, to report on the system. I asked if he had had their report. Yes, two or three months ago. Then a pause. I was wondering whether I ought to let myself get involved. In the event we both spoke together, I asking if he would like me to look at it; he saying he wondered if I would be able to. I said I should be glad to; and, after another pause, did he want me to comment. Yes indeed. Next morning I was given a copy, horrified at the length of it.

27 November 1957 12.00 to 1.00 with Federal prime minister and nine of the ten Federal ministers, all Nigerian. PM asked me to explain CDC attitude and policy as to Nigeria. I thought I should tell them about the White Paper with its embargo on government to government loans, even before independence, and the position after independence. Many of them expressed emphatic dismay and consternation; what could they do to have these sad decisions reversed or even modified. Communications minister said it was becoming increasingly clear to them all that to obtain financial help from UK they had 'to be naughty boys'; there was no reward for sincere endeavour and relatively stable government. If UK were unwilling to help then they would have to turn to other sources for financial help – USA or Russia. I said I would pass on their views, but meantime, supposing it was possible for CDC to put more money into Nigeria, where did they most want it? Finance minister and PM both said they had been hoping for about £5m from CDC all for railways. I asked would they really want it all for railways; CDC preferred to spread investments. Finance minister said that railway extension was the most important development of all, with absolute priority; they believed it would greatly facilitate raising of finance for their other projects from other sources official and private. At end of meeting PM hoped I would do everything I could to persuade UK government of urgent need of UK help to Nigeria.

In the evening there was a sherry party at regional controller's house. One hundred and fifty present; almost everybody who should have been was in fact there – African ministers, senior European officers and industrial leaders. I entirely agreed with the English chief justice in wishing that the Judicial Committee of the Privy Council should some-times hear territorial appeals in the territories concerned, with any and all its accustomed paraphernalia and formality. Those sort of happen-ings would have made all the difference all over the world; too late now.

Dinner-party at Government House. There is an advantage in the Moslem faith which I had not previously realized; it seems that when Moslem members get bored at any gathering they can depart en masse for prayers. This evening I was delayed on the stairs on the way to the drawing-room and then found myself shaking hands with all the Moslems of the party on their way out.

3 December 1957 We arrived at Benin at 20.45; we were to stay the night in the old Residency. There are now no residents in the Western Region and this fine old building is used only as a VIP lodging place. We were surprised to find only a Nigerian caretaker; and it was so forbidding a place that I visualized spending the night writing up reports near the front door in the least decrepit armchair one could find. The house must have been built soon after British occupation – commodious, dignified and most comfortable it must have been, well arranged and obviously at one time cared for; but now unkempt, undignified, pro-testing against its neglect and decay. Also it was spooky; Benin had been the scene of a frightful ambush and massacre of British troops for which two or three years later ample revenge was taken.[10] We had been warned we could not have anything to eat in this establishment but that dinner would be ready in an eating-house some distance off at 19.30. We were still all sitting near the front door at 21.15 wondering what to do when an Englishman, district administrative officer, appeared. Immediate question was where to have something to eat. We thought we had better go to the eating-house. He said he must first go and see what sort of a dinner they were putting up. He returned in a quarter of an hour, he thought the dinner would be all right – as indeed it was. And here I made the acquaintance of a Nigerian cat. We had a large plate of soup, then a substantial steak, then, to my horror, there arrived what turned out to be a fried lobster cutlet. I could do nothing with it but did not want to hurt the staff by rejecting it. A large tor-toiseshell cat had been sitting at some distance watching us; unseen, I held out a large piece of this, and the cat, in obvious fear, managed to take it from my hand, quickly withdrawing to its former stance. I addressed some kindly words to it; it seemed as if it had never been addressed before; it stood up; stared at me; turned to go away but then, after two or three false starts, came alongside again. It had the rest of the lobster cutlet, and, when we left, wished to accompany us, actually getting into the car. Getting to bed was a fearsome matter for me; thoroughly frightened I was; not of the spooks but of cockroaches.

[John Reith went from Benin, across the Niger, to Enugu in the Eastern Region of Nigeria. Here he was scheduled to meet the local prime minister and other ministers but was chagrined to find that 'premier Azikiwe was on the coast south of Port Harcourt, in-gratiating himself with the riverain tribes'. Nevertheless a meeting was held with the acting prime minister and all the other ministers except two, who were in England, and here John Reith made it plain that 'CDC's concern was for the good development of any territory in which it was operating, subject to covering its money; it was not interested in politics'. This straight talking was received with 'evident embarrassment' and John Reith moved on to Port Harcourt without attaining a confident relationship such as he had achieved in Lagos with the Federal ministers. From Port Harcourt he flew to Kaduna in the Northern Region where he arrived on 8 December.]

9 December 1957 [In Kaduna] Here it is quite different, I suppose, from any other part of the Commonwealth – the ancient aristocratic regimes,

romantic titles, animosities and jealousies between some of the Emirs. I talked with the premier for an hour before he left on a tour and then saw twelve of his ministers. I said I hoped CDC might do much more in the North, but suggestions must come from the region. They talk less easily in the North than in the South, but there were many questions. It was a very pleasant and friendly meeting with a good deal of laughing. On one occasion I asked which of them was responsible for a particular affair, and each of two ministers sitting together pointed to the other.

10 December 1957 One of the troubles in travelling about colonial territories and having meetings is that one has to take care about local records. A point had come up yesterday as to whether members of the House of Assembly should be members of public corporations. I explained what the position was in England, but was not prepared for the minute which emerged:

> Lord Reith stated that he felt the present membership of Northern Region Development Corporation was open to criticism. During his many years of experience he had come to the firm conclusion that board members should not be executives. He pointed out also that in the UK politicians were prohibited from membership of public boards. He added that this did not apply to members of the House of Lords because they were popularly regarded as being mentally defective.

11 December 1957 Off at 12.30 for Kano through Zaria, the first old Northern town I had seen; high, strong mud walls. Twenty miles from Kano the cars drew into a clearing in the bush for afternoon tea. Presently a boy of about twelve peered out of the bush, but seemed too frightened to come nearer. In a few minutes he was back with a tattered old blanket round him. He still did not come near; just stood watching. Ten minutes or so later one of the African chauffeurs held out a sandwich to him; the boy came running up, down on both knees, held out both hands to get the sandwich, then backed away. The chauffeur took it as a matter of course, but I thought it one of the most moving sights I have seen.

12 December 1957 [In Kano] Tour round the industrial area from 9.00 for an hour and a half and then back to the Residency to change for my call on the Emir of Kano. [John Reith had hoped to be able to show friendliness and respect without the formality of an audience. But the Emir had asked to see him.]

So now we were driving, resident and I, in a Rolls-Royce wearing a Jack into the ancient town. Eventually we drove under an archway into a large court; then under another archway into a smaller court with an impressive entrance to the palace at the far side. There was a large tree in the middle of this court, under it were several men reclining on the ground, dressed in all sorts of gorgeous clothes. They quickly jumped up, giving the Moslem salute. The car stopped by the tree and I noticed that in the doorway thirty yards off were two figures, one I recognized as the Mudaiki, the senior counsellor of the Emir whom I had met the previous evening. He was standing to one side, and in an attitude which, for all its dignity, conveyed subservience to the other figure. And this other figure was terrific. The Emir is about six foot three, magnificent robes, hat with wings of the aristocrat over the ears, shoes with huge rosettes of fur, and in his left hand two long spears. Resident introduced me; we shook hands, each bowing. Then I followed the Emir, resident walking beside me, into what I supposed was the audience hall – something like a private chapel, about sixty feet long and forty feet wide, very lofty, the roof going into a central point, with most striking and almost barbaric colouring of roof and walls. The Emir handed his spears to a retainer at the door. At the far end was a sort of golden bench, nothing at all on one side, three or four chairs in a line at right angles on the other. Reaching the bench the Emir turned and bowed me into the first chair on his right hand, resident sitting next me; on the other side the Mudaiki, for all his magnificence, sat cross-legged on the floor. As advised by the resident I said I hoped the Serriki was well (Serriki meaning King), that his family were well, that his people were well and that they had a good harvest. He seemed pleased, smiled and nodded. Then, speaking to the Mudaiki, I said would he tell Serrikin Kano that, being a Scot, I was particularly glad to be in the North and that I hoped the Development Corporation of London would be able to help the North. There was a short conversation between the Emir and the Mudaiki, and then the Mudaiki said the Emir had heard about the Scotch and I was all the more welcome. We talked about CDC for about seven minutes and I asked if the Serriki had any suggestions as to what we might do in the North. The Mudaiki said the Serriki thought houses were the chief need. While they were talking together I had asked the resident in a whisper if it were time to go; his reply, 'Not for a minute or two.' Eventually I got up, bowed and asked if we might now be excused.

The Emir came to the courtyard again with us, collecting his two spears and himself, in English, asked me to write my name in a book. Then we shook hands again, I gave the Moslem salute; turned and walked over to the car. When we reached it, I looked to see if the Emir was still watching us, as indeed he was; so, I gave another bow and salute which he returned with obvious cordiality. Resident was very pleased and said everything had gone very well.

After lunch in the Residency we drove to the airport and flew in the governor general's aircraft to Tiko in the Cameroons, arriving at 17.45; then three-quarters of an hour uphill 3500 feet to Buea. The absurdity of my itinerary will be apparent and should be explained. It had been arranged to come to the Cameroons from Port Harcourt and then to go to Kaduna and Kano in the north, and home. Governor general, had however, asked if I could go again to Lagos to talk with him after having been in the Cameroons. This was entirely sensible but it meant that I had to go north from Port Harcourt to Kaduna and Kano; then south again to the Cameroons; all the way west to Lagos; and all the way north again to Kano.

13 December 1957 [In Buea] They had told me to be sure first thing in the morning to pull up the blind and look at Mount Cameroon. I did so; and came into one of those rare occasions when one's eyes had been laid inaccurately and one found oneself increasing the angle of vision; then again; and a third time before one was satisfied that one was really looking at the summit.

No monarch had been to Buea. It is a German house built in German style; magnificent view in three directions, impressive terraces and gardens. Built in 1894, the kitchens may have been modernized (though I doubt it), but nothing else. Bathroom and lavatory fittings were original; and it was interesting to find oneself in the house of a British resident being instructed in German not to forget to pull the plug.

[In discussions on the possibility of CDC participating in the finance and management of the Cameroons Development Corporation (Camdev) John Reith repeated, what he had told the Federal prime minister in Lagos, that CDC would want extensive powers of management for a limited period, but that 'now I had seen the place, as far as I was concerned, the willingness and the desire to participate had increased'. Unfortunately, though provisional agreement on this was to be reached in July 1958, further action was held up, as the CDC Report for that year pointed out, 'by political uncertainties in the country'.]

16 December 1957 [Back in Lagos] Talked with governor general about Camdev. He is extremely anxious to have CDC in the Cameroons and he realizes that everything possible has been done to lessen the difficulties for him.

17 December 1957 Arrived London airport 9.00, three-quarters of an hour early. Interesting tour; great possibilities for CDC; vast potentialities in the country, sad that there should be such doubts and fears.

(e) *An unhappy ending, January 1958–March 1959*

[In the immediate aftermath of his return from Nigeria John Reith found that the better relations between CDC and the Colonial Office continued. He now hoped that he might be allowed to continue as chairman for at least one more year, until after his seventieth birthday, and possibly even for two. CDC was operating profitably and positively and, with the prospect of an early financial reconstruction, this would continue. He felt that having borne the burden of reorganization and recovery in the past he might now be granted the pleasure of supervising positive achievements. But in the summer of 1958 it became clear that this was not to be; the colonial secretary had resolved not to extend John Reith's tenure of the chairmanship of CDC beyond 31 March 1959, and on 23 September 1958 in an interview, which Reith subsequently described as 'the most humiliating experience I have been through', he told him so.

John Reith was deeply hurt. His first inclination was to cancel his tour of the CDC's Far Eastern projects which had been arranged for the autumn of 1958, but he thought better of this. Then, on his return at the end of that year, he found a fresh and even more painful development. His ultimate successor was not available to take over immediately and his own deputy and longest-serving colleague, Sir Nutcombe Hume, with whom he had been on close and friendly terms, was to become temporary chairman. He regarded this as disloyal and unjust. In February 1959 he went on his last CDC tour (to East and Central Africa where also his first visit had been in 1952) and on his return from this he learned that his replacement by his deputy had been confirmed. At the end of March he held his last, sad board meeting to sign his final report. Thus he left CDC, as he had left the BBC more than twenty years before, in bitterness and misunderstanding.

But there was one hopeful development in this unhappy period. In December 1958 he had been elected vice-chairman of British Oxygen, having been a director of that company since 1956. As he was to give up his directorship of Tube Investments in 1959 on reaching the age of seventy – another bitterly resented termination – this new responsibility at British Oxygen enabled him to concentrate his formidable talents once again.]

4 February 1958 Dinner with Lennox-Boyd in the House of Commons and talked till 10.00. Most agreeable, but I didn't ask about anything.

4 March 1958 Lord Home [Commonwealth Relations secretary of state] for tea and a talk about relationship with him and his office. Quite satisfactory talk; he wants every sort of contact with CDC, as CDC does.

20 March 1958 Day of signing Annual Report and Accounts [for 1957]. Board at noon and by 12.09 six items of agenda had been passed, the accounts had been signed by board and auditors, and also the Report by all the directors. I really think this must be a record.

11 April 1958 Annoyed that E. Black of the World Bank has been in London again without any communication with CDC. I shall have to do something about this. Of course Treasury and Colonial Office are to blame.

13 June 1958 Eugene Black for nearly an hour and most successful as to co-operation between World Bank and CDC. He said he always read the CDC Report – almost the only one he did.

14 July 1958 Hume in to talk about my end of term at 31 March. Sickening business it is – sickening.

[During July and August John Reith's fellow directors made every effort to persuade Lord Perth, minister of state at the Colonial Office, that his chairmanship should be extended for at least one year. Reith spent August in Scotland at his son's farm near Perth and on his return he was encouraged to hear from two of his colleagues that they thought 'they had made some impression'. But they misled him and themselves.]

23 September 1958[11] Saw Lennox-Boyd at 5.00. I knew from his manner that I was to be given *congé*; he was embarrassed; it seemed that he had gotten himself into a particular mood and attitude to enable him to go through an unpleasant bit of business. Abruptly and crudely he said he had better tell me what he had to say. By next March I would have been eight and a half years in CDC; that was quite a long while; did I not think it was time for a new long-term appointment? Of course there was no reflection on me; I had done very well for CDC; he was grateful; but he thought the time had come for a change. I must not think he was not very grateful for what I had done. I said I really did not look for gratitude. But was there any question that I was getting past what was required of a chairman? He certainly did not say Yes, but I do not think a flat negative came out. I was thoroughly sickened. Here there was involved one's natural pride and dignity. But I kept thinking I must carry this through; answer politely and quietly; carry on as if it were someone else whom I was discussing with an equal. So, to my disgust, I found myself saying that I thought I had done pretty well in my tenure of office and that my departure would be regretted by the directors and senior executives. It was a horrible experience. I have wondered how I got through it. I don't think I can carry on till the end of the term nor do another hand's turn for CDC. I don't know what to do. I did ask God that everything should be working for the best.

25 September 1958 Hume begged me to carry on, though fully appreciating how very difficult that would be. He was very decent.

[On 2 October John Reith, accompanied by his secretary Miss Molly Cotara, set out on his tour of the Far East which, in spite of its unhappy background, proved to be one of his most interesting and enjoyable journeys.]

2 October 1958 Off at 10.30 GMT. Arrived Frankfurt at 12.30 for an hour. Here spoke with Sir Cyril de Zoya, president of Ceylon Senate, rescuing him from a German policeman with whom he was in unilateral altercation through not having secured a receipt for a magnum of eau de cologne bought in airport shop. Made much of this; by saving him from jail we hoped we had cemented the bonds of what used to be called Empire. He said he was sure we had and he wished there were more of the Empire left.

5 October 1958 [In Singapore] Attended a Chinese dinner in the Cathay restaurant; not just Chinese food but the extremes of it, and a very inferior cabaret, but regional controller could not well have avoided this without giving offence. There were ten changes of dish; the muscles of my throat seemed set on rejecting almost everything that came to them – thoroughly unco-operative. Never so much juggling on one's dish to conceal what was really happening. And I was getting more and more hungry. Fortunately, item ten was a fraud; a splendid Lyons cake of which I had three slices.

6 October 1958 To Kulai, which I had been looking forward to. An hour and a half through the palm-oil plantations accompanied by two armoured Land-Rovers full of troops. When we came to the place where Gregoire and Gibson had been murdered, I said I would like to get out and see the memorial.[12] The troops immediately fanned out round the party, but, had there been any terrorists around, we would all have been finished. The memorial I thought awful; about twenty cubic feet of concrete, like an enormous piece of cheese, with the two names and the date of the murder. Nothing to tell what happened; no symbolism; no imagination.

7 October 1958 [In Kuching, Sarawak] We arrived at Kuching airstrip at 2.30 p.m. It was about twelve miles to Kuching town; suddenly the car taking us stopped on the edge of a big river, and we had to go down steps into a sampan; the Governor's house – formerly Rajah Brooke's – was on the opposite bank about three hundred yards off. How wise to preserve this prehistoric means of transport. There were three men to it; two sat cross-legged on a bit of deck forward of midships with paddles about five feet long. The third man sat aft with a steering paddle. According to tide and current an enormously varying course would be set, which invariably brought the sampan with minimum effort to the wharf at the other side; and always in complete silence except for the dip of paddles. Monstrous inefficient operation absolutely, extraordinary anachronism. But relatively, how refreshing; how utterly efficient. The house – Astana – is over a hundred years old, most attractive, with a fort built about the same time more or less constituting the front door.

8 October 1958 Regional controller and I had an hour with the governor [Sir Anthony Abell] before lunch. He had some definite suggestions to make about more contact between Sarawak and CDC. I welcomed his suggestions and said they were all in line with CDC's desire to work closely with and through local people and organizations; CDC to be considered part of the country rather than foreign.

At 7.00 p.m. I had a date – we all had – with Mr Peter Ratcliffe; better explain how it happened. Quite an early schedule indicated that this evening was to be his. 'Who is Mr Ratcliffe?' And when I heard I was both surprised and vexed. A civil servant; director of broadcasting; forsooth. But his name persisted in later drafts of the schedule; it was still there when I reached Singapore. There, I said to regional controller I was not going to broadcast or even go to broadcasting places. Plain enough; and yet here we were driving up at Broadcasting House, Kuching and three men were on the steps to receive us – Ratcliffe, the head of programmes and the chief engineer – the last two ex-BBC. We were conducted to a large studio; empty, it seemed, except for ourselves, the three officials and two hall porters. Well, there we were, myself wondering whatever was to happen next; all ready to be very annoyed; and Molly Cotara standing by, hoping I would be civil but obviously ready to extinguish the flames if I were not. Then Mr Ratcliffe: would I mind if he presented some others of his senior staff? All right, but where were they? Would I just come and stand near the door, please. 'Do be nice to them,' M.C. whispered. I went over to the door and looked out into the whole corridor. No one in sight; but by the time I had gone back into the studio there was a Malayan, smiling, waiting for a cue from Mr Ratcliffe. It was as efficient a reception as I have seen. While I was shaking hands and conversing with one, another appeared in the corridor. It seemed as if they came through a trap-door operated unseen by Ratcliffe, who in addition to naming each individual clearly, said also what he or she did. About forty of them, of a dozen nationalities. And then Mr Ratcliffe asked would I mind if he brought a few of them for a further talk? Go ahead – only I was going to sit down as otherwise I would not hear what they were saying. About twenty of them thus; sometimes in pairs. Altogether two and a half hours. What a doing – and for twenty years I had been trying to forget that I ever had anything to do with broadcasting. Most impressed I was – *malgré moi*; efficiency, zeal and pride. Mr Ratcliffe should go far.

10 October 1958 On a mound behind Astana there was what looked like a gravestone; I must investigate that before leaving. The three little children of the second Rajah had taken ship to go to England in 1872. They had all died of cholera and been buried at sea. I thought of the Rajah and his wife when that news had reached them.

11 October 1958 [At Tawau, North Borneo, the site of CDC's project, Borneo Abaca Ltd] To see the Iman rubber plantation. Before leaving I was asked to plant a rubber tree; all preparations had been made, so I thought I had better do it. I asked if anyone else had planted a tree. Yes. Who? The Earl of Perth and Mr Lennox-Boyd. 'Psalm I,' I thought, 'hasn't it something relevant to say?' And as I started to dig the lines came to mind:

> He shall be like a tree that grows
> Near planted by a river,
> Which in his season yields his fruit,
> And his leaf fadeth never;
>
> And all he doth shall prosper well.
> The Wicked are not so;
> But like they are unto the chaff
> Which wind drives to and fro.

Not quite relevant; but comforting.

13 October 1958 [At sea off Tawau en route to Kunak, site of another CDC estate] On board the governor's new yacht, *Petrel,* proceeding to sea, the Celebes Sea, blue sky and sunshine, every prospect pleasing. One felt that the Colonial Office and Treasury would probably disapprove; would find a clause in Overseas Resources Development Act which, turned upside down, would make it an offence for any Officer of CDC – chairman in particular – to go to sea in a governor's yacht; and that made the sea bluer and greener still.

About noon a four to five thousand ton ship appeared on the port bow; *Maradu* on course for Tawau, aboard which we would be two days later. I was sure *Maradu* would salute; wondered if our captain would know what to do. '*Maradu* will probably salute you, won't she,' I said, 'and then you will acknowledge in the same way. Is that right?' 'Yes,' he said; but it was an unconvincing affirmative. I thought I should make some arrangements on my own; went below to find a hat; and came on deck as *Maradu* and *Petrel* came level. I was vastly relieved when *Maradu* gave a tremendous blast and her ensign was dipped. No whistle from *Petrel* but her ensign was being dipped – thank heavens for that. And I tried to make up for the whistle. I put the glass on *Maradu*'s bridge, then ceremoniously took off my hat. Two figures on the bridge saluted in return. Something one's children can remember about their father – he was dipped to in the Celebes Sea.

16 October 1958 [On board SS *Maradu* bound for Sandakan] Berhala Island was passed at 8.00 a.m.; here the British from Sandakan were interned by the Japanese. Here there had been war unknown in England; all occupied by Japanese; experiences not relevant here; what is relevant is that these experiences have given the residents a close and compelling community of interest which the stranger cannot share – nor even understand. This is applicable throughout the whole region.

We went ashore [at Sandakan] at 10.15 a.m., were driven around for an hour and a half, given lunch and then seen off at the airstrip for Jesselton. Sir Roland Turnbull, the governor, was waiting for us there. I dined with him alone, which he wanted in order that he could talk frankly. He described the conditions when he came (in 1954); and the developments since. There was still no interest in politics; no sign of a desire for a hand in government; no desire to emerge; no doubt that would come. He felt that a great deal had to be achieved before there could be democracy in action.

17 October 1958 [In Jesselton] After tea the governor took me round the town, pointing out changes he had made, showing me plans of development approved. Practically nothing was left of Jesselton after the war and there were many pleasant and impressive features in the new Jesselton. I hope very much that CDC can stand in here [i.e. North Borneo]; I have seen no comparable enthusiasm and determination in any colony; and few places where I felt so anxious to help; and where there was so much incentive.

19 October 1958 Dined alone with the governor. He was greatly surprised and sorry to hear that I would not be long in CDC. I wish I could have helped him more. No Colonial Office minister has ever asked me to come and see him after these journeys. I had a great deal to tell.

20 October 1958   [en route for Kuala Lumpur, by air to Singapore, and then by train] I had not been looking forward to this train journey, but in fact it was one of the most pleasant of all the experiences, much smoother than anything ever experienced in England, despite narrow gauge; no jerking and jolting as at home; the permanent way must be very well looked after. When the Malayan customs officers came along they passed my cabin by. A minute later came a pathetic cry from down the corridor: 'Oh, but they were birthday presents.' Obviously Molly Cotara was in need of help, so I went along. The two Melanu hats given to her in Kuching had excited the curiosity of the customs officers and she was told she would have to pay duty on them. Hence the *cri de cœur*. I said I was the Tunku's guest and this lady was my secretary. 'Oh, your *secretary*,' said one; and in such a way as to make clear that the incident was closed. As I walked away I heard a hearty laugh. Next morning Molly Cotara said she had been shaken warmly by the hand by each officer.

21 October 1958 [In Kuala Lumpur] On arrival I was taken to the Istana Tetamu. I was the only occupant of this vast house – previously the King's House, residence of high commissioners. Very lonely and a bit eerie.

22 October 1958 Tea at the Residency with the prime minister, Tunku Abdul Rahman Putra, and Dato Spencer, economic adviser to the government. Dato Spencer, who had been trying to get the PM to have the railroad constitution looked into, told the Tunku that I had been impressed by my journey from Singapore. He added that despite all I knew about the public corporation system, I had never come upon a corporation which was, in fact, the incorporation of a single individual. This was quite true; the state appoints a general manager and he is the corporation; it was a dictatorship. The Tunku asked, did I think it a sensible arrangement? I replied that I would think it an extremely sensible arrangement if I were the general manager, but I would not expect anyone else in the country to agree. I said I was in favour of *de facto* dictatorships but not *de jure* ones, and this individual was pretty near to being *de jure*. Then the Tunku asked what I thought he should do and I said straightly that, if I were he, I would appoint a committee of inquiry to look into the present constitution and make recommendations. His reply was equally straight; he would do just that.

23 October 1958 Most everybody and everything is pleasant and agreeable here; most everybody seems to get on with everybody else and to like most everybody else – irrespective of race.

I had a few minutes today to walk round the garden at Istana Tetamu. I came on trees planted by the Duchess of Kent and the Duke of Edinburgh. Near the latter was a stone slab about three foot square, flush with the lawn. 'Rudi von Rosenthal,' it said. Then initials GWRT – EMT – and then two dates 1942–1954. Whoever was Rudi von Rosenthal? I made inquiries; nobody knew. Now, periodically, I had been aware of a senior servant, dressed differently from the others, superior in deportment, rig and manners. I inquired who he was; butler to the British high commissioners, I was told, for thirty or forty years. I got his name, Enche Rani, and this evening inquired if he knew what this mysterious memorial was. General Templer's dachshund; the initials were Templer's and his wife's.[13]

24 October 1958 Up early and watched the sun rise. I was sorry to be leaving this agreeable, friendly and interesting country – all the more agreeable that the Colonial Office had nothing to do with it. Istana Tetamu is on the crest of a hill and there are views on all sides round; foothills, then higher hills, forest covered, miles and miles of forest, farther away hills that are nearly mountains, range upon range. I could see tracks climbing and disappearing into jungle; and I wondered if, forgetting everything and everybody of the past, I might climb up one of the tracks and leave the rest to Osiris and the Sun.

[After travelling on to Hong Kong for a stay of three days, John Reith and Miss Cotara flew back to London arriving on the afternoon of 28 October.]

[Before the end of the year John Reith was aware that pressure was being placed on his co-directors to stay with CDC after his departure. This development pained, although it did not surprise him, and early in 1959 he released them from any promises they may have given to stand by him. Then at the end of February he set off on a brief journey to East and Central Africa.]

30 November 1958 Hume came to my room about 5.00 after seeing Lennox-Boyd again as asked by Lennox-Boyd. I suspected that he was being offered my job but that hadn't occurred to him. Obviously he is being hopelessly outwitted and they have him all anxious to please, just as they want it, except that he hasn't retracted on his refusal to stay on if I go. It is a sordid sickening turn that things have taken.

26 January 1959 Prideaux [a director of CDC] to see me. It seems now that there is a pressure on Hume to stay on in CDC till a new chairman has been found – trying to seduce him away from loyalty to me. I told Prideaux I couldn't understand why they were apparently in such a flap. There was still two months. The concern would go on quite well without any chairman.

27 January 1959 Hume to see me at 2.45. I said he could carry on if he wanted to; I certainly wasn't going to urge him to, but he had the green light. He was very grateful; and I didn't think much of him for the switch-over; he had so often been emphatic that nothing would make him change.

16 February 1959 Rang Hume to warn him that he was to be asked to be chairman for a year till the new man felt able to take the chair. I wouldn't be surprised if he really wants to.

17 February 1959 Hume at 5.00. He confirmed that he had been urged to take the chair for a year. Baring would go on the board in June but wouldn't be chairman for a year. Prideaux to be deputy chairman. I told Hume that I thought it would be absolutely wrong from every point of view if he accepted. His advice on fundamentals had been ignored and they were just assuming he would meekly do as required. It is thoroughly squalid and beastly.

22 February 1959 [en route to Nairobi] Two factors combined to set me on this trip; that I had told regional controller, East Africa, that I would try to come to the Njombe opening [of the new CDC wattle extract factory] as it would probably be his last function and I would like to do honour to him; and, secondly, that prime minister Welensky had asked me to come out to the Central African Federation as a Federation guest.

26 February 1959 [In Njombe, Tanganyika] The ceremony in the factory began at 11.30; speeches by regional controller, the governor and the bishop. There wasn't a word of Swahili and of course this was a bad blunder. Governor spoke very kindly of CDC and me. The bishop had asked me whether he should say a prayer. I said, yes, a prayer but not in the form of a prayer; follow the launching of a ship. He did that exactly after a few very good general remarks.

28 February 1959 [In Salisbury, Southern Rhodesia] Rough journey of one and an half hours to Kariba. I was very glad to be at this interesting job again but I felt that there had been no interest shown in what happens on a lowish or low level. So everything has been given European names – streets, ridges, roads; the Italian living quarters are shocking – windows half pasted over with newspapers which of course make the roads look beastly. The only imaginative item was a big bit of black and grey rock taken from the bed of the river and put at the entrance to the official hostel, Kariba House. I suggested that at the nerve-centre of the whole place – where the monarch is to do the opening ceremony in May 1960 – the commemorative notice be put on virgin rocks of which there is an outcrop there.

3 March 1959 Saw Welensky for three-quarters of an hour. He asked me what I thought of Kariba. I said I wished they had gone for African names more. He asked me to come to the Kariba opening with Muriel.

[John Reith arrived back in London on the morning of 5 March. Later that day he learned that his worst fears in respect of the chairmanship of CDC had been fulfilled. His final weeks were most unhappy.]

5 March 1959 To the office 2.45. After giving me ordinary papers, Molly [Cotara] handed me one saying she was very sorry to be giving it to me. It was a letter from Hume saying the Colonial Office wouldn't take No for an answer. I tore the letter into bits. His acceptance of the chairmanship is an endorsement of the Colonial Office attitude to me – and there is the supreme treachery as all the directors have signed the criticisms of Whitehall in the Annual Reports and he had always strongly defended the right and duty to report honestly.

22 March 1959 [Palm Sunday] I feel I must do something about the wretched Report. [John Reith's original inclination had been to have nothing to do with this.] I am extremely reluctant to let the politicians and civil servants and the traitors on the board get away with it. On the other hand I don't want to be beaten on it. I felt fairly sure about this at lunchtime but then changed after an hour or two, and felt right off seeing Hume. Muriel said whatever was the most distasteful thing to do was probably the right one to do, which is very wise.

23 March 1959 Sent a message to Hume saying I was willing to meet him today over the Report. We met in his office at 3.00; he was very civil. When I said I was here because of his *last* letter, offering to have another shot at the Report, he said he was hoping I was going to say because of his *first* letter (which hoped I would understand etc.). I said, No; that he knew one of my troubles was that I couldn't be in-sincere, and that if I felt strongly on something I just couldn't com-promise principle for the sake of peace. We agreed to go through Part] of the Report together tomorrow morning.

25 March 1959 Hume rang to say that my re-draft was 'absolutely first class' (which I knew, but that did not mean that he would like it). The revised Part I was sent out to all board members about 5.00 p.m.

26 March 1959 Weird board meeting at CDC at 10.00. I got there at 9.50; nobody in the boardroom when I came in but soon the others arrived. I had the Accounts signed at once; then said the Report was only ready yesterday afternoon but they would have read that. I would consider any suggestions that were not of fundamental principle; or were they willing to sign the Report as it was. Yes from all but one. I told him he would be expected to resign if he did not sign. He asked for the weekend to consider. I said No, it must be settled now and I asked him to sign. So he did. I think it was extremely good chairing on my part. And that is that. I went off without saying anything.

2. Epilogue, 1959–70

[When John Reith left the Colonial Development Corporation in March 1959 he wished to cut himself off completely from his Common-wealth interests as well as from the CDC and Colonial Office contacts. But his friends within the Commonwealth would not allow the first, while his friends at home did their best to end the second. So, Sir Roy Welensky invited him to open the Central African Trade Fair in April 1962 where he spoke with conviction for a middle and multi-racial course. He greatly deplored the break-up of the Central African Federa-tion which he believed he could have helped to prevent had he been granted the opportunity. Yet he would do little or nothing in these years to mend his relations with those concerned with Commonwealth affairs at home, who alone could have smoothed his path in this direction. Even when Mr Lennox-Boyd (now Lord Boyd of Merton and no longer colonial secretary) made generous efforts to end their differences in 1964, he remorselessly rejected him. In the same way he remained adamantly unforgiving towards Sir Nutcombe Hume and the CDC; and though, in 1962, he was much mollified by the Corporation's new chairman, Lord Howick of Glendale, it was not until Christmas 1964 that he returned to CDC's headquarters and lunched in friendly fashion with its new board. Nevertheless, his position as vice-chairman of the British Oxygen Company enabled him to make three last Commonwealth tours, to East and to South Africa in 1962, and to India, Pakistan and the Far East in 1963.]

Letter from Sir Robert Tredgold [chief justice of the supreme court of Rhodesia and Nyasaland] *29 May 1959*

(Received 22 June 1959)

Things are not good in the Federation and I don't myself see the way out, but there always is one that appears, sometimes when least expected. The Federal government has alienated the Africans to a point where reconciliation will be very difficult, not so much by anything it has done but by the things its leaders have said. There is an unfortunate tradition in politics here that you can say what you like to please the Europeans provided that you don't put it into practice. If it ever was true it certainly is no longer, for the African today is listening in.

7 July 1959 Talked with Hugh Gaitskell at 11.30 about his coming to the dinner [for Sir Roy Welensky] on Thursday [9 July]. Today he was off and on; frightened of getting into trouble with his colleagues if he came but wanting them to come.

Letter from Hugh Gaitskell, 8 July 1959

I am glad to hear that Patrick Gordon-Walker and Arthur Bottomley have accepted your kind invitation to dinner.

I should like to take this opportunity of thanking you for your kindness and help which has, incidentally, led to the meeting which I am to have with Sir Roy Welensky tomorrow afternoon.

[John Reith's dinner party for Sir Roy Welensky was held on 9 July in the Athenæum; in addition to the representatives of the Labour party the guests included the Editor of the *Manchester Guardian* and a representative of the *Economist*. 'Everybody,' Reith noted, 'seemed greatly pleased.' He continued to keep in touch with Sir Roy Welensky.]

Letter from Sir Roy Welensky, 12 January 1960

You know, John, I am very unhappy about what is happening on the African continent. I know that at the back of my mind I am quite an ardent imperialist and perhaps it is proving difficult for me to adjust my mental processes to what is happening. You see, I don't look upon this handing over of authority to states like Guinea, Ghana, Somaliland and Tanganyika as an act of faith. I don't even credit the people who inspire it with any generous intention. I frankly believe that in the main most of them are anxious to get out of the troubles and the responsibilities that advancing a continent like Africa brings. If ever there has been a time when guidance and assistance has been needed, it is now, and what does one see but the imperial powers busy scuttling out of Africa. It shames me. The problem of advancing Africa has hardly begun and I dread to think where the present steps are going to take us. If the Belgians get out of the Congo, as they now seem determined to do, one is going to see a blood bath in the near future.[14] My thoughts are not very pleasant companions these days.

24 March 1960 Garfield Todd to see me in the afternoon. He wants to set up a trust fund for Central Africa in London, but to be administered by his own party. I said it would be much better, if he were having a trust fund, to have it clear of any political party.

Letter from Garfield Todd, 2 April 1960

Things have been moving on the project whose boundaries you enlarged so greatly in our interview as to give it life.

Some general thoughts are:

That the aim of the organization be to create through education on the widest scale a climate in which racial harmony can grow and so make possible a true union of all our people in Central Africa.

Fear on the part of the Europeans is the great obstacle, as expressed by the belief that any advancement on the part of the blacks must bring down the white standard of living; and by the belief that white and black simply cannot work together, consult together, govern together, live together.

Therefore everyone should be told of the possibilities for the future, if the people were united.

5 May 1960 Lunched with Roy Welensky at Hyde Park Hotel. I asked if he would like me to be governor general because if he did, though I had never thought I would ever consider such a job, I might do it. He said 'Now you are talking.' But Dalhousie was appointed for five years, of which only two and a half have gone.

6 July 1960 At 4.00 I went to a meeting with Monckton[15] to go over the memorandum about Rhodesia and Nyasaland that I had put in. It was quite interesting and Monckton was most civil and friendly.

21 February 1961 Julian Greenfield, minister of justice, Central African Federation, spoke to me on the telephone tonight; he said he was going back fed up to the teeth with the United Kingdom government, and I do not wonder. I told him to tell Roy Welensky that I wished I could help; and that I was willing to do anything I could. I believe that, if I were suddenly asked what I could suggest towards some settlement of the frightful confusion and the really dangerous, or anyhow intolerable, situation that has arisen, I would say to send me out with plenipotentiary powers as governor of all three countries.

14 March 1961 Muriel and I went to a dinner in the Dorchester – Roy Welensky's farewell to Sir Gilbert and Lady Rennie [high commissioner for Rhodesia and Nyasaland]. I was digusted to find the wretched Hume there. He came up to me all smiling and deferential, and so delighted to see me, holding out his hand. As several people were standing about, I shook hands, made him a formal bow and said nothing. Welensky spoke quite well.

15 March 1961 South Africa has withdrawn from the Commonwealth which I think deplorable.

20 December 1961 The Central African high commissioner [Sir Albert Robinson] rang to say Welensky wanted me to open the Central African Trade Fair in Bulawayo on April 27. He had opened it last year and the Queen Mother the year before.

5 January 1962 Lunched at Brooks's Club with Lord Howick [Evelyn Baring]. He is chairman of the CDC now and had written two very nice letters to me recently, one urging me to go to the CDC annual party tonight; the other that he so much admired what I had done that he would like to meet me. He asked if I wouldn't come to lunch one day, no members of the board would be there. I thanked him but said it was better for me to keep clear.

Letter from Lord Howick of Glendale, 12 January 1962

I started life as an Indian civil servant, though I was invalided out long ago in 1934. My father [the first Lord Cromer] spent his life developing Egypt. I have always been deeply interested in the development of the poor and backward countries. It used to appear to me that Britain did much for education and social welfare and much also for the foundation of economic progress – what the Americans now call the 'infrastructure'. But then, as a governing country, we stopped, we lost interest and expected private companies unassisted by government to build on that 'infrastructure'. All right for India after 1947, hopeless for Swaziland, North Borneo or Dominica! So when the Labour government established the CDC I thought that a great step forward had been made. It was therefore a bit of a shock to find oneself dealing with a management which might have come out of Alice in Wonderland. The change brought about by you and Rendell was both complete and amazing and it was of enormous benefit to the Colonies. I well remember your two million pound loan to the Kenya Central Housing Board. We could raise the money nowhere else, yet it was needed for schemes in all towns other than Nairobi as part of our effort to prevent a small-scale civil war leading to lasting bitterness. I equally remember our inability to borrow one million pounds from the CDC for Kikuyu smallholders who had recently consolidated their scattered holdings and were open as they would never be again to ideas of agricultural progress. The absurd ban on 'finance house business' (since withdrawn) prevented this. The money was raised from the International Bank but only after two years damaging delay. No organization in this difficult field of development has ever accomplished so much with so heavy a millstone of interest rates tied round its neck as has the CDC since 1951.

So I enormously admire your work. Your ideas about running the CDC remain as they were, and are highly effective. The very good results obtained now, the good credit in the City, the high reputation of the Corporation in the regions, and the quality and morale of its staff are what you and Rendell made them. With the 'wind of change' in the old colonies our actions will have to change like everyone else's but we owe it to you that the Corporation is highly flexible and well placed to adapt itself with success to the new conditions.

In 1960 there was a definite effort made to wind the CDC up. This came from the Treasury. It was opposed by the Colonial Office and (very strongly) by Home at the Commonwealth Relations Office. This is now over and the need for the CDC becomes daily more apparent.

As a result we are now on good terms with the Colonial Office and have even, strange to say, slightly improved our relationship with the Treasury!

Letter to Lord Howick, 14 February 1962
I waited till you were nearly home again before sending a note to thank you for your most kind and interesting letter of January 12.
The Alice in Wonderland analogy is splendid. Your letter, and many special things therein, gave me great pleasure and comfort and I am more than grateful.

29 March 1962 Howick dined with me at Claridges and we talked 7.30 to 11.15. Most interesting. There is little difference of opinion between us as to politicians such as are now deplorably in charge of our affairs and destinies. Much talk about CDC.

13 April 1962 Letter from Howick telling me that CDC was to operate in ex-colonies. That is what I had the flaming row with Lennox-Boyd about; it has taken five years to bring people to my point of view.

28 April 1962 [In Bulawayo] At 2.00 we went to the Fair, received with much formality by about a dozen people. Then into the Royal Box. In the two previous years, the opener – Roy Welensky last year, the Queen Mother the year before – had spoken from the Royal Box, facing the arena, with about a thousand people sitting immediately behind them, and four or five thousand to right and left, and in front of them prize cattle and the like. Roy W. told me that in the middle of his speech one of the animals had given vent to a long, profound, and obviously resentful bray; fortunately he had thought of a good riposte: 'It seems,' he had said, 'that the Opposition is present in some force.' This year they had set up a tiny little dais immediately opposite the Royal Box and about fifty yards from it. On paper it looked quite sensible, as I did not have my back to anyone and was more or less facing the whole audience, but of course a great distance between me and the backs of the stands. The dais had an awning all over it, frills coming down on each side. I realized immediately that my face would not be seen by the audience, and that I would not see them. I pointed this out to the governor [Sir Humphrey Gibbs]; he immediately told someone they would have to go out when Sir Patrick Fletcher, who spoke first, had finished and either unship the awning or somehow fasten it back. Still worse, the loudspeaker system was quite awful; so

I do not think I was more than two-thirds heard. But they evidently heard enough to keep absolutely quiet. This was rather remarkable. I spoke quite slowly, but deliberately trying to avoid applause. At the end, they really did applaud. But then I had this fifty yards to walk back to the Royal Box and I could not help wondering whether the applause would last out. Actually, it did last the whole time.

After dinner [at Government House] both the governor and Lady Gibbs spoke with tremendous gratitude and even emotion about my performance this afternoon. There is no doubt that I said what wanted saying, and generally comported myself as I suppose not many could.

John Reith's Speech at Bulawayo, 28 April 1962

. . . Well – will you, for a few moments, look back two or three hundred years into history – the history of this land included. Looking back is often unprofitable, even dangerous; well do I know it . . . but if, in times of crisis perhaps, we can draw comfort and inspiration from the past, why then let us draw it. And I suggest that we might get help for ourselves now if we give to a particular past, a present and a future, and in thankfulness and pride remember those who made and managed what used to be called the British Empire . . .

It is surely right that we should on occasion remember and praise in heart and mind those famous men; the fathers that begat us; such as did bear rule in their Kingdoms; renowned for their power; leaders of the people. And despite their tremendous qualities of imagination, determination, endurance, courage and faith, I should think that the quality by which, here in Africa and everywhere else, they would most wish in the end to be judged, was that, to the people under their care, they were just, trustees of justice, even-handed, unpersuadable . . .

There has been much disparagement and denunciation recently of British imperialism and colonization; and presumably it will miserably persist so long as there is a single island called colonial. Perhaps nothing – in conception, policy or execution – has ever been subject to such vicious fabrication and distortion wherever chance or mischance offered scope – stygian and satanic . . .

But the heritage of colonial problems now remains almost entirely in those territories originally settled by a European minority, which may presently fear to be expelled, absorbed or oppressed by an African majority. Under what conditions can a European minority, which used to have some privileges related to the services which it was performing to the whole community, under what conditions can it hope to survive in countries ruled by other races and other confessions?

I do not believe that transference of full Westminster democratic institutionalism and practice all at once will solve the outstanding problems . . . Both the old Africa and the new Africa are authoritarian; and before any realistic and definitive policy can be settled and established, it is essential authoritarianism must be recognized . . .

Mr R. A. Butler will soon be here;[16] and I hope he will be welcomed by you, and helped. I believe that what he eventually suggests will be just, and safe, and settled; and to all concerned . . . And what is required of you beyond some vague goodwill towards Mr Butler when he comes? I will give the answer short and straight.

The first requirement – and I say it quite seriously – is the fear of the Lord which is the beginning of wisdom . . . The other is that there should be in fact be a new beginning; forgetting those things which are behind – reaching forth – pressing towards the mark. And the attitude of that reaching forth should be as of statesmen and not as of politicians; for this is not an occasion for disputatious arguing, nor for the petty triumphs of the public square. There is a common cause, and a mighty cause at that; and where there is a common cause, there is usually implicit some willing adjustments or concessions by the parties concerned . . .

Central Africa is, or anyhow very nearly is, and certainly before long in the care of Almighty God can be, a prosperous and mighty land, largely of your own making. But that demands dedication of you and from you all, to some degree and in some form . . . There being such dedication the peoples of Central Africa should be able to sing with the psalmist of old:

> According to her labours rise
> So her rewards increase;
> Her ways are ways of pleasantness
> And all her paths are peace.

[In August 1962 the government announced, what in April Lord Howick had warned John Reith was intended, that CDC was to be allowed to operate in ex-colonial territories and to change its name to the Commonwealth Development Corporation. As this represented the fulfilment of Reith's own policy he wanted to proclaim it in public and to dance, so to speak, upon the prostrate bodies of his defeated opponents. Sir William Haley, as always, guided him to wiser courses.]

Letter from Sir William Haley, 7 August 1962
I really do not believe that you will serve either yourself or affairs generally if you come out with all this now. No matter how you do it, there will be uncharitable people to take the wrong view of why you are doing it. There are many occasions in life when silence is wisdom, no matter at what cost to oneself. I am sure this is one of them. All this is behind you. What you have done is there for all to see. It does not need display or justification. Certainly not by yourself. Anything you said could only weaken the impression of the record, not strengthen it. Don't ever worry about that record or the record of anything else you have done. No man needs fewer monuments and you have plenty.

[At the end of October 1962 John Reith went on a swift tour of British Oxygen's subsidiary firms in Kenya, Tanganyika and Uganda.]

30 October 1962 [In Dar-es-Salaam] I was to have met the new prime minister at 3.00 p.m., but he had sent a message that he could not leave Tanga, which is as maybe and quite typical. At a cocktail-party later, to which three ministers had been asked, I was told that only one would be there – the sole European and maybe not likely to last long. Apparently this is recognized form – that ministers accept invitations but rarely attend. When I mentioned this later to the Kenya governor, he said he had recently had an advice from the Colonial Office that it would be a good thing to entertain more Africans; his reply had been that he had invited thirty-eight to dine at Government House in the last two months, and that only six had turned up, though all had accepted.

2 November 1962 [Staying at Government House, Entebbe] I had to go over the Mulago Hospital – 950 beds and a lot of oxygen installations in it. I talked for about half an hour with Dr Allardyce, an Australian. I was impressed with him and some of his senior Sisters whom I met. He astonished me by saying he was giving up at the end of the year (being only fifty) and he introduced me to his successor – a young African doctor.

3 November 1962 [Returning to London] The only suggestion I have to make is that the branches might be visited more often as there is too much of a qualitative gap between headquarters staff and branch managers; I wish this could be adjusted. It seemed to me that staff morale was very good. At the end of the week and indeed several times during the week, I tried – and despite kindly remarks without success – to imagine that I had been of some use to British Oxygen.

[In spite of his doubts about the utility of his visit to East Africa, John Reith was off again within a month, this time to South Africa, where he stayed in Johannesburg, Pretoria, and Durban, visiting the British Oxygen works in their vicinity.]

3 December 1962 [In Johannesburg] In the afternoon I spent about two hours with the five divisional heads [of African Oxygen, British Oxygen's subsidiary in the Union of South Africa]; it was rather heavy going. When I was told that firms were not allowed to put Africans in the way of training for skilled jobs, I said that would not last indefinitely. Apparently the chief objections to Africans being better trained is that they would put white men out of jobs; and there are 70,000 poor whites in the country. I remember saying in 1934 that the country was ruled by the poor whites; and there is still some truth in that.

6 December 1962 After visiting the Vanderbijlpark works we went to Vereeniging for lunch in the Riviera Hotel, overlooking the Vaal River – a most attractive setting. I found there was no memorial whatever of the meeting between Milner and Kitchener and the Boer leaders to stop the fighting, and to make arrangements for peace. I told them of my clear memory of my father, in the pulpit of the College Church in Glasgow, having a message from the *Glasgow Herald* editor one Sunday evening, and of his reading Milner's telegram, after which the organ crashed in with the Hallelujah Chorus. Dr Jacobs (managing director, Vereeniging Brick and Tile) said the signing had been on ground belonging to him; that the participants had walked about among the trees beforehand, and had then gone into a little cottage which had been prepared for the signing.[17] I had never been here before and was extremely interested.

7 December 1962 [In Pretoria] Went to the Voortrekker Memorial. I had been here before but it struck me still more how monumental, massive and oppressive and, from the outside, wholly lacking in any mystery or beauty, it was. I think I have never seen a less attractive and less inspiring memorial than this is, as seen from the outside. This is very unfortunate and sad, as there is a tremendous and heroic story to be displayed.

[The better part of a year was to elapse before John Reith went on his final journey on behalf of British Oxygen, this time visiting Pakistan, India, Ceylon, Malaya, Singapore and Hong Kong. Meanwhile he made contact, after a break of some years, with the Commonwealth Telecommunications Board.]

12 March 1963 Met the New Zealander, Donaldson, new chairman of the Telecommunications Board, and gave him lunch in the House of Lords. He had written on arrival saying he would very much like to see me and get advice on several points. I told him I had had nothing to do with the CTB since Sir Stanley Angwin's death.[18] Donaldson said that he was going to try to get it back where I intended it to be when I got it established. He urged me to come and lunch with them one day; said the members would be greatly pleased. He knew I hadn't been in the place for six or seven years. I was very glad to find that he was prepared to go into action against UK domination.

26 June 1963 Robbie [Sir Albert Robinson], high commissioner for Central Africa, to see me; he leaves London soon. What a squalid affair the dissolution of Empire has been.

29 August 1963 Lunched at the Commonwealth Telecommunications Board in 28 Pall Mall; everybody most civil to me. They have several extra countries now. I shook hands with about twenty in the board room. After lunch the chairman, Donaldson, made a kindly speech about me, and then I talked to them for about half an hour on origins and objectives: and I gave them a straight line for the future; also I said a thing or two about the UK attitude in the early days and was explicitly critical of the Treasury. A very pleasant meeting.

[At the end of October 1963 John Reith set off for his eastern tour.]

30 October 1963 [In Karachi] For anyone who has been in Pakistan or Indian towns and cities, there is a good deal common to them all. Pakistan and Indian slums can stand up to almost any competition, including those of Lagos, Nigeria. The nadir of this afternoon was not exactly a slum, but it certainly was a slummy exhibit. A holy place of some sort, I gathered, and part of the holiness was a muddy pond, around which, maybe in some simulation of worship, were a hundred or so men, women and children, with a glazed fixity, intensity and inanity of concentration – almost equal to that achieved by the television addict – gazing at godhead perhaps, or rather godheads; for here in what might have been elemental slime were a dozen or so wretched crocodiles. From there, not inappropriately perhaps but unwillingly, to Pakistan broadcasting HQ. First feeling on this trip is of something like fraudulence. I do all I can on these occasions to talk about Oxygen and not (repeat not) about BBC, BOAC, CTB, CDC or anything else irrelevant. I do not feel uncomfortable when being questioned about fundamental problems of organization, for one can easily bring in British Oxygen; often, though, I am almost saying, 'Hoi, will you remember what I am and not what I was?'

[After Karachi, John Reith flew first to Rawalpindi, taking a day off there to visit the North West frontier and having a picnic lunch near the summit of the Malakand pass. He then continued his tour with visits to Lahore, in West Pakistan; Dacca and Chittagong in East Pakistan (now Bangladesh); and Calcutta, Jamshedpur and Durgapur in eastern India. From Calcutta he flew to Delhi, arriving on 8 November.]

8 November 1963 [In Delhi] The last time I was here, I stayed for a week with the viceroy; on this occasion I was in a vast and new hotel belonging to government. There was a strike on; but we managed very well without waiters. I discovered an appointment had been made for me to see Dr Radhakrishnan [president of India] next morning. Deputy high commissioner (high commissioner was away from Delhi) said he would call for me.

9 November 1963 When we were quite near the entrance to the President's house, the old viceroy's house unchanged, a sentry signalled for us to stop. We had caught the sound of a military band; and as we stopped it came round the corner. Immediately behind was the president's bodyguard, exactly as I had seen it years ago. They then had the reputation of being the smartest body of cavalry in the world; and they had lost nothing of that smartness. But now something was happening; the officer commanding may have recognized the deputy high commissioner; anyhow while he was talking away to me I saw that the 'eyes right' command had been given. 'Look out,' I said, 'they are saluting you.' The officer at the rear had his sword at the ready and when he came alongside he gave what I have always regarded as the tremendously impressive officers' cavalry salute. Deputy high commissioner unfortunately had not a hat on which he could take off, so all he could do was to raise his right hand. I took off my hat; I always wear a hat when there is any chance of guards and sentries saluting.

We were taken into the president's room immediately; one wished that all presidents were such as he, with his tremendous background of philosophical learning. He invited me to sit beside him on a small sofa. His first remark was, 'The last time I heard your voice, Sir John – I beg your pardon, Lord Reith – you said, "This is Windsor Castle, His Royal Highness the Prince Edward." ' Conversation continuous without break; the usual trivialities to start with. I had asked whether there was any question I should put to the president. Deputy high commissioner had said he would be very much interested if I asked how democratic procedure was going down in India. I asked it flatly and the president immediately took it up. He said that of course, there were many defects in India's practice of democracy – India was not yet in a true sense democratic. But none the less the system was now accepted in India; it was a unifying force in the country and the people would not tolerate any other system. In spite of Mr Nehru's national leadership, Indian democracy had shown itself in the election to Parliament of three of his severest personal critics. In one way his own election as president was proof of some degree of democratic maturity; he had no personal political position; had never been a member of the Congress party; had never taken any part in politics; and, touching his forehead, had never worn a Gandhi cap. When I said the working of democracy depended greatly on the quality of the political leaders, the president said this was certainly true of India. There were many shortcomings deriving from divisions of caste and community, which would be very hard to overcome, but nevertheless the Indian people had in Mr Nehru a leader they trusted and who was capable of giving them the right inspiration. In answer to a question, he confirmed that though Mr Nehru was against outworn and irrational religious forms, he was certainly not an irreligious man and was constantly coupling science with spirituality in his speeches. Later, he said that a lot was said in this country about socialism but he begged me to understand that this was not to mean any invasion of personal liberties. India understood well that democracy existed for the enrichment of the life of the individual, and that anything that deprived him of liberty was the negation of what she stood for. At the end of half an hour I said I must go and he came with us to the door.

R.D.–2E

10 November 1963 [In Bombay] To the Taj Mahal Hotel. This is quite close to the Gateway of India archway – an impressive affair, but sadness on it now.

11 November 1963 Up at 7.00; when I drew back the curtains there was a magnificent view over the bay, the sun just about to rise, a great many ships including three warships of the Indian Navy. I could not help looking a good deal at the Gateway of India, and thinking of the people who had come into India that way, and that (*horresco referens*) I had wanted to do so myself.

[From Bombay, John Reith moved on via Bangalore and Madras to Ceylon and then to Kuala Lumpur.]

18 November 1963 [In Kuala Lumpur] To see the Tunku for half an hour – known of old. He did not seem seriously worried about Indonesian troubles and threats; indeed I not only expected him not to be, but saw no reason why he should be.

[From Kuala Lumpur John Reith went on to Singapore and thence to Hong Kong.]

21 November 1963 [In Hong Kong] This incredible place has greatly expanded since I was here three [in fact five] years ago. There are twenty or thirty new skyscrapers, including a gigantic Hilton hotel. The governor, Sir Robert Black, suggested we should go for a twenty-five mile drive round the island, which I was delighted to do. Seeing a big depression at the foot of some hills with what looked like a concrete bed, I asked whatever that was. He said, did I really not know? I said, no; and then it suddenly dawned on me – a reservoir absolutely dry. He told me there was only a four-hour weekly supply of water, and that he had laid on a water service in tankers from China. He said the drought was four months old, and there was no chance of rain now, so they were in for a year of it.

22 November 1963 The director of medical services for the colony took me to the new Queen Elizabeth Hospital, officially opened but not yet accepting patients. It took four years to build and is the largest in the Commonwealth and one of the most advanced in the world as to equipment. The visit, just over an hour, was carried out with military precision and efficiency. I was a good deal embarrassed, though I took care not to let this be noticed; they could not have treated royalty better.

[On 23 November John Reith returned home, flying home via Tokyo, Honolulu, San Francisco and New York, but not stopping more than a few hours at any. Back in London he soliloquized on his trip.]

23 November 1963 Is there too much of me and too little about British Oxygen's interests in this? Perhaps I expect people to give me more than they are capable of in the time. I never felt more 'on the job' and 'earning my pay' as when talking with the chairmen or chief executives [i.e. of British Oxygen's subsidiaries]. I wish there had been more of it; or that they could have talked more than they did. But I wish I could be sure that it is right in principle to continue the present arrangement of a fairly eminent chairman and a chief executive on whom a great deal must depend. One cannot generalize; it may be; but on the whole I think not.

[John Reith was to continue for another two years as vice-chairman of British Oxygen but he made no further journeys to the Commonwealth. His imperial interest in his last years was concentrated on the problem of Rhodesia.]

27 January 1964 I was unexpectedly asked to dine with the Southern Rhodesian high commissioner and prime minister, Winston Field. The wretched Lennox-Boyd was there but I absolutely ignored him, never even looked at him. Field, when I first talked with him, gave a most graphic account of the speech I made on my first visit to the Federation when I was staying with Huggins. He said everyone had enormously enjoyed it.

19 March 1964 Lunch with the Metal Box Company. Others there included the Southern Rhodesian high commissioner. He told me he had been tremendously pleased by the little note I had sent him about the casino to be erected near the Victoria Falls; that it was an insult to Livingstone, the Almighty, and the god of the river. He said he had sent it on at once to the prime minister with a covering note. 'Look what Lord Reith has to say about this job.'

28 May 1964 To the Dorchester Hotel for Southern Rhodesian high commissioner's dinner to Roy Welensky. Thirty there, worst instance of crowding at table that I have experienced. Very good dinner of course. Welensky made quite a speech afterwards, vehement warning of communist infiltration in the East, and condemnation of the government's dishonesty with him. Broke up at 9.45 and went on the terrace. Boyd had come to me before dinner to try to make peace with me; he was nervous and jerky over it. He referred to Roland Turnbull's dearest wish that we (Boyd and I) might be friends again. I remembered Turnbull's letter well, and it certainly had been a cry from the heart.[19] After dinner Boyd spoke to me again – didn't I think something might be done by such a gathering in support of Roy W. I said I entirely agreed, so we were all gotten inside to the ante-room, which just held the party. I tried to get the high commissioner to act as chairman, but he was too diffident. There was a major difference of opinion between Salisbury and Boyd as to communicating with the prime minister here. It went on for an hour – a most extraordinary affair.

15 July 1964 Dined in Quaglino's, private room, with J. F. Prideaux. I was thankful that we were away from the cacophony of the band. The objective was to persuade me to come to lunch or dinner with the CDC. He said it was my CDC in every way – senior staff, organization and all sorts of things of my origination. Everybody would be so awfully pleased if I went there again. I gave my reasons for not wanting to see the place again. He still kept on begging me to come. He was almost equally insistent on my agreeing to forgive Lennox-Boyd and to coming to the Goldsmith's Company to lunch one day, sitting between Lennox-Boyd (who is now Prime Warden) and himself so that everyone might know (what on earth does this mean, and what does it matter, whatever it means) that he and I (L-B that is) are on speaking terms again. I told him of Boyd having spoken to me at the Welensky dinner, and having asked me then to be friendly with him again; and I told him of the Turnbull effort (just before he died). Oh well, oh well. Of course Prideaux is a man of great importance already, and of much more importance to be, and it is kindly and complimentary of him to be so concerned. We talked till 11.30.

11 September 1964 Lunched at Savoy with Evan Campbell [high commissioner for Southern Rhodesia] to meet Ian Smith, the Southern Rhodesian prime minister. I sat next him. They (he and the UK prime minister) have agreed that Southern Rhodesia can have independence now, if he can show that he and his government have African support by a big majority. He said he wished I would come out to Southern Rhodesia. I said I would if he asked me to for some recognizable purpose.

10 December 1964 Lunched at 33 Hill Street [CDC headquarters] today, where I had not been since I left six years ago. They certainly made me welcome, Howick meeting me at the door, there being fourteen at lunch, Rendell on my right. It was a tremendous effort for me to go, and I would have given a lot not to go, but, from the time I got there, I behaved quite normally, and certainly everyone was most civil and friendly – neither individually nor collectively could they have been more kindly.

15 June 1965 I called at Rhodesia House to say goodbye to Evan Campbell. I asked if he were glad to be getting out of this country; he said in a way he was, but on the other hand he was not particularly looking forward to what was happening, and not happening, in Rhodesia. He said that just before Field was put out of office, Rhodesia was absolutely within reach of getting independence; but things had been mishandled at both ends. I asked him which country he was more annoyed with – Britain or Rhodesia; he said fifty-fifty.

Letter from Mr Evan Campbell, 10 May 1966
What a mess politicians make of problems that seem simple to ordinary folk. Both sides have left so little room for manœuvre that it now appears to be an exercise in saving face for them both. Let us hope that a formula to achieve this will be found soon. I think one of the saddest aspects of the situation is the hate that is being built up against Britain among the younger Rhodesians. Hate is such a sterile emotion that it makes one sad to think that it will grow.

Letter from Mr Evan Campbell, 13 June 1967
I know how interested you are in the future of Rhodesia. I know about the great prestige that you have in Britain. I write to ask whether you could intervene in this unfortunate and unnecessary dispute, which is doing neither your country nor mine any good at all.

Letter to Mr Evan Campbell, 17 June 1967
I haven't said anything in public about the deplorable situation for the simple, but maybe foolish, reason that I might be able at some time to do something about it, and that accordingly I had better stand off meantime.

I took a particular and unusual action on receipt of your letter. Maybe something will come of it.

18 June 1967 I told Hewitt [secretary for appointments to the PM] about Evan Campbell's interesting letter. I had often wondered if I would be asked to get things into order in Rhodesia. He spoke to someone at No. 10 with the result that this evening I dined with Sir Morrice James [deputy under secretary, Commonwealth Office]. We had quite an interesting talk and I think I gave him some new ideas, e.g. that it surely wasn't just a messenger with the UK's fixed terms that was wanted. But I also think that frightened him a good bit. Lord Alport has been sent out to Rhodesia 'to test the temperature'. He believes in the 'No independence before majority African rule' so he will be a welcome visitor, forsooth.

13 December 1967 Interesting talk with Welensky over lunch at the Hyde Park Hotel, 12.45 to 2.00. He was going off to the airport at 2.15. He said he could not go the direct way home as he might be seized and taken off as a prisoner if he went through Nairobi; he would not get to Salisbury till 12.30 tomorrow. I told him I immensely envied him getting there at all. He said that a suggestion he had made about Menzies coming in to arbitrate about Rhodesia wasn't really on because Menzies, for all his quality, was a cynic. It seemed from the way Roy was talking that he was going to suggest me as mediator. He said it wasn't a matter of the UK making a satisfactory deal now as its getting something out of the wreckage. One of the worst results of the situation was that the judiciary was almost bound to become politically influenced, and that was the ultimate shame.

Letter from Sir Roy Welensky, 23 April 1970
I believe that, had you been offered the governor generalship you might have been able to do quite a lot to help me in those difficult times. But I don't believe, any time after 1959, that it was really possible to have saved the Federation.

NOTES

1. The Gambia Poultry Farm was one of the worst of the inefficiencies which revealed itself when John Reith took over the CDC. Over £800,000 had been spent in three years on capital outlay with substantial revenue losses. The scheme was abandoned.
2. Sir Hugh Beaver, who had worked with John Reith at the Ministry of Works, was to be a director of CDC, 1951–60.
3. Tanganyika Territory had been German East Africa until 1918. John Reith's

acquaintance had presumably seen service there under General von Lettow Vorbeck during the first war.

4. Colonel Laurens Van der Post was one of an advisory committee appointed in 1952 to report on the Bechuanaland Cattle Ranch project.

5. Land at Crichel Down had been compulsorily purchased for use as a bombing range and had subsequently been sold to the Commissioners of Crown Lands despite the efforts of the previous owners to be allowed to repurchase or even to rent it. A public inquiry in 1954 revealed 'a most regrettable attitude' on the part of some of the civil servants involved who 'revealed a feeling of irritation that any member of the public should have the temerity to oppose or even to question the decisions of officials'.

6. John Reith actually wrote 1923 in his diary; he meant 1930.

7. Presumably this was Mr Kenneth Kaunda, then secretary-general of the African National Congress and subsequently president of Zambia (Northern Rhodesia).

8. The act of parliament to which John Reith refers was the Overseas Resources Development amending act of 1956. The 'moral obligation' which Reith felt arose from the fact that discussions on RISCOM had been held long before this act was mooted.

9. The CDC Report had concluded:

CDC has been assured on behalf of both Ghana and Malaya governments that it would be a great pity if emerging members of the Commonwealth were, at a critical stage, to be deprived of help of the experienced CDC personnel; of course 'Colonial' would have to come out of CDC title.

John Reith had had letters from Dr Nkrumah and Tunku Abdul Rahman Putra to sustain his case.

10. Eight Englishmen had been killed on 1 January 1897. Benin was captured a month later and a second punitive expedition dealt with the surrounding country in 1899.

11. This account was written on 1 October 1958.

12. Colonel Peter Gregoire, the Far East regional controller of CDC, and W. A. Gibson, manager of CDC's Kulai oil palms estate project, were killed in a terrorist ambush near Kulai on 25 July 1954.

13. General (later Field Marshal) Sir Gerald Templer had been high commissioner and director of operations in Malaya, 1952–4.

14. Events in the Congo were soon to prove Sir Roy right.

15. Lord Monckton had been appointed chairman of an advisory commission on the review of the constitution of the Federation of Rhodesia and Nyasaland in September 1959. The commission spent three months in Central Africa, February to May 1960, and reported in October that year.

16. Mr R. A. (now Lord) Butler was minister in charge of the Central African Office, 1962–3.

17. As the peace was signed on Saturday 31 May 1902 at 10.30 p.m. it is probable that the news of it was received in Glasgow on the Sunday. For the rest, John Reith and Dr Jacobs were romancing. Milner and Kitchener met the Boer leaders at Kitchener's headquarters in Pretoria, not at Vereeniging, and the peace was signed in his dining-room there. The conference of some sixty Boers which assembled at Vereeniging between 15 and 31 May 1902 to discuss and approve the peace terms met in a tent, not a cottage.

18. Sir Stanley Angwin, who had accompanied John Reith on his world tour in 1945, had succeeded him as chairman of CTB in 1951. He died in 1959.

19. Sir Roland Turnbull wrote:
It is near to my heart that two people whose friendship I so greatly value should not remain at a variance I am quite sure was desired by neither.

CHAPTER NINE

John Reith and Broadcasting (2)

After leaving the BBC 1938–70

John Reith left the BBC a month before his forty-ninth birthday. He had served as its effective director for nearly sixteen years. For the remainder of his active life which was to extend for almost double that period, he retained a deep concern for broadcasting policy as an aspect of national life; and at the same time he maintained, although with painful interruptions, his interest in the personnel, work and organization of the BBC. Throughout these years he consistently blamed himself for having agreed to give up his position as director general, partly because he felt that, if he had stayed, he would have avoided for himself the frustrations of his broken career between 1942 and 1950, but much more because he believed that he could have preserved the BBC's monopoly, prevented the establishment of commercial television and maintained the ethical and cultural standards of broadcasting which had been the primary objectives of his period of office.

As it was, Reith never again attained a formal position in the ruling hierarchy of the BBC, although he hoped on two occasions, soon after the war, to be appointed chairman of the governors. Nevertheless, he worked from outside in close contact with Sir William Haley at the time of the Beveridge committee, to which he gave evidence in 1950, and again, more than ten years later, he collaborated with Sir Arthur fforde and Sir Hugh Carleton Greene when he gave evidence to the Pilkington committee. His personal relationship with the corporation and its controlling members oscillated violently in these years between total separation, as in the seven or eight years following his departure and again in the later 1950s, and close co-operation, as throughout the last six years of Sir William Haley's period as director general. These variations in his attitude towards the BBC provide useful breaking points in the long story of John Reith's concern with broadcasting which can be found in his diary.

1. Separation in peace and war, 1938–46

[When John Reith left the BBC in June 1938 we have seen that he cut himself off completely. He refused to meet his successor, F. W. Ogilvie, until March 1939 and in May he would not attend the farewell dinner for R. C. Norman, who was finally retiring as chairman of the governors, although he contributed to his parting present. Even when he successfully intervened with the government to secure the offer to Cecil Graves of the position of director general of the embryonic Ministry of Information, he was enraged and frustrated by the refusal of Graves to serve. So, as war drew nearer, John Reith was in little happier a relationship with the BBC than he had been on his departure.]

26 August 1938 Miss Stanley telephoned. I was trying to determine whether I wished it was still the BBC she was talking from. For ease, yes; but I am sure I wouldn't really want it just because I would always know that it couldn't and shouldn't last.

12 January 1939 Muriel has replied to an invitation to stay the weekend – both of us – at New College [i.e. with H. A. L. Fisher] declining and saying that I really did not want to meet anybody from the BBC board.

24 January 1939 Long talk with Graves on the phone. I feel so bitter against the BBC. It shows a very unestimable trait in my character. Most worrying dreams about being back in the BBC building, chiefly I suppose due to the Graves call. I will try to avoid these in future.

8 February 1939 Lunched with Harold Brown [former vice-chairman of the BBC] at Brooks's and very glad to see him. Told him of the BBC situation and he was awfully vexed and anxious to square up. I told him I didn't want things patched up.

21 February 1939 Lunched with Harold Brown. He had apparently seen Norman lately. He wanted me to meet Norman and be friendly and go to the BBC and so forth. I tried to make him understand that I wasn't feeling unfriendly to Norman – just not friendly, negative attitude. I like Brown awfully.

13 March 1939 Letter from Ogilvie asking us to dine with him and his wife before the first Toscanini concert on 3 May and to come to an unveiling ceremony of my painting in the Council chamber.

15 March 1939 Wrote in reply to Ogilvie tonight, declining both but offering to meet for a talk.

23 March 1939 Show at the India Office for the French President, the quadrangle having been turned into a vast theatre auditorium. Met the director general of the BBC and wife. He was very civil and friendly and we are to lunch together on Monday.

27 March 1939 Lunched with Ogilvie at Brooks's – Ogilvie, director general of the BBC, asked my view of creating another controller of programmes for Empire work, and I gave it in favour of functionalism, not territorialism. Told him briefly the story of my leaving the BBC. I don't know what was achieved at all. He (and the silly governors) are all annoyed about the new chairman [Sir Allan Powell]! Well they might be. H. J. Wilson told Ogilvie that the prime minister had done it himself which, of course, wasn't true.

15 April 1939 I had a nice note from Ogilvie asking me to attend a farewell lunch or dinner to Norman – Control Board, Harold Brown and Mrs Hamilton – but I have declined.
[It was in April 1939 that John Reith was asked by Sir Samuel Hoare to advise the government 'on the wireless side of the Information Ministry'. Reith's answer was a brief memorandum dated 19 April.]

Memorandum on Ministry of Information [Extracts][1]

. . . It looks as if the Ministry has not so far been taken very seriously. If satisfactory arrangements and preparations are to be made a different and definite attitude is required. For the efficient conduct of public affairs we need the right men rightly circumstanced. Things go wrong if either element is lacking; in this case both may be.

The wartime director general should be chosen and put to work as quickly as possible. The home secretary must have someone to rely on and to do the work for him. A man of real ability, not necessarily full-time, should get things into shape in three to six months.

. . . All my present information leads me to recommend that [government] relationship with the BBC should be left as it is subject to the recommendation with respect to the DG post [i.e. Cecil Graves] which I think would solve all the problems.

[Graves declined to serve early in May.]

13 May 1939 Too much thinking and dreaming about the BBC. It will help if I have no more contact with Graves.

8 July 1939 It seems intolerably obvious that Ogilvie isn't managing the BBC at all, however nice he may be and people like him. Lochhead [BBC chief accountant and later controller of finance] (whom I told about my indignation with Graves) seemed to think that this was the reason for Graves turning down the M of I job.

16 July 1939 Mrs Hamilton told me that the BBC's reputation now, and that of the director general, was of 'genial incompetence'.

[The war brought about happier personal relationships between John Reith and the BBC chiefs. He renewed his friendly contact with Cecil Graves and he also ended his differences with R. C. Norman. While he was on his own (his family being still in America), he asked F. W. Ogilvie and his wife to stay at his home in Beaconsfield. But at the same time it was clear that the fears he had expressed in his memorandum of April 1939 about the possibilities of muddle and misunderstanding between the BBC and the newly established Ministry of Information were fully justified. He did his best to put this straight while he was, himself, minister of information in the first four months of 1940, but, as we have seen, his transfer to the Ministry of Transport came before his efforts could take effect.]

15 October 1939 Decided to speak to Graves. Wellington on the phone the other night urged me to do so. Long talk with him and he was very glad I had called up. He is disgusted with things in the BBC. Sleeps three nights on end in a studio. Three days 9.00 a.m. to 9.00 p.m., then three days and nights and then three days off. Ludicrous; he said it was Ogilvie's idea.

17 October 1939 [Returning from Lichfield after the installation of Iremonger as dean of the cathedral there] I left at 4.45 in Edgar's [midland regional controller, BBC] car as he was to guide us through Birmingham. He was awfully disgusted with things and said he would willingly leave the BBC now. There was no decision or control.

20/28/29/30 *October 1939* [20] Rang up Ogilvie to ask him and his wife to stay here.

[28] Met the Ogilvies and Mrs Hamilton.

[29] Ogilvies left. He made a very unfavourable impression on Mrs Hamilton – so indecisive and ineffective.

[30] I think Ogilvie is quite unaware of his own ineffectiveness.

1 November 1939 Lunched at Claridges with Harold Brown and R. C. Norman. Nothing special and no references to the past. Not embarrassing, as I had thought, but rather pointless.

8 November 1939 Lunched with Graves at Brooks's. He is very disgusted and told me various damning things about the lack of decision and control at the BBC. The chairman was dreadful. Ogilvie awful with his endless committees and meetings. Graves said both he and Ashbridge [controller of engineering, BBC] wished I were back. He seemed very pleased to be able to talk to me.

9 November 1939 R. C. Norman wrote on 6th that it gave him a lot of pleasure to meet me again and a lot more to get my letter written on 5th in which I said I was sorry I had been silly and unkind last year. He wrote:

> You need not be told, I am sure, that I have never ceased to have for you the warmest feelings of admiration and affection.

21 December 1939 Lunched with Graves, hearing of BBC unsettlements, especially of trouble between Ogilvie and Graves.

[John Reith became minister of information on 5 January 1940. In his interview with the prime minister on appointment he noted that Neville Chamberlain 'had said he supposed I would be gentle with the BBC; and that there was a lot of dissatisfaction with it and that Ogilvie was mostly responsible.']

11 January 1940 At 3.45 I received a formal call from the chairman and director general of the BBC. I showed them some courtesy, conducting them along the passage, down the stairs and to the inquiry desk. I subsequently concluded that this was four-fifths of courtesy to a departing visitor. Anyhow it impressed them enormously. I told them I had it in mind to appoint a broadcast functional director on the Ministry staff and asked if they would like to suggest somebody from the BBC.[2]

13 February 1940 An hour's talk with Halifax about Neutral and Enemy Propaganda which seemed to go satisfactorily. As I was going off, he said he had come to the conclusion that Ogilvie wasn't good enough for his job. I said I would hesitate to endorse that but that he certainly wasn't as good as he should be and lacked decision and control.[3]

23 February 1940 Visited Ogilvie in his offices – my first call in that building since I left. It was strange but not at all distressing. My room looked very different and so untidy and it had a bed in it. I told Ogilvie we thought he ought to be able to do far more on the Home Front – especially a nightly tonic talk which would deal with some special bit of news and with the more outrageous 'Haw-Haw' charges. I asked if he would like the BBC – the foreign language part – to be taken over and would that make things easier. I asked also oughtn't far more to be done in German. He spoke as if anything the Ministry wanted would be done. Odd.

2 April 1940 To Broadcasting House where I arrived early as my meeting with Churchill had to be put off. Graves fortunately turned up. I had found no one in the director general's secretary-room so I went into Graves *via* his secretary's and then through the waiting-room, trying to realize I had ever been there. We went along to see Lochhead and had some talk with him. Then Sir A. Powell and Ogilvie turned up and we all met Frossard [French minister of information] in the hall. I broadcast in French introducing him. I asked Powell to join the dinner-party in the House of Commons which was most successful.

22 April 1940 Kingsley Wood, H. J. Wilson, Lee [director general of Ministry of Information], Monckton and I interviewed the chairman and director general of the BBC about their news bulletins chiefly. They have a ridiculous organization change, Ryan becoming a controller responsible for the home spoken word and Tallents responsible for overseas programmes complete and overseas intelligence. I said what I thought about this and also that it wasn't courteous of them not to have consulted me. Pathetic meeting.

[In the middle of May 1940 John Reith moved to the Ministry of Transport. He now had no executive power in relation to broadcasting but he was aware that things were not going well with the BBC. He hoped that he would be consulted by the Cabinet on how best to set this situation to rights, perhaps even asked to return as director general. He was disappointed on both counts. In November 1940, by which time he had moved again to be minister of works, he discovered that a Cabinet committee had been established to consider the constitution and management of the BBC and wrote a memorandum on this, unasked, which he showed to Sir Kingsley Wood. It was ignored. His readiness to return was similarly turned aside. By the end of 1940 he was greatly distressed at the way the government was reacting to the BBC's situation.]

8 June 1940 Lunch with Tree and Peake [press adviser to the Ministry of Information] and then Wellington was in the carriage with me on the 3.10, so I heard plenty about the Ministry of Information and the BBC. The latter has gone all adrift and things are not at all satisfactory in the M of I.

17 June 1940 Lunched with Sir Kenneth Clark [director of the film division, Ministry of Information] and heard various things about the Information Ministry place – very muddled and lots of intrigue going on. BBC is being much criticized within and without. I even think I would be willing to go back to it and get it out of its rotten state. I told Clark so, and Wellington. Nothing to do. Nothing to do.

Letter from Ralph Wade [in charge of the BBC's London premises], *30 July 1940*
Your remark last night about the possibility of your returning here has literally put new life into me. There is a widespread need for real inspiring leadership here. My fear is that if your return is delayed too long the old BBC will be dead and the spirit of those who have tried to keep it alive will be dead too.

22 August 1940 Lunched with Ashbridge who spoke, as the others have, about the awful state of affairs at the BBC.

15 October 1940 Lunch with Ogilvie at the Athenæum where the windows have all gone – many clubs have been hit. Silly sort of talk as I said what I thought of Tallents and he said I mustn't think that. He referred to Graves as the rock he had leant on and was quite vexed when I questioned that.

[Early in November the question of commandeering Broadcasting House 'ground floor and downwards' for use by the government as a building capable of resisting bombing was raised by Lord Beaverbrook and considered by the Cabinet but rejected. John Reith was by now so disillusioned with the BBC's performance that he stood aside and offered no help.]

11 November 1940 Saw Walter Monckton to whom I had phoned on Saturday when he was staying with Halifax. I wanted to know if he would like to come to the Ministry of Works either as parliamentary secretary or otherwise. Halifax wants him to go to the BBC *vice* Ogilvie or to take F. Pick's place [as director general] at the Ministry of Information. Weird it all is. I told him I would hate to go back to the BBC but would do so if asked by the prime minister.

19 November 1940 I found in the Cabinet minutes that Kingsley Wood, Morrison and [Duff] Cooper had been told to report changes in consultation or management necessary to enable the State to exercise effective control over the BBC. Spoke to John Anderson about this.

20 November 1940 I dictated a long story about the BBC which I took to John Anderson after lunch. He advised me to let Kingsley Wood see it.

Memorandum on BBC [Conclusion]

When Mr Duff Cooper became minister of information, and on several occasions later when things in the BBC were going from bad to worse, I offered to help him, but he has never asked my view on anything. On the other hand I have been in receipt of increasingly urgent complaints and suggestions from senior people within the organization that I should intervene.

Whatever dissatisfaction there is with the BBC, there is much within it. The two major troubles are lack of leadership and decision in the director general and extreme dislike of Sir Stephen Tallents, who has had great influence with the DG from the start, gradually ousting Sir Cecil Graves, who in any event, was off ill from May till August.

25 November 1940 Talked with Graves on the telephone to Falloden. He was very distressed to learn that as Ogilvie might now be removed he was missing the chance of succeeding him. It is certainly very bad luck. I had also had a long talk with Wellington last night; [he said]

there was no one who could do what was required in the BBC except me.

3 December 1940 The senior staff have signed a note to Powell asking to be heard if there was any idea of appointing Tallents DG. This was my suggestion – instead of a protest afterwards. Broadcasting House certainly is in a rotten state.

4 December 1940 Walter Monckton called. He said D. Cooper had asked him that afternoon if he would go to the BBC and he had said (so he said) he would like to go if I were going also. I told him to insist on getting power of both Board and executive.

7 December 1940 Saw Kingsley Wood at my request. Told him about Graves and said I wished he would keep me in touch with what was happening about the BBC. That silly committee of his has only had one meeting.

31 December 1940 The blister Kingsley Wood has put in a report to the Cabinet[4] about the BBC without asking my views on it. It is utterly ludicrous – two 'advisers', foreign and general, to be in complete charge of the spoken word, immediately under Ogilvie but, in the event of disagreement with him, with direct appeal to the minister of information. The latter was also to hold weekly meetings with these officials and about a dozen others. Fantastic and puerile. And if Ogilvie had any pride I can't see his accepting it.

[Throughout 1941 and right up to his leaving the government in February 1942, John Reith was increasingly irritated by the turn of events affecting the BBC. He felt, for a time, that he might, if reappointed, stem the tide, but by January 1942 he had worked himself into such fury that he was ready to see the BBC 'smashed'. Then, by cruel irony, F. W. Ogilvie was removed from the BBC – just four weeks before John Reith himself was dismissed as minister of works.]

28 January 1941 Lunched with Ogilvie and told him all my train of complaints against him. Very decent he was. Said he was sorry for his Ministry of Information failures – when I was there, I mean. He seemed really glad of the talk. I told him I had not approved of his appointment but that I had not opposed it.

R.D.–2F

16 March 1941 Mrs Hamilton and Muriel and I walked to Jordans for tea with the Ogilvies. Quite considerable talk with him about the organization walking up and down by the village green. Lovely day it was and we enjoyed the walk.

28/29 March 1941 [28] Miss Stanley saw me off on the 9.50 for Newcastle where rather than wait an hour for a train (and we were an hour late as it was) I took an ordinary taxi to Falloden – forty-four miles off. I arrived about an hour before they expected to start to meet me. Beastly weather. I would have welcomed a cup of tea! Talked about the BBC. Graves is very down on Ogilvie – 'that bloody fellow' – I never heard him use that word before. I told him about conversations with Ogilvie and Wellington and others.

[29] More conversation about the BBC. He expects to go back in four weeks and to take real charge.

7 April 1941 The miserable BBC has Fraser and Mallon back as governors. Wretched choice that, and they are both Tallents supporters.

20 July 1941 My fifty-second birthday – how awful old. Tea at Cliveden. Geoffrey Dawson and wife were there – his retiral from the editorship [of *The Times*] was announced on Friday [i.e. 18 July] – and lots of others. Heard of changes in the Government – monstrous ones and the worst of all that Harold Nicolson becomes a governor of the BBC as if that were a political appointment.[5] Wicked. Spoke to Ogilvie on the telephone. He was very disgusted.

10 September 1941 Lunched with Welch, the BBC religious director. He is very disgusted with Ogilvie's lack of leadership. Carpendale turned up to tell me that the government are set on getting rid of Tallents and putting Kirkpatrick [soon to be BBC controller of European Services] in his place. Almost wish I could go back there.

11 September 1941 Met Monckton who is more and more all things to all people and very unreliable. He told me that Powell and Ogilvie had been to see him and Radcliffe[6] that day to recommend that Tallents should be deputy director general! This is a result of his getting pushed out of his present job to make room for Kirkpatrick.

3 October 1941 G. Dunbar [chief accountant of the BBC] to see me about the possibilities of commercial broadcasting after the war. I said I had never objected to the provision of programme material in return for a simple acknowledgement or even to an advertising period. What I had said all along was that the ether ought not to be at the power of money.

1 November 1941 The BBC latest humiliation is that the Gas Light and Coke Co. Manager [R. W. Foot] has been brought in for the war to advise on organization.

3 November 1941 Lunched with Graves. He said everything was awful at the BBC and getting worse and worse, and that Ogilvie was quite hopeless. He didn't know what to make of the new organization 'adviser' post. He said if someone else was made DG, if they pushed Ogilvie out, he would resign at once – someone other than himself.

15 December 1941 Over two hours with Lady Violet Bonham Carter, governor of the BBC. She is doing the sort of things that Lady Snowden did and she asked me what I thought about that. I told her exactly what I would have thought when I was there and made quite clear to her what governors should do and shouldn't do. But I said that circumstances alter cases and that things were in such a bad way now in the BBC that I didn't think she could do otherwise; but I advised her to have a proper talk with Graves. She said that people so often said to her that they always knew I was there, and I said that that supplied the answer to her question as to what was wrong with the BBC – lack of leadership.

21 December 1941 I am particularly infuriated by the thought of what Ogilvie has done (and the blasted board who appointed him) with the BBC.

19 January 1942 Saw Dunbar and Cartwright. They wished me to talk on commercial radio. I said the BBC, if it could be regenerated, would be able to do all that was needed, but that if it wasn't regenerated I shouldn't mind it being smashed, nor having a hand in doing so.

26 January 1942 Muriel phoned me to say that she had had a call from a man who wanted to tell me something before I heard it on the wireless. Ogilvie – I knew it was his resignation. He had told Muriel what it was and had said I had always been so kind to him etc. Rather a shock in a way, but of course what should have happened long ago. I rang him up to thank him and to say I was sorry for him.

27 Janaury 1942 Brendan Bracken [minister of information] telephoned to me to ask what I thought of Graves! I had spoken to him last night to ask what was happening and he told me of the dyarchy; he seemed quite pleased.[7] I rang him to tell him of Bracken's call and also to wish him good luck.

22 February 1942 [The day after he was dismissed] Phoned Ogilvie as he had phoned me in like circumstances and suggested we should go into partnership in a barrel organ.

[For more than a year after he was dropped from the government John Reith's diary contained virtually no references to broadcasting or to the BBC. It was a particularly unhappy time in his life. Then, in 1943, he began to pick up the threads again. Even so, he refused to take part in the BBC's celebration of its twenty-first anniversary at the end of that year and rejected an invitation to become an honorary life vice-president of the BBC club. When, in April 1944, Mr William Haley (as he then was) became director general, John Reith soon heard of his high reputation. Nevertheless, he continued to hold back from any contact and it required the ending of the war and the change of government that followed this to involve him once again in broadcasting questions. He now tried to influence the Labour postmaster general, Lord Listowel; he even hoped that he might be appointed chairman of the BBC in 1946; then, in the autumn of that year, he at last brought himself to make approaches to Sir William Haley. This was to lead once again to a period of close involvement with the BBC and with broadcasting problems, as well as to a deep and lasting friendship.]

29/31 May 1943 [29] Lunched with Mrs Hamilton to no purpose. She told me that things in the BBC were in an awful state – intrigues going on.
[31] I had a rotten night, dreaming I was back in the BBC.

12 July 1943 Gave Barnes [director of talks, BBC] dinner, seeing various BBC people, including Coatman [north regional controller] who seemed very pleased to see me. They all want me back there and say this is the only salvation for it – everything thrown away.

6 September 1943 Weird and disgusting announcement about the BBC: (1) that Foot is to be sole director general; (2) that someone (Haley by name) is to be brought in in charge of all output; (3) that he and Foot are to be jointly responsible to the Board; and (4) that an 'executive committee' is to assist Haley. And what is the difference between that and a joint DG-ship? Nicolls [controller of programmes, BBC] told me that the chairman had come in at the end of what used to be called the Enlarged Control Board, the day before, and had read them out a long statement with much puff about this Haley – of whom only Coatman had ever heard. Nicolls said that there was a lot of disgust about it which was very natural.

9 November 1943 Nicolls told me there was to be a BBC lunch-party of about three hundred to celebrate its twenty-first anniversary. I suppose I shall be invited – but perhaps not – anyhow I certainly shan't go. Not on any account. Muriel, to whom I mentioned the matter, only said when I asked her if she would want to urge me to go: 'I don't know; I should want to consider that.'

14 November 1943 Ogilvie told me at lunch yesterday in the Athenæum that he wouldn't go to the BBC lunch-party, but hoped to be invited in order to have the satisfaction of declining – which is what I feel too.

22 November 1943 I had the BBC lunch invitation today together with a very nice letter from the chairman. The lunch should have been given *to me*. I certainly won't go.

16 December 1943 Dinner in club, Mallon talking to me afterwards though I gave him no encouragement. He said Bracken was responsible for the humbug of the Haley appointment with its responsibility direct to the Board, as he had said it would be a mistake to let all the power get into one man's hands. At the lunch [on 8 December] Bracken had said he didn't interfere with the Corporation, which is a lie a hundred times over. The idea now is to have several competing regional concerns, which is of course fantastic. I told him I might have gone to the lunch if I had been chief guest and that this was the first communication I had had since I left. Also that everything I had done had been undone. He was very down on Ogilvie.

1 April 1944 Foot is leaving the BBC to be chairman of the Mining Association, a very important job in its way, but what a humbug he is to leave the BBC. It confirms what I have said all along about the position there. The man Bailey [i.e. Haley] is director general now. Feeling very depressed.

10 April 1944 I wonder what I would do if Bailey [i.e. Haley], the new sole director general of the BBC, made any approach to me.

16 May 1944 I had some conversation with Dr Welch of the BBC this morning after breakfast. He is to address the General Assembly next week. He thinks the new BBC man Bailey [i.e. Haley] might do well. He said they had been rudderless ever since I left.

5 July 1944 Lunched at Cable and Wireless. It was a big party and in the Board Room. I sat next Chancellor, who is one of the joint general managers of Reuters. He talked about Bailey [i.e. Haley] the director general of the BBC for whom he evidently has much regard. I said I thought he might have communicated with me on assuming the office I created. It always upsets me – this sort of talk about the BBC.

6 October 1944 I travelled home with Wellington and told him how cuckoo the BBC organization was now and he quite agreed.

19 October 1944 Feeling absolutely wretched about the past and future. Dreamt that I was back as DG of the BBC last night. I often do this.

[Between November 1944 and March 1945 John Reith was busy with the preparations for and the completion of his world tour in connection with the telecommunications of the Empire.]

28 May 1945 Nicolls joined me at lunch in the club and pointed out Haley (BBC) whom I had no desire to know even by sight.

[The Labour government took office at the end of July 1945 and immediately took under consideration the BBC's charter which was due for renewal in 1946. The decision was to procrastinate; the charter was renewed for five years pending a wider inquiry.]

29 August 1945 Lunched with Listowel who was most civil and agreeable. I thought he hadn't at all a good grasp of things. Talked about the BBC. Woolton's committee (which I thought it damnable that I wasn't asked to meet) had prepared a sort of interim report and now a new one has been set up.

23 November 1945 I have been reading the report on broadcasting done for the Cabinet by Morrison, Listowel, Williams [minister of information] and Noel-Baker which was sent to me by Morrison. It is a rotten document, not covering half what it should.

24 November 1945 Rang Listowel who entirely agreed about the inadequacy of the report – though he is a signatory of it. Offered to talk with him before seeing Morrison and he was very grateful.

25 November 1945 I rang Wellington as I decided I would like his views on some of the BBC points. He was here from 10.30 to nearly 1.00. It was very useful and I hoisted in for the first time the new system of programmes – light, so-called home (which may be all regions independently) and cultural. It is an absolute abandonment of what I stood for. Put in some more paragraphs into my comments. Apparently Haley, the DG, made some highly complimentary remarks about me.

27 November 1945 Rather fatuous and irritating meeting with Listowel and Gardiner [director general of the Post Office] (present on my suggestion) about the BBC paper. Frightened they both were.

3 December 1945 Saw Herbert Morrison from 10.00 till 10.55 about the BBC. He was very grateful and expressed himself as in entire agreement with practically everything I said. I don't suppose it is worth recording all the points I made. They covered ministerial control, board numbers, qualifications, pay, status and responsibilities of chairman. Treasury control and lots of other points. I did a very good job for the BBC anyhow.

27 February 1946 Lunched at the club and Nicolls talked to me about being chairman of the BBC. I said if I were offered it, which was inconceivable, I shouldn't accept unless I had first a satisfactory talk with the present director general.

3 April 1946 Periodic pointless and irritating conversations with Nicolls about the BBC chairmanship.

26 June 1946 To Lords for BBC debate which didn't begin till nearly 4.00. It went on till 6.15. I was very nearly intervening particularly at something Lord Sandhurst said [which was critical of BBC engineering]. The director general of the BBC was there with Farquharson [head of the BBC secretariat]. The PMG made a very feeble speech indeed. There will be another chance later.

7/8 July 1946 [7] I read up all the BBC stuff as I have to see the PMG tomorrow morning.

[8] Saw the PMG. He is a decent but very poor fellow and I really got nowhere with him.

[John Reith now sought to counter the criticism of BBC engineers he had heard in the Lords.]

23/24/26 July 1946 [23] Sarnoff [chairman of RCA] phoned in reply to my letter asking his view on BBC engineers.

[24] I managed to dictate over the phone a draft letter to *The Times* about BBC engineers for Ashbridge to vet.

[26] I had done some considerable amendment of *The Times* letter about the BBC engineers last night and as I wanted to get rid of it today I wondered if I could go to Broadcasting House on the way in and have Ashbridge vet it finally and get it typed. Anyhow I got off the lousy tube at Oxford Circus and while I was wondering what to do a BBC man addressed me. I got him to take me into Broadcasting House and straight to Ashbridge's room. Lochhead was with Ashbridge and they got a shock to see me walk in. Went through the letter and gave it out to be typed. Welcome cup of coffee. I got an awful shock in being told that I was in Carpendale's old room, next door to the DG, and a communicating door through. I had thought I was on a much higher floor. Fortunately he was away. Visited Nicolls who had of course heard I was in the building. I wouldn't look into my old room. I really hardly realized where I was or could conceive that this was the scene of so many years' work. Ashbridge was minded to accompany me to the door but I slipped out on my own. Quite an amusing and possibly pleasant experience.

[Early in September John Reith heard by chance that Sir William Haley had drafted a letter for him but had not sent it. He seems then to have decided to take the initiative himself and wrote to Haley offering to meet him. Sir William welcomed this.]

Letter from Sir William Haley, 19 September 1946
I was most happy to receive your letter. Thank you very much. It is a source of great pride to me to be trying to carry on the great traditions you founded and I have often wished we could meet. Diffidence kept me from approaching you.

Could we have lunch together? Would September 25, 27, 30 or October 1 suit you? If you could manage one of those dates and will let me know I will arrange a private room at an hotel.

30 September 1946 Lunched at Manetta's with Sir William Haley! He gave an awkward sort of bow when I went in. We talked from 1.00 till 4.30. He expressed on several occasions the utmost admiration for me and my work and said he wanted nothing better than to carry on what I had done and bring the concern back to what it had been. He was sure, however, that he wouldn't be there long if I were chairman. I had made it clear to him that my letter to him had nothing whatever to do with the vacancy for chairman. He satisfied me that he was trying to get back to a decent programme policy and also a better organization system.

3 December 1946 Dined at Lochhead's; very nice dinner and they were most agreeable. He was awfully anxious that I should be chairman of the BBC.

9 December 1946 Dined at Lady Reading's in Smith Square. Lady R. said Morrison had failed to have me offered the BBC chair. He had said I was too strong for Attlee. I don't at all know that I would have taken the job or been happy in it if I had, but this is certainly just another of the blows I have had so many of.

16 December 1946 I had lunch with Haley of BBC at Carlton Grill, my lunch. Talked a lot about organization and personalities. He was at great pains to assure me that he had nothing to do with my not being offered the BBC chair.

Christmas Day 1946 The BBC had put in a combined sound and television receiver on Monday [23rd] and we watched television after dinner.

2. Co-operation with Sir William Haley, 1947–52

[Just as the removal of his wireless and television sets in June 1938 had signalled John Reith's resolve to separate himself completely from the BBC, so their restoration at Christmas 1946 demonstrated that this separation was at an end. Throughout 1947 Reith and Haley were in close touch, meeting regularly, writing and telephoning often. In the early part of the year the unexpected resignation of the chairman, Lord Inman, who briefly joined the government, brought them together in the hope of securing John Reith's appointment in his place, but without success and Reith was disappointed for the second time in six months. Then the twenty-fifth anniversary of the BBC, which fell due in November, allowed some public demonstration of Reith's friendly reassociation with the institution which was largely his creation.]

3 February 1947 To lunch in my old room at Broadcasting House where I had only been once in early 1940. I washed in my old bathroom. It was all most harrowing. Lunch was done in great style in the room. Of course I was enormously envious of Haley with all the circumstances and amenities of a big office and organization. Talked till 3.30 mostly about personalities and organization system. One of the things he said was that the longer he was there the more he concluded that I was right, even though he had begun by feeling otherwise about this or that. I don't know that I was as much 'on the job' as I might have been, because it was so harrowing.

14 March 1947 I had lunch with Haley at the BBC. There I had a sort of royal reception which embarrassed me greatly. Talked till 3.15 and more definite subjects than before, especially about a small control board and a proper public relations officer who would take the whole matter of the broadcasting inquiry off his hands – build-up and preparation for it. He said the Board [of governors] wished to give the appearance that they were running the show, but that he didn't mind so long as in fact they didn't do so.

17 April 1947 Haley rang me at 10.30 p.m. to say he had just heard that the BBC chairman, Inman, was made lord privy seal. He has quite changed his mind and wants me to be chairman now. It was very interesting. And I should like to be that.

18 April 1947 Haley phoned that he had seen Barlow and Lady Reading. I cannot conceive being made chairman (a) not being Labour, and (b) not being weak and pliable. It would therefore just be another of the now innumerable disappointments.

22 April 1947 Lady Reading rang to ask me to look in on her tomorrow night. Said she was full of hope and very busy.

23 April 1947 Tubes and beastliness to Broadcasting House for lunch with Haley. I told him about Lady Reading's call. He said he had seen Bridges and Morrison's secretary and Listowel. Long talk all around it. I don't know that I'd be happy at all, but I am sure I shall be greatly cast down if it isn't offered after all this.

Lady Reading 6.30 to 8.00. She told me all she had done on her own and with Haley – he having seen Barlow, she M. Nicholson (Morrison's man), Bridges and Listowel. She was tremendously impressed with Haley's wanting me. But she told me the most harrowing stories about conditions at Broadcasting House and how worried the governors had been about many things, giving rise to two dinner-parties in her house. The chairman she could hardly find words to describe. I was left wondering what sort of job it would be more than ever.

24 April 1947 Haley had dinner with me and we talked till midnight. I told him more or less what Lady Reading had said to me. It was a great shock to him to know that the Board had been meeting on their own and were so dissatisfied with things.

I learned new things from him about the weird way Powell and Co. operated. He had been given the job before the rest of the board had heard of him and when the whole board was to see John Maud [now Lord Redcliffe Maud and then at the ministry of food]. Foot had had awful rows with them. I told him he ought to get in first with an organization chart and a memorandum about organization and devolution and such like.

Letter from Sir William Haley, 2 May 1947
On the all important matter there is little new . . . I saw Listowel at Lady Reading's house last night and gave him my views without any reserve. I hope it will do some good. The longer this goes on the more I am convinced that it is quintessentially right. Since I first heard of the vacancy I have never had a second's doubt, only increasingly ardent hopes.

23 May 1947 No word about the BBC. Surely must mean that I am out again.

24 May 1947 (*Whit Sunday*) After supper the bell rang and I saw from the pantry that it was Haley. I knew by his coming at all and by his manner that someone else had been chosen as chairman of the BBC. He didn't say who but it was someone who, failing me he said, was all right. I knew I should not have been at all exalted, if the job had been offered to me, but I certainly would have taken it; and I knew that I should be terribly cast down if it were not. The last straw it seemed; and that is how I do feel. It wasn't just a 'job' that might be offered and wasn't, like so many others. It was in a class by itself. I feel I absolutely *must* get away from this country.

4 June 1947 It is Simon of Wythenshawe [to become chairman of the BBC], exactly as I had expected. Letter from Haley saying my pre-science was uncanny. Long letter, very nice.

Letter from Sir William Haley, 4 June 1947
On a day which must occasion you some bitter reflections I want to write to you, if I may, as a friend. No matter of words can, of course, take away the lingering hurt of the disappointment and I will not attempt to do so. Nor, in view of all that might have been, can one remove the feeling of opportunity wasted. But having admitted these things, other facts remain.

The first is that nothing can take away your achievement . . . Your conception of what broadcasting should do was one of the great socio-logical and educational acts of all time.

The second is that this sense is most alive in the place where it is most to be valued, in the BBC itself . . . The feeling is not confined to your old colleagues. It is the driving force of the great body of us who never had the privilege of working with you . . . Today if the BBC does not house John Reith in body it does in spirit.

To ask the other man to take the long view is always easy. But both in history and in life it is the long view that counts . . . There must come other work for you to do. A nation even in the most vigorous health could not afford to let lie waste your powers. A country as sore beset as we are must sooner or later again call on them to their full extent. It is unthinkable that there should remain unextended one of the greatest capacities of our time.

16 June 1947 Lunched with Haley at Claridges. Usual sort of talk. He seems genuinely and urgently anxious that I should be on good terms with the BBC. I told him it was very hard on me to have these periodic exciting talks and find myself back in BBC problems again. He was very nice.

20 June 1947 Haley told me about their new national lecture idea; wanted to call them by my name. I don't like this much.

19 July 1947 Haley phoned me about the Reith Lecture business which he is to announce tonight; I don't like it.

1 October 1947 Lunched at Broadcasting House with Haley. I look forward to these meetings and at the same time dread them. Talked till 3.15. I gave him many good ideas for the BBC quarterly and a good many criticisms of programmes, including the announcers and the hawking the microphone about the streets.

6 October 1947 Rang Haley who was to have rung me anyhow to urge me to broadcast on November 9 – from home if I liked – at the beginning of their twenty-fifth anniversary week. I am sure I couldn't.

15 October 1947 Gave Haley lunch at the Dorchester. Talked with him till 3.45 – the Quarterly; the Reith Lecture panel; his party to me in November,[8] my broadcasting. There was no argument about my broadcasting; he accepted my abhorrence of that. As to his dinner to me, I wish I had stopped that when he first mentioned it. All most upsetting. We talked about all sorts of other things, particularly his attitude to and relations with the governors.

23 October 1947 Haley asked me to read the lesson at a special service on November 16 at which Woodward is to preach. I said I would.

27 October 1947 Went to BBC Dramatic show. Marston referred to me from the stage; he was with me in my last show. 'Our beloved director general' – I wished he hadn't, but it was very kind of him. Went behind afterwards and then to Broadcasting House with Snagge[9] where we had a long talk about announcers and such like.

[On 30 October the chairman of the BBC wrote to John Reith asking him to dine with the Governors as part of the BBC's Silver Jubilee celebrations on 11 November.]

4 November 1947 Wrote yesterday accepting BBC governor's dinner invitation. Simon of Wythenshawe rang this morning to say he hoped I was coming – wanted to keep in close touch etc.

11 November 1947 Governors' BBC dinner – in Broadcasting House *vice* Claridges owing to strikes. I felt disgusted at their doing it in this scudgy way. They should have had a big party with, I should have thought, the prime minister. They wouldn't have done even what they did but for Haley's suggestion. Dinner was in the Council chamber, most uncomfortable. No formality. Talk mostly about their trying to get a monopoly for television. Simon of Wythenshawe told me he had offered to do some job for Attlee; nothing came of it; then he joined the Labour party, was made a lord and given the BBC.

John Reith's message to the BBC, 14 November 1947

I am glad that your director general has brought me into touch with the BBC again and that old contacts are being renewed. I should like, therefore, to send a special message of greeting to those who served with me in the first sixteen years, particularly in the early pioneering days. The foundations that then were laid have carried all the load that later years required of them. And that should give us pleasure.

16 November 1947 [Sunday] We had to get up at 6.30 and left at 8.15 for Broadcasting House – an awful bore. Read *Romans* X, 9–18 and *Philippians* 4–8. Woodward preached. Too much orchestra in the service. I had to talk to the orchestra afterwards. Coffee in Haley's room with him and wife. Muriel of course hadn't been there since that ghastly day when I hadn't attended the last Board.

19 November 1947 Haley's party for me; he called for me at 6.45. Fifty-four there. Everything very well done. What I said when I spoke was worth a bigger audience. Carpendale and Graves both spoke. Lots of inquiries for Muriel.

31 December 1947 Lunch at Broadcasting House with Haley; I don't really think I want to keep up this contact; does me more harm than good.

[The closing entry for 1947 typifies John Reith's ambivalent attitude towards his renewed contact with the BBC and this dualism in his relationship was to dominate the next twelve months. So he re-remained in contact with Sir William Haley, who treated him always with gentle tact and understanding; he even attended further BBC celebrations in Glasgow and Birmingham; but he was also disapproving of certain programmes and methods.]

19 February 1948 Dinner with Haley at his flat. Uncomfortable of course. Talked about regionalism. Dinwiddie [BBC controller for Scotland] has bullied me into agreeing to go to Glasgow on March 5.

5/6 March 1948 Haley and Mrs collected Muriel and then me. 11.35 p.m. to Glasgow; good night but train one and a half hours late. Fine weather. Lord Provost's lunch at which I was made to speak. Muriel and I drove with him to Broadcasting House – a dreadful business there, being made to speak again though I had implored Dinwiddie not to call on me. Tea with the fifteen-year-olds [i.e. the senior serving BBC staff]. Very tired. Hour and a half rest then dinner jacket (tie forgotten but Dinwiddie and the hotel manager produced some) and 'staff floor show' 7.30 till midnight. Awful.

16 April 1948 Awfully disgusted at having to go to Birmingham. Collected by Nicolls at 1.50. Then to collect the Haleys, then home where Muriel (looking very nice) had coffee ready. Left at 3.30 and arrived in Birmingham at 6.00. Sunshine and some nice scenery but Birmingham is an awful place. We went to the BBC office – still the dreadful ones I knew. Having trailed up two flights we found Edgar and everyone else gone. My photograph was on Edgar's table still. Eventually got to the Midland Hotel, by the back door. The whole thing was second rate and badly managed. I managed to get out of speaking. We had to go on to a Lord Mayor's party which I didn't like at all. Home at 1.30.

20 May 1948 Lunched with Haley and was thoroughly wretched there. I don't want to go there any more.

> [Lord Simon of Wythenshawe also did his best at this time to woo John Reith on behalf of the BBC. At the end of May he wrote to say that he was having Reith asked to a series of sherry parties which the governors were giving to 'the senior staff in all the various sections of the BBC'. Then, in June, he invited him to dinner but though he went, he was not to be won.]

18 June 1948 Charabanc [with Commonwealth Communications Council delegates] to BBC for lunch. I had fixed the seating. Quite good. The CCC gave Lady Reading a lift in its charabanc afterwards and she told me she was much concerned about the chairman [Lord Simon of Wythenshawe] – crashing about. One of his latest ideas was that his governors should each have special oversight of a region. Most outspoken she was.

25 June 1948 Dinner with Haley at the Club and talked on the verandah till 10.50. It was mostly about his relations with Simon. I gave him very good advice on various matters for which I think he was grateful. He seems to have some affection for me.

15 July 1948 Haley came to tell me about the situation as to television and cinema. Ridiculous muddle. He wanted me to know all about it and to be able to comment as the consequences might be very serious.

14 August 1948 [On holiday in Scotland] Almost every night I dream that I am in the BBC again. Absolutely sickening.

2 September 1948 [On the way home] I am thankful that we shall be home tomorrow night. I have continued with bad nights and of course dreams about being back in the BBC.

18 November 1948 I am feeling awfully anti-BBC and very fed up with Haley and with everybody. There was a war memorial unveiling this evening to which all the crooks of old – Duff Cooper, Bracken, Foot etc. were asked. Insult to ask me too. I had declined without knowing of the others.

15 December 1948 Wrote to Haley saying I couldn't go on with a superficial and intermittent involvement in BBC affairs.

26 December 1948 Listened to the first 'Reith Lecture' by Bertrand Russell, forsooth. He went far too quickly and has a bad voice anyhow. And it was actually recorded which depreciated its value greatly. However, I wrote him a civil note which is more than Mr Romanes or Mr Rede could do.[10]

29 December 1948 I am feeling sick of the BBC and all its works – somewhat softened by a nice and very long letter from Haley this evening.

Letter from Sir William Haley, 28 December 1948
. . . I have derived real help from you. And while I can understand your feeling that because by the very nature of your work you once knew everything down to the smallest detail you are now conscious of

John Reith as Lord High Commissioner addressing the Assembly of
the Church of Scotland, May 1967

John Reith as Lord High Commissioner (John Knox looks on),
May 1968

all you do not know, I do wish you to appreciate that I *have* derived great help from you, that I should be distressed if because of your dissatisfaction we were to grow apart, and that I shall always value and seek to foster our association.

. . . [referring to a review in the *Listener* to which John Reith had taken exception] Here, I suppose, I am a greater believer [than you are] in editorial independence. All my life I have been brought up to the idea that in all matters of day to day judgement the editor should be trusted implicitly and that only in the event of a succession of misjudgements [or disagreements about judgement] did one act, in which case you chose a new editor because you could trust the old one no longer. I still think it is the right idea. It must lead to what one feels are odd happenings at times, but the gain is far greater than the loss.

I think, incidentally, that some of the same difference in approach lies at the root of your feeling about our programme policy at present. There are things I do not like; I seek to eradicate them by general influence, guidance, and progress, reserving the individual ukase for the really objectionable. I am satisfied the standards are being reestablished and the programmes steadily being raised. But I seek to achieve this by working on the whole rather than on the parts.

[During 1949/50 John Reith's contacts with the BBC became happier and more constructive once again. The reason for this, apart from Sir William Haley's personal sympathy, was the challenge of the committee of inquiry which the Labour government appointed under Lord Beveridge to consider the future of broadcasting in Britain. Reith and Haley had discussed the need to prepare for an inquiry of this sort as early as March 1947. Now they worked together in close association. For, while John Reith might criticize programme policy or internal organization within the BBC, he was determined to defend its monopoly and its independence from any attack from without.]

30 January 1949 Wrote to Haley in reply to his of December 28. His saying that he worked on the whole rather than on parts is very feeble since it is only by his commenting on parts that people can synthetize into the whole he says he wants. I permitted myself a cynical PS about the Tommy Handley[11] funeral orgies – roads blocked and the crematorium swamped; a special service in St Paul's conducted by the Bishop of London and mobs outside. A sociological comment on the age. Dreadful.

R.D.–2G

8 February 1949 Haley came at 6.20 and was here till 7.50. Three things to talk about: (1) Would I bring him and Iremonger [Dean of Lichfield, former head of BBC religious broadcasting] together; (2) Would I explain whole inquiry committee procedure; and (3) What exactly did chairmen do in my time. As to the third, Simon is interviewing people all day and every day – utter nonentities like the *Daily Mirror* radio correspondent. Haley wants to have it out with him.

Letter from Sir William Haley, 10 February 1949
   I agree the whole will come right only as the parts come right but the important thing is who is going to put the parts right. I feel it should be the programme people themselves acting under the stimulus of a steady influence. They must see of their own volition what is wrong. Then they will not be so likely to go wrong again.

23 May 1949 Lunched with Haley at the club; don't like lunching there but hadn't thought in time that I might go to Broadcasting House. Talked about the inquiry committee and the possibility of my being put on the board at the end of this year.

1 June 1949 Received BBC memorandum of evidence to inquiry committee. Haley rang. He is very sorry that Radcliffe cannot be chairman. I thought he never should have been appointed.

20 July 1949 [John Reith's sixtieth birthday]. Lunch in Broadcasting House to which I wasn't at all looking forward, but it would have been ungracious to refuse. It was in a tower room now used for such purposes and very well rigged. Haley made an extraordinarily kind speech about me – most moving. I was hopelessly confused and embarrassed in replying. They gave me a signed book.

   [As the moment for Sir William Haley to give evidence to the Beveridge committee of inquiry drew near John Reith urged again his view, first put forward more than two years earlier, that the BBC should mount a public campaign in its own interest under the supervision of a public relations officer. Haley was troubled by the practical difficulties involved in this.]

Letter from Sir William Haley, 9 September 1949
   I am sure your experience is right in this matter. But so far as I personally am concerned I find a large gap between planning the kind of campaign you mention and the process of day by day actually carry-

ing it out. There are some people who have a gift for the manipulation of other people. I am afraid I have little.

. . . I know you will say this leads all the more forcibly to the argument in favour of a good public relations man. But what is the answer to this triple dilemma (if that isn't a solecism):

(a) If such a man is to carry any weight with people who matter he must himself be a man of almost equal weight with them;

(b) If you told me of such a man I would have to put him right in the top rank of directors and I believe that has serious dangers to programme policy and purpose;

(c) If I don't get such a man and if I don't put him in the top rank, I am just adding one more to what I believe are on the whole a pretty ineffectual brigade.

. . . What I think it all comes to is this: I see the force of the argument for the kind of PRO you have in mind but I don't in fact think so high-powered a figure can be good for the BBC as a PRO.

. . . We have now got through the final batch of Beveridge committee papers . . . Would it interest you to glance through them? . . . I would value an evening with you if you can spare one.

17 September 1949 Haley's car at 9.00 and to his house at Hampton and then home by 12.45. He had sent me several special papers for the inquiry committee and I had read them all last night. Made several suggestions for improvement. He also questioned me closely about several organizational principles of mine – especially the proper reestablishment of the old 'executive' system. I told him what I did as between creative and business, getting men to rely on, clearly understanding what was required of them. He is obviously worried about uneconomic expenditures – especially in television.

Letter from Sir William Haley, 25 October 1949

. . . There is a steady recapturing in the BBC of the old traditions, and I think it will strengthen and accelerate. And it is because that is so that the two birthday lunches[12] have seemed so natural and in keeping. People, that is your people, are feeling at home once more; that is why it gives them such a genuine lift of the heart to see you about the place.

3 November 1949 Muriel and I went to the BBC amateur dramatic show at the Fortune Theatre. I went because Wade and Snagge and company so much wanted it; but I was tired and bored. The three plays were very good indeed. They had wanted me to go and make a speech on the stage.

Letter from Sir William Haley, 26 November 1949

I have been thinking over what you said last night [at the BBC Club's twenty-fifth anniversary dance at Earl's Court]. I do think that one of your greatest services was the type of men you brought into the BBC who really are in their loyalty, devotion and competence, the salt of the earth – they are the real riches you stored up for the BBC. And there is nothing more pleasing – because there could be nothing more just – than the strong feelings they still all have for you . . . 'Sir John *is* coming,' one of the old hands said to me when we arrived at Earl's Court. If you could have heard the ring in his voice as he said it, you wouldn't ever talk of the BBC being a Pyrrhic achievement . . . I keep thinking about the year ahead for in it so much will be decided for the BBC. Surely at last our foundations will be secured for a reasonably long time to come and we shall be allowed, undistracted and with our whole attentions really free, to concentrate on the work, to re-vivify and to re-build. We have never been free to do this these last six years. One cannot say that they have been six years that were wasted, but they have been years when so much has had to be slowed up that might have gone quicker, when so much that should have carried conviction and assurance has had to carry the ghost of a question mark. The disturbing influence seeps everywhere; regions (that is the people in them outside the BBC) wonder if they cannot get more of the spoils; television (some of them inside the BBC, alas) wonder if they cannot create an Empire of their own; the crooks and the cranks come out of their holes into the hospitable columns of the newspapers; even the well-wishers become amateur constitution makers. And it all takes up so much time.

[In December 1949 Lord Beveridge invited John Reith to give evidence to his broadcasting committee. Reith accepted at once and a date was fixed for February 1950 'subject to the risk of being displaced by a General Election'. As, in fact, the election was held in February it was not until April that he appeared before the committee. Meanwhile, early in February, Sir William Haley had had to enter the London Clinic for an operation. John Reith was deeply concerned. Fortunately, Haley made a quick recovery and they were soon in correspondence again, by now, as Reith noted with satisfaction 'on Christian name terms at last'.]

Letter from Sir William Haley, 14 March 1950

I do hope you will make up your mind to go [i.e. to the Beveridge committee]. Your voice about what the BBC created by you stands for and the vital need to preserve the constructive moral purpose in broadcasting is bound to be most powerful. And I think you owe it to the band of pioneers you collected who are still here and those of us who are, with them, trying to re-build the tradition. The BBC needs your help. You can't deny *that* call.

Letter from Sir William Haley, 29 March 1950

Beveridge is now reaching what I hope is the final flurry. I have just finished a batch of fifty-one papers sent to us by the committee for observation and comment.

19 April 1950 I went to Town and had over two hours with the Beveridge broadcasting committee. Beveridge had the courtesy to come out and fetch me in. Quite interesting; very hard work and rather harrowing of course.

Letter from Sir William Haley, 25 April 1950

It will be a relief to be rid of Beveridge. I do envy you your early days, when it is true you had to fight every inch of the way, but you could feel a fundamental continuity and security for what you were doing.

I think the real battle will centre round whether we keep television or not. A good deal of private lobbying of MPs is going on about this. And some people are being very assiduous in putting stories about. I hope they will shoot their bolt too soon. Personally, if the monopoly were to be destroyed, I would prefer it to be replaced by bodies doing both sound and television than by divorced services. For I am sure that sound and television will to a large extent come together into one programme in the end.

21 May 1950 We went to the Haleys' at Hampton arriving at 1.00 and leaving at 4.45. Haley and I talked for an hour or so; nothing special except that he has won a victory over Simon who had tried to resurrect a paper limiting the DG's functions got out for the benefit of Foot. He said he was sure that they would need a television man on the management committee, which I think wholly and dangerously wrong.

1 June 1950 Lunched with Haley and talked about organization: he is dreadfully muddled; says himself he only knows about a small newspaper office. I said I could see some rationality in a management board composed of service general managers and functionalism somewhere below, but not in the present mix-up of regional and functional. Also told me that the lord chairman [i.e. Lord Simon of Wythenshawe] is trying to get the Whitley paper [about governors and DG] abolished. I had a specially trying dream last night about being back in the BBC.

17/21/22 June 1950 [17] Really worked on the BBC memorandum this morning; typed it after lunch.

[21] Got the BBC memo: considerably improved; Haley had suggested a few things and I altered many more.

[22] Got the BBC memo off to Beveridge; Haley was very pleased with it.

A note on some of the major issues for the Broadcasting Committee
21 June 1950 [Extracts]

. . . If the initiative passes from the BBC, if the decline in serious listening is not arrested, it will be very unfortunate.

I do not suggest that nothing other than 'output benefit' matters; nor that any means to that end are justified. But I do think output benefit matters most; matters so much as to justify some adjustment of attitude, some compromise and tolerance as to some of the means involved in its fulfilment.

Monopoly. It was the brute force of monopoly that enabled the BBC to become what it did; and to do what it did; that made possible a policy in which moral responsibility – moral in the broadest way; intellectual and ethical – ranked high. If there is to be competition it will be of cheapness not of goodness. There is no reality in the moral disadvantages and dangers of monopoly as applied to Broadcasting, it is in fact a potent incentive. Incidentally, if there ever were competing concerns, the restriction of any one of them to sound broadcasting would surely be unnatural as well as uneconomic and unfair.

Charter term. A fifteen or twenty year term would be very welcome; great disruption attends an inquiry.

Assessment of listener opinion. Listener research on the scale and system now in operation is a waste of time and money; its results are unreliable and misleading; it is inevitably a drag down; it causes producers to look to itself for criteria of success; for the last two reasons it is wholly subversive. But listener opinion must have a place; and however assessed – and there are many ways – there should be adequate representation of it on high level at headquarters and in the Regions.

Regions. The Regions have a contribution to make; they should have adequate opportunity to make it. But the criterion should be interest and merit, not vague assessments of what, in quantity, should be justifiable. There is too much regional material at present; the cause of regionalism would positively gain from its reduction.

Governors and Director General. Public corporation boards vary – some part-time 'trustee' as in the BBC, some full-time and executive, some half and half. I feel that the BBC system is probably the most satisfactory in general, and that it certainly is so for broadcasting. But an executive board of governors is a possibility; at least it makes sense even if not the best sense. I do not think it can be half trustee and half executive. So I hope the Whitley paper will be preserved [with 'the sort of functioning thereby envisaged'] . . . The governors should *de jure* have all the authority and responsibility; the director general nothing *de jure* but as much as possible *de facto*.

Conclusion. It is in terms of moral effect that the influence of broadcasting will eventually be judged – whether more harm than good. To this end the Corporation must not shrink from clear leadership and decision in the formulation of programme policy and in its prosecution; must be helped and encouraged thereto. This means that the committee may be willing to condone, indeed approve and recommend, what otherwise they might dislike as out of phase with modern practice and trend. But deliberately; for a special and high purpose; one of immeasurable significance to the country.

27 July 1950 [On holiday in Scotland] Letter from Beveridge yesterday about my note to his committee; quite good; and he wants to see me again.

23/24 August 1950 [23] Lunched with Lord Beveridge and talked about various matters of his BBC report.

[24] Lunched with Haley and talked at home 2.30 till 7.15. I told him of my talk with Beveridge yesterday. Also talked BBC organization and then his assurance that I was to do some big work and must be in the mood for it – serene of mind now. All very impressive.

5 October 1950 Haley rang; there is apparently a tremendous row on about the cancellation of a play because it was anti-government. It was

Simon's doing against Haley's strong advice. He thinks that the governors will have learned a lesson and that it was worthwhile.

19 October 1950 Letter from Lord Simon of Wythenshawe this morning asking me to a party he was giving to governors and earlier governors and a PS about wanting me to talk to him about the cancellation of the play. I went and was there for an hour. I told Simon there were three points:

(1) Whether the play should have been permitted;

(2) Whether the chairman should ever have to override the director general on a matter like this; and

(3) Whether it should have been cancelled – irrespective of other considerations – after the appearance of an attack in a newspaper.

I said straightly what I thought on each. Later on he asked if I thought he had damaged the BBC. Yes. Later still, after he had said he didn't really think he had been motivated by party political views, I said he had acted wrongly, not evilly but stupidly.

6 November 1950 Dinner with I. A. R. Stedeford[13] at the Athenæum and talked from 6.45 till 10.00 about BBC affairs. The Beveridge committee report should be out by the end of the year. I got from him most of the important recommendations. Simon has been working on Beveridge to get the chairman's position improved, which it doesn't need at all, and my suspicion is that Beveridge wants to succeed Simon as chairman. Wicked this would be.

[Although Lord Beveridge asked John Reith in November 1950 to comment on certain historical paragraphs in the report, which Reith gladly did, it was not until early in 1951 that the report itself was published. There were recommendations in it with which John Reith profoundly disagreed and when Herbert Morrison, then still lord president of the Council in Attlee's second administration, asked him for his comments he was able to develop his case supported by 'a most moving letter' from Sir William Haley. It seemed at first as if their views had prevailed. In April he heard that the objectionable recommendations were to be disregarded. Then, in July, a government White Paper was issued including some of them. But before any action could be taken the Labour government fell. The new Conservative administration established a cabinet committee to consider the whole broadcasting scene, and by the early summer of 1952 it was clear that the Conservatives intended to make possible a break in the BBC's monopoly in respect of television. John Reith was outraged and said so in the House of Lords and in the Press. To no avail. To add to his discomfiture, Sir William Haley was appointed Editor of *The Times*. John Reith was delighted for his friend but greatly disturbed for the BBC. It was the start of his second long period of separation from the BBC and broadcasting in general.]

18 January 1951 Beveridge report out and utterly fantastic suggestions in it; position of director general is made into that of a secretary-general – or head clerk as Haley said.

22 January 1951 Dinner with Haley at Broadcasting House. I convinced him that he was all wrong in thinking that the paragraph on the director general was so dreadful. It only says what was said in 1925 – that the governors should be in the foreground, not the director general; that he ought to accept that; that the position of the director general is not 'laid flat' by this, as he said, but by the monstrous practical suggestions that are made.

23 January 1951 Letter from Herbert Morrison asking for my comments on Beveridge's tripe.

Notes on Beveridge Committee's Report sent to Mr Herbert Morrison *31 January 1951* [Extracts]

The Chairman seems to have had two objectives:
(1) to produce a BEVERIDGE report;
(2) to uncover abuses.
He had a personal motivation; was prejudiced.

To him, as an academic, the monopoly was anathema; that anyhow had to be broken.

Soon he found himself beaten on the monopoly issue; but there are long pages of effort to excuse and justify. And after all, no abuses to uncover. Seldom such travailing of the mountain.

Unfortunately the report does not leave it at that; there are specific recommendations deriving from the failure to disrupt the monopoly; expedients to take the sting out of monopoly.

They are:
(1) regional commissions;
(2) charging of individual governors with special responsibilities – in particular for overseas services;

(3) the special position of the new public representation director;
(4) public showing of television.

These are lethal safeguards against hypothetical monopolistic abuse; they would eventually destroy the purpose and justification of the monopoly – the exploitation of broadcasting as an integrated service to the maximum advantage.

. . . The Whitley document is to be abolished; I think that unfortunate; it was not devised to strengthen the director general's position at the expense of the governors', it was devised to avoid trouble of a sort that had seriously threatened. A dictatorial director general is not desirable; but he cannot be a dictator since he can be dismissed; since he is under observation by an omnipotent board.

. . . Here now is what it comes to: the position of chief executive has been virtually abolished by the report; anyhow made impossible; in that great office there would in future be found only a harassed corrector-general.

. . . The Third Programme, positively and negatively is objectionable. It is a waste of a precious wavelength; much of its matter is too limited in appeal; the rest should have a wider audience. When overall programme policy and control was abandoned, the Third Programme was introduced as a sop to moral conscience, a sort of safety valve. Odd that this vital issue has been ignored.

It is disappointing that there is no comment on the programmes broadcast on Sundays.

18 April 1951 Lunched at Broadcasting House with Haley. The government's decision about Beveridge's report is very largely satisfactory to the BBC. I shan't have to make a speech in the Lords – for which I am thankful.

[As the external attack on the BBC seemed to be beaten off so John Reith returned to his worries about its programmes. 'I am so unhappy,' he noted on 30 May 1951, 'about so much the BBC puts out.'

Early in June he wrote to Sir William Haley expressing these feelings and once again Haley replied fully and sympathetically.]

Letter from Sir William Haley, 4 June 1951
. . . It seems to me there are two problems:
(1) To differentiate prejudice from principle;
(2) to distinguish means from ends.
Anyone in charge of anything so vital as broadcasting must be doing these two things all the time.

What do I mean by the first? Well, I mean not taking people off the air because one personally disagrees with what they are saying.

. . . I am sure the greatest need of the nation is to keep the greatest freedom of responsible expression. I acknowledge the difficulty of making the true equation between liberty and standards. But I believe the equation can be, and largely is being, made. There are enough critical forces always playing on the BBC for it to know if it were getting the equation wrong.[14] Of course, there will always be things one quite serious person or another will hate. But one of the responsibilities of the BBC seems to me to be to preserve tolerance . . . for me to prevent this or that speaker going on the air because I, or my closest friend, dislike him seems to me to be wrong. If there is a broad consensus of opinion in all serious and responsible quarters in the land, then that is another matter.

. . . I believe one of the greatest safeguards to the BBC is that while serious-minded opinion knows we will uphold moral values, fight for all that is best in our western way of life, and seek to use broadcasting to raise public taste and not to lower it, it also knows we will not seek to do these things in an authoritarian or Draconian spirit; that we will realize reasonable liberty of opinion and conduct is part of that very western way of life we are defending.

. . . All the internal pressures from the top in the BBC are one-way, towards raising taste. But they seek to make people act from conviction, not from ordinance.

That brings me to the second point, the distinguishing of means from ends. Do not please ever doubt my ends. I am as anxious to have as high and serious and moral a system of broadcasting in this country as you are. But I seek to do it within the concept of an agreed serious body of opinion, both inside and outside the BBC, and not by means of purely personal predilection or ukase. I think it can be done. I think it is how you yourself would do it if you were here now.

11 July 1951 The government issued a White Paper on the BBC yesterday; Haley sent me a copy with a note of his views. There are actually to be the regional commissions after all; and fifteen per cent of the BBC's income is to be docked. I should have been sickened and infuriated if I had had anything to do with it.

[John Reith now had to make up his mind whether to speak against the White Paper recommendations in the House of Lords. After much brooding, he put himself down and then decided at the last moment not to speak. His dilemma was that while he disapproved the Labour government's proposals, he suspected the Conservative opposition's motives.]

25 July 1951 An awful day this, and after all no House of Lords speech. I sat in the Lords from 2.35 till 6.15. Woolton led off – superficial, patronizing, hollow; I was thoroughly disgusted with him. I had put myself down to speak at the end but left.

[After his summer holiday John Reith reverted to his programme worries, but the change of government in the autumn soon brought him back to general broadcasting policy.]

28 September 1951 The Third Programme is having a fifth anniversary and I was *very* disgusted by a *Times* leader this morning. It might be that my views and my doings over broadcasting will be completely distorted in future because I don't approve of the Third Programme – for the very reason that its adherents would most approve, if they understood it.

1 October 1951 Wrote to Haley about the Third Programme racket.

Letter from Sir William Haley, 2 October 1951
. . . I must honestly say that I think you read into *The Times* leader things that are not only not there, but not even thought of or intended . . .

What it seems to me *The Times* man was saying was that as broadcasting is now, it would be incomplete without the Third Programme It is perhaps a superficial point, because in fact nothing is ever complete. And even without the Third Programme there would be more than enough in the Home Service and indeed in the Light Programme to keep the BBC above the level of the cinema.

But I think it is fair to make two points. When I took over in 1944 (and even more in 1945 when people's minds began to turn away from the war to other things) the BBC did not have any longer *The Times* circulation among its audience. They wanted nothing of what we had to offer except perhaps the news bulletins. The two great universities had grown unconscious of us. They neither listened nor, in the main, contributed to our programmes . . .

You may not have agreed – indeed you have all along been very frank that you don't – with my remedy to this particular problem. I do not myself think any other remedy would have put right *that* state of affairs so quickly. I do not believe the climate of opinion in those post-war years would have allowed the BBC to carry through so large an influx of high and serious material into the existing programme compass. And when I say public opinion I am not thinking of the penny press – as it then was – or listener research, but of Parliament itself and influential, responsible opinion. So in came the Third Programme. And frankly, in came into broadcasting things that had not been there before. There can be two views whether they are desirable or not; whether they have a large enough audience to sustain them or not. But just as the years 1938-44 had appallingly extended the range at the lower end of the scale, I think it is fair to claim that 1944–50 has seen it extended at the other . . . We *have* cleared out a good deal of that lower end. We have doubled the serious content of the Light Programme. And we are all the time trying to carry on the process while keeping listeners away from sponsored radio elsewhere.

6 October 1951 Wrote to Haley in reply to his; the fact remains that the standards on the Home and Light programmes are nothing to what they should be; and he either doesn't mind or just isn't able to give the necessary orders to bring things right. On the whole I think the major trouble is his not caring to 'interfere' with his subordinates.

[A general election was held at the end of October and the Labour government was replaced by a Conservative one. John Reith now hoped to influence the new government's thinking on the problems of broadcasting.]

5 December 1951 Balfour of Burleigh rang last night to say that he had seen Salisbury as promised and that I would find things as I hoped; and that Salisbury would be asking me to come and see him soon. This meant that Salisbury would be chairman of the Cabinet committee to recommend about the BBC and not Woolton as we had feared. I rang Haley and he was very pleased. Tonight he rang to say I had been entirely right about the committee being appointed soon and getting to work; Lord Simon had heard today that this was so. Salisbury, chairman, Woolton, Maxwell Fyfe, James Stuart and the postmaster general.[15] Very good.

Letter from Sir William Haley, 27 January 1952
. . . I do not regard the talks we have as jocular or light-hearted where the BBC is concerned. To me they are one of the most valuable

and vital parts of the inner process of trying to discern not only one's duty but the true way to discharge it.

28 January 1952 Saw Lord Salisbury for about an hour at his request about what is to be done with the BBC. Interesting but not very impressive.

16 February 1952 Haley here 3.00 till 5.45 to consult about Salisbury's committee which he is to see on Monday. [i.e. 18 Feb.] His worst worry is about the film people and television.

[In March Lord Halifax wrote to *The Times* to deplore the 'disturb‐ ing rumours' that the new government was planning to break the BBC's monopoly, apparently in the belief that 'better broadcasting will be provided by competition' although, as Halifax wrote, this belief was 'against all the evidence we have'. John Reith was pleased that the BBC should have this support but could not stop himself from complaining that Halifax had not included any commendation of his personal part in the development of British broadcasting but had attributed its excellence to 'gradual growth' under the guidance of Parliament and public. Sir William Haley begged him to see things in better perspective.]

Letter from Sir William Haley, 24 March 1952
. . . If there were any question, or had ever been any question, of all you did in creating and inspiring the BBC being fully acknowledged I could understand your being hurt by some particular omission. But this is just not so. Your work has been acknowledged time and time again . . . It will be referred to in more ways than one can imagine and by more people than one can conjecture for a generation and more to come . . . But there are bound to be occasions when achievements are not specifically referred to because knowledge of them is taken for granted. That you should feel hurt on such occasions distresses me very much . . . because it springs from an unhappiness really based elsewhere, something not really in the BBC, or in your relations with the BBC, but in yourself . . . I just feel that someone serene would not worry about such things, but would regard them of small moment against the great perspective of life.

29 March 1952 I wrote a long letter in reply to W. Haley and I think I made my point of view clear to him; my disgust at this toadying to the Mother of Abominations [i.e. Parliament].

15 April 1952 M. Nicholson from lord president's office to see me, and I got a lot out of him about the BBC White Paper. It seems there was an utterly contemptible flapping about; he said Salisbury began it, but now things have come out reasonably well but with a lot of irritating stuff in the document that can be read in different ways – real politicians' jiggery-pokery – door left open to advertising, regional chairmen and boards, and lots more.

20 April 1952 [*Sunday*] Muriel and I went to Cherry Cottage, Prestwood – C. R. Attlee and Mrs for tea. He said he didn't think they would break the BBC monopoly; I said I thought they would as it was Woolton who was in charge. He said Woolton used to come to him during the war saying he found it 'very difficult to work with these Tories'.

[It was at this moment that the first approaches were made to Sir William Haley to become the Editor of *The Times*.]

25 April 1952 Lunched with Haley in the Lords, talking till 3 o'clock. The Cabinet yesterday didn't deal with the BBC at all – shocking it is. Haley did not know this; nobody had thought to tell him, which is very bad. I asked him if he had nothing at all on his conscience about the smash up of the BBC – which looks like coming; and went over the main issues I have with him – the lack of programme policy or control, and the failure to plan as for a military campaign against the present troubles. But we spoke of *The Times* job mostly; I said it was *sui generis* in the world, and whether the BBC director generalship was at nadir or zenith, I could not imagine his hesitating. He of course emphasized the uncertainties and frustrations attending on the BBC job, deriving from the unknown governors.

29 April 1952 Lunched with Pakenham [later Lord Longford] at House of Lords. Salisbury spoke to me afterwards about the BBC – said he thought the White Paper would be out in two to three weeks, and he would let me know as soon as possible; thought my debate should be on the same day as the House of Commons one. I said I would give way if the government would prefer to make the debate themselves, but he didn't think so.

13 May 1952 Tea with PMG [Lord De la Warr] in House of Lords. He gave me the White Paper to read. It is as expected – *de jure* sponsored television, *de facto* none; a clever but really contemptible sort of compromise. De la Warr said he regretted it; later Salisbury implicitly likewise. Trying to arrange that I should have my motion debated on 22nd.

14 May 1952 From 2.50 to 4.20 with Salisbury, De la Warr and others on the broadcasting debate. Having said last night that they didn't want to introduce the debate, they now do – partly to prevent Woolton speaking, De la Warr having the right to reply if he initiates, but more I think to obviate my having a division. They are obviously frightened of what might come of a motion by me.

Eventually decided that they couldn't introduce a motion without asking approval which of course they don't want to do ahead of the Commons.

[John Reith was thus left to take the lead in defending the BBC's monopoly in the House of Lords which he did with passionate sincerity. The debate spread over two days and he met with wide support, notably from Lord Halifax. But the government was not to be shaken. Lord Simonds made this plain when winding up the debate as lord chancellor. He castigated Reith and his supporters for their 'holier than thou' attitude and he called on the peers, with unconscious irony, to 'trust the people'. Even before he heard this speech, John Reith had swallowed his pride and appealed to the prime minister, his *bête-noire*, Winston Churchill, to be allowed to make his case in person. There was no reply for several weeks. Impatient, as always, Reith returned to the attack with an article in the *Observer*, this time aimed at the Conservative party as a whole and at the lord chancellor in particular. Churchill now replied with icy dignity rejecting Reith's appeal for an interview. The game was lost.]

19/21 May 1952 [19] Worked all night at my House of Lords speech for Thursday [22nd] on broadcasting. Vastly relieved to have it done.

[21] I told the Archbishop of York [Cyril Garbett] that it would be dreadful if nobody spoke for the Church of England, so he hunted up the Bishop of Sheffield; it is Ascension Day tomorrow, which makes it difficult for bishops.

22/23 May 1952 [22] Lunch in House of Lords. I spoke for twenty-eight minutes; it certainly was listened to and I had many congratulations.

[23] Walter Monckton congratulated me on my speech; said he

Sir Gerald Kelly's portrait of Reith for the BBC, 1967

John Reith filming *Lord Reith Looks Back*, February 1967

didn't agree with the White Paper (he is a member of the Cabinet) and that the Leader of the House of Commons [H. F. C. Crookshank] didn't either.

Letter to the Prime Minister [Winston Churchill] 25 May 1952
There is a general and a particular purpose in this note.

The general is to remind you that I am still around; busy but ready to be a lot busier.

The particular is the White Paper on broadcasting.

I do not suppose you can have read what I said in the Lords last Thursday; and more important is what Halifax said:

(a) if I were to divide the House (which he was glad I was not to do) he would have voted with me;

(b) he thought the government decision 'profoundly wrong';

(c) he was 'profoundly sorry' it was his party which had made it.

I am sure, from every point of view, that there should be second thoughts.

Perhaps you will ask me to come and see you sometime; the last occasion was ten and a half years ago.

26 May 1952 Sat in the House of Lords from 2.30 till 7.15. Some of the speakers were utterly revolting. And the lord chancellor was shocking also – talking like a socialist on the hunt for votes about liberty and Milton's *Areopagitica* and all. Very tired and *very, very disgusted*.

29 May 1952 William Haley to see me, 10.30 to 11.45. He had rung up yesterday to say 'the egg had been officially laid' and that he would like to see me as soon as possible. It was the editorship of *The Times* of course – which I had astounded him on three occasions by forecasting. He had much to say about the BBC and himself. He thought though he might in time have brought the BBC back to what it was in my time without television, television would beat him. I told him (what I had said before) that I couldn't imagine his hesitating. Gosh, how lucky he is. I greatly appreciated his coming to talk to me about it.

11 June 1952 In the House of Commons 3.15 till 6.00 – BBC sponsoring debate – wretched affair.

12 June 1952 I worked till 4.45 a.m. mostly reading Hansard and drafting a short article for the *Observer* about sponsored broadcasting.

R.D.–2H

15/17 June 1952 [15] Article in *Observer*[16] seemed all right; main feature it was.

[17] Many letters about my *Observer* article, but I don't suppose the Tories will let that go without reprisals.

Letter from the Prime Minister [Winston Churchill] 20 June 1952

I have now found time to read both your speech in the House of Lords and the article you wrote in the *Observer* on Sunday, June 15. In view of these I cannot feel that an interview between us would be useful at the present time.

Letter to the Prime Minister [Winston Churchill] 7 July 1952

I am sorry.

I had done all I could before the Lords' speech [with Salisbury and De la Warr] to avoid having to speak at all; or if I did, to make suggestions they might take up.

I wrote you immediately after the Lords debate; and nearly three weeks passed between that writing and the Commons' debate, without sign from you.

I enormously hoped the government attitude might be modified before the Commons' debate, and was ready to help in any way.

But I felt deeply on the matter; and as there was no change, and still no sign from you, I wrote the June 15 article.

I really am sorry about your last sentence.

3. Separation again, 1952–9

[John Reith's reassociation with broadcasting and the BBC had in large measure been the personal achievement of Sir William Haley and naturally his departure as director general removed the most important bond between Reith and the BBC. This situation was later to be made worse by his disillusion at the political defeat over the preservation of the BBC's monopoly. So, it seemed to John Reith in the summer of 1952 that much would turn on two new appointments, one, to be made by the government, of the new chairman of the BBC in succession to Lord Simon of Wythenshawe whose term had just expired, and the other, to be made by the governors of the BBC, of Haley's successor as director general. In the event he was bitterly disappointed by both. The government chose for the first Sir Alexander Cadogan, a man whom Reith came later to respect and love but who at this time, as a retired diplomat, seemed to typify that subordination of the BBC to government influence of which he particularly disapproved. Just as in 1938 he had opposed the appointment of a civil servant as director general, so now he deplored the government inserting into the vacant chairmanship someone whom he feared would be the catspaw of Whitehall. Then the BBC governors appointed as their new director general, Sir Ian Jacob, a distinguished soldier but a post-war recruit to overseas broadcasting and not one of Reith's own men. Both chairman and director general made friendly advances before the year was out but John Reith would not respond. It is true that his regular meetings with Cadogan on the board of the Phoenix Assurance Company from 1953 onwards laid the grounds for their personal friendship but not for co-operation over broadcasting. So Reith opposed the government's plans for the introduction of independent television at the end of 1953 without any collaboration with Broadcasting House. Sir Ian Jacob, for his part, made further approaches in 1953 and early in 1954, but John Reith saw no common ground between them and broke off contact.

For the next four years John Reith was as much cut off from broadcasting and the BBC as he had been between 1942 and 1945. It was not until the end of 1958 that Sir Arthur fforde, Cadogan's successor as chairman of the BBC, attempted to end this separation and another year was to pass before this was fully to take effect under Sir Ian Jacob's successor as director general Mr (now Sir Hugh) Carleton Greene.]

20 July 1952 Sixty-third birthday. W. J. Haley rang to wish me happy returns and I learned from him that the new BBC chairman was likely to be Cadogan, the retired civil servant. Having been quite ineffective at the Foreign Office he was sent to be UK representative at United Nations; having been quite ineffective there he was brought home, given £5000 p.a. for life from the Suez Canal and the OM – which of course was a bad let-down for the OMs and the first time a civil servant got it. And now the BBC; absolutely *shocking*. Spoke with Clark of the *Observer* and I hope he can start some trouble about this.

[John Reith hoped that Sir Basil Nicolls would be made director general, at least for a year or so, and expressed this view to two of the governors in August. But by the time he returned to London in October, after his tour in Africa the previous month, he learned of Sir Ian Jacob's appointment.]

7 October 1952 Day I was [nearly] killed thirty-seven years ago; a pity.

Lunched with Nicolls in Café Royal. He had heard about the two board meetings since I went away. The opposition [i.e. to Nicolls] had got agreement to Jacob being appointed DG next June and then, of course, procured his immediate release.[17] And Cadogan had said that Haley had put him off consulting me because I was fifteen years out of date.

8 October 1952 Lunched with Haley at Carlton Grill. I asked him if it was consistent or decent that he should have boomed Cadogan off consulting me about Nicolls.

29 October 1952 Lunched with Barnes [BBC director of television]. I said, and with emphasis, what I felt about the standard of output now and that perhaps it was now coming to this – that the BBC no longer deserved its monopoly. In my time it had been deserved in terms of what was done with it. The use was the justification. As there was no longer that use the monopoly might no longer be justified. He is sure commercial television is coming, does not think the BBC can possibly hold its pre-war attitude and wants to lower standards still further to compete with commercial television. Miserable attitude.

11 November 1952 I had a civil note from Sir A. Cadogan, now BBC chairman forsooth, inviting me to a BBC party to mark the thirtieth anniversary of broadcasting and the beginning of a new charter term. I replied, civilly, asking to be excused.

17 December 1952 I went to lunch with Camrose, after trying to get out of it yesterday, enormously regretting it because I just hate this *galère* and felt I had let myself down by going – but I had given my word. Sir A. Cadogan among those there. He came round the table to speak to me at the end. He said he was a humble admirer of my great work. I said there wasn't much of it left. He was sure there was; oh yes. He asked if I knew Jacob; I said No, only met him once or twice casually. He asked, didn't I think it was the right appointment. I said I didn't know; but had they really searched the country before appointing him; oh yes. I said it was a pity he had allowed himself to be put off seeing me by Haley. He first said it wasn't Haley; I told him Haley had admitted it; he then said he ought to have seen me but to tell the truth he had been frightened, frightened that I would influence him too much. GOSH . . .

18 December 1952 Christmas card from Sir I. Jacob this morning and a letter asking me to a management board anniversary dinner on January 5 – anniversary of the 'establishment' of it by Haley – I having established it thirty years ago, it lapsing from 1940 to 1948 when on my advice Haley 'established' it again. I shall write a civil note but I won't go.

[In spite of his growing estrangement from the BBC, John Reith prepared a note at the end of 1952 marked 'given to a governor of the BBC on request'[18] which showed him still to be hoping for developments in keeping with his ideals of management and output.]

Note dated December 1952

Whatever governors may be prepared to leave to the executive, they must decide and direct policy, and they must have a lively, comprehensive and continuing care for the product of the organization they are appointed to govern.

This is the more so when no straightforward, commercial profitability criterion can show them how things are going.

. . . These notes are about the product – what the Corporation exists for; and certainly our chief responsibility.

There are four chief questions:

(1) Is there a programme policy? If so, what? Are we 'giving the public what it wants', or have we any formulated and approved policy deriving from a sense of responsibility – general and specific, music, talks, drama, variety etc., television of course included?

(2) Are we satisfied with the methods of operation? Is there much wastage of time and money and effort?

(3) Are we satisfied that what is turned out is in accordance with policy in (1), if there be a policy, and with the best traditions of the BBC . . .?

(4) To what extent does listener research, rather than policy . . . determine what is done?

Perhaps a paper might be prepared for us by the executive dealing with these four questions . . .

21 January 1953 Dinwiddie wrote inviting me to go to Glasgow for their thirtieth anniversary of broadcasting and to record an introduction to the special programme and to write a foreword for a pamphlet. I thanked him but said I could have nothing to do with it; there was practically nothing of policy, procedure or practice as I had put them there.

7 February 1953 Dinwiddie rang at 7.00 as he had advised in an express letter received this morning – I said it was a sort of refinement of bullying because he knew I wouldn't want absolutely to refuse to do what he wanted; but it was utterly distasteful to me, and I should have thought quite improper, in view of what I felt to the BBC, that I should write anything for his thirty-year brochure. He persisted and I said he could send me a draft.

20 February 1953 Lunched with Sir I. Jacob at Army and Navy Club. I hadn't at all been looking forward to this; felt much inclined to call it off. We met at 1.10 (he being ten minutes late) and parted at 2.35 without mention of broadcasting or the BBC. This is exactly what I had wanted and what Muriel had suggested; I was afraid that if broadcasting had come up I should be rude. Talked mostly about defence.

[Sir Ian Jacob wrote to John Reith at the end of February suggesting a talk but unfortunately, Reith took offence at some remarks made in the same letter on an article he was writing, and ignored this approach. Sir Ian now, understandably, left things be. For the remainder of 1953 Reith's disillusion with the BBC continued unchecked. In July, after returning from his South African tour, he noted 'we haven't had the wireless on since we returned and hope we never will'; in August he would not attend a BBC farewell party to Sir Basil Nicolls; and in October he refused to record a message or go to a dinner in connection with the twenty-first anniversary of external broadcasting. Then in November the government revealed its plans for commercial television and John Reith momentarily abandoned his Achilles posture.]

13 November 1953 De la Warr handed me, at 2.00 p.m., a copy of the White Paper about competitive TV – his own copy. They are to have another corporation! I am so disgusted with the BBC that I don't care.

16 November 1953 Busy on the television debate mostly. Haley rang and I spoke to Lord Brand [a member of the BBC's General Advisory Council] in the country and then to Lord Halifax in Yorkshire. Halifax wasn't at all anxious to take my motion; he seemed afraid that Anderson (Waverley) would resent his doing so because he (H.) hadn't joined Lady V. Bonham Carter's television society and W. had. We are to meet on Wednesday [18th]; and after all this I got my motion moved to 25th.

17 November 1953 Telegram from Lord Halifax that he had 'flu and couldn't come to town as arranged. He said he would accept whatever I and the others decide so I phoned Lord Brand and said it was up to him to assemble a meeting.

18 November 1953 Went to the House of Lords even though Halifax wasn't to be there. Brand, Hailsham, Samuel, Jowitt and Waverley there. Half an hour to choose a subject and then I left. Brand rang this evening to say he had already done all that was necessary, and a good deal that wasn't. I am sorry in a way [not to be speaking] as there would be some fun and great publicity and interest about the motion.

20 November 1953 Having resolved not to take part in the Lords debate on commercial TV, I felt I must get something out of my mind about it, so I inquired yesterday morning of Clark of the *Observer* if he would like a short article. Yes. So I had to leave it along tonight; it wasn't ready till 7.00.

22 November 1953 Article very prominent in the *Observer* – 'The Precedence of England'. [John Reith argued that the champions of independent television were 'trying to promote commercial interests under the guise of Miltonic precepts and at the cost of this country's precedence in a vital sphere'.]

[Although John Reith attended the first day of the debate in the Lords he was not present on the second when the lord chancellor, Lord Simonds, made an attack on him alleging that Reith's article of June 1952 had impugned his honour by saying he had been speaking to a brief. Reith's friend Lord Balfour of Burleigh was very anxious that he should make a personal statement disowning this.]

30 November 1953 I sent Balfour of Burleigh what I supposed he would want me to say. I made it clear that I was much more inclined to do nothing at all, and next to that to have a row with Simonds. I asked Muriel if she thought I should make a statement in the House of Lords tomorrow and she did.

1 December 1953 Lunched alone and then to the Lords where I read the personal statement; I had made it stronger by saying that I was exceed-

ingly sorry I wasn't in the House last Thursday but that now I was only
going to deal with one of the lord chancellor's personal remarks. Lord
chancellor in reply said he understood it was an apology and as such
accepted it gratefully and he hoped bygones could be bygones. But they
cannot.

Letter from Sir Ian Jacob, 15 January 1954
    ... If I may speak frankly the sadness is in the BBC because so many
feel keenly that you do not seem prepared to mingle at our gatherings
where your presence would be so very welcome. I have no doubt that
you do not approve of a great deal that we do. That seems to be inevitable in any activity as the years go by and many different minds
apply themselves to the difficult problems that arise. There are bound
to be sharp differences of opinion on the policy that should be pursued.
But we are all trying our best to maintain the standards you set, in a
constantly changing world. We would gladly have your criticism and
advice and would like to show you that warm feeling for its founder
persists in the Corporation. We may misunderstand your attitude and
you may misunderstand ours. Can we not try to dissipate these mis-
understandings by meeting and talking?

19 February 1954 Lunch at Connaught Hotel with Jacob of BBC and
talked till 4.00. The more I think of it, the less point there seems to be
in it; he is just fundamentally different in outlook to me, and in practically every way. Not worth taking the space and time to describe the
conversation.

21 February 1954 The more the Jacob conversation comes back into
my mind, the more utterly hopeless does the situation between me and
the BBC seem; he and I really agree on no vital issue at all.

Letter to Sir Ian Jacob, 5 March 1954
    Our conversation a fortnight ago today has been often in my mind,
by day and night. I do not think I ever lost half an hour's sleep in all
the vexed sixteen years of my association with the BBC, but I have in
the last fortnight.
    I mentioned I was often more influenced by personalities than by
policies (so-called); having for instance stood quite clear of broadcasting and the BBC (because of contempt for my successors and what
they did) from 1938 till 1946, I then got to know Sir William Haley ...
I found he approved what I had done and was minded to restore some

anyhow of the principles and procedures of early years. I was greatly surprised at some things (and some people) he tolerated, but that was his business, not mine. Whatever he did or did not do, it seemed we were fundamentally *ad idem*.

I do not think you and I are; and I am indeed sorry. I do not think you have any particular regard for what I did . . .

There is nothing left in broadcasting of what I put there and cared mightily about, is there? . . .

If there is nothing left, if you are entirely satisfied, if we do not agree fundamentally, well there is nothing I can do to help you, is there; or the BBC, or broadcasting; and no point in any contact.

Tell me if I am mistaken.

23 March 1954 Very unwillingly to Town. Lunched with Sir I. Jacob at Army and Navy Club and had a more or less agreeable talk. He said I was entirely mistaken in what I had said in my letter; he spoke as if he definitely wanted to ask my views about things. I really don't take him seriously – though I think he may be trying.

[Some time after this, John Reith noted on the copy of his letter of 5 March: 'lunch 23rd, but it was a farce and an intolerable bore. I shall see him no more. He is utterly wooden.']

24 June 1954 I went unexpected to a meeting in the House of Lords about the TV bill – Anderson [Waverley] in the chair. Halifax, Hailsham, Archbishop. On being asked for views I said the thing was evil and one shouldn't compromise with evil; so I wasn't interested in tinkering amendments; but there might be a clause putting off the operation of the bill for two years. That was a bit of a shock.

20 July 1954 My sixty-fifth birthday. Sat in the House of Lords for about twenty minutes, report stage of TV bill. Absolutely nauseating; Jowitt asking courteously and cogently for a change in the title of the Independent Television Authority and De la Warr just feebly saying it couldn't be done and giving no reasons. And the three palsied old hags, Woolton, Swinton and Salisbury, yapping away on the front bench. I left in disgust.

28 August 1954 After I wrote to Sir I. Jacob to tell him about Carpendale's eightieth birthday on 18 October he replied at once that he was very grateful and would invite Carpendale; he hoped he could say I would be present as it would make all the difference etc. . . . I replied thanking him but please to excuse me. Letter from Miss Singer asking me earnestly to reconsider which I did and wrote attitude unchanged and that it would be horribly insincere to go to Broadcasting House feeling as I do.

21 October 1954 BBC reported to their General Advisory Council yesterday that there was a notable decline in serious listening – just as I expected.

[Broadcasting and the BBC now virtually disappeared from John Reith's diary except for occasional keening references to the decline of standards on the air. So he was distressed by the absence of any references to moral law in Sir Oliver Franks' Reith Lectures which he found 'most disappointing; all about sterling-dollar balances and such like'. Six months later he noted a comment in a book review of his work in the 'BBC *horresco referens*'. When independent television began in September 1955 and Mr Norman Collins sent him a kindly letter, he replied, in thanking him, 'I try hard not to let myself think about the BBC or anything relating thereto.' The same lugubrious tone continued throughout 1956 and 1957. His work in broadcasting was 'all gone for nothing'. When he went to a lunch for the prime minister of South Africa in June 1956 and found Sir Ian Jacob among the other guests he noted, 'I hated having to meet Jacob'. Even the death of his friend and former colleague, Sir Cecil Graves, in January 1957 was used as an occasion to dig up old differences and his flowers were accompanied with a card inscribed 'from the first director general of the BBC in grateful memory of the man who should have been the second'. When in August 1958 he heard that the BBC were broadcasting betting prices he noted, 'that is about the last trace of my management gone.' This was still his frame of mind when towards the end of 1958 he met Sir Arthur fforde who had become chairman of the BBC the previous year.]

12 November 1958 [CDC dinner for the Duke of Edinburgh] I had some conversation with fforde who seemed very pleased that I had spoken to him – chairman of the BBC forsooth.

Letter from Sir Arthur fforde, 24 November 1958
My chief feeling is one of inadequacy, one should be younger and with more available energy so as to do what is possible to prevent a further slide in the direction of commercialization.

. . . On the face of it the question will boil up on a discussion of the renewal of the Charter. But we feel that it is quite possible, unless the proper steps are successfully taken, for that position to go by default and get prejudged before the inquiry really starts. The dilemma is that

(a) If we turn our backs on all blandishments in the way of 'entertainment' or 'background music', and lose the large audiences in those fields, it will be said that we are not giving the public, en masse, what they pay their licence fee to get.

(b) If we don't, it will be said that there is no distinction between the BBC and the 'Independents', so why have a BBC?

. . . I'd like to have a talk with you about all this.

[John Reith does not appear to have taken up the offer of a talk. He contented himself with writing, mostly a summary of his resentments over the previous twenty years, and with enclosing a copy of his note of December 1952 on the duties of the governors of the BBC. It seems that it was not until the summer of 1959 that they made contact.]

1 July 1959 Muriel and I lunched in the House of Lords with Oliver Whitley. Macdonald [of Gwaenysgor, a governor of the BBC] came for coffee and asked Whitley who, if anybody, in the BBC could succeed the present director general, who is apparently leaving soon. Whitley said if anybody Carleton Greene, which horrified me; I wondered if there could be anyone better than himself, and he would have his father to help him. I rang Sir Arthur fforde as a result of what Oliver Whitley had said, and he would like to talk with me.

6 July 1959 Sir Arthur fforde at Lollards Tower 4.00 to 6.00; very agreeable and interesting; talked about who should be director general when the wretched Jacob leaves.

20 July 1959 My seventieth birthday and I suppose one of the unhappiest days of my life. Among letters there was one from Sir Arthur fforde. It was to tell me that the decision about the new director general of the BBC was one that I wouldn't approve [i.e. Hugh Carleton Greene]. I wrote that the appointment of a divorced man, remarried and an unbeliever would be an immense delight and encouragement to those set on the paganization of the country. I said I thought his letter had been a greeting on my seventieth birthday and that there had been a lunch-party in Broadcasting House on my sixtieth. I also said I had thought that he was determined to get some sort of reconciliation between me and the BBC. How ridiculous.

8 October 1959 Feeling absolutely awful about things. The Tories are back in office and power and I found I regretted this enormously.[19] It is not at all that I would like the Socialists to be in. It is that I hate the core of the Tories, especially because of Churchill and Eden and Woolton and Selwyn Lloyd and Lennox-Boyd and such like and because of their breaking the BBC monopoly. Incidentally I wrote a civil friendly note to Beadle [BBC director of television] saying I couldn't come to see over the television place.

Letter from Sir Basil Nicolls, 14 December 1959
I sat next to Hugh Carleton Greene at dinner one night last week. He is taking over the BBC on January 1st.

He talked with the highest respect and admiration about you and asked me if I could possibly arrange for him to meet you. He wants to feel that in his new onerous job he will have, to some extent at any rate, the backing and background of the BBC . . . Greene is a man of some force of character and I think he will prove to have the right perspective on things.

Letter from H. Carleton Greene, 31 December 1959
Although we have never met I feel that one of my first duties on taking over from Ian Jacob is to write and pay my respects to you as the founder of the BBC . . .

I have heard from Sir Basil Nicolls that he was proposing to bring us together in the New Year and I very much hope that this can be arranged.

Although I did not have the honour of serving under you myself, I have always during my years with the BBC been impressed by the feeling of loyalty which you still inspire among those who did. It would be a great satisfaction to all of them if we could have you with us from time to time.

4. Indian Summer, 1960–3

[In January 1960 John Reith decided to accept the olive branch which was skilfully and flatteringly extended to him from the BBC. Thus began a period of four years of renewed association at every level. He **was** regularly in touch with chairman and director general and at one moment in 1960 seems even to have suggested that he be made a governor. He visited Broadcasting House and the Television Centre in London, as well as regional centres in Birmingham, Cardiff and Glasgow. He spoke on several occasions at the BBC's staff training centre at Uplands. He gave evidence to the Pilkington committee of inquiry, he wrote in the Press, he spoke in the Lords – all in defence of the BBC. He even agreed to expose himself to public probing on television in a *Face to Face* programme with the then Mr John Freeman. Yet for all this appreciation, almost adulation, John Reith was not at ease in the way he had been in the time of Sir William Haley with whom he had shared a genuine identity of purpose. He came to feel that the flattery and attention paid to him by Sir Hugh Carleton Greene, as he was soon to become, cloaked the rejection, indeed the total reversal, of all his ideas for the best development of BBC programmes. This feeling grew on him throughout the second half of 1963 and in January 1964 he ended, as abruptly as he had begun it four years before, his third and final period of close involvement with British broadcasting.]

2 January 1960 Rang Nicolls in Cornwall to say he could tell the new BBC director general that I would meet him if he was sure he wanted it. This was largely the result of a well-reasoned letter from Andrew Stewart [BBC controller for Scotland] in Glasgow urging me to do it.

17 February 1960 Lunched with Carleton Greene, or rather he with me. I got a private room at the Dorchester and we had quite a good meal, and, I suppose, quite a good conversation; but I really don't know if I am glad that this meeting has taken place or not; he said it would make a tremendous difference to him in his work if I would go to the office – and all the old hands would be so very pleased; also would I come to a party in his house to which he would invite about twenty of the seniors. I really don't know what to make of it all, because I don't think I have any interest in the BBC and there seems to be nothing left of what I put into it. I learnt from him that they are definitely concerned about the sound monopoly, there being a tremendous agitation to let the commercial organizations do it too. He asked if I had any suggestions to make about the chairmanship of the committee of inquiry which would be set up quite shortly.

2 March 1960 At 4.30, as a result of a particularly cordial letter from Sir Arthur fforde, I went to see a film about the BBC in the Grand

Committee Room off Westminster Hall. I really would much rather have not gone to this, but I was received very courteously by the chairman and director general. I didn't like the film, it was entirely at the operations end, dozens of reporters and producers and such like, it seemed; a great deal of noise and no recognizable sequence.

31 March 1960 Lochhead was at Lollards Tower for an hour this afternoon before we both went to Carleton Greene's house in Addison Avenue [to meet about a dozen of his 'old hands']. Strode [general manager, BBC publications] who is retiring this week, and who wanted me to see the new Marylebone Road building, persuaded me to have my name put on the circulation list [of BBC publications] again. They all seemed extremely pleased to see me; it really was quite moving; I was glad that I had accepted Greene's invitation and his approach in the first instance, and invited him to lunch.

14 April 1960 After lunch I went to the BBC publishing department in Marylebone High Street, at Strode's request. It is the same place as in Goldsmith's day but vastly bigger. Quite impressive. They seemed very glad to have me go round.

10 May 1960 To lunch at Bush House with Sir B. Clark [director of external broadcasting], T. Lean, his deputy, European controller Monahan, and Overseas controller Hodson. It was a very amusing lunch party, with an immense amount of talk, and I seemed to give them great amusement, particularly in exchanges with Hodson who, they said, was not accustomed to being worsted in argument; they deriving great satisfaction from this. We talked from 1.00 till nearly 2.30, then there was a quick trip through various parts of the building, particularly the central news room, also the control room and several studios, including the Arabic one, because Arabic was the first foreign language started by me.

12 May 1960 Broadcasting House at 1.00, the DG on the pavement on arrival. On the first floor I saw for the first time Lady Scott's bust of me, in the corner by the door into the DG's room; here also were Harman Grisewood [chief assistant to the director general] and John Snagge. We went into my old room for a few minutes, but it was much deteriorated; they had not replaced the painting above the fire, and there were several odd sizes of maps hanging about, as well as an ugly series of rolled up ones. He has a small table with drawers down each side; it all looked most unsatisfactory. Went into the dining-room, all very nice indeed, sat down at about 1.20 and didn't get up till about 2.45. Everything went very well indeed; a lot of talk towards the end about public relations – this being the only serious part. There was a lot of fun about the two private lavatories, one of which had been for the woman governor in my time; I had let my secretaries use it, and H. A. L. Fisher had walked in one evening by mistake when one was in an advanced state of undress before a party. [After lunch] we went to the old concert hall, where, to my delight, Leslie Woodgate was conducting an enormous choir; they were doing Verdi's *Requiem*, but when he saw me he stopped immediately and came rushing over; he introduced me to the choir and seemed to have forgotten all about the rehearsal till I asked him to let us hear him at work; he did quite a long part which was thoroughly enjoyable . . . It was really a most pleasant party throughout, ending in the DG's office at 5.45 and tea there, Mrs DG turning up.

20 May 1960 Went to Lime Grove to lunch with Beadle and Tudsbery [consulting civil engineer to the BBC]; a very good lunch and most enjoyable in every way; then by car to the new building and was there from 2.30 till 6.30. Of course it was very interesting and impressive.

5 July 1960 To Lime Grove, where Beadle and Burnett were waiting: they ran through the Adlai Stevenson *Face to Face* before an extremely good dinner and then Welensky after. I had agreed to do this *Face to Face* before I had seen these two, and I certainly wouldn't have been much encouraged to do it by what I saw tonight.

26 July 1960 Harman Grisewood to see me and quite an interesting talk about the BBC and public relations. Apparently the chairman and DG are both very chary of spending any money on entertainment on the scale that is required because of the coming inquiry. Moreover they are both frightened that the BBC might displease the government – PMG [J. R. Bevins] in particular forsooth – if they propaganded on their own behalf. Meantime a public service broadcasting association is being formed; when asked what I thought of this, I said it was idiotic and would never come to anything; also that to stand off propaganda for the reasons given was cowardly. It is a most pathetic situation.

10 August 1960 Harman Grisewood came for me at Lollards Tower at 7.15 and I gave him a glass of sherry and then dined with him at

Claridges, talking till 10.30. I had had a letter from the DG before he went on leave saying he was glad I had seen Grisewood and hoped the conversation would be carried on in his absence [i.e. about public relations and preparations for the Pilkington committee of inquiry]. I said I felt a bit bored at the prospect of having to argue with the chairman and DG, and what *locus standi* had I anyhow? It was far too much like pushing at a haystack, which was far more irritating than dealing with positive opposition; I said I really didn't quite see why I should, and there seemed little chance of persuading sceptics and timorous folk; however I said I would ring up the chairman and get a meeting with him, and say directly what I felt about things.

18 August 1960 Lunched with the BBC chairman, Sir Arthur fforde, at Broadcasting House. Talked till 2.45. I found that he was far more inclined to favour a serious public relations campaign than I had understood; he hoped very much I would write an article for the *Guardian*, as had been suggested by Hetherington [editor of the *Guardian*] and I said I would, provided I could be given adequate material from Broadcasting House.

Letter to Sir Arthur fforde, 19 August 1960
As to the general (and very important) matter we discussed, I will await further word; but I am ready to help if help be desired; more than ready. I feel that what is eventually decided [i.e. about broadcasting and the BBC] will depend largely on what is done or not done in public relations in the next year or two – working, I imagine, to a maximum activity after publication of Pilkington's report. The overthrow of the major Beveridge recommendations, and the adoption of some silly ones, is an impressive though melancholy precedent.
[It was at this time that John Reith seems to have suggested to Sir Arthur fforde that he be appointed to the board of governors, and his letter continues . . .]
I do not know whether I was serious or not in the Board membership suggestion. It derived from your desire to reserve your right to disagree with anything I might suggest. Such a reservation certainly would not be necessary between a chairman and a member of his board; whatever my position might be today, as a member it would be clearly subordinate.

30 September 1960 I had a letter from Sir Arthur fforde two days ago asking me if I would advise them about public relations and saying that either would I form my own terms of reference, as widely as I cared, or else would I take the director general's plans and make suggestions thereon. He said I should do whichever I was more inclined for, and would I let him know what my ideas were as to the strategy and tactics the BBC should follow, on the footing that the wider the terms of reference the more the BBC was likely to gain from my advice and experience. I rang him today but he was not in the office, so I spoke to the DG, who was obviously hoping that I would work on his plans; but, when I said I would, and would he please send them along, he had to admit that he had no plans in writing at all, and that he had hoped to discuss the situation with me on October 11 when I am to dine with him. He damned well ought to have plans by this time, and pretty extensive and detailed at that.

11 October 1960 To 25 Addison Avenue [Hugh Carleton Greene's house] from 8.00 to 11.00; I was astounded at the complete change of front on Carleton Greene's part about propaganda in connection with the BBC future; I am quite certain that his point of view had radically changed as the result of the Broadcasting House lunch, and I wished he could have said so; as it was he tried to make one feel that he had always meant to have a lot done, and he told me things that he had started up, but I felt sceptical as well as annoyed.

[John Reith now found himself participating in a *Face to Face* programme as promised earlier in the year.]

Sunday 30 October 1960 Here was a long-dreaded day. A very good dinner at the television place; then at 8.45 I had to go and meet Freeman. He and I talked for about twenty minutes; then we went upstairs. I was sitting in the chair under the terrible lights and surrounded by cameras and microphones for about forty minutes before the programme was due to start. I was told to look at Freeman all the time, and not into the cameras, but in fact I had determined to look into the cameras periodically, because it seemed quite stupid not to – it is the sort of thing BBC producers can go so utterly wrong about, and apparently no one dare disagree. Someone had told me to smile sometimes and it seemed to me that I smiled most of the time, often positively laughing. It all went extremely easily and there was nothing that I regretted at the end of it, except that I hadn't been given the opportunity to say quite a lot of things that I had gotten into my mind in the course of the afternoon – about the vote, about religion, about ambition (though I said a little about this), about Central Africa and lots of other

R.D.–21

things. Several people had rung up this morning, and most of them said they hoped I would put Freeman in his place, but in fact I thought he was entirely courteous and considerate.

[Over the next two years John Reith remained in close touch with the BBC and thought constantly of broadcasting problems and policy. But much of what he thought and said was repetitive of the past. It was a time when he was suffering from severe depression. His article in the *Guardian*, which appeared at the end of 1960, summarized his evidence to the Beveridge committee given ten years earlier. His evidence to the Pilkington committee in April 1961 was equally much concerned with looking back – his recollection at times playing him false as on the details of the 1932 imbroglio over the proposed talk by a German U-boat commander – although, here, he felt he had not been asked very good questions. Even when he spoke in the Lords in May 1962, just before the publication of the Pilkington report, he concentrated his efforts on an attack on Lord Woolton and the Conservative party for their part in launching commercial television in the 1950s. So it was fitting that these middle two years of John Reith's final period of active reassociation with the BBC should have ended with celebrations of the past, this time of the fortieth anniversary of the founding of the BBC in November 1962.]

16 March 1961 I could not have been feeling in much worse form. I have often wondered what a nervous breakdown was, but I still do not know the form it takes. At 5.35 I arrived at Uplands for a visit to the BBC training school. I do not know how I got through the evening, but it was obviously regarded as very successful. I spoke for about ten minutes, and answered questions for an hour and a half. I think I must have been functioning almost automatically because there were frequent roars of laughter at my replies, and much appreciation at the end particularly from Arthur fforde who had come to take the chair. I think everyone of the thirty-odd participants came to speak with me either before or after.

7 April 1961 Lunched in the office and then to the Pilkington broadcasting committee where I was for nearly two hours. I had had quite lengthy conversations with Harman Grisewood and Carleton Greene this morning. It was not as much fun at the committee as I had thought, because I was not asked very good questions; and the questioning was done almost entirely by Pilkington; very unusual. They were all very polite, all getting up when I went into the room, and when I went out, I giving a formal bow on each occasion.

25 May 1961 I managed to get a letter off to Bernstein [chairman] of Granada [TV] declining an invitation to open their headquarters in Manchester. I would have done this, maybe to an extent in cussedness, but I knew it would be quite inconsistent and that I ought not to; Carleton Greene told me that they would be very sorry indeed.

8 June 1961 To the BBC place, Uplands, arriving early and having to do a detour to get there at 6.45. This time dinner was before the talk. The director general was in the chair, but the chairman was there also. I spoke for about half an hour, and I think quite differently from the last time, and definitely better. I did not think the questions were so good as before, but everyone seemed very pleased. The meeting finished at 10.15; then an extraordinary episode – a game of golf croquet, the director general and I against Arkell [BBC director of administration] and de Lotbinière [BBC controller of television programme services]. DG and I won, three up and one to play, and by that time it was quite dark.

> [In July 1961 a book was published by Professor H. H. Wilson of Princeton University entitled *Pressure Group*. It gave a detailed account of the breach of the BBC monopoly and the launching of commercial television.]

25 July 1961 Lunched at Claridges with Isidore Ostrer and Wilmot [of Selmeston] one of the very few Labour lords whom I know to say hullo to. The *Pressure Group* book was mentioned and they both asked why I was not going to raise the matter in Parliament. I said I had thought of doing so, but had given up the idea because the BBC were frightened their relations with government might be badly jolted if I were to do so; I was not even to put down a motion.

26 July 1961 About the Pressure Group affair. I had not followed up a conversation with St Aldwyn, the Chief Whip, by putting down a motion for the next session; and to my astonishment, I had a letter from him this morning saying he hoped I would do so. Accordingly I spoke to Grisewood in Broadcasting House. He wanted me to speak with the DG, but I said I would rather he did it and that they had a good argument about it. He rang back and said they had completely changed their minds and thought I should register a motion.

[The nervous and mental tension which John Reith had endured for much of 1961 now intensified, nor was it much relieved by the medical treatment prescribed at the end of November. Nevertheless, in spite of a characteristic spurt of anger over the manner of his invitation to the dinner celebrating the twenty-fifth anniversary of television, he remained on good terms with the BBC.]

17 August 1961 I had a letter from Farquharson [secretary] of the BBC enclosing an official invitation to a dinner on 7 November to mark the twenty-fifth anniversary of TV.

I had heard nothing about this and was of course most angry. I cannot imagine how fforde and Carleton Greene could let this happen; the same thing happened over the twenty-first anniversary of the BBC. The Lord Mayor is to be the chief guest and the prime minister is to propose the toast to the BBC. I certainly did not accept the invitation.

30 August 1961 Carleton Greene rang me yesterday and the day before and again today. I did not at all want to speak to him because I knew what it was about; but I had to speak to him today. I thought he made a very poor showing saying that 7 November was the day the prime minister could do and it was all fixed up in a great hurry. He said he hoped very much I would come; and that if there were any fault on his side, he would of course apologize, and was doing so. I did not feel in the least bit minded to go, but I told him I would think it over.

5 September 1961 There was an extraordinarily nice letter from Arthur fforde, apologizing for not having told me about the BBC dinner a long time ago.

24 October 1961 I lunched with Carleton Greene and Harman Grisewood at Broadcasting House. They seemed very much to appreciate what I said about BBC public relations. Oliver Whitley to see me about my going again to Uplands and I agreed at last.

31 October 1961 Long letter today from Hailsham about a motion against Pressure Group. I think he is taking a very feeble line. I don't now feel inclined to do anything about it. And I ought to.

7 November 1961 BBC TV affair in Grocer's Hall. I didn't want to go at all – especially with decorations on. Prime minister spoke nicely of me, and many others also. I had been most reluctant to go to this dinner, but I must say everybody was very civil and friendly.

8 November 1961 Saw Hugh Gaitskell at his request. He asked if I would take on a sort of royal commission on money expenditures during elections.[20] I said I would but that I would want Tory members as well as Labour and I tried to point out to him how much more valuable this would be. He was very scared and not at all intelligent. Then I saw Longford and A. V. Alexander about the shocking *Pressure Group* book which none of them, not even Gaitskell, had heard of. Quite shocking this.

12 December 1961 Arkell of BBC came at 3.30 and we left at 3.45 reaching Uplands exactly at 5.10. Meeting till 7.00 and it went very well. Arkell's introduction of me was most flattering.

19 February 1962 Saw Harman Grisewood for about an hour about my Lords speech [i.e. to be given on Pressure Groups] and about the fortieth anniversary doings of the BBC. Then saw Hailsham who was most friendly and courteous about my House of Lords motion.

21 February 1962 Talked with Albert Alexander and Lucan [Labour chief whip in the House of Lords] telling them I had managed to get Wednesday, 9 May, agreed by Hailsham [for debate in the Lords]. I had found out from Pilkington that his BBC report will not be published till the end of May. So it was more of an achievement than I had at first realized. Then a BBC film, meeting Carleton Greene and Kenneth Adam [BBC director of television]. It wasn't bad, but too long and too much alike all through – television in many countries.

[In March Sir Arthur fforde wrote inviting John Reith to attend a dinner as 'guest of the evening' as part of the celebrations of the BBC's fortieth anniversary in November. He accepted gladly. In the intervening months he continued to keep in touch with the BBC.]

21 March 1962 A most disagreeable drive to Uplands arriving exactly at 7.00. Dinner and then 8.15 with the governor [Sir Robert] Lusty, in the chair. He spoke extremely kindly about me in the introduction. I suppose this was the most successful and impressive evening I have had here. The questions went on for one and three-quarter hours, and they were very good.

3 May 1962 Harman Grisewood to see me about the Lords debate next week about Pressure Group and commercial television. Then to the House of Lords to meet the Labour lords who were likely to participate in the debate; nothing much came out of it and I got contrary advice – some wanting me to be very fierce, others wanting me to be mild. I was told they were going to move an amendment for a select committee, which, of course, I would be very glad to see, but I am sure the Tories would never agree.

[On 9 May John Reith introduced his motion in the House of Lords asking for papers in respect of the work of 'a political pressure group for the introduction of commercial broadcasting'. He certainly was not 'mild'.]

9 May 1962 I got myself to the House of Lords by 2.30. I was feeling angry with the BBC over the total failure of their public relations in connection with this debate. They had not been able to mobilize one single person who was prepared to put decency, honesty and honour of country – apart from the interest of the BBC – above party loyalty, forsooth. I spoke for about thirty minutes from the back cross bench, and was listened to in absolute silence. I was beginning to get sick of hearing my own voice and nothing else when fortunately I got to the end. I wish I could have spoken in easier circumstances, as I might have done from the oppostion box, but which on the advice of several people, including the BBC, I did not do. Woolton spoke after me, and frothed away about vulgar abuse, and what did I mean when I said he had 'sold the BBC down the river'; was I suggesting that there was any cash involved? I jumped up at this, but, instead of saying that he was asking a ridiculous question and of course I was not suggesting that there was any cash involved, I said, 'If the cap fits, wear it,' because I wanted to be more rude than the other. I rarely heard such utter rot talked as by most of the Tory speakers. They all, but particularly Woolton, vehemently repudiated charges that had never been made; and this was as clear a proof as one could wish for that the charges I had made had gone home. I find it quite impossible to say what I was feeling like. A lot of people congratulated me on a magnificent speech, but I did not feel I had made a magnificent speech, and still less that I had damn-blasted Woolton as forcefully as it was thought I had done. I dealt with him extremely mildly compared with what I might have said; but I was glad he was so angry with what I had said, and that people generally felt I had given him a terrific dressing down.

[The Pilkington report was eventually published at the end of June. It contained some sharp reflections on commercial television which angered the government as well as the television companies. John Reith's diary, however, contained few references to any of this. He felt, as he told Sir Arthur fforde, that 'it was all there to be read'. So he rejected an invitation from the *Evening Standard* to write an article giving his impressions of the report; and even privately he was little moved by Sir William Haley's congratulatory letter. It was a time when he was still in a state of great nervous tension – 'most awfully bothered about my future – nothing to come by way of proper work'. Sir Arthur fforde showed a sensitive appreciation of his tortured state of mind and spoke and wrote kindly in an attempt to help him. Sir Hugh and Lady Carleton Greene showed comparable kindness in entertaining him and helping to turn his mind outwards. By the end of the year, then, he was able to enjoy and enter into the BBC's fortieth anniversary celebrations.]

Letter from Sir William Haley 26 June 1962
I do hope you enjoy the Pilkington report. I have only skimmed it so far but it seems to me to be the most forthright vindication of all you said broadcasting should be . . . I can well believe that ministers are taken aback. It is the most root-and-branch condemnation of *their* creature that there has been. It is heartening to find someone restoring purpose into broadcasting. The Tories never accepted that.

26 July 1962 Collected Muriel at 12.40 and went to Broadcasting House to lunch with Sir Arthur and Lady fforde. Both chairman and wife very cordial. Lady fforde and Muriel went off at 2.15 with John Snagge, but I didn't get off till 3.30 as fforde had several things he wanted to ask me about in connection with propaganding re Pilkington's report. I said I thought Pilkington shouldn't have talked so much after publication; I wouldn't have said anything as it is all there to be read. Also that the BBC shouldn't itself appear as propaganding but should stimulate maximum propaganda on its behalf, and over the whole report and all issues involved.

Letter from Sir Arthur fforde 28 July 1962
[John Reith had enclosed in a letter to Sir Arthur a copy of his note prepared in 1952 asking 'four chief questions' of the governors. This letter gave Sir Arthur's answer to each.]
    . . . I think on (1) [=is there a programme policy?] that there is a

recognizable difference between Sound and TV. I hope it will gradually fade out, but at present it is discernible . . . The TV side hasn't yet got – though I think it is getting – the sensitivity, the instinctive ethos that the Sound chaps have inherited. There *is* a policy, but it is extremely hard to define it.

. . . As to (2)[=is there much wastage in the methods of operation?], the situation is pretty good; wastage I would say 'no, not much.' Impossible to say 'None.'

. . . As to (3) [=are programmes in accordance with the best tradition of the BBC?] Why, certainly.

. . . As to (4) [=to what extent does listener research determine what is done?], the figures certainly affect what is done, but I don't think they determine it. I believe they are an essential check on results. I do not believe they determine the setting of the next course. Certainly not when a question of substantive programme policy gets to the Board, as from time to time it does.

Letter from Sir Arthur fforde 29 July 1962
[In this letter Sir Arthur followed up the attempt he had begun in conversation three days before to guide John Reith into a better frame of mind about himself.]

I was not telling you that you should be content with what you have done. Goodness knows it is enough for most men. But what right have I to tell you it is enough for you? Moreover, I don't see the question in these categories.

Nevertheless in common with one, two or three other admirers of yours, it is a grief that you should continue to suffer this distress at 'not being properly occupied', and anyone of us, if anything we could say might help, not to *console*, but to offer grist to the mill of your mind, would say it.

. . . You said at one point early in our conversation that you were finding it hard to accept having reached an age at which it seemed that the job that stretched you would no longer come your way . . . Then, later, when we were talking of BBC affairs, you said a slightly different thing. It was hard, you said, not to be so completely busy as to have no time to think about your own problems.

. . . Putting side by side your first remark and your second one it was in my mind at the time and has stayed there since – believing as I do that God in his mercy really does decide things in his own time, however hard it is for us at times to see it – it was in my mind to ask whether this your distress can be anything but preparatory to a τέλος not yet seen? and whether when you say

(a) I want a job that will stretch me to the limit, and

(b) I want to be so busy that I have no time to think about my distress, the message may not be, 'the time is now accomplished during which you were to serve Me in those busy ways. You are being stretched by your distress. You are being stretched of a purpose. When you can stop thinking in the former categories, this new purpose, in new categories, I will shew you. And as for wanting not to have time to think, what then becomes of *Philippians* IV, 4.8?' (which leads on to verse 9 of the same).

As I say, this is not an assertion, it is a question, asked in humility by one who has hesitated much whether or not to ask it . . .

One other thing I want to say. You really do fail to realize how much you help people. You seem to think that the measure of the help you can give is involved in the degree to which you go into the full technical, legal, accountancy, etc. etc. works. But it is not so. It is what you are, that helps.

Sunday 12 August 1962 At my table again all day. Managed to finish a reply to Arthur fforde's really wonderful letters of 28 and 29 July. He suggested, with much diffidence, that I was being fully stretched by God now, just as things were . . . and this is apropos τέλος and μοναι.

[In the autumn, Sir William Haley, as ever concerned for his friend, pursued a more active course than Sir Arthur fforde but to the same purpose.]

Letter from Sir William Haley 10 October 1962

I had a session with the prime minister [Harold Macmillan] last night. I told him straightforwardly of your desire. He was interested and we talked about you. I have no idea whether anything will come of it. One never does on such occasions.

[In November John Reith attended numerous celebrations of the BBC's fortieth anniversary. Unfortunately Sir Arthur fforde was prevented by ill health from being present.]

14 November 1962 BBB/LCC lunch, I sitting on the chairman's left - Mrs Dean – very civil to me she was. Then BBC reception at Grocers' Hall, 6.30 to 8.30, though I didn't get there till 7.30. Too many people to talk to but I did my best.

15 November 1962 10.10 Paddington. Pullman to Birmingham, travelling with Carleton Greene and some others. Visited a BBC exhibition in the Town Hall, then to luncheon by the Lord Mayor who spoke most kindly. In reply I made quite a score by saying this was Carleton Greene's fifty-second birthday. To BBC new office and then 4.00 train, being seen off by the stationmaster. Travelling with several BBC people reminded me of the old days.

20 November 1962 [In Manchester for a dinner to mark the BBC's forty years of broadcasting] I was going to bed at midnight, but met Carleton Greene in the passage, and we talked for nearly an hour about there being a lay head of the BBC religious department, and secondly what did I think of Oliver Whitley succeeding Lindsay Wellington and even himself as DG when the time came. I gave a cordial approval about both points about Oliver Whitley, but did not think a lay head would be right, though I was quite in favour of their taking on an ordained head for a limited term, such as five years.

21 November 1962 Broadcasting House dinner, and this, I think, is the part of the celebrations which I most feared. All the governors were there except the chairman. Speeches about me and then the deputy chairman, Sir James Duff, made me a presentation of twenty-four volumes of the OED and a television set. I was sitting opposite my own portrait which was not very congenial, but before the speeches began I got the lights turned off except two in the centre which was a tremendous improvement. I suppose I spoke for about ten minutes. (Next night, at the Lord Mayor's party, Muriel said that every BBC person she spoke to said how wonderful it had been and what a hold I had on them all, not during this ten minutes but seemingly through all the years.) Of course, afterwards, I thought of many things I might have said and how much I could have made them all laugh by going round the room, commenting on each individual whom I knew in turn. What an extraordinary evening it all was.

22 November 1962 Rang Lady fforde to tell her how enormously I had appreciated her husband's letter and how much he had been missed through all the celebrations.

Lord Mayor's dinner at the Mansion House at 6.40. There were about two hundred at the dinner. There was tremendous ceremony about the affair, Muriel and the Lord Mayor walking immediately behind the City Chamberlain with his spurs clanking (and how I envied him), and then myself and the Lady Mayoress to the applause of the other diners who had been sent ahead of us. I spoke for seven and a half minutes and it seemed that I got on very well. Then there was a reception in the Guildhall. It really was a most satisfactory sign of the City of London's approval of the BBC – and I suppose incidentally of me, though that is not worth anything – and moreover an encouragement to carry on as in the past. I said this when I spoke.

[The goodwill aroused by the celebrations at the end of 1962 carried John Reith forward into 1963 and in the early months of that year he continued much as before, attending more celebrations, speaking at Uplands, dining with the director general and his wife. But it was about this time that he began, once again, to feel strongly that the standards of the BBC's output were being allowed to sink. Owing to his attack of acute appendicitis in June and the operation this entailed, it was not until August that he formulated this dissatisfaction. In October, John Reith tried to indicate the intensity of his feelings to Hugh Carleton Greene; then at New Year 1964 he could contain himself no longer, formally breaking his links, yet again, with the BBC and its director general.]

24 January 1963 Rang Sir Arthur fforde's house as he was back at work yesterday and today for the first time. Lady fforde said, quite incidentally, that they had been at a party in Broadcasting House the night before to unveil General Jacob's picture. Well, well . . . I said if his picture was in the Council Room, I would like mine to come out of it. He came on the line and I said the same to him. He was much distressed. I feel quite furious about this.

13 February 1963 To Cardiff. BBC exhibition and then I unveiled a plaque commemorating the first BBC premises. Then lunch, I sitting on the Lord Mayor's right hand. I had to speak after the loyal toast. Talked to J. B. Clark (KCMG) [i.e. Sir Beresford Clark] all the way back. Quite interesting, if I have to talk about the BBC.

6/7 March 1963 [In Glasgow] [6] Lord Provost's dinner at 7.15. fforde said all sorts of things about me. Then I spoke for about six minutes and seemed to be approved.
[7] BBC governors lunch in Central Hotel – far too many people at the top table. I had to speak; fforde was almost pathetic about it, admitting that I had made my coming conditional on not having to speak. I

spoke again for six minutes or so, and it went down very well. To a BBC exhibition in the Maclellan galleries, but a rough sort of teddy-boy crowd there.

4 April 1963 To Uplands, arriving at 5.50 and giving them the best yet. The session lasted from 6.00 till 7.50. Carleton Greene was there and Arkell.

18 April 1963 Oliver Whitley has written asking me to Uplands in June, and I really don't think I can do that.

20 June 1963 Left for Uplands at 5.00. All there as usual save that it seemed definitely that it was the best yet. They were very good in their questions and very loud in their acclamation at the end.

[The next day John Reith was taken ill while at Ascot in the BBC box. He had acute appendicitis; but he made a rapid recovery after the operation and was able to celebrate his seventy-fourth birthday on 20 July on the river at Henley where Mr J. H. Arkell was his host.]

6 August 1963 Rang Hugh Carleton Greene about 6.00 and found he and Mrs were up from Suffolk for two days. I don't know why I rang him. There are more and more complaints about BBC staff – it is terribly sad; and, quite apart from moralities, the indignities increase, especially hawking the microphone about the streets, and what they did about the Dr Ward trial.[21] Terribly sad that the BBC has lost all I put into it.

9 August 1963 Most welcome letter from Arthur fforde this morning and most significant. I am so glad that at last he is going to try to save the BBC from the terrible state it has gotten into.

18 August 1963 Arthur fforde rang this evening. He had sent me his twelve-page statement that he was going to send to key people in the BBC with a view to getting better quality material and less vulgarity and cheapness. I said it was a splendid document but that I didn't see it being turned into executive orders. In my view it is far too erudite and involved and vague ever to be effective.

I watched a BBC television item on India – such an opportunity it was; but it was utterly tawdry and left-wing; a terribly cheap affair. This was one night last week, and I mention it because it is so very uncommon for me to look or listen to any radio. The only thing the wretched producer wanted to get across was Amritsar.

Letter from Mr Oliver Whitley 20 August 1963
. . . What do I think of things nowadays? I think thoughts of dismay but not despair at the corrupt, misguided society . . . Government appears nowadays to imagine that its job is done when it seeks material advance and adopts a neutral stance in morals and ethics. Like Goethe's *Faust*, it creates by its neutrality between Heaven and Hell, simply a new kind of Hell in the form of society without meaning for the soul . . . NOT despair because I know this has happened often before. Wilberforce, I read yesterday, said he saw around him all the signs of Empire in decay, but your father and mine weren't yet born when he wrote that.
. . . These things one tries to disseminate atmospherically rather than didactically at BBC management conferences and on other occasions in the BBC, contending against the 'Faustian' thesis that the BBC's job is simply to inquire, inform, expose without adopting an unequivocal attitude on the side of what humanists and Christians must, if they think hard enough, both recognize as the right if in the long run life is to be worth living.

22 August 1963 If I were not committed (as it were) to friendliness with the DG I am pretty sure I would make a serious attack on the BBC in the Lords.

7 September 1963 Long letter from Sir Arthur fforde in reply to my long and rather angry one. He seems to agree with everything I say, but to be too weak or frightened to give orders to the staff. The BBC, particularly in television, has utterly discarded everything I did. And the vulgarity of the *Radio Times* week by week makes me sorry I ever started it. I had a good talk with Oliver Whitley on the telephone. He saw that I couldn't go to the next Uplands meeting without being extremely critical or else somewhat hypocritical.

12 September 1963 Dined with Elaine Greene. After the meal she asked me to talk about the BBC. Was I not going to Midhurst on 10 October? I said I wouldn't decide till after Hugh C.G. returns, as he was intending to go. But she knows what I feel as I spoke about the *Radio Times* and various disgusting things that came across – mostly television. I said that, apart from anything else, the dignity of the BBC has utterly departed. The DG is far too much away. She told me, what I hadn't heard before, that when he was asked at one of his sessions at Uplands what he regarded as the most important or significant thing he had done as DG, he had replied, 'Getting Lord Reith back into association with the BBC.'

8 October 1963 Went unwillingly and in some apprehension to lunch with Carleton Greene in his room at Broadcasting House today.

10 October 1963 Drove to Durnford near Midhurst in Sussex to Cobden's house. It is now a YMCA hostel. Carleton Greene was there and Arkell and, of course, Oliver Whitley. I was there from 6.45 to 10.15. The evening seemed to go very well. I was light with my distress about the way the BBC had fallen – or rather, though I made my attitude quite clear, I did it in a delicate way to Carleton Greene, and indeed in a way that was most respectful to him.

1 January 1964 I don't think I am going to have anything more to do with Carleton Greene or Lady – as she has become today. They had both written lately about our getting together after Christmas.

8 January 1964 Mrs Hugh Carleton Greene put through to me (telephone) this morning. Most embarrassing. She went straight to the point: why had I sent such a cold message on my Christmas card; why hadn't I rung up or written to Hugh about his knighthood . . . I said I was pretty disgusted at what was happening on the BBC and that anyhow I wasn't very well. Sickening.

10 January 1964 Lunched with Mrs Carleton Greene. I just took it as a sort of philosophical discussion. I made my point of view absolutely clear – that Hugh and I were fundamentally in complete opposition of outlook and attitude. I lead; he follows the crowd in all the disgusting manifestations of the age. I say I lead – all through my time in the BBC, and it all comes from the Manse. Without any reservation he gives the public what it wants; I would not, did not and said I wouldn't. I am very annoyed that I ever got on to terms with him. It was of no avail and has probably done a lot of harm.

5. Final detachment, 1964–70

[John Reith's detachment from the BBC in his last years was not as complete or as bitter as his previous periods of separation. While he personalized his disapproval of the BBC's programme policy by maintaining a total breach with Sir Hugh Carleton Greene – much in the same way as he had done with Sir Ian Jacob in the later 1950s – he preserved many of his other BBC friendships and ties particularly with those who had worked under him, as he demonstrated by his special Christmas messages to BBC retired staff. In the summer of 1964, thanks to the good offices of Sir Michael Adeane, he extended his contacts farther when he agreed to meet Lord Normanbrook, the new chairman of the BBC. He sent him a copy of the memorandum on governors' duties which he had first prepared in 1952 and then revised for Sir Arthur fforde ten years later.

For the next year and a half he continued from time to time to meet and to write to Lord Normanbrook but with little practical result. For by this time John Reith's mind was virtually closed to rational argument in respect of broadcasting policy; even Oliver Whitley, the son of his former chairman J. H. Whitley, could not penetrate the armour of his disapproval. Increasingly he dwelt in the past, seeming to feel that only the complete reversal of the social and intellectual changes of twenty-five years could bring the BBC back to the path of virtue. This longing for the past was accompanied by the extraordinary illusion that, at the age of seventy-five, he might yet be made chairman (this was before Lord Normanbrook's appointment was announced) or even, when two Conservative backbenchers called for the replacement of Sir Hugh Carleton Greene, director general. Yet for all his disgust, John Reith steadfastly refused to attack the BBC in public. He was prepared to offer his views confidentially to the new Labour government, but he would not write his criticisms in the Press nor speak in the Lords. In keeping his disapproval to himself in this way he earned the respect and gratitude of his many friends in the BBC.

In 1967 Lord Normanbrook died and Lord Hill of Luton was appointed to succeed him as chairman of the BBC. John Reith greatly disapproved, but nine months later he yielded to the pleas of his friend Lord Muirshiel and agreed to meet the new chairman. He felt that he had made even less genuine contact with Lord Hill than he had with Lord Normanbrook; further, he felt that his offer to help with advice was ignored. Fortunately, his active interest in broadcasting was to end on a happier note. In 1969 Sir Hugh Carleton Greene was succeeded as director general by Mr (now Sir) Charles Curran. By now John Reith had little new to say, but Mr Curran wrote kindly to him and after some months' delay, caused by John Reith's serious fall in the summer of that year, they met for lunch early in 1970. A second lunch was proposed but John Reith, feeling that there was 'too much at variance' between him and the BBC, begged to be excused and Mr Curran sadly accepted this. This exchange took place a year before his death and is a fitting place to end.]

Letter from Mr Oliver Whitley 5 January 1964
. . . Granted that the BBC is less dignified than it was, and that it commits lapses of taste or judgement from time to time, and that it is incomprehensible to you that chairman and DG allow all this to happen, I still think that there is a tendency for you to become a focus for criticism of the BBC by some people at least who are wide of the mark and whose discontent is really born less of BBC error than of their own lack of imagination, charity and understanding. In other words there is enough *really* to worry about in the BBC for you or me; and I am sad that you are told things – which you haven't heard or seen yourself – which make it seem a good deal worse than it is.

Letter to Mr Oliver Whitley 16 January 1964
. . . The director general of the BBC and I are, I have only recently and regretfully realized, poles apart.
He is, in fact, in favour of what is a negation of almost all that I stood for. He gives the public what it wants. That is his price. It is exactly what I utterly repudiated . . . this determining aim and objective of giving the public what it wants really is the all-important and all-operative factor. *I lead* – arrogantly maybe; he not only *follows* but seeks to follow.
I don't mean this as an attack or a denunciation *ad hominem*. As to the *policy* – yes, and as fierce as I can make it.
You have elected to side with the regnant lord. All right. But I wouldn't think it profitable or effective to essay to reconcile irreconcilables – e.g. The O.J.W. of today and of twenty or thirty years ago.

Letter from Mr Oliver Whitley 18 January 1964
. . . There is no question of my 'siding' with or against anyone in general terms or of my changing as compared with myself earlier on. I

simply tried to say, and I say again, that there is something wrong when you, not apparently having any direct knowledge whatever of a programme – e.g. *Juke Box Jury* – accept that it is *evil*, a very strong word . . . Rather than admit the possibility that you may be wrong you begin to attribute to me in your mind such things as transfer of loyalty, change of attitude, abandonment of principle.

. . . Why do you do this? The reason seems to me to be that you are determined to make the evidence fit your picture of the BBC and the DG, rejecting any suggestion of good and accepting any suggestion of bad.

[Ill health forced Sir Arthur fforde to retire as chairman of the BBC early in 1964. John Reith appears to have written to Sir William Haley indicating his readiness to take over this position, if asked. Sir William wrote kindly to warn him not to build any hope of this.]

Letter from Sir William Haley 15 March 1964
. . . Your name has not come to me otherwise [than in your letter]. This leads me to say – don't bank on it too much. If it comes, that will be fine; nothing could be finer, more heartening for the country, or more appropriate. (There would be some querulous outcries from the popular press and from little men, but these need not deter you in any way.) I would welcome such an appointment as I would no other. So would most people who care desperately about what the BBC can do for the education, culture and moral health of the country. But, alas, so often in public affairs – and above all in public appointments – the right thing is not done. So do not set your heart on it too much. I would not have you heartbroken.

30 March 1964 I feel immensely sad (and more than that) at the eclipse, or rather complete overthrow and destruction, of all my work in the BBC. It was my being prepared to lead, and to withstand modern laxities and vulgarities and immorality and irreligion and all. No one was ever in such a position as I; I did what my father and mother would have wished – to universal amazement. All gone. Feeling most melancholy.

2 April 1964 The Dean of Westminster wrote asking me to come to a service on the 19th to signalize the start of the Number Two television BBC. I wouldn't on any account go to that, nor to anything associated with the BBC.

R.D.—2K

Letter to Sir Arthur fforde 18 May 1964

. . . The BBC has lost dignity and repute; in the upper reaches of intellectual and ethical and social leadership it has abdicated its responsibility and its privilege.

Its influence is disruptive and subversive; it is no longer 'on the Lord's side'.

I am sorry I ever had anything to do with it.

14 July 1964 Buckhouse Garden Party – I went three times all round by myself, trying not to see anyone and mostly succeeding. Muriel was much annoyed with me for not staying with her; I thought she was all right with Mrs Adeane and Daisy Bigge.[22] I had some conversation with Michael [Adeane]. He had been lunching (or dining) with Lord Normanbrook at the BBC. He asked if I knew him and I said hardly, and I very much object to a civil servant being put into that job. I said if this Normanbrook had had the sense to write to me on appointment that would have committed me to help him. M.A. immediately said, 'Is it too late now?' Before I could answer some female burst in on us, and I went off.

[The next day John Reith wrote to Sir Michael Adeane with his answer to the question 'Is it too late now?' It was characteristic; he was ready 'to respond favourably' to an approach from Lord Normanbrook on the assumption that Lord Normanbrook 'was sorry he had not made overture to me in the first instance'. It was on this occasion that he sent the copy of his memorandum on governors' duties for Sir Michael Adeane to pass on 'if so minded'. Lord Normanbrook took up this opening with great courtesy.]

22 September 1964 Went with Muriel to the opening of the Whitehall Banquet Hall after reconditioning. Very impressive place, though too much white; it was all white except the Rubens painted roof. I accepted the invitation because Muriel wanted to go; but I was awfully embarrassed by it:

(1) because of the number of people who knew me but whom I can't remember, though perhaps I should do; and

(2) because of the number of people I dislike and don't want to meet.

A great many people came to speak to me including, to my astonishment, Normanbrook; and most polite he was; could he come and call on me. I don't know yet if the letter and enclosure I sent to Michael Adeane have been sent on to him.

29 September 1964 Normanbrook to see me 10.00 to 11.15. I asked if Michael Adeane had anything to do with his speaking to me; he said not. He read the guide to governors which I drew up years ago at the wretched Stedeford's request. It all seemed to go very well, but I can't imagine anything coming of it.

20 January 1965 House of Lords with Muriel, sitting there for about five hours (Muriel leaving after about three). Normanbrook and the wretched man Hill were there; the latter was next me for most of the time but I ignored him. Ferrier (Conservative) and Peddie (Labour) were vehement in attack on BBC. C. P. Snow [parliamentary secretary, ministry of technology], winding up for the Government, made much the most significant reference to me: 'No one in the history of this kind of communication has really had a coherent view of what he wanted to do with it, with the single and startling exception of the noble lord, Lord Reith. He began with a vision . . . of what can be done with such a medium. In the process of carrying out his vision . . . he raised the tone of our national life. Of this we are quite clear. We are not so sure that the same vision is easy to sustain at present.'

[After this debate John Reith wrote to Lord Normanbrook partly to explain his silence in the House of Lords which, he said, arose from 'decency to yourself and a sense of dignity for myself', and partly to follow up their talk of the previous autumn. He asked in particular whether Lord Normanbrook approved the view recently advanced by the then head of BBC radio drama that it was the duty of the BBC as a public service 'to reflect opinion . . . not to dictate or mould it', a view which John Reith saw as 'an absolute negation of what made the BBC respected throughout the world'. In his reply Lord Normanbrook reassured him that he rejected this statement 'if it meant that public service broadcasting has no responsibility for moulding public opinion or public taste'. He then went on to a more general consideration of the BBC's situation.]

Letter from Lord Normanbrook 11 February 1965

. . . It troubles me that so much of the current dialogue about the BBC is conducted by people who take extreme positions on either side. On the one side are those who disregard all the changes which have taken place in our society in the last thirty years and seem to believe that the BBC could proceed today as it did in the days when there was no television and the Corporation had a complete monopoly of broadcasting. On the other side are people who are so preoccupied with the facts of the new situation that they can see no place for principles, or as you would say, for leadership. Between those who start from these extreme positions rational discussion is very difficult, for there seems to be no common meeting ground.

. . . I do not think that our audience is divided between these extremes. For many, the arguments of the extremists are largely irrelevant, and our service must concern itself with the many. If we do not seek to make our appeal to this middle group, we must abandon the concept of public service. Leadership which discards relevance to those whom it seeks to lead is of no purpose. Therefore I believe that within the BBC constructive policies can only be formulated by people who try to find a middle position – who take account of the facts of life in our contemporary society, however much they may deplore them, but are ready to seek new ways in which broadcasting can bring a healthy influence to bear in this society.

12 February 1965 Lunched with Harman Grisewood in the House of Lords. I showed him the letter I had written to Normanbrook after the BBC debate and his reply just received. I said it was jesuitical, apologizing for the use of this word to a Catholic. I am wondering whether I will reply to it in a few words or try to deal with it properly; it will almost certainly be the former.

[John Reith's reply, written on 22 February, followed the course he had forecast. He thanked Lord Normanbrook for his trouble but added that his disagreement was so complete and vehement that it was better for him to say nothing at all.]

7 March 1965 Yesterday's *Times* had a middle page half column about a demand for the BBC director general's dismissal.[23] I concluded, without hesitation whatever, that if in fact the director general were dismissed, and if inconceivably I were offered the job, I would take it; and I could do what was required more or less in my sleep. I would insist on being director general, not on the board. I think this would be better and wiser than my being executive chairman even.

15 May 1965 I was in a sickening bad mood over the weekend. I was feeling profoundly depressed about myself – past, present and future, and several things are happening to increase such a feeling, particularly the definite, deliberate and sustained sabotage and subversion in religion and every sort of morality by the director general of the BBC.

21 May 1965 BOAC lunch, arriving 12.25, Sir Giles Guthrie coming out of the board room, and, to my horror, saying he would like me to meet the directors. Normanbrook was one of them. I said I hoped he had not resented the reply I had sent him to his long jesuitical letter as to what was happening in the BBC. He said now, with what had happened since, he imagined he and I saw eye to eye about things. I said I was glad to hear that, and that I would be ready to help him if I could.

18 June 1965 Lunched with Harman Grisewood in the Oriental Club where I had not been since about the time my memoirs were published. Grisewood particularly wanted to tell me that there were two suggestions for the BBC in order to make up their considerable deficit – one was to give them a grant in aid, the other to admit commercial broadcasting. He asked me which I thought the worse evil. I said that of course I had not the slightest doubt that, if I were involved, I would choose the grant in aid as the lesser of two evils since the ill effects of a grant could be conditioned and controlled; in other words the Government and civil service kept in their places; whereas the evils of commercial broadcasting were absolutely inevitable under the present management.

2 July 1965 Wrote to the lord president [Bowden] at H. Grisewood's emphatic request. The issue is the future of the BBC. I said that I wasn't asking or suggesting anything – no indeed – only indicating a willingness to be consulted which I don't suppose he has the courage to do.

[John Reith's expectations were confirmed. His offer was acknowledged with polite procrastination . . . 'at a later stage we may wish to avail ourselves of your experience'.]

6 August 1965 [Attending the funeral of Sir Basil Nicolls] Gillard [BBC director of sound broadcasting] asked if I would give the address if there were a memorial service for Benjie in London. I said NO, for two reasons: that I didn't approve of these addresses, and that I would not do anything at a BBC service – not read the lesson either. I had expressed myself with considerable clarity about the BBC as it now is – the leader of agnosticism and immorality among young people particularly.

27 September 1965 Called on Tangye Lean at Bush House – he succeeded Sir Beresford Clark recently. Lean said he was most honoured to have me call on him. It was in continuation of the talk with John Arkell last week about my sending a message to the South African Broadcasting Corporation for the opening of their new short wave transmitters. The BBC is most anxious that I shouldn't do so, but I shall, because it is right that they should be able to tell their own story.

4 October 1965 Lunched with Lord Normanbrook about my letter to him asking for no BBC tribute to me on departure. Very courteous he was. I said I objected to it absolutely – dislike of publicity; and relatively – the abominable way the BBC is behaving now. In the end I said I would leave it to him; he knew my views but I realized his points also. But, incidentally, he must not allow C. Greene or the beastly Muggeridge in on it.

He knew I was going to make a record for South Africa, and he came with me to 1 Portland Place. I think I did all right – saying what I wanted to say but not saying what I knew Tangye Lean and others wouldn't like.

26 October 1965 Lunched with Gillard of BBC at Lords. He tried hard to persuade me that things weren't nearly so bad in the BBC as of course I know them to be.

[In November 1965 John Reith was elected Lord Rector of Glasgow University and the preoccupations of this office turned his mind away from the BBC and broadcasting for a space. Over the next six months his only contact with these matters was in a sharp correspondence with Lord Normanbrook but the issue here was purely historical – the extent to which he had *created* the BBC as a public corporation. In a public lecture Lord Normanbrook had reasonably and rightly followed the work of Lincoln Gordon and Asa Briggs on this point. But John Reith would have none of them; he had persuaded himself that it was he who first put to the Crawford committee in 1926 the idea of the BBC as a public corporation. Normanbrook agreed that he wanted it and that he had worked for it; but he maintained that John Reith did not speak for it in evidence before the committee. John Reith would not accept this: 'Whatever others say,' he wrote, 'I alone know.' He appealed to his diary. But his diary proves him wrong. On 1 February 1926 he wrote: 'It [i.e.

the future constitution of the BBC] must be put on a public service basis, *but I cannot say this definitely in evidence* [Editor's italics].']

10 June 1966 Quite an argument on the telephone with one Hugh Massingham about my rejection of a request from him to write two articles for the *Sunday Telegraph*. His opinion of the BBC coincides with mine. Cheap and trivial and that it was largely responsible for the vast increase in sex and violent crimes and for the general very heavy decline in morality of all kinds. He wouldn't admit any justification for my not going into action against the BBC, nor that, if I were to do it, the House of Lords would be the place.

6 September 1966 Today I had lunch with the director of the BBC Overseas Services [Tangye Lean] and his five controllers. It was most interesting really. They assured me that I was held in greater respect than ever, and that the newest and youngest members of the staff were quickly aware of the Reith tradition. We talked on till nearly 3.00. I wrote to thank Lean for having me there and in his reply he said there was a unanimous cabinet view in the BBC that 'my restraint from public criticism contributed very greatly to my stature'. He said he was sure that there was no risk that my silence might be taken to imply identity of view or any similarity of view.[24]

[In the autumn of 1966, Mr Malcolm Muggeridge put forward the idea that John Reith should agree to another television programme along the lines of the *Face to Face* interview of six years before. At first Reith was marginally in favour; then, in November, he said he was 60:40 against; but by the end of January 1967 it is clear that it was firmly agreed.]

9 February 1967 Someone from BBC television going through my Diary Enclosure volumes to get points for the Muggeridge broadcast affair, which I am exceedingly sorry I ever agreed to do, and I have tried hard this week to cancel it altogether. If it weren't that I am on friendly terms with John Arkell, I would cancel it.

17/18 February 1967 [17] In my Glasgow University office at 9.00 and then 10.00 to 3.30 in the robing room doing a sort of *Face to Face* with Muggeridge.

[18] Rain all day yesterday and then today actually sun. We did all the morning filming in the Med. Quad and then to the High Drive where we walked about quite a lot. Extraordinary to be there again

recalling childhood and youth. After lunch to the Manse, much 'shooting' and talking on the outside steps and in the hall and in the dining-room and in Father's study. I took Muggeridge upstairs to see my room and I was in most all the others. Oh dear. I am glad some part of the filming is done.

20/21 February 1967 Both these days occupied all day by the television affair. Twelve men, eight arc lamps, two or three cameras, two microphones and the most awful turn-up in the sitting-room. Muggeridge asked me to finish the whole affair by reading the closing passage from my father's sermon on his fiftieth anniversary. Extraordinary to think of the tremendous publicity that this sermon will have.

27 July 1967 Almost incredible news that the new BBC chairman was Lord Hill of Luton, forsooth.

[Malcolm Muggeridge's filmed interviews with John Reith were turned into three fifty-minute programmes which were transmitted towards the end of the year. They were called 'Lord Reith looks back' and the title was well chosen. For, in spite of his active summer in Edinburgh as Lord High Commissioner, John Reith was by now increasingly occupied with his recollections. He noted in his diary in August 1967: 'I find myself more and more slipping into ruminations about the past.' So while he still heard news of the BBC it was now only from time to time. Then, early in 1968, he developed heart trouble and had to enter hospital for an operation for the fitting of a 'pace-maker'. He left hospital at the end of March.]

9 April 1968 [Dictated on 25 July] An unusual meeting tonight with Lord Hill, the BBC chairman. I was most reluctant to do this but was so much urged by Jack Maclay [Lord Muirshiel] that I eventually agreed. We started in Boodles, then went to a private room at the Turf Club and talked till 11.30. Hill was most forthcoming. He said he was very glad to have met me, and when, after a good deal of thought and very mildly, I said I was prepared to help him, he said he was most grateful both for this meeting tonight and for this offer.

[John Reith followed up this meeting by asking Lord Hill to come to Holyroodhouse as one of his guests during his second period as Lord High Commissioner in May 1968. He hoped that this gesture would lead to further talks between them on BBC matters, but he was disappointed; as he wrote to Lord Muirshiel in July – 'not a word about the BBC, or anyone in it, or anything about it since the little dinner-party at the Turf Club'. He continued to brood on this, more particularly because of the announcement that Sir Hugh Carleton Greene, on giving up as director general in March 1969, was to become a governor of the BBC. He regarded this as a public confirmation of the policy followed by Sir Hugh in respect of programmes and, therefore, as a public rejection of his own principles.]

1 July 1968 Today it was announced on the BBC that the wretched director general was retiring in March, and three months after that was joining the Board. Greene said in an interview about three months ago that he was going to stay in the BBC till he was sixty-five; now he says that he has come to the conclusion he has done all he can in the BBC. Hill said the same sort of thing, that Greene had done a very good job and so forth – absolutely nauseating.

Letter to Lord Muirshiel 20 February 1969
. . . You will remember that [in our talk with Lord Hill] . . . I said that whereas I had been determined that the intellectual and ethical standards of the community were not to be made lower than they already were by the operation of broadcasting, in other words that the BBC had a heavy and serious responsibility on this score, the present director general [Sir Hugh Carleton Greene] not only did not accept this but definitely rejected it; it was not his business to be concerned with the intellectual or ethical standards of the community, it was his business to reflect life as it was, and to give people what they wanted.

There was his policy in a few words, directly opposite to mine, for I had often said that the BBC did not 'give the public what it wanted', but what it would come to want.

Shortly before we broke up I made a remark which I had not expected to make and which it took me all evening to say: 'If I can help you in any way I shall be pleased to do so.' Having made that remark I would of course have confirmed it by action if any appeal were made to me.

No appeal has ever been made; nor ever, I think, will; I have had no contact with Lord Hill except, casually, at Holyrood.

I expect you were as shocked as I to find that he had agreed to the director general's appointment as governor after three months. It is usually a mistake to have an ex-chief executive appointed to the board on retirement; it is generally thought to be at least embarrassing, if not unfair, to the chief executive.[25]

And would you not have thought that the Lord Hill might have said something to me about getting that terrible McKinsey firm[26] in, and to have asked me to discuss their report with him?

I am most sorry that I offered to help him.

12 March 1969 Lunched at the Athenæum with Jack Maclay [Muirshiel]. I had written him about Hill's ignoring me and I certainly wasn't going to any jubilee affair in 1972. He said he was sure Hill was frightened to talk with me, just as Sir A. Cadogan said he had been frightened to consult me as to who should be director general when Haley left. Jack Maclay is a very decent fellow but he had no suggestion at all to make. I am extremely disgusted with all I hear about the BBC.

(Just as I was writing this Lusty rang to say he had been at Greene's farewell dinner in Broadcasting House last night and the new DG, Curran, had asked him to arrange for him to meet me. He assured me that the idea originated entirely with Curran. I got out of it by saying I would consider the suggestion.)

[On 5 July 1969 John Reith fell heavily and so damaged a knee that he had to go into St Thomas's Hospital where he remained until 13 August. The last entry in his diary before the accident was for 29 June. It appears that Mr John Arkell successfully interceded with him, when entertaining him at Henley on 26 June, to persuade him to meet the new director general of the BBC, but owing to his fall and his poor health they did not finally meet till 20 February 1970.]

20 February 1970 I did wish I hadn't to go out to meet Curran of BBC today; however the conversation went all right once I had got properly started, 3.00 till 6.00 p.m. Curran was very civil to me and said it had been a great honour to have had such a talk. There were some things that he clearly didn't see fully with me, but not much. I don't suppose anything can come of it.

21 February 1970 I wasn't feeling that I wanted to get up. I think it is the disgusting behaviour of BBC people that is having a quite serious effect on me. There is a debate in the House of Lords but I can't see any point in my going there.

25 February 1970 In the House of Lords 3.00 till 6.30 with half an hour for tea. Miserable affair and extremely disappointing. The whole thing was despoiled of any effect by the concentration on the wretched Third

Programme instead of dealing with the general utter surrender of any principle in ethical or intellectual standards. Terribly sad – and some appreciable degree of responsibility is with me in leaving the concern in 1936 (or 35 was it?) [It was in 1938.] I left when I was under fifty – I could have been in complete charge for fifteen more years – till just before I went to the CDC to save it from disaster.

1 March 1970 The BBC director general has written a civil note inviting me to lunch with him; he says he would be very glad if it could be in Broadcasting House, but after very short thought I have decided that I will not do this; and I don't wish to be on terms with anyone there, except, as far as I can see, with this director general and within narrow limits here.

Letter to Mr Charles Curran 23 May 1970
. . . After careful thought I feel you are much too occupied to take on an additional complication such as this one – as I see it. I think we should postpone any discussion *sine die*. I think there is far too much at variance between us.

In the unlikely event of your feeling there is anything I could possibly do to help, then the door is open.

[John Reith's diary ended as a continuous narrative on 28 May 1970. He took it up again in November after moving from his flat in Lollards Tower in London to his grace and favour house in Edinburgh in the autumn, but there were now, as he himself noted, only 'disconnected entries'. Before he left London, however, Mr Curran successfully restored his good relations with Broadcasting House which endured for the remaining months of his life.]

Letter from Mr Charles Curran 26 May 1970
I have received your letter of 23 May, and I read it with not a little sadness. I have clearly failed to convince you that I hold you in considerable reverence, even though you may be critical of some of the things which now come from the BBC. I think that you underestimate the decisive influence on our present work of the foundations which you so truly laid. We have changed, but I do not think that all the change has been for the worse. Much has been simply the change of times.

I shall not press you, if you are reluctant, but I note particularly that if I should feel there is anything you could do to help, then the door remains open for me. The scriptures tell us that not everyone who cries

'Lord, Lord' shall enter into the Kingdom of Heaven. I assure you that when I express the honour in which I hold you, it is no mere formality. If therefore I feel that you can help I shall ask.

Letter to Mr Charles Curran 24 June 1970
. . . I only want to say that I think your letter is as impressive and delightful as ever I received. It is immensely appreciated and treasured.

NOTES

1. A longer, but verbally inaccurate, excerpt from this memorandum is given in *Into the Wind*, p. 342.

2. [Sir] Lindsay Wellington was chosen.

3. In the memorandum which he wrote in November 1940 John Reith stated:
I gave Lord Halifax a written reply on February 15. The gist was that I would help the director general to stay in his job.

4. John Reith had given a copy of his memorandum to Kingsley Wood on 22 November. His chagrin at being ignored led him to overlook the first and most important recommendation made by the cabinet committee, which said:
We do not recommend that the government should assume complete control of the BBC.

5. Harold Nicolson had been dismissed from his position as parliamentary secretary to the Ministry of Information on 18 July 1941 and was compensated with a governorship of the BBC which he was to hold *in commendam* with his parliamentary seat and salary.

6. Sir Cyril [later Lord] Radcliffe was soon to succeed Monckton as the fourth and final war-time director general of the Ministry of Information.

7. Graves and Foot had been appointed joint directors general.

8. Sir William Haley planned a dinner at Broadcasting House for all who had worked under John Reith as director general.

9. John Snagge entered the BBC in 1924 as one of Reith's earliest appointments and for forty years was a loyal exponent of his ideals within the corporation.

10. John Reith's allusions are to the Romanes Lecture given annually at Oxford which was founded in 1891 by G. J. Romanes and first given by Mr Gladstone in 1892; and to the Rede Lecture given annually at Cambridge since 1858 which commemmorates the benefaction of the sixteenth-century chief justice Sir Robert Rede.

11. Tommy Handley, the radio comedian, had died on 9 January 1949.

12. The *dinner* of November 1947 and the *lunch* of July 1949 are probably meant here.

13. (Sir) Ivan Stedeford was a member of the Beveridge committee and subsequently a governor of the BBC. John Reith worked under him in Tube Investments between 1953 and 1959. For much of this period they were on friendly terms but towards the end John Reith felt that Stedeford had withdrawn his confidence. So by the time he left Tube Investments he 'disliked and distrusted' Stedeford and later placed him on his black list of enemies he would not forgive.

14. John Reith pencilled the word 'No' against this sentence.

15. In the new Conservative government Lord Salisbury was lord privy seal, Lord Woolton was lord president of the Council, Sir David Maxwell Fyfe (later Lord Kilmuir) was home secretary, James Stuart (later Lord Stuart of Findhorn) Scottish secretary and Lord De la Warr postmaster general.

16. John Reith called his article 'The force of Money'. He wrote in it:

It is the BBC and its friends who are fighting to preserve the freedom of the ether; Lord Woolton, the lord chancellor, Mr Profumo and his associates who would surrender it to the brute force of money.

17. Sir Ian Jacob had been seconded from the BBC to be deputy secretary of the Cabinet during 1952.

18. The governor for whom this was prepared was Sir Ivan Stedeford; see below 29 September 1964.

19. The general election of October 1959 had increased the Conservative government's majority.

20. This approach from Hugh Gaitskell turned into John Reith's special commission of inquiry (into advertising) on behalf of the Labour party.

21. Dr Stephen Ward had been charged with living on immoral earnings and his trial took place between 22 and 31 July 1963. He was found guilty but had committed suicide before sentence could be passed.

22. Mrs Adeane and Miss Bigge were the daughters of Lord Stamfordham and had long been friendly with John and Muriel Reith. See chapter 3.

23. Two Conservative MPs, Mr James Dance and Sir Leslie Thomas, tabled a motion demanding the immediate replacement of Sir Hugh Greene as director general of the BBC. This was in protest at a sketch shown in the television programme *Not so much a programme, More a way of life* which made offensive references to Roman Catholics on Merseyside and to birth control.

24. In December 1966 Tangye Lean entertained John Reith again, on this occasion in his home, and gave him:

a silver drinking cup of the sort used in All Souls; he had used one of these recently marked John Thornhill, *Nulla dies sine linea*, and he had had this one marked, Johannes Reith, *Nulla dies sine linea*. I had never known before that the line was an artist's line. Most extraordinarily kind of him.

25. This had not been John Reith's view in 1938 when he hoped to be placed on the board himself on moving to Imperial Airways.

26. The business efficiency firm of McKinsey's had been consulted on the question of cost efficiency in the BBC's work and organization.

Index